Second Edit

TRAINING ESSENTIALS FOR ULTRARUNNING

JASON KOOP

WITH JIM RUTBERG AND
CORRINE MALCOLM

Copyright © 2021 by Koop Endurance Services, LLC

All rights reserved. Printed in the United States of America.

No part of this book may be reproduced, stored in a retrieval system, or transmitted, in any form or by any means, electronic or photocopy or otherwise, without the prior written permission of the publisher except in the case of brief quotations within critical articles and reviews.

Acute Training Load, Chronic Training Load, Training Stress Balance, Normalized Pace, and Training Stress Score are trademarks of Peaksware, LLC.

Ironman® is a registered trademark of World Triathlon Corporation.

Library of Congress Control Number: 2021924148
Library of Congress Cataloging-in-Publication Data

Names: Koop, Jason, author. | Rutberg, Jim. | Malcolm, Corrine.

Title: Training essentials for ultrarunning, Second edition / Jason Koop with Jim Rutberg and Corrine Malcolm

Description: Colorado Springs, CO, Koop Endurance Services, LLC [2021]

Subjects: LCSH: Marathon running—Training. | Ultra running.

This paper meets the requirements of ANSI/NISO Z39.48-1992 (Permanence of Paper).

Cover design by Abby Hall, cover photograph by Keith Ladzinski
Interior design by Abby Hall

TO ACCESS A DIGITAL VERSION OF ALL OF THE FIGURES AND TABLES FROM THIS BOOK, VISIT THE QR CODE ABOVE.

For David, the most selfless person I have ever known.

May we all follow in your footsteps.

See you on Hope Pass!

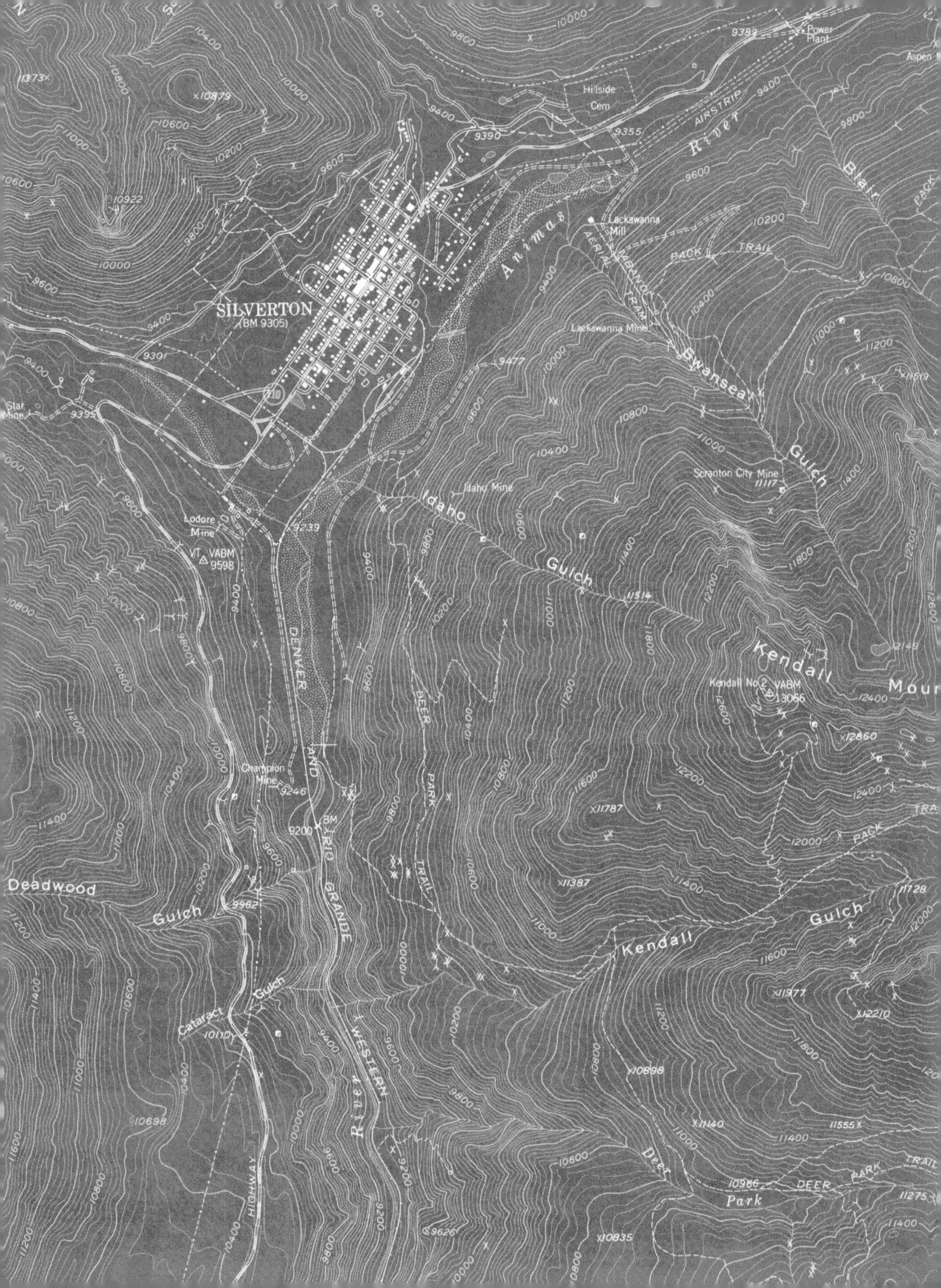

SILVERTON
(BM 9305)
Hillside Cem
Power Plant
AIRSTRIP
Animas River
Lackawanna Mill
AERIAL TRAM
Lackawanna Mine
PACK TRAIL
Swansea Gulch
Blair
Scranton City Mine
Idaho Mine
Idaho Gulch
Kendall Mountain
Kendall No. 2 VABM 13066
Star Mine
Lodore Mine
VT VABM 9598
DENVER AND RIO GRANDE WESTERN
Champion Mine
DEER PARK TRAIL
Deadwood Gulch
Cataract Gulch
Kendall Gulch
HIGHWAY
River
Deer Park
DEER PARK TRAIL

TABLE OF CONTENTS

Foreword

BY KACI LICKTEIG

"I want to win Western States."

Jason Koop was the first person I said that to. It might have been the first time I'd even said it out loud. It was the summer of 2014, and although I'd already achieved some success in two seasons as an ultrarunner, taking aim at the top step of the podium in the granddaddy of them all seemed like a giant leap. Putting it out there made it real, and having Jason in my corner made it feel possible. That's what a coach does for you: they help expand your vision of what's possible, not by telling you what you're capable of but rather by guiding you to discover it within yourself.

My journey started in 2013, my first season running ultramarathons. I had transitioned from road marathons to trail running and experienced some success pretty quickly, but I could also tell that what I was doing wasn't sustainable. I didn't truly understand how to train for ultrarunning. Road marathons and trail ultras were very different, and I had a lot to learn.

When I won the 2013 Bear Chase 50 Mile outright, people started to take notice. I was introduced to Scott Jaime, who recommended that I contact a coach named Jason Koop. At the time, I had no idea who either of them was, so I didn't act on the recommendation right away. As I continued to train on my own, however, I found myself wanting guidance and accountability, so I decided to reach out to Jason.

We had a great initial conversation. He asked me a ton of questions about my background, current and previous training, accomplishments, and goals. I similarly dug into his background and was reassured by his use of the latest scientific research, his coaching certifications, his personal experience as an athlete, and his rejection of "cookie cutter" training plans. What I truly loved was that he personally trains the same way he trains the athletes who work with him. He's not a "do as I say, not as I do" coach. He does the workouts, runs the races, crews for runners, volunteers, and is active in the community.

I was excited to work with Jason, particularly because I had just earned a coveted spot into the 2014 Western States Endurance Run. As with any relationship, it took some time and patience for both of us to learn and adjust to each other. I was training at sea level, without a mountain in sight, for a 100-mile run featuring 18,000 feet of climbing, 23,000 feet of descending, and a peak elevation over 8,000 feet above sea level. I questioned plenty of things about his plan, and at every step he had solid science to back up what we were doing. Any remaining questions or doubts were put to rest on race day, when I ran around the Placer High School track to finish 6th in my first Western States.

It was shortly after that when I privately told Jason my ultimate goal and dream was to win Western States.

We went to work, and Jason was there through plenty of ups and downs. Two years later, on June 25, 2016, I achieved my dream. After 17 hours and 57 minutes, I ran around the track in Auburn, California, to win the Western States Endurance Run. I will never forget that moment, and I owe it to Jason for preparing me both physically and mentally for it. He will never take credit for his athletes' accomplishments, but the performances speak volumes.

The Koop you'll "meet" in this book is the same Koop I talk with on the phone. He's a direct, brutally honest, no-nonsense scientist and coach who also has a tremendously compassionate, empathetic, and supportive side. He can be stern when it's warranted, but he's also the first person you want to see in an aid station when your day is going sideways, and he'll be leading the cheering section when you cross the finish line. All of that passion, expertise, and perspective comes through in the pages of this book, which is why *Training Essentials for Ultrarunning* has helped so many new and experienced ultrarunners discover what they are truly capable of.

Galena Mountain
Turquoise Lake
Tennessee Park
St Kevin
Grandview Shaft
Hagerman Pass
Sugarloaf Mountain
Bald Eagle Mountain
Campgrounds
Leadville Junction
Leadville
Evergreen Cem
Gravel Pit
Venture Shaft
Gaging Sta
Radio Tower
Thespian Mine
Colorado Mtn College
Stringtown
California
Malta
County Airport
Twin Mounds
LEADVILLE
FEDERAL FISH HATCHERY
FOREST
NATIONAL
WILDERNESS
MOUNT MASSIVE
Mount Massive
Iowa
Gulch
Thompson
Empire
Union
Substa
Campground
Halfmoon
Arkansas
DENVER
AND
RIO GRANDE
SAN ISABEL
French Mountain
Iron Mike Mine
Mount Elbert
PACK TRAIL
Mt Elbert Forebay
Kobe
T 10 S
T 11 S
R 81 W
R 80 W
Bull Hill
Dayton
Gulch
Fidelity Mine
Little Joe Mine
Twin Lakes
Powerplant
Radio Tower
Holmes
Twobit

CHAPTER 1

The Ultrarunning Revolution

As this book finds its way into your eager hands, I will be well into my third decade of being a professional coach. During that time, I've worked with thousands of individual (and very different) athletes. I've helped guide marathon runners, cyclists, triathletes, ultrarunners, mixed martial arts fighters, motorsports athletes (NASCAR, motocross, and Formula One), various winter sports athletes, and a host of other athletes looking to develop their endurance. Some of those sports were familiar to me at the outset. As a lifelong runner, I had a background in the traditional distance events (5K, 10K, and marathon) and could readily adapt to other sports like cycling and triathlon. Running, cycling, and triathlon also had rich histories of peer-reviewed physiological research, as well as books like *Daniels' Running Formula* to draw upon. In working with any moderately fit marathoner, I could use a combination of my previous running experience, scientific literature, and other coaches' guidance to comprehensively inform training. Thankfully, as a young coach I wound up in an environment that forced me outside sports I was familiar with, and that has made all the difference.

You learn the most when you are out of your comfort zone, and working with MMA fighters and NASCAR drivers was way out of my comfort zone. I didn't know anything about those sports, which makes it pretty hard to improve athlete performance based on sheer experience. These sports also had relatively little scientific literature to draw upon and few points of reference to inform training. As a result, I was forced to learn about the sports from the ground up. In order to figure out how endurance training could be applied to sports not traditionally mentioned alongside marathon running, cycling, or triathlon, I developed a method of first meticulously learning about the sport before diving into the x's and o's of coaching. I would peel apart the physiological and psychological demands of the sport using a combination of old-school observation and best practices borrowed from similar sports.

When our coaching team started working with NASCAR drivers, we'd never been inside of a race car, never attended a race, and didn't even knew the basic rule structure. So, our first order of business was to attend a routine practice alongside the engineers, pit crew, and the rest of the support system required to operate a NASCAR team. We rigged the drivers up with heart rate monitors and observed their breathing patterns over race radio to determine the cardiorespiratory stress during a race. It turns out that their heart and lungs are working as hard as any marathoner, so we designed training strategies for these athletes that leveraged proven training methods from other endurance disciplines. We had them train like marathoners and triathletes, complete with intervals, threshold runs, and long runs. We measured the temperatures in the car and inside the drivers' specially designed suits and quickly determined that the conditions are similar to a summer day in Death Valley (which ironically would be another environment I became quite familiar with). As a result, we also had them perform heat stress protocols in the sauna, not too dissimilar to any athlete preparing for a hot-weather event like the Western States 100 or Badwater 135. And you thought all there was to NASCAR racing was to sit down and turn left.

The results provided proof that endurance training techniques can improve performance in sports outside the traditional endurance sports. Reducing the physical strain on the drivers though improved cardiovascular fitness and heat tolerance improved their driving. The drivers were able to better control their cars and communicate with their team because fewer of their physiological resources were dedicated to fighting the demands of the event. All of these interventions were developed through observation and borrowing protocols from other sports, a tactic that would serve me well as I entered into the realm of ultramarathon coaching.

As ironic as it might sound now, ultrarunners were actually very late to the table when it came to adopting and accepting coaching. And it was not from a lack of trying. In the early 2000s I spent frustrating amounts of time trying to convince elite ultrarunners that coaching would be a good thing for them. Ultrarunning is a complicated affair, so in my mind it seemed clear that some professional guidance would do the sport's elite athletes some good. Alas, my pitches fell on deaf ears in those early years, and I got laughed out of more than several meetings.

Finally, in 2004 some of these athletes started to turn the corner and seek out professional coaching. Being that this was a new sport group to work with, I did what I always did with a new sport: I dug through copious amounts of research and looked for guidance. Except in this case, there was little to be found. The same year I started working with ultrarunners, there were exactly six research papers on the subject. No books on ultramarathon training existed. Any guidance I could find had to be mined from blogs, anecdotes, and the infamous ultra listserv (a message board for ultrarunners that the old-timers will remember fondly). So, absent any scientific guidance, just like with the NASCAR drivers, I went and observed. I went to races, paced athletes, spoke with those who were successful, and started running ultramarathons myself, all in an effort to understand the sport better. I also borrowed best practices from cycling, triathlon, and even cross-country skiing, because in many cases the demands from those sports overlap with ultrarunning.

Developing training strategies through observation and educated guessing works to an extent, particularly when it is all you have. And I have to say, the athletes I worked with in those early years did far better than anticipated. They thrived, won races around the globe, and achieved success that far outpaced their peers. People started to notice, so much so that a cottage industry for ultrarunning coaching sprouted and blossomed. As the sport grew and elite performances improved, the pace of research into what constitutes ultramarathon performance increased. All of this was good for athletes. Better information led to evolutions in coaching practices across the entire sport and more information for athletes to use on their own . . . but it was scattered. I wanted a way to consolidate it all. I wanted something that would present the training methodologies I had observed and curated side by side with emerging research. I wanted something that could synthesize best practices, the art of coaching, and emerging science to provide a comprehensive guide for ultramarathon athletes and their coaches. And for the first fifteen years I coached ultrarunners, this amalgamation failed to emerge.

The first edition of this book was written, in large part, to create the book I wanted as a coach and athlete. I sought to create a reference that would inspire, inform, and guide ultrarunners and coaches along their journeys. I wanted to create a book that I personally would have turned to when I first started working with ultrarunners, much like I used *Daniels' Running Formula* and *The Lore of Running* early in my coaching career. By any measuring stick, that effort was a success. Ultrarunners all along the spectrum of novices to elites finally had a book that blended science and practice. They had a manual to guide them, regardless of whether they were training for a 50K in the desert, 200 miles in the mountains, or any distance and terrain in between. Tens of thousands of copies of the first edition of this book have been sold. It's been translated into multiple languages, and I've traveled around the world to give lectures on its contents. I've even had to recruit, screen, and train an entire ultrarunning coaching department (which at the time this book is published sits twelve coaches strong) to satiate the demand for athletes wanting to be coached.

Despite that success, the first edition of this book had some detractors. The training methods came under scrutiny, as they rightfully should, and at times by influential and well-known coaches. In 2016, just before the first edition of this book went to press, I was profiled by *Trail Runner Magazine* for a feature in their annual "Dirt" edition. The feature contained the normal Q&A-style interview, complete with a tour of my office and physiology lab, as well as interviews with many of the athletes I have worked with. Unbeknownst to me at the time, the author also gathered the opinions of trail running coaches David Roche, Ian Torrence, and Ian Sharman. Mr. Roche described some of the training strategies I use as chasing "marginal gains," which is a contentious strategy that aims to compound many small incremental improvements to potentially create a larger meaningful benefit. Mr. Torrence and Mr. Sharman were critical of some of the strategic underpinnings I use for ultrarunners that are derived from different sports such as cycling.

Since the first edition of this book was published, some of those criticisms have echoed. I've been told "you don't believe in strength training," "ultrarunners are not cross-country skiers," and the like. The fact of the matter is that most of these criticisms are ill-informed, shortsighted, poorly thought out, and lacking context. For example, anyone who has followed the hundreds of articles, interviews, and other pieces of content I have posted over my career knows that I preach a consistent theme of focusing on what matters most for improvement before chasing any "marginal gains." Additionally, there are certain, limited circumstances where many marginal gains *can* mean the difference between an athlete winning and losing, or making a cutoff or not. Ultramarathon training is highly nuanced and rewards coaches and athletes who are open to new information and willing to accept that there may be multiple paths to a successful outcome.

The contents of this book exemplify this way of thinking. As you will come to find out, you can weigh the benefits you get from a sauna, strength training, or any other "marginal" intervention against one another and make choices on which gains to chase and which to forgo. Furthermore, while ultrarunning is a unique sport, it is not so dissimilar from cycling, cross-country skiing, triathlon, marathon running, or any other endurance sport that we can't borrow and adapt research and best practices to better train ultramarathon runners. The fact of the matter is, there is far more information on training athletes in those traditional endurance sports than training ultrarunners, and there likely always will be. The key is finding the nuance in what can be applied across different endurance disciplines, what needs to be adapted from one sport to another, and what doesn't apply at all.

Our understanding of ultramarathon running continues to evolve, and this book had to evolve as well. We know far more now about ultramarathon performance than we did at the time of the original publication. We've learned more about concepts like how neuromuscular fatigue likely plays an important role in ultramarathon performances, low-carbohydrate diets impact running economy, and hyponatremia (low blood sodium) is more often caused by overdrinking fluids that do not contain sodium than not consuming enough sodium. The six scientific papers published in 2004 have now expanded to more than one hundred per year, providing a growing trove of information coaches and athletes have the opportunity to digest and synthesize into their training.

With that as a backdrop, here's what's new in the second edition of *Training Essentials for Ultrarunning*: almost everything. In fact, more than 75 percent of the content has been revised, expanded, or written anew. Among other additions, there is a section devoted to low-carbohydrate diets, an entire chapter on the benefits (or lack thereof) of strength training, a chapter on mental skills for ultrarunning, and an in-depth section devoted specifically to considerations for female athletes. And to make sure I, as a male coach, wasn't unconsciously biasing the recommendations for female athletes, as has often happened in various areas of research, I brought in my coaching colleague Corrine Malcolm to specifically pen that section. This book also went through greater scientific scrutiny from Nick Tiller, PhD, and Stephanie Howe, PhD, both ultrarunners who are well respected in their fields. This expands upon the scientific guidance provided by pre-eminent biomechanist Rodger Kram, PhD, and former Western States medical director Martin Hoffman, MD, in the first edition of this book. There are nearly 400 references to scientific literature, all of which can be found in the book's references section.

Despite the additions, you still will not find a stock training plan in this book. If you are expecting to see a page you can tear out, put on your refrigerator, and blindly follow for the next twenty weeks, you are going to be sorely disappointed. So, don't say I didn't warn you, and please ask for your money back now before you leave a one-star Amazon review. Better yet, read the book, and at the end, if you hate it, email me and I will gladly refund you, no questions asked.

This book will walk you through the steps of solving your personal puzzle of ultramarathon performance. It will take you on a journey, step by step, on how ultramarathons work, what you can do to better prepare for them, and how you can thrive during the process. At the end of that journey, I want you to come away well informed and confident about whatever ultramarathon adventure you have chosen. I want you to understand what it takes to make yourself a better ultrarunner. I want you to have enough information and wisdom to create and adjust your own training, nutrition, and ultramarathon game plan, and to be confident with the process. I want you to dog-ear the pages in this book that have particular meaning to you and scribble notes in the margins. Above all else, I want you to be inspired by the training processes you uncover and the realization that you are ready to crush your most audacious goals. After all, ultrarunning is a ridiculously difficult sport, one that is rife with pitfalls and hazards that confound even the most seasoned athletes. Preparation is your greatest ally and most powerful resource, and the information in this book will help you be as prepared as possible when you step up to the start line.

Finally, I would be remiss not to mention that this book does not have any sponsors, endorsers, or other sources of financial or business entanglement. In 2018, I made the conscious decision to alleviate myself from any such conflicts of interest, real or perceived, and I have to say that the move was quite liberating. In today's world of paid partnerships, Instagram influencers, and implied endorsements, it is nearly impossible for the end consumer to ascertain fact from fiction. While there are many athletes and influencers that authentically use and endorse the products they are peddling, there are just as many that wear a different brand of shoes on their feet, have a different drink in their bottle, or are just taking the endorsement money and running. So, I decided to avoid these conflicts altogether and turned down every endorsement opportunity that has come my way since (much to the dismay of my bank account). As a consequence, if I recommend something it is because I believe in the product or method based on its merits, not because someone is paying me to do so. This freedom also allows me to opine on products and practices that are, quite frankly, junk and pseudoscientific garbage. And I certainly don't mind calling them out as such.

To take it a step further, I acquired the rights to self-publish this book in order to make it as long, detailed, and accurate as possible. (Plus I wanted to say whatever I pleased, which is problematic with even the most liberal of publishers.) Make no mistake, these actions cost me a copious amount of time and a fair amount of money. I hired and paid editors, contributors, printers, and the like out of my own pocket in order to get this edition of the book off of the ground. But the trade-off is worth it, and I wouldn't change a thing. In my profession, I am ultimately a purveyor of advice. Athletes trust in the words I write and say. Based on that trust, they take action from those words. I honor that trust as a sacred bond between me and the athletes reading these pages. So, rest assured the content that follows contains the truth, the whole truth, and nothing but the truth in a pure, raw, unentangled, and unadulterated fashion all the way down to the last sentence.

So, if you are ready, willing, and able, let's get right into it!

Oro Mine
Anderson Pit
Bowen Mine
Franklin Pit
Franklin Pit
BM 4067
Volcano
HAWK
BREECE
West
East
CODFISH
Drummond Pit
Spring
TRAIL
Air Shaft
CHICKEN
ROAD
DITCH
WHEELER
Turkey Hill Mine
Manhattan Mine
Spring
El Dorado
CHANCE
DEADWOOD
FORK
Golden Gate Mine
Daniel Webster Mine
El Dorado Hill Mine
Footbridge
Rainbow Land Mine
LAST
CHICKEN
Burns No 1 Mine
Poor
Canyon
BLUFF
Cem
Sugar Loaf
Burns No 2 Mine
Eastman Mine
Michigan Bluff
Cem
Historic Marker
BM 3531
Mans
MICHIGAN
Anna Sue Mine
Cem
Canyon
BIG GUN
DIGGINGS
Mary Anna Mine
AMERICAN
FORK
MIDDLE
Skunk
BM 2731
ROAD
Mosquito Ridge Lookout
3509
FORK
Canyon
Spring

CHAPTER 2

The Physiology of a Better Engine

The human body is an incredible machine. You take in food, an all-encompassing term that covers everything from fresh berries to a Big Mac, and within minutes convert it (or at least some of it) into usable energy. When it comes to accessing that energy, you are able to go from the sedentary state of reading this book to sprinting, if necessary, at a moment's notice. And as you run longer or change your pace, your body seamlessly adjusts how it produces energy based on how quickly you are demanding it and the energy sources available.

To do this, the human body has three primary energy systems that produce adenosine triphosphate (ATP), which is the energy currency the body uses to power all activities. The quickest source is the immediate energy system of stored ATP and creatine phosphate (ATP-PCr), followed by the glycolytic (anaerobic) system and the aerobic system. All three energy systems produce ATP, which releases energy when one of its three phosphate bonds is broken. The resulting adenosine diphosphate (ADP) is then resynthesized to ATP so it can be broken down again, and again, and again. All three energy systems are always working together synergistically in varying amounts (Figure 2.1); there is no on/off switch, and at any given time the amount of energy produced by each system is based on demand. These three energy systems are fundamental to endurance training, and although you don't need a physiology degree to be a good ultra-runner, it is nonetheless helpful to understand the systems you're training.

The Immediate Energy System: ATP-PCr

The ATP-PCr system supports high-power efforts that last less than eight to ten seconds. You use it when you have to jump out of the way of a speeding bus, and from an athletic standpoint it's most important in power sports like sprinting, mixed martial arts, or powerlifting. In endurance running this system is used mostly for explosive movements like jumping across a creek or bounding up a series of boulders. During those few seconds, you demand energy faster than either the glycolytic or aerobic energy system can deliver it. The ATP-PCr system yields immediate energy because ATP, the energy-yielding molecule, is stored directly in the muscle. This very limited supply that is stored in your muscles is available for immediate use because it doesn't require the multiple steps that the anaerobic and aerobic systems require to produce ATP. Endurance athletes don't rely heavily on this system, and it is typically adequately developed through normal training.

The Lactic Acid System

The lactic acid system is the high-speed express lane for delivering energy quickly in times of heightened demand. This is the system people often refer to as "anaerobic," which literally means "without oxygen." This terminology causes confusion because it implies that the body has stopped using oxygen to produce energy, which is not the case. As exercise intensity increases, there comes a point at which the demand for energy outstrips the aerobic system's ability to produce ATP in working muscles. Then comes a hill. Or you spot a fellow racer and pick up the pace. The demand for energy increases further, and in order to meet the demand, the mitochondria's aerobic functions are supported by energy derived from anaerobic processes. Although the actual process involves many steps, to put it simply, where aerobic metabolism delivers all of the energy available from a molecule of glucose (sugar), glycolysis converts glucose into lactate through a process that delivers some of the energy available in glucose, but more quickly.

Lactate is a normal by-product in the breakdown of carbohydrate (glucose) to ATP during glycolysis. As lactate is produced via glycolysis, 75 percent of it enters the bloodstream and is shuttled to the mitochondria, where it can be utilized as a substrate for energy production (Brooks 1986). The remaining 25 percent is sent to the liver to be repurposed into glucose via a process called "gluconeogenesis," literally "creating new glucose." Lactate has been misunderstood for years. It has been blamed for the burning sensation in your muscles when you surge above your sustainable pace. It has been blamed for delayed-onset muscle soreness. People have tried to massage it away, flush it out, and buffer it in (largely failed) attempts to enhance or prolong exercise. We now understand that increases in lactate are not the cause of fatigue, they merely coincide with it, and the best way to utilize lactate is to reintegrate it back into normal aerobic metabolism to complete the process of breaking it down into energy, water, and carbon dioxide.

Under normal conditions, when aerobic energy supply meets energy demand, lactate clearance from the blood occurs at a rate faster than it accumulates. Once lactate production outstrips the body's ability to buffer it, lactate begins to accumulate in the blood. This is referred to as the "lactate threshold" and indicates a change in the way energy is being derived from predominantly aerobic means to now include a greater contribution from anaerobic sources. In short, this threshold is the intensity at which an athlete can sustain his effort for an extended period of time. By increasing the intensity or pace at which this occurs, an athlete is able to improve performance. Thus, this is one of the primary outcomes of endurance training. This training adaptation also enables you to recover from hard efforts more quickly, because deriving energy from glycolysis is like buying energy on credit. You're getting the currency you need as you need it, but you don't have unlimited credit, and sooner rather than later you're going to have to pay back every cent you borrowed. What's more, you have to cut back on spending while you're paying it back, which means you have to slow down.

As an endurance athlete, one of the key adaptations is an improvement in the ability to integrate lactate into aerobic energy production so it can be oxidized completely. The faster you can process lactate, the more work you can perform before fatigue-inducing anaerobic metabolites (not lactate) accumulate in the muscle and blood. Or, in the financial analogy, a stronger aerobic system puts more cash (aerobic metabolism) in your pocket so you're not so quick to use credit.

The Aerobic System

The aerobic system is remarkable. It produces the majority of the energy we use for daily life and exercise; can burn carbohydrate, fat, and protein simultaneously; and can regulate the mixture it burns based on fuel availability and energy demand. It can even burn protein, although that's not used as a significant source of energy unless you have very low energy reserves. The aerobic system is a flex-fuel engine that's clean and efficient; when the aerobic system is done with a molecule of carbohydrate, the only waste products are water and carbon dioxide. In comparison, the lactic acid system discussed earlier produces energy faster but can only utilize carbohydrate, produces less ATP from every molecule it processes, and produces metabolites that lower body pH and interfere with muscle contractions.

For an endurance athlete, increasing the amount of oxygen the body can transport and utilize is one of the primary goals of training, because oxygen is the limiting factor in how quickly you can produce energy aerobically. On the transportation side, your body's amount of hemoglobin, which is a component of your blood, largely dictates how much oxygen you can take from your lungs and deliver to working muscles. Once oxygen has been transported to the muscles, it is then utilized by the mitochondria during the process of energy conversion. The mitochondria are a muscle cell's power plants. They harness the oxygen and fuel (carbohydrate and fat) and convert those substrates into useable energy. Training improves both the transportation and utilization sides of the equation.

VO_2 Max

When the body is delivering and utilizing as much oxygen as it possibly can and exercise intensity reaches its absolute peak, you're at VO_2 max. VO_2 max, or maximum aerobic capacity, is measured in liters of oxygen per minute taken up and utilized by the muscles. Since VO_2 max varies by body size and muscle mass, the measurement unit mL/kg/min is used to compare across different athletes because it takes body weight into account.

VO_2 max is one of the indicators (but not the only indicator) of your potential as an endurance athlete. And while a higher VO_2 max is generally a good thing for any individual athlete, an exceedingly high VO_2 max doesn't automatically guarantee you'll become a champion. All it means is you have a big engine. You need a big engine to be an elite athlete, but no matter what size engine you start with, you can optimize your performance with effective training.

It takes a great effort to reach intensities near VO_2 max, and VO_2 max-specific workouts generate an enormous amount of lactate and burn energy tremendously fast. But the reward is worth the effort, because increasing your pace at VO_2 max (the pace you can run while utilizing the maximum amount of oxygen possible) and your absolute VO_2 max (how many liters of oxygen you can utilize per minute) give you the physiological underpinnings to run faster at any distance. Ultramarathon athletes sometimes suffer from a one-pace mentality. When your goal is to keep moving for fifteen to thirty hours, it seems to make the most sense to primarily use endurance and some lactate threshold workouts to get to the fitness level necessary to sustain that effort. It's the sustainable aspect that keeps too many athletes from venturing into more intense efforts. The perception is that the sport is all about making steady forward progress and that one only needs longer long runs to ensure success. While volume is important, intensities at and near your VO_2 max are also critical for building your engine.

The Endurance String Theory

Delineating the various ways your body can produce energy is both a blessing and a curse. On the positive side, knowing how each system works gives us the information necessary to design training that maximizes the specific physiological adaptations we desire. On the downside, the same information has inadvertently led people to believe that these systems operate independently of each other. Sports scientists, coaches, and even the folks who made your heart rate monitor have told you that training in "zone something-or-other" will target your lactic acid system and increase your pace at lactate threshold. And although that is true, the lactic acid system isn't the only one doing the work at that intensity, nor is it the only one that will reap a training benefit.

Energy production is always coming through all possible pathways, but your demand for energy determines the relative contribution from each. At low to moderate intensities, such as 40 to 50 percent of VO_2 max or an easy endurance run, the vast majority of your energy comes from the aerobic system (mitochondria breaking down primarily fat and some carbohydrate). As the intensity level increases, a greater amount of energy is derived anaerobically. Energy contribution from glycolysis ramps up even further as you approach intensities near and above your lactate threshold, which can be anywhere from 65 to 85 percent of VO_2 max for a particular athlete. Because glycolysis uses only glucose, the overall percentage of energy coming from carbohydrate rises dramatically as intensity increases from lactate threshold to VO_2 max. The body is still using fat, but at a lower rate because the breakdown of fat into energy is much slower.

Rather than seeing your various energy pathways as separate and distinct, it's better to think of them as segments of one continuous string, arranged based on the relative contributions of energy derived from each as the duration of an all-out task increases. At one end of the spectrum, for very short efforts lasting eight to ten seconds, is a small segment represented by energy contributions primarily from the ATP-PCr system. After that is the lactic acid system, which can provide a lot of energy at full gas for efforts

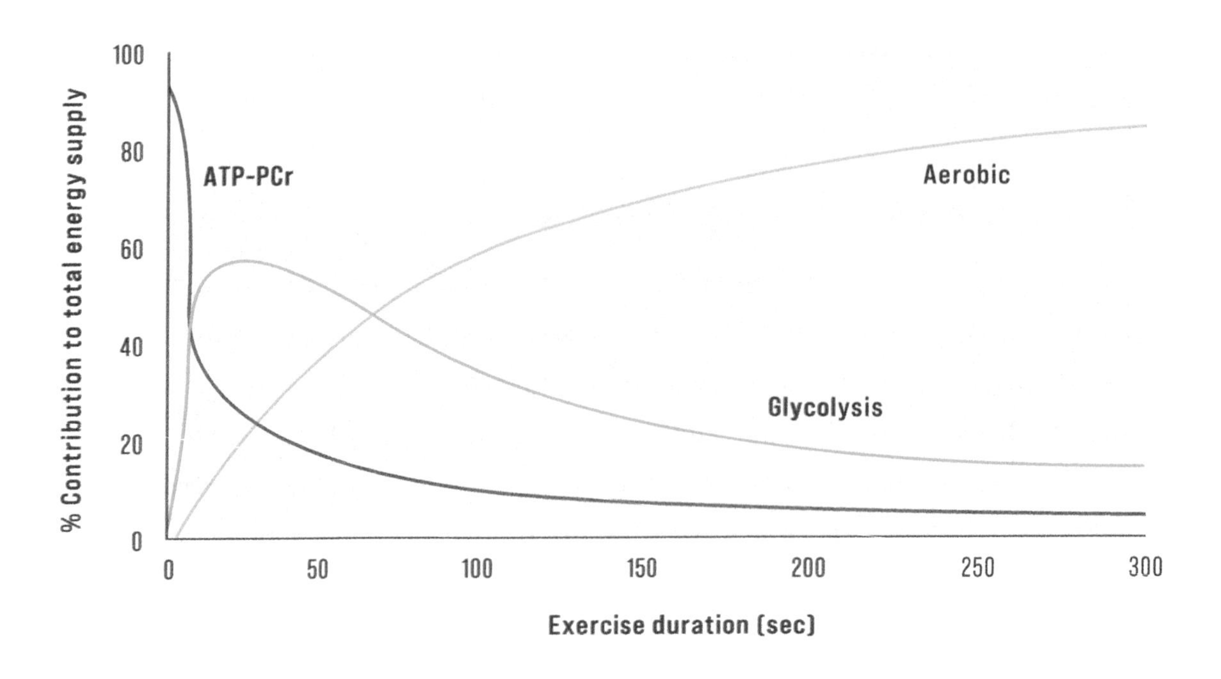

FIGURE 2.1 The contributions of the three energy systems (ATP-PCr, glycolysis, and aerobic) to energy production over time (seconds) during an all-out effort. Adapted from Gastin 2001.

WHAT ABOUT AEROBIC DEFICIENCY SYNDROME?

THE TERM "AEROBIC DEFICIENCY SYNDROME" (ADS) was coined by Phil Maffetone as a deleterious condition whereby your aerobic system is "deficient" (Maffetone 2015). He has described it as a "devastating" condition for athletes that affects "millions of people." The result of this syndrome, according to Maffetone, is "reduced endurance," "quickened fatigue," "loss of aerobic speed," and "a variety of chronic conditions." Sound pretty terrible? Yeah, I'd be afraid of it, too.

This apparent syndrome has also been regurgitated among writers, bloggers, coaches, athletes, and anyone else that can't think for themselves as a justification for avoiding high-intensity intervals and only performing very low-intensity exercise.

Let's examine these claims.

First, as of this book's publishing, the term "aerobic deficiency syndrome" appears nowhere in any scientific literature. It's not in any textbook or scientific journal article. Contrast that with overtraining syndrome (oftentimes referred to as underperformance syndrome), which has been extensively described in scientific literature and has a robust consensus among athletes, coaches, and sports scientists.

Furthermore, as the name implies, people "suffering" from ADS apparently have a deficient aerobic system stemming from too much high-intensity work. The fact of the matter is, after you get past just a minute or two of an all-out effort, nearly 100 percent of the energy contributions will come from an aerobic pathway (see Figure 2.1). Thus, for any endurance athlete, even if you are doing high-intensity interval work, you are still deriving almost all of that energy aerobically. So, the notion that your "aerobic system is deficient" is complete and total nonsense. Aerobic deficiency syndrome is just a fictitious combination of words, is not described anywhere in any scientific literature, and does not accurately describe anything in endurance training.

Bottom line, this is just a made-up term. Don't be fearmongered into not doing high-intensity work because of a fake syndrome.

lasting less than about two minutes. Finally, as duration increases further, there is a large segment representing the aerobic system, which theoretically could power your muscles at a moderate intensity level forever if it had sufficient oxygen and fuel. Improving fitness in one system is like lifting the string in that region—all other areas of the string rise, too. The extents of these ancillary improvements vary based on the system you initially targeted. For instance, targeting VO_2 max has a greater lifting effect on lactate-threshold fitness and aerobic endurance than training at aerobic intensities has on lifting lactate threshold or VO_2 max. Ultimately, all of the systems are interconnected, and even the most narrowly focused training will have upstream and downstream effects on your physiology.

Fundamental Principles of Training

No two athletes are exactly the same, but we all use the same mechanisms to produce energy. Similarly, no two athletes adapt to training the exact same way, but effective training is based on a common set of principles. When you distill the world's most successful training programs across all sports, you arrive at five distinct principles of training:

1. OVERLOAD AND RECOVERY
2. PROGRESSION
3. INDIVIDUALITY
4. SPECIFICITY
5. SYSTEMATIC APPROACH

OVERLOAD AND RECOVERY

Fundamentally, training is designed to leverage the body's normal response to stress (or overload). The human body is designed to respond to overload, and as long as you properly overload a system and allow time for recovery, that system will adapt and be ready for the same or greater stress in the future. To achieve positive training effects, this principle must be applied both to individual training sessions and to entire periods of your training. For instance, an interval workout around your lactate threshold must be intense enough and long enough so that the total stimulus is great enough to make your body say, "OK, I got it. I need to be bigger, stronger, and faster than I am right now so that the next time this happens, I am more equipped for the task."

Proper overload and subsequent recovery are incredibly important for ultrarunners. Most ultrarunners will come into the sport with some running background. The significance of this is that they have previously gone through the early stages of development where improvement and PRs seemingly happen every week. Runners with more than four years of experience (most ultrarunners fit into this category) will know that as you gain experience, improvement is harder and harder to come by. Striving for those gains means finding ways to increase overload, often within limited training time, while also scheduling adequate recovery. As a result, training and workout architecture will matter more for an experienced athlete than for a novice athlete who can improve simply by not screwing it up. The various workouts, short-range plan, and long-range plan described later in this book are designed so that you can realize an appropriate amount of overload and then combine that with appropriate recovery in order to continue to see improvement regardless of your experience level.

Many novice athletes start out with haphazard or scattered training, but they nevertheless make steady gains because they are beginners. Just the act of training leads to significant improvement when you're starting out. But that progress stalls relatively quickly because you reach the point where the stimulus applied with each individual workout is not high enough or consistent enough to lead to further adaptation. Focusing your training on one area for a number of weeks, as you can do with a block of lactate threshold training, concentrates workload and training time to create a stimulus large enough to improve performance in that area. This becomes even more important for ultra-endurance athletes, because you are already adapted to a high overall workload. To make progress in any one aspect of fitness, you not only need to focus on it but also need to reduce focus on other areas during the same period. For example, when working on VO_2 max it's important to reduce overall volume to adequately recover between sessions and maintain the quality of each workout.

On the other end of the spectrum, there's recovery. Recovery, which is covered in

HOW LONG SHOULD INTERVALS BE?

POP QUIZ: EACH OF THE INTERVAL SETS BELOW features the exact same duration of work, but only one is the most effective for improving VO_2 max. Which one?

A. 12 x 1 minute at maximum intensity with 1 minute recovery between intervals

B. 4 x 3 minutes at maximum intensity with 3 minutes recovery between intervals

C. 2 x 6 minutes at maximum intensity with 6 minutes recovery between intervals

Intervals that work are long enough to stress the desired physiology and separated by recovery periods that let an athlete repeat the effort. Intervals that don't work are either too short or too long and separated by recovery periods that are too short or too long. They might be hard but don't have a focus in a way that is productive. You get tired but ultimately not stronger or faster.

The point of intervals is to maximize the body's exposure to intensity over time. For intervals where the primary purpose is to improve VO_2 max , they need to be long enough to achieve and sustain an effort above 90 percent of your VO_2 max (as measured by oxygen consumption), which takes anywhere from sixty to ninety seconds. The figure below is from a study that examined the physiological response to one-, two-, four-, and six-minute intervals with 1:1 work-rest ratios. Though each combination represents twenty-four minutes of interval work, you can see the differences in cardiovascular response as the intervals get longer. They found that athletes achieve their highest oxygen consumption during the four-minute intervals. In practice, intervals between two and four minutes are long enough for an athlete to ramp up to VO_2 max intensity and maintain it for the duration of the interval. When athletes pace themselves through six-minute intervals, they don't reach as high an intensity.

OPTIMAL WORK-REST RATIOS

The interval duration is one thing to get right; the work-rest ratio is another. For intervals targeting VO_2 max improvement, two to four minutes at a 1:1 work-rest ratio works best, as it maximizes recovery from the previous interval without extending the overall workout duration and thus compromising the intensity you can achieve during

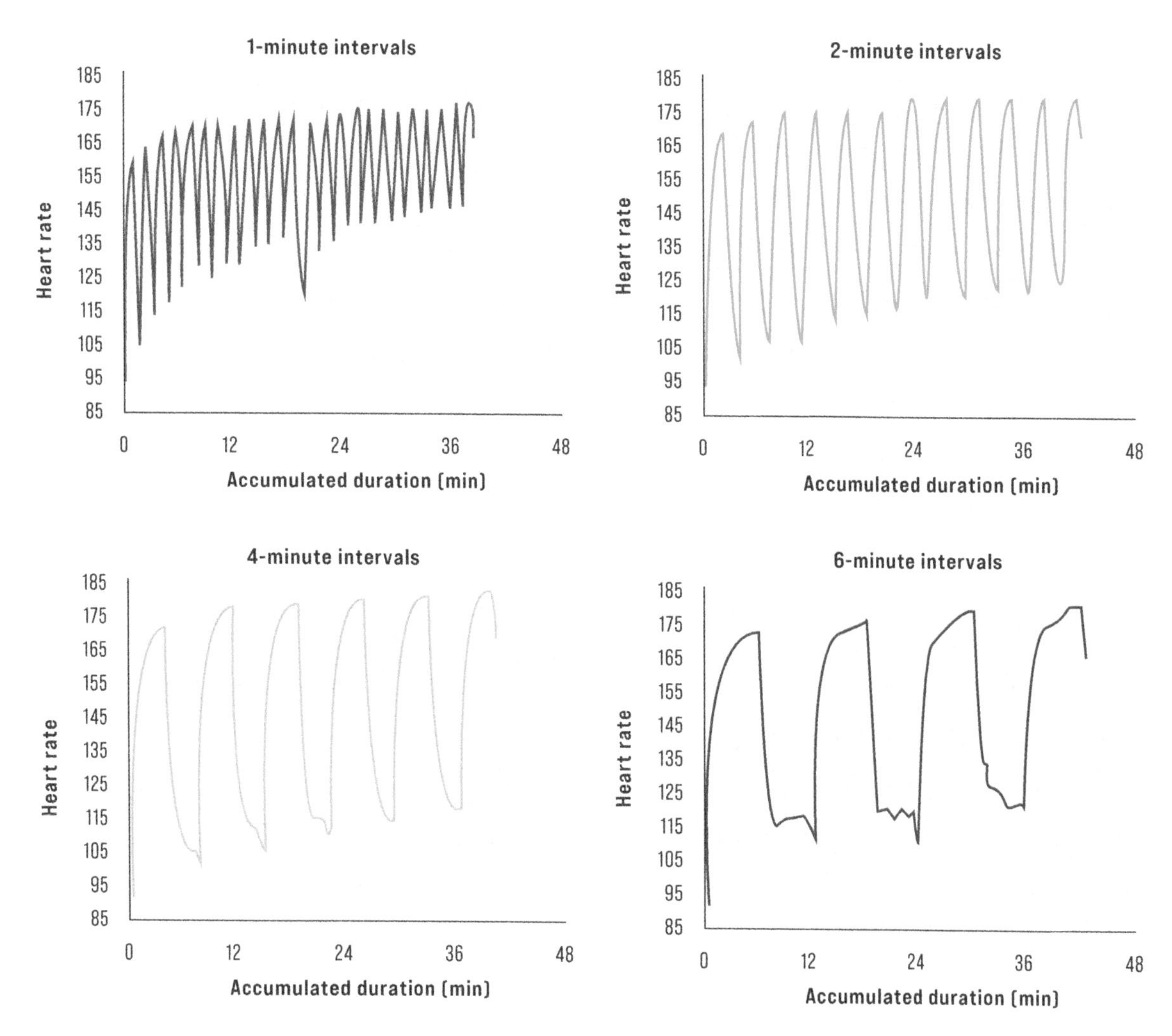

FIGURE 2.2 Mean heart rate responses during (A) 1-minute, (B) 2-minute, (C) 4-minute, and (D) 6-minute intervals. Adapted from Seiler and Sjusren 2004.

the rest of the interval set. As intervals get longer and the intensity drops, athletes don't need as much recovery relative to the interval length before they are ready to repeat the effort. That's why the work-rest ratio for intervals at lactate threshold (TempoRun) is 2:1 and grows even greater for high-end aerobic intervals (SteadyStateRun). (TempoRuns and SteadyStateRuns will be further defined in Chapter 9.)

Getting back to the original question on the most effective VO_2 max workout, the answer is B (4 x 3 minutes). The intervals in A are too short to reach VO_2 max and stay there long enough to be effective. The intervals in C are so long most athletes would pace themselves at too low an intensity to optimally train VO_2 max.

depth in Chapter 8, is not merely the absence of workouts but rather a crucial component of training. Days off should not be viewed as missed opportunities to get in another run. In reality, the periods between your workouts are when the really important adaptations such as plasma volume expansion, mitochondrial biogenesis, and red blood cell volume increases happen in your body. When you're in the middle of a training run, you're not improving your fitness; you're just applying stress and accumulating fatigue. But when you kick up your feet, sleep, hydrate, and provide your body with adequate and proper nutrition, that's when your fitness improves. It's not possible to train hard and gain fitness without proper rest and recovery. So, the next time your Type A buddy who's trained every day of the past four years chastises you for sitting on the couch or going for a walk with the dog instead of a sixty-minute run, just smile and tell her you're busy adapting.

PROGRESSION

Training must progressively move forward for continued gains in performance to occur. Time and intensity are the two most significant variables you can use to increase your workload. For instance, you can increase the number of hours you devote to training (which is training volume) or increase the overall intensity of your workouts. You can use time and intensity to manipulate training in a near limitless combination. No matter what you choose, the end result must generate a training stimulus great enough to elicit adaptions from your heart, muscles, blood vessels, bones, gut, connective tissue—basically everything. These are not static adaptations, however. Once you adapt and grow stronger, you have to again manipulate the time and intensity variables to further increase workload and generate another training stimulus. In other words, it will take a bigger workload to overload a stronger system.

The timeline for progression can take several forms. Many novice marathon training programs will use a weekly progression structure, meaning the volume (the amount of time or miles you do) and volume of intensity (the amount of time spent doing hard efforts) increase every week with periodic recovery weeks. Practically speaking, these runners would do a thirty-minute Tempo workout one week, a forty-minute Tempo the next week, and a forty-five-minute Tempo the week after that assuming that some sort of positive adaptation takes place in those intervening weeks that enables the athlete to handle higher and higher workloads.

This type of architecture, while fine for many athletes, has a few glaring flaws upon further examination. First, for most cardiovascular- and endurance-related adaptations, the time course of said adaptations takes weeks, not days, to complete. That being said, there are very few things going on physiologically that would result in any meaningful improvement between weeks one, two, and three. Second, the hardest Tempo workouts (forty-five minutes) would be happening during the week of the most cumulative fatigue, presenting a potential "worst of both worlds" scenario (highest level of fatigue coupled with the hardest workout). Finally, the athlete is set up to do their easiest hard workout (as oxymoronic as that sounds) at the time when they are the freshest (week one, presumably after a recovery week). It is for these reasons that I primarily prefer that volume and/or volume of intensity generally decrease throughout a phase, then increase (or progress) subsequently after a recovery week. Using the above example, the forty-five-minute Tempo run would be on week one, forty-minute Tempo on week two, and thirty-minute Tempo on week three when the athlete has the most cumulative fatigue. In this way, progression can be viewed through the lens of a few or even several weeks at a time. This concept will be discussed more in Chapter 12.

Neither training time nor intensity is limitless, even for professional athletes. There are only twenty-four hours in the day, and the human body can only be pushed so hard. Professional athletes—across the range of endurance sports—are pretty much maxed out in terms of the annual hours they can accumulate while still performing at a high level. While some case studies have shown that simply adding low-intensity training volume for highly trained or elite athletes results in continued improvement (Solli et al. 2017), others contradict this, suggesting that for athletes who are already trained, adding more volume may not lead to additional improvements in VO_2 max, power at lactate threshold, or mitochondrial density (Laursen et al. 2002).

Unlike professional athletes who can design their lives around training, most amateur athletes are limited in terms of the time they can devote to training. For almost everyone lining up at an ultramarathon, running is a priority that has to be balanced with—and almost always comes after—many other priorities. The other commitments in your life mean you have to do what you can in the time you have. To achieve progression within the weekly training hours you have available, you have to manipulate all of

SEQUENCE OF TRAINING

PROGRESSION IS OFTEN CONFUSED WITH "FASTER" in the context of the sequence of training. In other words, as the year progresses, most athletes think that their training should progress to higher and higher intensities, which is common with runners training for events like the 5K, 10K, and marathon. In those disciplines, beginning with a slower "aerobic base" followed by higher intensities and ultimately culminating with intervals at a race-specific intensity is the norm. However, that does not mean that the sequence of training has to progress from lower-intensity aerobic training to medium-intensity training and finally to higher-intensity training. Rather, progression should be thought of as occurring within each intensity so that the system gets stronger and needs a bigger stimulus (volume and intensity) in order to adapt.

Starting off with low intensity and moving to higher intensities is a stereotypical—and flawed—way of organizing training, particularly for ultrarunners. As will be discussed in Chapter 10, an ultrarunner's training does not have to move through this order of low to medium to high intensity. Rather, it should move from developing the least-specific aspects of your ultramarathon physiology to the most specific.

the tools you have available at some point or another. This means increasing the overall training time, types of intensity, and volume of intensity.

Individuality

The individuality principle simply states that the training program that works for you, right down to the individual workouts and interval intensities, has to be based on your physiological and personal needs. Training is not a one-size-fits-all product. All parts of your program—the total mileage, the number and type of intervals, and even the terrain—must be personalized. That doesn't mean that you can't train with your friends or training partners; it just means that while you're with them, you have to stay true to your own program.

The individuality principle is another reason there are no full-length training plans in this book. As I'll say many times throughout the book, ultrarunning is not just a longer marathon. If I were writing a marathon running or Olympic-distance triathlon training book, I'd include training plans, because a generalized training plan can work for events of those lengths. Whenever I have tried to write generalized training plans for ultrarunning events, they just don't work that well. A training plan for Western States 100-Mile Endurance Run, Hardrock, Wasatch Front 100 Mile Endurance Run, and similar races would have to be thirty weeks long, minimum. With a time frame that long, a prewritten training plan is bound to under- or overestimate an individual runner's response to training and her ability to stick to the schedule. It will end up being way too hard and will run you into the ground, or way too easy and will not adequately prepare you for the demands of the event. In addition, it's impossible for a static training plan to fully consider the milieu of other training considerations including nutrition, equipment, psychological preparedness, environmental considerations, pacing strategies, and the like.

Ideally, every athlete would work with a coach and get a training program built from scratch, but personal coaching is not an option for everyone. The workouts and concepts in this book are rooted in the principles I use to coach my athletes, and you'll be able to apply the individuality principle to these workouts as well when you establish your personal training program and fit the workouts into your busy work and family schedules.

Specificity

Your training must resemble the activity you want to perform. In a broad sense, this means that if you want to be a runner, you should spend the vast majority of your training time running. In a narrower sense, it means you have to determine the exact demands of the activity you wish to perform and tailor your training to address those demands, particularly as any critical races draw near. Conversely, it also means that your training is going to prepare you optimally for specific events and activities.

The importance of specificity becomes clear when you look at how competitive ultrarunning has evolved over the past decade. The speed at the front of the pack has increased dramatically, so much so that running a course record pace from a decade ago might land you well outside of the top ten now. Is this because today's runners are that much more talented than runners from ten years ago? Are they running more miles than athletes did ten years ago? Are the shoes that much better? Are the energy bars that much better? No, none of the above. Athletes at the top of the sport are getting faster because their training has become more specific to the unique demands of the events they are training for. And the more we have learned about tailoring training to those demands, the more athletes of all ability levels can benefit from the same knowledge.

Systematic Approach

When it comes to achieving high-performance fitness, you need a training program that integrates and addresses all the principles of training. A systematic approach to training integrates all the crucial components: overload and recovery, progression, individuality, and specificity. Focusing on any one of the principles while neglecting others will take your training off course.

Ultrarunners devote a lot of time to training, so it is unfortunate when I see athletes wasting much of that time with ineffective workouts (see the earlier sidebar "Sequence of Training") and poorly planned programs. Workouts that are neither hard enough to contribute to positive adaptations nor easy enough to provide adequate recovery just contribute to fatigue. Scattered training plans that jump from one intensity to the next before anything has substantially developed make athletes work hard without creating meaningful progress. It's all bang, but very little buck.

In order to leverage the benefits of each of the previous four principles of training, they need to be combined into a systematic approach to improvement. Appropriate levels of overload and recovery must be established based on your individual needs and manipulated so that you achieve progression. And a training program doesn't do you much good unless it prepares you for the specific and unique demands of your goal event.

You can apply any of the previous four principles individually, but you're not likely to be satisfied with the results. A common failure of training is achieving mastery of overload and recovery and progression while completely neglecting individuality and specificity. I see this most often with the data junkies, the athletes so focused on numbers, graphs, and training logs that all they care about is the trend of the data, even if it's leading them away from the fitness they need to perform at their best in their goal event.

Another problematic scenario is created by neglecting individuality and progression.

This is typically an issue for social runners, athletes who value the social environment of the running community so highly that they substitute socializing for progression and individuality, which causes their training progress to stall or even collapse. These athletes are essentially going through the motions or treading water. Preparing for an ultramarathon requires a lot of focus for a significant period of time, and that level of focus may not be sustainable year after year. Therefore, a balance between focused training and some social running is ideal for most runners. I would much rather see runners reduce their focus on individuality and progression for a while and focus on staying active in the running community than drop out or burn out completely. In the former situation, they feel less pressure to keep pushing their fitness upward but still experience the satisfaction of training and being an active athlete.

Some people seem to be able to remain fit regardless of what they do or how much they do. These people are the fortunate anomalies. Most athletes, even those of you who like to think of yourselves as rebels, thrive with structure and benefit significantly from approaching training systematically. As you plan your training and get ready for your ultramarathon, remember that with limited training time, every hour and every interval counts, and all workouts are connected through the principles of training.

Special Considerations for Female Athletes

> **AUTHOR'S NOTE:** I am the first person to admit that I don't know everything. I am in a constant pursuit of diving down the next rabbit hole to figure out the best ways to improve athletes. In that endeavor, I rely on a combination of research and experience to form best practices. So, it should come as no surprise that when it comes to special considerations for female athletes, I am woefully underexperienced. Can I coach and advise female athletes? Absolutely. But I felt that this section of the book would be best penned by a female coach who can accurately and authentically combine areas of research and personal experience. Fortunately, I have just the person for the job in fellow coach and co-author of this book, Corrine Malcolm. The following section was written directly by Corrine. It follows a framework from another contributor to this book, Nick Tiller, PhD, whose original research can be found in the References section (Tiller et al. 2021).

Women's participation in endurance events has come a long way. In 1928, several women collapsed upon completing the Olympic 800m race. For decades after that race, women were deemed "too fragile" to compete in distance running events. That belief was held so strongly that it took until 1960 for the women's 800m to be reinstated. It took until 1972 before women were allowed to compete in the Olympic 1500m, the same year eight women were "legally" able to run the Boston Marathon for the first time. Fast-forward to 1980 when the American College of Sports Medicine finally came out in defense of women, with a consensus statement advocating for women in competitive running (ACSM 1979). This led to women finally being allowed to compete in the Olympic Marathon for the first time in 1984. Despite these delayed beginnings, women's running has been on the rise, to the point that women now make up over half of all worldwide marathon finishes. However, in contrast to traditional road races, trail and ultrarunning still have a ways to go in closing the gender gap. Women only represented 23 percent of all ultramarathon finishes worldwide (Knechtle and Nikolaidis 2018). That number is steadily rising, but we still have some catching up to do.

Sadly, exercise physiology research has followed the same disproportionate trends as ultrarunning. Historically, research involving human test subjects has predominantly utilized college-aged males, and that's not just because you can pay college guys next to nothing to do crazy things. The truth is, college-aged males make really convenient volunteers. Females do not, as real and perceived complications stemming from hormonal fluctuations during the menstrual cycle upset the research process. Studies designed with female test subjects generally take twice as long and involve exceptionally precise planning to control for each volunteer and her individual cycle. Throw birth control into the mix and things become even more complicated. All of this costs time, money, and effort, which is not a good excuse, just reality.

This issue is not limited strictly to exercise physiology. The wider scientific community is facing pressure from organizations like the National Institutes of Health to not only include female test subjects in end-stage research but also in pre-clinical trials. So, given the historical lack of research on female athletes, despite the rapid increase in female participation in road running, trail running, and ultrarunning, what do we know about the nuances of female physiology?

Pertinent to the following discussion, we want to set up the differences between the terms "sex" and "gender." These terms have traditionally, and incorrectly, been used interchangeably. For clarity we will be using the descriptions set forth by the National Institutes of Health, wherein "sex" refers to biological, genetic, cellular, and molecular differences (male vs female), and "gender" refers to the social construct comprised of values inherited by society (men, women, and people who identify as nonbinary).

PHYSIOLOGICAL SIMILARITIES AND DIFFERENCES

Although males and females are similar in many regards, we are also biologically complex. This leads to specific sex differences from the metabolism of certain substrates to your body composition and the fatigability of your muscles. In that vein, it would be naïve not to acknowledge these important anatomical, physiological, and hormonal differences. Some differences might not end up being that impactful on performance outcomes, others may be performance defining, and a few may be just a logical extension of the research (which is my polite way of saying we don't know). We know that endurance performance up to the marathon distance is heavily influenced by factors such as VO_2 max, lactate threshold, and running economy and that these factors explain much of the ~10 percent difference between male and female performances. However, these

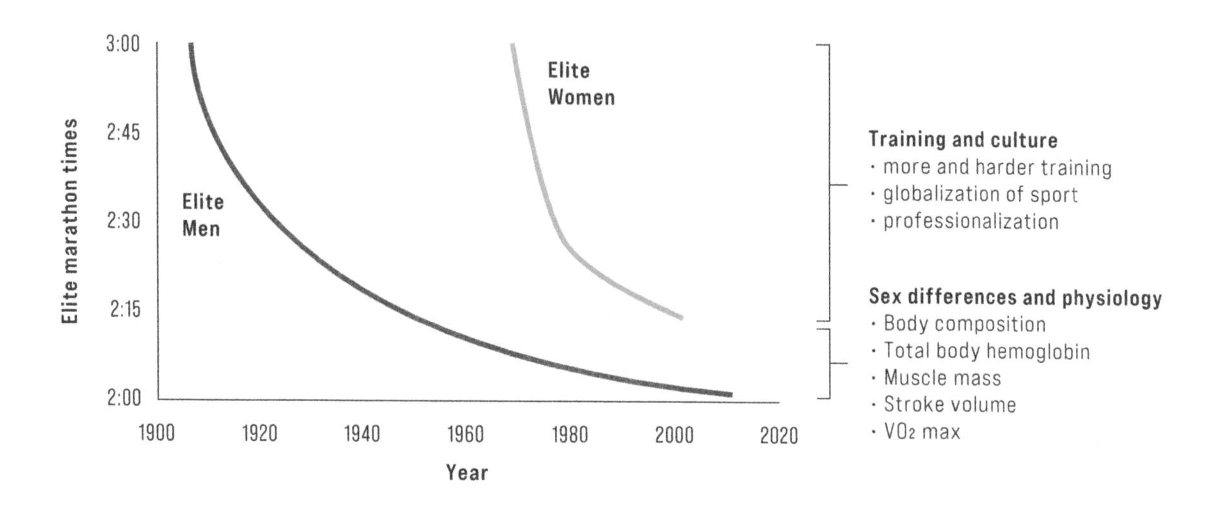

FIGURE 2.3 Many of the initial differences between male and female performance can be attributed to social factors like training and cultural support. The remaining differences that contribute to differences in performance are body composition, total body hemoglobin, muscle mass, stroke volume, and VO_2 max. Source: Joyner 2017.

factors have been shown to be less impactful on ultramarathon performance (Davies et al. 1979). This opens the door for the interplay between other physiological attributes that directly impact performance outcomes, such as substrate utilization and efficiency, fatigue resistance, muscle structure, hormone regulation, gastrointestinal (GI) function, and even decision-making (Knechtle et al. 2018; Millet et al. 2011). But how are these factors swayed by sex, and which ones might be responsible for closing the performance gap between males and females in ultra-endurance events?

SUBSTRATE UTILIZATION

We know that carbohydrate and fat provide the majority of the energy required to get down the trail, and this is particularly true during prolonged, submaximal work performed in ultra-endurance events. As races increase in distance and intensity decreases, we rely more and more on the utilization of free fatty acids (fat) to provide energy to working muscles (Waśkiewicz et al. 2012). Doing this can spare our limited store of carbohydrate (glucose stored in muscle and the bloodstream) and stave off the dreaded "bonk" (sudden fatigue due to overdrawing that account). It turns out endurance-trained females exhibit greater rates of fat oxidation (24 to 56 percent more) compared to their male counterparts, even at rest (Melanson et al. 2002). This continues to hold true while exercising. Females tend to utilize more fat as a percentage of total energy expenditure, have higher rates of fat oxidation relative to their body weight, and reach maximal fat oxidation at higher intensities as compared to male athletes (see Figure 2.4; Knechtle et al. 2005; Tarnopolsky et al. 1990; Venables, Achten, and Jeukendrup 2005). Why? Well, it turns out females have at least two things working for them here. The first is that females exhibit greater expression of genes that code for fatty acid metabolism, including a specific protein (CD36) that makes transporting and utilizing free fatty acid more efficient (Kiens et al. 1985; Monaco et al. 2015). Additionally, females have more estrogen than males, which may enhance lipid oxidation and which downregulates glucose utilization (Isacco et al. 2016). It's these factors, in combination, that seem to give females a distinct metabolic advantage during ultra- and extreme ultra-endurance events. Interestingly, one of the reasons "fat-adapted" strategies are generally ineffective for females is because they are already efficient fat burners (not to mention the potential negative health side effects).

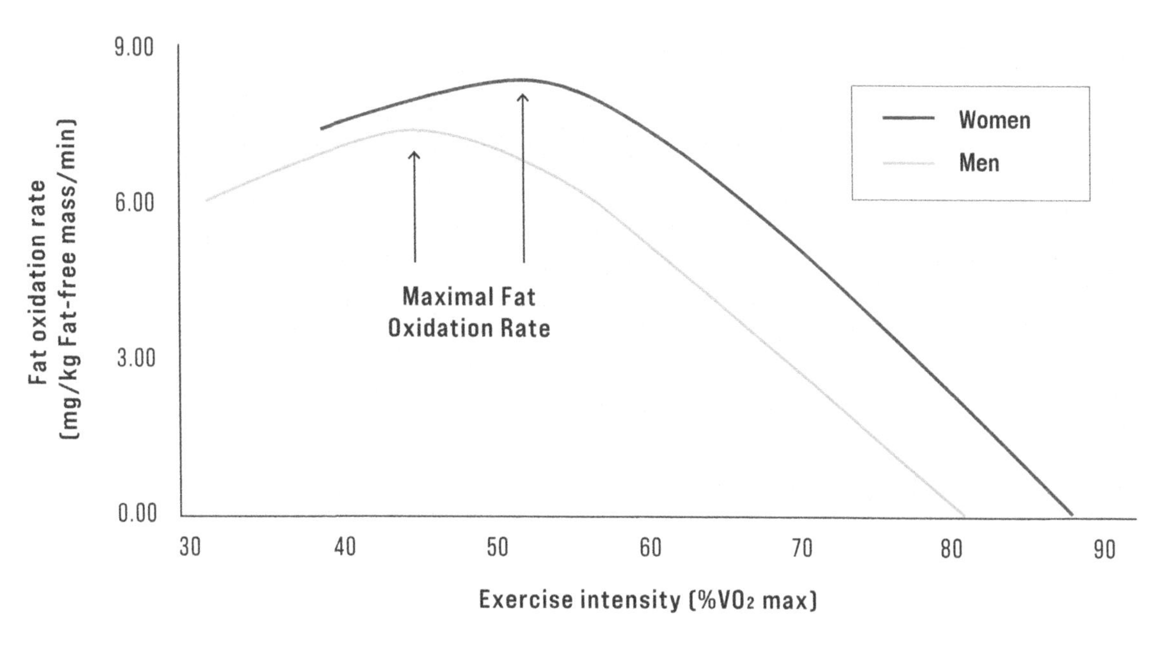

FIGURE 2.4 Women exhibit higher rates of fax oxidation relative to their body mass. Adapted from Venables, Achten, and Jeukendrup 2005.

FATIGABILITY AND MUSCLE STRUCTURE

When it comes to fatigue, in the context of performance limiters, we are specifically addressing neuromuscular fatigue rather than "feeling tired." Neuromuscular fatigue is what happens when, over the course of a long run, race, or other exhaustive exercise, you experience diminished ability to voluntarily activate and/or contract muscles (Millet 2011). In both the lab and the field, at submaximal intensities, females typically outperform their male counterparts when it comes to muscular fatigability (Hicks et al. 2001; Hunter 2014). At a mechanistic level, there seem to be three factors that are favorable for females in this area: muscle fiber type, muscle mass, and neuromuscular control (Hunter 2014).

You have likely heard about type I and type II muscle fibers (slow-twitch and fast-twitch, respectively), with type II fibers further broken down into oxidative and glycolytic based on their preferred energy pathway (Brooke et al. 1970). Type I fibers are considered more fatigue resistant and are best at long aerobic work due to their high mitochondrial content (Zierath et al. 2004). Interestingly, in a study by Staron et al., they found that females naturally had a higher percentage of type I fibers compared to males (Staron et al. 2000). Additionally, males are more likely to have a higher percentage of glycolytic type II fibers compared to females (Welle et al. 2008). Males are also more likely to have greater muscle mass than their female counterparts, but interestingly this is because their individual muscle fibers are generally larger in diameter (Miller et al. 1993). What this means is that males have less blood flow to their individual muscle fibers during submaximal contractions, making them more fatigable and prone to faster rates of neuromuscular fatigue (Hunter 2014). Combined, these factors create greater demand on the cardiorespiratory and central nervous systems, giving women and their larger percentage of type I muscle fibers a theorized advantage when it comes to long endurance events.

GASTROINTESTINAL DISTRESS

Gastrointestinal (GI) distress is one of the top reasons cited for dropping out of an ultramarathon, next to undertraining (Hoffman et al. 2011). GI distress comes in many flavors, ranging from nausea and vomiting to cramping, reflux, bloating, and diarrhea (Costa et al. 2019; Wilson 2019). Any of these could end your day early from pain or discomfort. As we discuss in Chapter 14, the causes of GI distress during ultramarathons are generally multifactorial and are most commonly exacerbated by taking in more food or fluid than you have practiced, running harder than you have trained for, and failing some element of managing thermoregulation. So, why do females runners report a greater propensity for GI distress?

Two of the main factors that could influence GI distress in females are the physical size of female stomachs and gastric emptying rates. In general, females have 10 percent smaller stomachs than their male counterparts, which would make them less capable of accommodating larger volumes of food (Cox 1945). Additionally, we know that compared to males, females have slower transit times (the time it takes food to go in one end and out the other; Probert et al. 1993) as well as slower gastric emptying rates (how long it takes food to leave the stomach; Mori et al. 2017). The mechanism for this is not exactly understood, but it's thought to be related to concentrations and interactions of estrogen and progesterone (Datz et al. 1987). Essentially, this is one of the logical extensions of the literature: it is not fully understood why females have higher instances of GI distress, but it is apparent that it could be a limiting factor in ultra-endurance performance. The end result is the same, so training the gut is an important factor to consider in your training plan.

HORMONE REGULATION

As mentioned above, males and females have drastically different hormones that regulate their respective reproductive systems. However, those same hormones act on your nonreproductive tissues as well. They play distinct roles in bone and tissue health and even affect exercise performance in various ways (hello muscle mass). These hormones, often referred to as "sex hormones," are estrogen, progesterone, and testosterone. We'll talk more about estrogen and progesterone and specifically the menstrual cycle in a little bit. One interesting thing to consider is estrogen's role on the elastic properties of muscles and connective tissues (Joyner 2017). These changes are thought to put female athletes at an elevated risk for connective tissue injuries compared to males (The Female ACL 2016), which is something to consider depending on your injury history (e.g., ACL tears). Additionally, it's plausible that running economy might fluctuate for women throughout the course of their menstrual cycle as hormonal levels fluctuate (Casey et al. 2014; Fletcher et al. 2013).

Testosterone has been considered the leading physiological factor in the gap between male and female athletic performances. However, there's a caveat, as testosterone's advantage is seen more in speed and power disciplines compared to endurance sports. This is because testosterone, and exposure to higher circulating levels of it from puberty onward, is responsible for developing greater muscle mass and subsequent strength and power (Storer et al. 2003). It also lowers body fat, altering body composition; creates higher hemoglobin concentrations (Bhasin et al. 2001); and increases protein synthesis to aid in recovery (Griggs et al. 1989). Interestingly, the one area where high testosterone might not be as advantageous is decision-making. Females, on average, are reported to be much better at pacing themselves over the course of ultra-endurance events. This is in no way a slight toward males. I'm blaming the literature here, but higher testosterone levels are generally associated with impulsiveness and greater risk-taking behavior (Goudriaan et al. 2010). Potentially because of this, albeit speculatively, males tend to overestimate their abilities compared to females and therefore have a greater decline in pace over the course of a race (Hubble et al. 2016). Maybe it's testosterone, maybe it's psychology, but that's a topic for another day.

MENSTRUAL CYCLE

It's pretty well established that exercise physiology and performance research focusing on women has not kept pace with the rapid rise of female participation in sport (Mcnulty et al. 2020). The truth is that science sometimes lags behind what is already being applied in the field. If you are or have been a menstruating female, you can probably self-identify "times of the month" that feel better vs days that feel fairly dreadful. So, what exactly is going on physiologically during your individual menstrual cycle that might cause you to feel better or worse? And what, if anything, can you do to work with your individual cycle in order to avoid surprises during training or on race day?

The menstrual cycle is a critically important biological rhythm whereby you experience large cyclical fluctuations in endogenous sex hormones, specifically estrogen and progesterone, approximately every twenty-eight days (Mcnulty et al. 2020). These fairly predictable changes in concentrations of estrogen and progesterone across your menstrual cycle create significantly different temporary hormonal phases of your cycle. Although there are distinct phases of every menstrual cycle, typical cycle duration can vary widely between individuals, from twenty-one- to forty-day-long cycles. However, independent of

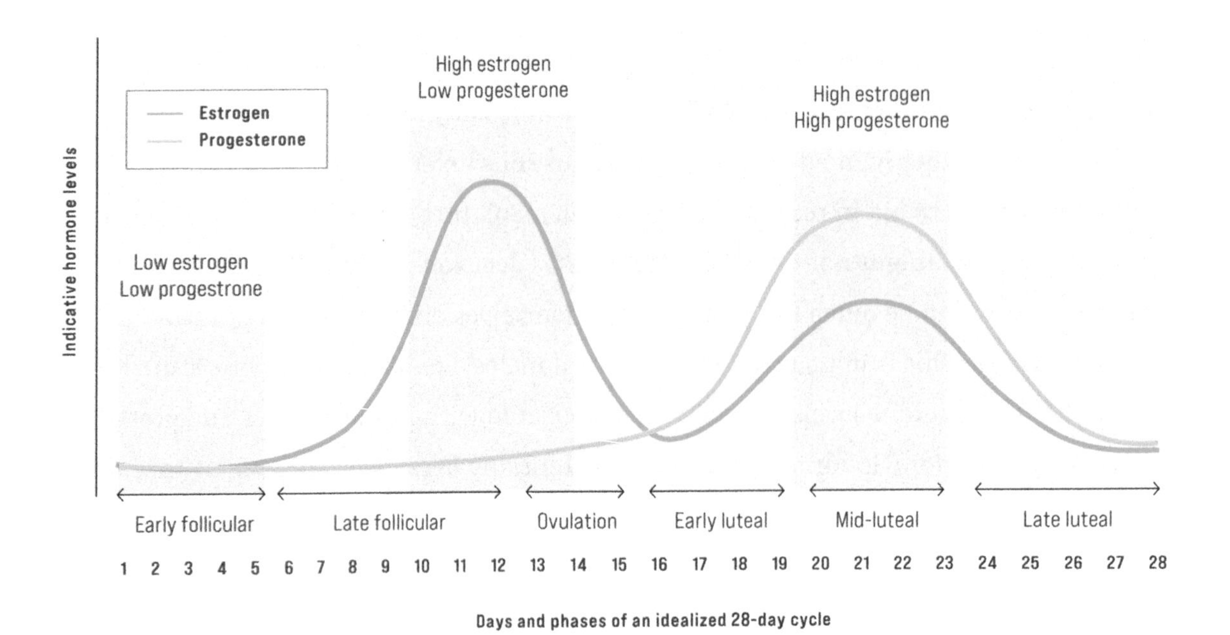

FIGURE 2.5 Representation of the hormonal fluctuation across an idealized twenty-eight-day menstrual cycle.

cycle duration, there are three common and sequential phases: the early follicular phase characterized by both low estrogen and progesterone, the ovulatory phase characterized by high estrogen and low progesterone, and the mid-luteal phase characterized by both high estrogen and high progesterone (Mcnulty et al. 2020). Like anything in physiology, I'll say it again and again: it is important to remember that there is a lot of individual variability.

According to the current literature (which still has a long way to go), menstruating females are most likely to report negative symptoms when estrogen is at its lowest. This time period generally falls within your early follicular phase and means that females often feel their best immediately following this phase, as estrogen rises. Why is estrogen so important? Estrogen has numerous known positive impacts on athletic performance, including regulating glycogen use (and sparing it), protecting against muscle damage and reducing inflammatory response (and thus speeding recovery), and increasing voluntary activation of neural pathways (Mcnulty et al. 2020). Additionally, progesterone is believed to have a dampening effect on estrogen, so as progesterone rises through the luteal phase you might not feel the same estrogen boost as during your follicular phase. Again, for the people in the back, this is based on an idealized cycle; your own individual cycle might create different trends.

We are using a lot of words like, "believed," "likely," and "might" to talk about menstrual cycles in relation to athletics, and there are unfortunately two good reasons for that. The first reason is that the research on how the menstrual cycle impacts exercise performance still has too much variance, largely due to methodological issues. The second reason is that, for a long time, coaches and sports scientists have looked at the menstrual cycle in a confined setting and through the lens of a predetermined and static "normal," when the truth is there is a large amount of individual variability in both cycle duration and hormonal concentration/phase duration. This means the current recommendation, which comes from a group of researchers far more qualified than me, is to approach training and competing independent of the different phases of your menstrual cycle in as personalized a way as possible (Mcnulty et al. 2020). From a practical standpoint this means that, as an athlete, you should be tracking your individual menstrual cycle and keeping a log of how you feel and perform at different phases. This should allow you to track trends of when you feel good and when you might experience symptoms and to make individual adjustments to training accordingly. For example, I know that in my early follicular phase I am more likely to experience GI distress. This doesn't mean I can't race during this time, but it does mean I go into training and racing ready to troubleshoot. Over time, as trends may emerge, you can hopefully avoid getting caught off guard by seemingly avoidable surprises.

It's important to acknowledge that this topic area (broadly the topic of females in endurance sport) will need continued research in order for meaningful comparisons to be made, but hopefully this will happen as female participation in ultra-endurance events increases. For now, we can infer that there are several attributes that differ between sexes that might predispose females to find success in ultra-endurance events. Those characteristics include greater fatigue resistance, possessing a greater distribution of type I (oxidative) muscle fibers, a greater efficiency for oxidizing lipids, and the ability to generally pace themselves better than their male counterparts. On the other side of the coin, physiological attributes that might impede female performance include having a higher prevalence of GI distress and the impacts of hormonal fluctuations on metabolism and tissues.

BIRTH CONTROL CONSIDERATIONS

How does birth control impact the menstrual cycle? To start off, there are many different types of birth control, and birth control is used and prescribed for many things aside from contraception. The most common forms of birth control can be divided into two groups: oral contraceptives and intrauterine devices (IUDs). Oral contraceptives are usually taken in a twenty-one-day block followed by a seven-day "contraceptive-free" phase, which allows for a very controlled cycle. This has been touted as a good thing because it means there are generally no surprises. But how does this influence your natural (endogenous) hormones? It turns out intaking exogenous or externally derived estrogens and progestins impacts your natural feedback systems, which results in a chronic downregulation of your hypothalamic-pituitary-ovarian axis (the connection between your hypothalamus, pituitary gland, and ovaries; Elliot-Sale et al. 2020). Basically, it's telling your command center for regulating estrogen and progesterone, "I've got this covered; you can relax." This means your body is no longer in control.

Additionally, one of the biggest differences between a natural cycle and a cycle affected by oral contraceptives is that the daily ingestion of a pill creates a daily surge in hormones, causing mini pseudo-phases. This alteration of your natural hormones has various side effects, but one of them seems to be producing a chronic hormonal profile that is closest to the early follicular phase where both estrogen and progesterone are low. As we suggested earlier, this is generally when females saw the greatest negative impact on their training and racing performance (Elliot-Sale et al. 2020; Mcnulty et al. 2020). The current consensus in the literature is that being held in that chronic hormonal profile by oral contraception causes slightly impaired exercise performances compared to females who are naturally menstruating. This is consistent with previous studies that suggest that the use of oral contraceptives can lower VO_2 max by ~4.7 percent (Lebrun et al. 2003).

It is important to recognize that there are many times when the best course of treatment for a female athlete may be oral contraceptives. These include: managing the symptoms associated with dysmenorrhea (cramps and pelvic pain) and menorrhagia (heavy bleeding), symptomatic fibroids, functional ovarian cysts and benign breast disease, polycystic ovarian syndrome, premenstrual syndrome, and pelvic inflammatory disease, and decreasing the risk of ovarian and endometrial cancers (Elliot-Sale et al. 2020). On an individual basis, the lessening of those symptoms may far outweigh the small performance decreases associated with taking an oral contraceptive.

The other common contraceptive is IUDs. An IUD can be either hormonal (low-dose progesterone) or nonhormonal (copper) and are popular choices because they are good for three to eight years and do not require remembering to take a daily dose of medication. But wait, didn't we just say that progesterone can blunt the effects of estrogen and mess up our natural hormonal cycles? Generally speaking, yes; however, low-dose hormonal IUDs keep the hormone localized within your uterus, which means it does not impact your circulating hormone levels the way ingesting an oral contraceptive would.

One risk that comes with either form of contraceptive method is that it can potentially mask amenorrhea. Oral contraceptives can give you a "fake period" while hormonal IUDs cause approximately 20 percent of females to lose the bleeding portion of their menstrual cycle. Both outcomes take away one our warning signs of poor health and should be taken into account, particularly if you are at risk for relative energy deficiency in sport (RED-S). Finally, if you have any doubt or concern about any aspect of your menstrual cycle or contraceptive options, you should speak with your primary care provider or OB-GYN.

RED-S

I'm not going to mince words—despite many myths, losing your period (the bleeding portion of your menstrual cycle) is not normal, even for endurance athletes. You can think of your period as the canary in the coal mine; if it disappears, that should be a red flag that something is not quite right. Unfortunately, just because you know you shouldn't lose your period doesn't mean that it'll stick around. In fact, amenorrhea (the absence of the menstrual cycle for ninety days or more) and oligomenorrhea (cycles lasting longer than thirty-five days) are reported at rates of up to 70 percent of women participating in sports compared to 2 to 5 percent in the general population (Jacobsson et al. 2014; Nazem et al. 2012).

For a long time amenorrhea, or menstrual dysfunction, was considered one pillar of the Female Athlete Triad, along with low energy availability and decreased bone density. However, more recently the International Olympic Committee and other research groups have coalesced around a similar concept called Relative Energy Deficiency in Sports (RED-S). RED-S still covers the interrelationship between energy availability, reproductive function, and bone health but expands it to acknowledge that males can also fall prey to low energy availability and its associated complications.

Put most simply, your body's job is to keep you alive, and to do that it needs energy to maintain all your basic physiologic functions, from cellular maintenance and growth to thermoregulation and reproduction. When your body doesn't receive adequate energy to meet the energetic cost of your exercise, it directs energy away from things like metabolism and reproduction in order to survive. Over time, low energy availability decreases athletic performance and can also can impact bone and musculoskeletal health, cardiovascular disease, and neuroendocrine abnormalities like thyroid dysfunction (Clark et al. 2018; Mountjoy et al. 2018). This might sound a little scary, but that is exactly why it is so important. You need to diligently take care of yourself.

It should be noted that you can be in a state of low energy availability and menstrual dysfunction without struggling with restrictive or disordered eating. As endurance

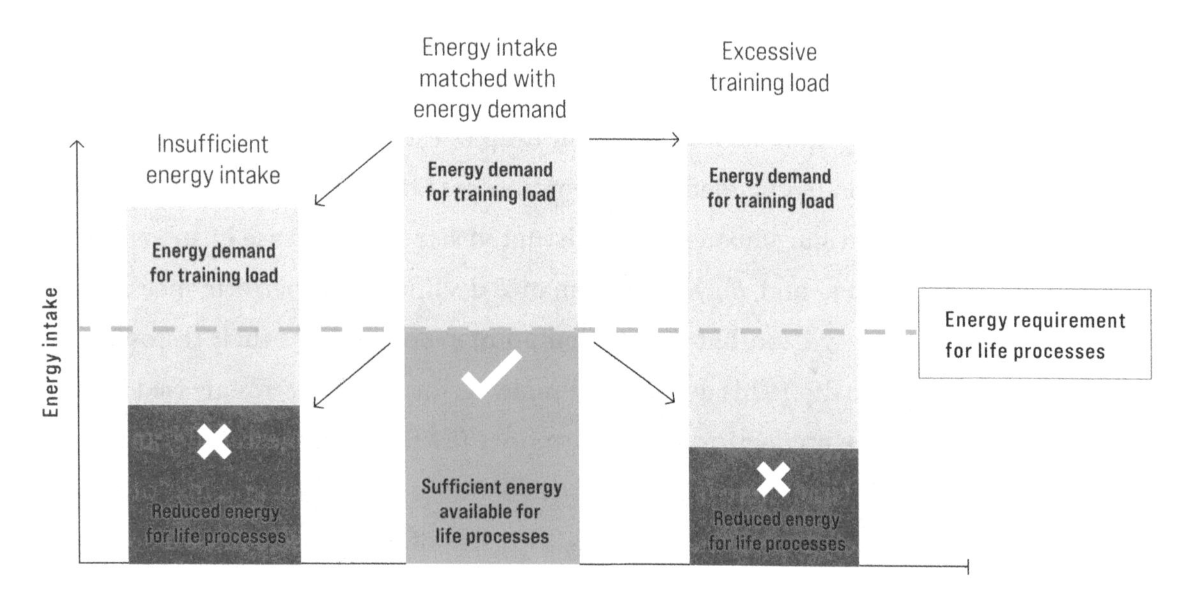

FIGURE 2.6 Matching energy intake to demand. Adapted from Keay 2018.

athletes, and especially ultra-endurance athletes, it's easy to fall behind on the nutrition demands of your day-to-day training. This is particularly true because energy expenditure is not static; rather, it's incredibly dynamic in nature. The ever-changing demands of training mean that you can't simply balance the calorie checkbook at the end of each calendar day. As a result, you will likely have days of overcompensation, like that on rest day after a long training run over the weekend. Falling into the trap of "limiting your calories" because you are not training that day overlooks the likelihood that you are still behind from a day where your energy expenditure was too much to make up in a twenty-four-hour window.

MENOPAUSE

You've hit your stride, and you have time for your ultrarunning pursuits as you revel in the eagerly anticipated "midlife," but then . . . menopause. It doesn't seem fair, does it? So, what exactly is going on, and how can you get the best out of your running as the ebb and flow of your hormones changes?

Often striking while the iron is hot in your mid-forties (between 36 and 45 years of age, on average), perimenopause, or "menopause transition," is the time when your ovaries gradually start to make less and less estrogen. This time period starts on average four to five years before you reach menopause, which is the point at which your ovaries stop releasing eggs and you experience a complete cessation of your period. In the last one to two years leading up to menopause, your drop in estrogen speeds up, and this is when you typically begin to experience the common dreaded menopause-related symptoms like hot flashes; fatigue; mood swings; disrupted sleep; an increase in subcutaneous and intramuscular fat; and, oh yes, performance decline. (Sure, performance declines for males as they age, too, but their falloff point occurs later, as their testosterone concentrations begin to dip.) This decline in female performance is strongly tied to the definitive slowing in the production of key hormones (estrogen, progesterone, and testosterone). During this time there is a gradual acceleration of atrophy and loss of skeletal muscle, predominately type 2 muscle fibers. This loss of lean muscle mass also comes with a reduction in oxygen utilization and a subsequent drop in VO_2 max at a rate of 5 to 10 percent per decade after 30 years of age (Hawkins and Wiswell 2003).

So, as you find yourself looking at this seemingly new biological self, what can you do to dampen the blow of a new hormonal profile?

FOCUS ON SLEEP HYGIENE.

As estrogen and progesterone levels decline, your ability to fall asleep and stay asleep declines, too. Combine that with struggles to regulate your body temperature at night due to changes in melatonin and cortisol levels, and you're exhausted. To counter this, exercise early in the day and do everything you can to practice good sleep hygiene, like sleeping in a cool, dark room away from screens and avoiding alcohol consumption before bed.

LIFT HEAVY THINGS.

I know you are an endurance athlete, but crashing into midlife comes with a gradual and steady loss of lean muscle mass that unfortunately starts sooner for women than for men. This is because that dip in estrogen is accompanied by a dip in testosterone and other growth hormones, making building muscle harder and harder as we age. The best way to counter this and to boost testosterone naturally in the process is to add in ergogenic strength training (see strength training in Chapter 11) combined with adequate protein consumption postexercise. This style of training will also help to maintain healthy bone density.

WATCH OUT FOR THE HEAT.

Hot flashes cause blood to rush to the surface of the skin in an effort to cool you off, which can be annoying when you would prefer your blood to be going to your working muscles or to your stomach to aid in digestion. Additionally, as we age, our sweat rate changes, starting a little later in exercise. This is important because sweating is a primary form of cooling, so slower onset of sweating may lead to increased heat storage at the start of your runs (so a longer warm-up before hard efforts is worth considering). Finally, as we age, our thirst mechanism dulls, making us less in tune with our hydration needs. This means we need to be even more cognizant of our hydration needs during training and racing.

AVOID RUNNING FOR THE BUSHES.

Declining estrogen levels make the body more sensitive to carbohydrates and insulin, while our ability to absorb fructose declines to the point that products with added fructose might send us running to the bushes midrace. This can be managed by avoiding foods with added fructose and looking to sources of energy with simpler sugars such as glucose, dextrose, and sucrose.

DON'T BE AFRAID TO REST.

Recovery takes longer as we age, so don't be afraid to alter your training periodization in both the macro and micro sense. This might mean moving to a ten-day training block instead of following the traditional seven-day week to allow for more rest between hard sessions. Another option is adding in more recovery weeks, thereby moving from a 3:1 or even 4:1 ratio to 2:1.

EAT MORE PROTEIN.

Metabolically, the dramatic slowing and decline in hormone production decreases your insulin sensitivity and your reliance on carbohydrates. This, combined with increased muscle catabolism (the breakdown of muscle tissue), means your ability to maintain lean muscle mass relies heavily on the timing of protein consumption in your post-activity window and, as mentioned above, your ability to lift heavy things.

KEY POINTS ON THE PHYSIOLOGY OF A BETTER ENGINE

- You have three pathways with which you can derive energy:
    - The ATP-PCr system
    - The lactic acid system
    - The aerobic system
- All three of these are in use all of the time. There are no on-off switches.
- There are five basic principles of training:
    - Overload and recovery
    - Progression
    - Individuality
    - Specificity
    - Systematic Approach
- Females compared to males are predisposed to excel in ultrarunning events in some ways, but not in others.
- Female ultrarunners may benefit from tracking their menstrual cycle, along with other variables, and adjusting their training accordingly.
- Some women will see performance decline with oral contraceptive use. Use of oral contraceptives should be balanced with the individual goals of each athlete.
- Post-menopausal athletes should:
    - Pay extra attention to their sleeping environment
    - Lift heavy things to avoid loss in muscle mass
    - Use extra precaution in hot environments
    - Factor in additional recovery
    - Pay extra attention to their postexercise and race-day nutrition programs

CHAPTER 3

The Anatomy of Ultramarathon Performance

Ultramarathon performance is an enigma. It's elusive and hard to understand, and even when you are successful, you look back at the performance and wonder how exactly you accomplished what you did. Sometimes you don't even remember much of the ordeal, chalking the experience up to "ultra-amnesia" or some other concocted disorder. The difficulty of defining exactly what underpins ultramarathon performances shows up in the wide array of reports from runners at the end of an ultramarathon: "My legs were shot." "I got too hot on the exposed section." "My stomach went south." "I was really good on the climbs, but not so good on the descents." This array of experiences and associated tales have led ultrarunners and coaches to adopt a barrage of training strategies to combat those ailments. And, just like the event postmortems you'll hear at the finish line, basic training components like training volume, the proportion of time spent training at a certain intensity, supplemental training like strength training, and even coaching philosophies will vary wildly.

Even elite ultrarunners, who should be a more homogenous training cohort, show vast differences in training strategy. In 2018, I profiled *Ultrarunning Magazine*'s

"Ultrarunners of the Year," Jim Walmsley and Courtney Dauwalter. My aim was to uncover a bit of what made them successful that particular year. They both had excellent seasons with multiple wins across a wide variety of ultradistances, punctuated by wins at the famous Western States 100. Since I did not coach either of these athletes, I recreated their training from interviews I conducted, publicly available information on Strava, and other sources such as their social media accounts and prior interviews they had given. I've illustrated their training in Figures 3.1 and 3.2. Some aspects of their training, like annual training volume, were quite similar. (Note: Through the course of this book, I will refer to training volume in terms of hours per week as opposed to miles per week. This is because a time-based method of capturing volume is more consistent compared to a mile-based method. As any trail runner will know, the time and effort it takes to run a mile can vary wildly depending on if you are going uphill, downhill, or over technical terrain.) Courtney's 719 hours of annual training was quite comparable to Jim's 745 hours. They both used the principle of specificity and tailored the vertical gain and terrain of their training to a race as it approached. Yet other training variables were markedly different. For example, Jim's amount of vertical gain accumulated during the year (926,906 ft) nearly doubled Courtney's vertical gain (453,000 ft).

You see these types of discrepancies in training strategies throughout the pack. Some athletes will use high-volume strategies, running in excess of thirty hours per week, while other athletes will focus on intensity, doing three or four hard workouts per week. Some athletes swear by strength training, while others couldn't tell you the difference between a trap bar and a Snickers bar.

Some of this discrepancy is fueled by ultrarunning's history. Weird, obscure, and rooted in anecdote, training methods from ultrarunning's past have been indecipherably passed down from person to person in a decades-long game of telephone. The now defunct Ultra-list, a message board popular in the 1990s and early 2000s, was filled with endless iterations of "here's what I did" successes and failures from the early pioneers of ultrarunning. With each subsequent telling of the tale, the training pattern described moved further and further away from the truth and eventually resembled something closer to a fishing tale than a training log.

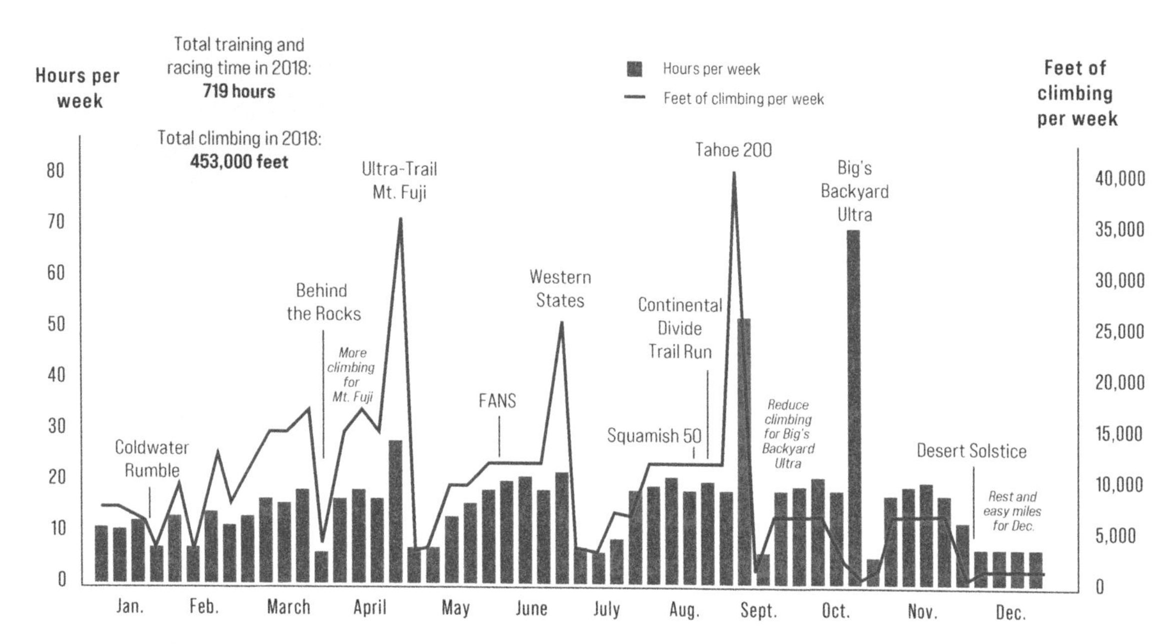

FIGURE 3.1 Courtney Dauwalter's 2018 training. Source: Koop 2019.

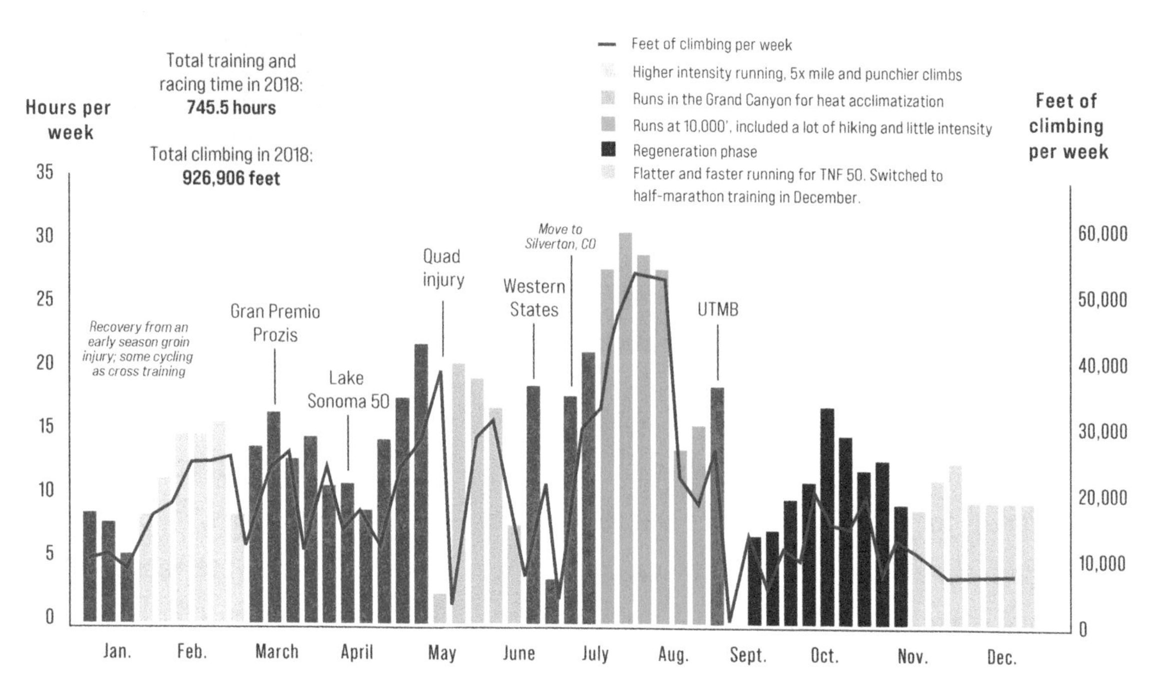

FIGURE 3.2 Jim Walmsley's 2018 training. Source: Koop 2019.

Other parts of these training discrepancies can be chalked up to our individual adaptations to training. "It worked for me," while a pure anecdote, has legitimate physiological roots. According to the principle of individuality that I described in Chapter 2, different people respond to different types of training differently. Coaches have known this for decades through simple observation. Within a group of athletes given the exact same training program (like in a collegiate cross-country setting), individuals adapt differently to speedwork, high-volume training, and other training components. In more recent years, physiologists and coaches have attempted to tease out precise mechanisms that create these individual variations. They've determined that differences in muscle fiber type distribution (Bellinger et al. 2020; Leivens et al. 2020) and genetic coding (Bouchard 2012; Sarzynski, Ghosh, and Bouchar 2017) can influence how athletes adapt differently to a particular training protocol and even that our psychological response to training is different from one athlete to another (Wahl et al. 2013). Going down this rabbit hole, coaches have attempted to tailor training plans based on these narrow underpinnings, altering training for their "fast-twitch" vs "slow-twitch" and "tough" vs "not-so-tough" athletes. These narrowly focused attempts to individualize training ultimately miss the mark, as one single point of difference is unlikely to explain the whole cascade of physiological changes that result from training. It is the constellation of many different individual variances, not any single one of them, that ultimately constitutes the individual variability of a particular training protocol.

THE PROBLEM WITH ANECDOTE

WE'VE ALL HEARD TALES, TIPS, AND TRICKS from fellow ultrarunners on what has worked for them. Exclamations such as "Chew gum to alleviate a sour stomach—it worked for me," "I drank some soup at mile 70 and it worked wonders," and "These toe socks are the only socks that won't give me blisters" abound in pre-race meetings, aid stations, and Facebook groups alike. While true and well-meaning, these anecdotal tales are a poor way to construct any ultramarathon plan. Why? First off, you can always find anecdotes both for and against any intervention. For every runner that magically turned their day around with a grilled cheese sandwich, there is another runner who threw it up immediately after leaving the aid station. So, is runner #1's anecdote more valuable than runner #2's? Furthermore, many anecdotes do not equal data. Just because your Facebook straw poll indicates that everyone is wearing HOKAs does not mean that they are the right shoe for you. You can find similar sentiments across a wide variety of interventions ranging from low-carbohydrate diets to what type of gel is best and even if an altitude tent works.

As coaches, we are trained (or at least we should be trained) to use a hierarchy of evidence when evaluating such claims. At the top of the food chain are systematic reviews and meta-analyses. These studies of studies take dozens and sometimes hundreds of similar research studies and filter through the findings to ascertain interventions that have worked and not worked in sports science. We can then use these types of interventions and have a reasonable degree of confidence that they are going to have some positive effect on the athlete. Adjunctive training like strength training, use of a sauna, block training, and altitude training (all of which are discussed in this book) fall into this category. They have all had systematic reviews and meta-analyses performed, and we can use those findings to inform training.

Next, we use randomized controlled trials and case-controlled studies. These singular studies look at the effects of a specific intervention across a homogenous group of people. For these two categories of research, we can take the findings and create applicable extensions by combining them with the fundamental aspects of physiology to create reasonable ways to train athletes.

Finally, on the hierarchy of evidence, we have anecdotes and field reports from athletes and coaches. These tales of "it worked for me" often become the basis for designing a randomized controlled trial or case-controlled study. However, they should not take precedence over information gleaned from randomized controlled trials, case-controlled studies, or meta-analyses. Anecdote can add context to those findings, but if you are going to supersede a finding from a meta-analysis with a tale from one of your running friends, you might as well admit that you are throwing a dart at a dartboard while blindfolded.

Cracking the Code of Ultramarathon Performance

When I first began coaching ultrarunners, I examined research-based models to try and identify the limiting factors for performance. In the marathon world, well-established research described performance being limited by three factors:

1. VO_2 max, or the maximum amount of oxygen an athlete can utilize in one minute of maximal exercise
2. The fraction of that VO_2 max an athlete can sustain over the course of the marathon
3. The oxygen cost of running, or how much oxygen it takes to go a given distance

Manipulating any or all of these three variables can influence marathon performance. This performance prediction was simple and robust enough that in 1991, Dr. Michael Joyner boldly predicted that the upper limit of marathon performance was 1:57:58 if one were to optimize all three of those variables (Joyner 1991). Fast-forward twenty-six years, and a team of scientists, product developers, and athletes decided to test the hypothesis. Led by Brad Wilkins, PhD, and the Nike Performance Laboratory, the team sought athletes with the greatest combination of the aforementioned physiological characteristics and then placed them in an environment with the equipment and conditions that would exploit those variables and maximize their chances of breaking the two-hour marathon threshold. They found a pool of over a dozen athletes who simultaneously possessed very high VO_2 max values, the ability to utilize a large fraction of their VO_2 max, and an extremely low cost of running (meaning that they required less oxygen to run a given distance).

Finding the athletes was not enough. After all, athletes race marathons all the time, and up to that point, no one had come close to breaking the two-hour mark. So, the team started to push and pull on other parts of the sub-two-hour equation. They researched the optimal temperature so the athletes could utilize a greater fraction of their VO_2 max for forward motion rather than dissipating heat. Advanced nutritional interventions were designed with precision, to be delivered to runners by bicycle in order to avoid any wasted motion. They sought the ideal conditions that would further drive down the cost of running by selecting a flat course at sea level that had very few turns. Teams of pacers would rotate to the front of the pack of runners to reduce the amount of aerodynamic drag, driving down the cost of running even further. As if that weren't

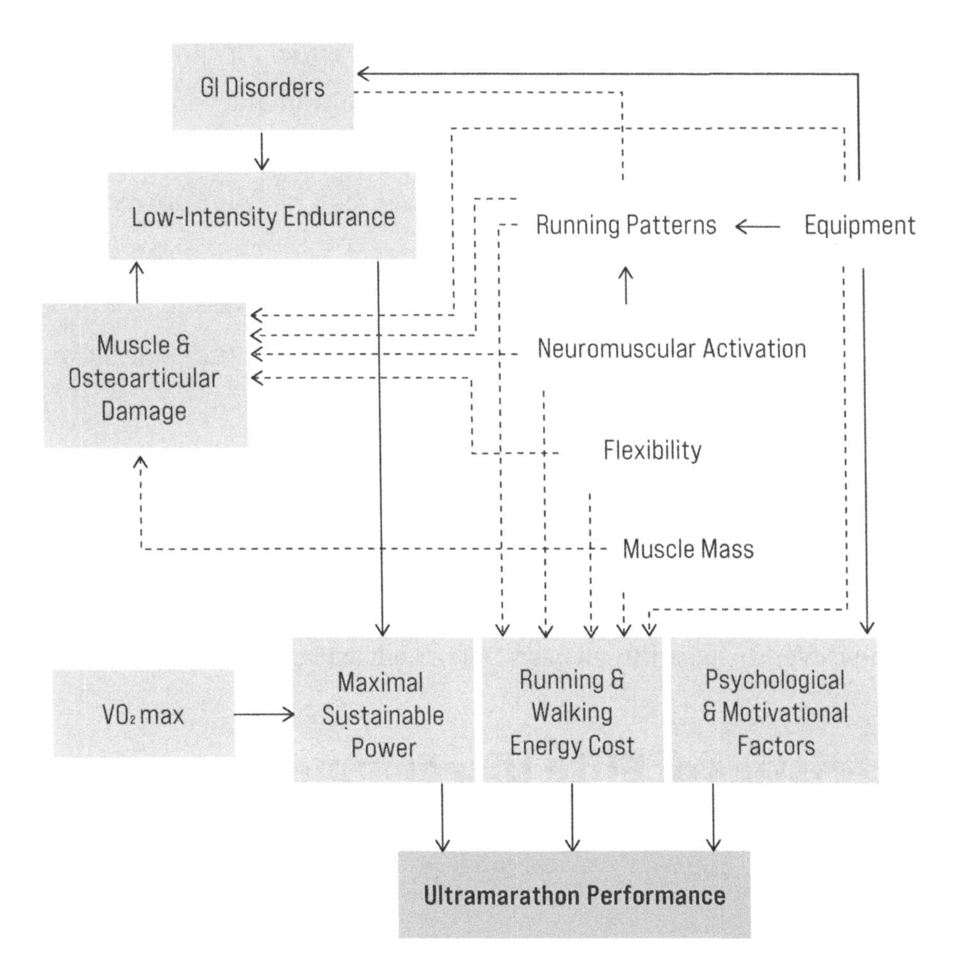

FIGURE 3.3 Proposed determinates of ultramarathon performance. Adapted from Millet 2012.

enough, the entire entourage of athletes and their pacers ran behind a Tesla with a giant video board mounted on top in an attempt to squash what little wind resistance remained. Finally, Nike introduced the controversial Vaporfly shoes into the scenario, putting a final stamp on the cost of running reductions. I shouldn't need to tell you how this story ends.

I would love to tell you ultrarunning is that simple. Push a little here, pull a little there, reduce this variable, and you'll magically run faster. Ultrarunning is not marathon running, and if I sound like a broken record repeating that basic fact throughout this book, it's for good reason. In fact, I will go on record right here and now and say that the marathon is likely the longest race where pure physiology is the main determinate of performance. In ultrarunning, physiology is still important, but your body will have to overcome markedly more obstacles that have greater potential for cataclysmic failure.

For what it's worth, researchers heavily invested in ultramarathon performance have started to make headway in finding the ingredients that make up the goulash of ultramarathon performance (Garbisu-Hualde and Santos-Concejero 2020; Knechtle and Nikolaidis 2018; Millet and Millet 2012, 2020; Millet et al. 2011; Thompson 2017; Knechtle and Senn 2011). And I have to say, while we've made a lot of progress in this area, we're a long way from a three-variable formula that describes the upper limits of ultramarathon performance (see Figure 3.3).

One way we can look at what optimizes performance is through the lens of the elite athletes who dominate the sport. Ultrarunning is now competitive enough, with a sufficient number of elite athletes, that we can look at that landscape and discern general trends and traits that drive elite performance. Fortunately for you, I've had a front-row seat to that show over the past fifteen years. Here's what I've learned.

Characteristics of Elite Ultrarunners

Despite their diverse backgrounds, elite ultrarunners share three common characteristics. You have them, too, to varying degrees. Not only do you share these characteristics with elite runners, but all three can be developed by any runner to improve performance!

TALENT.

Elite ultrarunners (and elite endurance athletes in general) have a high genetic potential for aerobic power and other variables that constitute ultramarathon performance. This potential is trainable, so the takeaway for any runner is that no matter your starting point, working to optimize the talent you have will make you a better ultrarunner.

MENTAL SKILLS.

Elite ultrarunners possess supreme mental skills. They thrive not only on their best days, but at times on their worst days. The good news for all runners is that anyone can harness mental skills with focused training.

EMOTIONAL ENGAGEMENT.

Ultramarathons are hard. The best runners have an emotional attachment to the races they compete in; they care about the race and the community surrounding the event, not just their own performance. I encourage my athletes to pick races they have genuine, visceral attractions to, the type of attractions that makes you excited, giddy, and just a bit scared all at the same time. I would encourage you to do the same.

It is the harmonious intertwining of these qualities that ultimately enables elite ultrarunners to perform at their peak. While we all wish to run as fast as an elite athlete, reality dictates that most of us will be much slower. (Sorry to break the news.) The key is to optimize what you have by tapping into, leveraging, and developing your own innate talent, mental skills, and emotional engagement.

Talent

My formal education is in biochemistry and genetics. I spent the better part of five years toiling away in labs, behind pipettes, graduated cylinders, and beakers, studying gene expression and its role in the development of living organisms. Thus, it is with a bit of bias that I consider talent to mean your genetic predisposition for athletic performance. All elite ultrarunners are born with a high degree of innate talent. This gift bestowed upon them by their parents is completely out of their control. Genetics sets some of the parameters and physiological limits of athletic potential. It plays a large role in determining the height of your highest-possible jump and the speed of your fastest-possible run, even if we could optimize everything else, like training, nutrition, and recovery.

For an endurance athlete, physiological talent is largely (but not exclusively) measured through the amount of oxygen one can utilize, represented as VO_2 max. This measure, the maximum volume of oxygen an athlete can consume, transport, and use, is usually expressed as milliliters of oxygen per kilogram of body weight per minute (ml/kg/min). Typical VO_2 max values for elite athletes in a variety of sports are shown in Figure 3.4. For endurance athletes, the rate of oxygen consumption is your most significant limiting factor, or your greatest advantage. The oxygen you take in is used to release energy through the breakdown of carbohydrate and fat (and, in dire circumstances, protein). The more oxygen you can utilize, the more rapidly you can deliver energy and, therefore, the greater the work capacity you have for an ultra.

To be an elite endurance athlete, you have to be able to utilize the oxygen required

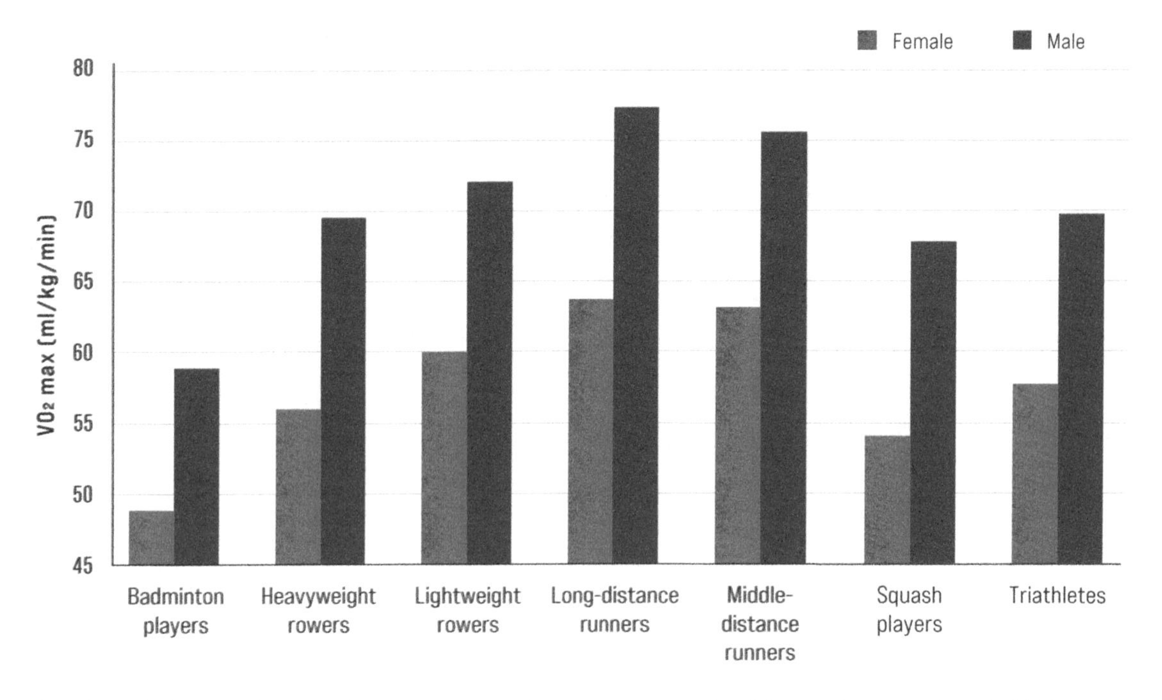

FIGURE 3.4 Typical VO_2 max values for elite athletes in various sports. Adapted from Nevill et al. 2003.

to keep you at the front of the pack. When an athlete has the necessary VO_2 max values, we typically say they are "in the club." In long-distance running, for example, a typical elite male will have a VO_2 max around 77.4 ml/kg/min (Nevill et al. 2003). This does not mean that all elite runners have this level of maximum aerobic output, nor does it mean that one can't be an elite runner with less than a 77.4 VO_2 max. Instead, it means that in order to be an elite male runner, you have to at least be close to that number. Someone who comes into a physiology lab and tests at only 40 ml/kg/min has no realistic chance of "getting into the club" in elite distance running.

Elite ultrarunners don't have to have VO_2 max values as high as elite marathoners, but they still have to be able to consume oxygen at or above a certain rate in order to compete at the top of the sport. In my testing of elite ultrarunners, successful males typically have VO_2 max values of approximately 60–70 ml/kg/min, and successful female competitors typically have VO_2 max values of approximately 55–65 ml/kg/min. This means simply that if you want to win a big, competitive race like the Western States 100, Leadville Trail 100, or Lake Sonoma 50, your VO_2 max values need to be in those neighborhoods.

In spite of how much emphasis I put on the aerobic system, I am the first to admit that an athlete's aerobic power is not the only physiological variable to consider. If races could be won simply by having a higher VO_2 max, athletes could skip the running part and just show up with VO_2 max test results to claim their prizes. To be a contender to win any major ultrarunning competition, an athlete needs a more diverse set of physiological talents compared to athletes in other running events. (I expand on this concept in Chapter 4.)

Elite ultrarunners are naturally skilled over varied terrain and equipped with good balance, reflexes, and an innate sense of where to put their feet. They have a talent for coping with environmental stressors and are able to consume food and fluid in great quantities in the middle of intense competition without getting sick. The fact of the matter is, elite ultrarunners are elites because they are talented across many physiological and psychological variables, not solely because of their aerobic power.

It is important to note that these aspects of talent are trainable. For novice runners, VO_2 max can improve by well over 20 percent. Even an elite athlete with a very high VO_2 max can still improve VO_2 max ~5 percent with proper training (although for these athletes, VO_2 max improvements are not nearly as important as improvements in other areas). Other aspects of innate talent can be similarly improved. You can train to consume more food, run over technical terrain, and handle hot and cold conditions. In these respects, all athletes are working to maximize their innate talents; elite athletes just have a higher ceiling.

WHY TALENT MATTERS

Very few athletes have the constellation of physical gifts required to be an elite ultrarunner, but talent is nevertheless important for all of us. Every athlete has some level of talent, and it is important to identify the areas where genetics and predispositions are well suited to ultrarunning. Maybe you don't have a world-class VO_2 max, but you have a better-than-average ability to maintain your lactate threshold pace for long periods. This ability is useful for events with long climbs, as well as many other areas. Maybe you adapt remarkably well to high altitude, so your performance and pace don't drop as much at higher elevations. Or perhaps you are able to sustain a heavy training workload week after week because you recover and adapt to training stress quickly. These are all innate traits you can optimize and leverage in training and competition.

When elite ultrarunners line up at the start of a major race, they are very similar to one another in terms of talent. On paper it would appear to be a race among equals, yet the runners' real-world performances vary greatly on any given race day. Where these athletes differ is in how much they have closed the gap between their actual performance level and their maximum potential. Because the athletes have very similar levels of talent, those who can operate closest to their physiological ceiling have the advantage.

No matter where your own physiological ceiling is, the goal of training is to close the gap between your current performance level and your maximum potential. The great thing is that there is always room for improvement, because none of us, not even Olympic-caliber endurance athletes, operate at our maximum. We can get very, very close to that theoretical maximum, but we always come up a little short. That persistent gap is the reason we can all improve with proper training.

MENTAL SKILLS

Four to one is my typical rule of thumb: for every four workouts I give an elite athlete, I'm holding them back in some way on one of them. This is because elite athletes are naturally very mentally tough. All too often, they are too tough for their own good. They have a tendency to push through injury and illness, sometimes to the point where these problems become unnecessarily serious. This can be a bad thing in day-to-day training, but toughness is a golden quality on race day. Elite ultramarathoners train a lot. That's one of the bigger advantages they have over the rest of the pack. They organize their lives so they can train for many hours. However, even elite athletes can only prepare so much for race day. The goal is always to be 100 percent prepared, but reality dictates that they will show up at the starting line with at least a few chinks in their armor. Maybe they left mileage on the table. Sometimes they couldn't get in enough vertical. In these instances, mental skills can provide strength in areas training left vulnerable. Elites reduce or eliminate these vulnerabilities better than the rest of the pack.

WHY MENTAL SKILLS MATTER

No matter how well you prepare for an ultra, it is nearly impossible to be fully ready for everything the race will throw at you. The elites have the mental skills to maintain a performance level that will keep them in contention for victory. Sometimes, when victory is no longer within reach, they have to rely on those skills just to keep moving forward. For a non-elite ultrarunner, mental skills may be even more important because you are out on the course longer, so there's more time to be affected by adversity, for unfavorable weather to creep in, and for your stomach to turn against you. While you're battling through fatigue at hour 23 or 27, the elites crossed the finish line hours earlier. Fortunately, mental skills can be developed and honed. They are forged through day-to-day training and through learning to endure specific challenges as you prepare for your ultramarathon event. You develop mental fortitude and grit by rising to those challenges, like pushing through difficult workouts and working through bad patches during long runs. This is such a crucial aspect of performance that I will spend an entire chapter on the subject (Chapter 15) later in this book.

EMOTIONAL ENGAGEMENT

Elite athletes have a high level of emotional engagement in the events they choose, and it shows. They have a tendency to care about the community surrounding the event, not solely their own performance on race day. During interviews, the elites demonstrate having a sense of history, past winners, and every rock, nook, and cranny of the racecourse. Many times, they know the aid station captains by name. And after they are done competing, they often volunteer for the races they have won and come to love.

In 2015, Western States 100 winner Rob Krar ran the final mile with the last finisher, in flip-flops. Think about that for a second. After running 100 miles and resting for about fourteen hours, this guy had the energy and emotional investment to escort the final finisher all the way to, and around, the Placer High School track. He could have easily sat in the bleachers with the rest of the crowd and perhaps mustered the energy to join the standing ovation. But he did so much more. He took his emotional engagement several hundred steps farther. He cared about the overall race, and he cared about that last finisher. He has an emotional engagement with the Western States 100 that surpasses his own planning, preparation, and the rigors of race day.

A large part of success in any elite competition is the athlete's emotional engagement with the event. We have all seen extremely talented, well-trained athletes underperform on the field of battle because they were "checked out." It happens in every sport and at every level of competition, even in elite ultrarunning. The elites I work with are able to go to almost any race on the planet. When I sit down with them at the beginning of every season, the number of opportunities on the table is unmanageable. During this process of picking and choosing events, it is easy to identify the characteristics of the races that would best suit the athlete's physical abilities. It is easy to look at a race and consider how much climbing and descending it includes, how hot or cold it will be, and whatever other variables exist and say, "Well, you are good at X, Y, and Z, so go do the races with X, Y, and Z." However, I always begin with finding events that have the most emotional pull for each athlete. I put my athletes in a position for success by first encouraging them to train for events they genuinely care about and then building their physical tools around that event, not the other way around.

WHY EMOTIONAL ENGAGEMENT MATTERS

For the last several years, I have been working with an athlete who has been attempting to complete the Leadville Trail 100 within the required thirty-hour cutoff. As of this book's publication, she unfortunately has been unsuccessful in this endeavor. Based on her innate talent, the thirty-hour cutoff for that race is within the limits of her physical capabilities, but only by a razor-thin margin. For her to be successful, everything has to go right. In training she has to make the most of every day, completing each workout to the fullest and resting with purpose. During the race she needs perfect weather and flawless race execution, and she has to dig into her training-honed well of mental skills deeper than ever before. If, and only if, all these things go right, she has a chance to be successful.

On her very best day in her very best year, this athlete is capable of a 29:45:00 finish. For the last four years she has been on the other side of that coin, yet she continues to go back, and I wholeheartedly encourage her to do so. I could easily coax her into an easier race with a more generous cutoff—perhaps a 100-miler at sea level. There are numerous events that would greatly increase her chances of finishing her first 100-miler, on paper at least. Yet, despite what I know from the rudimentary mathematical exercises of cutoffs, paces per mile, and probability ratios, I refuse to talk her out of racing Leadville. The sole reason for this is that she is 100 percent head over heels all-in infatuated and in love with the Leadville Trail 100. She is more emotionally engaged with that event than with any other race. So, even though on paper another event might be "easier" for her, I would argue that her best chance of success in a 100-mile footrace is in the race she's most passionate about.

Many people race in events they have no attachment to. I honestly don't know why. Even when you love the sport and the event you're preparing for, at some point you will want to quit. When you're exhausted, wet, cold, and nauseated, a part of your brain will tell you it's just not worth it, and you will quit. Training for and running an ultra are extremely hard. You'd better care about what you are doing.

TRAINING TIES TALENT, MENTAL SKILLS, AND EMOTIONAL ENGAGEMENT TOGETHER

Because this book centers on training for an ultramarathon, I'd be remiss if I neglected to tie together how training affects talent, mental skills, and emotional engagement. Quite simply, training is the catalyst that maximizes these qualities. You can improve by training more. You can improve by training harder. However, the most successful athletes also train smarter than their competitors. They use training to harmoniously maximize their innate talent, hone mental skills, and reinforce their emotional engagement for the event they are training for.

Training maximizes talent by pushing your raw physical capabilities ever closer to their predetermined genetic limits. Even rudimentary training moves you in the right direction, and training that is well designed further enhances your progress. The better, more intelligent, and more precise the training design, the closer you will get to your physical talent ceiling.

As for mental skills, their importance cannot be exaggerated. As much as I am an advocate for intelligent, precise training, I still want my athletes to work hard, push themselves when required, and be mindful of the work they have accomplished. After all, physical adaptation to training is Darwinian in nature. Training should be difficult because you need to impose enough stress in order to adapt. In this way, training hones your mental skills. The deliberate act of pushing yourself in training reinforces and builds the mental skills you will draw upon come race day.

Training is elective; with rare exceptions, we are not running to earn our next paycheck, which is all the more reason that emotional engagement is a key part of training. You choose to lace up your shoes, head out the door, and put in the miles. This ritual is a daily reminder of what you are ultimately training for and serves to reinforce the emotional engagement you have with your goals. Do you post the elevation profile of the race you are training for on your wall or refrigerator? That is a form of emotional engagement. The hills you run, the intensity of your efforts, and nearly all aspects of training should remind you of the event you have chosen to undertake.

KEY POINTS ON THE ANATOMY OF ULTRAMARATHON PERFORMANCE

- Successful ultrarunners have used a variety of different training pathways to success.
- While marathon performance can be described by VO_2 max, the fraction of that VO_2 max you can utilize, and the oxygen cost of running, ultramarathon performance depends on a broader array of variables.
- Elite ultrarunners exhibit three distinct characteristics:
  - High levels of genetic talent (physical, psychological, and otherwise)
  - Highly developed mental skills
  - Strong emotional engagement with the events they have chosen
- All athletes can leverage these three attributes to better their ultramarathon performance.
- Training ties talent, mental skills, and emotional engagement together.

MC DOWELL MOUNTAIN

REGIONAL PARK

Lousley Hill

10

11

12

15

14

13

22

23

24

27

26

25

TRAIL

JEEP

Pemberton Ranch

RESERVATION BOUNDARY

CHAPTER 4

Failure Points and How to Fix Them

There is a simple and elegant equation that is traditionally used to determine running velocity in endurance events. It states that velocity is determined by how big your aerobic engine is (VO_2 max), the fraction of it that you are utilizing (F), and the oxygen cost it takes for you to run a given distance (cost of running [Cr]). (These three variables should be familiar, since we covered them in the previous chapter.) The equation explains why a runner with a bigger aerobic engine can run faster than one with a smaller engine when they are equally economical. It also explains why the cost of running is important, particularly if you have maximized your aerobic engine. Consequently, innumerable hours of scientific research have been dedicated to studying how these three simple variables are affected by body weight, temperature, shoe mass, genetics, elastic energy return, flexibility, running cadence, stride length, training, gender, age, biomechanics, and many other factors.

$$Velocity = F \times Vo_2max/Cr$$

The equation is extremely versatile, allowing us to predict and explain performance in endurance events from 5Ks to marathons (Di Prampero 1992). Furthermore, improving performance for running events ranging from the 5K to the marathon has been rooted in optimizing these three variables. Improve your VO_2 max and the fraction that you can utilize, and you will run faster. Reduce your cost of running, and you can run faster still.

But beyond the marathon distance, the validity of this equation in predicting performance starts to break down. Ultrarunning is not a marathon. It's not even a long marathon. It's a different sport altogether, and the variables associated with it mean that performance can no longer be determined solely by oxygen consumption and the cost of running.

The Science of Ultrarunning

While other endurance sports such as triathlon, marathoning, and cycling have an abundance of scientific research to draw upon, ultrarunning has very little by comparison. It's a difficult proposition for a researcher. Finding subjects who are willing to run on a treadmill for the necessary durations is understandably challenging. And because of the remote nature of most ultras, fieldwork and race-day biological assessments are difficult to attain. Plus, taking postrace measurements involves poking and prodding athletes who in many cases have just finished the most difficult race of their lives. With all these obstacles, the scope of what can be studied will always be somewhat limited.

When I first started working with ultrarunners in the early 2000s, I followed a similar framework for any new sport group that I worked with: study the game, understand the athlete, and do research on the sport. The first two I could accomplish on my own. I could look at race profiles, dig into race reports, attend events, and even do races myself to better study ultrarunning as a sport. Then, the process of understanding the athlete was universal across runners, cyclists, and triathletes, so I had that down pat, too. However, when it came to finding research in the early 2000s, I was grasping at straws. There was quite simply very little research to draw upon that was specific to ultramarathon running. Fortunately, that has changed. Ultrarunning's popularity and interest in the sport continue to grow, and with that comes academic research specific to the sport. The amount of research is still dwarfed by what has been published on

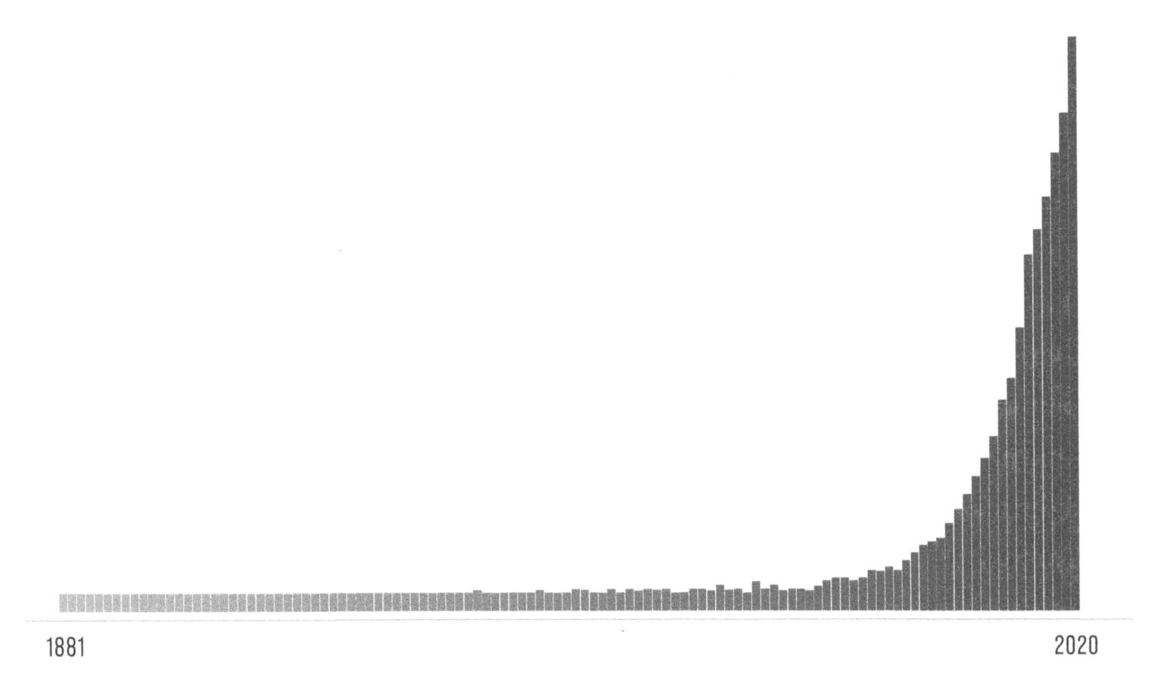

FIGURE 4.1 A PubMed search for the word "ultramarathon," "ultra marathon," or "ultra endurance." Accessed March 2021.

the traditional sports of road and track running, cross-country skiing, cycling, and triathlon, but it's a start.

Much of the research that has been conducted is based on pre- and postrace questionnaires asking things like: Why did you drop out of the race? What was your biggest issue? How long was your longest training run? While the answers to these questions offer a glimpse into a runner's trials and tribulations during an ultramarathon, their usefulness is limited. They are the runner's own interpretations of what happened, not necessarily clear explanations for why it happened. Take, for example, a commonly cited reason for underperformance in an ultramarathon: nausea. "I had a queasy stomach" and "I couldn't tolerate any food" are certainly important sentiments to capture, but then what do you do about them? Very little research exists into why that nausea happened to that particular individual in the first place in an ultramarathon setting. Did she take in too much food? Not enough fluids? Too much of a particular type of carbohydrate? Was the gut actually damaged and leaking endotoxins into the bloodstream? Did her vision become altered late in the race, causing disequilibrium and nausea? We know that nausea is in fact an issue, but no one knows for sure what the key triggers for nausea are in an ultramarathon setting. Make no mistake: we're getting closer and closer to finding helpful answers for this and many other questions. But you would be hard-pressed to find a singular "aha" discovery that would prevent nausea from happening in every case.

So, what do we really know about the science of ultrarunning? In 2011, Martin Hoffman and Kevin Fogard published an article titled, "Factors Related to Successful Completion of a 161-km Ultramarathon." Their study explored the characteristics and issues that affected the performance of runners during the 2009 Western States 100 and 2009 Vermont 100 via pre- and postrace questionnaires. One of the more interesting tables in their article outlined the main problems self-reported by both finishers and nonfinishers (Table 4.1).

Through this lens, we can look at many of the failure points and limiting factors of performance and what the science has to say about them. Nausea, blisters, exhaustion, and muscle pain top the list of ailments runners mentioned as performance limiters.

PROBLEM	FINISHERS (%)	NONFINISHERS (%)
Blisters or "hot spots" on feet	40.1	17.3
Nausea and/or vomiting	36.8	39.6
Muscle pain	36.5	20.1
Exhaustion	23.1	13.7
Inadequately heat acclimatized	21.0	28.1
Inadequately trained	13.5	15.1
Muscle cramping	11.4	15.8
Injury during the race	9.0	10.1
Ongoing injury	7.5	15.8
Illness before the race	6.0	5.0
Started out too fast	5.1	6.5
Vision problems	2.1	3.6
Difficulty making cutoff times	1.8	27.3
Other, not categorized	11.7	26.6

TABLE 4.1 Comparisons of problems that impacted race performance.

PROBLEM	%
Nausea and/or vomiting	23.0
Unable to make cutoff times	18.7
Other, not categorized	12.2
Ongoing injury	7.9
Injury during the race	7.2
Inadequately heat acclimatized	7.2
Blisters or "hot spots" on feet	5.8
Muscle cramping	5
Muscle pain	4.3
Exhaustion	3.6
Illness before the race	2.9
Vision problems	0.7
Started out too fast	0.7
Inadequately trained	0.7

TABLE 4.2 Main reasons given by nonfinishers for dropping out. Source: Hoffman and Fogard 2011.

Surprisingly, being inadequately trained represented only 13 to 15 percent of the complaints among both groups as a reason for diminished performance (Table 4.1) and was the least-cited reason (at 0.7 percent) for dropping out among non-finishers (Table 4.2). It would be easy to dismiss this data point, but for me it is crucial.

I would argue that if you are nauseated, are unable to make the cutoff times, and have muscle pain that forces you to drop out or causes you significant issues, above all else, you are inadequately trained. A successful training process for an ultramarathon addresses all of those issues. Any ultramarathon will still be hard, and even the most well-prepared ultramarathon runners encounter issues, but training either mitigates or alleviates them altogether. The striking fact is that while runners often are able to identify the acute causes of their discomfort, they usually do not correlate those sensations with being inadequately trained. This is important because it means runners are focusing on the symptoms and not the root cause of the problem: inadequate training.

Using nausea as an example, you absolutely can and should train to have a stronger stomach (and I'm not talking about six-pack abs). Your digestive system is a combination of muscular and cellular machinery, and it adapts to stress just like the heart and skeletal muscles. That being the case, you can train your gut and digestive machinery to absorb calories from carbohydrate faster, to digest food more rapidly, and to resist damage caused by bacteria (Carrio et al. 1989; Costa et al. 2017; Cox et al. 2010; Harris,

Lindeman, and Martin 1991; Jeukendrup and McLaughlin 2011). Furthermore, as part of the training process, you can and should use different types of calories to see what does and does not work for you.

Nausea is particularly accentuated in ultramarathon running because the event is long enough for consistently poor nutritional choices to significantly affect performance. You can eat poorly and hang on long enough to finish a four-hour marathon or maybe even a 50K. But add another twenty hours of running, and those mistakes will catch up to you. Training for the gastrointestinal stress of racing will produce positive gut adaptations, just as interval work will improve your cardiovascular system. If you are too nauseated to keep running, quite frankly, you are inadequately trained for that stressor of an ultramarathon!

Blisters, dead legs, muscle pain, and all the remaining items on the list in Table 4.2 are similar. They are all stressors in an ultramarathon, and they can all be trained. The key is that you have to know what the science says in these areas in order to know how to train them. So, using Hoffman and Fogard's list, let's take a look at these limiting factors for performance, what the science says about them, and how to properly train for them.

Limiting Factors

"What does success look like to you?" I routinely ask this of all of my athletes, whether they are just starting out, attempting to finish their first ultra, or trying to win races. This question allows me to get a comprehensive view of what they are trying to accomplish. Inevitably an athlete's answer includes some outcome goals ("I want to finish Leadville in under thirty hours") and some process goals ("I want to be able to actually run at the end of the race"). As a coach I learn a whole lot more from "I want to be able to run at the end of a 100-miler" than from "I want to finish the Leadville Trail 100 in under thirty hours." Why? Because when it comes to the outcome goal, determining the range of performances of which an athlete is capable is a matter of simple math. How they become the most adept at achieving that goal is a much bigger—and more vexing—question. By asking what success looks like, I get the color and context of the entire athlete, not just the end goal.

In my experience, most ultramarathon athletes, even the elites, find success through a lack of failure on race day. They achieve their goals, win races, and get those coveted belt buckles not because they ran one section very well but because they prevented the negative. They prevented time spent at 0 mph. They prevented themselves from becoming a nauseated, sore, blistered, battered, and stumbling mess. They continued to be able to eat, drink, and locomote down the trail, even if it was not very fast. Because so many things can go wrong and the penalties for failure are high, "success by lack of failure" is a key element in successful ultramarathon running. These failure points are somewhat universal, as indicated by Hoffman and Fogard's research, and help define the limiting factors for ultrarunning. (The very small exception is elite athletes competing in 50Ks, 50-mile distances, and flat 100Ks. This is because the finish line for elite athletes in those races often comes before the failure points discussed in this chapter have a chance to impact performance.)

All reasonably healthy individuals can locomote at the necessary speed to beat the cutoffs for any ultramarathon. I say this not as an opinion but as a biomechanical fact. The preferred walking speed for the average human is around a nineteen-minute mile (Browning and Kram 2005; Levine and Norenzayan 1999; Mohler et al. 2007). With a little effort, one can easily achieve eighteen-minute miles, which is a pace that would yield

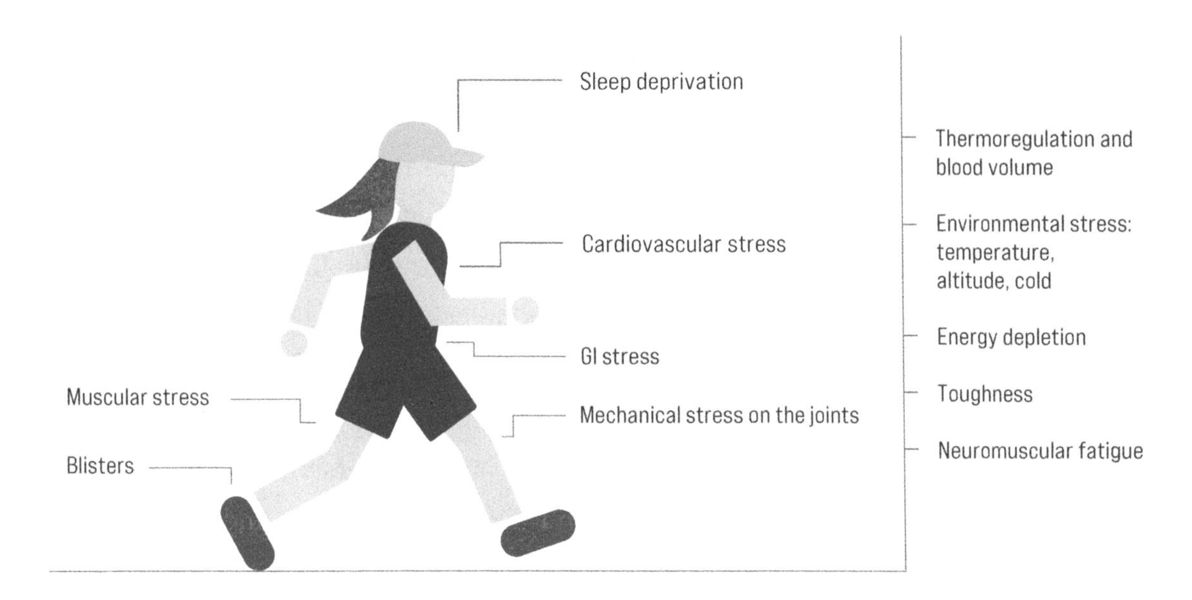

FIGURE 4.2 Ultramarathon race stressors.

a thirty-hour 100-mile finish.

Former Western States record holder Timothy Olson ran 14:46:44 in that coveted race. This time works out to about 8:50/mile. When we tested Timothy in our lab, his lactate threshold pace was under 6:00/mile. At a pace slower than 6:00/mile, his aerobic system can keep up with his energy demand, delivering oxygen to his muscles at a rate that is sustainable with few negative by-products. Having coached Timothy since he set that record, I can attest that on any given day, an 8:50/mile pace is not challenging for his cardiovascular system, even on terrain similar to Western States. Yet if you look at his Cal Street section (from mile 62 to mile 78), you will see that he ran for 16 miles with a net elevation loss at a pace of nearly 9:00/mile. From the standpoint of cardiovascular fitness, that 9:00/mile pace, which is more than 50 percent slower than his lactate threshold pace, was easy. It was essentially a normal recovery-run pace for him. So why on race day, sixty-two miles into a record-setting performance, couldn't Timothy run faster than his normal recovery-run pace? The answer lies in the fact that there are many stressors on race day, and success in an ultramarathon has far more to do with your ability to cope with the sum total of those stressors than with the capacity of your cardiovascular system alone.

Figure 4.2 illustrates the major limiting factors experienced by ultrarunners. They are not all equally limiting, but they all play some part in any ultramarathon. Your goal is to arrive at the starting line as a 100-percent-ready athlete, meaning your training has fully prepared you to handle all the potential stressors of the event.

This sounds like a simple task. However, distinguishing fact from fiction in today's world makes finding good information on how to train for these limiting factors problematic. Particularly because of the proliferation of social media and worldwide connectivity, there is more information (and misinformation) than ever about how to prepare for any endurance sport. The minute another study comes out, the popular press jumps on any new and unique angle. The 280-character version is posted on Twitter; the highlights of the article are "shared" and "liked" on Facebook; and athletes read said interpretation of the study and chase it accordingly. How can you not? You might read, "Study shows that breathing through the left nostril improves endurance performance by 12 percent" and think, Then why the heck do I need a right nostril in the first place? Some of the research is better than the rest, some is outdated, and some is very good, but how do you wade through it all? One of the failings of popular media is that they can always find some research to support an idea on how to improve endurance performance. Additionally, like any other area of science, sports science is constantly evolving. What we knew to be true several years ago may no longer be considered true now or in the future.

With this limitation in mind, I developed my training strategy for ultramarathoners by combining research specifically done with ultramarathoners, research in other endurance disciplines that can be applied to ultrarunning, and practical coaching experience. Academics and journalists would lay out all the studies, strategies, and philosophies side by side and leave you to figure out what to do with them. That's like having a doctor hand you textbooks when you go into the office feeling like death warmed over. When you're sick, all you want to know is what to do to get better. As an athlete you want to know how to use the best that science has to offer to improve your performance. I'm going to do both—explain the science and show you how to practically use it to optimize your performance.

Hydration, Sodium, and Thermoregulation

Although an ultramarathoner will face many stressors on race day, much of the associated duress is fundamentally determined by two very simple physiological factors: hydration status and fuel availability. Of the two, hydration status is far more important. The fact of the matter is, fueling errors are easy to fix, but your hydration status is not. You can pop a gel, drink a Coke, or eat some noodles and within minutes add fuel to the fire. Your body's process for this is simple: eat, get sugar into your bloodstream, and deliver it to your muscles and brain. Even if you eat the "wrong" thing, you will still get sugar into your body relatively quickly.

If you screw up your hydration status, the fix is not so simple. Compared with fixing a bonk, the remedy involves far more complex mechanisms that include hormonal regulation, electrochemical gradients, and other ridiculously complicated-sounding phenomena. At times, staying hydrated sounds more like an engineering project than just talking about water. In addition to being more complicated than "eat sugar and let it digest," these mechanisms of regulating hydration (and therefore blood volume) are indeed slower. They take hours to rectify if disturbed, and the series of steps an athlete may need to follow is often complicated.

More importantly, the penalty for screwing up your hydration (and therefore blood volume) is far more severe than bonking. If you run low on energy, you simply slow down and eat. At worst, you get disoriented, which in extreme cases can lead to nausea and vomiting. Don't get me wrong, those are not good outcomes, but a drop in blood volume can be much more catastrophic. I'm not trying to scare anyone off from running an ultra, but if you screw up your hydration enough, you could end up in the hospital or even die. The magnitude of the "penalty for failure" in this respect is precisely why hydration, sodium, and thermoregulation are the most important nutritional aspects to understand while preparing for an ultra.

Over the past several years, it seems like more sports science research has been done in the area of hydration and sodium consumption than in any other. This makes sense given the aforementioned importance and the overall complexity of the issue (not to mention the financial incentive for for-profit companies to demonstrate the efficacy of their drinks). In ultramarathoning, sodium supplementation has gone from being demonized to in vogue and back again. Even the most basic measurements, such as an ultrarunner's body weight (which can fluctuate based on hydration status), goes in and out of favor. As an example: for many years, high-profile races such as the Western States 100 and Wasatch Front 100 used body weight to determine if a runner was fit to continue. While that practice is no longer followed at those races, the fact that one of the simplest tools available, one that physicians have used for hundreds of years, was deemed essential and then disappeared in the matter of a few years emphasizes how complicated the practice of monitoring hydration can be.

The current battle between "drink early and often" vs "drink only in response to thirst" adds more confusion for ultrarunners. It is important to realize that in the context of hydration, water, sodium, and carbohydrate need to be considered simultaneously. These components are intertwined, with one always affecting the others. Therefore, the recommendation for when to drink always needs to begin with the answer to an earlier question: What should you drink? While some physiological aspects of fluid and sodium balance are still debatable, research has provided athletes with key recommendations for maintaining hydration and sodium balance and ultimately for improving performance. This is such a large topic that rather than getting bogged down in it here, I have covered it in greater detail in Chapter 13.

Fueling and GI Distress

For the last several years on April Fools' Day, GU Energy Labs designed elaborate pranks that revolved around a nutrition "breakthrough." One year it was the flavor of their gels. Their lineup of "savory" flavors like Pimento Loafer, Lard Dart, and Savory Sardine was simultaneously funny and vomit-inducing. One memorable prank, though, struck a particular chord: DermaCharge, a gel that you smeared on your skin that delivered energy and electrolytes. The gag was hilarious, complete with scents of Tenacious Tomato, Sultry Cucumber, Intense Butter, and Furious Avocado, and, of course, photos of a fitness model smearing the goop on his six-pack abs. I got a good laugh out of it, but that day the questions I received by email ranged from "What do you think of this? Is it going to work?" to "How come you never mentioned this to me?" Some athletes were actually upset that they learned about this breakthrough from social media and not from their beloved coach.

At first I was stunned at how easily the wool had been pulled over their eyes. I mean, come on, a goop that you rub on your skin that smells "furiously" like avocado and delivers a wallop of carbohydrate and electrolyte? Really? Besides the lesson to be wary of marketing, their reactions reemphasized an important point: athletes are always looking for a better way to fuel. If one thing is drilled into ultramarathon runners' heads more than any other concept, it is that you must fuel in order to be successful. Even for my athletes, who have worked considerably on their nutrition strategies to minimize the stomach distress referenced in Hoffman and Fogard's research, any conceivable way to take in calories without eating sounded too good to pass up . . . even if it was as silly as rubbing avocado-scented goop on their bellies.

WHAT THE SCIENCE SAYS

At a fundamental level, digestion is a relatively simple process. When you eat a gel, cookie, or anything else at the aid station table, you must first mechanically break down the food by chewing it in your mouth, where it comes into contact with enzymes in saliva, and by churning it in your stomach. Then your stomach and intestines chemically break it down further with gastric juices, acids, and more enzymes. Finally, the intestines absorb the nutrients from the broken-down food and transfer them into the bloodstream. The key is that both a mechanical and a chemical process are in play when properly digesting and absorbing foodstuffs. Both phases of this process are central to understanding fueling and nausea.

YOUR STOMACH AND INTESTINES ARE MADE OF MUSCLE, TOO!

As I just described, your stomach and intestines are essential for digestion. Because your stomach and intestines are muscular organs, they require blood flow to do their job, just like any other muscle in your body. The problem is, blood flow is a hot commodity when you are running. At any point in time, the blood volume you have available is a fixed resource, and blood is needed to deliver oxygen and nutrients to your working muscles (including your stomach and intestines), and it also needs to move to the surface of your skin to dissipate heat. This creates a fierce competition between the aforementioned processes of digestion, oxygen and nutrient transport, and cooling. And guess which competitor wins? Ding, ding, ding! If it has to, your body prioritizes cooling, in order to protect vital organs, over delivering oxygen to working muscles (thankfully so, I might add). When this happens, blood flow to the stomach and intestines decreases, movement of food through the gut slows or stops, and pretty soon you start experiencing gastrointestinal distress. In this way, training to become more fit increases your body's ability to process food during an event. The reason is that training increases your overall heat tolerance and reduces the blood flow required by skeletal muscles at the same running pace, both of which free up blood to be sent to the gut.

The number one recommendation when you have a queasy stomach is to "slow down and cool off." Besides being easy to remember and implement, this advice is effective because both actions redistribute blood flow from other areas back to the stomach. Slowing down reduces the oxygen and nutrient demands from your working skeletal muscles, thereby freeing up blood for digestion. Cooling off does the same by reducing your body's need to send blood to the skin in order to cool you down. You get the greatest bang for your buck by doing both because slowing down also reduces the heat generated by skeletal muscles and helps you cool down more quickly.

DAMAGE TO THE GUT

In addition to creating a competition for blood flow, endurance running causes damage to the gut as a by-product of digestion, blood flow reduction, and constant jostling up and down (Heer et al. 1987; Lucas and Schroy 1998; Øktedalen et al. 1992; Papaioannides et al. 1984). Recently researchers at Monash University studied the naturally present bacteria (endotoxins) that leak into the bloodstream as a result of this damage. They found that most individuals participating in an ultramarathon had markers in their bloodstream equivalent to those found in hospital patients experiencing an acute infectious episode (Gill et al. 2015). This means the gut is so damaged that it leaks endotoxins and triggers an immune response that is as severe as if you had a life-threatening

TO EAT ON THE UPHILLS OR DOWNHILLS?

WHEN AND WHAT YOU ARE DOING while you eat can affect food tolerance and calorie absorption. The less jostling you are experiencing and the more blood flow you have available, the better you will tolerate food. Furthermore, eating smaller portions of food means less blood flow is required by the gut for digestion, and you will have less stuff bouncing around in your stomach that could potentially damage it. So, when considering your next cookie, pretzel, or gel, think first about the ideal time to eat it. If you do have to take in a bigger caloric punch, do it when you have the greatest blood flow available and the least jostling—in other words, during a slower uphill hike. The goal is to have as much of that food as possible digested and into your bloodstream by the time you return to higher intensity or more jostling. Depending on the length of the climb, try to finish eating at least ten minutes before the summit. Taking in your bigger portions of calories during the slower, less intense sections of any ultra may help stave off the gut distress that can be caused by reduced blood flow and damage to the gut.

infection. Although the researchers concluded that the damage was significant and that the gut was impaired, little evidence was presented for how to alleviate or avoid the condition. The one correlating factor suggested by the research team was that the individuals who had simply trained more exhibited less damage (Monash University 2015). Further research is needed to better understand why this extreme amount of damage to the gut occurs, but the current takeaway suggested by the research team is simple: better training equals less damage to the gut and less damage to the gut leads to less gastrointestinal distress which literally fuels better performance.

Blisters

My very first ultramarathon experience was as a crew member for Dean Karnazes during the Badwater Ultramarathon. Talk about jumping into the deep end. I was extremely nervous and legitimately underqualified. Assisting a well-known athlete in a big, demanding race in a completely foreign environment was way over my head. Therefore, before the race, I did copious amounts of research on the course, what to expect, the limiting factors for performance, and how the race worked (Badwater is unique in that the crew can accompany the runner nearly the entire way). Through that research, two things stuck out: Death Valley would be hot as hell (duh), and runners often end up with mangled feet. I immediately made three purchases: an ice bandana, a prepackaged blister kit, and the book *Fixing Your Feet* by John Vonhof. When I opened up the package and started rifling through the contents of the blister kit, I had no clue how all the powders, lubricants, tapes, adhesives, and bandages worked. So, I read, and I practiced. I would read through a section of my new book, contort my legs like a tenth-degree yogi to gain access to my foot, apply some concoction of adhesive and tape, and then go run to test out the technique. Every day, I tried something different. As the race neared, I was obsessed. To put some of these newfound techniques to the ultimate test, and to mirror the conditions of the race—specifically the condition of constantly pouring cold water over yourself and your runner—I routinely soaked my laced-up feet with the garden hose before setting out on a run. Though this process of trial and error, I was able to refine my technique and tools and find what combinations would work for my feet in those conditions (which in this case was a combination of KT tape and tincture of benzoate).

As it turned out, I got to use my newfound skills in the wee hours of the morning in Death Valley, as Dean managed to get a blister smack-dab on the ball of his right foot. Somehow my tape job held up for the remaining forty miles of the race. After Dean's race and our celebratory dinner were over, we staggered into the Dow Villa Motel in Lone Pine, California. The motel is on the racecourse (mile 122) and is used as a medical checkpoint and communications hub for the event. A constant stream of runners ran (or staggered) past the motel throughout the night, illuminated by a union of street-lights, headlamps, multicolored safety lights, and reflective vests. Curious and hopped up on far too much caffeine, I stayed awake all night watching the battered runners gradually make their way down the course. Most of them looked awful, limping and moving very slowly through the darkness. They were dealing with a variety of issues: tired legs, fried brains, hyponatremia, bonking, hallucinations, you name it. However, one prevailing issue bound them together as brothers and sisters of this race: collectively, their feet were destroyed. Runner after runner stopped at the motel to get their feet patched up, sometimes by professionals and sometimes by their crews. Some foot issues were relatively benign. Most were dreadful. All night and into the next day, the runners came in, got patched up, and left ready to tackle the final thirteen miles of the race.

Upon returning home, I decided to reinforce my blister prevention and treatment arsenal and purchased a red plastic toolbox from Home Depot. I filled the box with an array of products to help repair feet when they become battered, bruised, bloodied, and blistered. Admittedly, the toolbox was a bit makeshift—its contents were somewhere between the basic necessities and a full-blown medical kit—but it was mine, and I knew how to use every product in it. More than fifteen years later, I still have this same box. I bring it with me whenever I attend an ultramarathon as a coach or as an athlete. Often it remains idle. At other races it is a lifeline for athletes. I take comfort in knowing that if athletes do run into trouble with their feet, I have some level of skill to patch them up and get them on their way.

Hoffman and Fogard's survey of participants in the Western States 100 and Vermont 100 demonstrates that blisters remain a prevalent issue and do limit performance. Quite simply, your feet propel you forward. When your foot is damaged, it affects the entire kinetic chain from the ankle to the knee and through the hip. You might be able to limp through for a while on a sore foot, but chances are that the change in biomechanics will eventually catch up with you and compound the issues you face. In many cases, it's not the blister that leads to the DNF. The blister just starts the process by changing the way you run, and over time those changes lead to other biomechanical problems that slow you down, knocking you off your nutritional strategy, exposing you to the elements longer, and so forth. This does not have to be the case. Blisters can be largely prevented through training, prevention, a little treatment know-how, and better race-day management. Treatment is relatively easy, requiring a few basic products and skills to fix the majority of issues. It takes practice, but it's worth it.

PREVENTING AND TREATING BLISTERS

Whenever you stress an organ or a structure in your body beyond its capabilities, you cause damage. Ultramarathons normally represent a longer, more difficult run than your day-to-day training, complicated by the fact most ultramarathon events occur in areas away from your home training grounds. The trail surface, camber, dirt, dust, and debris your feet encounter are undoubtedly different during the race than at home. Furthermore, your biomechanics are different depending on the properties of the trails, placing stresses on different areas of the foot—and, of course, the skin covering those areas. Consequently, the shoe/sock/powder/tape/lubricant/insole combination that worked in training may not always work during the race. Just as training on flat ground will not completely prepare you for a mountainous ultra, training on your home trails might not fully prepare your feet for the rigors of race day. Therefore, a combination of education, preventive measures, and wound care skills offers the most comprehensive way to ensure that your hard-earned training is not negated by the unraveling of your feet on race day.

WHAT THE SCIENCE SAYS

What runners commonly refer to as a blister is clinically termed a "friction blister" because friction is the primary culprit. Although heat and moisture are contributing factors, friction and the underlying shear forces (forces parallel to the ground) are what ultimately cause the dreaded blister (Figure 4.3). As I will discuss later in this chapter, with each and every foot strike, you apply shear forces parallel to the surface of the

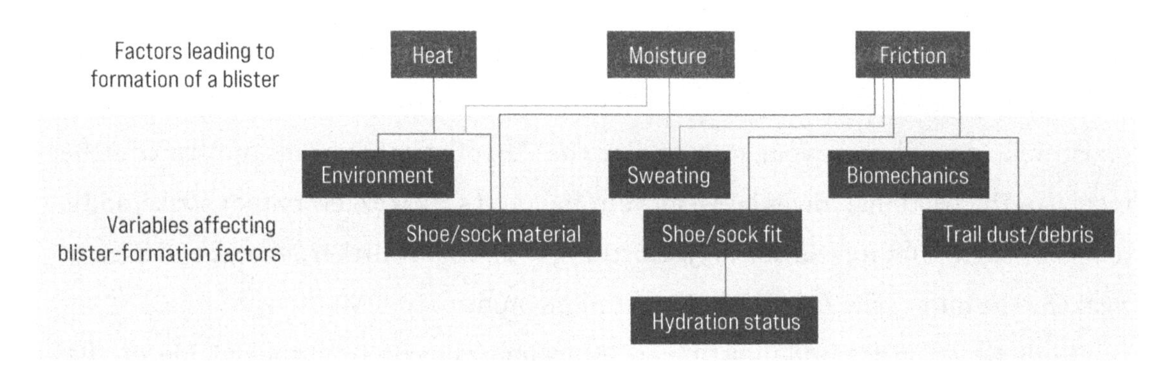

FIGURE 4.3 Heat + moisture + friction = blister.

ground in both the anterior-posterior (forward-backward) and the mediolateral (side-to-side) directions. As you hit the ground, the ground pushes backward on your shoe, your insole pushes backward on your sock, and your sock pushes backward on your skin. Then as you push off the ground, these forces between your skin and sock, sock and insole, and shoe and ground all reverse direction.

The problem is that the surface of your skin is pliable (after all, it is called soft tissue). As your body applies these shear forces, your soft tissue (skin on the feet) moves more than your skeletal system (rigid bone). These out-of-sync movements between your skeleton, soft tissue, sock/shoe, and shoe/ground are what ultimately cause the frictional force that leads to a blister. Your shoe and sock move against your outer layer of skin (epidermis) more than your outer layer of skin moves against your inner layer of skin (dermis). As the bump and grind between these two skin layers continues, the layers eventually separate. Once this separation occurs, fluid fills the void due to hydrostatic pressure. The result is a fluid sac between the newly separated layers of skin bordered by yet-to-be separated layers along the edges.

The addition of heat and moisture exacerbates blister formation. Heat accelerates the blistering process primarily by loosening the bond between the dermis and epidermis. Research has demonstrated that an increase in skin temperature of 4°C will accelerate blister formation by 50 percent (Hashmi et al. 2013; Kiistala 1972b). Increases in foot skin temperature, heat from the environment, metabolic response, and heat from frictional forces all add to the heat within your shoes. Plus, the warmer your feet are, the more they sweat. The more your feet sweat, the more saturated your socks, shoes, and skin become. Dumping water on your head, running through a river crossing, and running in the rain all accomplish the same feat (excuse the pun): they increase the moisture in your shoe, in your sock, and on the skin of your foot. This moisture further increases the frictional forces between your foot and sock with every foot strike, adding to blister susceptibility (Naylor 1955; Worthing et al. 2017). Furthermore, the moisture weakens the outer layer of skin, making it more prone to injury.

While heat, trauma, and moisture are attacking your skin from the outside, on the inside your hydration status can also make you more susceptible to blisters. If a runner becomes even slightly hyponatremic (having low blood sodium), one of the body's protective mechanisms—long before blood sodium levels are dangerously low—is to pull water out of the plasma and into the extracellular space, thus increasing the concentration of sodium in the blood. As a simple by-product of gravity, this fluid in the extracellular space pools in the extremities, commonly resulting in puffy hands or feet. Unlike your hands, your feet are subject to the rigors of propelling you forward. The increased fluid in the extracellular space in the skin of your feet accelerates the blistering process: it causes your feet to get bigger, turning your once perfectly broken-in shoes into friction-laden traps. It also loosens the skin layers, enabling fluid to be pushed between the dermis and epidermis more easily.

TRAINING, GEAR, AND PROTECTION

Each of the three aforementioned blister factors of friction, heat, and moisture can be alleviated with the right combination (in order of priority) of training, gear (shoes and socks), race-day preventive measures, and finally treatment.

How Training Influences Blister Formation

Training is the first level of prevention in blister formation. Your skin adapts to stress just like any other organ in your body. Many studies, primarily involving the military, have demonstrated that gradual exposure to frictional forces on the foot (through hikes and marches) decreases the skin's susceptibility to blisters (Allan 1964; Hodges, DuClos, and Schnitzer 1975; Knapik et al. 1995). As you train, your epidermal skin cells become thicker and in theory more cohesive, making them more resistant to blistering. How

SHAVE DOWN YOUR CALLUSES

SHOULD YOU KEEP YOUR CALLUSES or shave them down? Proponents of keeping the callus say the extra-thick skin is less prone to damage and therefore acts as a protective layer. Although there is some truth to this, the far greater risk is that the callus will continue to grow and become an anomaly in the foot/shoe interface (i.e., it sticks out). Remember that a blister forms when an outer layer of skin moves out of sync with an inner layer of skin. A callus can act as the outer layer and still separate from the inner layer of dermis, leading to a blister under your callus! When this happens you generally lose the entire callus, which defeats the purpose of building up this protective layer of extra thick skin.

Because allowing calluses to become overly thick greatly increases the likelihood of forming a blister under the callus, I encourage athletes to keep calluses shaved down to maintain a smoother, more uniform skin surface. That doesn't mean you should remove calluses entirely. Use a pumice stone or metal callus shaver and file down the callus so that it is flush with the surrounding skin. Shaving them is a matter of maintenance, not removal.

does this happen? As you run, you slough off skin cells faster than normal. These are rapidly replaced by new skin cells, but the young cells don't get the chance to differentiate into layer-specific cells (epidermis, dermis) before they are stressed by another run (Kim et al. 2010). When this happens frequently over a relatively short time, it results in overthickened skin, otherwise known as a callus.

How Shoe and Sock Choice Influences Blister Formation

Your shoe and sock combination is the next level of blister prevention. With respect to blister prevention, your shoe/sock combination should serve the dual purposes of (1) reducing frictional forces between your skin and sock and your sock and shoe and (2) managing moisture transfer from your foot into the air. Some socks that segregate the toes (toe socks) also aim to reduce the skin-to-skin friction between the toes. Overwhelming research has shown that a well-fitting wicking sock offers the best blister prevention strategy (Herring and Richie 1990; Knapik et al. 1995, 1996). Fortunately, most sock companies are now wise to this idea and are moving away from thicker, bulkier, and less wicking socks for runners and ultrarunners. Shoe companies are following suit. Materials for shoes are constantly becoming more pliant and breathable, and shoes are available in a wider variety of shapes and sizes. Perhaps blister prevention is not the shoe manufacturers' end goal, but the improvements in materials and fit do help.

You should test your shoe/sock combination in training and conduct shoe trials early in the season. It is important to figure out what works and what doesn't far out from your event so you can ramp up your training without fear of damaging your feet. Along these lines, once you find the combination that works for you, I recommend investing in enough shoes and socks to get you through the entire season. Ultrarunners burn through shoes and socks, and designs or availability can change unexpectedly. You don't want to be searching for new shoes or having to switch to a new model or design in the middle of the season when your training workload is very high.

Race-Day Preventive Measures

One lesson I've learned from racing and crewing ultramarathons—and from watching that parade of mangled feet at Badwater—is that athletes use an incredibly wide range of techniques to prevent blisters on race day. Some use tape, some use lubricants, and some use powders. The more creative ultrarunners will use elaborate combinations and concoctions of all of the above, sometimes taking hours to apply. In many cases, two runners will use techniques with opposing goals (keep the skin from moving vs encourage the skin to move with less friction), and both techniques may (or may not) work. This reinforces the "find what works for you" advice from the bible of blister prevention and treatment, *Fixing Your Feet,* which makes the point by providing numerous personal "n of 1" anecdotes from athletes. From a scientific standpoint, this advice rings true. In fact, there is little scientific evidence that any of the aforementioned strategies work. Furthermore, there is conflicting research indicating that some preventive measures actually exacerbate the problem by adding moisture and thus increasing skin friction (Figure 4.4; Allan 1964; Allan and Macmillan 1963; Knapik, Reynolds, and Barson 1998; Knapik et al. 1995; Nacht et al. 1981; Quinn 1967; Reynolds et al. 1995).

This is an area where less is more. The prevention strategies we know work are

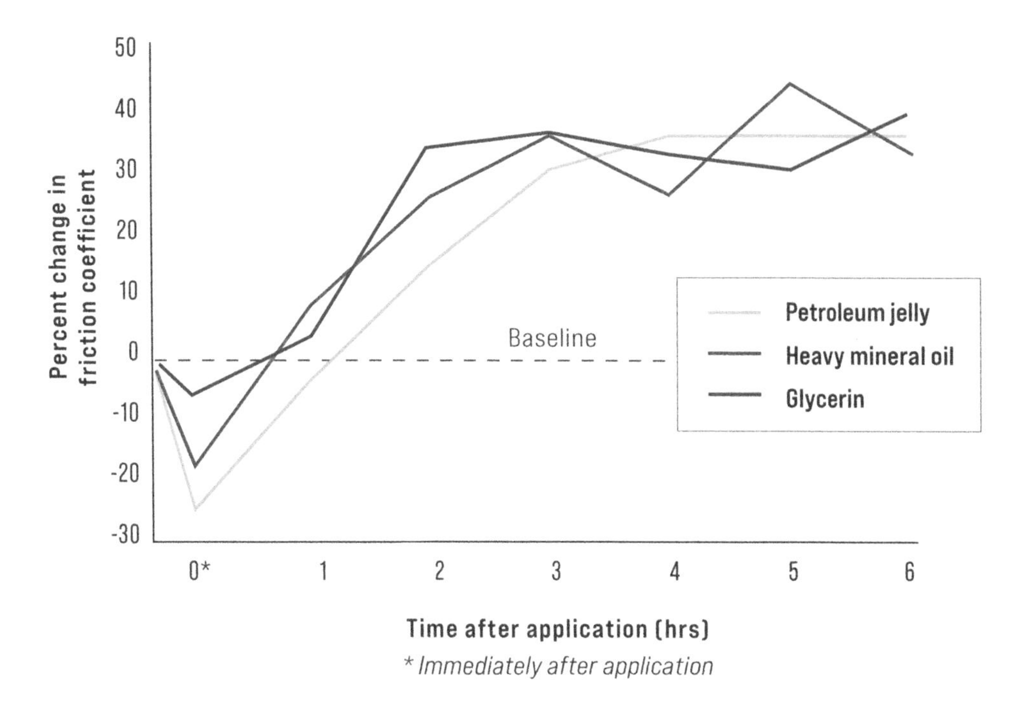

FIGURE 4.4 Graph showing an initial decrease, then increase, in friction of common lubricants when used on the skin. Source: Nacht et al. 1981.

training (conditioning the feet to handle the stresses of long miles) and an effective shoe/sock combination. These should always be your starting points. Adding other techniques like tape, lubricant, powder, or antiperspirant increases complexity, adds more variables to the training or race-day situation, and might exacerbate the problem.

It is also important to realize there is no combination of equipment or amount of training that will entirely eliminate the risk of developing blisters during training or on race day. You can minimize these risks as much as possible, but you also have to learn to patch and repair a blister in the field when things go wrong.

Blister Patch and Repair

If you do get a blister (or the precursor, which is referred to as a "hot spot"), you have a decision to make: you can save some time and continue running, or you can stop and lose some time treating your feet. In making this decision, you need to balance your race-day goals, performance expectations, safety, and race situation. Generally speaking, the more time you have left to run and the bigger the problem could become, the more it is worth your while to take a few minutes and fix what is wrong. Don't let little problems become big problems. My advice is to always err on the side of caution and fix problems early, particularly at the 100K and 100-mile distances, where there is a lot of ground to cover.

If you are in a situation where you choose not to stop and fix a blister, or you are many miles from the next aid station and you have no products to treat the blister, it is time to suck it up. Blisters hurt because the foot is highly innervated, and runners tend to find relief by changing their gait or foot-strike pattern. While this is a logical strategy ("I have pain there; I am going to try to avoid it"), the ramifications of changing your gait too much can have consequences up the kinetic chain. Your foot, ankle, knee, and hip are all connected and constantly affect one another. Although I am an advocate for manipulating gait and biomechanics in an effort to combat muscular fatigue (as you will see in the next section), I do not advocate doing so in the context of a blister. In this case it's time to be tough and keep your gait as normal as possible. Running with your normal gait may make the blister worse, but that's still only one problem and one

WHAT A BLISTER KIT SHOULD CONTAIN

THIS SMALL ASSORTMENT OF PRODUCTS will be enough to fix minor and moderate blisters out in the field and keep you moving. It is manageable for your crew to carry or to pack in a drop bag. It is neither a substitute for a full medical kit nor what you would use to treat skin injuries after a race.

- Adhesive felt sheet or moleskin
- Needles or small scalpel (size 11)
- Alcohol pads or Betadine swabs
- Gloves
- Kinesio Tex Gold tape, Elastikon tape, and/or Leukotape (to patch or prevent)
- Scissors
- Adhesive such as tincture of benzoin
- Lubricant such as Body Glide, BlisterShield, or Squirrel's Nut Butter
- Gauze pads

you can treat and get under control. Changing your gait to "run around a blister" can lead to pain or injuries you can't effectively treat and control while continuing to race. Of course, while you might have to tough it out and run on a blister on race day, it's not a strategy to rely on. Blisters can and should be prevented and treated.

Blisters come in a variety of shapes, sizes, and levels of discomfort. Treatments also come in many shapes and forms. Unless you are a medical professional with many years of blister management experience, a simple solution is always best. I have found success with the following nine-step plan:

1. Clean the surface of the blister and the surrounding skin. If an alcohol pad or disinfectant is available, use it. If not, it is still usually best to proceed to step 2. You are less prone to infection if you can properly manage the blister while it is small and treatable. Large broken blisters will become prone to infection more readily than small broken blisters because there is more opportunity to become infected through the larger area of damaged and exposed skin.
2. Puncture the blister with a sterile needle, sharp scissors, or scalpel. (I prefer the scalpel, as you can use it to create a window or hole for the blister to drain better.) Take care to puncture the blister enough to allow fluid to drain but not so much that the blister roof becomes detached. If you are using a needle (sterilized safety pins from a race bib also work well), put three to four holes in the blister so that it will drain. Ideally, position the punctures such that fluid can continue to drain while you keep running.
3. Squeeze the fluid out of the blister.
4. Clean and dry the surface of the blister and the surrounding skin. You are now prepping the skin to apply a patch, so ensure that it is dry and free of debris. You can choose to add a very small dab of lubricant to the blister roof. This is to prevent the patch from sticking to the blister roof when you eventually peel the tape off.
5. Size up the area you are going to dress and cut a piece of tape or bandage to cover the blister. It should be large enough so that it can stick to the surrounding undamaged skin. If the blister is on a toe, this might mean wrapping the entire toe. If you do have to wrap a toe, it's usually best to wrap the adjacent toes as well so that the tape does not rub directly on adjacent skin.

6. Apply a tape adhesive such as tincture of benzoin to the area surrounding the blister. Although the tape has its own adhesive backing, using an additional tape adhesive will ensure a better stick.
7. Place the tape down on the skin from one edge of the tape to the other. Be careful to avoid folds and creases. If you do get a fold or a crease, start over.
8. Lightly press down on the patch to ensure the adhesive completely sticks to the skin.
9. Put your socks on, lace up your shoes, and run!

If you are particularly blister prone, practice various techniques at home. Cutting and placing the patch on the surface of the skin can be the most frustrating part of the process during a race. The tape is sticky and adheres to itself and to your fingers. You're in a hurry. You're sweaty and dirty. And you're working in a dirty, dusty environment. Finding a routine and learning some simple skills goes a long way toward making the process smoother and faster in race conditions. As with any other skill, practice makes perfect!

Muscular Breakdown and Fatigue

The overall concept of muscular breakdown and fatigue incorporates several areas of physiology. Physical trauma to the muscle, depleted energy stores, neuromuscular dysfunction, central vs peripheral fatigue, and myriad other phenomena fall under this umbrella. To avoid recreating a muscle physiology textbook, I will focus specifically on the aspects of ultramarathoning that lead to muscular breakdown and fatigue.

ULTRAMARATHONS AND MUSCULAR BREAKDOWN

It is well documented that a significant amount of muscular breakdown occurs during an ultramarathon. Researchers have studied the blood parameters that indicate muscular trauma, particularly creatine kinase (CK), from finishers in Spartathlon, the Ultra-Trail du Mont-Blanc, and the Western States 100, among others. With respect to muscular breakdown, all the research comes to the same conclusion: there's a lot of it in ultrarunning. Additionally, there's tremendous variability among individuals. Blood markers for CK after an ultramarathon range from relatively normal to more than 100 times normal values (Fallon et al. 1999; Kim, Lee, and Kim 2007; Millet et al. 2011; Overgaard et al. 2002). That's a lot of muscular tissue turnover. This is all obvious to ultrarunners, even if they've never heard of CK or any of the other biochemical markers associated with pain, fatigue, and muscular breakdown, because they run slower at the end of a race.

Although it's clear that muscular breakdown and fatigue are significant, there's so much individual variability that it is difficult to determine ways to prevent them (Figure 4.5). Correlations between muscular fatigue and training components such as volume and vertical gain/loss are scant. The same goes for correlations between any race-day phenomenon (nutrition, pacing, hydration) and muscular fatigue or damage. Whenever this is the case, it is important to rely on best practices and research in other areas to help guide training principles.

With that as an introduction, a quick biomechanics lesson is in order.

During the course of running, your muscles can only pull, or contract, to move your limbs. They cannot push. When muscles pull, you generate positive force. This positive force is what pushes you off the ground and propels you forward. However, during the course of a step on level ground, you need to generate an equal amount of negative force (or counterproductive force) as your foot initially hits the ground and your body is lowered. During this initial phase of foot strike, many of your muscles are actively being lengthened, or pulling against a force in the opposite direction. Make no mistake: they

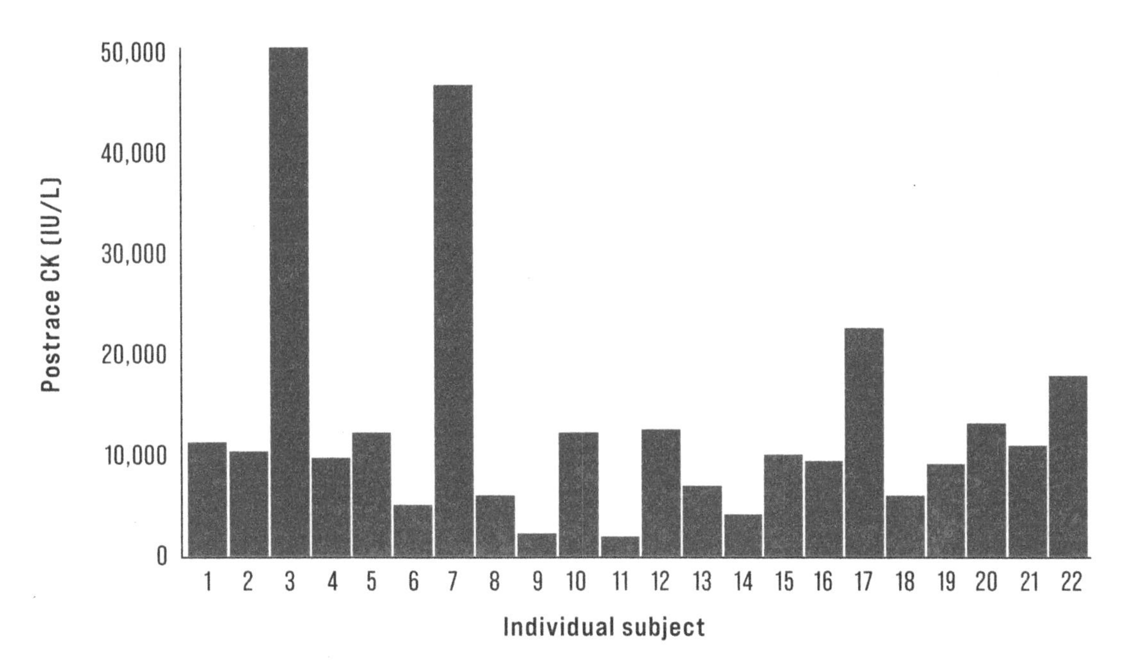

FIGURE 4.5 Postrace creatine kinase (CK) levels in Ultra-Trail du Mont-Blanc finishers. Adapted from Millet et al. 2011.

STEP VS STRIDE

FOR YEARS THE WORDS "STEP" AND "STRIDE" have been used interchangeably (and thus incorrectly) in popular literature. For the purposes of this book and to be accurate, I am going to use these terms correctly. A step is defined as one foot strike to the opposite foot strike, in terms of either length or time (i.e., the distance between your left foot hitting the ground and your right foot hitting the ground, or the time that passes between the two footfalls). A stride is defined as one foot strike to the same foot striking the ground (i.e., the distance or time from your left foot hitting the ground to your left foot hitting the ground again). Therefore, your stride length will be double your step length, because two steps essentially equal one stride.

- Step length: the distance between the initial contact of one foot and the initial contact of the opposite foot
- Step rate: the total number of right and left foot strikes per minute
- Stride length: the distance between the initial contact of one foot and the next initial contact of the same foot
- Stride frequency: the total number of the same foot strikes per minute (e.g., the total number of right foot strikes per minute)

FIGURE 4.6

are still pulling; they are just doing so against a larger force and are therefore lengthened. This active lengthening is what is oxymoronically referred to as an eccentric contraction. Such contractions are unavoidable, whether one is running or walking (DeVita, Helseth, and Hortobagyi 2007; Enoka 2008).

Whenever an eccentric contraction happens, a certain amount of muscular breakdown occurs. The amount of breakdown varies with the individual and with velocity, force, and the total repetitions that are produced (Chapman et al. 2006; Nosaka and Clarkson 1996; Tiidus and Ianuzzo 1982)—all of which is fine and dandy to know, but what do you do about it?

HOW TO COMBAT MUSCULAR BREAKDOWN

Eccentric contractions and the muscular breakdown associated with them have long been villains in the coaching and training world. The victims are your muscles, which lose their ability to function when you have stronger, more frequent, and a higher total number of eccentric contractions (Bontemps et al. 2020; Chapman et al. 2006; Ebbeling and Clarkson 1989; Eston, Mickleborough, and Baltzopoulos 1995; Proske and Allen 2005; Proske and Morgan 2001). By its very nature, an ultramarathon creates these conditions because of the hundreds of thousands of steps and associated eccentric contractions required to reach the finish line. Adapting your physiology and finding strategies to handle this huge stress can be a big advantage. Failing to do so can result in a catastrophe—so much so that ultrarunners have contrived numerous techniques to solve the problem. Equipment such as trekking poles and highly cushioned shoes have been used in attempts to minimize the damage. Additionally, training techniques such as strength training and hard downhill repeats have also been utilized by ultrarunners to combat this phenomenon. While many of these efforts deserve credit for trying, problems arise when you look at the science and the practicality of dedicating your precious time and effort specifically to some of these interventions.

While the science is not crystal clear on this aspect of performance, most research points to the rationale that a little eccentric training will go a long way in preventing muscular breakdown and that those adaptations last a long time (Clarkson et al. 1992; Nosaka et al. 2001). What is not clear is what the curve of diminishing returns looks like in this area and how we should determine the optimal amount of eccentric training.

ARE WOMEN MORE FATIGUE-RESISTANT THAN MEN?

EVERY YEAR, SOME ULTRAMARATHONS are won outright by women, leading certain people to ask, "Are women better at ultradistance events than men?" Adding fuel to the fire are anecdotal tales from expedition-length adventure racers about the women commonly outperforming the men on mixed teams late in the race. Many in the ultrarunning world have speculated that women are more psychologically and physically suited for ultramarathons than men, and scientists and researchers have debated whether women should or should not be able to outperform men in ultrarunning, noting the statistical performance differences between men and women at different distances. Early in this statistical debate, it was theorized that women could, in fact, outperform men as the distance increased (Bam et al. 1997). Later statistical analyses, however, contradicted those initial theories (Peter et al. 2014; Zingg et al. 2014). Bringing this argument full circle, recent research into the difference in fatigue resistance between men and women might now actually begin to turn the initial statistical speculations into physiological reality.

Researchers examined different variables related to fatigue for male and female finishers of the 2012 version of the Ultra-Trail du Mont-Blanc (that year's race was shortened to 100K due to inclement weather). What did they find? While both men and women demonstrated similar amounts of central fatigue and muscular damage and inflammation (CK, C-reactive protein, and myoglobin levels), they differed in the amount of peripheral fatigue (fatigue within the muscle itself) measured after the race. The 100K race negatively affected men more than women specifically in the amount of voluntary force produced in the knee extensor and the evoked mechanical response in the plantar flexor (Temesi et al. 2015). Simply stated, within these muscle groups, women fatigued less than men after 100K of mountainous running. Does that translate to women being better ultramarathon runners than men? At this point, no. But the door is certainly open!

SHOULD I CHANGE MY STRIDE?

RECENT RESEARCH HAS SUGGESTED that one way to cope with the massive amount of muscular breakdown is to vary your stride throughout the course of the race (Bontemps et al. 2020; Rowlands et al. 2001). If you are a heel-striker, you would intentionally run with a forefoot strike periodically and vice versa. The theory is that the slight changes in biomechanical patterns will spread the work and subsequent damage out among different muscle groups. In trail running, with its varied terrain, this happens to a certain extent naturally. But in events where the terrain is more homogeneous, consciously altering your gait could prove to be a useful tool to help prevent muscular breakdown.

Additionally, some academic research has suggested that downhill running prowess has more to do with movement coordination than with oxygen consumption or force tolerance (Minetti et al. 2002). Thus, training to run downhills harder (at higher cardiovascular intensity levels and higher forces) might not have as much of an effect as training to run downhills with better technique.

In contrast, we know a lot more about the recovery from large bouts of eccentric training and associated muscular breakdown, and we can use that information to evaluate

RESEARCHERS WANT YOU!

THERE IS A LACK OF COMPREHENSIVE RESEARCH in ultramarathon running. While there are a few dedicated research teams delving into the science of ultrarunning, they are in a vertical kilometer's worth of an uphill battle finding subjects to poke and prod. This does not have to be the case! You can help. I encourage you to participate in the research being done in ultramarathon running. Some of this is done at races, and some is conducted in the lab. If you come across a researcher asking for subjects, please consider participating. Your involvement increases our understanding of the discipline. It might even help to save a life.

and compare eccentric training with other training components. The more you descend, the longer recovery times you will need. Additionally, the faster you descend (the higher forces you apply), the longer recovery times you will need. Comparing foot for foot of elevation change, it will take longer to recover from descending than from ascending, even though ascending requires more energy to perform and a longer time to complete.

Practically, we need to look at this from a cost-benefit ratio standpoint. It doesn't take a lot of descending to achieve the desired adaptation, and more descending requires disproportionately long recovery periods. It is for these reasons (and a couple more I will explain in the next chapter) that my philosophy for coping with muscular fatigue and breakdown revolves around a singular strategy: match the grade and speed of your training to what you will experience during the race. This concept is examined further in Chapter 5.

KEY POINTS ON LIMITING FACTORS

- We are learning more and more each year about ultramarathon performance. We can now lean on practice and science to drive training.
- Ultramarathon stressors are not the same as marathon or other traditional endurance stressors. Performance will be dictated by more than one's VO_2 max, lactate threshold, and the cost of running.
- Ultramarathon performance can be limited by interrelated factors such as hydration, thermoregulation, muscular damage, and gut function.
- Any ultramarathon limiting factor can be trained! That's what this book is for.

BM 1598
Ackerman Sch
North Fork Dam
Gaging Sta
35
36
AMERICAN
RIVER
FOREST
HILL
CANAL
PIPE
BM 1495
BOARDMAN
1
2
1486
PLACER CO
EL DORADO
MIDDLE
FORK
New York Bar
Louisiana Bar
NORTH
FORK
GRADE
BM 1395
AUBURN
11
12
1460
RAILROAD
OLD
Ravine
Warner
Sta
BM 1359
Pointed Rocks
1658
Highland Gen Hosp
PACIFIC
College
Ford
Roble Pt
13
1608
14
GRADE
BM 1539
CANAL
RAILROAD
OLD
Tamaroo Bar
PLACER CO
Creek

CHAPTER 5

The Four Disciplines of Ultrarunning

Many ultramarathons are run over challenging terrain. Some courses have massive amounts of elevation gain, while others are contested over more benign, rolling terrain. Still others are contested on tracks and bike paths. Most ultramarathons contain a mixture of level running, uphill running, downhill running, and walking (which ultrarunners affectionately refer to as power-hiking). It does not take a rocket scientist to know that level running, uphill running, downhill running, and power-hiking are fundamentally different. Much as a swimmer can train for different strokes, these can be viewed as four different disciplines for which runners can train, each with its own set of specificities. If you know some key biomechanical differences among these disciplines, you can better tailor your training for any event. Looking at them side by side will make it easier to see why I prefer uphill interval work, avoid downhill intervals, and recommend trying to match the average grade and locomotive specificity in training to the course you will be running.

Biomechanical Differences

While running uphill, running downhill, running on the flats, and power-hiking are four different disciplines of ultrarunning and should be trained as such, I see athletes neglect the differences between these four disciplines all too often. They run too much when preparing for a mountainous ultra which will require copious amounts of hiking. They focus on "speed work" by hammering out intervals on the track, but at the wrong phase of training or in pursuit of the wrong adaptations.

The best way to differentiate among the four disciplines of ultrarunning is along three facets:

- Differences in ground reaction forces
- How muscles propel you forward or slow you down
- Differences in joint segment angles

MAY THE (GROUND REACTION) FORCE BE WITH YOU!

Each time your foot hits the ground, the ground pushes back with an equal amount of force. Biomechanists refer to these forces as your ground reaction forces (GRFs). With every step taken while running on a flat, level surface, you strike the ground with a force of about 2.5 to 3 times your body weight in the vertical plane (Cavanagh and Lafortune 1980; Chang 2000; Kram et al. 1998; Yack et al. 1998). Running faster increases these forces (Hamill and Knutzen 2006; Munro, Miller, and Fuglevand 1987; Nilsson and Thorstensson 1989). As you run uphill or downhill, these forces change yet again in both magnitude and pattern for the normal (perpendicular to the trail) plane (Gottschal and Kram 2005b). As indicated in Figure 5.1, peak vertical forces for running uphill and downhill at the same speed are only slightly different, with forces for downhill being slightly greater (Gottschal and Kram 2005b). But in the real world, you go downhill a lot faster than you go uphill, right? In which case, here's what's important to note: at the same effort level, running downhill produces much larger forces than flat, level running or uphill running because you are running faster (Figure 5.2).

Walking is a whole different kettle of fish. As can be seen in Figure 5.2, the forces in walking are utterly benign compared to running. The force patterns do not resemble running in the slightest, and peak GRFs are much lower, at 1.2 times body weight (Browning and Kram 2007; Margaria 1976) when walking on level terrain.

These differences in GRFs represent one way the four disciplines of ultrarunning are indeed different. Within each discipline, you strike the ground with a different pattern and peak force.

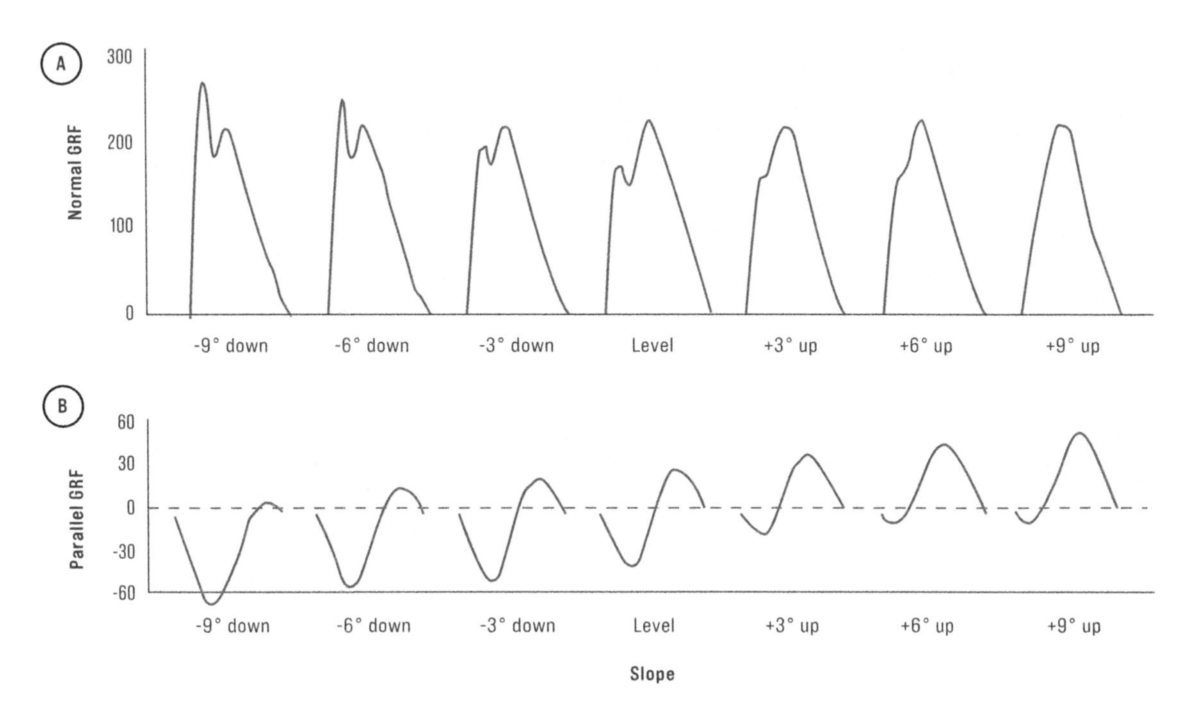

FIGURE 5.1 (A) Normal and (B) parallel ground reaction forces vs time traces for a typical subject (73 kg) running at 3 m/s (~9 min/mi) on different slopes. Adapted from Gottschall and Kram 2005b.

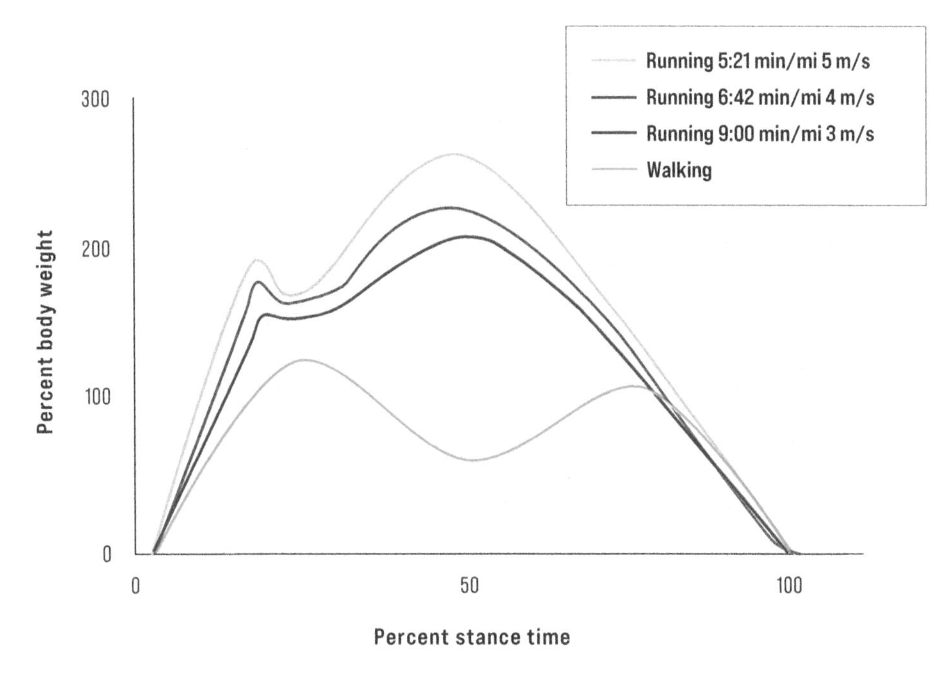

FIGURE 5.2 Vertical (normal) ground reaction force (GRF) for running at different speeds and walking. The running GRF increases with speed, and the walking GRF is noticeably less.

Adapted from Browning and Kram 2007; Gottschal and Kram 2005b; Grabowski and Kram 2008; Keller et al. 1996; Nilsson and Thorstensson 1989.

MUSCLES AND JOINT SEGMENT ANGLES

Just as GRFs differ across the four disciplines, the ways your muscles and joints are used also vary. Scientists measure this activity in two ways. First, they look at the muscles' activity via electromyography (EMG), which involves measuring the electrical activity in surface-level muscles. The more forceful the muscular contraction, the higher the EMG reading. The second way to measure how your muscles and joints operate is to look at your limbs under a high-speed three-dimensional video while running/walking and measure the angles between different joints (known as joint segment angles). This latter analysis provides a physical look at how the limbs move through three-dimensional space and therefore provides clues as to how the underlying musculature is working.

With both of these types of analyses, pictures are worth thousands of words. You certainly do not need to know the minutiae of EMG data and high-speed video analysis to interpret the results. I present Figures 5.3 and 5.4 simply to show that there are obvious and noticeable differences in the data patterns created by each of the four disciplines, demonstrating that you utilize muscles differently for each discipline.

Figure 5.3 summarizes the results of a study in which researchers placed subjects on a treadmill and had them walk, increased the treadmill speed to a run, and then decreased the speed back to a walk (all in a level condition). The researchers then analyzed the resulting EMG data and lower limb angles at these different speeds. Obviously, lower limb angles changed from walking to running. Additionally, nearly all the lower leg muscles exhibited more electrical excitation during running vs walking (see Figure 5.3A). This should come as no surprise, because running generally requires more muscular force than walking. A more important finding as it pertains to ultrarunning is that the actual pattern of muscular activation changed significantly when the subject went from walking to running and from running back to walking (see Figure 5.3B). So not only was there a change in electrical excitation, but there was also a shift in the pattern of how muscles worked together to complete the task.

Similarly, on a whole-body level, joint segment angles can tell the story of the interplay between flat walking, flat running, uphill running, and downhill running. Figure 5.4 visually summarizes how the hip, knee, and ankle angles change during these different disciplines.

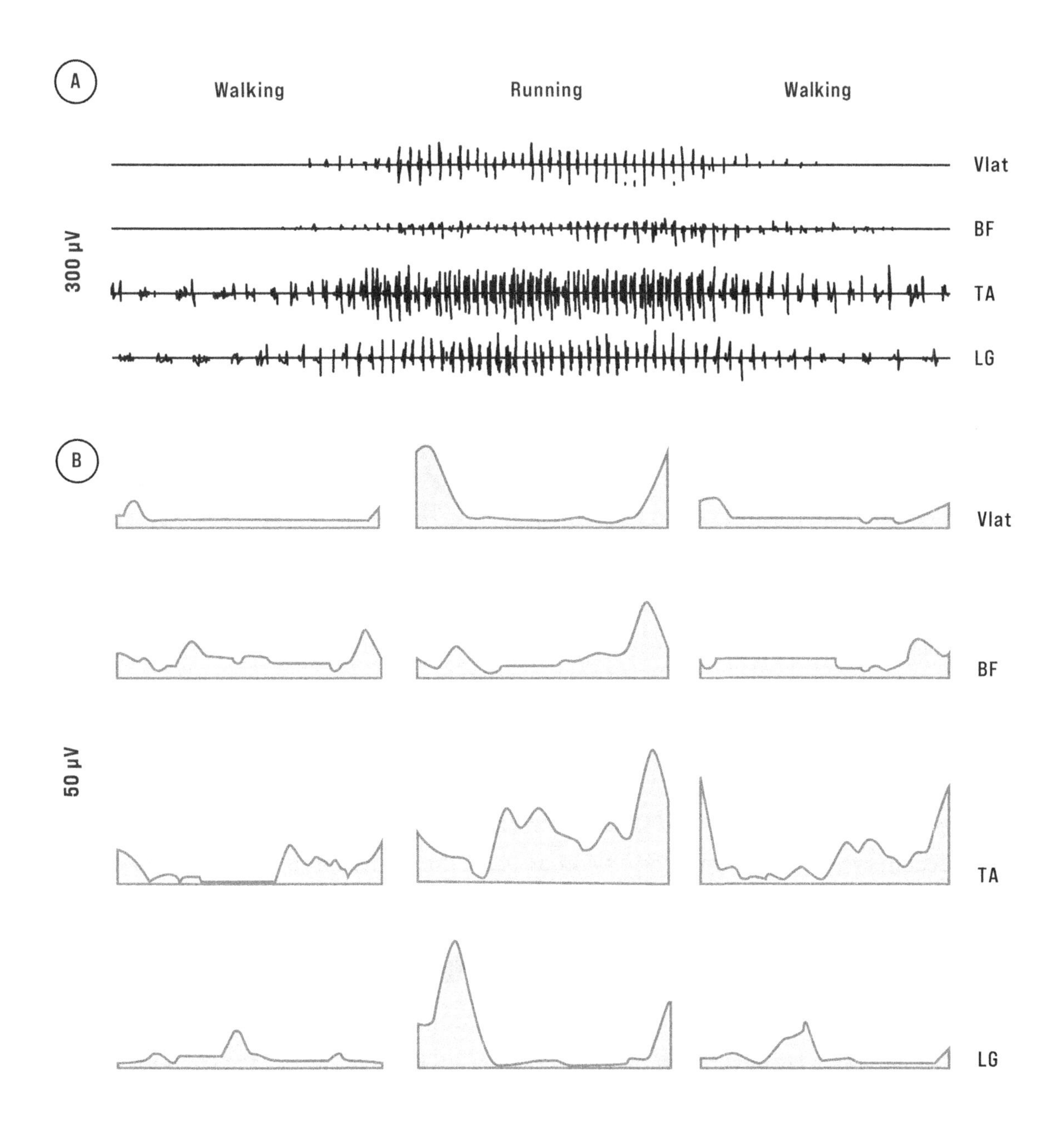

FIGURE 5.3 (A) EMG activity for various muscles in walking, running, and returning to walking. The higher the EMG amplitude, the greater the muscle activation. (B) EMG patterns for various muscles while walking, running, and returning to walking. The patterns of activation are different for walking, running, and then returning to a walk.

Note: Vlat = vastus lateralis; BF = biceps femoris; TA = tibialis anterior; LG = gastrocnemius lateralis. Adapted from Cappellini et al. 2006.

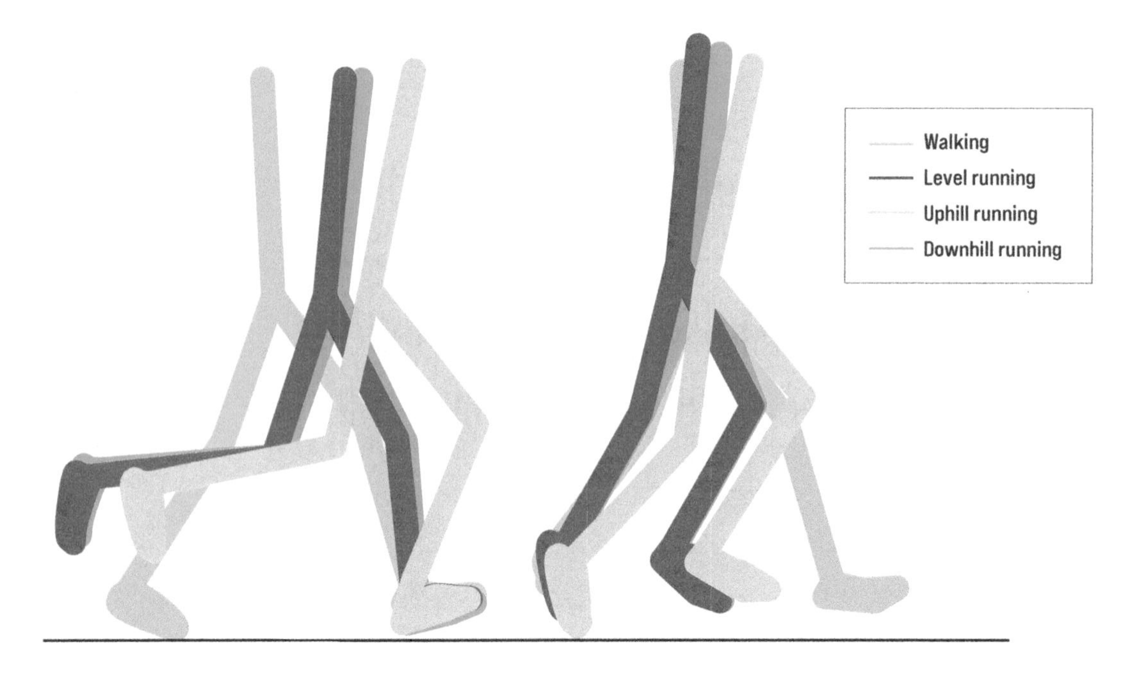

FIGURE 5.4 The hip, knee, and foot are all in different positions when walking or running on level ground, running uphill, and running downhill. Adapted from Guo et al. 2006; Hicheur et al. 2006; Yokozawa 2006.

As can be seen from the force EMG and joint segment data, the four disciplines of ultrarunning serve up different biomechanical stressors. While the cardiovascular system links them all together, the patterns of movement are distinctive enough that I consider them akin to separate sports and hence address them individually in training.

How to Train for the Four Disciplines

Knowing that each of the four disciplines of ultrarunning is unique and requires specific training, you can now put that knowledge into action in your day-to-day training. The simplest way to do this is to determine your event's average elevation change per mile and then try to recreate that elevation change over the course of a week's worth of training, particularly on any non-recovery run and in the last several weeks before an event. (See Chapter 10 on why this latter point is particularly important.)

The average elevation change per mile is determined using this simple calculation:

total elevation change in feet/total miles

For example, the Western States 100-Mile Endurance Run boasts an elevation gain of 18,090 ft and an elevation loss of 22,970 ft over 100.2 miles. Therefore, the average elevation change per mile for the course is the following:

$$(18{,}090 + 22{,}970)/100.2 = 410 \text{ feet of elevation change/mile}$$

Granted, this is the average for the entire course, including the steepest of climbs, level terrain, and varying descents. There are obviously sections that are more or less steep. However, if you attempt to match this average elevation change per mile in a week's worth of training, you'll be on the right path.

If you want to take this concept even further, you can break the course down into the major climbs and descents, find the average grades of those particular components, and search out local trails that are analogous. Finally, if you can anticipate the amount of power-hiking you will do during the race (as a function of the steepness of the climbs and your anticipated pace), you can incorporate that percentage of power-hiking into your training.

If you live near the course, consider yourself lucky. Some ultrarunners have the exact terrain and grade specificity they need to be optimally prepared. Most do not. But, with some background research on the course you are preparing for and a little simple math, you can better tailor your training to the demands of the event and more specifically prepare yourself for the four disciplines.

Flat running, uphill running, power-hiking, and some downhill running can all be done as specific workouts. At Carmichael Training Systems (CTS) we use a specific nomenclature for workouts, and I will use that throughout the book. TempoRuns (TR), SteadyStateRuns (SSR), and RunningIntervals (RI) are all specific workouts that can be done at a variety of grades depending on the goals for the training phase (see Chapter 9). When building fitness early in the season, it is preferable to do these intervals uphill to maximize their aerobic benefit. Later in the year, during training for the specific demands of the event, a mixture of uphills, downhills, and flats can be used, particularly for TR and SSR intensity. RunningIntervals are almost always best completed on flat ground or uphill terrain, as it is difficult to reach the required intensity running downhill, and doing so carries high risks for injury.

MATCHING WORKOUT ELEVATION CHANGE TO RACE ELEVATION CHANGE: AN ATHLETE EXAMPLE

THE FOLLOWING LIST SHOWS several critical workouts from an athlete's final training phase for the Ultra-Trail Mt. Fuji (UTMF). Note that the elevation change per mile on most (but not all) workouts is close to that of the UTMF course (487 feet of change per mile). It's not perfect, nor should your training be!

WEDNESDAY, MARCH 28TH	Miles	11.3
1:45 hour EnduranceRun with 1 x 35 min TempoRun	Vertical gain/loss (ft)	5,544
	Change/mile	491
THURSDAY, MARCH 29TH	Miles	14.7
2:30 hour EnduranceRun	Vertical gain/loss (ft)	7,304
	Change/mile	497
SATURDAY, MARCH 31ST	Miles	22.9
2:40 EnduranceRun with 2 x 30 min SteadyStateRun, 5 min recovery	Vertical gain/loss (ft)	6,738
	Change/mile	294
SUNDAY, APRIL 1ST	Miles	26.1
5:00 hour EnduranceRun	Vertical gain/loss	8,988
	Change/mile	344
WEDNESDAY, APRIL 4TH	Miles	10.6
1:45 hour EnduranceRun with 1 x 35 min TempoRun	Vertical gain/loss (ft)	5,250
	Change/mile	495
THURSDAY, APRIL 5TH	Miles	13.5
2:00 Hour EnduranceRun	Vertical gain/loss (ft)	6,752
	Change/mile	500

Should I Use Poles?

The use of poles in ultramarathons has become increasingly popular. Once largely confined to European races, ultrarunning-specific trekking poles can now be seen in many of the more mountainous ultras in the United States. Advancements in materials and construction have helped to make poles lighter and easier to carry and stow. Poles can be used to aid in propulsion and stability, as well as to redistribute some of the force of running uphill and downhill from the legs to the lesser-used arms.

The use of poles is always a personal choice. Consider these factors before deciding to use or not use poles in your ultra:

- Generally speaking, the more you are going to power-hike and the greater the amount of vertical change on the course, the more aid you will get from using poles.
- You should train with poles for at least four weeks leading up to the race. This is to acquire the necessary skill, strength, and stamina in your arms to use the poles effectively. It will also give you time to decide if you want to use the poles only when moving uphill or in both the uphill and downhill portions.
- The use of poles in all but the steepest instances will be less economical and thus will require more energy and oxygen. You should be able to mitigate some of this economy penalty by training with poles consistently (Figard-Fabre et al. 2009).
- Nevertheless, it might be worth the economic penalty if the use of poles results in saving your legs from the ensuing muscular damage or mitigating localized fatigue.
- You can use your poles for stability (uphill and downhill), for propulsion (uphill only), and as a means of coping with the forces associated with downhill running. You will get the most benefit if you learn to use them for all three.
- Find the right pole size. Your elbow should be bent at a ninety-degree or slightly greater angle when your elbows are at your sides and the poles are touching the ground. You should be able to grasp the handle grip higher or lower, depending on the situation. Alternatively, some research suggests taking 68 percent of your height in centimeters to find the right pole size

(Hansen and Smith 2009; Pellegrini et al. 2105).

- If using your poles for propulsion, align and time the pole strike with your foot strike, step for step or on alternating steps. This will maximize the work done by the upper body.

When to Hike and When to Run

"When should I run and when should I hike on steep terrain?" Ultrarunners have asked this question for years, yet the answer has proved to be elusive. Recently, researchers at the Locomotion Laboratory at the University of Colorado Boulder wanted to better answer that question. To confront the problem, they built a one-of-a-kind treadmill capable of reaching a slope of forty-five degrees. To put that in context, the back side of Hope Pass on the Leadville Trail 100 course is roughly a ten-degree slope (18 percent grade). Dubbed the "steepest treadmill in the universe," it's part research tool and part torture device for any who dare to crank it up to its limit.

Coaches and athletes have suggested that the transition point from run to walk should be based on grade, speed, feeling, strategy, and combinations of all of the above. The aforementioned steep treadmill plays a key role in solving this riddle, as researchers can conduct metabolic and EMG testing at a variety of speeds and slopes. While the research is currently in its infancy, there are some initial findings of interest.

IT'S NOT ALL ABOUT RUNNING ECONOMY

Recently, the lab has been studying both the metabolic demands and the muscular activity of steep uphill running across different grades and speeds. The fact that the lab is studying multiple aspects of uphill locomotion is a testament to the fact that, ultimately, the run-to-hike transition is not determined by one singular factor but by many. All too often, runners and coaches focus on running economy as a predictor of performance and determinate of improvement. While running economy is important, it is also important to note that performance in ultramarathons is not as linked to aerobic power and economy as it is in other endurance disciplines (like the marathon, for example). Localized neuromuscular fatigue, supraspinal input (your brain sending signals down to the rest of your body), muscular damage, and a host of other maladies outside of the cardiovascular system (i.e., running economy) will also impact performance. Together, these factors can impact performance more than can be explained by changes in running economy alone.

BOTH SPEED AND GRADE WILL DETERMINE WHEN TO RUN AND HIKE

While the data points are few, one clear aspect of the run-to-hike transition has emerged: the decision to run or hike will involve both grade *and* speed. From the initial data, there will not be a universal grade where all runners will be more economical switching from running to hiking and vice versa. If you have seen or heard absolute black-and-white advice, like "always hike on grades over 10 percent," you can wholeheartedly dismiss it. Similarly, there will not be a universal speed at which it is more economical to hike vs run that works across all grades and runners. That said, my current working theory is that the range of speeds where it will be more effective to hike vs run is relatively small on most normal grades (~4 to 16 percent). Time will tell if that (somewhat) educated guess is right or if I have to eat crow.

WHAT WE ALREADY KNOW: WHEN TO RUN AND WALK ON LEVEL GROUND

The relative impact of grade and speed is still being figured out, but we have good data from running and walking/hiking on level ground. Here's the nitty gritty of what we know from previous studies and what the University of Colorado Boulder lab has explored thus far: for decades, locomotion scientists have studied the preferred walk-to-run transition speed. They have quite literally traveled the world to ascertain the preferred walking speed of people in different locations and from different cultures. When you plot out walking speed vs cost of transport (the amount of oxygen it takes to go a given distance), what results is the U-shaped curve in Figure 5.5. As it turns out, people are lazy (and smart) and prefer to walk at a speed that corresponds to the lowest point of this curve (minimal oxygen consumption, and hence minimal energy expenditure). This point, labeled preferred walking speed (PWS) in the figure, is ~1.5–1.6 m/s, or about 16:45–18:00 min/mi across large population studies (i.e., athletes, non-athletes, sedentary people, active people, you name it).

As we begin to walk faster, the transition point where people will prefer to run instead of walk is at a slightly higher speed, about ~2 m/s (~13:30 min/mi). Interestingly, this preferred transition speed (PTS) is a point at which walking is still more economical than running, indicating that the preference for walking or running depends on more than just oxygen cost. In Figure 5.5, the intersections of the red and blue lines is the point where running becomes more economical than walking. This area between the PTS and the most economical walk-to-run transition illustrates the consternation trail runners face during a training run or race: there's a difference between the point at which you *want* to run and the most economical point *to* run. This phenomenon also helps explain why it is unlikely there will be one magical hike-to-run transition speed that's proven to work best for all runners.

WHAT WE ARE LEARNING ABOUT RUNNING AND WALKING FROM STEEP TREADMILL RESEARCH

To assess when to run and when to walk on steeper terrain, the research team at the University of Colorado Boulder brought in high-caliber runners and tested them at different speeds on a thirty-degree slope (58 percent grade). For context, a thirty-degree slope is steeper than the infamous Manitou Incline in Colorado and about equal to the slope of the vertical kilometer course in Fully, Switzerland, where the current vertical

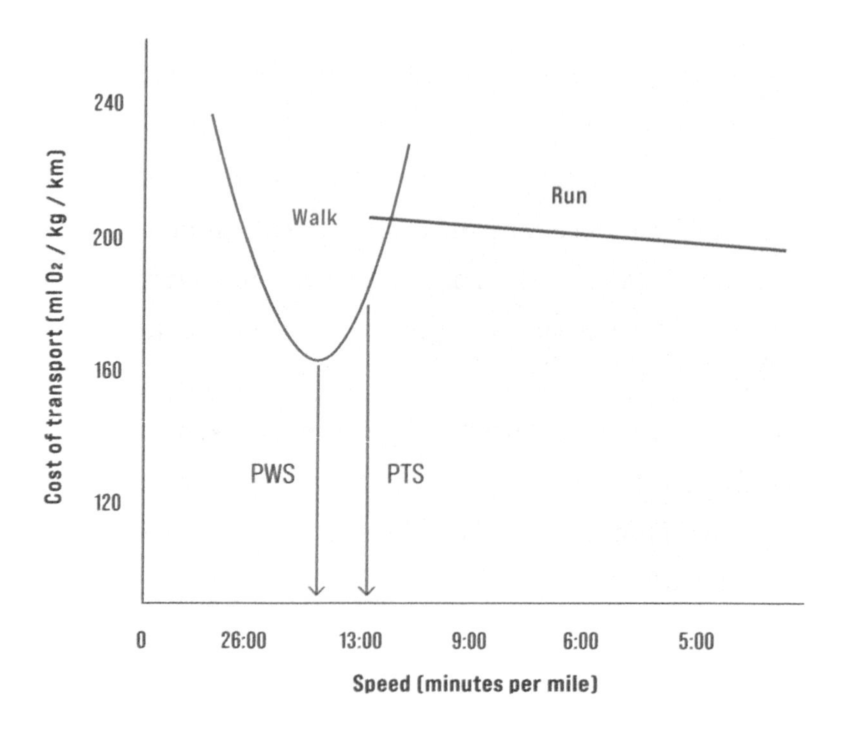

FIGURE 5.5 Representation of the metabolic cost of transport for walking and running as a function of speed. The vertical arrows represent the preferred walking speed (PWS) and preferred transition speed (PTS). Adapted from Bramble and Lieberman 2004.

kilometer world record was set. In Figure 5.6, we see that metabolically, all runners were more economical at speeds below 0.9 m/s (just under 30 min/mi), meaning that on ridiculously steep terrain, only the very best runners at the very highest speeds will be better off running than walking.

We also know from earlier data (see Figure 5.7) that when the vertical speed (the amout of vertical gain per unit time) is kept constant, walking is more economical across a range of speeds (which are still ridiculously fast) and grades, with the exception of a ten-degree slope (17 percent grade) at a speed of 2.14 m/s. To put that into context, that's running a 12:30 min/mi pace up the back side of Hope Pass (which is slightly less than an 18 percent grade). In other words, it's really fast and, like the trials in the lab at the University of Colorado Boulder, only applies to the fastest of runners on the steepest of grades.

What is starting to emerge from studies of elite runners at high speeds on steep grades is that there is some combination of grade and speed at which it will be more economical to walk vs run and vice versa. The relationship will hold true for all runners, superhuman or not. At this point in time, though, we just don't know exactly what those combinations are for all runners.

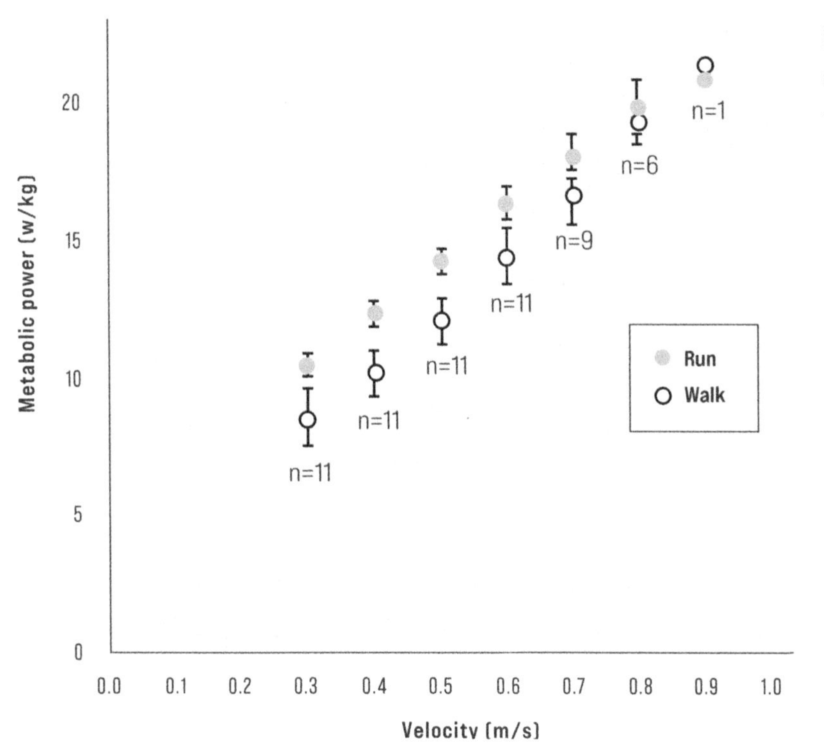

FIGURE 5.6 Metabolic power as a function of velocity for walking and running on a 58 percent grade. Adapted from Ortiz et al. 2017.

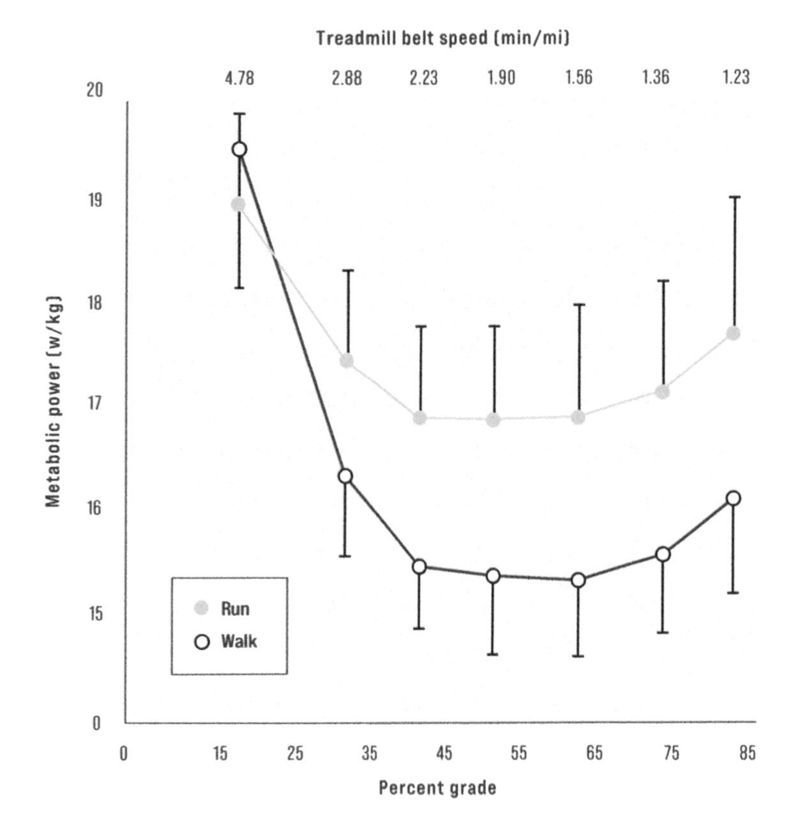

FIGURE 5.7 Metabolic power as a function of slope when the vertical speed is constant. Adapted from Giovanelli et al. 2015.

THE TAKE-HOME MESSAGES

Here's what we know and some reasonable assumptions:

1. There are certain combinations of grades and speeds where it will be more economical to walk vs run and vice versa.
2. We don't know quite what those combinations are yet.
3. A good run-to-walk transition point on flat ground is ~13:30–14 min/mi. This means if you are walking faster than that on flat ground, it's more economical (costs less oxygen and energy) to run. If you are running slower than that, it's more economical to walk.

Whereas heart rate or pace zones on your GPS watch can tell you when to speed up or slow down during a marathon, I think we are a long way off from your GPS watch telling you when to walk and when to run in an ultramarathon. Nonetheless, I have a few practical recommendations for all ultrarunners, from the front of the pack to the back, about choosing when to run or walk:

1. Practice walking in training. This is something I don't think enough runners do.

Particularly for the longer ultras with more elevation gain, walking is going to be a big part of your race plan. Just like nutrition, gear, etc., it is better to practice it in training. So, if you have climbs available to you, dial down the intensity and hike them in training sometimes, even though you could run them if you wanted to.

2. Use rating of perceived exertion (RPE) during the race to determine when you are going to hike and when you are going to run. You should have a reasonable RPE plan going into any race. When executing that plan, hike when your RPE is exceeding your race plan (and hike slower if you need to), and run when you can keep your RPE in your desired range. Simple, but not easy!
3. When in doubt, prioritize hiking if the race or the particular climb is longer, and prioritize running if the race/climb is shorter. With the shorter climbs and/or races, you can take a risk and run slightly harder during the uphill, knowing that the effort is short and there is (likely) a downhill on the other side where you can recover.

WHAT'S SO GREAT ABOUT UPHILL INTERVALS?

ROUGHLY 80 PERCENT of all the intervals I prescribe are uphill. Why?

- Uphill running, in most cases, elicits a higher cardiovascular response than level running. This why many standardized running VO_2 max tests will increase in grade in order to measure maximal oxygen consumption.
- Uphill running is a hedge against injury. It slows you down, therefore decreasing the peak GRFs on every foot strike.
- More time is spent climbing than descending in ultrarunning. If you can improve by 1 percent on the uphills, it's worth more time on race day than a 1 percent improvement on the downhills.
- A little downhill work goes a long way, and the effects last a long time, so the focus needs to be on the uphills (see "How to Combat Muscular Breakdown" in Chapter 4).

I would like to send a special thanks to Jackson Brill for his assistance with this chapter.

KEY POINTS ON THE FOUR DISCIPLINES OF ULTRARUNNING

- There are four distinct disciplines of ultrarunning:
  - Flat running
  - Uphill running
  - Downhill running
  - Power-hiking or walking
- These disciplines are distinct enough that they need to be explicitly trained for.
- Your weekly training should contain roughly the same amount of vertical gain and loss per mile as your race, particularly in the final weeks leading up to the race.
- Poles can be advantageous particularly if your race contains a lot of hiking and if you can use them in training.
- Walking will be a more effective form of locomotion as compared to running in certain situations.
- If you plan on walking/power-hiking during your race, you should also do so in training.

CHAPTER 6

Tracking Training in Ultrarunning

I killed a lot of trees when I first started coaching. Throughout the course of a workday, I received numerous faxes and email attachments of training files from my athletes. I printed out every single one of them, and then I'd pore over each file, examining the critical data. Yellow, orange, and pink highlights would adorn the sheets, denoting intervals, critical heart rate values, and anything else I found significant. I'd fill the margins with notes from conversations and debriefs on each workout from the athlete. Finally, I'd place the sheets of paper in individually labeled folders, one for each athlete.

At the conclusion of a training phase, I'd spread the contents of an athlete's folder out on a table. My preferred canvas for this exercise was a large, round table in our conference room, but that seldom gave me enough space. Papers were everywhere—on the table, floor, and chairs and in the adjoining rooms; no horizontal surface was safe. Once the documents were strewn about to my liking, I'd try to make sense of it all. Was the athlete improving? Were they hitting the correct intensities? Was it time for rest? The colors, highlights, notes, and scribbles all provided clues; the conclusions, however, I had to determine myself. As rudimentary as this system was, it did its job, and I could get a good fix on what was going on with the athlete. It was not perfect, but it was all I had.

Over time, training-related technology and software has improved and is now quite sophisticated. Sheets of paper collected in file folders gave way to electronic storage and access. The device manufacturers, motivated to differentiate their products from the rest, all created ways of organizing and making sense of the information collected from their widgets. Each system has its own spin. Some are very good at taking individual files and breaking them down. Others are better at aggregating many files to identify trends. All have been helpful to coaches trying to understand it all.

As heart rate training gave way to power-based training (in cycling) and GPS-based training (in running), some of our previously unidentified training flaws started to show. We could now see pace and power decoupled from heart rate (renowned endurance coach Joe Friel developed terms to describe this phenomenon: "aerobic decoupling" and "efficiency factor"). We could quantify and aggregate training load and see how various loads affected performance. Myriad other insights ensued, none of which would have been possible from staring at 8½ × 11-inch sheets of paper, no matter how much highlighter I used.

As a coach working with endurance athletes, I took to this evolution, which helped me gain greater insight into how my athletes were training. In road running, triathlon, and cycling, the data acquired in the field could be meaningfully interpreted in order to analyze and adapt training for athletes. I had tangible quantifications of workload, and improvements could be easily identified. I wish I could say the same kind of data existed for trail ultrarunners.

In ultrarunning, particularly trail ultrarunning, the tangible quantification of workload and work rate that exists in road running and cycling becomes inconsistent and blurry. Improvement markers are also difficult to come by, particularly in mountainous areas where the properties of the trail surface can change from one run to the next or even during a single run.

Nonetheless, when I started working with ultrarunners, I realized I needed to solve the same problems I'd faced with other athletes. I needed a way to quantify workloads and work rates and to compare one workout to the next. I needed a way to determine if an athlete had improved. Harking back to my earlier experiences with folders and highlighted sheets of paper, I hacked together a way to use the available tools and data to better coach ultrarunners. Is it perfect? Hell no. Does it do the job? You bet. Technology and software will continue to evolve, but in the meantime, people still have to run and train, and I—and you—have to figure out ways to make sense of it all.

Tools to Track Your Training

GPS monitors are the primary tracking devices for recording day-to-day ultrarunning performance. Several manufacturers produce them, and ultrarunners have to pick the features and price point that best suit their needs. This technology is constantly evolving, so rather than focus on specific brands and the differences between them, I will focus on the key features to look for when selecting and using a device to track your training.

GPS ACCURACY

Much of what you can do to train for the specificity of any particular ultra is rooted in the exercise of matching the grades and surfaces you train on to what you will experience on race day. This being the case, GPS and altitude accuracy are important considerations in choosing a watch. The quality of GPS data is fundamentally determined by the strength of the satellite signal, how many satellites are acquired, the position of the antenna within the watch, and how frequently the satellite information is collected. Most of the traditional watch manufacturers do a great job with this aspect, and there are few notable differences among high-quality watches.

BATTERY LIFE

Battery life on many GPS watches hinges on the quality and size of the battery and the amount and quality of data samples collected. Many of the device manufacturers are becoming wise to the fact that athletes are going longer, so they are engineering their watches and batteries to last as long as possible and providing a reasonable footprint for the watch to wrap around your wrist. Battery technology is improving all the time, stretching the life span of what a watch can record in a single session. Some watch manufactures are even embedding small solar panels into the watch as a means of extending battery life.

Taking battery life a step further, device manufacturers also provide options for athletes to manipulate the GPS recording variables of the watch. The user can opt to save battery life by recording data at less frequent intervals or by manipulating how the GPS signal is acquired. The watch then uses non-GPS movement data to fill in the gaps and determine speed when GPS position is not being recorded. Some GPS devices come with this as the only recording option to minimize the watch's physical size and bring it down to a less expensive price point. It is a classic compromise that prioritizes the battery life (and sometimes price point) over the accuracy of the data collected.

As another approach, some manufacturers give athletes the ability to improve GPS quality by utilizing GLONASS and GALIELO satellite capabilities and other GPS signal-strengthening tools. This decreases the battery life for any one particular workout but improves the accuracy of the data collected.

As a coach, I prefer to have the highest-quality data possible. In analyzing files, it makes a difference looking at information that was collected every second vs information that was collected every few seconds, particularly when evaluating intervals that are just a few minutes in length. From a practical standpoint, interval recording options of one second are necessary for any trail-running GPS watch. Furthermore, because trail running is done where terrain and trees can interfere with satellite signals, a premium must be placed on acquiring the most precise position possible at all times. Therefore, while the option of sparing battery life at the expense of lower-quality data is a good one (particularly for longer races), in day-to-day training it is best to stick to the highest-quality data and most frequent data collection rate possible.

Logging Your Training

After you choose the right device to monitor and track your training, the next step is to home in on the software that is going to harness the data and give you actionable information you can use to better guide and focus your training. As a coach, I have thousands of hours of practice aggregating and analyzing training information. I don't ask my athletes, and I would not ask you, to delve that deeply into the data. However, with a few key insights into how concepts like total workload, work rate, fitness, and fatigue work, you can use the information collected by your GPS watch, as well as personal feedback, to better monitor your training.

THE TOOLS OF STRAVA AND TRAININGPEAKS

While each device manufacturer (Garmin, Suunto, COROS, etc.) has developed its own software to harness and present data, third-party developers have spent the last several years showing us that they can do a better job in this role. Garmin, for example, makes numerous GPS devices (and even cameras) for use in running, golf, boating, driving, aviation, and other activities. Suunto, Polar, and other GPS device manufacturers similarly make a range of different products. All of these manufacturers are experts in making devices that can capture information on a miniature computer (like, in the case of running, a watch). Meanwhile, software-specific companies focus solely on taking the data acquired from a training device and presenting actionable information. They are experts in taking information from the tiny computers and making sense out of it for athletes and coaches. So, it is not surprising that the better platforms for monitoring and tracking training come from the software-specific manufacturers. In my view, Strava and TrainingPeaks are currently the go-to platforms for endurance athletes.

COMPARING WORKLOAD AND WORK RATE

Determining total workload (kilojoules) and work rate (power) is one of the long-standing challenges in coaching trail ultrarunners. While volume quantifies the amount of training (in time or miles), and intensity describes the effort of training, total workload and work rate are more useful in determining how much training stress an athlete incurs.

According to simple Newtonian physics, work is a product of force and distance. A bigger force applied over a longer distance leads to more work done. In level running, the amount of work performed is a function of your weight (which, as was discussed in Chapter 5, influences ground reaction forces) and how far you ran (distance). Therefore, for level running, workload can be well represented by how many miles you ran and how much you weigh. A heavier runner will have a higher total workload than a lighter runner who covers the same number of miles.

Work rate is the total amount of work done divided by the time it took to perform it. On level ground, running a mile takes approximately the same amount of work regardless of how long it takes to run it. You can see this manifested in caloric expenditure equations (total calories = 1 calorie per kilogram per kilometer); caloric expenditure is a function of distance and weight, not speed. Your work rate, however, is dependent on speed. The faster you run any given distance, the higher your work rate. For flat running, work rate can be represented by pace and weight. Similarly, a heavier runner will have a higher work rate than a lighter runner at the same speed.

For a runner who is training primarily on flat terrain, workload can be represented by miles, and work rate by pace. These two values can even be compared among different runners who have the same mass. In cycling, work rate and workload can actually be measured by devices called power meters. At the time of this writing, nothing analogous is available in trail running. (Sit tight before you yell at me about running power meters like Stryd, RunScribe, and Garmin.) The differences in trail surface and elevation gain and loss make capturing workload and work rate problematic at best. There are tools out there that trail runners and ultrarunners can use, but to properly evaluate training, it is important to know the basis for and limitations of such tools.

NORMALIZED GRADED PACE AND GRADE ADJUSTED PACE

Both Strava and TrainingPeaks have developed algorithms to convert running on uphills and downhills to flat, level running (Table 6.1). TrainingPeaks' Normalized Graded Pace (NGP) and Strava's Grade Adjusted Pace (GAP) take your running and "grade" it as if you were running on flat, level ground. For example, if you are running up a 6 percent climb at a 12:00 min/mi pace, your NGP or GAP would be 9:21. In other words, running 12:00 min/mi on a 6 percent uphill is comparable to running 9:21 min/mi on the flats. This gives athletes the ability to compare paces on different climbs and descents with the equivalent pace for flat, level running.

	GRADE	-10%		-6%		-2%		0%		2%		6%		10%	
		NGP	GAP	NGP	GAP	NGP	GAP	NGP	GAP	NGP	GAP	NGP	GAP	NGP	GAP
PACE PER MILE	8:00	15:18	11:27	11:13	10:05	8:51	8:40	8:00	8:00	7:19	7:22	6:14	6:16	5:26	5:21
	10:00	19:07	14:19	14:00	12:37	11:04	10:50	10:00	10:00	9:09	9:13	7:48	7:50	6:47	6:42
	12:00	22:56	17:11	16:48	15:08	13:17	13:00	12:00	12:00	10:59	11:04	9:21	9:24	8:08	8:02

TABLE 6.1 NGP and GAP for different grades and paces.

TrainingPeaks' NGP takes the paced algorithm a step further (see what I did there?) and "normalizes" the pace to its physiological equivalent had the runner perfectly paced the entire run. For example, if you do a workout comprising of six sets of three minutes hard, three minutes easy, where the hard parts are at six-minute pace and the easy parts are at ten-minute pace, your average pace for that workout will be just under seven minutes per mile for thirty-three total minutes. But, the workout will certainly feel harder and have more physiological impact than thirty-three minutes at seven-minute pace. So, TrainingPeaks' NGP "normalizes" undulating paces seen in training and racing and calculates a physiological equivalent.

Both of these algorithms do a decent job of comparing the respective paces (and therefore work rates) of climbing and flat, level running when performed on similar surfaces and at normal gradients. You can go out and do intervals on flat sections and on climbs, compare the efforts, and determine which effort was harder or easier. However, there are two glaring flaws in utilizing these algorithms for trail runners.

Flaw 1: When the Surface Is Different

Neither GAP nor NGP has the ability to account for the difference in work associated with running on different surfaces. You intuitively know that running through sand is more difficult than running on a track. Similarly, running over technical terrain requires more effort than running over smooth terrain. However, the raw paces and calculated GAP and NGP will not account for the differences between those surfaces.

Flaw 2: Descents

The calculations for GAP and NGP use the difference in energy/oxygen cost between uphill, downhill, and level running to arrive at the equivalent pace for level terrain. While on flat ground, your pace is directly related to work rate. Your cardiovascular system has to work harder in order to go faster, which means a higher pace requires a higher work rate. But remember that for downhill running in particular, energy cost tells only part of the story. For downhill running, other factors outside of the energetic cost combine to significantly affect the overall stress. These include changes in foot speed, coordination, and musculoskeletal stress, all of which are different in downhill running than in level or uphill running. Neither GAP nor NGP takes these additional stresses into account, and as a result those two algorithms underestimate the overall stress of downhill running. In a single or shorter run, the misestimation may not be a big issue. For ultrarunners, however, it represents a greater flaw as you try to sum up cumulative training stress during a very long run or over a longer period of training.

Total Training Stress

Total workload and work rate can be used to quantify the amount of training stress for any particular run. This is important because it gives an apples-to-apples comparison of how stressful different runs were. Hilly, undulating runs with wild differences in pace can be compared with flat runs with little deviation in pace on the basis of their total amount of stress. Similarly, interval workouts can be compared to EnduranceRuns. In TrainingPeaks, these values are referred to as Training Stress Scores (TSS), of which there are three flavors depending on how you want to delineate intensity (either by power denoted by TSS, pace denoted by rTSS, or heart rate denoted by hrTSS). Strava's version of this is called Relative Effort. All of these scoring systems are trying to do the same thing, albeit by different methods.

On the TrainingPeaks platform, training stress is calibrated using an algorithm anchored to a sixty-minute run at lactate threshold being equal to one hundred points. Recovery runs will be less than 100 points, and longer endurance runs will typically

PLATFORM	NAME	INTENSITY DETERMINANT	METHOD OF SCORING
Strava	Relative Effort™	Heart rate	Threshold heart rate, duration of run, time spent at different intensities
TrainingPeaks	TSS™	Running Power	Threshold power, duration of run, NGP for run
TrainingPeaks	rTSS™	NGP	Threshold pace, duration of run, NGP for run
TrainingPeaks	hrTSS™	Heart rate	Threshold heart rate, duration of run, NGP for run

TABLE 6.2 Training stress scoring systems.

be more than one hundred points. This gives you a basis to determine how stressful a short, high-intensity run is compared with a longer, lower-intensity run (see Table 6.3 for examples). Additional formulas can utilize pace (in the case of rTSS), heart rate (in the case of hrTSS), or power (in the case of TSS) as the intensity determinant in order to let the user decide which flavor to use for a particular workout. The reason TrainingPeaks uses this 100-point calibration system is that one hour of running at lactate threshold intensity (what they term Functional Threshold Pace) is about the maximum that most normal people can sustain. (Elite athletes can sustain more than an hour at threshold and beginner athletes less, so they split the difference.) The effort would essentially be an all-out time trial. Therefore, when a coach or athlete looks at a particular run, using 100 points as an anchor for an extremely difficult, high-intensity effort, the score for the particular run is immediately put into a broad context.

On Strava's platform, Relative Effort was inspired by Dr. Eric Bannister's TRIMP (Training Impulse) system (Bannister and Calvert 1980). It uses heart rate and the time spent across different intensities to score a workout.

If you are caught up in the weeds right now, fret not. Here's the bottom line: TSS/rTSS/hrTSS and Relative Effort use your lactate threshold intensity (defined by running power, pace, or heart rate) and the time you spend at your relative intensities (endurance, lactate threshold, VO_2 max, etc.) to score each workout using a point-based system. The higher the score, the more stressful the workout.

TYPE OF RUN	TSS/rTSS/hrTSS POINTS
60-min RecoveryRun	50-80
90-min EnduranceRun with 3 x 10 min TempoRun	100-150
90-min EnduranceRun with 6 x 3 min RunningIntervals	100-150
2.5-hr EnduranceRun	150-200
50-mile race	400-600

TABLE 6.3 Training stress scoring systems.

There are ton of caveats to these scoring-based systems. Before we get to those, though, let's dive into how to leverage these training load metrics a bit more.

AGGREGATING TOTAL TRAINING STRESS

Within TrainingPeaks, your TSS/rTSS/hrTSS can be aggregated and trended over time. This provides one of the more valuable pieces of feedback when analyzing training load. Acute Training Load (ATL) and Chronic Training Load (CTL) provide snapshots of the long-term (more than seven days) aggregate training load.

Acute Training Load is a seven-day rolling weighted average of the TSS/rTSS/hrTSS for each particular day. Chronic Training Load is the same thing but over a forty-two-day period. (The time frames for CTL and ATL can be customized.) Over time, these numbers offer a big-picture view of historical training that provides clues as to when an athlete is the most fit (highest CTL), most fatigued (highest ATL), and most ready for performance (highest Training Stress Balance, or TSB, which is the difference between CTL and ATL). TrainingPeaks provides useful charting capabilities of these metrics that athletes can use simply by uploading their training files on a day-to-day basis.

Figure 6.1 is an analysis of an athlete training for the Western States 100. You can see the athlete's CTL was highest just before Western States, indicating that they were at peak fitness for that race. You can also see the consistency with which the athlete built their training load over the course of the season, as indicated by the ramping gray area.

Strava, Garmin, and other companies offer similar, albeit more rudimentary, tools to aggregate training stress. Strava's version, for example, is called "Fitness and Freshness." If you are interested in tracking your training load and gleaning valuable insights, these tools are not quite up to the task, and athletes are better served utilizing TrainingPeaks' ATL/CTL/TSB system for analysis.

BEWARE THE FLAWS

Unfortunately, the flaws with TSS/rTSS/hrTSS, ATL, and CTL mirror those with NGP (which is unsurprising given that NGP is used in the equations). Changes in surface and large amounts of descending make it difficult to compare one run with the next. However, if your training generally contains the same trail surface and amount of climbing and descending from day to day, rTSS, ATL, and CTL can give you a ballpark idea of how hard or easy one run is compared with the next and how these training loads stack up over time.

Also bear in mind that point for point within any training scoring system, points are physically more difficult to a runner the further they are into a run. In other words, fifty TSS points (equivalent to a short RecoveryRun) when accumulated at the beginning of a one-hour run are not nearly as difficult as when accumulated at the end of a six-hour run, yet they will be calculated at the same Training Stress. In addition, training scoring systems are essentially combining stress from endurance and intensity into one metric, which is inherently problematic. For example, a sixty-minute TempoRun (which is essentially an all-out effort) will accumulate approximately the same number of TSS or Relative Effort points as a two-and-a-half-hour EnduranceRun, although they have markedly different effects on the body and require different amounts of recovery (more recovery will be needed after a sixty-minute TempoRun).

MONITORING IMPROVEMENT

How do you know you if are becoming more fit? In the road-running world, your day-to-day paces and workouts can provide answers to this question. In trail running, the

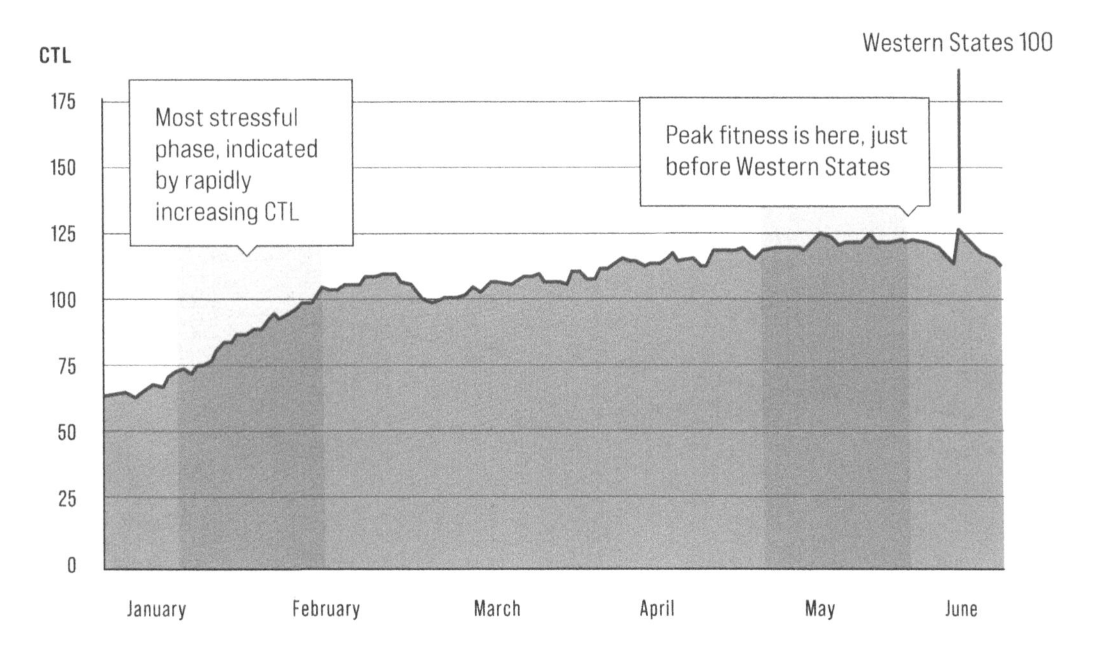

FIGURE 6.1 Analysis of an athlete's training for Western States. The CTL (blue-shaded area) is highest just before the Western States 100. This indicates that the athlete was most fit just before the race. The CTL also ramps up fastest during the tempo phases, indicating that they are generally the most stressful phases.

process is similar, though the answer requires more investigation, particularly if you are doing your specific interval work on trails (as you should be).

Both Strava and TrainingPeaks provide tools to help you understand how your fitness is trending. These tools do not provide stoplight answers that turn green when things are good, red when they are bad, and yellow for somewhere in between. Rather, they provide general trends you can interpret to see if your training is on the right track and if you are making improvements over a period of weeks or months.

Strava Segments

One of the great and convenient features of Strava is segment tracking. Strava segments are marked-out sections of road and trail, created by users. You can even create your own segments for sections of trail you commonly use for specific interval work. Every time you run across that section of trail, your segment time is recorded for everyone to see (you can change this setting if you wish to keep your run or your segment private). Results are ranked and stacked on a leaderboard, and you can see where your time fits in with the rest of the pack or in relation to your previous runs. While you should not try to set a PR every time, the general trend line can provide clues to how your fitness is trending, particularly if the segment of trail is one you use frequently for training (Figure 6.2). The great thing about these segments (other than being addictive) is that they

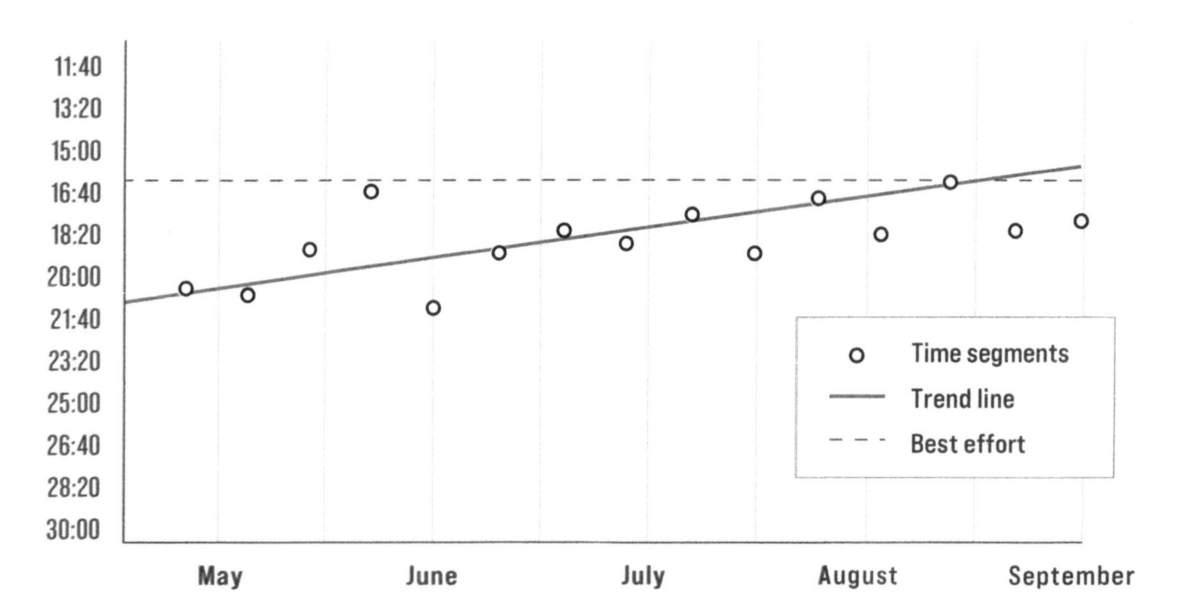

FIGURE 6.2 Strava segments with the trend line generally getting better over time.

are automatically calculated and tabulated once you have uploaded your run—no need to print out pages and mark them up with a highlighter.

NGP Between Efforts

TrainingPeaks provides fitness tracking via the capability to break down files and create laps once the file is uploaded. In this way, after doing specific workouts, you can come back to the file and analyze the NGP of specific segments. You can use these data to gauge the quality of your workouts from interval to interval (Figure 6.4) and to compare intervals across several days or weeks.

Measuring and Personalizing Training Intensity

If you are going to use interval training to accumulate time at intensity and target specific areas of your fitness, you need a way to figure out how hard you are working. In some sports like endurance running and swimming, this is simple. Ultrarunners don't have it so easy. For a long time, runners have tried to use heart rate to gauge intensity, creating intensity ranges based on percentages of lactate threshold heart rate or the average heart rate recorded during a 5K time trial. Others have used pace ranges based on time trials or goal race paces, or a combination of heart rate and pace ranges. Prescribing intensity based on either heart rate or pace is notoriously difficult in ultrarunning, and after trying all manner of methods, I found the greatest success in a remarkably simple, nontechnical, yet scientifically accurate method: rating of perceived exertion (RPE).

Why Heart Rate Is Not a Good Training Tool for Determining Intensity

The heart rate value you see on a watch is a measurement of your body's response to exercise. It's not a direct measure of the work being done; instead, the work is being done primarily by muscles, which in turn demand more oxygen from the cardiovascular system. Because that oxygen is delivered via red blood cells, heart rate increases in order to pump more oxygen-rich blood to the muscles as their demand for oxygen rises. It's an indirect observation of what's happening at the muscular level, but in the absence of a direct way to measure workload, heart rate can provide valuable information. Research has shown conclusively that there's a strong correlation between heart rate response and changes in an athlete's workload, and that research allowed sports scientists and coaches to start creating heart rate training zones back in the 1980s. However, as sports science has evolved over the past thirty-plus years, we have learned that many factors affect an athlete's heart rate, and those factors reveal that heart rate response is not reliable or predictable enough to be an effective training tool.

FACTORS AFFECTING HEART RATE

Core Temperature

As your core temperature increases, heart rate at a given exercise intensity will increase. Your circulatory system carries heat from your core to your extremities to aid with conductive and radiant cooling. Because part of your blood flow is redirected in this manner, your heart has to work harder (pump faster) to deliver the same amount of oxygen to the muscles.

Caffeine and Other Stimulants

When you consume caffeine, either from your morning cup of coffee or from a caffeinated gel during a training session or race, your heart rate increases.

Excitation/Nervousness

A race is an exciting event (or at least it should be if you have the right emotional engagement), and that causes a release of epinephrine and norepinephrine, which increases your heart rate. Other emotional responses, including frustration, anger, and anxiety, can also affect heart rate.

Hydration Status

Although hydration-based changes in heart rate are often concurrent with impacts from core temperature, your heart rate can increase from dehydration with or without a rise in core temperature. As your blood volume diminishes, your heart needs to beat faster to deliver the same amount of oxygen per minute.

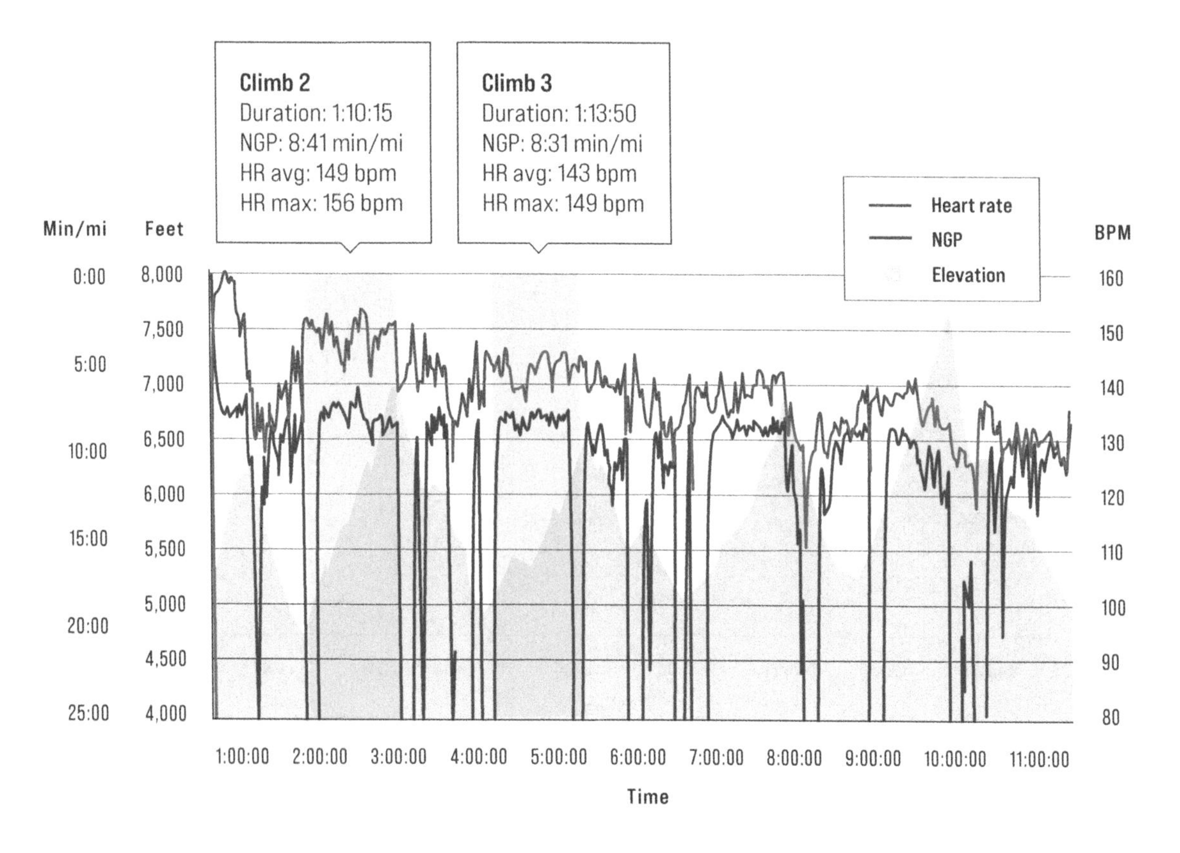

FIGURE 6.3 Example of how fatigue affects heart rate. Heart rate (red line) starts high due to freshness and then drops as fatigue sets in, even though NGP remains roughly the same for the first three climbs.

Altitude

Most athletes train within a small altitude range in their local area, but goal races may feature dramatically different elevation profiles. Heart rate and respiration rate increase at altitude, starting at about 5,000 feet above sea level. This occurs because the reduced partial pressure of oxygen in the air you're breathing means there are fewer oxygen molecules in each lungful of air.

Fatigue

While many of the factors that impact heart rate act to increase it, fatigue often suppresses it. When you are fatigued, your heart rate response to increasing energy demand is slower and blunted. A tired athlete will see heart rate climb more slowly at the beginning of an interval or hard effort and will struggle to achieve the heart rate normally associated with a given intensity level.

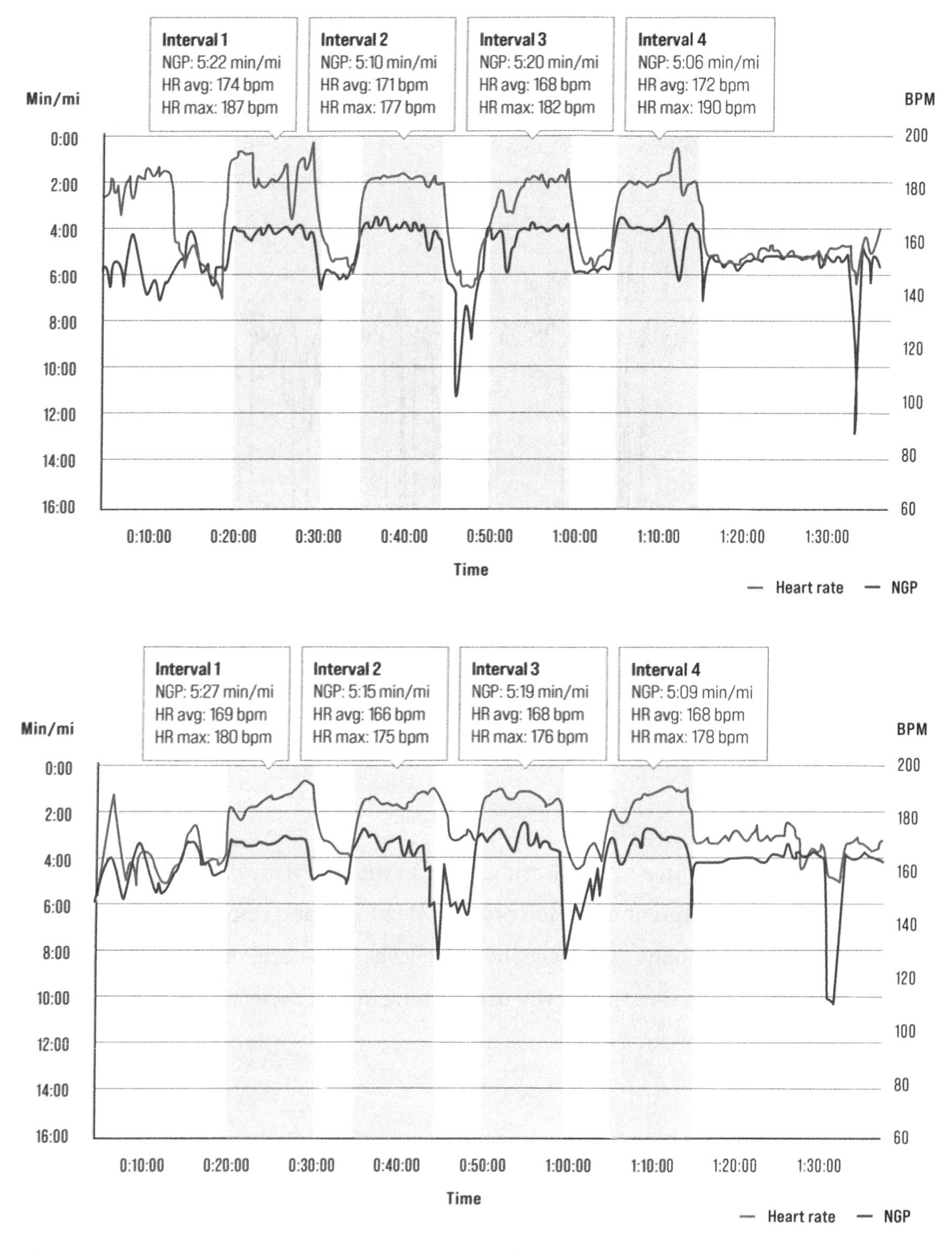

FIGURE 6.4 Two consecutive days of TempoRun intervals. While the normalized paces are similar, the heart rate is generally depressed on the second day. Had the athlete been training using heart rate, he either would not have been able to do the workout or would have pushed too hard.

Of all the factors that affect heart rate, fatigue can get an athlete in the most trouble. When heart rate response is exaggerated and heart rates are higher than expected, athletes who are training or competing by heart rate tend to slow down. If your ranges say to run at 150 beats per minute (bpm) to sustain a pace without exceeding your lactate threshold, but your heart rate response is being boosted by 5–8 bpm due to elevated core temperature and caffeine, running at 150 bpm will result in a slower actual pace. Meanwhile, when fatigue suppresses heart rate, you may push even harder in an effort to achieve your goal intensity of 150 bpm.

Figure 6.3 is from an athlete in a 100K race. The first three climbs of the race were paced perfectly at similar NGP. However, the heart rate on the first climb is markedly higher due to the athlete's initial freshness and adrenaline rush at the start of the race. The heart rate on the third climb is suppressed because of the accumulated fatigue. Had the athlete tried to target a specific heart rate on the first climb, she would have been much too slow. Had she tried to match her heart rate from the first two climbs on the third climb, she would have run far too hard, particularly that early in the race.

There are two problems with pushing harder in response to a suppressed heart rate response. The first is that a suppressed heart rate at a given effort level or pace doesn't always mean you aren't performing as much work. Athletes who are fatigued can often perform the same workout two days in a row but experience suppressed heart rate response on the second day.

Figure 6.4 shows a runner performing interval work on back-to-back days. On the second day, the athlete is able to perform the workout at a similar NGP but at a generally lower maximum and average heart rate due to the accumulated fatigue. This phenomenon plays into the second problem caused by suppressed heart rates. If you are gauging the success of your workout by your ability to run at a specific heart rate—or within a small heart rate range—and that heart rate is difficult to achieve because of fatigue, you may just push yourself harder to achieve the heart rate number you want to see. The effort feels harder than it should, but you push through anyway. If you are truly fatigued, you're just digging the hole deeper.

CARDIAC DRIFT

One of the greatest disadvantages of using heart rate alone to gauge training intensity is "cardiac drift." Because up to 75 percent of the energy produced in muscles is lost as heat, your body has to work to dissipate that heat to keep your core temperature from rising out of control. As you exercise—especially at higher intensities—your body uses your skin much like your car uses its radiator. Heart rate increases not only to deliver oxygen to working muscles but also to direct blood to the skin so it can supply fluid for sweat and cool off through convection (provided that the ambient temperature is lower than your core temperature). The sweat is released onto the surface of the skin so it can evaporate, which carries much of this excess heat away from the body. Much of the fluid that appears as sweat on your skin was most recently part of your bloodstream. As you lose blood plasma volume to produce sweat, your heart has to pump even faster to continue delivering the same amount of oxygen to working muscles. As a result, your heart rate will increase slightly as exercise duration increases, even if you maintain the same level of effort. The impact of cardiac drift will be lower if you are able to stay well hydrated: you're replacing the fluid lost by sweating and helping to maintain a higher overall blood volume. However, no matter how diligent you are about consuming fluids, some level of cardiac drift is unavoidable during intense endurance exercise.

You can see the impact of cardiac drift in Figure 6.5. In this heart rate file from a lactate threshold interval workout, the athlete performs three intervals at roughly the same pace, but his heart rate gets progressively higher for each effort. When athletes train by heart rate alone, they are instructed to maintain the same heart rate range for each interval. Ideally this would result in efforts of equal intensity, but as a result of cardiac drift, the first interval is actually completed at a faster pace than the subsequent ones. To the athlete, heart rate seems right on target, but they don't realize that workload is actually falling, and as a result, the workout loses some of its potential effectiveness.

Why Ultrarunners Should Embrace Perceived Exertion

As much as I embrace the role of technology in enhancing the precision of training, there's an incredibly simple measure of workload that continues to hold its own against new gadgets and software applications. Rating of perceived exertion is the ultimate

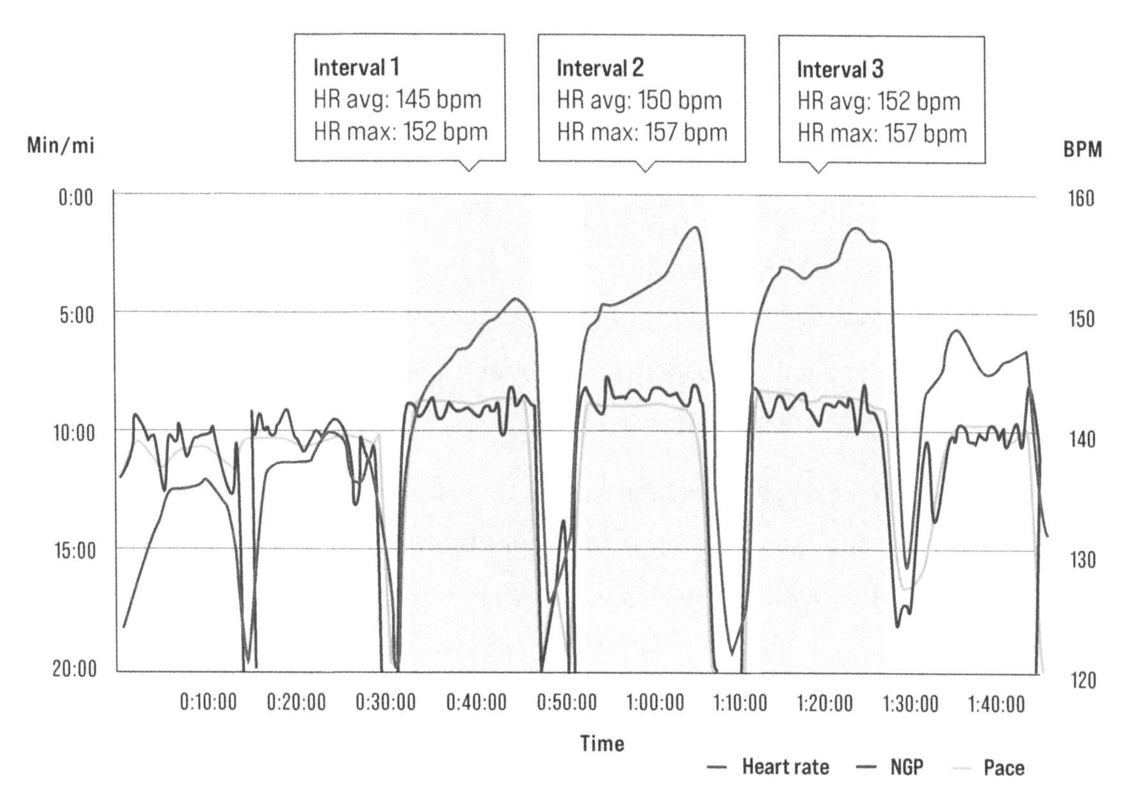

FIGURE 6.5 Impact of cardiac drift during a 3 × 10-minute TempoRun workout where the heart rate increases throughout each interval and from interval to interval.

in simplicity: it is nothing more than a scale of how hard you feel you are exercising. There's not one single piece of data collected, and you don't need any special equipment. All you need is a numerical scale.

In the physiology lab, I use the Borg Scale, which ranges from 6 to 20 (with 6 being no exertion at all and 20 being a maximum effort). Why 6 to 20? Borg's research has shown that there's a high correlation between the number an athlete chooses during exercise, multiplied by 10, and her actual heart rate at that time. In other words, if you're on a treadmill during a lactate threshold test and tell me that you feel like you're at 16, there is a pretty good chance your heart rate is around 160 bpm. This isn't absolutely true of all athletes, but you'd be surprised at how accurate the 6 to 20 scale tends to be.

Outside the lab, however, the Borg Scale isn't as helpful for athletes, most of whom find it easier to relate to a simpler 1 to 10 scale (with 1 being no exertion at all and 10 being a maximum effort). Using this scale, an endurance or "forever" pace would be a 5 or

WHAT ABOUT LACTATE THRESHOLD AND VO_2 MAX TESTING?

OVER THE YEARS, I have brought most of the elite athletes I work with—and many other runners—into a physiology lab for lactate threshold and VO_2 max testing. There is a sentiment that this type of testing lacks value, as VO_2 max values are not useful by themselves. This is true, but physiological testing is less about finding one particular end point and more about what is happening during the continuum of intensities that are studied.

I mostly use the tests as benchmarks to establish baseline physiological values for an athlete and then build a profile of her progress through subsequent testing. On a practical level, however, I don't use the test results to create training intensity ranges for ultrarunning athletes, as I do for other types of endurance athletes. I think the most valuable thing an ultrarunner can learn from testing, and the most valuable thing I've learned from testing many ultrarunners, is that ultrarunners have lactate threshold values that represent a higher percentage of their overall VO_2 max. In other words, a cyclist might come into the lab, and his lactate threshold power is 78 percent of his power at VO_2 max. An elite cyclist might increase that to about 85 percent. Most marathon runners are similar. But an elite ultrarunner will frequently record a lactate threshold value at 95 to 97 percent of VO_2 max!

What does that mean? For the most part it means ultrarunners have traditionally done a poor job of training to improve VO_2 max and a good job of developing their physiology at lower intensities. Their training has improved performance at aerobic and lactate threshold intensities but has not had much effect on their maximum capacity to take in and deliver oxygen to working muscles. Normally I'd say having a lactate threshold at 95 to 97 percent of VO_2 max is great, but in the context of ultrarunners, what it actually shows is where most ultrarunners are underdeveloped. VO_2 max is your maximum potential—the ceiling or roof of the building. If you want to fit more stuff in the building (more endurance, greater performance capacity), then raise the roof!

6, a challenging aerobic pace would be a 7, medium-intensity interval work that approximates lactate threshold intensity occurs at about 8 or 9, and high-intensity intervals—which I call RunningIntervals—are the only efforts that reach 10. Just as the Borg Scale multiplies the perceived exertion number by 10 to correlate with heart rate, the number chosen on the 1 to 10 scale, multiplied by 10, seems to correlate closely to the percentage of VO_2 max that an athlete is currently maintaining.

With GPS-equipped heart rate monitors providing more detailed pacing information for runners, some athletes are tempted to relegate RPE to the trash bin of sports science history, but RPE remains critically important because it provides valuable context for the data files from a heart rate monitor or GPS watch. When you're fresh, 9:00 min/mi may feel like a moderate pace, but when you're fatigued, you may feel like you're having to work harder than normal to run that same pace. It turns out that RPE is a great early-warning device for recognizing fatigue: your body is telling you it can still do the job but that the effort to complete it is greater.

In addition, RPE can indicate progress. For example, at the beginning of the season, a ten-mile run at 9:00 min/mi pace may feel strenuous enough to rate a 7 or even an 8. Later in the season, when your fitness has improved, running that same course at that same pace may take less out of you and feel more like a 6. To reach an RPE of 7 to 8, you may now need to hasten your pace to 8:30 min/mi.

Although many of my athletes have access to the best training technologies and gadgets on the market, I base the vast majority of their training on perceived exertion. The main reason is because everything else is irrelevant during an actual competition. When you are scrambling up a 25 percent grade in a cold thunderstorm at 10,000 feet above sea level, 65 miles into a 100-mile ultramarathon, what heart rate would define lactate threshold pace? What minute-per-mile pace should a midpack ultrarunner aim for in that scenario?

Your brain is the most valuable tool you have for monitoring and evaluating your intensity, and it's the only training tool yet designed that can determine the correct interval and racing intensities for an ultrarunner. Your job as an athlete is not to find the gadget that will give you the information you seek but, rather, to master the ability to gauge intensity and workload by perceived exertion. It's the only information you need, which is good, because it's also the only accurate information you have.

To use perceived exertion to accurately gauge your workload, you need a good understanding of what you're trying to accomplish at each intensity level, the impact that intensity level has on your body, and the ways you can detect or interpret those impacts.

RPE AND BREATHING RATE

The respiration rate in healthy individuals is highly attuned to the amount of carbon dioxide in your blood. Interestingly, in normal conditions at rest, your involuntary respiration rate is more controlled by the carbon dioxide you're trying to get rid of than the oxygen you need to survive. As your energy demand increases and your muscles break down fuel for energy, the carbon dioxide levels in your blood increase. To keep carbon dioxide levels from rising too much, heart rate and breathing rate increase so more venous blood transports carbon dioxide to the lungs. There, pressure gradients transport carbon dioxide out of the blood (and oxygen into it), and you exhale the carbon dioxide. Table 6.4 shows how different types of workouts affect RPE and breathing rate.

Because exercise increases both your oxygen demand and your production of carbon dioxide, it makes intuitive sense that increasing exercise intensity leads to faster and deeper breathing. It's so intuitive that it's largely ignored, but you can monitor your breathing as a gauge of intensity. At a recovery pace (RPE 4 or 5), you should be breathing only a bit faster and deeper than when you walk at a brisk pace. If you have just finished an interval, your breathing will of course be much faster and should come down to this 4 or 5 level during your recovery period. The exception is during high-intensity interval workouts, where the recovery periods are purposely too short to allow full recovery.

The amount of carbon dioxide you produce in response to energy expenditure does not increase linearly, and this is the phenomenon athletes need to pay attention to. You produce more carbon dioxide when you burn more carbohydrate for energy. Furthermore, a higher percentage of your energy comes from carbohydrate as your exercise intensity increases because glycolysis (the partial breakdown of carbohydrate that provides energy quickly but also results in lactate production) breaks down only carbohydrate, not fat.

At rest you normally exhale less carbon dioxide than you inhale oxygen. This respiratory exchange ratio (RER; volume of CO_2 expired/volume of O_2 inspired) is indicative of the fuels you are burning; an RER of 0.7 to 0.85 is normal at rest or low activity levels and is associated with burning a mixture of fuels. With more intense exercise, your RER rises as you start exhaling more carbon dioxide. RER approaches and can exceed 1.0 as the rate of carbohydrate utilization increases from glycolysis.

RPE	ACTIVITY	TALKING ABILITY
1–3	Sitting on the couch	Uninhibited
4–5	Easy run	Story time!
5–6	Normal run	Comfortable conversation
7–8	Hard workout	2–3 sentences at a time
8–9	Very hard workout	5–7 words at a time
9–10	Extremely hard workout	Single word, probably four letters

TABLE 6.4 RPE and the Talk Test.

RPE AND THE TALK TEST

HOW FAST YOU'RE BREATHING impacts how easily and comfortably you can speak. I call recovery pace "story time" because you should be able to tell your training partner all about last weekend's epic adventure without pausing. When you bring the pace up to endurance or "forever" speed, you should be able to have a comfortable conversation, but you're probably not talking for very long before having to pause. As intensities increase, your ability to converse will dwindle to two or three sentences before you need to focus full-time on breathing. When you are running at or near your lactate threshold pace, you should only be able to say one complete sentence, maybe five to seven words. If someone tells you they are running at lactate threshold yet they are carrying on a normal conversation, they are lying to you (or they don't know any better). Finally, there's no talking at intensities near VO_2 max, unless you count four-letter expletives and grunts.

Because higher levels of carbon dioxide drive you to breathe faster and deeper to get rid of it, and a dramatic increase in carbohydrate utilization leads to a big increase in carbon dioxide levels in the blood, your breathing rate can give you a good (not perfect) indication of when you have reached lactate threshold.

As you progress from recovery pace to an endurance or "forever" pace (RPE 5 or 6), your breathing becomes deep and rhythmic; it is faster than at recovery pace but not labored. When you step up the intensity to target the high end of your aerobic range (RPE 7), your breathing will remain deep, but you should start to feel that you are laboring to breathe fast enough. The next intensity level is the tricky one: lactate threshold (RPE 8 or 9).

The easiest way to use your breathing to find lactate threshold is to go beyond it. When you exceed lactate threshold intensity, your breathing will go from deep, labored, and in control to short and rapid. The intensity or pace you want to hold during a lactate threshold interval is below the point at which your breathing shifts from controlled to short and rapid. In contrast, when you are doing RunningIntervals (RPE 10), you want to exceed this ventilatory threshold; your breathing should be short and rapid.

WHAT ABOUT RUNNING POWER METERS?

In the early 2000s as I was ramping up my coaching career, I had the good fortune to be privy to the power meter revolution that took over cycling. The concept of cycling power meters was simple. A cycling power meter works by measuring the force being produced either on the crank arms, pedals, or hub. By measuring the force, as well as the speed of what you are measuring (the pedals, cranks, or hub), it's a quick calculation to mechanical power (power = force × velocity).

Early power meter models were expensive, clunky, and heavy—all of which made power meters rare outside of the small circle of the best Grand Tour and track riders. Yet, they were a powerful-enough tool that many of the top riders in the world used them to inform training. Fast-forward a few years to the mid- and late 2000s, and these devices became more affordable, more streamlined, and lighter. Those innovations paved the way to widespread adoption not only by elite athletes but by everyday cyclists. This revered tool, once reserved only for training, could now also be used for racing to glean valuable insights into the demands of the sport.

It is in no way a stretch to say that this transition revolutionized the way we approached training cyclists. As coaches, we had a direct way of measuring intensity and race demands as well as a simple way of transferring and analyzing all of the information. Coaches subsequently had to "learn" how to read, analyze, and aggregate power meter files to better inform their coaching practice, and I am proud to say that I helped lead some of the first coaches to be fluent in this new language. I was also present to witness power meter failures, ranging from misinterpretation of the data to design flaws of the devices (and sometimes both). All of this experience continues to shape how I work with data to better coach athletes.

Jump to present time. Companies like Stryd, RunScribe, and Polar, among others, have recently attempted to replicate the cycling power meter revolution in running. It's a novel attempt, but in my opinion it will ultimately either fail or at least take on a different meaning. While cycling power meters directly measure the force exerted on the crank arms, pedals, or hub, running power meters have had to interpret power through a few degrees of separation. Some companies use the movement of the foot to determine the mechanical work required for the activity and thus calculate mechanical power through a proprietary algorithm. Others take a different approach altogether by reverse engineering the metabolic power (oxygen cost) required to run. Throughout it all, the key thing to keep in mind with a running power meter is that the devices are deriving power using various algorithms, none of which is a good surrogate for directly measuring force and speed like a cycling power meter. The differences are so great that even the phrase "running power" is essentially meaningless, both in terms of its biomechanical interpretation as well as its practical use with athletes.

So, where does this leave the average trail runner when it comes to "running power?" First off, in a trail running application, determining running power is problematic because the surface cannot be accounted for (similar to the NGP issue discussed earlier). Your running power meter does not know if you are running on pavement, sand, or an alpine ridge. Therefore, regardless of how good the algorithms are or if the running power meter is providing information about your mechanical or metabolic power, interpreting the data as an intensity surrogate is a meaningless exercise. Using running power meters that measure movement at the level of the foot might have utility to inform trail runners on effective training technique or form by analyzing the precise movement

HEART RATE VARIABILITY (HRV)

LIKE MANY PEOPLE, it's possible you got into running because it's simple. All you need is a pair of shoes, maybe a watch, and you're out the door. Despite that aspiration, the running world is saturated with gadgets and measurements that promise to make you better, faster, fitter, and stronger. Enter heart rate variability (HRV).

HRV is the measure of inter-heartbeat variation for a given period of time, reflected by what is known as the R-R interval (see Figure 6.6). What I mean by this is that even though your heart might beat at a rate of sixty beats per minute, those beats do not happen perfectly every second on the second. There is variability, and that variability of the timing within each heartbeat is both good and important. Measuring this variability gives us a noninvasive window into how well your autonomic nervous system is functioning. The autonomic nervous system is your body's regulator, with the important job of helping to maintain homeostasis. When you are fatigued, your autonomic nervous system cannot adjust to internal and external stimuli as efficiently, and that is reflected in your inter-heartbeat variation being more regular (which in this case is negative).

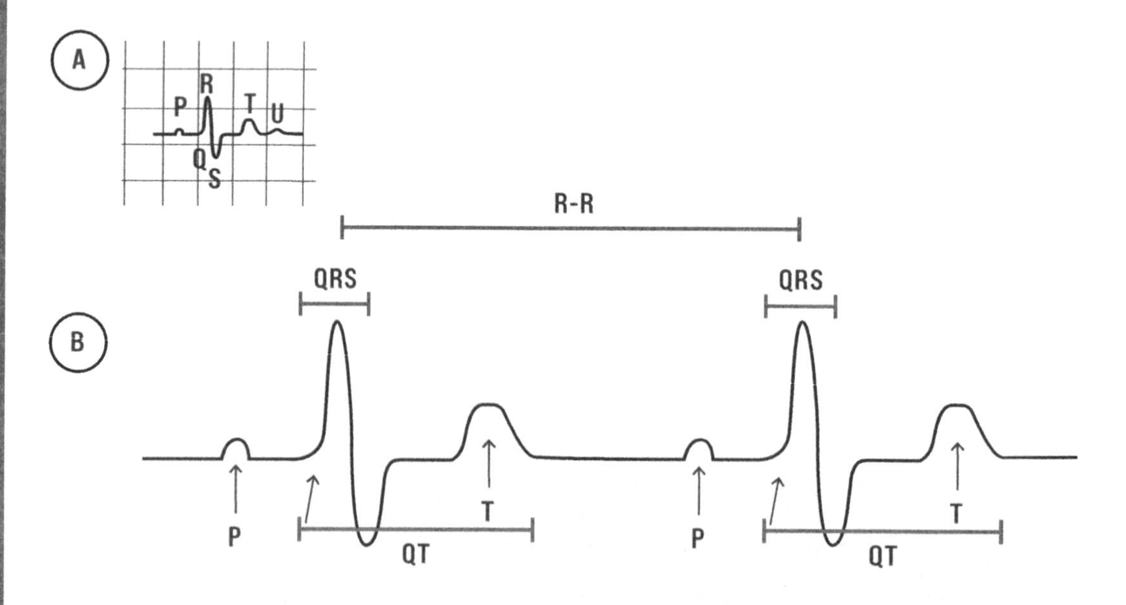

FIGURE 6.6 An EKG reading of the R-R interval across two heartbeats. Adapted from Dong (2016).

In this line of reasoning, we can utilize HRV to monitor training load, fatigue, and potentially how well you are adapting to training. Negative adaptations to long-term training would then be associated with reductions in HRV, and an increase in fitness (positive adaptation) would be associated with increases in HRV indices (Dong 2016).

What does that all mean? In order to utilize HRV, you need to do a few things:

- **Establish a baseline.** HRV does not provide valuable information with one singular reading but instead carries the most weight when you can monitor positive and negative trends. As with many other metrics in exercise physiology for performance, context is key.
- **Take effective readings.** Aside from daily readings, it's important to also utilize the best measurements possible. This means taking the readings upon waking first thing in the morning and opting for longer measurements than the default sixty-second options most applications will give you. Clinicians opt for five-minute readings. If you can fit that into your morning routine, five minutes gives you the likelihood of getting cleaner recordings.
- **Understand HRV is not cut-and-dried.** Like any training metric, HRV is not perfect. An increase in your HRV is not always positive, and a decrease is not always negative. Peaking for an event with a taper, an artificial rebound value forty-eight hours after a hard effort, or an overworked immune system while you fight off illness can send your daily HRV readings into uncharted territory. Therefore, it's important to utilize context and monitor trends over time; if you start using HRV, commit to gathering data for at least four weeks before making big decisions.

of the foot over the course of a run. But as a means of determining intensity, the promise of running power meters has yet to prove its worth.

SUBJECTIVE FEEDBACK

Out of all of the tools I use on a day-to-day basis with my athletes, subjective feedback is the most important. Descriptions of how you felt during a workout should be incorporated into your training log, and a premium should be placed on capturing this information consistently. You can record whatever you wish, but at a minimum write down how you felt (was the workout hard, easy, did you feel particularly fast, etc.), any challenges you encountered along the way, and any significant nutrition strategies you used. You will end up using the subjective feedback to help decide when to take a recovery phase (see Chapter 10) and to determine your nutrition plan (see Chapter 14), as well as to illuminate patterns and trends in your training. Finally, deliberately capturing subjective feedback makes you more aware during the run, which in turn can drive mental and psychological development that is also critical to success (more on this in Chapter 15).

What the Coach Uses

I will let you in on a secret: very little, if any, of this information is actionable by itself. In all my years as a coach, I cannot recall a time when I have taken one piece of such information and used it to decide what an athlete should do. Rather, action is determined by the aggregate of the information, combined with feedback from the athlete. From a practical standpoint, I utilize the following system to drive the creation of and adjustments to an athlete's training. I encourage you to do something similar.

- Use TrainingPeaks to schedule workouts (see the short-range plan, as described in Chapter 12).
- Use NGP, rTSS, and Strava segments to evaluate and compare workouts.
- Use rTSS/CTL/ATL to track training load.
- Use subjective feedback from the athlete to further gauge fitness, fatigue, and motivation.
- Use knowledge and experience to synthesize the information and drive action.

No Magic Bullet

Unfortunately for trail runners, there is no magic bullet for tracking workload or work rate or for monitoring progress. There is an amalgamation of approaches you can use to get a better handle on these aspects, but no single one will give you a definitive answer. Even when better tools emerge, coaches and athletes will continue to take their training and analysis beyond the realm of what the data can provide. Soon enough, running workload and work rate will become the norm. These will replace pace, NGP, and GAP just as those metrics have largely replaced the heart rate monitor. Even when that happens, don't expect to see stoplight answers. The training picture will never be green or red, nor will it be encapsulated by my quiver of highlighters. Instead, it will be a blur of many different colors, altogether subject to interpretation. As technology progresses, expect to be able to train more precisely and with greater knowledge—but don't expect the information to do the training for you.

Many of the training file graphs produced throughout this book were done through TrainingPeaks' WKO5 software. I would like to thank Frank Pipp and Mike Bonenberger at TrainingPeaks for their assistance.

KEY POINTS ON TOOLS TO TRACK YOUR TRAINING

- GPS watches are going to be the primary tool to track your training.
    - Choose the most accurate settings when recording intervals.
- Tools like TrainingPeaks, Strava, and Final Surge can harness the information collected on your watch and make it informative and actionable.
- Track volume by time, not miles.
- TSS can be used in concert with volume to inform you about training load, fitness, and fatigue.
    - Realize the limitations of TSS, and don't let it dictate your training.
- Heart rate is not a good tool for determining intensity. You can use it after the fact in training analysis as long as you know what factors confound it.
- RPE should be used to calibrate intensity during workouts and races.
- Subjective feedback is also critical to capture during day-to-day training.
- Synthesize all of the information available to drive training.

CHAPTER 7

Environmental Conditions and How to Adapt

Difficulty is part of ultrarunning's appeal. The length of the event, the unknown time it will take to get from aid station to aid station, and running over varied terrain at night all present challenges to even the most experienced ultrarunners. However, two conditions in particular strike fear into ultrarunner's hearts: heat and altitude.

Heat and altitude affect runners similarly: they strain your body's finite resources (oxygen and blood, primarily) to the extent that runners turn to special, and at times peculiar, adaptation strategies. Runners training for the Badwater Ultramarathon will wheel their treadmill into the laundry room, disconnect the hose from the dryer vent, and then turn the appliance on at full blast during training runs in order simulate the "hair dryer" effect, named for the notorious furnace-like winds runners face in Death Valley on July afternoons. More-daring runners will take it up a notch and layer on extra clothing, too. The ultra-paranoid will turn on a space heater in the room for good measure. Meanwhile, ultrarunners concerned with altitude deploy tents, masks, training camps, and all other methods of acclimation in order to prepare for racing through the thin air.

While all of these training interventions are well intended, few actually work. Some will have a net-zero effect, and several are actually counterproductive. So, before you go out and unhook your dryer in an attempt to battle Death Valley heat, let's paint some perspective on how heat and altitude actually affect performance and what you can do about them.

Fitness Is Your First Weapon

First things first: fitness is your primary weapon for optimal performance both at high altitude and in searing heat. The more fit you are, the more effective your natural cooling mechanisms are for hot environments and the more red blood cells you have to carry oxygen in high-altitude conditions. I mention this up front because it's important; none of the training interventions discussed below should be undertaken at the expense of building fitness. I mean it (so much so that I will repeat the point several times throughout this chapter). If your fancy altitude tent compromises your sleep and therefore your ability to complete (or recover from) hard workouts, skip sleeping in the tent. Similarly, running hard intervals in the middle of a hot day might provide a heat acclimation boost, but it will also limit that workout's effectiveness, so don't partake in that nonsense either. As you will see in Chapter 10, the total volume of workload you can do and the quality of the workouts you do are far more important than specific heat and altitude protocols. Yet, they are not mutually exclusive. So, if you can get the right amount of work in *and* perform either or both of these interventions, great! But, if you have to compromise workload or quality to do so, it's likely not a good trade-off.

With all of that said, let's dive into considerations and interventions for high-altitude and extreme-heat situations.

Altitude

Aside from heat (which I will talk about later in this chapter), altitude might be the scariest environmental factor for many trail and ultra-athletes. We host a running camp in May every year in Colorado Springs, Colorado, and the most common thing we hear going into camp is, "I'm from sea level. I'm worried that I will be too slow at the camp because of the elevation." While altitude is not everyone's friend, it doesn't have to be your foe either.

"There's not enough air up here!" is something I myself have yelled while running in the mountains, and while it's an incredibly popular phrase, it's not entirely true. Despite a change in altitude from sea level to 8,000 feet, the composition of gases that make up the air around you remains the same: 20.93 percent oxygen, 0.03 percent carbon dioxide, and 79.04 percent nitrogen. So why does it feel so terrible up high? As you go up in elevation, there is a decrease in the partial pressure of oxygen, and your lungs rely on a pressure gradient for both inhalation and exhalation as well as the gas exchange between your alveoli (the small air sacs in your lungs) and capillary beds (Sinex and Chapman 2015). Basically, there isn't "less air," there's less oxygen in a lungful of air due to changes in partial pressure at higher elevations.

PHYSIOLOGY AT A GLANCE

Despite these environmental challenges, our bodies are incredibly adaptable at the multisystemic and cellular levels to not only survive but thrive and perform at a high level. The research literature on human survival and performance is rich: from military interests to mountaineering feats, altitude has been inspiring physiologists for generations. This fascination with performance at high altitudes was heightened even more heading into the 1968 Summer Olympics in Mexico City (located at ~7,350 feet), where performing well at altitude meant the glory of Olympic medals for the countries and athletes competing.

So, what happens when you travel to higher altitudes? When you travel to altitude, your body needs to go through a series of adaptations very quickly to counter your decreased ability to transport oxygen efficiently. Remember that oxygen moves from the lungs to the bloodstream because of a pressure gradient, so the reduction in partial pressure means it's harder to get oxygen into the bloodstream and then to both working muscle tissue and your brain. The adaptations you undergo are generally two-pronged: some take place in the first twenty-four hours at altitude, while others may take several weeks to fully develop. And while we may think we are limited by our lungs and respiratory system, the adaptations take place throughout our bodies and affect our cardiovascular and metabolic systems as well.

At a cardiovascular and hematologic level, changes can take place almost immediately.

This is because your body is trying to artificially boost the density of your red blood cells through a process known as hemoconcentration. When this happens, your plasma volume can decrease by 10 to 25 percent, which in turn increases your hematocrit (the percentage of red blood cells—which contain hemoglobin, the oxygen-carrying component—per unit of blood). Ramping up hematocrit helps your body temporarily improve its ability to transport oxygen until you can produce more red blood cells to get the job done (Beidleman et al. 2017). This is also why your heart rate tends to be elevated for the first few days at higher elevation. As blood volume decreases, so does stroke volume (the amount of blood pumped out of the heart per beat), and your heart rate has to increase to keep cardiac output stable (cardiac output [Q] = HR x stroke volume). This will normalize at rest and at lower aerobic intensities more quickly, but it is why you generally feel your worst from twenty-four to seventy-two hours after arriving at altitude. This is also why athletic programs recommend you keep your training intensity low (below 70 percent of VO_2 max) when you first arrive at altitude to avoid increased fatigue or maladaptation (Sinex and Chapman 2015).

At a respiratory system level, the decrease in oxygen coming into your bloodstream from gas exchange in your lungs causes an increase in ventilation rate and depth of breathing. This increase in ventilation is important because of its downstream effects. When you breathe faster you exhale more carbon dioxide than normal. This in turn means there is less carbon dioxide in your blood and can eventually lead to respiratory alkalosis, or a pH imbalance (Sinex and Chapman 2015). Because our bodies like to operate within very finite parameters, this increase in blood pH causes our kidneys to get involved to correct-course and bring our body back to equilibrium. The kidneys do this primarily by increasing urine volume. The other things your kidneys do in response to hypoxia are produce and release more erythropoietin (EPO; Goldfarb-Rumyantzev and Alper 2014). EPO might sound familiar due to its illicit use as a performance-enhancing drug, but EPO is also naturally produced to help stimulate the body to make more red blood cells. The process of erythropoiesis (the production of red blood cells), stimulated by EPO, takes at least one week and as many as two to three weeks to allow red blood cells to mature and become fully functional (Garvican-Lewis 2017). It is this long-term response that allows your blood plasma volume to not only return to normal but to also

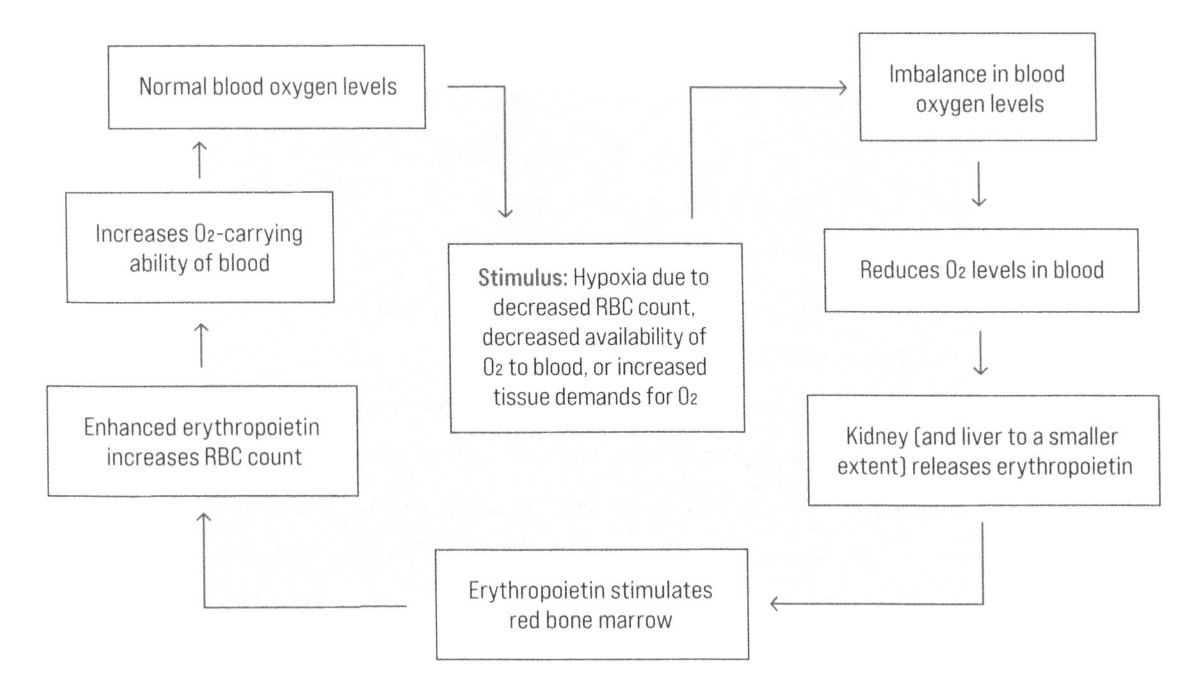

FIGURE 7.1 Hematologic effects to altitude exposure.

expand, and with this increase in red blood cells there are also increases in your hematocrit and hemoglobin and ultimately the desired adaptation of carrying more oxygen. This entire cascade of events is described in Figure 7.1.

ACCLIMATION PROTOCOL FOR ALTITUDE

When it comes to methods for altitude acclimation, there are two primary contenders: "live high, train high" and "live high, train low." If you have the ability, time, and means to either put together your own high-altitude training camp, or if you live at moderate to high altitude, you might be interested in understanding what the ideal setup is. The general consensus in the research community is that the "live high, train low" method will lead to the greatest hematologic and performance benefits (Constantini, Wilhite, and Chapman 2017). This is because you get both the long-term altitude exposure throughout the day and overnight and the higher-quality workouts performed at lower elevations. Of course, if you are really lucky, you fall into the "live high, train high/train low" camp, in which you live high, do low-intensity workouts up high, and then do high-intensity workouts down low, allowing you to perform high-quality workouts while utilizing maximum recovery. However, there are fairly few training sites that allow this type of training to be done conveniently (living high with a short commute to running low). These sites include Park City, Utah; Flagstaff, Arizona; Mammoth Lakes, California; Big Bear Lake, California; Lake Tahoe, Nevada/California; Cloudcroft, New Mexico; and Sierra Nevada, Spain (Constantini, Wilhite, and Chapman 2017). They might sound familiar, as many professional running groups use them as training hubs, fulltime residences, or high-altitude camps.

What does all of this mean for you as you get ready for the Leadville 100 while living in the Midwest? First, don't worry, you are not alone. Second, there are few things to consider. When we think about altitude acclimation, there are two primary methods: using an altitude tent or finding a natural high-altitude environment. No matter which one you use (or have access to), effectiveness often comes down to dosage: how high for how long.

If you can use a natural environment, it is important to have your chronic exposure take place above 5,900 ft (1,800 m) and below 9,840 ft (3,000 m). It's important to point out that there isn't anything inherently negative about being above 9,840 ft; there just do not appear to be any added benefits, hematologically speaking. Additionally, with an increase in elevation, there comes an increased risk of acute mountain sickness, so think

	LIVE HIGH, TRAIN HIGH	LIVE HIGH, TRAIN LOW	LIVE HIGH, TRAIN HIGH / LOW
Living	Living between 6,840–8,050 ft	Living between 6,840–8,050 ft	Living between 6,840–8,050 ft
Training	Training at or above 6,000 ft	Training below 4,100 ft	Train at low intensities between 6,840–8,050 ft, and high intensity workouts below 4,100 ft*
Duration of Protocol	~21-28 days	~21-28 days	~21-28 days

TABLE 7.1 Different altitude training protocols.

*Living between 6,840–8,050 ft is optimal for hematological responses while not impairing recovery and sleep. Moving high-intensity runs below 4,100 ft is also optimal because it allows you to preserve the ability to effectively deliver oxygen to working muscles, maintaining the quality of higher-intensity sessions.

of the altitude cap as balancing optimal adaptations with relative safety.

As far as dose is concerned, the general recommendation is a minimum of two weeks, and ideally up to four weeks, to reap maximum performance benefits (Constantini, Wilhite, and Chapman 2017). This might not be realistic when you are looking at travel plans for your upcoming A race, and that's where the one-week minimum recommendation comes into play. This recommendation is not based on maximizing performance benefits but rather avoiding feeling terrible on race day. As I mentioned earlier, athletes generally feel worst during the twenty-four- to seventy-two-hour period after arriving at altitude, so getting over that hump will at least spare you the added hindrance of your body trying to make its initial adaptations.

Finally, it's important to note that traveling to altitude above 8,202 ft (2,500 m) does not come without general health risks such as developing acute high-altitude illness, which covers several syndromes such as acute mountain sickness (which usually resolves without treatment) or, more seriously (potentially fatally), high-altitude pulmonary edema (swelling of the airway) and high-altitude cerebral edema (swelling of the brain). Because of this, it's important to consult with your primary care provider if you have any questions or concerns before traveling to altitude.

When it comes to using an altitude tent, the time course for adaptation remains fairly constant, with three to four weeks of exposure needed to produce any hematological changes. However, the biggest concern around this strategy is that you're not actually spending a full three to four weeks in the altitude tent; at most you are probably spending eight to ten hours a day exposed to hypoxia. Researchers are still struggling to discern meaningful hematological changes in athletes utilizing altitude tents while living at altitudes lower than 5,900 ft. That said, if you live at the cusp of the minimum elevation required for chronic altitude exposure (~5,500–6,500 ft), several studies have shown that utilizing an altitude tent for nine hours a night at a simulated altitude (8,200–9,840 ft) was enough exposure to produce positive adaptations (Carr et al. 2015; Garvican-Lewis et al. 2015).

What does that mean for altitude tents? I think the verdict is still very much out. But as a coach I weigh the following questions before recommending them on an individual basis: Can the athlete afford the tent? Does it decrease their training quality by impacting their quality of sleep? At what elevation do they currently live? And, can they make it out to their race at least one week prior to the gun going off?

IS AN ALTITUDE INTERVENTION A GOOD IDEA?

There is one more important piece of this puzzle that is worth mentioning. Like everything else in physiology, there is some degree of individual variation when it comes to altitude acclimation. Over the past twenty years there have been terms tossed around like "responders vs nonresponders," and while it does appear that people are affected differently by chronic exposure to altitude, oftentimes it's because we are missing an underlying cause. These underlying causes can inhibit an individual's ability to produce a normal response to altitude exposure, including the expected increases in EPO and hemoglobin. This does not mean an individual may never be a responder to altitude, but it does reinforce the importance of context when looking at research outcomes.

Factors we know can easily inhibit your ability to adapt to altitude include injury, illness, and iron status. Injury and illness can both create inflammation in the body that naturally reduces your hemoglobin at sea level, before you even leave for altitude. Additionally, injury and illness can elevate cortisol levels, which blunts adaptation. This is largely why physiologists recommend avoiding high-intensity training (which also raises cortisol levels) in the days before traveling to altitude. Finally, low iron status, specifically stored iron measured as serum ferritin, can impact your body's ability to create hematological adaptions at altitude. In studies evaluating runners at high-altitude camps, researchers found that athletes whose serum ferritin was less than 35 ng/mL could not produce an increase in red blood cell mass even after four weeks of altitude exposure (Constantini, Wilhite, and Chapman 2017).

PRE-RACE ALTITUDE STRATEGIES

This is where I remind you that the absolute best thing you can do, no matter the elevation of your hometown, is to make sure you are as fit as possible before going to a high-altitude race. No amount of magic, sleeping in a tent, prayer, or time at altitude is going to make up for a lack of fitness and other race-specific factors. Along with great fitness, here are three things you can do to optimize your race-day performance:

GET AN IRON PANEL THREE MONTHS OUT: Three months before going to elevation, meet

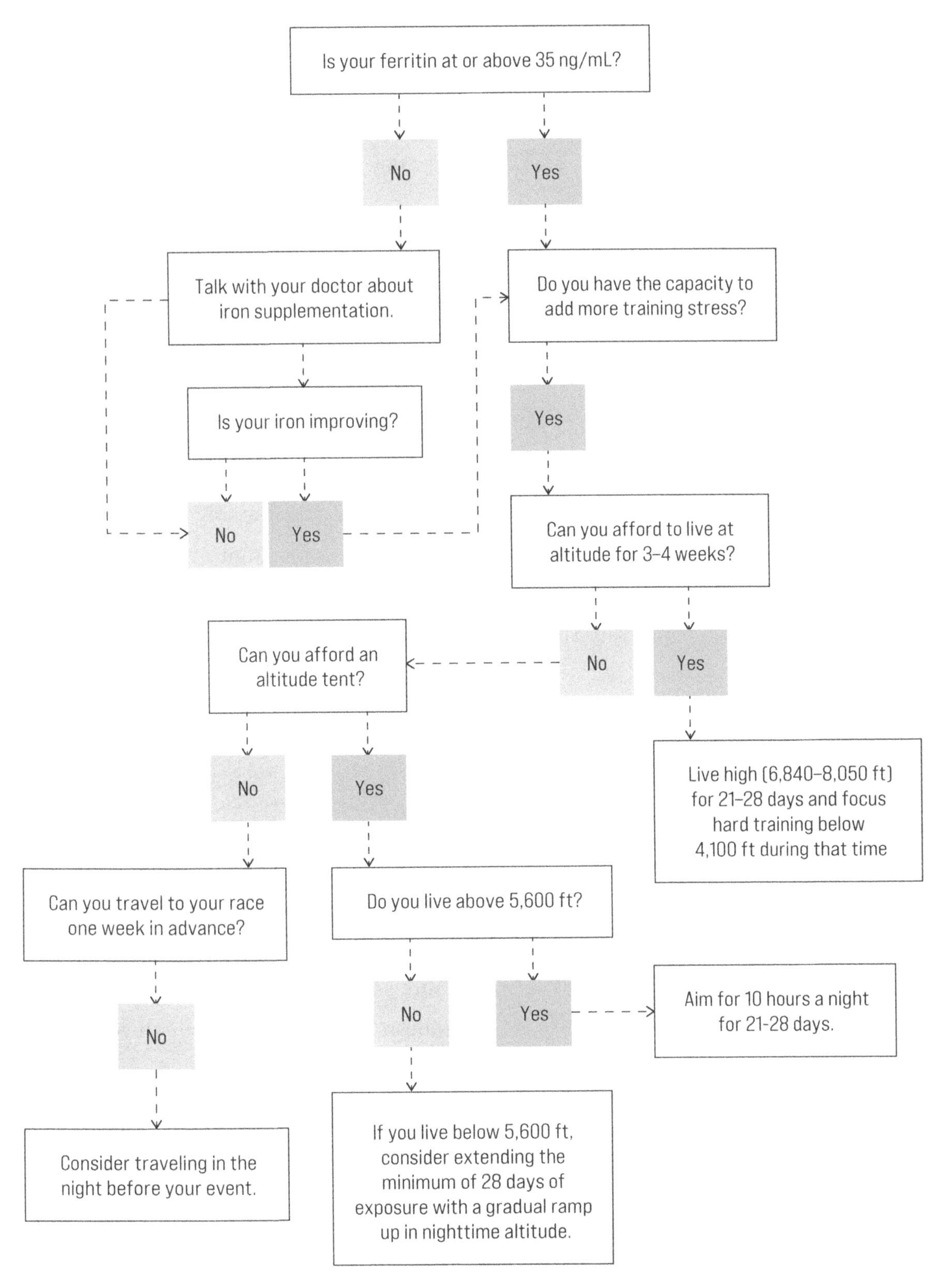

FIGURE 7.2 Are you a good candidate for altitude training?

with your primary care provider and get an iron panel done. (This should be done before taking iron supplements, because consuming too much iron can be toxic.) Three months gives you time to benefit from increased iron intake (if necessary) so you have the tools to adapt to altitude for a race, training camp, or time spent in an altitude tent.

TRY TO ARRIVE AT YOUR RACE EARLY: If you can't get there early, arriving the night before or morning of the event might allow you to fit your race into that twenty-four-hour window before your body ramps up the responses to altitude that make people feel miserable. General recommendations are to arrive three to five days early for races at 1,640–6,561 ft, one to two weeks for races at 6,561–9,842 ft, and at least three weeks for races over 9,842 ft (Chapman, Stickford, and Levine 2010).

ORGANIZE A TRIAL RUN: If possible, go to altitude for a camp ahead of a high-altitude A race. The benefits are mostly experiential, giving you an understanding of how your body responds to running at altitude. This is also a good time to figure out the adjustments you'll need to make to both fueling strategies and pacing strategies in order to (hopefully) avoid any unpleasant surprises come race day.

Heat

Many of you have probably thought or heard someone say, "I'm bad in the heat." I've read it in training logs and seen it in the eyes of runners coming into Michigan Bluff during the Western States 100. But here's the thing: although you might not love the heat, your body is clever and can definitely get better, both physiologically and psychologically, at running in hot conditions. Additionally, there are strategies you can employ before and during your event to make sure you don't melt, crumble, or end up in the medical tent. As with altitude, the heat doesn't care about how tough you are. How well you prepare for heat can make the difference when it comes to finding the finish line.

PHYSIOLOGY AT A GLANCE

As humans we are inherently inefficient beings. The truth is, only a fraction of the work you do ends up propelling you down the trail; the majority of it simply generates heat

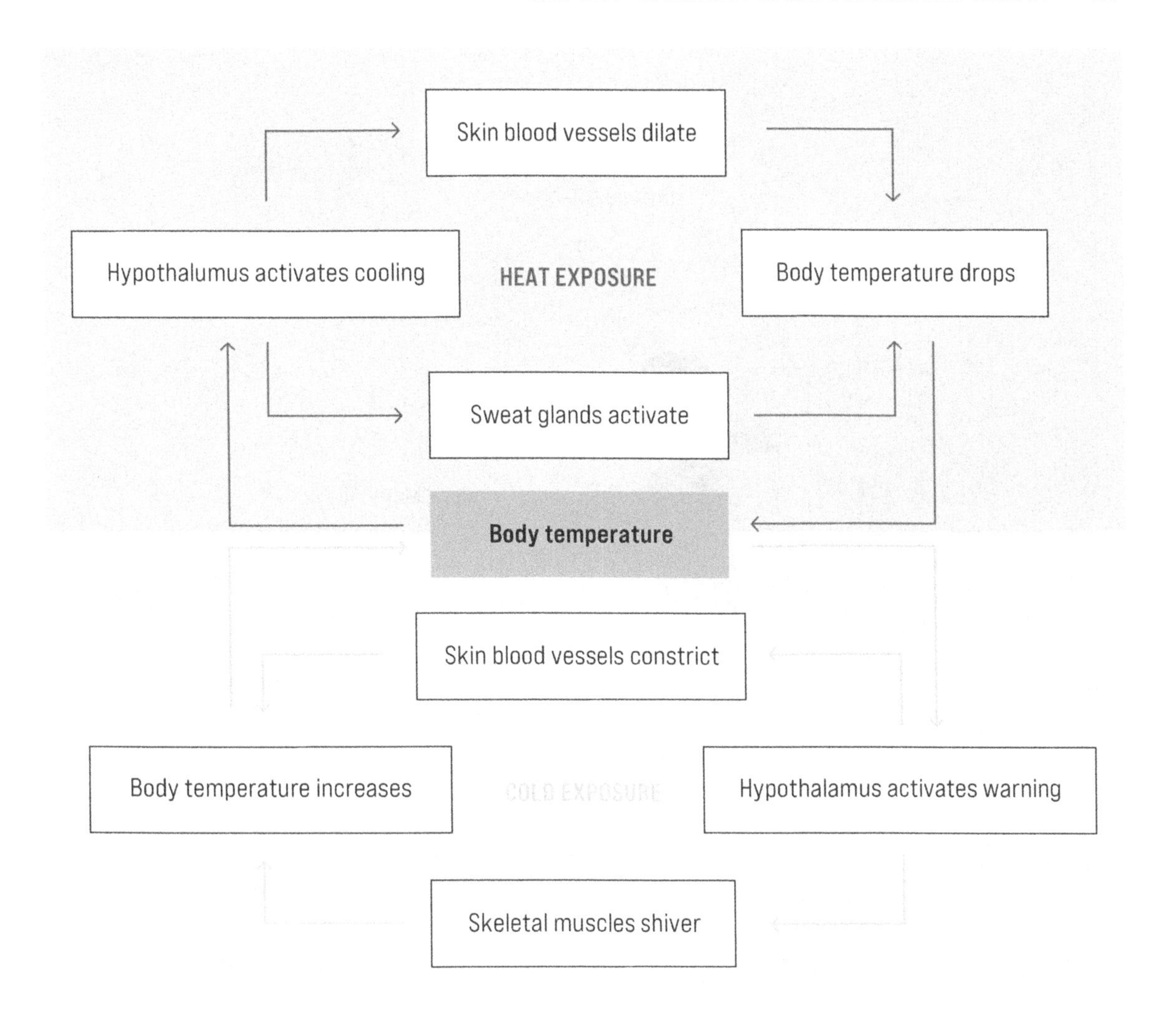

FIGURE 7.3 Physiological response to temperature change.

that doesn't really have anywhere to go. As a result, we rely first and foremost on our body's internal capacity to maintain our ideal core body temperature (37°C/98.6°F), and then we can then supplement that capacity with actions like putting on more or less clothes, etc. When your body temperature drops, your blood vessels constrict, keeping warmth near your core to protect your vital organs, and you begin to shiver in order to produce heat. In contrast, when your body temperature rises, your blood vessels dilate, sending more blood to the surface of the skin to dissipate heat into the environment and activating your sweat glands to provide water for evaporative cooling.

Again, there are two major factors at play when exercising and racing in the heat:

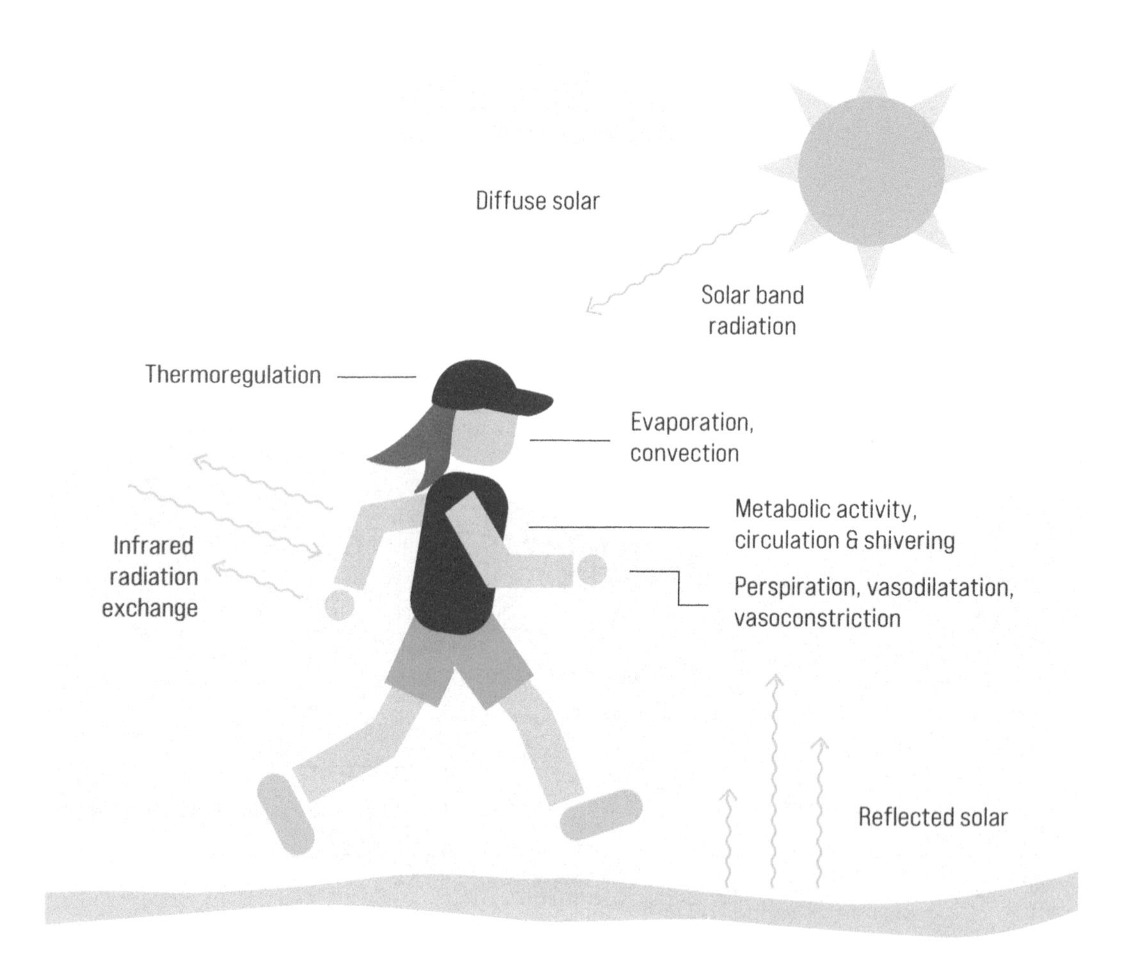

FIGURE 7.4 Thermoregulation of the human body.

the heat you create and the heat you're exposed to. Like I mentioned before, your body produces a lot of heat doing metabolic work when you run—as much as 5 to 15 times more than at rest—and it will try to dissipate as much of that as possible to maintain a relatively stable core temperature (Sawka et al. 1993). Additionally, you are running in a hot environment, which adds more heat strain to your metabolic mess.

Where you are running matters too. Some examples include an environment where ambient air temperature is greatly influenced by the surface you are running on (like at the Badwater 135 where the pavement reflects the heat of the sun), you're in direct vs indirect sunlight, or you're exposed to wind from varying directions. The environment impacts the four categories of heat transfer: conduction (direct transfer of energy), convection (air or water moving over your skin), radiation (direct or indirect transfer of

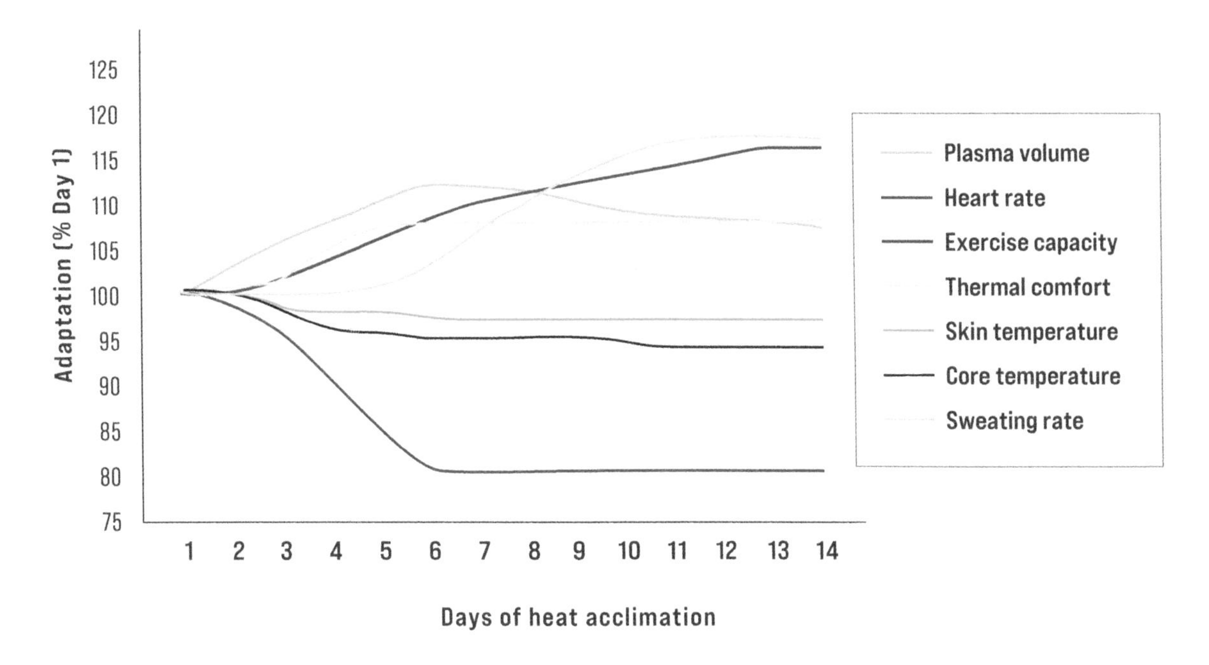

FIGURE 7.5 Time course of adaptations from heat acclimation. Adapted from Périard, Racinais, and Sawka 2015.

heat from electromagnetic waves), and evaporation (conversion of liquid to gas; Sawka et al. 2011). These methods of transfer work together to either heat you up or cool you off, but their effect is largely dependent on the temperature gradient between you and the surrounding environment, because heat moves along a gradient (high to low).

Acclimation, the process of your body getting more efficient and adjusting to your environment over time, applies to both altitude and heat. It is our clever capability to maintain, survive, and thrive across a wide range of environmental conditions. Heat acclimation leads to internal changes that enable the body to function better in hot environments. The key changes that your body makes after chronic, daily heat exposure are an earlier onset of the sweat response, an increase in sweat rate and a corresponding decrease in sweat sodium concentration, better reabsorption of sodium and chloride through the sweat duct, lower skin and core temperature thanks to blood plasma volume expansion, lower heart rate during exercise (or, rather, a return to normal heart rates), increased fluid and cardiovascular stability, and a decrease in the metabolic cost of exercise (Périard, Racinais, and Sawka 2015; Rivas et al. 2017). Combine all these factors and you have the most important adaptation of all: the ability to tolerate and feel more comfortable in the heat come race day.

ACCLIMATION METHODS

You might be looking to heat acclimation to perform better at a hot race or to jump-start your summer training as the temperature creeps up, so what methods are available to you? As a coach I ask myself, "How do I elicit the adaptation I want with the lowest dose or minimum intervention possible?" This is important, because anything we add to your training is stress, and when adding stress there are always trade-offs. What do we take away to make room for this additional stress? We know from the literature that all of the following strategies can work, but the one that is best for you has a lot to do with what you have at your disposal and what you can tolerate.

What we know is that if you repeatedly, day after day, increase your core body temperature through exercise, environmental stress, passive interventions (sauna or hot-water immersion), or all of the above, you induce physiological adaptations that will increase your thermal tolerance (Minett et al. 2016).

The methods most commonly used by athletes are natural heat acclimation (exercising in hot ambient conditions), controlled hyperthermia (overdressing), controlled intensity (use of exercise in a climatic chamber), and passive heating (postexercise heating via sauna or hot-water immersion; Daanen, Racinias, and Périard 2017). All of these methods work but take varying amounts of time to increase your core body temperature to ~101°F (38.5°C), where it should stay for approximately ninety minutes. Additionally, some of these methods are time-consuming and inherently uncomfortable and could even be dangerous.

There have been numerous studies dating back to the 1960s that look at sessions ranging from 50 to 100 min of daily heat exposure, twice-daily heat exposure, trials lasting anywhere from five to twenty-seven days, and combinations of the aforementioned methods. The summary of this research is that the end results were more or less the same: they all work, and most importantly, more is not better.

PRIORITY OF METHODS

There is a hierarchy of heat acclimation protocols, and it's a little bit like "Goldilocks and the Three Bears": The one that fits just right is the one that allows you to maintain the highest-quality training. Like everything in a performance physiology setting, we are looking to

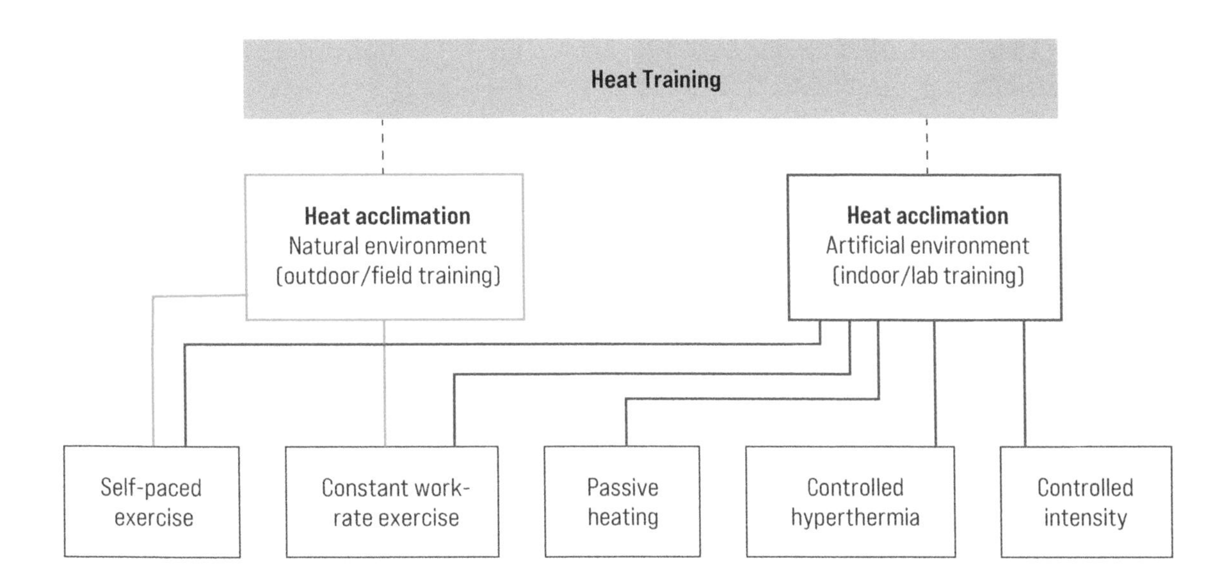

METHOD	ACTIVITY EXAMPLE	WORK RATE	CONDITIONS	DURATION
Self-paced exercise	Football, or running	Variable, or self-selected	Variable outdoor, or indoor 40°C/104°F, 40% relative humidity	60–90 min
Constant work-rate exercise	Cycling ergometer, or marching	60% VO_2 max (185 W) or 6 km/h	Indoor 40°C/104°F, 40% relative humidity, or variable outdoor	60–90 min
Passive heating	Water immersion, or sauna bathing	N/A	Water 40–42°C/104–107.6°F or sauna 70–90°C/158–194°F	45–60 min, or intermittent for 30 min
Controlled hyperthermia	Resting and/or exercising to maintain core temperature at 38.5°C	Variable	40°C/104°F, 40% relative humidity	60–90 min
Controlled intensity	Cycle ergometer	65% VO_2 max heart rate (145 bpm)	40°C/104°F, 40% relative humidity	60–90 min

FIGURE 7.6 Different heat acclimation methods. Adapted from Daanen, Racinais, and Périard 2017.

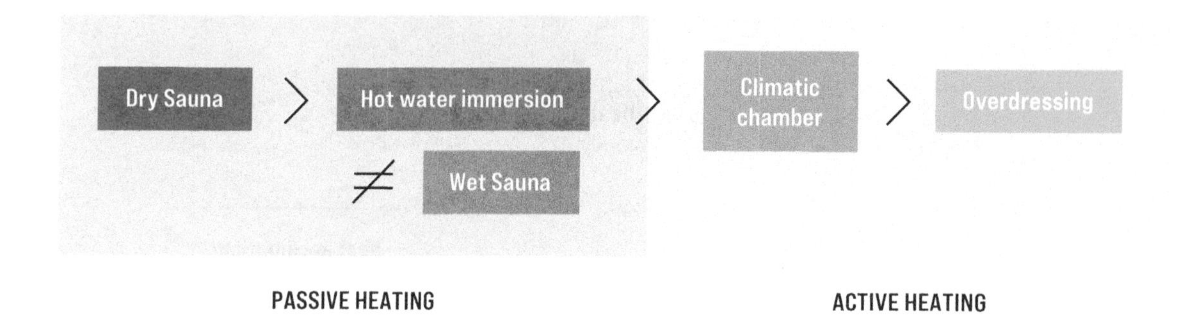

FIGURE 7.7 Hierarchy of heat acclimation protocols.

achieve the desired adaptations (boost performance) with the smallest dose possible.

Active heating by overdressing or by exercising in a controlled environment like a climatic chamber is effective, but are you sacrificing workout quality by cutting the volume or intensity? Likely both. You can also spend a long time (sixty to ninety minutes broken up as needed) in a dry sauna, wet sauna (a steam room), or hot tub to get the desired effects of heat acclimation, but that's a lot of additional time and stress added to your daily training regimen. When we take these two factors—dose and time needed—into consideration, passive heating (dry sauna, wet sauna, or hot tub) immediately postexercise rises to the top of the pile. This strategy allows you to maintain the quality of your workouts in the natural environment and spend less time in the actual heat because you are entering "pre-warmed" by the exercise.

It's important to note that inducing hyperthermia has inherent risks, and it is important to monitor yourself throughout any protocol. This can include monitoring core body temperature and hydration status (either by weighing yourself pre- and post-sauna to account for water loss or by using urinalysis strips to ensure you rehydrate adequately post-sauna). Additionally, you should consult your primary care provider if you have any questions or concerns.

ACCLIMATION PROTOCOLS

Passive heating best combines the temperature threshold needed for adaptation to take place with a small and manageable additional stressor on top of training workload. The following protocol illustrates how we help athletes as they prep for hot races like Western States 100, Transgrancanaria, and The Coastal Challenge.

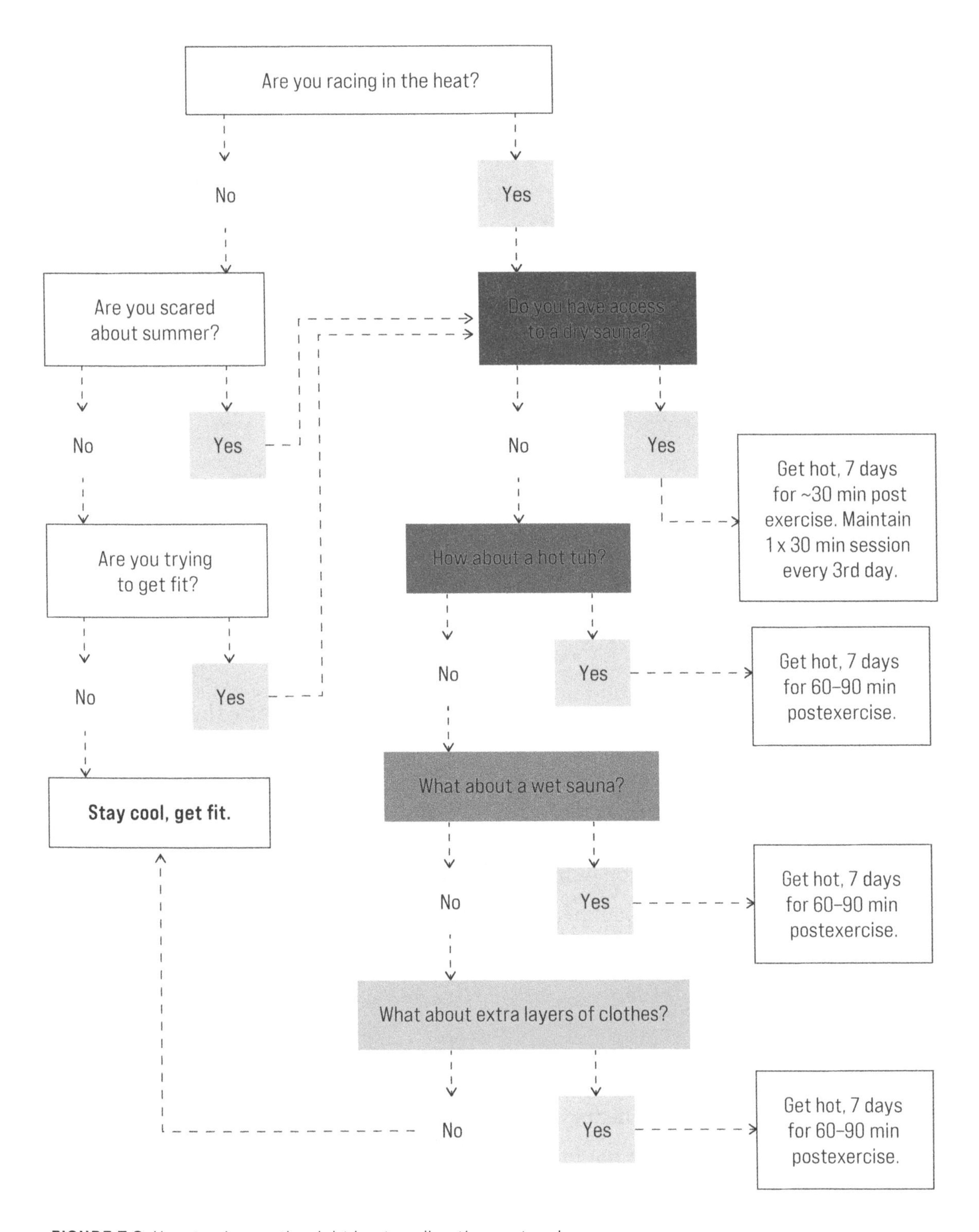

FIGURE 7.8 How to choose the right heat acclimation protocol.

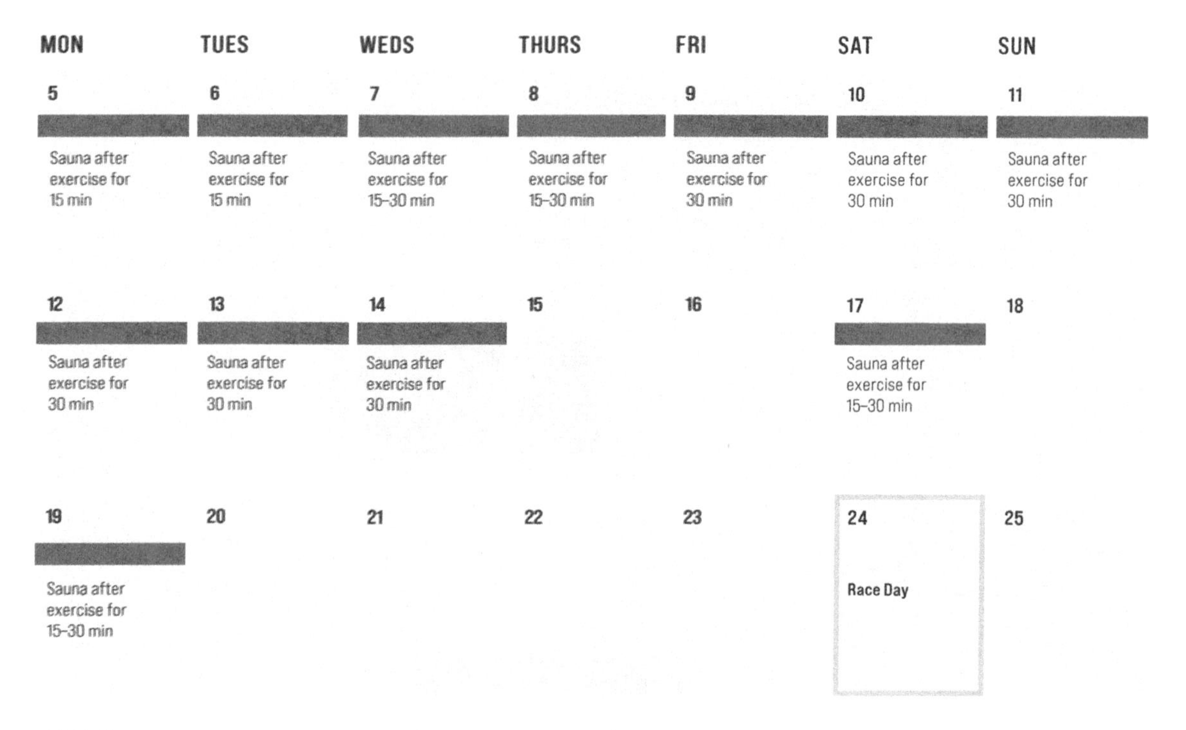

MON	TUES	WEDS	THURS	FRI	SAT	SUN
5 Sauna after exercise for 15 min	6 Sauna after exercise for 15 min	7 Sauna after exercise for 15–30 min	8 Sauna after exercise for 15–30 min	9 Sauna after exercise for 30 min	10 Sauna after exercise for 30 min	11 Sauna after exercise for 30 min
12 Sauna after exercise for 30 min	13 Sauna after exercise for 30 min	14 Sauna after exercise for 30 min	15	16	17 Sauna after exercise for 15–30 min	18
19 Sauna after exercise for 15–30 min	20	21	22	23	24 **Race Day**	25

FIGURE 7.9 An example of a heat acclimation protocol using a sauna.

Things to keep in mind:

- Heat acclimation will make you tired. Our aim is to minimize this consequence.
- You need seven to ten days in a row, ideally, to elicit positive adaptations.
- After heat acclimation is achieved, you can maintain these adaptations by adding exposure to heat again once every three days.
- The average degradation of heat acclimation is ~2.5 percent a day after the first forty-eight hours without heat exposure. If you were to do a two-week taper with no heat exposure, you could expect a decay in heart rate control of ~35 percent, a decay in core temperature control of ~6 percent, and a decay in sweat rate improvements of ~30 percent. If you are traveling to an event in a hot environment, it is important to know you can generally reacclimate in as little as four days.
- A heat acclimation schedule can be adjusted to align with the "most manageable" training (i.e., it's not ideal to do this on top of peak volume training).
- In the following examples, I use "sauna" as the preferred method of choice. This is because of its efficacy, utility, and accessibility. A hot-water immersion bath would be a close second choice.

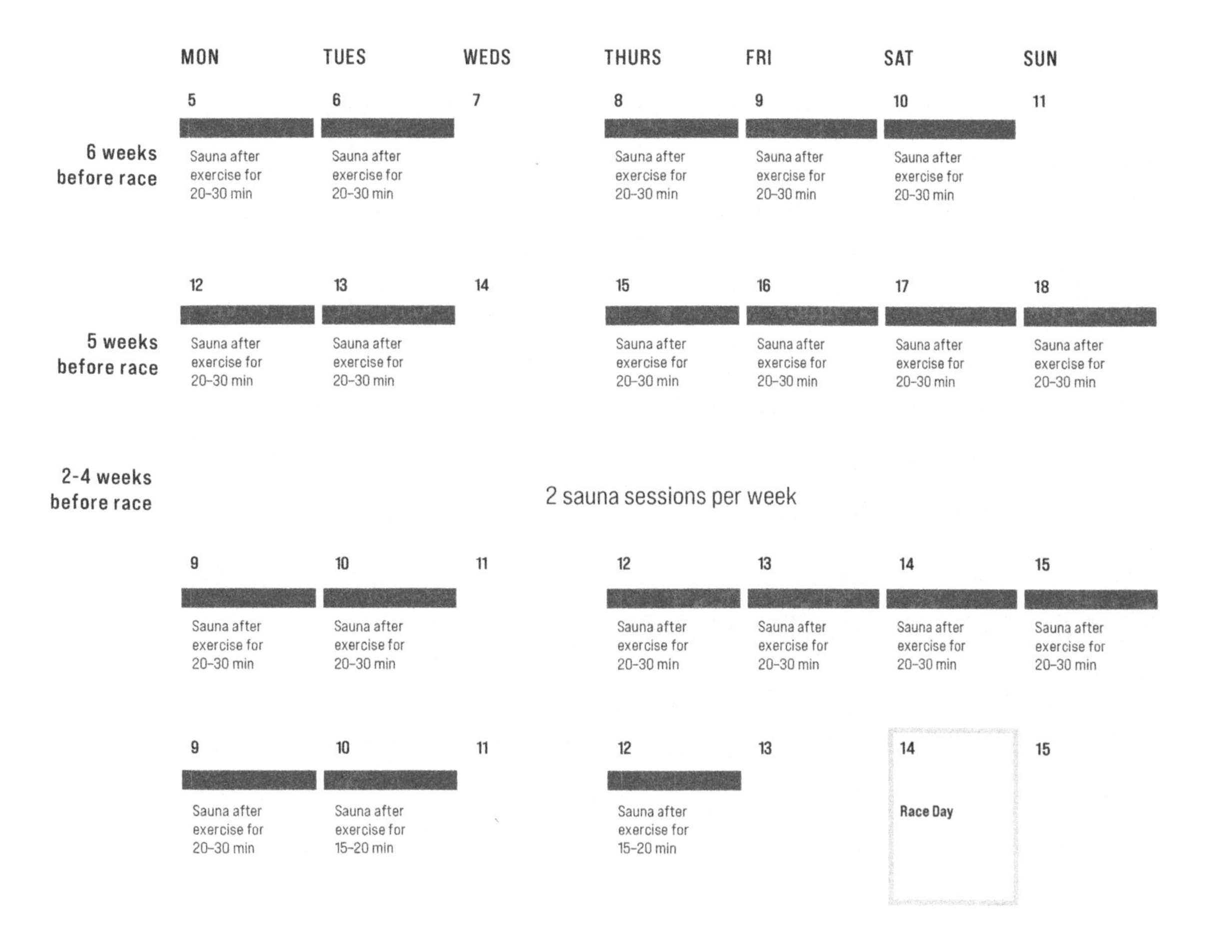

FIGURE 7.10 Two-phase sauna acclimation protocol.

Protocol #1: Single Exposure Leading up to the Race

If you have limited time and resources to gain access to a sauna, adding in a heat acclimation protocol in the several days leading up to an event is going to be your best choice. However, take extra precaution that you taper more than you normally would, as the sauna will add additional stress on your system, which is contraindicated for the taper.

Protocol #2: Repeated Exposure

If you have more regular access to a sauna and if your training leading up to an event is going particularly well, this protocol might be more effective for you. This protocol, while more complicated, mitigates the risk of overdoing the sauna exposure close to the race. For this protocol, you take full advantage of a longer period of time by acclimating in two separate bouts. One occurs approximately six weeks out from the event, and the second occurs in the final week of the event. In between, you will have several heat "maintenance sessions" approximately every third or fourth day so that when you are ready for the final re-acclimation period it can be faster and more effective. These maintenance sessions also partially mitigate the ~2.5 percent per day decay in heat acclimation mentioned previously. Additionally, we know that repeated exposure to hot environments have an additive effect. So, you might get a slightly better adaptation from this protocol. The downside of this protocol is that the first acclimation period (about six weeks out from an event) can coincide with heavy and important training. If this is the case for you, consider protocol #1 so you are not adding so much stress all at the same time.

Race-Day Considerations

So, you've done the work, you're fit, and you've spent the time to be as ready as possible to handle the heat. Now what about when you're actually racing? Even after effective heat acclimation, there are still strategies you can employ to both improve performance and avoid a medical emergency like heat stroke. We refer to these strategies as "during-event cooling."

During-event cooling strategies all aim to rapidly remove excess heat from the body in hopes of creating more heat-storage capacity (Bongers, Hopman, and Eijsvogels 2017). The goal is not so much to actually lower your core body temperature, but rather to keep your skin temperature low enough to maintain a temperature gradient between your core and skin. This encourages blood to be sent to your skin (via vasodilation) to release heat into the environment. Maintaining this delicate balance is like walking a tightrope.

Strategies you can employ in your next race include packing ice on your torso, icing your neck and head (ice bandanas, collars, and hats), icing your peripheral arteries (ice down your arm sleeves), wearing loose and light-colored clothing to facilitate heat dissipation, limiting conductive heat (wearing light colors), increasing evaporation (dump water on yourself), and drinking cool fluids (Tyler, Sunderland, and Cheung 2013). Not to be outshone by more exciting strategies, I cannot stress enough how important it is to maintain proper hydration status—it is of utmost importance to keep your sweat response intact so you can utilize evaporative cooling and keep your core temperature below critical levels. Finally, a really effective way to cool down is to stop running (because remember, you are actively producing heat when you run). If you need to, you can save your race by walking slowly or stopping for ten, twenty, or thirty minutes to ingest fluids and food while you get some ice or cold water on your body.

KEY POINTS ON ADAPTING TO THE ENVIRONMENT

- Ultramarathons are frequently contested in hot and high-altitude environments. Heat and altitude are both worth taking into consideration for training.
- Fitness is your first weapon in combatting heat and altitude.
- Your body will adapt to altitude through a host of activities, primarily by producing more red blood cells and expanding plasma volume.
- When initially arriving at altitude, your body will respond with an elevated heart rate, which normalizes after twenty-four to seventy-two hours.
- There are three methods of acclimating to altitude:
    - Live High, Train High
    - Live High, Train Low
    - Live High, Train High/Train Low (low-intensity sessions at high altitude, high-intensity sessions at low altitude)
    - Each of these protocols can last from twenty-one to twenty-eight days.
    - The most efficacious is the Live High, Train High/Train Low protocol.
- Not all athletes are good candidates for altitude camps. Athletes with low ferratin levels (< 35 ng/ml) have room to improve through normal training, and athletes who cannot logistically orchestrate an altitude camp should focus on improving through other means.
- No matter what elevation you are training at, if you are going to a race at altitude you should conduct an iron panel three months out, try to arrive at the race early (how early depends on the altitude of the race), and organize a trial run at the altitude of your race to see how you react. (Keep in mind there are real risks associated with the development of acute high-altitude illnesses at elevations above 2,500 m/8,202 ft).
- You produce five to fifteen times more heat when you run vs at rest. Your body will dissipate as much of this heat as possible through conduction, convection, radiation, and evaporation.

- Commonly used methods to acclimate to the heat are natural heat acclimation, over-dressing, exercising in a climatic chamber, and passive heating via a sauna or hot-water bath. (Keep in mind it's important to monitor core temperature and hydration status during any protocol.)
- All of these methods work, but passive heating (sauna or hot-water immersion) will be the most practical and efficacious and will interfere with training the least.
- Even if you are heat acclimated, athletes competing in hot environments should employ race-day cooling methods such as packing ice on your neck/torso, dousing in cool water, and consuming cool drinks.

GTON CO
CHESAPEAKE AND OHIO CANAL NATIONAL HISTORICAL PARK
POTOMAC RIVER
Shepherds Island
Neck
Terrapin
Spring
Cem
Horseshoe Bend
ROCKHOUSE
RIVER RD
POWELL ROAD
Snyders Landing
WEST VIRGINIA
MARYLAND
BM 462
CHESAPEAKE AND OHIO CANAL

CHAPTER 8

Recovery Modalities and When to Use Them

There are 168 hours in a week, and even at the high end of the training spectrum, it is rare for any endurance athlete to exercise more than thirty-five hours in a big week or more than twenty-five hours on an ongoing basis. Exercising—inclusive of running, strength training, yoga, Pilates, or other complementary activities like cycling, swimming, soccer, etc.—between twenty-five and thirty-five hours per week is 15 to 20 percent of the total time available in a week. It is far more common for ultrarunners to exercise for a total of ten to fifteen hours per week, some even fewer, which represents only 6 to 9 percent of the week. That means most ultrarunners, unless you have a particularly active job, are basically inactive 91 to 94 percent of the time.

When I lay this scenario out for some runners—particularly those with Type A personalities—their instinct is to view it as a challenge: "How can I increase the percentage of time I spend exercising?" They get standing desks, do lunges for no reason, and include a calf raise or two every time they encounter a set of stairs. But that's not the challenge. As I will hopefully show you throughout this book, the time you spend running is rarely the limiting factor for performance, and just spending more time running is rarely the most effective or time-efficient way to improve performance. The challenge is how to use all that time you're not running to maximize the quality and effectiveness of the time you are.

The Consequences of Doing Too Much

In order to make progress, stress and recovery have to work in harmony. That doesn't always mean a perfect balance between the two. There will be times when your lifestyle, career, personal relationships, and training tip the balance toward more stress and less recovery. At other times, you may purposely reduce your sources of stress and tip the balance in favor of recovery. There are consequences to both directions. The simpler consequences come from too much rest and recovery; at first, performance will improve as physical and mental stress recede. However, when training frequency drops or time between training stimuli becomes too long, your workouts stop building upon one another. Your fitness and progress stagnate and can even start to slide backward.

Fortunately, studies examining the time course of detraining show that markers of fitness are quite resilient. While complete training cessation (meaning zero training) for several weeks can result in performance declines of >20 percent, adding in as few as three sessions (~50 percent training reduction) per week can keep those losses in the 5 to 10 percent range, even if the detraining phase is several weeks in length. In other words, if you cut your training in half, you are only going to pay a single-digit penalty for it. Furthermore, your return to your previous fitness will not take all that long (Bosquet, Laurent, and Mujika 2012; Lacour and Denis 1982; Mujika and Padilla 2000; Neufer 1989; Pallarés et al. 2009).

At the other end of the spectrum, it can be more difficult to identify the consequences of tipping the balance toward too much work and not enough recovery. In order to create a training stimulus sufficient to induce a positive adaptation, you need to stress a physiological system to the point that performance starts to decline. The stress from an individual training session causes a small decrease in performance but is often not great enough to lead to significant long-term adaptations. You need a way to make training sessions additive. After individual training sessions, when you take adequate time for recovery, there's a short-lived "supercompensation" effect that allows for increased performance. Consistent and proper training architecture schedules repeated bouts of exercise to take advantage of this cycle. Over a period of weeks, this cumulative stress leads to a decrease in performance known as functional overreaching, which is reversed by taking adequate time for recovery and is a normal part of the training process.

Pushing functional overreaching too far is what gets athletes in trouble. Instead of training to the point where performance diminishes and then letting up to allow for recovery, some athletes keep piling on the fatigue. Eventually, overreaching progresses to a scenario where more than two weeks of complete rest aren't enough to reverse extreme fatigue, disrupted sleep, irritability, and lack of desire to train. Some coaches and athletes refer to this scenario as "overtraining syndrome" (OTS), but training isn't the root of the problem—recovery is. The term "under-recovery" is more accurate, and the even newer term "unexplained underperformance syndrome" (UUPS) encourages athletes and coaches to look beyond the training plan to consider all sources of stress and rule out other possibilities, like RED-S, anemia, hypothyroidism, and acute or chronic illness (Lewis 2015).

Symptoms of OTS/UUPS include:

- Unrelenting feeling of fatigue
- Acute performance decline
- Sleep disturbances
- Elevated resting heart rate
- Low HRV
- Mood disturbances
- Loss of libido
- Low motivation to train
- Loss of appetite
- Frequent or persistent minor injuries and illnesses

The tipping point between functional overreaching and OTS/UUPS is highly individual and difficult to quantify, particularly because individual OTS/UUPS symptoms can be part of an athlete's normal response to hard and effective training. To the body, stress is stress, whether it comes from a workout, a hard day at the office, an argument with your partner, or an infection. The appeal of a multimodal approach to recovery is that it provides a wide range of tools to chip away at the monolith of stress.

The Goals of Recovery

Recovery is a broad term that encapsulates complete rest, restorative activities, and sometimes complex interventions, with the end goal of enhancing future performance in training and competition. It can be as simple and free as taking a nap, or it can be extremely complicated and expensive. It can also be very difficult to measure, and its effectiveness is often subjective and open to interpretation. This is why there are so many products, supplements, and modalities vying for athletes' attention and money; people want to believe these things work, the placebo effect is real, and it can be difficult to convince athletes to trust science over intuition and emotion.

To evaluate whether a recovery method is valuable, we need some criteria to test it against. We also have to recognize that recovery is very individual; what works for you may not work for someone else, and vice versa. There are a few products or methods that are utterly nonsense, but the vast majority provide varying levels of effectiveness for most athletes. I encourage athletes to test a potential recovery method against the following criteria:

- Will it promote muscle repair and growth, or any other adaptive response?
- Will it replenish something that training has depleted?
- Will it enhance your readiness for your next workout?
- Will it support immune system function?
- Will it be any more effective than getting more sleep?

That final question is perhaps the most important. As I'll explain shortly, sleep is the gold standard for recovery. For many athletes, adding activities in order to get more or better rest is counterproductive, and the best thing they can do is optimize their sleep behaviors.

Recovery Modalities

My goal here is not to go a mile deep into every possible method, supplement, and product purported to aid in recovery. For an in-depth treatise on the science of recovery, I recommend reading *Good to Go* by Christie Aschwanden. For the purposes of this book, I'm going to cover the recovery modalities my athletes use most and the ones athletes ask about most frequently.

TIME BETWEEN TRAINING

Proper scheduling of workouts and training phases is one of the most basic forms of recovery. This topic is covered extensively in Chapter 9 in the section on key workouts and in Chapters 10 and 12 in the sections on long-range and short-range plans, respectively. Nonetheless, it is important to mention here because a well-thought-out training strategy can be rendered ineffective without adequate recovery, and it will absolutely fail if it is both poorly structured and deficient in rest.

SLEEP

As I alluded to earlier, sleep is the gold standard and fulfills all the criteria for effective recovery. For starters, the physiological repair and growth that actually makes you better happens when you rest, and predominantly when you sleep. It improves motor learning (learning a new skill) and cognitive function. Additionally, better sleep can lead to better emotional well-being. Unfortunately, the converse is also true: a lack of sleep can lead to a decrease in optimism and mood.

None of this should come as a shock to athletes. You have experienced it firsthand when you woke up in the middle of the night to a crying child, barking dog, or unruly neighbors and felt slow and groggy the next day. You may have even snapped at your significant other for something trivial. It's OK, we've all been there. Because sleep has a major effect on training and recovery, it's important to understand how you can optimize your sleep to optimize performance.

Sleep Restriction Research

Many early studies into sleep restriction indicated that a few days of a few hours of sleep restriction had little to no impact on varying measures of strength and endurance performance. A 2015 review paper from Fullagar et al. noted that skill and precision sports are affected to a greater extent by sleep loss compared to endurance sports. The takeaway for athletes is if you have one or two terrible nights of sleep, you can probably just suck it up and get in a decent workout. You also have no excuse for a disastrous race due to one poor night's sleep.

As a coach, I rarely change an athlete's workout due to one night of poor sleep unless there is some other confounding factor like being on the verge of injury or illness, at the end of a long training block, or any other negative combination of objective and subjective measures. All this being said, it would be easy to look at this combination of research and practice and say, "Well, if it is not affecting performance, restricted sleep really does not matter."

Au contraire!

Effect of Sleep on Illness and Injury Risk

While missing out on a few hours of sleep for a few nights might not affect acute endurance performance much, the effect that high-quality sleep has on your immune system and your ability to recover (or not) is quite astounding. Both of these matter in the long run, as they affect week-to-week consistency, which is a far better indicator of success than any one workout.

A 2016 study by von Rosen et al. found that sleeping more than eight hours per night reduced the chance of injury by 61 percent in adolescent elite athletes. As a comparison, strength training, which has long been lauded for reducing injury risk in endurance athletes, reduces the chance of injury by about the same amount, according to a 2018 meta analysis by Lauersen et al. The studies did not provide apples-to-apples comparisons, but the takeaway is that sleep has a profound effect on recovery and injury prevention and should be considered a vital component of any athlete's program.

Sleep affects your immune system similarly and just as dramatically. According to research from Cohen et al. (2009), adults who sleep fewer than seven hours per night for a prolonged period are nearly three times more likely to develop a cold. More recent review studies not only confirm the link between sleep disturbance and immunosuppression but also indicate that shorter sleep duration (less than six hours) may decrease the acute response to and lifetime protection from standard vaccines like influenza and hepatitis B (Irwin 2015; Walsh 2018). The effect of sleep on vaccine response gained even more importance in 2020 as the world pinned its collective hope on a vaccine to end the COVID-19 pandemic.

The simple takeaway is that sleep matters. It matters a little bit on the acute performance side of things, but more importantly, it matters more for long-term health, injury prevention, and training consistency.

The Architecture of Sleep

Your long-term habits around sleep make more of a difference than whether you slept well last night. As a result, I encourage athletes to think of "sleep hygiene" as habits to adapt to rather than a short-term issue to fix. In order to understand sleep hygiene, it is important to understand the basics of what goes on before, during, and after you sleep.

Figure 8.1 below illustrates how three critical areas—core body temperature and the hormones cortisol and melatonin—are affected just before, during, and after sleep. Cortisol is a hormone that prepares you to deal with stress, and melatonin is a hormone that helps regulate the sleep-wake cycle. Notice that core body temperature and cortisol go down and melatonin goes up right as sleep onset occurs. The key to unlocking powerful sleep lies in setting up your room and your habits to take advantage of the constellation of these changes.

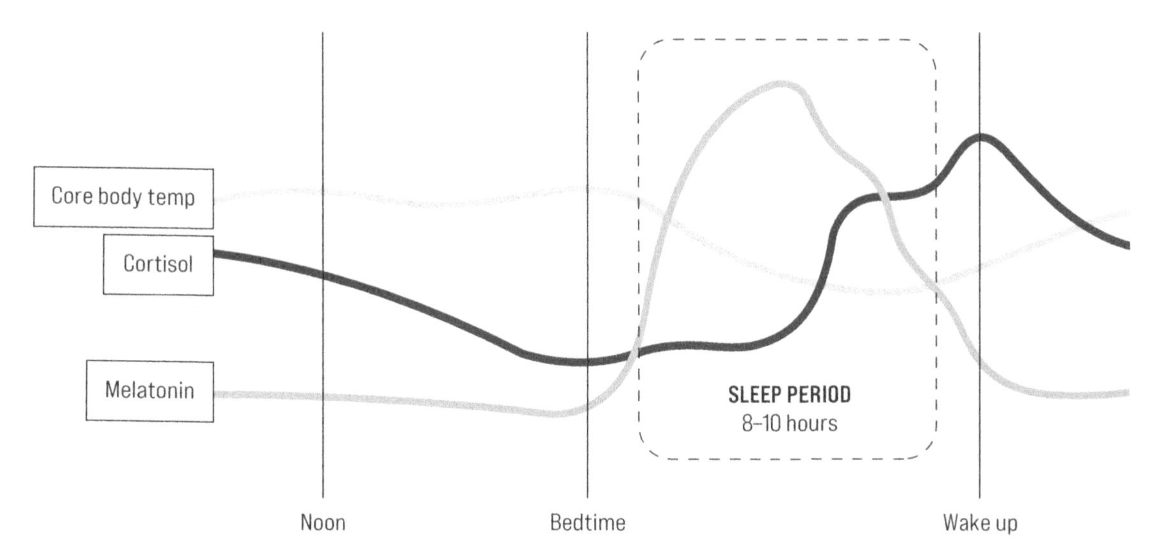

FIGURE 8.1 How core body temperature, cortisol, and melatonin fluctuate throughout the day.

Steps for Better Sleep Habits

STEP 1: SET UP YOUR ROOM

You should be able to describe your bedroom with the following words: calm, cool, dark, and quiet (Venter 2012). Optimizing these factors not only helps you get to sleep faster, it also helps increase sleep efficiency, which is your total sleep time divided by the time you're in bed. Sleep efficiency can have a big impact on immune function. According to a 2009 study on sleep habits and susceptibility to the common cold, "participants with less than 92% efficiency were 5.50 times more likely to develop a cold than those with

98% or more efficiency" (Cohen 2009).

- **CALM**: Minimize clutter and remove TVs, handheld screens, and bright alarm clocks.
- **COOL**: Ideal room temperatures are between 60°F and 67°F, which may feel cold but facilitate the natural drop in body temperature described above. Using blankets in a cooler room allows you to more easily establish and maintain a core body temperature conducive to sleep than a warm room and lighter sheets.
- **DARK AND QUIET**: Light (and the absence thereof) has the biggest effect on telling your body when it is time to sleep and time to be awake. Use blackout curtains to minimize light and sound seeping through the windows. Remove or cover objects with indicator or power lights.

STEP 2: ESTABLISH YOUR BEDTIME ROUTINE

A consistent sleep/wake time, combined with enough sleep (more than eight hours), will establish much of the routine. The rest is comprised of turning off any electronics—and your brain—ninety minutes before bedtime. Blue light emitted from your smartphone suppresses the release of melatonin (see above why melatonin release is important), and blue light filters on your phone and tablet only go so far. Bright lighting suppresses melatonin, too, so lower the lights or partially darken the room even before starting to get ready for bed. Create a routine where, instead of checking e-mail or Twitter, you journal, read for pleasure, meditate, or take a warm shower just before bed.

STEP 3: ESTABLISH YOUR WAKE-UP ROUTINE

Your wake-up routine is just as important. Regardless of workout schedule or traveling to a new time zone, try to wake up at the same time every day. What happens if you stay up late? Take a nap. This will maintain your bedtime and wake time routine. If you can't take a nap, then modify your normal wake-up time as best as you can so it can stay consistent.

STEP 4: ESTABLISH YOUR MORNING ROUTINE

Your routine after you rise (whether it's morning or another part of the day) is just as important as your routine before you sleep and can follow the subsequent steps: seek light, move, and nourish. As previously mentioned, light will have the biggest effect on signaling to your body that it's time to lay down or to rise. Therefore, seek light (preferably sunlight) when you rise. If you get up before sunrise, turn up the lights in the room where you get ready for the day.

After you are up and have some light, it's time to move. This can be your morning workout or preworkout routine or simply getting some chores done around the house. I recommend getting in ten to twenty minutes of movement first, before settling down to read the morning paper or heading out the door for your run. While you are getting in this first-of-the-day movement, or when it is done, nourish yourself with some fluids (because you will be dehydrated after sleeping) and your preworkout snack or breakfast.

ENERGY BALANCE

If sleep is the gold standard for recovery, energy balance is next in order of priority. Put simply, total energy intake is the linchpin for achieving adequate recovery and getting a positive response to training. Regardless of the macronutrient composition of what you eat, you will not significantly improve your running performance unless your total energy intake is high enough to support your basic bodily functions, your daily activity level, and the energy expenditure of training.

Athletes get into trouble with energy balance by undereating, overexercising, or a combination of both. Often, the mismatch between energy intake and energy expenditure stems from efforts to lose weight or maintain a low body weight, but the reason behind the mismatch can be more complicated than not eating enough after workouts. Athletes in sports that place a premium on being lightweight (see "The Body-Weight Conundrum" sidebar) can feel internal or external pressure to lose weight or look a certain way. This can be a factor in the development of behaviors and beliefs that can lead to negative self-image, disordered eating, overexercising, and a long list of physical and psychological problems. From a training perspective, RED-S (discussed in Chapter 2 in the "Considerations for Female Athletes" section, but applies to both males and females) poses the greatest risk to athletes who are acutely or chronically undereating, overexercising, or a combination of both.

RED-S was originally referred to as the Female Athlete Triad based on three key

THE BODY-WEIGHT CONUNDRUM

BODY WEIGHT HAS AN IMPACT on the energy cost of running, but lighter isn't always better for performance, recovery, health, or emotional well-being. To understand the relationship between body weight and performance, let's take a look at what happens when you lose weight:

Energy Cost of Running: Normally on flat ground the energy expenditure of running is independent of speed. When you run faster, you burn more calories per minute, but you also cover distance more quickly, so the overall caloric expenditure per kilometer or mile stays relatively constant. When you lose weight, you reduce the energy cost of running by 1 percent for each 1 percent reduction in body weight. It might not seem like much, but over the course of 160K (100 miles), a 5 kg weight loss translates to an 800-calorie savings.

Ground Reaction Forces: From Chapter 5, remember that vertical GRFs are typically two-and-a-half to three times your body weight, so any reduction in body weight will lower GRFs.

Muscle Damage: We know a lot more muscle damage is incurred during an ultramarathon than during a marathon. To a point, athletes carrying more muscle may be able to spread the damage across more tissue and hence cope with the damage better than lighter athletes with less muscle mass. This may partly explain why top athletes in ultrarunning have more muscular builds than extremely lean marathoners.

VO_2 max: The maximum amount of oxygen your body can take in, transport, and utilize per minute is often expressed relative to your weight. When we say a 70 kg elite ultrarunner has a VO_2 max of 65 ml/kg/min, it means he can utilize 65 ml of oxygen for each kilogram of body weight in a minute. When you reduce body weight, absolute VO_2 max stays pretty constant, but relative VO_2 max goes up. Increasing VO_2 max, whether through weight loss or intervals or both, impacts performance at all levels of intensity. Not only does being lighter make you faster at the very highest intensity you can achieve, but your aerobic pace and your lactate threshold pace get faster, the length of time you can sustain a given pace increases, and you recover from efforts above lactate threshold more quickly.

While the list above seems to favor being as light as possible, the bigger picture shows that proactively working to lose weight often does ultrarunners more harm than good. Carrying more muscle mass in the legs can correlate with faster ultramarathon finishing times (Knechtle, Rosemann, and Lepers 2010), although it is worth noting that training volume and finishing times at the marathon distance were better predictors of ultrarunning performance than any body measurement (Knechtle et al. 2009; Knechtle, Rosemann, and Lepers 2010; Knechtle and Senn 2011). This supports my preference to focus on cardiovascular development and the limiting factors for performance outlined in Chapter 4. By doing so, weight management tends to take care of itself as a result of increased training volume and intensity. Coaches who focus on weight loss as a means to improve performance risk creating abusive environments and almost always forego meaningful performance improvements that would result from better training.

symptoms: amenorrhea, low energy availability, and decreased bone-mineral density. The change in terminology is more than words; it reflects an expanded understanding that energy deficiency is a problem that affects both males and females, and that it has far-ranging consequences. The host of performance complications illustrated in Figure 8.2 include decreased muscle strength, decreased bone mineral density, increased injury risk, and decreased training response, to name a few.

Athletes don't need to have every symptom of RED-S to be negatively affected by undereating or trying to maintain an excessively light body weight. When you are losing weight because you are not sufficiently supporting your training workload with calories and nutrients, you will lose both fat and lean muscle mass. Because some of this muscle mass is important for coping with the metabolic stress of running long distances, losing weight by losing muscle is problematic. Athletes who are too lean cannot train as effectively because they cannot recover from hard efforts as quickly. Being too lean also puts additional stress on the immune system, leaving some athletes more susceptible to illness. When I encounter a runner who is not responding positively to training,

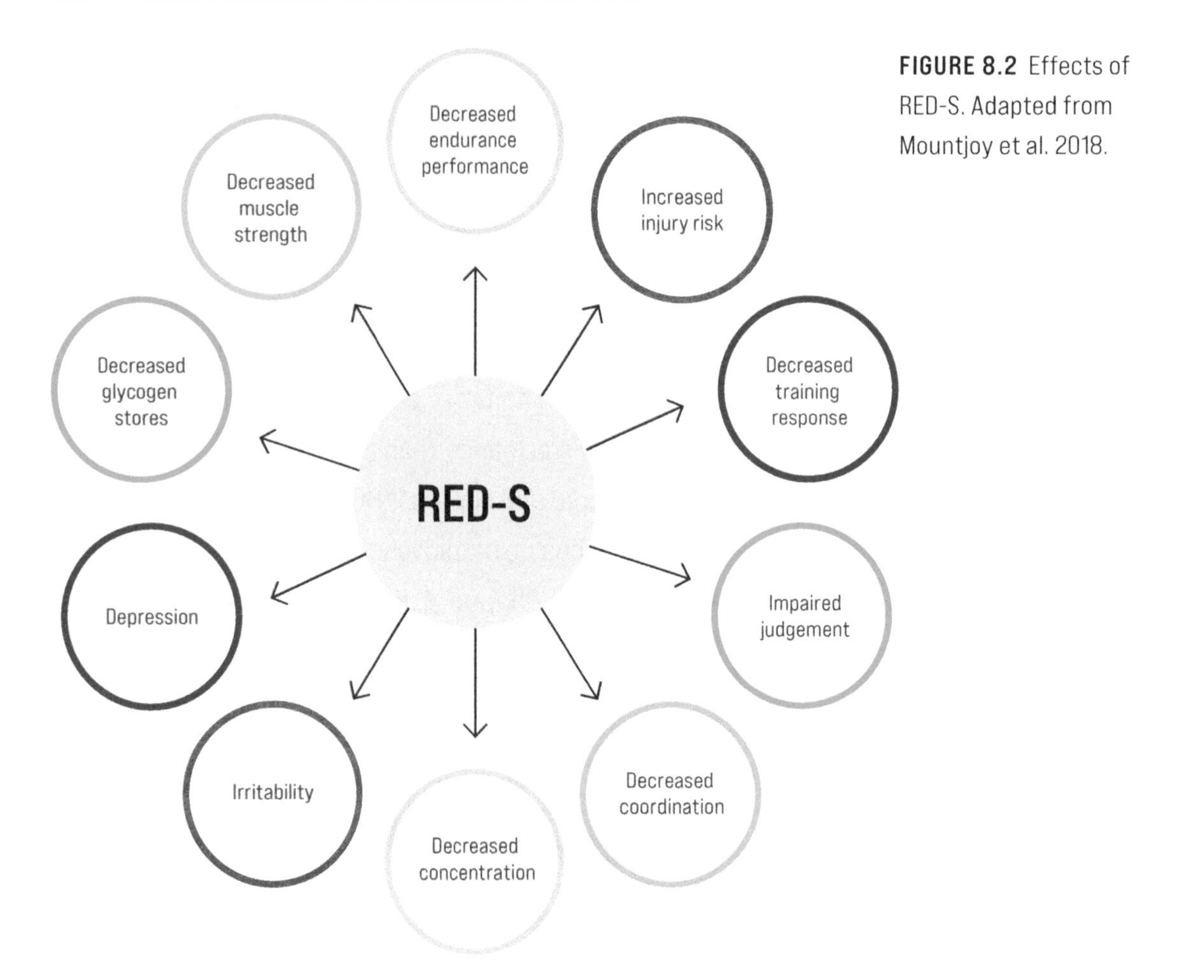

FIGURE 8.2 Effects of RED-S. Adapted from Mountjoy et al. 2018.

is struggling to finish races or training sessions, and is constantly dealing with small colds, gastrointestinal bugs, and nagging injuries, the first thing I look at is the athlete's nutrition program. It is likely the athlete is not consuming enough calories to support his training workload.

Postworkout Cooldown

Ultrarunners who have limited training time sometimes cut their warm-up or cooldown short or eliminate the cooldown altogether. From a recovery perspective, "active recovery" or reducing your pace to a light jog or walk for ten minutes at the end of your workout is time well spent, particularly after higher-intensity sessions. While you are exercising, skeletal muscle contractions assist the circulatory system to pump blood throughout the body. Blood has a lot of jobs, from delivering oxygen and fuel to muscles to dissipating heat, producing sweat (from plasma), redistributing lactate, and removing metabolic waste. During exercise, demand for all these functions increases, and that demand doesn't return to baseline levels the moment you stop your GPS watch.

Active recovery at the end of a workout maintains somewhat elevated circulation, with the notion that this eases the body's transition back to baseline conditions. A 2018 review of active and passive recovery studies indeed showed that active recovery can accelerate recovery of lactate in blood and can bring core temperature down to normal more quickly (particularly if the activity maintains airflow over the skin). However, on balance, the review found that active recovery—including stretching—didn't improve actual performance in training or competitions the following day, compared to passive recovery. Put another way, active recovery delivered some benefits more quickly after exercise, but by the next day the recovery effects evened out (Van Hooren and Peake 2018).

While the physiological advantages of active recovery over passive recovery are more pronounced following high-intensity training than EnduranceRuns, I still incorporate active cooldowns at the end of athletes' workouts. They are perhaps most useful as a means to transition from the focus and intensity of a hard workout to the next parts and priorities of your day. I don't, however, prescribe a specific set of cooldown activities, because one isn't particularly more useful than any other. The main takeaway from the research is that the performance penalty for skipping or shortening your cooldown is likely minimal.

Compression/Massage/Foam Roller

I'm grouping these modalities together because they broadly do the same thing: apply pressure. Compression clothing and pneumatic compression devices aim to facilitate circulation of blood back to the heart and reduce swelling by moving lymph or preventing it from pooling in your extremities. Massage palpates muscle groups, sometimes superficially and sometimes more vigorously, often with the stated goals of pushing lactate and/or waste products out of the muscle, increasing blood flow to bring in nutrients, and addressing adhesions between layers of fascia (the connective tissue that surrounds muscles). The goals of foam rolling are virtually identical to massage, although the self-massage aspect may impart additional neural benefits on sensations of muscle soreness.

The research doesn't point to a clear physiological benefit from any of them, or at least no benefit that consistently improves performance. Compression garments and devices are absolutely effective for people following surgery, who are bedridden, or who have clinically poor circulation, but for healthy individuals the circulatory system doesn't really need extra assistance. Similarly, lactate clearance from muscles happens naturally, whether you rub the muscle or not (and the rate of lactate clearance is not important for recovery anyway). And while it is physiologically plausible for layers of fascia to stick to one another, the necessity or benefit of breaking those adhesions with massage or foam rolling hasn't been proven (Groner 2015; Wilke 2017; Zaleski 2016).

Compression, massage, and foam rolling make people feel good, enhance mind-body connection, and provide a relaxing time to pause. And there's a big placebo effect. These benefits are valuable on their own and meet the criteria of enhancing readiness for the next workout or competition by reducing stress. However, as with active recovery activities, the research indicates you won't be at a distinct disadvantage by skipping massage, compression, or foam rolling if you don't like them or they're not available.

THE LONG-HAUL FLIGHT HOME

THERE ARE INCREDIBLE ULTRARUNNING EVENTS all over the world, and as ultrarunners travel far and wide to participate, it is important to look at strategies for optimizing health, performance, and recovery on long-haul flights. For people with underlying health problems, sitting for long periods (especially more than four hours) increases the risk of deep vein thrombosis (DVT, characterized by a blood clot, often in the lower leg) and venous thromboembolism (VTE, when that blood clot travels through circulation and can end up in the lungs as a pulmonary embolism). Dehydration from the dry (1 percent humidity) cabin environment exacerbates the potential for DVT. These risks do increase for everyone somewhat, but for healthy populations and athletes, even the increased risk is extremely low and can be lowered still by staying hydrated and occasionally walking around the cabin (Bartholomew 2011).

Compression socks are recommended to help prevent VTE in people whose underlying health issues put them at higher risk for blood clots. Otherwise healthy endurance athletes can also be at increased risk for VTE, particularly after hard and/or long workouts or competitions, based on Virchow's triad: venous stasis, damage to veins, and hypercoagulability (Kushner 2020). The stasis comes from sitting still. The damage to veins can result from microtraumas during training and competition. And the hypercoagulability results from a disruption of hemostatic balance, which is the interaction of factors that promote clotting (coagulation) and factors that prevent it (fibrinolysis). Markers for both increase during and after exercise, a phenomenon known as hemostatic activation (Kupchak 2016; Zaleski 2015). Normally, markers go up and come back down, and you're none the wiser. The risk for VTE increases when your actions (sitting still for long periods, dehydration) and intrinsic factors (damaged veins, predisposition to clotting) tip the balance toward coagulation.

There's more research on the effect of compression socks on running performance when the socks are worn either while traveling to a race or during a race. There is little direct research on the effects of wearing compression socks on airplanes after a race. Findings are mixed, but there is some evidence that compression socks when worn during a race or hard workout could reduce subjective perceptions of delayed-onset muscle soreness and could attenuate hemostatic activation (thus reducing blood clot risk) in the hours after long and hard runs (Zaleski 2016). The only thing the research seems to consistently agree upon is that compression socks are safe for athletes before, during, and after hard exercise.

The upshot: on long-haul flight, or any long-duration travel after an ultramarathon, it is important to address the problems of Virchow's triad. Get up and walk at regular intervals. Stay hydrated. And if you want to use compression socks, they might help.

Cold Therapies

Before and during exercise in hot weather, ice baths, cold water immersion, ice vests, ice socks, ice slurry beverages, and cold wet towels are all effective ways to lower skin and core temperature and keep athletes from overheating. After exercise, these same options can be used to reduce body temperature if necessary, but assuming body temperature is normal or just slightly elevated from exertion, ice baths, immersion, and cryotherapy won't enhance recovery in a way that will improve performance tomorrow.

Exposure to cold was once thought to aid recovery by reducing inflammation. Ice baths, cold water immersion, and a few minutes in a chamber chilled to -140°F all rapidly lower skin temperature, leading to dramatic vasoconstriction in the extremities. There is evidence that cold exposure can lessen the inflammation caused by exercise, but it turns out that reducing inflammation is counterproductive in terms of long-term adaptation to training stress (Peake 2017). Your body's response to the inflammation caused by training is integral to making the fitness gains you're seeking, and blunting that response hinders adaptation.

Cold exposure also has an analgesic effect by numbing pain temporarily. For athletes performing repeated bouts of exercise with limited recovery, like track runners competing in preliminary and final heats, ice baths or other forms of cold exposure can provide temporary pain relief but may reduce force output in subsequent efforts. This is less of a concern for ultramarathon runners who rarely—if ever—perform multiple high-intensity track sessions in a single day.

Ice baths and contrast baths have such a long tradition in sports that I don't expect athletes will stop using them, and we will still see athletes getting into cold, picturesque mountain streams after runs. Like the other modalities discussed in this chapter, people like them because they believe they work and because they are part of the rituals of their sport.

Stress Relief

Goal-oriented athletes sometimes view recovery as the absence of physical activity, but there's a difference between sitting at peace and sitting still while stressed out or anxious. Psychological stress from the pressures of your life, career, relationships, and finances have to be taken into account when adding up the total stress that needs to be balanced through rest and recovery. This includes anxiety or runaway thoughts about your training, an upcoming workout, a previous workout, or the event you're preparing for. Feelings of stress can lead to frequent or continuous stimulation of the sympathetic nervous system (SNS)—the "fight or flight" one—which then leads to chronically elevated levels of hormones like cortisol.

Your parasympathetic nervous system (PSNS) regulates the "rest and digest" functions and unwinds the sympathetic nervous system's responses to stressful conditions. When athletes track HRV, the desired outcome is higher variability in the intervals between heartbeats. This is a sign that the PSNS is effectively modulating minute changes in excitability without disturbing heart rhythm. When HRV is low, it is a sign an athlete is not recovering well because the SNS is still overactive and causing minute fluctuations in the intervals between heartbeats.

Recovery modalities seek to re-establish homeostasis by activating the PSNS to dial back SNS activity. Remember that a drop in cortisol is part of the process of falling asleep, and the steps recommended for promoting sleep include a cool, dark, uncluttered, and quiet environment. These calming steps tune down the SNS and tune up the PSNS so you can get a good night of restorative sleep. The plausible mechanisms of action for active recovery, yoga, massage, compression, and cold therapies all include some level of PSNS activation as well.

Your brain is the ultimate modulator of long-term balance between the SNS and PSNS, so it is critical to address the brain's role in stress relief. Mental skills training, meditation, breathing exercises, counseling, spending time with a pet, or floating in a sensory deprivation tank can all be effective for dialing down the stress response, restoring balance, and hence improving your ability to recover from training and make positive adaptations. No two brains or sets of life experiences are the same, so the stress relief strategies that work best for specific athletes are also highly individual. The biggest takeaway is that non-exercise stress is inescapable, but when you are better prepared to cope with non-exercise stress, you create a greater capacity to recover from exercise stress, which allows you to increase training workload and achieve greater physiological adaptations.

Pills, Potions, and Supplements

Effective and safe (and legal) recovery rarely comes out of a bottle. Yet that doesn't stop companies and athletes from advocating the use of nonsteroidal anti-inflammatory (NSAID) medications, opioid and non-opioid analgesics, cannabidiol (CBD), and entire warehouses full of nutritional supplements. Here's how to approach these pills, potions, and supplements in terms of recovery.

NONSTEROIDAL ANTI-INFLAMMATORY (NSAID) MEDICATIONS

There is quite literally a stack of research on NSAIDs—which include naproxen (Aleve), ibuprofen (Motrin/Advil), acetylsalicylic acid (Aspirin), celecoxib (Celebrex), and others—and their effects on endurance athletes. The findings and sentiments can be summarized as follows:

- The use of NSAIDs increases the risk of hyponatremia (low blood sodium) in endurance athletes.
- The use of NSAIDs increases the risk of acute kidney injury in endurance athletes.
- The use of NSAIDs is prevalent amongst participants in triathlon, cycling, running, and ultrarunning events.
- Athletes generally do not know the risks of NSAID use.
- NSAIDs have not been shown to improve performance.
- There is very little evidence that demonstrates NSAIDs improve injury outcomes.
- NSAIDs can perpetuate existing musculoskeletal injuries, primarily through masking pain but also by affecting the biochemistry of the healing process.

I am not going to mince words here. The use of NSAIDs in endurance and ultra-endurance sports is dangerous. The research is unequivocal. Even seemingly benign use (i.e., the recommended dosage on the bottle), when compounded by the stress of the race or training, can exacerbate existing musculoskeletal injuries. Of greater consequence though: NSAID use increases the risk of hyponatremia and acute kidney injury, particularly in hot environments. Both can cause serious, if not fatal, medical complications.

Used outside of sports and following the recommended dosage on the bottle or the instructions of your doctor, NSAIDs can alleviate occasional pain, inflammation, or fever with only low to moderate risks for stomach bleeding or kidney injury.

ANALGESICS

Pain is part of sports, and ultra-endurance athletes often pride themselves on how much pain they can tolerate. It is important to recognize that temporary soreness is part of the normal process of training and competing, and an accurate assessment of pain is essential for understanding how well or quickly you are recovering and hence how much or how soon you can go again. That doesn't mean you have to be a masochist and reject all manner of pain relievers, but it does mean that masking pain with strong analgesic medications can encourage athletes to accumulate an inappropriate amount of training stress or cause them to exacerbate a minor injury until it turns into a major one.

Acetaminophen is a common over-the-counter analgesic that is neither an NSAID nor an opioid. It is a pain reliever and fever reducer, but not an anti-inflammatory. Like NSAIDs, the occasional use of acetaminophen for pain relief or fever reduction following recommended dosages or your doctor's instructions carries few risks for negative side effects. The same cannot be said for the other major category of pain relievers: opioids.

Opioid and synthetic opioid medications, including morphine, fentanyl, tramadol, and oxycodone, are powerful analgesics that can play an important role in the acute and chronic management of severe pain. Sadly, athletes have been suspected of using opioids, particularly tramadol, as performance-enhancing drugs to mask the pain of competition. While tramadol is not on the World Anti-Doping Agency's List of Prohibited Substances as of 2020, it is in their monitoring program, and individual sports—including cycling—have banned its use in competition.

The exponentially greater problem with opioids is that they carry a significant risk for addiction and fatal overdoses. According to the US Centers for Disease Control and Prevention, in 2018 opioids contributed to the deaths of more than 46,000 Americans. Therefore, put simply: if an athlete is experiencing pain so intense it can only be managed with opioid analgesics, they are not healthy enough to continue training. An exception could be made for an athlete using opioids, under a doctor's supervision, in order to participate in physical therapy or post-injury rehabilitation.

CANNABIDIOL (CBD)

CBD is everywhere these days, in everything from tinctures and skin cream to food and shampoo. It is a phytocannabinoid found naturally in Cannabis plants, including *Cannabis sativa* (hemp) and *Cannabis indica* (marijuana). Unlike tetrahydrocannabinol (THC), which is also found in cannabis, CBD is not psychoactive.

Cannabinoids exist naturally in your body, and the endocannabinoid system is thought to modulate the activity of neurons by selectively inhibiting the release of certain neurotransmitters. For instance, when CBD is used to treat epilepsy, it may reduce seizure activity by, in part, reducing the buildup of glutamate, an excitatory neurotransmitter (Grewer et al. 2009). Proponents of CBD contend that consuming it could be thought of as supplementing or increasing the activity of your body's existing endocannabinoid system.

CBD is primarily marketed to athletes as a pain reliever, anti-inflammatory, sleep aid, and anti-anxiety aid—or, taken collectively, as a recovery aid. The research into the validity of these claims is still evolving. As a result, I approach CBD with a healthy dose of skepticism. It has bioplausible mechanisms of action that could prove useful, but there isn't enough evidence yet that it actually delivers meaningful benefits for athletes. That said, research shows that the effectiveness of several of the recovery modalities mentioned in this chapter is debatable, so as with those, if you believe CBD works and it makes you feel better, that may be enough for it to have a positive effect on recovery.

Effectiveness aside, there are bigger reasons I encourage caution when it comes to CBD:

- **YOU DON'T KNOW WHAT YOU'RE GETTING:** A 2017 study published in the *Journal of the American Medical Association* tested eighty-four different CBD products from thirty-one companies. They found that 21.4 percent of the CBD products tested also contained appreciable amounts of THC and only 31 percent contained accurate amounts of CBD compared to the label (Bonn-Miller et al. 2017). Ideally, market competition should gradually solve this problem, but one look at the ongoing inconsistency of ingredients and labeling in the much more mature nutritional supplement market suggests mislabeling will be a persistent issue. And the risk is real. Even though the World Anti-Doping Agency has increased the legal limit of THC for athletes in an effort to lower the risk of positive tests due to accidental or recreational use, exceeding that limit—even accidently—will still result in a ban.

  CBD producers can ask a third-party lab to perform an analysis on their products and produce a certificate of analysis (COA). Companies that have taken this step will typically have these COAs listed on their website. Look for companies who have taken this extra step to ensure that their products have what they say they have in them.

- **YOU DON'T KNOW WHO YOU'RE GETTING IT FROM:** Choose a CBD product manufacturer who can tell you where their CBD is coming from. States where recreational and medical marijuana is legal (like Colorado, California, and Oregon) have higher regulatory standards than other states. Currently there's a lot of clutter in the CBD marketplace. There are (relatively) established players with good processes and manufacturing procedures that *could* produce an efficacious product, but unfortunately there are also, shall we say, seedy players in the marketplace.

- **IT'S BEING MARKETED AS A PANACEA:** This should be a red flag, whether you're considering CBD or any other supplement. When you can't really prove what a product can do, it is hard to disprove what it can't do. Hopefully the industry will become more regulated, production will become more standardized, and research will home in on a reasonable set of effective use cases. We're just not there yet.

NUTRITIONAL SUPPLEMENTS

There's a lot of money to be made selling busy people drinks, pills, and powders that are supposed to replace what's missing from their diets or provide enhanced benefits they can't get from food. There are absolutely cases where supplementation is necessary to correct a clinical nutrient deficiency, but the consensus of reputable federations and sports science organizations is that few supplements provide performance-enhancing benefits that can be supported by solid science (International Olympic Committee Consensus Statement 2018). In 2016, the Academy of Nutrition and Dietetics, the American College of Sports Medicine, and the Dietitians of Canada released a position paper that stated, "Relatively few supplements that claim ergogenic benefits are supported by sound evidence" (Thomas, Erdman, and Burke 2016).

The Australian Institute of Sport (AIS) developed a system to categorize supplements based on their safety, their legality in sport, and the strength of the scientific evidence supporting their efficacy. The 2019 AIS Sports Supplement Framework features an ABCD classification system. Foods and supplements in the A category are "supported for use in specific situations in sport using evidence-based protocols." Category B foods and supplements are "deserving of further research and could be considered for provision

GROUP A

OVERVIEW OF CATEGORY	SUBCATEGORIES	EXAMPLES
Evidence level: Supported for use in specific situations in sport using evidence-based protocols	**Sports foods** Specialized products used to provide a convenient source of nutrients when it is impractical to consume everyday foods	**Sports drink** **Sports gel** **Sports confectionery** **Sports bar** **Electrolyte supplement** **Isolated protein supplement** **Mixed macronutrient supplement** (bar, powder, liquid meal)
	Medical supplements Supplements used to prevent or treat clinical issues including diagnosed nutrient deficiencies. Best used with advice from an appropriate medical/nutrition practitioner	**Iron supplement** **Calcium supplement** **Multivitamin supplement** **Vitamin D supplement** **Probiotics**
	Performance supplements Supplements/ingredients that can support or achieve an enhancement of sports performance Best used with an individualized and event-specific protocol, with the advice of appropriate sports science/nutrition practitioner	**Caffeine** **B-alanine** **Bicarbonate** **Beetroot juice/nitrate** **Creatine** **Glycerol**

TABLE 8.1 Various supplements and evidence. Adapted from "Supplements." Sport Australia. www.ais.gov.au/nutrition/supplements accessed September 2020.

GROUP B

OVERVIEW OF CATEGORY	SUBCATEGORIES	EXAMPLES
Evidence Level: Deserving of further research and could be considered for provision to athletes under a research protocol or case-managed monitoring situation	**Food polyphenols** Food compounds which may have bioactivity including antioxidant and anti-inflammatory properties May be consumed in food forms or as isolated chemicals	**Cherries, berries, and black currants** **Quercitin, ECGC, epicatechins, and others**
	Other Compounds which attract interest for potential benefits to body metabolism and function	**Collagen support products** **Carnitine** **HMB** **Ketone supplements** **Fish oils** **Phosphate** **Curcumin**
	Sick pack Multi-supplement approach to address an issue of health or well-being Best used with advice from an appropriate medical/nutrition practitioner	**Zinc lozenges and Vitamin C**
	Amino acids Constituents of protein which may have effects when taken in isolation, or may be consumed individually by the athlete to fortify an existing food/supplement that is lacking in this amino acid	**BCAA/Leucine** **Tyrosine**
	Antioxidants Compounds often found in foods which protect against oxidation or reactions with free-radical chemicals May be consumed in food forms or as isolated chemicals	**Vitamin C and E** **N-acetyl cysteine**

to athletes under a research protocol or case-managed monitoring situation." In other words, they might work, but research hasn't proven they do work. Category C foods and supplements "have little meaningful proof of beneficial effects." The vast majority of supplements fall into this category. The AIS summarizes this by saying, "If you can't find an ingredient/product in Groups A, B or D, it probably deserves to be here." Category D, by the way, is reserved for performance-enhancing drugs and supplements that are "banned or at high risk of contamination with substances that could lead to a positive drug test."

The supplements in Category A and Category B can be found in Table 8.1. I didn't include Category C or D because they can be summarized as "everything else" and "performance-enhancing drugs and prohibited substances," respectively.

From a recovery standpoint, my biggest concern with supplements is that they can give athletes a false sense of confidence that makes them less vigilant about things that we know work. For instance, if taking a supplement makes you think you don't have to be as conscientious about making good food choices, the negative consequences of poor food choices are going to outweigh any benefits from the supplement. Replace "food choices" with "sleep" or "fundamental training" and the statement remains just as true. The effects of supplement use go beyond the efficacy of the substance you're consuming; they change an athlete's perception of what is valuable and impactful for improving performance. Some of my athletes consume supplements, but only after we have thoroughly investigated the physiological necessity, the athlete's motivations, and the anticipated outcome.

Nutrient Timing

Athletes inherently know that workouts burn energy and that eating is required to replenish that energy and provide fuel for adaptation. The logical extension is that coordinating the timing of your calorie and/or macronutrient intake with your training must be beneficial. There are instances where this is true, but overall, the importance of nutrient timing has been oversold.

Remember the research that indicated that active recovery provided benefits more quickly following exercise, but that with or without it athletes were equally recovered and ready for training the following day? The same is essentially true for the effect of nutrient timing on recovery. As I'll discuss more in Chapter 13, consuming carbohydrate and protein within thirty to sixty minutes after exercise (long referred to as the "anabolic window") can increase the initial rate of muscle glycogen replenishment, but the "window" doesn't slam shut after sixty minutes. Assuming an athlete's daily diet provides adequate total energy and a variety of macronutrients, muscle glycogen levels will be completely restored by the following day.

Similarly, there is research all over the map that claims to show performance, metabolism, recovery, or weight-loss benefits to eating breakfast, skipping breakfast, eating most of your calories for dinner, eating fewer calories late in the day, eating small meals more frequently, eating bigger meals less frequently, or restricting feeding hours to create fasting conditions. Some of the research is well done, and some of it has flaws in methodology or small sample sizes, but taken collectively the reasonable conclusion is that none of these nutrient timing strategies promotes enhanced performance or recovery for everyone all the time.

When it comes to the effect of nutrient timing on performance and recovery, here's what I tell my athletes:

1. Eating enough total energy each day is more important than how you distribute your energy intake.
2. When possible, protein consumption should be spread across the day rather than concentrated in one or two big feedings. You utilize protein around the clock for recovery, physiological adaptation, and immune function, but unlike carbohydrate and fat, protein can't be easily stored in the body for later use.
3. Rapid postworkout carbohydrate replenishment (leveraging the "glycogen window") is more important if you have fewer than eighteen to twenty-four hours before your next training session or competition. Otherwise, you can eat as you normally would, and the results will be the same.
4. Specific carbohydrate-availability strategies—either in the direction of carbohydrate loading or exercising with low carbohydrate availability—can play a role in training or competition but should not take priority over fundamental, high-quality, fully fueled training.

5. The eating pattern that works best for your lifestyle, personal preferences, and performance really is the one you should stick with. Be open-minded and try different patterns to see how they make you feel, but trust that what feels right probably is right.

KEY POINTS FOR RECOVERY

- More activities aren't necessarily better for recovery than simply doing less between training sessions. Don't mistake being busy with being effective.
- The two best things you can do to optimize recovery are getting more sleep and making sure your total daily energy intake is high enough to support your total daily expenditure.
- Active recovery, nutrient timing, massage and compression, and/or cold therapies can make you feel better sooner, but within twenty-four hours the recovery benefits are roughly equal to passive rest, sleep, and adequate caloric intake.
- NSAID pain relievers are dangerous for endurance athletes. Opioids are effective analgesics but have a high risk for abuse, addiction, and overdose.
- Despite physiological plausibility, there isn't enough high-quality research yet to say whether CBD is an effective and consistent recovery aid. Nevertheless, it is here to stay.
- The vast majority of nutritional supplements have little to no solid science to back up claims of improving performance, recovery, or health

W A S A T C H

N A T I O N A L F O R E S T

Big Cottonwood

Honeycomb Fork

South Fork

Giles Flat

Cottonwood Canyon

Mill F East Fork

Little Dollie Tunnel

Scottish Chief Mine

Solitude Ski Area

Tunnels

Woodlawn Mine

Prince of Wales Shaft

Solitude Tunnel

Silver Lake Forest Camp and Rec Area

Brighton

Mt Evergreen

Black Bass Shaft

Davenport Hill

Michigan-Utah Mine

Brighton Ski Area

Mt Millicent

Mt Wolverine

Mt Tuscarora

Big Cottonwood Mine

Pioneer Peak

Alta Ski Area

Albion Basin

Sunset Peak

SALT LAKE CO

WASATCH CO

UTAH CO

Shafts

Steamboat Tunnel

CHAPTER 9

Train Smarter, Not More: Key Workouts

It's not that athletes were training incorrectly at the beginning of ultrarunning; it's that there wasn't really any specific training going on at all. Fit and very hardy individuals took on outlandish challenges and managed to finish them. More people became interested in these modern-day feats of endurance, and events became more organized and recognized. Through a lot of hard work and dedication from men and women we now know as icons of the sport, the events grew, course records were established, and a little bit of money came into the sport in the form of sponsorship and prize purses. However, as the winning times in the big ultramarathons started dropping, the sport developed beyond the point where "go run more" was a viable training strategy.

Ultrarunning isn't the only sport to experience this evolution. In fact, it's an evolution common to many sports. Triathlon, for instance, originated in 1977 in Mission Bay, California and in the early years the sport's top athletes were the ones who could endure the greatest workload. The sports science that had previously shaped the accepted practices in triathlon's component disciplines—swimming, cycling, and running—didn't catch up to the unique demands of triathlon until several years later. Training techniques, equipment, technology, and nutritional strategies all evolved—and continue to evolve—and course records continue to be broken.

One of the milestones for any sport occurs when training becomes organized and sport-specific, i.e., when "go run/train more" is replaced by specific kinds of activities that are separated by rest and organized into a schedule. Consider the concept of periodization, which has been around in various rudimentary forms for thousands of years. The modern and almost universally accepted version of periodization—systematically changing the focus and workload of training to maximize the positive impact of overload and recovery on training adaptations—was constructed by Tudor Bompa and other Eastern Bloc coaches in order to win Olympic medals in the 1950s, when the Olympics were as much about the battle of East vs West as they were about athletic achievement.

Before Bompa, German scientist Woldemar Gerschler took the relatively informal but highly effective training practices of Swedish running coaches and, in the 1930s, refined them into what you and I recognize today as interval training. At the time, the Swedes were using changes in terrain to interject periods of intensity and recovery into their longer runs. They referred to the practice as "fartlek" running, a term and technique which is still widely used. But Gerschler eliminated the unpredictability of fartlek training by adding structure—in the form of precise times, distances, and paces—so he could quantify both the work being done and the recovery being taken between efforts.

Neither Bompa nor Gerschler had you in mind when he was pushing the boundaries of sports science. Bompa had to earn Olympic medals to show the world the power of the Soviet system, and Gerschler was working to find a way to help his athletes, including eventual record-holder Roger Bannister, break the coveted four-minute barrier in the one-mile run. But the science they discovered changed the face of endurance training for athletes at all levels.

Interval training is effective for improving performance because it enables you to accumulate time at specific intensities, and it is time at intensity that is the most critical aspect to achieving positive adaptations. The interval workouts described in this chapter are designed to apply the principles of training—overload and recovery, progression, individuality, specificity, and a systematic approach (discussed in Chapter 3)—to individual training sessions. These workouts are in turn governed by five components of training: intensity, volume, frequency/repetition, environment, and stride rate. By manipulating these components, you can create a workout to target just about any physiological demand found in sport.

The Five Workout Components

When you get ready to head out for your training sessions, you can address the five principles of training using use the following variables:

1. **INTENSITY**
2. **VOLUME**
3. **FREQUENCY AND REPETITION**
4. **ENVIRONMENT (TERRAIN, SURFACE, AND AMOUNT OF VERTICAL RELIEF)**
5. **RUNNING CADENCE AND STRIDE RATE**

You can change the goal of a workout by changing one of its components. The clearest example of this is found in changing the intensity. Two ten-minute intervals can target completely different aspects of your physiology if you simply change your pace. You can maintain a pace at the high end of your aerobic intensity to develop greater aerobic endurance, or you can run at your lactate threshold pace to increase your ability to produce and process lactate. You can also manipulate the environment for your workout (i.e., running uphill vs running on flat ground) to change its purpose.

INTENSITY

Intensity is a measure of how hard you are working, and the impact of a workout is directly related to the intensity at which you are working. Measuring intensity is notoriously difficult in running, particularly trail running. Unlike cycling, where athletes can utilize power meters to directly measure workload, or road running, where runners can generally use pace, trail runners can at best observe the body's response to workload in the form of RPE. Even gauging intensity by heart rate is problematic for trail runners, as explained in Chapter 6. New technologies may soon enable us to measure power or normalized pace in running, but until then the best measurement tool we have is RPE.

VOLUME

Volume is the total amount of exercise you're doing in a single workout, a week of training, a month, a year, or a career. The most important concept related to interval training volume is volume-at-intensity. One of the purposes of intervals is to break hard efforts into smaller bites so you can accumulate more time at a specific intensity than you would be able to sustain in one longer effort. For instance, if the goal of a workout is to spend sixty minutes at lactate threshold intensity, but currently you can sustain that pace for only forty minutes, you can organize the workout into six ten-minute intervals, separated by recovery periods. By the end of the workout, you have run at your lactate threshold pace for sixty minutes and generated a training stimulus that will increase the amount of time you can stay at your threshold pace in a single effort. You can also schedule two or three of these workouts in a single week and accumulate up to 180 minutes of volume-at-intensity targeted at your lactate threshold pace.

To properly quantify volume, you have two choices: miles or time. Volume in an ultrarunning or trail running setting is best prescribed by time. This is because a five-mile run can take you one, two, or even three hours depending on the terrain. When you view volume as a volume of time (rather than as a volume of distance), you can more accurately quantify training.

FREQUENCY AND REPETITION

Frequency is the number of times a workout is performed in a given training period, whereas repetition is the number of times an exercise is repeated in a single session. Frequency and repetition are used to ensure the quality of your training sessions. Intervals are effective only if they are performed at the prescribed intensity, volume, frequency, and repetition based on your current fitness. It is the correct combination of all of these variables that leads to the most effective training, not the dominance of any one variable over the others.

Let's say your lactate threshold pace is 9:00 min/mi, and you can sustain that pace for forty minutes. You might be able to run 8:30 pace for three minutes during a RunningInterval workout (defined later in this chapter), which would be closer to your pace at VO_2 max. There's no point in trying to complete a twenty-minute RunningInterval because your pace would fall so dramatically after the first three to five minutes that the rest of the effort would no longer be VO_2 max-type intensity. It would still feel ridiculously hard, but that effort would no longer be addressing the goal of a RunningInterval. In contrast, if you do seven three-minute RunningIntervals at 8:30 min/mi, separated by three minutes of easy running at a recovery pace, you'll accumulate twenty-one minutes at 8:30 pace.

Frequency gives you another way to accumulate workload, by repeating individual interval sessions during a given week, month, or even year. For instance, a week with two RunningInterval workouts like the one just described means forty-two minutes at 8:30 pace. The harder the intervals, the more recovery you need before you'll be ready to complete another high-quality training session. In any effective training program, workouts are spaced out to provide adequate recovery between sessions. I will discuss the relationship between interval workouts and recovery days later in this chapter.

ENVIRONMENT

You can use environmental factors to manipulate your workouts. In some cases, you can increase or decrease the workload of particular efforts, as with performing intervals while going uphill. As discussed previously, I prefer certain intervals, especially RunningIntervals, to be done uphill to maximize the aerobic benefit and to contribute to race-specific training, particularly if the goal race is hilly. Running your intervals uphill can also be useful as a hedge against injury and to overcome flagging motivation. Sometimes it can be difficult to push yourself through maximum-intensity intervals on flat ground, but a hill adds resistance and a visible challenge, which can be the little something extra you need to make your workout more effective.

Environment has a big impact on specificity in all sports. The surface you run on can make a difference in your pace and in the amount of stress you apply to your body. Even trail ultramarathons almost always have a mixture of surfaces, including trails of varying technical difficulty, dirt roads, and some pavement. Training is not just about developing cardiovascular fitness; it's also about preparing the musculature, joints, bones, and connective tissues for the challenges of competition.

You can use treadmills to your advantage in training. The suspension found in treadmills means that treadmill running typically has less impact on your feet and legs than running outdoors, and it even has less impact than running on some trails. For athletes who have a history of foot or knee problems, running on a treadmill may enable you to complete more running with less pain. Running on the treadmill can also make interval training more convenient because you can program in the appropriate paces and durations and let the treadmill adjust your pace and hold it steady for the duration of the interval. This is often helpful for athletes who have trouble motivating themselves to maintain a fast-enough pace on their own for difficult intervals. In the end, you'll have to find that motivation to push yourself if you want to succeed on race day, but if you sometimes need the treadmill to provide that motivation, that's OK. Regardless of whether or not you will use a treadmill for interval workouts, EnduranceRuns, or RecoveryRuns, you can set the incline at various degrees depending on your goals.

RUNNING CADENCE AND STRIDE RATE

Decades ago, Cavanaugh and Williams (1982) showed that runners naturally gravitate toward the stride length that is most economical for them in terms of oxygen consumption. Numerous other investigations on running economy have reached similar conclusions. While your natural stride rate might change in the early phases of your running career, once you're a reasonably proficient runner, your biomechanics will settle into a sweet spot that is right for you.

For an ultrarunner, there are advantages to developing the ability to run at different stride lengths and rates. It may seem counterintuitive to purposely change your stride, given that you have gravitated toward the one that is optimal for you, but this makes sense in ultrarunning because changing your stride and foot-strike patterns changes the ways you are stressing your body. A faster stride rate with a shorter stride length, even if it is not your naturally chosen stride, changes the stresses on the muscles and ligaments in your legs. This shortened, rapid stride can be useful for maintaining a solid pace early on while sparing your legs for harder terrain in later miles.

Stride length and frequency can also be manipulated during drills to prepare you for harder work in interval sessions. For instance, during a warm-up, a series of twenty-second RunningStrides (drills from a standing start, focusing on a constant twenty-second acceleration) helps to develop the neuromuscular pattern for higher-speed running before you have the fitness necessary to maintain those higher speeds. Similarly, when used during a warm-up before a hard interval workout, RunningStrides get your body ready for the hard work that is ahead.

Key Running Workouts

Workouts such as endurance, tempo, and steady state are used by many coaches and athletes. Yet all too often, these words can be confusing and fail to precisely describe the workout in question. In fact, here's a quick test: go ask five of your running friends, "How long/hard should a tempo run be?" You'll certainly get different answers, but what should strike you most is the range of answers. Over the course of my coaching career I have seen durations from one minute to two hours used to describe a single type of workout. At CTS we use these words as well, but with very specific definitions so our coaches can communicate with each other and with their athletes consistently and precisely. Throughout this book, I use the following terminology to describe workouts and their associated intensities.

	RPE	TYPICAL INTERVAL TIME	TOTAL TIME AT INTENSITY	WORK : REST	TYPICAL WORKOUT	FREQUENCY PER WEEK
RecoveryRun (RR)	4 to 5	NA	20–60 min	NA	40-min RR	2-3
EnduranceRun (ER)	5 to 6	NA	30 min–6+ hours	NA	2-hr ER	2-6
SteadyStateRun (SSR)	7 to 8	20-60 min	30 min–2 hours	5 to 8:1	2-hr ER with 2 x 30 min SSR, 5-min recovery between intervals	2-4
TempoRun (TR)	8 to 9	8–20 min	30–75 min	2:1	2-hr ER with 3 x 12 min TR, 6-min recovery between intervals	2-3
RunningIntervals (RI)	9 to 10	1-3 min	12–24 min	1:1	90-min ER with 6 x 3 min RI, 3-min recovery between intervals	2-3

TABLE 9.1 The five critical workouts.

Table 9.1 presents a summary of the five key running workouts and their associated ranges of duration, frequency, interval length, rest between intervals, RPE, and breathing rate. In each individual section below, I will outline how you can tailor these interval combinations depending on your experience level.

RECOVERYRUN (RR)

To be effective, a RecoveryRun needs to be very easy. All you're trying to do is loosen up your legs and increase circulation and respiration with some mild activity. Your RecoveryRuns should be no more than sixty minutes; the typical duration I prescribe is about forty minutes. Perceived exertion for a RecoveryRun is about a 4 or 5, so it's not a leisurely walk, but it should be substantially easier than an EnduranceRun. The frequency for RecoveryRuns depends on your training schedule, since this workout needs to be balanced with your harder training sessions, but I frequently have athletes run two or three of them in a week.

ENDURANCERUN (ER)

You're going to spend much of your running time in the EnduranceRun intensity range. This is the moderate-intensity running time surrounding your focused interval sets, as well as the "forever" intensity for your EnduranceRuns that contain no specific intervals. Perceived exertion for this intensity is 5 or 6 and will naturally vary with uphills and downhills. EnduranceRun durations range from thirty minutes to more than six hours. A typical workout would be a two-hour EnduranceRun. When you are running at this intensity, however, it is important to slow down when you begin going uphill. It can be easy for your intensity level to creep up into SteadyStateRun or lactate threshold territory, and then you are adding training stress and using energy you may need and want later.

STEADYSTATERUN (SSR)

A SteadyStateRun pushes you to a challenging aerobic pace but keeps you below your lactate threshold intensity and pace. This intensity plays a very important role in developing a stronger aerobic engine because you are maintaining an effort level greater than your normal "forever" pace. SteadyStateRun intensity is very close to your everyday EnduranceRun intensity. Most runners find that they naturally fall into this intensity when doing continuous climbs longer than twenty minutes. SteadyStateRun intervals should be as continuous as possible, with individual intervals ranging from twenty to sixty minutes and total time at intensity for a single workout ranging from thirty minutes to two hours. A typical SteadyStateRun workout might be two thirty-minute SteadyStateRun intervals separated by four minutes of easy recovery. The recovery period is intentionally short as compared to the total duration of the interval in order to facilitate the right intensity, which will be well below lactate threshold. The RPE for a SteadyStateRun is 7 to 8, and it will take a bit of extra attention to keep your intensity level from creeping up toward TempoRun territory on climbs. SteadyStateRuns can be done on flat, uphill, or slightly rolling terrain.

RUNNER EXPERIENCE	WORKOUT STRUCTURE	RPE	TOTAL TIME AT INTENSITY
Beginner	1 x 40 minutes hard	7 to 8	40 min
Intermediate	2 x 25 minutes hard with 4 minutes recovery	7 to 8	50 min
Advanced	2 x 30 minutes hard with 4 minutes recovery	7 to 8	60 min
Pro	2 x 45 minutes hard with 4 minutes recovery	7 to 8	90 min

TABLE 9.2 SteadyStateRun examples.

TEMPORUN (TR)

TempoRun intervals are a crucial workout for making you a faster and stronger runner. The pace and intensity for these intervals are strenuous, and you will be running slightly below or at your lactate threshold intensity. These intervals help drive the process of increasing the size and density of mitochondria in your muscles, which improves your ability to process and utilize lactate as fuel. They also can increase plasma volume, giving you greater ability to manage your core temperature and increasing mitochondrial enzyme activity, which helps you produce more energy faster.

The critical component of TempoRuns is the time spent at the particular intensity. Therefore, the design of the interval structure is imperative. The intensity will be too low if there is too much interval volume combined with prolonged interval length and not enough recovery. Intensity might be too high if there is too little volume with a protracted interval length and copious recovery. As a rule of thumb, most trained runners could sustain TempoRun intensity for forty to ninety minutes if you were to do an all-out time trial. That's a big range, but, in the laboratory and in the field, we see this range play out. Less-experienced runners start out only being able to tolerate forty to fifty minutes at their lactate threshold pace. As they become more trained, they can increase this tolerance to an hour or even longer, even when adjusting for the increase in pace to accommodate their increase in fitness. In other words, training both makes your lactate threshold pace faster and increases your tolerance for longer durations at this intensity.

Accordingly, the total amount of interval time for a TempoRun workout will be between forty and ninety minutes, divided up into intervals of eight to fifteen minutes. Rest between intervals should be half the duration of the interval, meaning a 2:1 recovery ratio, or six minutes of recovery between twelve-minute intervals. TempoRun intervals should be run at an RPE of 8 or 9 with the rate of perceived exertion gradually creeping up throughout the course of each interval and throughout the set. TempoRuns can be done on flat, uphill, or slightly rolling terrain.

RUNNER EXPERIENCE	WORKOUT STRUCTURE	RPE	TOTAL TIME AT INTENSITY
Beginner	3 x 12 minutes hard with 6 minutes recovery	8 to 9	36 min
Intermediate	4 x 12 minutes hard with 6 minutes recovery	8 to 9	48 min
Advanced	4 x 15 minutes hard with 7 minutes recovery	8 to 9	60 min
Pro	5 x 15 minutes hard with 7 minutes recovery	8 to 9	75 min

TABLE 9.3 TempoRun examples.

RUNNINGINTERVALS (RI)

If there were a workout ultrarunners are allergic to, it would be RunningIntervals. The lung-searing intensity these intervals induce is seemingly incompatible with the long, slow nature of an ultramarathon. Combine that with the sheer discomfort these intervals elicit, and even the most seasoned ultrarunners will avoid these like the plague. Yet, ultradistance athletes can reap important benefits from this type of work. RunningIntervals improve your heart's stroke volume and maximum cardiac output, and consequently your VO_2 max. But the benefits do not end there. Like TempoRuns, RunningIntervals can also increase your blood plasma volume, giving you the ability to tolerate heat better as well as improving muscle capillarization, which helps deliver blood and oxygen to working muscles.

RunningIntervals are performed at an effort coaches call "VO_2 max" intensity. The quotes are intentional, as you are only at your true VO_2 max for part of the workout. More importantly, and what drives most of the adaptation, is that you are accumulating more than ten total minutes running at an effort that elicits 90 percent of your VO_2 max oxygen consumption. Most of the research behind this specific time at intensity (ten minutes at 90 percent of VO_2 max) was done by French researcher Vérinoque Billat, who interestingly enough won the famed Sierre-Zinal race in 1982.

RUNNER EXPERIENCE	WORKOUT STRUCTURE	RPE	TOTAL TIME AT INTENSITY
Beginner	4 x 3 minutes hard with 3 minutes recovery	9 to 10	12 min
Intermediate	5 x 3 minutes hard with 3 minutes recovery	9 to 10	15 min
Advanced	6 x 3 minutes hard with 3 minutes recovery	9 to 10	18 min
Pro	5 x 4 minutes hard with 4 minutes recovery	9 to 10	20 min

TABLE 9.4 RunningIntervals examples.

Now that the history lesson is over, let's get into how to structure a workout to drive this critical time at intensity. In order to drive the critical amount of time (more than ten minutes) at the specific intensity (>90 percent of VO_2 max oxygen consumption), I target intervals that are two to four minutes in length and add up to twelve to twenty-four minutes of total work time, with a 1:1 work to recovery ratio between intervals. The RPE for these efforts is between 9 and 10.

Although these intervals can be completed on any terrain or on a treadmill, I recommend doing them uphill if possible. The incline is helpful for increasing the workload and enabling you to reach 90 percent of your VO_2 max more consistently. RunningIntervals should never be done downhill, as it will be nearly impossible to achieve >90 percent of your VO_2 max in this condition.

Peak and Fade RunningIntervals

Peak and fade RunningIntervals are an advanced training technique I use with many of my athletes who have experience doing interval work. While you don't need to be an elite runner to partake, you do need to have a moderate amount of training experience under your belt (two to three years running ultras), as well as experience with interval work. If you fit the bill and are up for the challenge, buckle up. Peak and fade intervals will test even the heartiest of athletes. As the name implies, you go as hard as you can during the initial part of the interval (aka the "peak") and simply fade as you become fatigued further into the interval.

HOW TO DO PEAK AND FADE INTERVALS

Start with the same RunningInterval workout you would normally do (six sets of three minutes hard, three minutes easy, for example). As you begin each interval, take the first fifteen seconds to ramp up to the highest intensity you think you can sustain for sixty to ninety seconds. Hold that intensity for as long as you can. Because the interval is greater than ninety seconds, the pace/intensity will not be sustainable (intentionally), and for the last half of the interval you will gradually slow down while hanging on for dear life. Rinse and repeat for the remainder of the workout. If you are running these on a track or flat ground, you will likely be about 10 percent faster at the beginning of the interval compared to the end. Yet your heart rate will increase throughout the set of intervals.

These intervals can be intimidating. After all, you are intentionally starting each interval at an unsustainable intensity. In reality, they are not all that frightening once you give them a chance. You will never get the pacing perfect, and that's sort of the point. As long as your pace is faster at the beginning than at the end (which you might not be able to measure if you are doing this workout on trails) and they are literally a struggle to complete, you're doing it right.

WHY PEAK AND FADE INTERVALS WORK

Peak and fade intervals can be superior compared to their evenly paced interval counterparts because they drive a higher absolute amount and average of rate of oxygen delivery to the working muscles—and that higher oxygen demand will in turn produce a more robust adaptation. This was elegantly demonstrated in a study by Brent Rønnestad

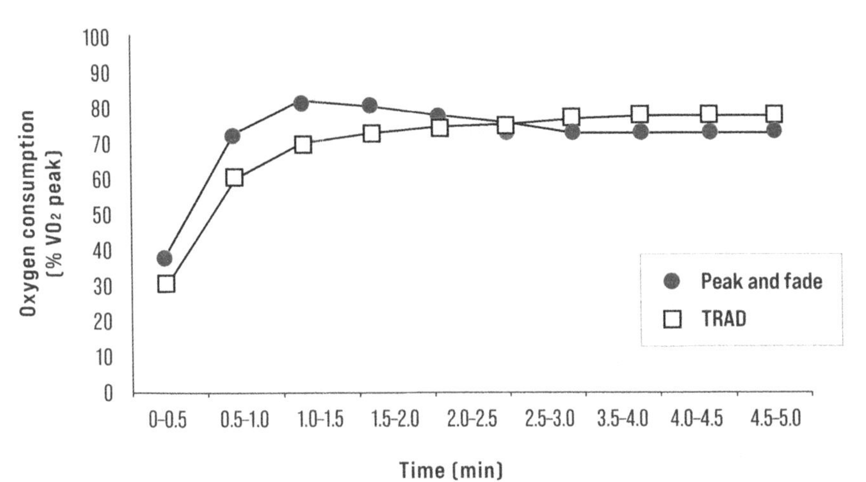

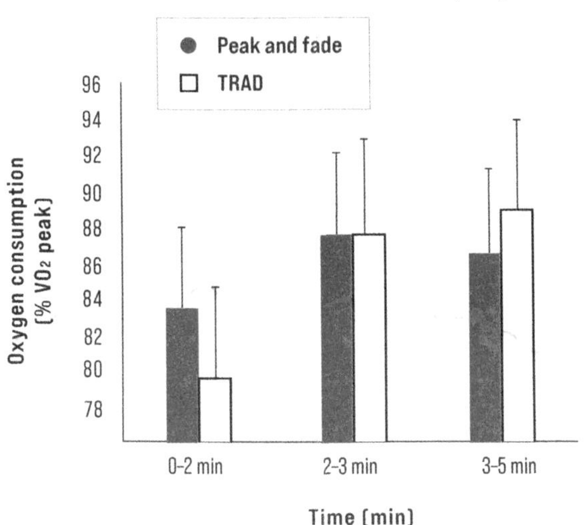

FIGURE 9.1 Oxygen consumption response from traditional, evenly paced intervals (TRAD) and peak and fade intervals. Adapted from Rønnestad et al. 2019.

from Inland Norway University of Applied Sciences (Rønnestad et al. 2019). In the study, they had a group of well-trained cross-country skiers complete a workout (five sets of five minutes hard, with three minutes recovery) using a peak and fade model and compared the results with the same workout that was evenly paced. What they found was that the peak and fade intervals produced higher mean and absolute VO_2 levels, indicating that subjects' aerobic systems were stressed more despite the workout construction being identical.

I also feel there is a toughness component at play with these intervals. Psychologically they are difficult to wrap your head around, as you are not saving anything for the end of the interval or subsequent intervals. However, I feel that once athletes get through this aspect and get comfortable being uncomfortable (even while running slower), it facilitates a new level of grit and determination they can tap into on race day.

Racing Intensity	Ultramarathon Zone		Maybe if you are an elite			
% VO_2 max	50	60	70 75	80 85	90	
Workouts	**RecoveryRun**	**EnduranceRun**	**SteadyStateRun**	**TempoRun**	**RunningIntervals**	**Traditional speed workouts** (e.g., 6 x 200 m)
Adaptation						
Plasma volume	✓		✓✓	✓✓✓	✓✓✓✓	✓
Mitochondrial enzyme activity	✓✓		✓✓✓	✓✓✓✓	✓✓	✓
Lactate threshold	✓✓		✓✓✓	✓✓✓✓	✓✓	✓
Capillarization	✓		✓✓	✓✓	✓✓✓	✓
Conversion of Type IIB muscle fibers to Type IIA	✓✓		✓✓✓	✓✓✓	✓✓	✓
Stroke volume and cardiac output	✓		✓✓	✓✓✓	✓✓✓✓	✓
VO_2 max	✓		✓✓	✓✓✓	✓✓✓✓	✓
Lactate tolerance/ anaerobic capacity					✓	✓✓
ATP/PCr stores						✓✓
Muscle glycogen storage	✓✓		✓✓✓✓	✓✓✓	✓✓	
Neuromuscular power						✓✓

TABLE 9.5 Physiological effects of different workouts.

What about Intervals Shorter Than One Minute?

Intervals shorter than one minute have their time and place, with the right workout construction. Short intervals are good for athletes' physical tools *and* mental skills. Are they ultimately superior in every way, shape, and form to their longer-interval counterparts? Certainly not. You can easily construct a workout with very short intervals that achieves a similar time at intensity to any RunningInterval workout. In a six by three minutes hard, three minutes easy example, you could easily substitute thirty-six times thirty seconds on, thirty seconds off to achieve the same time at intensity (eighteen minutes), provided you can count that high. Seriously, could you actually do that while motoring up a trail at breakneck speed? I have athletes who can't count to five at this type of intensity.

Shorter intervals are fine if you are looking for a different stimulus or just something novel to do. The benefit at the end of the day, *as long as the time at intensity is equivalent,* is likely negligible. Personally I prefer the longer style (one- to three-minute) intervals in trail running, as it's more specific to the sport and the workout is easier to manage.

Why Workout Construction Matters

When we as a coaching staff review workout designs, one critical element emerges to determine the efficacy of the intended workout: time at intensity. For each of the aforementioned critical workouts (SteadyStateRun, TempoRun, and RunningInterval), I have gone through the painstaking task of determining how much exposure is needed to elicit a particular adaption. It's not a task to be taken lightly. After all, you want the work you do to result in improvement. Too much time at intensity and your workout gets shortchanged by the resulting reduction in the intended intensity. Too little time at intensity and there is not enough exposure to elicit the adaptation you want. However, when done correctly these workouts will result in a wide range of physiological adaptations that you can target depending on your goals.

Similar to the energy systems concept introduced in Chapter 2, these adaptions do not turn on and off like light switches. Rather they are tuned up and down like volume knobs depending on the workout. I've summarized the specific physiological responses expected from all of the workouts described in Table 9.5. I have also overlaid common racing intensities seen in the ultramarathon world so that you can relate the workout intensities to what you can expect on race day. Additionally, I've added a separate column to summarize the adaptations from more traditional distance running speed work like 200 m and 400 m repeats.

A Word on Recovery

All this talk about interval RPE, duration, number of intervals, and terrain might make you think, "What about the intensity of the recovery period?" Don't complicate this. Do the work periods hard and the easy periods easy. This means that the recovery between intervals can be easy running or even walking. Remember, the structure behind these workouts is specifically designed to target an amount of time at a physiological intensity which then drives a certain adaptation. Increasing the intensity of the recovery period will normally shift the entire workout to an easier intensity and therefore might force you out of this critical time at intensity you are trying to target.

That last sentence might seem counterintuitive, but it's true. When the intensity of recovery periods is too high, it results in lower intensities for your work intervals, which reduces the effectiveness of the whole workout. Easier rest yields stronger intervals.

The Right Warm-Up for Trail Running

Many run-training programs define precise warm-up and cooldown periods to bookend specific interval work. Typically, and somewhat arbitrarily, the warm-up and cooldown periods are exactly fifteen minutes each. The fifteen-minute number is not magical. The background for this structure is rooted in track and field, where the warm-up and cooldown can be done on roads near the track (and can thus be exactly fifteen minutes in duration). In trail running, I find this approach impractical. I am far more interested in the specificity of the intervals, which should include both the intensity and appropriate environment (either surface or grade characteristics) for the desired adaptation. Many times, this will require the athlete to run for seventeen or nineteen or twenty-two minutes to get to the section of trail that is ideal for the task. Therefore, when I prescribe a workout that includes intervals, I use the EnduranceRun duration to define the total time of the workout, and I intend the intervals to be completed within that time. For instance, a two-hour EnduranceRun with three by ten-minute TempoRuns and five minutes of recovery between intervals means "run a total of two hours, and within those hours complete three ten-minute TempoRun efforts separated by five minutes at RecoveryRun pace." This gives the athlete a flexible amount of time for the warm-up period and allows additional training time to be accumulated on the back side of the interval portion. My only parameters are that the warm-up lasts between ten and thirty minutes and that the cooldown lasts at least ten minutes. Often I also prescribe four to eight RunningStrides of twenty seconds each after the warm-up and before any intervals.

FIGURE 9.2 The right structure for warm-up, workout, and cooldown.

What about Weight Vests or Other Contraptions?

If you have been following the trail and ultrarunning game for any appreciable amount of time, you have undoubtedly seen your fair share of weighted training devices intended to add resistance during running. These come in the form of weighted vests, sleds, carrying rocks in your hands, and other contrived forms of training. Athletes who live in flatter regions often look to these alternative sources of resistance as a means of preparing for a mountainous event.

Weighted vests and other derivatives might have their place in ultramarathon training, but there are some misconceptions about what they are good for and how to use them.

HOW TO USE A WEIGHTED VEST FOR HIKING

There's a lot of hiking in ultramarathons, so from a sport-specificity standpoint it is important to incorporate hiking into training if it is warranted by your goal event. The tricky part, especially for athletes who have limited time to train and who live in flatter areas, is achieving enough cardiovascular stress to create an aerobic training stimulus during hiking and walking. Weighted vests can help deliver the cardiovascular stress of an endurance run while you are hiking.

LOAD UP YOUR RUNNING PACK

Rather than going out and buying a tactical vest with pockets for lead weights or sandbags, load up the pack you intend to use in your event. Fill the hydration bladder with more water than you'll need. Put full bottles in the front storage on your chest. Carry your heavier gear instead of going light. I recommend this because using your pack is more sport-specific—you're distributing the weight as it would be distributed during your event.

DON'T OVERLOAD

When training with a loaded pack, more weight is not necessarily better. Bending forward and slowing cadence is the natural response to shouldering an unnaturally heavy load. That's problematic for a runner because it significantly changes your biomechanics and defeats the purpose of inducing a hike in the first place. The much bigger risk is that it leads to injury.

AIM FOR <10 PERCENT OF BODY WEIGHT OR JUST ENOUGH TO INDUCE A HIKE WHEN YOU WOULD NORMALLY RUN

The primary result of the <10 percent recommendation is that it generally keeps packs under 20 lb as well as ensures more sport-specific biomechanics. For beginners, you might want to start out with ~5 percent of your body weight and then work up/down from there depending on your initial tolerance. Once vests get above 20 percent of body weight (>30 lb for a 150-lb runner), the sport-specific benefits typically decrease due to altered biomechanics, and injury risk increases.

BE CONSERVATIVE GOING DOWNHILL

You're probably going to run and hike downhill wearing your pack during your event, so you should do it in training. However, if you are carrying a pack that is purposely heavier than you're going to use in your event, be cautious about running downhill. As discussed in Chapter 4, downhill running is more stressful from a musculoskeletal standpoint than running in a level or uphill condition. Adding weight to your pack only adds to this stress, which could lead to injury. If convenient, you can load up your pack with extra water for the uphills, dump the water as you head downhill, and repeat the process as you cross streams or return to a refill point.

SKIP PUSHING SLEDS AND PULLING TIRES

A weighted hydration vest is not the only way runners can add resistance, but it's the only one that's really applicable to ultramarathon running. Dragging a tire harnessed to your waist or chest makes it harder to move forward and increases aerobic and muscular workload, but you're not going to drag the tire for miles, and you certainly are not going to see one in any ultramarathon. Pushing or pulling a sled is similar in that the biomechanics are vastly different from ultramarathon running. Both of these activities could be great strength-training activities, but ultrarunners who wish to strength train would be better off doing some heavy squats or reverse lunges. Chapter 11 will have specific recommendations for strength-training activities for ultrarunners.

The Time-Crunched Ultramarathoner

How much time do you really need to train? Most of us are limited by time, with our training somehow crammed into busy lives. Taking an hour at lunch or waking up an hour earlier to get a run in is more often than not the way most normal people with jobs, friends, and a family fit in their training. It is extremely easy, particularly if you are an aspiring ultrarunner, to conclude that you don't have enough time to train. But I find most athletes overestimate the amount of time truly required to train for an ultramarathon.

They tend to linearly expand their marathon training to accommodate longer distances: "If I trained eight hours per week for a marathon, I need to train sixteen for a 50-miler."

On the surface that type of thinking is entirely logical, so I don't blame athletes for approaching the idea of training for an ultramarathon with trepidation. The fact is, though, the relationship between the training required for a marathon and the training required for an ultra is not linear. A 50-miler does not require twice the amount of training as a marathon, nor does a 100-miler take twice as much training as a 50-miler. And even if those volumes of training were ideal, the reality is that most people are limited by available time. Therefore, reality dictates that most people devote a similar amount of time to training volume, irrespective of the distance they are training for. This limitation underscores the need for high-quality structure in your training. After all, if you ain't got much, you better make the most of what you do have.

There is, undoubtedly, a minimum amount of training time required to be successful at an ultramarathon, although it's not the same for everybody or for every distance. I always present this concept in terms of the minimum amount of time you need to be able to devote during your period of highest training volume. This "minimum maximum" sets a reference point for what you can expect to achieve on race day and helps you determine if the distance you have chosen is reasonable. While you do not need to always have this "minimum maximum" amount of training time available, you do need to have it for key weeks during the season:

- 50K and 50 miles: minimum maximum of six hours per week for three weeks, starting six weeks before your goal event
- 100K and 100 miles: minimum maximum of nine hours per week for six weeks, starting nine weeks before your goal event

Outside of this three- or six-week period, you can have a lower volume and be perfectly successful as long as you also do higher-quality training. Although this formula does not guarantee success or maximum performance, not being able to achieve these critical minimum maximums can lead to failure and underperformance.

When setting goals for a season, you need to carefully consider this minimum maximum concept. You need to understand that, according to your goals, you will need to meet these minimum time requirements in key training weeks in order to achieve success. If you can't commit the time, you are less likely to meet your goals. It's that simple. However, if you do have the required time—six hours per week for three weeks, or nine hours per week for six weeks—you have every reason to believe that you can be successful. How successful you are with that time depends entirely upon how effective your training is!

KEY POINTS FOR THE KEY WORKOUTS

- There are five key components to a workout: intensity, volume, frequency/repetition, environment, and cadence/stride rate. You can manipulate any or a combination of these components to achieve a desired effect.
- The key running workouts used in this book are: RecoveryRun, EnduranceRun, Steady-StateRun, TempoRun, and RunningIntervals.
- Each workout type has its own specific structure. Tampering with that structure runs the risk of failing to achieve the desired adaptation.
- Interval workouts should be performed with a proper warm-up of ten to thirty minutes that includes easy running, dynamic stretching and strides.
- If you are a time-crunched ultrarunner, you can apply the minimum maximum concept to see if you have enough time to train for an ultra: six hours per week for three weeks (50K and 50-mile races) or nine hours per week for six weeks (100K and 100-mile races).

CHAPTER 10

Organizing Your Training: The Long-Range Plan

Ultramarathon (\'əl-trə-'ma-rə-thän\ n.): a footrace longer than a marathon

Ask any runner what an ultramarathon is, and this is the definition you're likely to hear. While it may technically be correct, from a training perspective, an ultramarathon cannot be thought of as merely longer than a marathon. Ultramarathon runners cannot merely extend marathon training programs found in books and lay publications because the stressors and success factors in an ultramarathon are not solely greater those in a marathon. Successful preparation for an ultramarathon incorporates correct mileage, volume, and intensity—all key pieces of training in any footrace. However, unlike marathon training, ultramarathon training needs to include vertical specificity, terrain specificity, training of the gut, adaptation to environmental stressors like heat and altitude, familiarization with equipment like packs and poles, and other considerations not routinely considered in marathon training.

Despite all of these unique needs, organizing your season does not start with the demands of the event, a specific type of interval, or any other physiological phenomenon.

It is actually quite the opposite. Yes, training over the long term and how you organize it are important, and I promise I will get to that. In fact, since the launch of the first edition of this book, this chapter has proven to be the most popular, talked about, and discussed. When I go to speaking events, more questions, comments, and discussion revolve around when to do what workout than anything else. However, before you start that first workout, take some time to organize the nontraining picture. I trust you will put in the work—so before that, put the pieces in place that will maximize the results of the physical work you will do down the road (or trail, as it might be).

Choosing Your Event

Every winter, thousands of ultrarunners eagerly await the results of the coming summer's race lotteries. Some athletes take a "throw your hat in all the rings" approach, entering every conceivable lottery option and letting fate sort it out. Others hedge their bets on one lottery, trying to stack the odds in their favor for a singular desired outcome. Whatever your approach, organizing your training should always start with one question: "What events deeply resonate with me?"

The answer to that question has many facets. You can't control the random outcome of the major ultra lottery processes, but you can control which events you focus on. Ultrarunners these days have their pick of different racing options. Some events have elaborate race management and support systems; others are more low-key. Some are "fast"; others are "slow." Some are in high alpine environments; others are in the desert. Whatever your preferences regarding an event's management style, terrain, and environment, chances are you can find a race that suits your desires. Organizing your training starts with choosing the events you have a deeper connection with, because those will enhance your emotional engagement with the training process. The event might attract you because of its difficulty. Maybe you have a history in the region or an attraction to its flora and fauna. Whatever the case, take the time to ensure that the race is meaningful to you on an emotional level, not merely a box to check.

After you have determined what events are going to rile you up, it's time to bring the people you live and run with into the loop. Rarely does one run an ultra without support from other people. Your family, friends, colleagues, and running groups can all enhance the outcome of the events you have chosen. You may even depend on these people to crew and pace you come race day. So, get some firepower in your corner. Tell your family, friends, and fellow runners what you are training for and what your goals are. If your colleagues know what the heck you are doing with your free time, it will make sense when you walk into the office still wearing your headlamp from your morning run. Your chosen peer group can help you out, even if they don't run a step with you in training.

Strategies for Long-Range Planning

When I was in college, we had the following weekly routine:

- **MONDAY:** rest day
- **TUESDAY:** 5 x 1000 meter repeats around a grass field (similar to RunningIntervals)
- **WEDNESDAY:** 75-minute EnduranceRun
- **THURSDAY:** 6-mile TempoRun
- **FRIDAY:** 60-minute RecoveryRun
- **SATURDAY:** 8K cross-country race or 5K race on the track
- **SUNDAY:** 90-minute EnduranceRun

Without fail, our entire team had this routine on repeat for nine months during the cross-country, indoor, and outdoor track seasons. Sure, every once in a while we would add some trivial wrinkle, like substituting an eight-mile TempoRun for the six-mile TempoRun, or 400 m repeats instead of 1000s. But the general weekly architecture remained the same, keying in on one RunningInterval workout, one TempoRun, a race (where the intensity would resemble the RunningIntervals), and a long run. This is commonly referred to as a "mixed-intensity micro-periodization cycle," which is an overcomplicated way of saying that your key workouts during the week are at a variety of intensities (RunningIntervals and TempoRun, in this case). Just about every collegiate cross-country program uses some small variant of this training strategy. It works well for college-aged athletes, partially because they are early in their training arc and partially because their twenty-year-old physiology will adapt to just about anything. That mixed-intensity training structure has been passed down post-collegiately for generations and made its way into the marathon and even ultramarathon realms, albeit with small caveats and nuances that claim to be markedly superior (like substituting 800 m repeats for 1000s or using a progressive TempoRun as opposed to a standard TempoRun).

While this type of training structure is almost universal in the running world, it is far less common in other endurance sports like cycling and triathlon. I have never understood why. Cyclists, runners, and triathletes all prosper under the same type of endurance phenotype: a robust cardiovascular engine. A strong cardiovascular engine that can process copious amounts of oxygen and deliver it to working muscles is a universal requirement for all endurance sports, even if the modalities are different. Logically, the training structure means to the cardiovascular end should be equally universal. Yet, this has historically not been the case. While many runners have used the mixed-intensity architecture I experienced in college, cyclists over the last twenty years have leaned more on a "block" structure, focusing each month or training phase on one type of intensity (TempoRun, for example). Triathletes took a different take entirely, using a

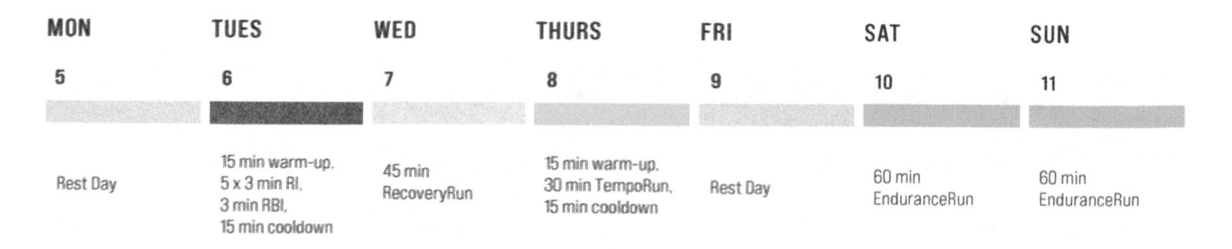

FIGURE 10.1 Example of mixed-intensity periodization: a way of organizing training where an athlete does workouts at a few or several different intensities during the week.

MON	TUES	WED	THURS	FRI	SAT	SUN
5	6	7	8	9	10	11
Rest Day	15 min warm-up, 5 x 3 min RI, 3 min RBI, 15 min cooldown	45 min RecoveryRun	15 min warm-up, 5 x 3 min RI, 3 min RBI, 15 min cooldown	Rest Day	60 min EnduranceRun	60 min EnduranceRun

FIGURE 10.2 Example of block intensity periodization plan: a way of organizing training where an athlete does workouts at similar intensities during the week.

hybrid of both to balance development across the three disciplines.

So, which of these strategies will give you more bang for your training buck? Advocates for a mixed-intensity periodization commonly boil it down to a "use it or lose it" philosophy—meaning if you don't stress your physiology in any one specific area (i.e., RunningIntervals that predominately stress VO_2 max) for as little as a few weeks, you will lose your hard-earned fitness across that specific piece of your physiological spectrum. Advocates for block-style architecture point to the fact that because you are concentrating the physiologic stress in one area, the adaptation is likely to be greater. Research slightly favors block-style architecture in both laboratory and field settings for sports such as cycling, kayaking, and cross-country skiing (García-Pallarés 2010; Mølmen et al. 2019) and has a biological basis of support (Goutianos 2016; Issurin 2018), although the extrapolation for ultramarathon runners remains a source of debate.

For athletes I work with, and for the remainder of this book, I will generally favor a block-style training structure. Experientially I have found block-style training superior for well-trained, experienced athletes, which nearly every ultrarunner is. In addition, most ultramarathon races are performed in a very narrow range of intensities, and therefore it behooves an athlete to maximize development across that specific range, even if it is at the expense of some other area of physiology. In other words, you should be OK with the "lose it" criticism levied at the mixed-intensity philosophy because what you are losing is not deterministic in ultrarunning, so long as your long-range plan is structured correctly.

Creating a Long-Range Plan

Open any book on endurance coaching and training and you are sure to see three words: "foundation," "preparation," and "specialization." The history behind these words goes back many decades to some of the founding fathers of periodization who used these terms to compartmentalize training into discrete sections. These books describe the foundation phase as being reserved for building an aerobic base, similar to laying the foundation for a house. The preparation phase "develops your cardiovascular fitness, readying you for higher-level work." Finally, the specialization phase is reserved for higher intensities that are "specialized" to the event.

I dislike these generalizations and get enormously frustrated with the labels, which don't accurately describe the process. First off, building an athlete is not like building a house, where certain things have to be done in a very specific order. Secondly, isn't an athlete always "preparing?" I would rather name each training phase based on what it is—specifically by referring to the particular aspect of physiology the athlete is focusing on the most: endurance (EnduranceRuns and SteadyStateRuns), lactate threshold (TempoRuns), or VO_2 max (RunningIntervals). Make no mistake, you are always training all aspects of your physiology. However, for the purpose of organizing a season, I prefer to define the segments of the year by the workouts you are doing and, thus, the primary physiological adaptation you're after during each period of time.

STARTING AT THE END

When I design training plans for athletes, it is always a "pick and choose" exercise based on what is going to benefit the athlete the most. I have an unlimited number of workouts to choose from: speed workouts, long runs, fartleks, ladders, progressive tempos, strength training, cross-training, plyometrics, downhill intervals, uphill intervals, and more. However, after the planning process is all said and done, I end up using only a small handful of the arrows in my quiver, defined primarily by the five workouts described in Chapter 9. You always have far more options for how to improve than you have practical ones. These five primary workouts set the framework of how to organize a season.

Once athletes pick their goal events and determine the time frame they have available for preparation, I begin the process of designing a long-range plan (LRP). These plans offer a season-long snapshot of what I want an athlete to focus on at any point during the season. The plans are generalized in the sense that their level of detail is limited to weeks (not days), overarching training intensities (RunningIntervals, TempoRun, and SteadyStateRun), and other miscellaneous components of training such as the amount of vertical, type of surface, or environmental adaptations like heat or altitude. At this stage I do not outline the specific days per week or the specific combination of intervals I want the athlete to do; that is reserved for the short-range plan, explained in the next chapter. The purpose of the LRP is to ensure that an athlete employs proper strategies throughout the year. It keeps a check on when to do peak volume and how much, when to incorporate intensity, and how the race-and-recover cycles fit into the year.

Like many aspects of training, there is no one-size-fits-all approach. Each LRP I develop is for an individual athlete based on her goals. Despite this individual nature, I rely on three common principles (in order of priority) for putting together the LRP for each of my athletes.

PRINCIPLE 1:

Develop things that that are the most specific to the event closest to that event, and develop the things least specific furthest away.

Figuring out the demands of an event is a very large part of what I do as a coach. The analysis starts from the very high-level cardiovascular physiology that is specific to the event and extends all the way down to the surface characteristics of the trails or roads, the distance between aid stations, the environmental conditions, and how one copes with the stress of eating and drinking. Even though the practical applications might be overly broad or extremely narrow, the principle is the same: if an aspect is highly specific to the event, develop it closer to the event.

A classic example of this can be seen in connection with the Hardrock 100. Hardrock is very specific in that hardly anyone actually runs the uphill portions of the race. Even the fastest "runners" hike the majority of the uphill and then run the descents. Therefore, applying Principle 1, I have my athletes do the majority of their hiking training in the several weeks leading up to the event because it is so specific to the race in question. You can extend this thinking to many other areas such as workout intensity, surface, environmental conditions, and the average grades of the course. Most runners who go out and recon a course in the weeks leading up to an event are applying this principle correctly. They are training specifically for the grades, surface, and environmental conditions they will face on race day.

In contrast, I have my athletes do the least specific aspects of training as far away from the event as they can logistically manage. Again, using Hardrock as an example, I cannot think of anything less specific, or inconsequential, in that race than a runner's velocity at VO_2 max. In other words, a Hardrocker's pace at VO_2 max is likely the least important factor in the whole scheme of success. But it is still important to develop (as you'll see in Principle 2). Being the least important should not be confused with being unimportant! This is why, from a practical standpoint, many of my Hardrockers do flat, fast, high-intensity running very early in the training season.

PRINCIPLE 2:

At some point during the season, incorporate each of these three critical workouts: SteadyStateRun, TempoRun, and RunningIntervals.

It is important to visit all the various intensities, because over the course of months athletes will reach a point of diminishing returns for any one adaptation. The various intensities build on each other throughout the year, allowing the athlete to achieve better fitness. I once had a colleague ask me why it was important to train at various intensities if the event in question had a very low intensity—say, a thirty-hour Leadville finish. To him it made all the sense in the world to train at that very low but specific intensity for as long as possible during the entire course of training. As I've discussed previously in this book, the flaw in this logic is that all the energy systems are connected, and there are improvements to be made at the relatively easy aerobic pace that can be achieved only by raising an athlete's maximum sustainable intensity (lactate threshold) and maximum aerobic capacity (VO_2 max). To illustrate this concept, I pointed out some of the lab data we have collected from elite and amateur ultrarunners throughout the years. One of the common themes we find in ultrarunners we test just as we start coaching them is that their sustainable intensity is very, very close to their maximum intensity. In other words, their lactate threshold intensity is nearly identical to their VO_2 max intensity. Sometimes this difference is as little as 3 percent.

Practically speaking, this means that only a handful of seconds per mile separates the pace they can maintain for long periods of time (hours) from the pace they can handle for only a few minutes. Normally, as a coach, I would do a backflip if I got this result from my athletes; I'd love it if their sustainable intensity were as close to their maximum intensity as possible. That is a much-coveted outcome of the training process and, if you remember earlier in this book, running speed is a product of the fraction of VO_2 max you can sustain and the cost of running ($Velocity = F \times VO_2\ max/Cr$). It would be a huge win from a training perspective if you could sustain 80 to 90 percent of your VO_2 max like some elite marathoners can for up to two hours. However, where do you go from there? Certainly your sustainable pace cannot exceed your maximum pace.

When we see this situation in our physiology lab, the training protocol becomes quite simple: the athlete needs to first raise VO_2 max and then work on lactate threshold and other lower intensities. This will give the athlete a little room between VO_2 max and other intensities before they go back and work on other aspects of physiology. Targeting different intensities throughout the year allows you to make measurable gains in each area, and each time you get stronger in one area, you also gain the tools to make further improvements in the other areas.

PRINCIPLE 3:

Work strengths closer to the race and weaknesses further away.

Most runners are aware of their natural strengths and weaknesses. We come to these realizations during group runs and races; anytime you run with a companion, you get an immediate barometer. If you are passing people on the climbs and getting dropped on the technical descents, then your strength is climbing and your weakness is technical running. Therefore, according to Principle 3, you should try to improve your technical running as far away from your key event as possible and your climbing as close to the event as possible. This principle is far more applicable for elite athletes who will generally win races that are closely aligned with their strengths. For other runners, the focus should be on improving your weaknesses as far out from the race as possible.

A CLOSER LOOK AT THE LONG-RANGE PLAN

The template for the LRP is a simple color-coded spreadsheet that delineates the specific types of workouts (RunningIntervals, TempoRun, and SteadyStateRun), higher-volume and lower-volume periods, critical events throughout the season, and other variables of training like amount or rate of vertical gain and loss, trail vs road, etc. I have supplied an example of this for an athlete training for the Western States 100 and also provided a blank LRP template in the Appendix.

The LRP offers me a season-long picture of what the athlete needs to work on at any given point. It also gives the athlete a heads-up on when to expect higher volume and higher intensity and when to focus on other aspects of the event such as nutrition planning.

MONTH	January	February	March	April	May	June
RACE NAME		Rocky Raccoon 100		Lake Sonoma 50	Silver State 50; Western States Training Camp	Western States 100
RACE PRIORITY		A		B	B	A
PHASE GOAL		Short round of RIs		Fitness build, 4 x 15 T	SSR and EnduranceRuns	
RECOVERY						
ENDURANCE						
STEADYSTATERUN						
TEMPORUN						
RUNNINGINTERVALS						
TAPER						
NOTES			Develop initial nutrition strategies	Pick training back up quickly after Lake Sonoma; Use Silver State as a training race	Highest volume, lowest intensity	Race nutrition strategies during all long runs; Sauna protocol

FIGURE 10.3 An example of a Long-Range Plan.

However only so much detail can go into the plan at this point. You will always need to adapt as the season goes along. Nevertheless, starting out with a solid plan from the get-go will ensure that you're keeping your priorities straight during the year, so when push comes to shove, you know what to push and what to shove!

When you are developing your LRP, think broad brushstrokes, not minutia. Find the things that are most important for you to be successful, and develop those aspects in the several weeks leading up to the race.

Applying the Three Principles of Long-Range Planning

PRINCIPLE 1:

Develop the physiology that is most specific to the event closest to the event, and develop the least specific physiology furthest away.

The Western States 100 is notorious for being a long, hot day in the mountains. Long, as in it typically takes even the best athletes over fifteen hours to finish. Hot, as in temperatures commonly exceed 100°F in the middle part of the course. And mountainous because of the 400-plus feet of elevation change per mile. Therefore, the most specific pieces of physiology this athlete needed to develop were the ability to run at a relatively low intensity (EnduranceRun for her), to withstand the heat, and to be able to cope with the climbing and descending on the course.

In contrast, VO_2 max-type RunningIntervals represent the least specific intensity for the Western States 100. There was very little chance any athlete would be running anywhere close to this intensity during Western States. Therefore, this extremely high, unsustainable intensity was "least important" (not unimportant).

Application of Principle 1

Perform SteadyStateRuns and EnduranceRuns closest to the race and RunningIntervals furthest away. Focus on heat acclimation and specific nutrition strategies closest to the race.

While this athlete did not have the opportunity to train regularly on mountainous terrain like she would encounter during Western States, she seized opportunities to overcome this by going to the Western States training camp, using the Silver State 50 as a training race, and using the 100- to 200-foot climbs in her local area as much as possible. This confluence of targeting the right intensity, heat acclimation, and training on terrain as close to the race environment as possible during the last eight weeks of training ensured she was optimally prepared for the conditions of the race.

PRINCIPLE 2:

At some point during the season, incorporate each of the three critical workouts (SteadyStateRun, TempoRun, and RunningIntervals).

The athlete's early-season RunningInterval work and late-season EnduranceRun/SteadyStateRun work bookended the process so, naturally, the middle could easily get filled in with TempoRun. In many five- to seven-month LRPs, a good way to facilitate the flow of training from one phase to another is to figure out the bookends first, then fill in the middle with whatever is left.

WHAT INTENSITY DO I RACE AT?

IT IS MOST COMMON FOR ULTRARUNNING race intensities to be SteadyStateRun/EnduranceRun, with VO_2 max intensity at the other—least-common—end of the spectrum. This holds true for even "shorter" ultramarathons lasting four to six hours. Exceptions are rare and consist of skyrunning races as well as 50K and 50-mile events for elite runners. Elites in those race distances run for a shorter duration (because they are faster) and can run at higher intensities for longer periods. In these races, the elites can actually run within 10 to 15 percent of their threshold intensity for much of the race.

Application of Principle 2

The bookends of this athlete's physiological demands mirror her strengths and weaknesses (see Principle 3). Thus, accomplishing all three principles was an easy task, as it was a function of determining what to do last, determining what to do first, and then filling in the middle.

PRINCIPLE 3:

Work strengths closer to the race and weaknesses further away.

I knew from the onset that one of this athlete's strengths was her physiology at EnduranceRun intensity. I could tell this from her performance at 100-mile competitions compared to marathon and 50K distances, as well as data from her day-to-day training.

She can tolerate high training volume very well and can seemingly run forever at lower intensities. By contrast, she is not as good at races like the 5K and 10K (which rely more on VO_2 max intensity), and we typically see fatigue set in quickly when she is prescribed a phase of RunningIntervals. All of this points to her strengths being more rooted in lower intensities and weaknesses rooted in higher intensities.

Application of Principle 3

Since the athlete's strengths and weaknesses lined up with the most and least important aspects of her physiology, the flow from RunningIntervals to TempoRun to SteadyStateRun was a natural one. This is not always the case. Sometimes, the time frame or other mismatch dictates that you have to pick and choose among the three principles, even leaving one of them out. More often, you skimp on one to develop another. These are judgment calls, and thus there are few right and wrong approaches. In general, though, I tend to favor training for the demands of the event as an ever-so-slightly higher priority than the other two principles.

Training Phases

Generally speaking, each training phase should last approximately eight weeks. This athlete's ultimate LRP conveniently fits into this time frame, with the exception of the early season RunningInterval phase. That phase was intentionally shortened for reasons I will describe below. If you are designing your own LRP, I encourage you to go through the following process:

Begin planning by identifying what training phase will be last. This will be the intensity that is most specific to your race and/or your strength(s). Make this final bit of training two phases of four weeks each.

Next, plan your first training phase with what is least important and/or the weakness you want to work on. Make this two phases of four weeks each.

Fill in the middle with the intensity that is left over.

Adjust your time frame for each phase based on the aspects I will soon describe.

Add in any nuance for nutrition training, heat/altitude acclimation, or any training camps.

In reality my athletes are switching the intensity of their training every four to twelve weeks, with the number of weeks based on three distinct facets: intensity, significance, and rate of adaptation.

INTENSITY OF THE PHASE

Typically, higher-intensity phases can be shorter than lower-intensity phases. I commonly have athletes go through a VO_2 max phase that is as short as two or three weeks. It is equally common for an endurance phase that includes SteadyStateRuns and EnduranceRuns to lasts twelve weeks, with rest at appropriate times. This is because your physiology at high intensities adapts over a shorter time course and vice versa. Stephen Seiler (2006) has developed a useful theoretical curve to visually explain this phenomenon and its impact on performance (Figure 10.4). It neatly describes how an athlete's VO_2 max and lactate threshold can improve and plateau over time.

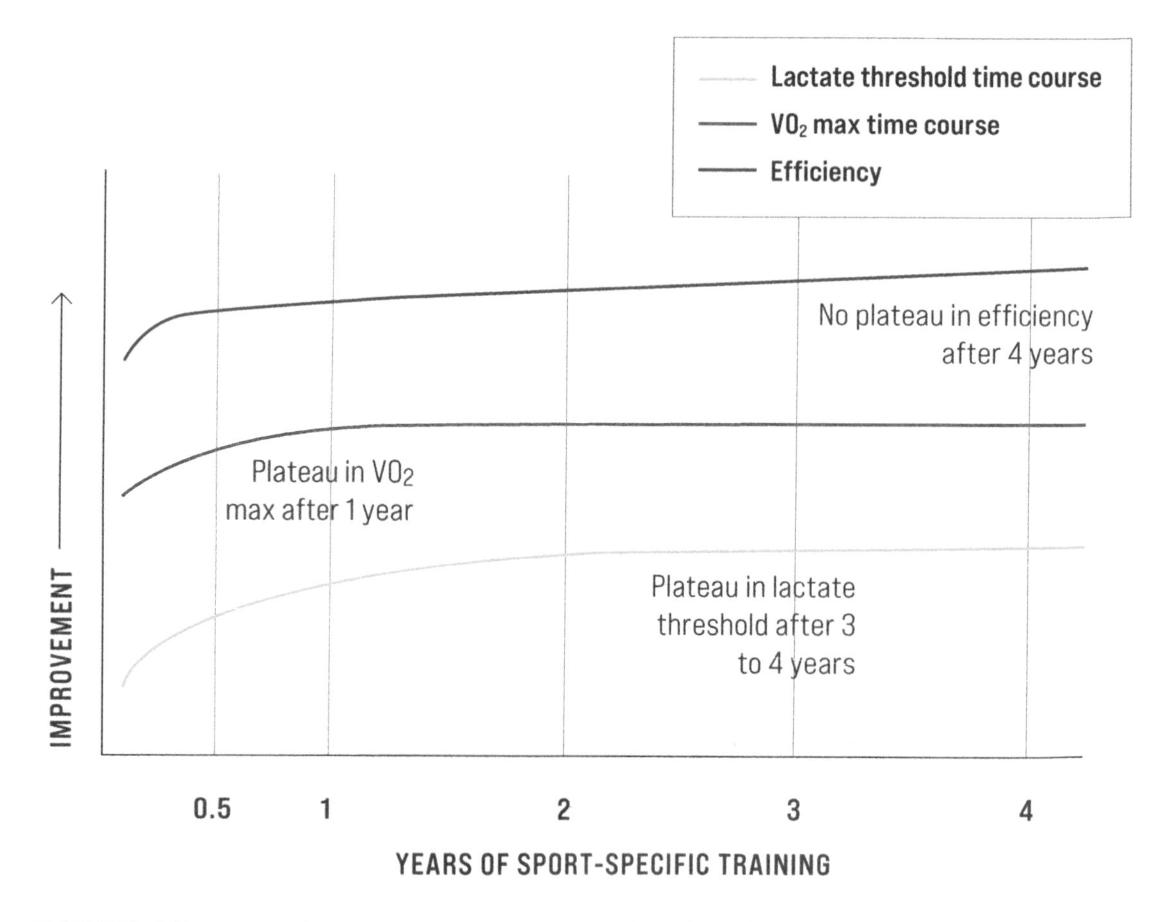

FIGURE 10.4 Time course for training adaptation. Adapted from Seiler 2006.

SIGNIFICANCE OF THE PHASE IN THE OVERALL PLAN

Significance is quite easy to determine and correlates to Principle 1 from designing the LRP. Quite simply, if the training aspect is more critical to success, I will have an athlete develop it closer to the race and also for a longer period (typically eight weeks or more). If the aspect is less important, I have the athlete work for a shorter period (eight weeks or less) and typically further away from the event.

POINT OF DIMINISHING RETURNS

The concept of diminishing returns can be illustrated by the example of eating cookies. The first cookie is delicious, melting in your mouth with a warm, buttery, sugary goodness. By the time you eat the fourth or fifth cookie, meh, it's OK but not nearly as satisfying as the first. The enjoyment you get from the treat diminishes as each subsequent cookie is devoured. Physiologically speaking, the concept of diminishing returns applies to training: the returns on your hard work diminish as time and training move forward. Additionally, as you become more fit, it takes a longer amount of time to improve less (again, see Figure 10.4). This is generally a good thing, as it means you are becoming stronger and faster. Depending on the type of stress, this point of diminishing returns can come after weeks, months, or even years. Figure 10.4 also illustrates that even though these physiological phenomena can reach their points of diminishing returns, the athlete's efficiency (and therefore performance) can still improve.

While the figure specifically describes physiological changes at lactate threshold and VO_2 max as we would measure them in a lab, the basic idea is that higher intensities produce changes in an endurance athlete more quickly but to a lesser extent, and they reach the point of diminishing returns sooner as compared with lower intensities. By knowing this simple physiological phenomenon, you can better gauge when you've reached this point of diminishing returns, which is the third facet in determining how long to focus on what stress.

BALANCING SIGNIFICANCE AND DIMINISHING RETURNS

While the general intensity of the phase can inform how long or short a phase should be, the aspects of significance and diminishing returns need to be balanced when actually constructing the details of the phase. During the planning process, significance takes priority. How important is the phase to the end result? This dominates the phase-duration philosophy because the reality of training has yet to take place. You as an athlete, and I as a coach, have yet to see how the training and adaptation actually unfold. So, we make an educated guess about when our neat little blocks are going to begin and end when we formulate the LRP. Sometimes those nice, neat blocks run true to form, but sometimes they change.

Once reality takes hold we can prioritize training based on what we observe about the aspect of diminishing returns. As a coach, I evaluate training on a daily basis, looking at how fresh and fatigued an athlete is. Even more important, I use that information to determine whether an athlete is better after a rest phase, and I either keep the original LRP or alter it accordingly. It's a tricky balance, because I want to see the athlete fatigue during the course of training and then improve just after coming out of a recovery phase. Athletes need to literally get worse before they rest and thus get better; they need that amount of stress in order to adapt. Yet needing an athlete to get worse before getting better can only be taken so far before the stress is too great.

When I see an athlete fail to improve shortly after a recovery phase, it's one indication that they are ready for a different stimulus. For athletes who are designing their own training programs, I encourage you to switch in and out of training phases more quickly, rather than forcibly wringing out every last ounce of improvement. This errs on the side of caution, keeping the training stimulus novel and helping to prevent burnout. For the athletes I coach, I look at a range of variables to indicate that a change is needed and appropriate, including interval metrics, cumulative training load, acute training load, training stress scores, qualitative feedback, and workout comments from the athletes' training logs. I have outlined some of these variables in Chapter 6.

An Ultrarunner's Hierarchy of Needs

My alma matter's code of conduct was "Aggies do not lie, steal, or cheat, nor do they tolerate those that do." As we Texas A&M Aggies are a cheeky lot, we would routinely add an addendum to the code that stated: "They just exaggerate, collaborate, and borrow." Little did I know that the "collaborate and borrow" tongue-in-cheek piece would actually come in handy as I became a professional coach.

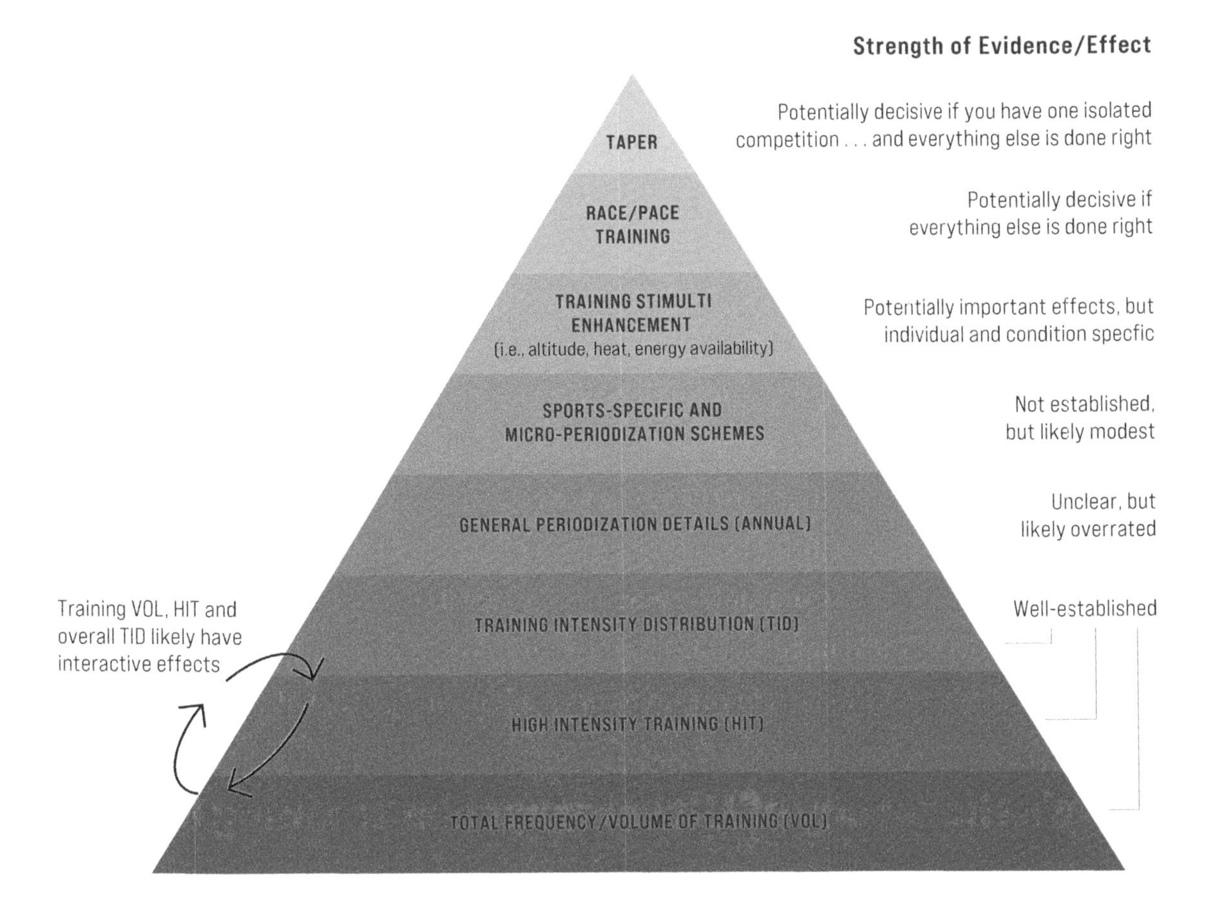

FIGURE 10.5 Hierarchy of Endurance Training Needs. Source: Seiler and Sjusren 2004.

In a 1943 paper, Abraham Maslow described human beings' basic needs and arranged them in a hierarchy, proposing that some basic needs (food, water, security) have to be met before "higher" needs (social relationships, ego, self-esteem) are addressed. Maslow's hierarchy of needs has been taught in psychology classes and re-envisioned for other purposes for decades. As a student of sports science, I was enthralled by Dr. Stephen Seiler's application of this concept to physical training. He refers to the pyramid below as the "hierarchy of training priorities for endurance athletes."

The basic premise of Seiler's hierarchy is that athletes need to accumulate a lot of training time—and lots of time at intensity below and around lactate threshold—before adding more specialized techniques. I completely agree and have preached the notion of "first things first" for years: go after the big 20-percent performance gains from hours of fundamental endurance training before you try to squeeze out a 1 to 2 percent improvement from "marginal gains." Don't add altitude training until you've done the work to develop your aerobic engine first.

As a coach, I felt the need to "collaborate and borrow" Dr. Seiler's hierarchy a step further. While his hierarchy describes the priorities that must be addressed to increase athletic performance, I think there is a separate hierarchy that describes the priorities needed for ultramarathon athletes, and coaches working with them, to reach their full potential. As you work through your LRP, keep the following "hierarchy of ultramarathon training needs" in mind. Focus on the things that matter more. Training concepts near the big base of the pyramid will matter much more than the nuance of whether you spend eight or ten days in the sauna. The hierarchy of ultramarathon training needs is also a good reminder to include the "other" things in training that are often forgotten. Aspects like building your team and training the gut are important but often get lost in the desire to design the number of miles, amount of vertical, and timing of intensity. Do not neglect these; include them in the notes or an additional section of your LRP.

Koop's Hierarchy of Ultramarathon Training Needs

Athletes are not science experiments, and they are not machines. Human physiology can be predicted and measured using various formulas, equations, and tests, but human performance cannot. There's no equation for mental toughness. There's no formula for learning to adapt when Plan A, Plan B, and Plan C all go out the window. I've always said coaching is a combination of art and science, and when I view the concept of a hierarchy of needs through an ultramarathon coaching lens, here's what I come up with:

TOTAL VOLUME OF WORKLOAD

As with Seiler's hierarchy, the first thing athletes have to do is put in the time. If you ask me what you should do to improve your performance, I'll almost always say "train more over long periods of time." The "over long periods of time" piece is important, because it de-emphasizes the single long run or single-week volume in favor of annual volume, which is far more impactful and mitigates injury. From a coaching perspective, this means helping athletes find or create more training volume throughout the year. I try to increase the number of sessions per week or overall number per month.

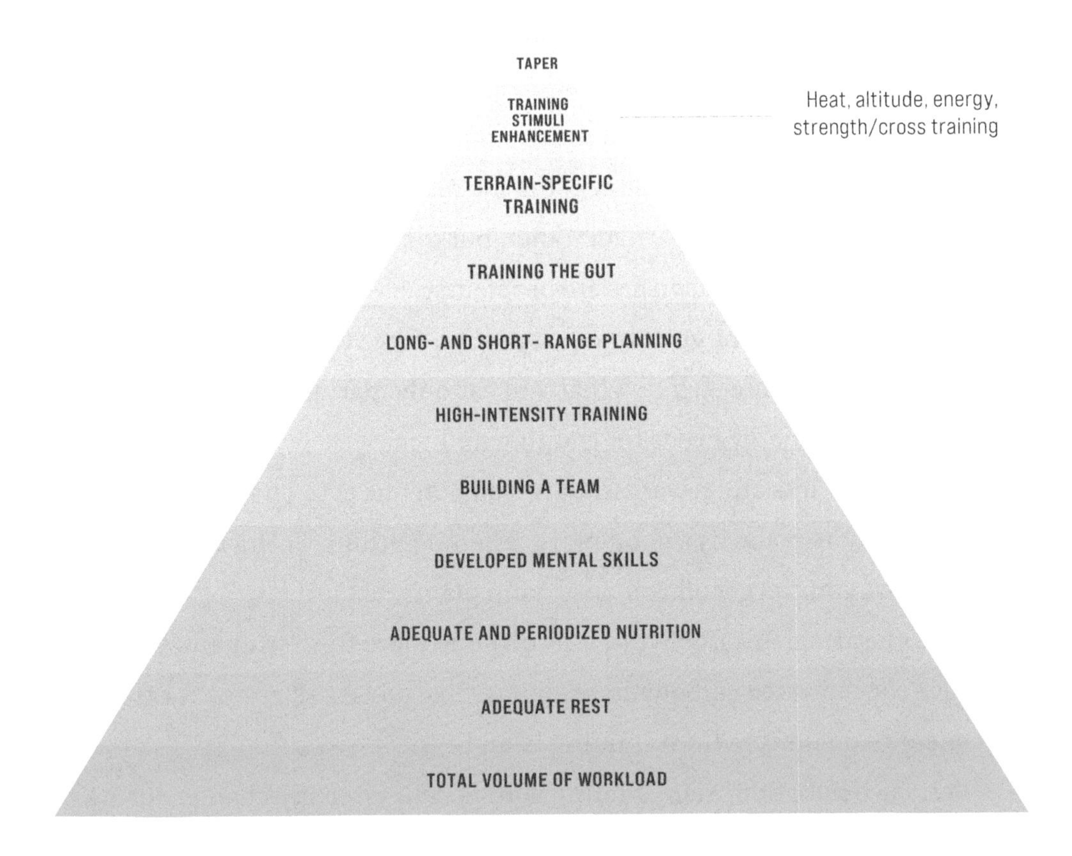

FIGURE 10.6 Koop's hierarchy of ultramarathon training needs.

For time-crunched athletes who can't increase total weekly hours or the number of training sessions per week, I try to make some runs longer. Longer runs are helpful for generating a bigger stimulus, and for people with tight schedules I sometimes reduce the number of runs per week by consolidating two shorter training sessions into one longer run. They get the same number of hours per week, but rearranged to add duration to an individual session.

ADEQUATE REST

Rest is implicitly included in Seiler's hierarchy because it is integral to structuring training, but I break it out into a distinct coaching need because it is typically harder to get athletes to rest than it is to get them to go full gas during an interval workout. Rest is boring, and high-energy, driven athletes have trouble taking it easy. When I ask a roundtable of CTS coaches the number one thing they wish their athletes would do more, it's rest.

WHOLESOME NUTRITION, MOSTLY PLANTS, PERIODIZED A PLUS

If an athlete is putting in the time and following the plan in terms of work and recovery, they also need to make sure they're fueling to meet the demands of training. The foodstuff you ingest literally becomes the fuel for the machinery in your body that propels you forward. I don't preach any particular diet, but diets that eliminate or demonize particular food groups or macronutrients are problematic for athletes at best and harmful at worst. The most important guidelines I try to reinforce with endurance athletes are:

- Consume adequate energy. What you eat only matters once you're meeting your overall energy needs for training and recovery.
- Eat more plants and fewer animals. You don't have to be solely plant-based, but adding more plants is a good move. There's nothing wrong with animal protein, but you can get all you need from plants, too.
- Don't be afraid of carbohydrates. Consume more fresh fruit and vegetables, and save concentrated carbohydrate sources like processed grains for times when energy expenditure from training is highest.
- Periodize nutrition. Your training volume and intensity change during the year, and your caloric intake—and your food choices to a lesser extent—should change, too.

DEVELOPED MENTAL SKILLS

Your physiological characteristics determine the maximum amount of exercise capacity you ultimately have. Your psychological skillset determines how much of that total capacity you can utilize. This goes far beyond being "tough," "gritty," and the cliché descriptors we assign to athletes who outperform their physiologically equivalent peers. Mental skills for ultrarunning are an imperative part of the sport and are described in further detail in Chapter 15.

BUILDING A TEAM

There is only so much an athlete can accomplish on their own before they need to build a strong support system. This includes some or all of the following: family, friends, training partners, a coach, a physical therapist, a massage therapist, a nutrition professional, and a physician. Many athletes resist this step, thinking they are "not enough of an athlete" to warrant substantive support. As a coach, one of my roles is to help an athlete build a support network, actually utilize it, and recognize the value it delivers. I routinely build relationships with my athletes' families and support networks because I know it is all part of the big wheel that keeps them going. When everything is going great, it may seem unnecessary. But when everything goes sideways, athletes without an established support system get swept way off track.

HIGH-INTENSITY TRAINING AND DISTRIBUTION OF TRAINING INTENSITY

High-intensity training is an important component of training for endurance athletes—even ultra-endurance athletes—but from the time-at-intensity standpoint it actually accounts for maybe 20 percent of training sessions and only about 10 percent of total training hours *per year*. If you run ten hours a week (six-hundred minutes), you'd have to average sixty minutes of work above lactate threshold just to hit 10 percent. Even though I am a coach known for—and sometimes criticized for—using VO_2 max interval workouts with ultramarathon runners, the actual distribution of training intensities I prescribe is heavily weighted toward low-intensity training with strategic use of high-intensity workouts.

LONG- AND SHORT-RANGE PLANNING

Long- and short-range planning is essentially the application of variety in training in order to change the stimulus. On an annual basis this means training aspects of fitness that are less specific to your goal event farther out from the event, and then training more event-specific aspects of fitness as the event draws closer. On a phase or weekly basis, this gets down to how individual workouts are arranged on days of the week. Planning plays a role in fine-tuning an athlete's performance for events, but coaches have to be careful not to give rigid schemes more importance than they are due.

TRAIN THE GUT

Gastrointestinal distress is a leading cause of DNFs in ultramarathon events, and I view that as a consequence of inadequate preparation. The gut can and should be trained to handle the volume of food and fluids an ultramarathoner needs to consume over a six-, twelve-, or thirty-hour period. If you've done everything right in terms of training, rest, and support, you'll be able to reach the point in an ultra-endurance event where your gut may be the weakest link. If you haven't done those other things first, you won't last long enough in the event for your gut to be an issue.

TERRAIN-SPECIFIC TRAINING

2016 Western States winner Kaci Lickteig is a great example of why terrain-specific training occupies an advanced step in the hierarchy of ultramarathon needs. She trains in Nebraska, without access to big mountains, yet she's won the Western States Endurance Run and other ultras with tens of thousands of feet of climbing. Spending all your time running in the mountains doesn't automatically make you a great mountain runner, especially if your training is not addressing the fundamentals first. As a coach, my goal is to put the fittest athlete on the start line, because fitness is an athlete's most important tool for creating the ability to adapt to the specific challenges of an event. If you can match a goal event's elevation gain and climbing in training, that's awesome, but develop the biggest aerobic engine you can before worrying about terrain-specific training.

TRAINING STIMULI ENHANCEMENT

Training stimuli enhancements like altitude training and heat acclimation sit near the very tip-top of the pyramid, after everything else has been done. Does altitude training work? You bet, but only if the athlete is healthy, already fit, and well rested. Is heat acclimation important? For races in hot weather, yes. But it doesn't take that long or that much effort to achieve most of the benefits from heat acclimation, so it shouldn't displace fundamental training months before your event. The same can be said for strength training (more on that in Chapter 11). The trouble is, chasing improvements in these areas, sometimes referred to as marginal gains, is sexier than going out for another four by ten-minute TempoRun workout. And coaches fall for the appeal of marginal gains, too, often to their athletes' detriment.

TAPER

"Taper tantrums" are real and derail many athletes right before major events. Keeping an athlete on track in the final two weeks before a major race is perhaps a coach's most important role, but not because of the potential 1 to 2 percent improvement in performance

SLEEP DEPRIVATION TRAINING FOR 200s?

THE EMERGENCE OF 200-MILE RACES has raised the collective eyebrows of the ultramarathon world. Events like the Triple Crown of 200s (the Bigfoot 200, Tahoe 200, and Moab 240 all in the same year) as well as the Tor des Géants have drawn the eyes of ultrarunners looking for their next great challenge. Indeed, as ultramarathons are not simply long marathons, 200 milers (and beyond) are not simply longer ultramarathons in terms of training, preparation, and race strategy. You can't just run more and expect that to translate into success at longer and longer distances. So, while the general preparation outlined in this chapter can apply to any ultramarathon, there are some specific considerations athletes should take note of for runs of 200 miles and longer.

One of the more challenging characteristics of 200-mile races is that sleep deprivation will eventually become a factor, for nearly all runners, in the outcome. This has led to the logical notion that ultrarunners preparing for these events need to undertake some type of sleep deprivation training to better cope with that stress. Anecdotal strategies have emerged and range from training sessions performed overnight or after a short sleep to training after being awake for twenty-four hours. All of these strategies attempt to condition the body to a lack of sleep. They are all novel and worthy attempts to solve a critical performance problem for these events. However, there is very little, if any, scientific evidence indicating that any sort of sleep deprivation training has any meaningful physiological effect on an athlete's ability to tolerate a lack of sleep. If anything, some of these training techniques will familiarize an athlete with how it feels to run overnight and operate with little sleep, but the extent of any benefit is limited to just that: the familiarization of locomoting with little sleep.

In addition to this, sleep deprivation training comes with a cost. You are interrupting and compromising normal training by intentionally introducing a sleep-deprived state. The quality of sleep-deprived sessions is compromised on the order of about 2 to 10 percent (Oliver et al. 2009; Roberts et al. 2019; Skein et al. 2011). Training needs to be altered before and after the sleep-deprived session in order to accommodate pre- and postworkout rest. Athletes also might be more vulnerable to injury and illness after training in a sleep-deprived state. All of this effort costs valuable training time and begs the question, "Is it even worth the effort?" In my opinion the balance between advantages and potential downsides of sleep deprivation training favors normal day-to-day training as a means of maximizing the athlete's physical capacity. If anything, an overnight session or two might be warranted simply to test lighting and other equipment, as well as to have some degree of familiarization with running for prolonged periods with a headlamp.

Specific sleeping strategies for 200-milers will be discussed in Chapter 16.

that might come from a perfect taper. Early in 2018, *Dylan Bowman won the Ultra-Trail Mt. Fuji* by a mere couple of minutes. The percent he won by was in this cliché 2 percent area. Did the taper make the difference? Maybe, but it is certainly not the whole picture.

The more important part of the taper is not screwing up everything the athlete worked so hard to build. Every year I see runners training on the track in Chamonix in the days before Ultra-Trail du Mont-Blanc. This is silly because it is the least event-specific activity they could do. It's a coach's job to prevent athletes itchy for competition from being their own worst enemies. In an ideal world, the athlete enters their taper period confident they have done all the work necessary to be at their best, and that confidence allows for relaxation and stress reduction, all of which enables them to arrive at the start line rested and ready to turn all their preparation into action.

LAST WORD ON THE HIERARCHY OF ULTRAMARATHON TRAINING NEEDS

Athletes rarely achieve breakthrough performances purely because of their physical training. Getting to the start line with the best possible conditioning is important, but it's not everything. To realize your full potential, you have to go to the start line with a full toolbox of mental, physical, and emotional skills so you are as prepared as possible to deal with the unpredictable nature of endurance sports. Some of those tools are more or less fundamentally important for success, and some take more or less time to develop. The hierarchy of ultramarathon training needs provides a visual guide to rank ordering seemingly unrelated aspects of preparation into one hierarchy. Your best day doesn't happen because you have the highest VO_2 max or because you have optimized fat oxidation; it happens because you have prepared yourself for whatever a race can throw at you, and you have prepared more for the things that matter more.

KEY POINTS FOR LONG-RANGE PLANNING

- Block periodization will be superior to mixed periodization for most ultrarunners.
- When you are working on your LRP, start at the end (your goal event) and work backward chronologically.
- Do the things that are most specific to the race closest to the race. Do the things that are least specific to the race further away. This normally results in a plan that moves from high intensity and low volume to high volume and low intensity as the season progresses.
- At some point during training, do one training phase of each critical intensity (SteadyStateRun, TempoRun, and RunningIntervals).
- Work your weaknesses earlier and your strengths later.
- Start with eight-week training blocks, divided in half with a recovery week every fourth week, working one intensity at a time.
- Shorten a block if:
  - The intensity is high
  - The intensity is less important
- Lengthen a block if:
  - The intensity is low
  - The intensity is more important
- If you are designing your own training, err on the side of short training cycles and switching the intensity more frequently.
- You have a hierarchy of needs as an ultrarunner. The total amount of work you do and adequate rest are the most important.

CHAPTER 11

Strength Training for Ultrarunning

In the first edition of this book, I made an egregious error regarding strength training and cross-training. I had a whole section like the one that follows laid out, only to leave it on the cutting room floor and replace it with a small sidebar. The reader reviews stemming from that omission were brutal. While the conclusions made in that sidebar are almost identical to the section that follows, I regret not taking the time to expand fully on why strength and cross-training may be good, how to implement them, and when they might be counterproductive for you.

Some might say that I think strength training is a waste of time, and based on the previous rendition of this book, that's a fair critique. Honestly, we paint the term "strength training" with an overly broad brush. It can mean anything from bar-bending Olympic-style lifts to benign glute activation exercises. Thus, there should be some reasonable calculus to deciding the ultimate goal of strength training for a specific athlete, what exercises to incorporate into that athlete's regimen, and how they are going to incorporate the exercises into their training and lifestyle.

For the purposes of this book, I am going to divide strength training into two distinct categories: "strength training" and "corrective exercise training." In the most basic sense, "strength training" is training for strength. You are literally training in a manner that makes your muscles and tendons stronger so that they will produce more force. This is primarily accomplished by resistance training with progressively heavier loads in order to improve muscle strength, power, hypertrophy, and/or endurance. "Corrective exercise training," on the other hand, is focused on correcting some sort of imbalance or movement pattern, primarily through the use of lighter weights, resistance bands, body weight, and unstable surfaces. While there is some overlap between the two, they are distinct in the fact that strength training will leave you fatigued and corrective exercises, while taxing to specific muscle groups, usually will not. This has programming considerations that will be discussed in short order.

Strength Training as an Ergogenic Aid

Strength training has long been used by long-distance and marathon runners as a way of improving performance and preventing injury (which has the tangential benefit of improving performance through increased training availability). It is a universally accepted practice at the high school, collegiate, and post-collegiate levels, and for good reason. Many studies have looked at the performance benefits of concurrent strength and endurance training in endurance athletes. A quick PubMed search of "strength training and endurance" will yield hundreds of results, all of which add their own twist on prescription, timing, duration, and outcome measurements. Nearly universally, these studies show improvements in running economy (the steady state rate of oxygen you consume and utilize at submaximal pace), increases in VO_2 max, improvements in real-world performance, and reductions in injury rates (Balsalobre-Fernández et al. 2016).

However, even with a universally accepted practice, a closer look is always warranted. How big are these improvements? A few percent, maybe. Are they applicable to real-life situations? Probably not. Do they come at a cost of time and effort? Usually. How important are the improvements for *ultramarathon* performance? That's the question we are after.

STRENGTH TRAINING AND RUNNING ECONOMY

One of the primary benefits lauded by strength-training advocates is the improvement in running economy. Traditional strength training should improve your running economy by improving spring stiffness (the ligaments and tendons) in your legs and via better neuromuscular recruitment. Essentially your legs are springs, and you propel your body with those springs. Some of this movement is the energy needed for muscular contraction, but a lot of that energy is also "free." Your muscles and tendons stretch during your gait cycle, like a rubber band being stretched, and that elastic energy is harnessed before being released again. The spring stiffness you acquire from jumping and moving heavy weights (creating a thicker rubber band) improves how effectively you can push against the ground as you propel your body forward on the trail. Awesome, right? Well, potentially, but strength training can mean a lot of work for a 2 to 4 percent improvement in running economy (Balsalobre-Fernández et al. 2016), and there is still uncertainty about whether it will matter over the course of a 100-mile effort.

STRENGTH TRAINING AND INJURY REDUCTION

A compelling reduction in injury rates is another big potential benefit of strength training for endurance, according to the scientific literature. One meta-analysis (Lauersen 2018) suggests that athletes who strength train experience a ~66 percent reduction in injury risk. This is important when we factor in training consistency over the long haul, which is a predictor in ultramarathon performance and finishing rates. The calculus is simple: if you miss fewer days of training every year from injuries, you can train more, and more training generally (not always) improves performance. However, there are a lot of other things that lower injury risk, including rest days (Ristolainen et al. 2014), sleeping eight or more hours a night (O'Donnell 2018), and avoiding RED-S. The point is that more is not always better, and when you add something to your workload, that often means having to take something else away.

So, where does this fit into your ultramarathon training? Unfortunately, there is not a simple binary "Yes, do it!" or "No, don't do it!" answer. Just like any piece of your training puzzle, individuality is key. As mentioned above, this kind of strength training is hard, meaning there is a demand on the body and subsequently a higher overall workload or training stress. In nearly all cases, adding this kind of training means eliminating another quality session during your week, like that second interval session. There are times of the year when that is of much less consequence and might even have a lot of benefit. What that means is it's important to look at your LRP, decide on the most important aspects of your training goals for each block, and ask yourself, "What do I prioritize, and what do I sacrifice?"

ARE YOU A GOOD CANDIDATE FOR STRENGTH TRAINING?

Not all ultramarathon runners are good candidates for strength training. While there are gains to be made in the weight room, there are also gains to be made out on the trails. If you are looking at improving your race time or finishing chances by a few percent, you can choose to do so by adding more miles, incorporating more recovery, or hitting the gym, but not necessarily all three, because they will be mutually exclusive at times. For example, if you decide to add two hours of strength training per week, that's two hours you could have spent simply resting. If you have enough rest and recovery time built into your schedule, that might not be a big deal. But, if you are burning the training candle at both ends, you might be better off just taking that time to lay on the couch. Time and energy are limited commodities, even for elite athletes, so you must choose wisely.

When I work with athletes, I go through a flowchart similar to Figure 11.1 to determine if they are good candidates for strength training. After completing this exercise, some are good candidates, but many are not.

PRESCRIPTION FOR STRENGTH TRAINING

You've determined that you're a candidate for strength training—great! The key now is to develop a smart and efficient program that supports your running volume and intensity while allowing for appropriate recovery. Although the reps and sets (volume) will change depending on where you are in your training phase, there will always be five basic movement patterns you should perform:

1. **PUSH:** includes exercises like push-ups, bench press, and other types of upper body push presses
2. **PULL:** includes exercises like bent-over rows and pull-ups
3. **HINGE (OR HIP HINGE):** includes exercises like a Romanian deadlift
4. **SQUAT:** includes exercises like a squat (go figure), lunge, or reverse lunge
5. **CARRY (OR OTHER TYPES OF DYNAMIC CORE WORK):** includes a farmer's carry, woodchoppers, and medicine ball slams

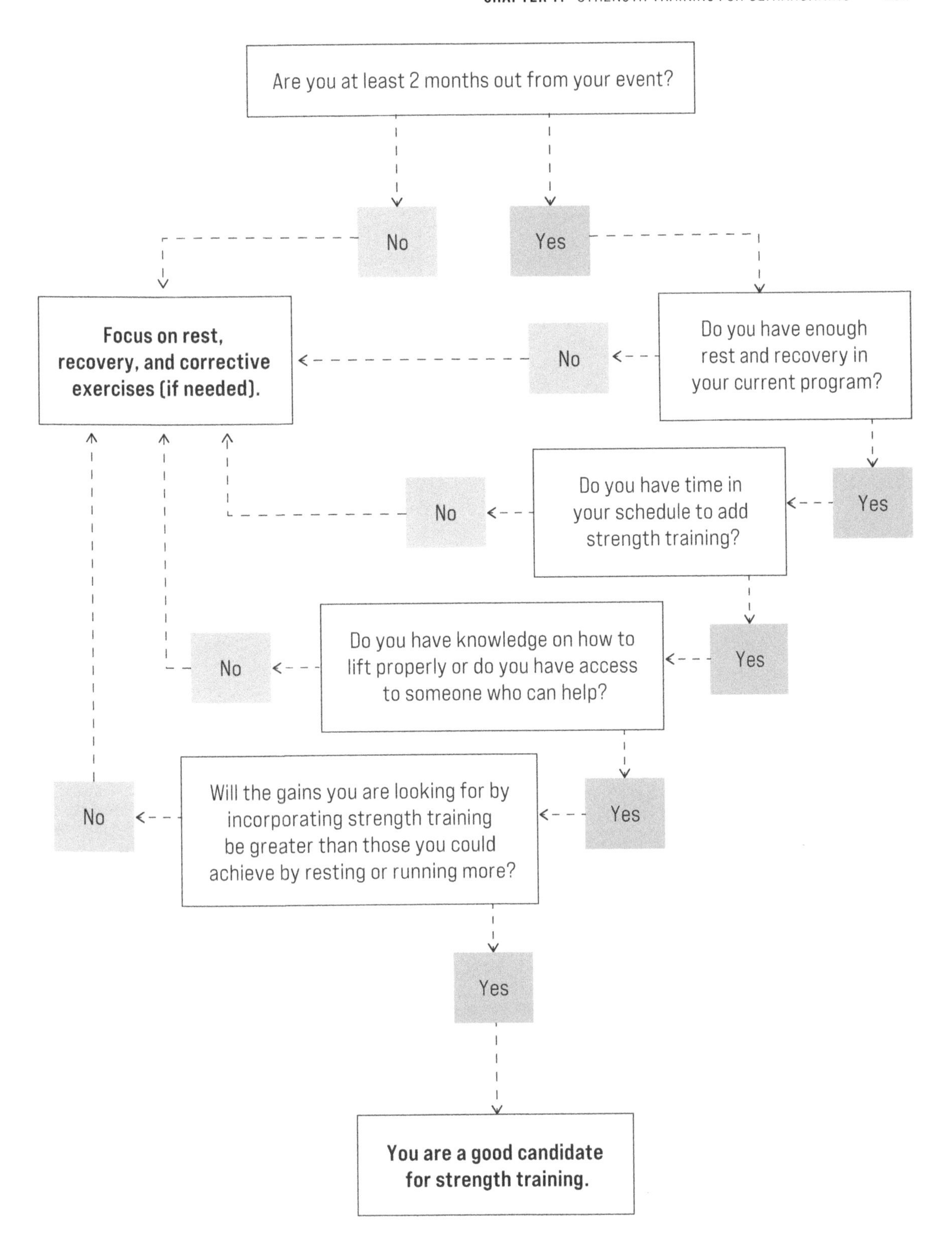

FIGURE 11.1 Are you a good candidate for strength training?

These exercises can be organized into a two- or three-days-per-week strength program. An example follows, using Day A as the first day and Day B as the second. If you choose to have a three-day-per-week strength program, you can repeat your preference of either Day A or B.

Day A

- **PUSH-UP**
- **DUMBBELL ROW**
- **ROMANIAN DEADLIFT**
- **SQUAT**
- **FARMER'S CARRY**

Day B

- **OVERHEAD PRESS**
- **PULL-UP (WITH ASSISTANCE IF NEEDED)**
- **HIP THRUST**
- **REVERSE LUNGE**
- **MEDICINE BALL SLAM**

Now, how do we structure these training days into the overall architecture of your weekly schedule? Remember that strength training should complement your run training, not detract from it.

Looking at the calendar in Figure 11.2, you will notice a few things. First you will see that your strength days are scheduled as far away as possible from your next long run and/or hard runs. This will allow you to go into those workouts as fresh as possible so you can have the best workout. In addition, pairing your strength-training days on the evenings of where more intense work is programmed allows you to truly take your easy days easy. On the days when you lift and run on the same day, it is important to prioritize your run training, taking care to program your runs prior to your strength work.

For your particular schedule, you might be forced to do your long runs in the evenings or on a different day, but in any case, the overall strategy of placing your strength- training days such that you have as much recovery as possible should reign supreme. Things get particularly tricky if you add a third strength-training day to the week, and normally I don't advise that for athletes focusing on ultramarathon performance.

FIGURE 11.2 Example training week with two scheduled strength-training workouts.

ORGANIZING STRENGTH TRAINING THROUGHOUT THE SEASON

When determining how often and how much strength training to do within your running season or year, the best advice is to look at where you are in your run programming and then see where your strength training lines up and fits in. Remember, your priority here is to achieve appropriate run volume balanced with recovery, and strength training should *complement* this balance of training and recovery, never detract from it.

With that in mind, a good guideline is to look at the entire season of training before your event as a big pie, and divide the pie into three segments: an early season, a mid

PART OF TRAINING	SETS	REPS	REST	FREQUENCY
Early	1–5	1–5	90+ sec	3x week
Mid	3	8–12	45–60 sec	2–3x week
Late	2–3	10–15 or time-based	As needed	1–2x week

TABLE 11.1 Overview of strength-training programming.

season, and a late season. For the purpose of this example we are going to assume that you begin your training in January for a race in September, so you have nine months to train. The early season is the very beginning of your training, and this is usually months 1 to 3 of the pie. Your mid season would be months 4 to 7, with the late season (the last two months before your event!) being months 8 and 9.

The Early Season

The early season is before either run volume or intensity has increased dramatically. This is when you build the foundations for the coming phases. In some cases, you start the early season by coming off a bit of a break or a period of decreased run volume. In this season of running, your strength training should be made up of one to five sets of one to five reps of big compound movements utilizing heavier weight, with longer recoveries between sets. The focus here is heavier weights and lower reps and sets. Because run volume is nowhere near its peak, you have more time to balance the stress and load of strength training with your running while still having adequate time to recover.

The Mid Season

The mid season is when you will start to see an increase in intensity or volume of running, depending on your training block. In any case, your run training will be harder and consume more of your physiological bandwidth. Because of this, strength training will begin to emphasize moderate sets and reps, with a goal of three sets of eight to twelve reps, lifting weight that is a challenge but leaving one or two reps in the tank—so not to failure.

The Late Season

At this point you are zeroing in on your event, and all of your body's resources should be dedicated to the specific demands of that event. Rest and recovery days are at a premium, and you want to reduce or eliminate adding any unnecessary stress to the body. Therefore, this is the phase to concentrate more on corrective and restorative exercises (see next section). This type of work is minimally taxing on both your body and your time. It is a time to shore up any areas of weakness, work on mobility, and allow for more recovery in the place of longer, more intense strength-training sessions. Higher reps are more appropriate with the exercise selection and can also be time-based (i.e., thirty seconds per exercise or stretch). The programming of these sessions should be one to two days a week of work that complement your run training.

In all of these prescriptions, the set/rep range should be ~70 to 80 percent of what you feel is your maximum. For example, on a set of five reps, you should feel like you could do one or two more repetitions before failure.

Corrective Exercise Training

Corrective strength training is perhaps the most common form of strength work we see in the endurance community. Akin to physical therapy, the goal of a corrective exercise program is to target specific movements that address minor weaknesses and imbalances particular to your anatomy, movement patterns, and strength. This style of training has a low cost of effort and is less time intensive compared to traditional strength training. Exercises that fall into this category generally include body-weight exercises, clamshells, banded walking drills, and exercises done on balance balls or other unstable surfaces. These exercises potentially protect athletes from injury by correcting imbalances, but it's unclear if this style of training could influence injury risk in the same way as traditional strength training. The benefit of this style of training is that it has little impact on the quality of focused interval workouts and long runs. This means corrective exercise training is a low-risk addition to your training cycle that "could" have the added benefit of minor injury prevention.

ARE YOU A GOOD CANDIDATE FOR CORRECTIVE EXERCISES?

Being that most corrective exercise programs have little to no impact on higher-quality run sessions, most runners would assume that everyone is a candidate. After all, if there is no harm, you might as well do it, right? Still, there is a time cost involved with incorporating even the most basic corrective exercise program. If you have the ability to overcome this time cost, a simple corrective exercise program could be for you. More importantly, if you are a runner who is constantly injured, investing time in a corrective exercise program, along with managing your overall running workload, is essential. In these cases, I suggest seeking out and working with a qualified physical therapist.

WHAT ABOUT LEG CIRCUITS AND BODY-WEIGHT EXERCISES?

STRENGTH TRAINING HAS ALWAYS BEEN a tricky element to program for ultramarathon athletes. High running volume and copious amounts of climbing and descending leave trail runners with tired legs on a daily basis. The last thing many of them want to do is add additional workload to their legs, particularly if it's hard and heavy (as strength training should be). This has led many coaches and athletes to come up with an "in-between" solution using leg circuits, body-weight squats, and other high-volume/low-weight programs. Some of these are even timed, have clever names, and are encouraged to be performed daily.

High-repetition and low-weight strength-training exercises work only very temporarily and primarily in a corrective setting. Just like run training, strength training should be purposeful. It should be hard and require recovery in order to reap adaptation. The issue with frequent high-repetition leg-circuit exercises is that after the initial adaptation phase (usually just a few short weeks), there is no further progress to be had, as there is no source of progressive overload. It is literally the worst of both worlds, as the resistance is not high enough to elicit a strength adaption, and the cardiopulmonary stress is not specific enough to translate into running performance. Additionally, in the cases where the circuits are timed, the emphasis is put on speed or volume because the number of repetitions performed serves as a score that needs to be improved. This sacrifices technique and increases the likelihood of injury. So, even if you are crunched for time, you are better off redirecting your efforts into a few heavy squats as opposed to several dozen body-weight squats, lunges, and matrixes.

PRESCRIPTION FOR CORRECTIVE EXERCISE TRAINING

When it comes to corrective exercise training there are many areas runners in particular can benefit from, including:

- Posterior chain exercises for the glutes, hips, and hamstrings: These can include ball bridges, traditional bridges, and banded glute work.
- Exercises to strengthen weak feet: These can include barefoot balance work,

foot stretches and activation, and top-of-the-foot and calf stretches.

- Exercises for hips and pelvic stability: These can include monster band walks, lateral step-ups, and the pelvic list.

Most of these exercises can be done on alternating days throughout the week, up to three days per week. Work up to completing two to three sets of up to twelve reps or fifteen to thirty seconds. If you are just starting out, pick one from each category and rotate the exercises each session.

But Won't I Gain Weight That Will Slow Me Down?

The most common concern I hear from endurance athletes is often the worry that they'll bulk up from strength training. The reality is few of the endurance athletes reading this book are going to look like a professional bodybuilder from a couple of days per week of strength training. In most cases, there is nearly no muscle hypertrophy when performing concurrent strength and endurance training. In fact, in long-term studies (twenty-four to forty weeks) looking at concurrent strength and endurance training, there were no signs of muscular growth despite improvements in strength measurements (Blagrow, Howatson, and Hays 2017). This happens because of what occurs at the molecular level when practicing concurrent training. On one hand, strength training induces an upregulation in protein synthesis and releases a specific protein, called mTOR, that in a normal strength-training setting would help you build your beach muscles. However, when concurrent endurance training is taking place, you release an enzyme called adenosine monophosphate-activated kinase that blunts the effects of mTOR. What this means is that as an endurance athlete it is possible to increase muscular strength, your ability to generate power, and your muscle-tendon stiffness without the potentially negative side effects of mass gain.

Aging Athlete Considerations

Aging athletes are in a battle against the natural age-related loss of muscle mass that starts somewhere north of 40 and accelerates rapidly as you cross the 60-year threshold. From a performance standpoint we also know that this decrease in muscle mass is one of the main culprits when it comes to declining performance, as age-related decreases in VO_2 max are directly related to the loss of muscle mass. So, for aging athletes, strength training isn't just corrective or ergogenic, it's essential for general health and well-being. Trying to build and maintain muscle mass is of utmost importance and should be taken into account when you look at your training availability each week. For younger athletes, strength training might take a back seat for much of the year, but as we age we are all encouraged to shift some priority away from running time and toward moving heavy objects a few times a week.

A Place for Cross-Training

If you only have time to run, you should be spending that time running, not cross-training. Yoga, CrossFit, Zumba, and cycling might make you a better, more well-rounded athlete, but will it make you a better ultramarathoner? Probably not. Running is what will make you better at running.

However, there may be a time and place for cross-training sometime in the course of a year or season. Utilizing other training modalities can make sense when you can't run due to an active injury, when you're coming back from injury, or when your goal races are far off. Additionally, if you are a workload-capped runner (you have more available time to train, but adding more running workload leads to injury), using a bike, skis, or a pool to add training can be effective. Furthermore, if you simply like getting on your bike once or twice a week, go ahead and give it a whirl. Just don't think that it will automatically make you a better runner. The same goes for yoga, swimming, rowing, and the like: if you enjoy doing these activities, then great! But in the vast majority of cases, translating those activities to being a better, faster trail runner is a stretch. From a physiological standpoint, fitness and specificity of training are the most important things come race day, so keep the big picture in mind if you choose to supplement your training with nonrunning activities.

I would like to thank Sarah Scozzaro for her contributions with this chapter.

KEY POINTS FOR STRENGTH TRAINING FOR ULTRARUNNERS

- Ultrarunners can use strength training to acutely enhance their performance through running economy and/or injury reduction.
- Not all ultrarunners are candidates for strength training.
- Strength training comes at a compromise of time and energy, which must be balanced depending on your goals.
- Corrective exercise training is a low-cost, low-effort training adjunctive that can be used to mitigate injury risk.
- If you like other forms of cross-training, that's great. Just don't expect them to improve your ultrarunning performance in any meaningful way.

Winfield
Cemetery
Mine
Prospect
Prospect
Winfield Peak
Virginia Peak
Banker Mine
S A N I S A B
Brown Peak
Huron
Mines
BM 10226
WILDERNESS
BOUNDARY
North Fork
Creek
Gulch
4WD
20
29
28
32
33
10531
10358
10435
12342
13077
13089
13523
12300
11160

CHAPTER 12

Activating Your Training: The Short-Range Plan

The short-range plan is where the rubber meets the road. It is what most people refer to as their daily schedule, although some will refer to it as a single "block" of training. This schedule lays out the specific workouts and rest periods for the days and weeks to come. Your short-range plan contains the precise volume, intensity, intervals, recovery, and terrain specificity on a day-by-day basis.

Many coaches and athletes arrange their short-range plans in tidy four-week periods of three weeks "on" and one week "off." Generic twelve-week plans available in magazines or online are often arranged in this fashion, and while this offers a convenient way to organize a typical four-week month, I've always found this approach to be lazy and uneducated. The fact of the matter is that various stressors affect the body differently. It takes a different amount of time to recover from high volume compared to high intensity. Similarly, your body adapts along a different time course for various intensities. You cannot pigeonhole the process into rigid four-week time frames for every single training phase.

The 3:1 work-rest paradigm is a good reference point, but to get the most from your hard-earned training, this time frame needs to be adjusted to suit the adaptation you are seeking. The question is: How do you know what to adjust and in what ways? I use three primary concepts to design short-range plans, and when you apply these concepts to your training and your goals, you'll find that your training better suits your individual needs, is more precise, and most likely breaks the 3:1 paradigm.

Concepts for the Short-Range Plan

DO THE BIGGEST TRAINING LOAD WHEN YOU ARE THE MOST RESTED.

You run the best when you are fresh. This is why we taper before races (though tapering tends to drive ultrarunners stir crazy) and will often have our best workouts right after a rest week. When we are fresh and rested, we can run faster for longer periods of time. If we extend this concept to training, you are the most ready to handle the biggest training load right after a recovery phase. Following that strategy, your short-range plan should start with the workout(s) with the biggest training load. Regardless of the phase you are in, you should aim to do the hardest workout you will do for the phase

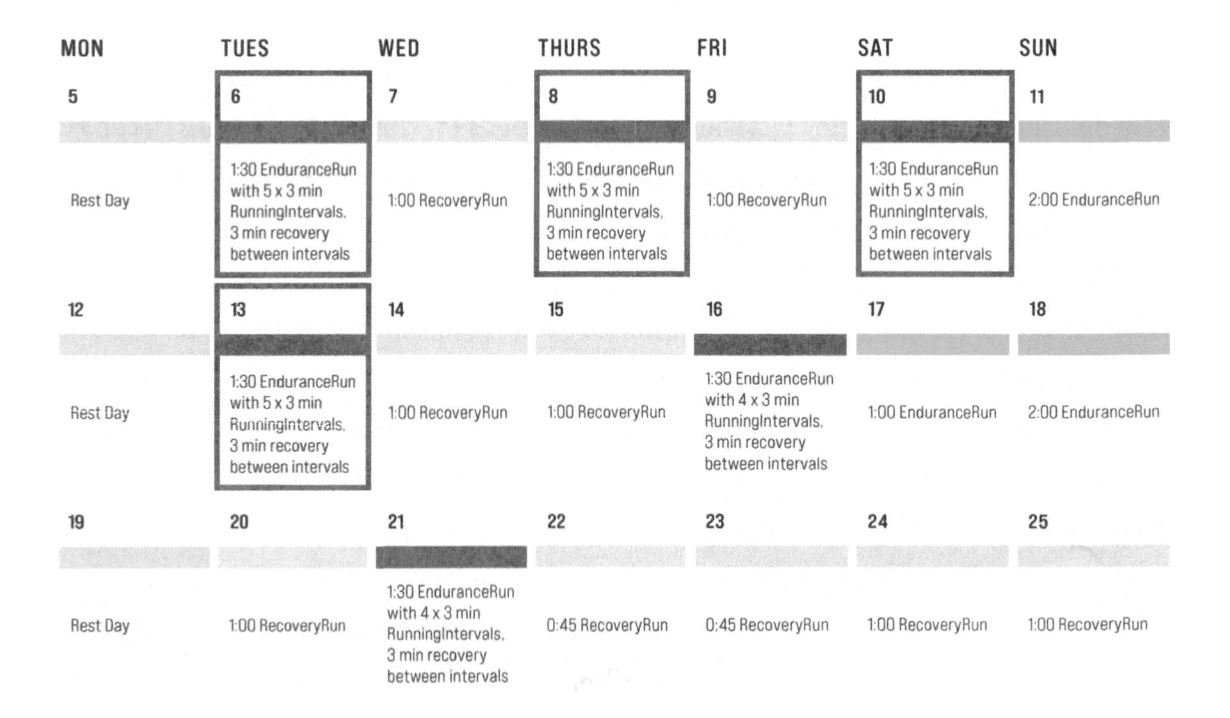

MON	TUES	WED	THURS	FRI	SAT	SUN
5	6	7	8	9	10	11
Rest Day	1:30 EnduranceRun with 5 x 3 min RunningIntervals, 3 min recovery between intervals	1:00 RecoveryRun	1:30 EnduranceRun with 5 x 3 min RunningIntervals, 3 min recovery between intervals	1:00 RecoveryRun	1:30 EnduranceRun with 5 x 3 min RunningIntervals, 3 min recovery between intervals	2:00 EnduranceRun
12	13	14	15	16	17	18
Rest Day	1:30 EnduranceRun with 5 x 3 min RunningIntervals, 3 min recovery between intervals	1:00 RecoveryRun	1:00 RecoveryRun	1:30 EnduranceRun with 4 x 3 min RunningIntervals, 3 min recovery between intervals	1:00 EnduranceRun	2:00 EnduranceRun
19	20	21	22	23	24	25
Rest Day	1:00 RecoveryRun	1:30 EnduranceRun with 4 x 3 min RunningIntervals, 3 min recovery between intervals	0:45 RecoveryRun	0:45 RecoveryRun	1:00 RecoveryRun	1:00 RecoveryRun

FIGURE 12.1 A RunningIntervals phase where the hardest workouts are the first four.

right off the bat. For example, for athletes who can handle a maximum of sixty minutes of SteadyStateRun, I will have them do that workout at the beginning of the phase, when they are the most rested. They might not be able to do a workout of that caliber for the remaining weeks of the phase, but that is fine. Many times, the hardest workout is actually a "B" race. You race hard, and the subsequent training stimulus of the race is far bigger than the stimulus you can achieve on any of the remaining training days. In any case, the fatigue induced from the initial few workouts will eventually lead to the desired adaptation. In this way, you must accept the fact that during the training process, you will get worse before you get better. If you do the right things in training, this is intentional (Figure 12.1).

WEEKLY PROGRESSIVE OVERLOADS HAVE CONSEQUENCES

TAKE THE TRAINING PROGRAM IN FIGURE 12.1 and flip it around. I see this type of training architecture time and time again, even with elite athletes. Each week builds off of the next with progressively more and more time at intensity. There is a huge glaring issue when athletes do this, and one that I think goes underappreciated in the endurance world. When athletes apply this type of weekly progressive workload training model, they end up attempting the **hardest and/or longest workouts when they are most fatigued**. This is a huge problem and a mistake many athletes and coaches make. It can be a costly mistake as well, since doing the hardest workout last can lead to insufficient recovery, maladaptation, or injury.

HIGHER INTENSITY MEANS A SHORTER ADAPTATION PROCESS, LONGER RECOVERY, AND LOWER WORKOUT DENSITY.

Most ultrarunners are intensity-averse, which means they do anything they can to avoid running very, very hard. If you are among the ultrarunning crowd that fears high-intensity work, the type of work that makes your lungs sear and your legs burn, the next paragraph will be a relief.

One of the saving graces of high-intensity work is that it takes very little of it to produce an adaptation. Hooray! The time you work at that intensity during any particular workout and the total number of consecutive weeks necessary to produce an adaptation are relatively small compared to the amount of moderate and lower-intensity work. Because of this, I never hesitate to work with "time-crunched" ultrarunners, because I can take their most time-crunched periods and still get excellent adaptations at high intensities. You can see that concept reflected in Figures 8.2 and 9.1, which show the time course for training adaptation.

But wait, there's more! It takes longer to recover from high-intensity work, which means that, workout for workout, you need more rest and recovery between sessions to get your body ready for the next hard session. From a practical standpoint, most high-intensity phases, particularly RunningIntervals, need to be only two or three weeks long to elicit an appropriate adaptation. So, the total number of "hard" workouts is markedly smaller because the length of the phase is shorter and the density of the hard workouts is lower. See Figure 12.2A (SteadyStateRun) and Figure 12.2B (RunningIntervals) for a comparison between a higher-intensity phase and a lower-intensity phase. SteadyStateRun is at a lower intensity, and therefore that phase can be longer than a RunningInterval phase.

LOWER INTENSITY MEANS A LONGER ADAPTATION PROCESS, SHORTER RECOVERY, AND HIGHER WORKOUT DENSITY.

Workouts like EnduranceRuns, SteadyStateRuns, and to a lesser extent TempoRuns are typically at low enough intensities that it takes many weeks to accumulate enough training stress to produce an adaptation. Most ultra-athletes intuitively realize this, as their day-to-day training is mainly a compilation of EnduranceRuns ad nauseam. It is important to realize that even at the slightly higher intensities of SteadyStateRun and TempoRun, this can still be the case. Given the right construct, you should be able to handle back-to-back SteadyStateRun and TempoRun days for at least some of the phase and be able to stay in these phases for more than three weeks. At the TempoRun intensity, I have my athletes do these workouts two to three times per week, often scheduling two of these workouts on consecutive days. For SteadyStateRuns, that workout density gets pushed to four times per week in certain weeks.

During the long-range planning process, I always alert my athletes to what the hardest phase will be. The purpose is to better prepare them for what is to come. During that

(A)

MON	TUES	WED	THURS	FRI	SAT	SUN
5	6	7	8	9	10	11
Rest Day	1:45 EnduranceRun with 2 x 30 min SteadyStateRun, 5 min recovery between intervals	1:00 RecoveryRun	1:45 EnduranceRun with 2 x 20 min SteadyStateRun, 5 min recovery between intervals	1:00 RecoveryRun	2:00 EnduranceRun with 2 x 30 min SteadyStateRun, 5 min recovery between intervals	3:00 EnduranceRun
12	13	14	15	16	17	18
Rest Day	1:45 EnduranceRun with 2 x 30 min SteadyStateRun, 5 min recovery between intervals	1:00 RecoveryRun	1:45 EnduranceRun with 2 x 20 min SteadyStateRun, 5 min recovery between intervals	1:00 RecoveryRun	2:00 EnduranceRun with 2 x 20 min SteadyStateRun	3:30 EnduranceRun
19	20	21	22	23	24	25
Rest Day	1:45 EnduranceRun with 2 x 20 min SteadyStateRun, 5 min recovery between intervals	1:00 RecoveryRun	1:45 EnduranceRun with 1 x 30 min SteadyStateRun, 5 min recovery between intervals	1:00 RecoveryRun	1:30 EnduranceRun with 1 x 30 min SteadyStateRun	4:00 EnduranceRun
26	27	28	29	30	31	1
Rest Day	1:00 RecoveryRun	1:00 RecoveryRun	1:00 RecoveryRun	1:00 RecoveryRun	2:00 EnduranceRun with 2 x 30 min SteadyStateRun, 5 min recovery between intervals	3:00 EnduranceRun

(B)

MON	TUES	WED	THURS	FRI	SAT	SUN
5	6	7	8	9	10	11
Rest Day	1:30 EnduranceRun with 5 x 3 min RunningIntervals, 3 min recovery between intervals	1:00 RecoveryRun	1:30 EnduranceRun with 5 x 3 min RunningIntervals, 3 min recovery between intervals	1:00 RecoveryRun	1:30 EnduranceRun with 5 x 3 min RunningIntervals, 3 min recovery between intervals	2:00 EnduranceRun
12	13	14	15	16	17	18
Rest Day	1:30 EnduranceRun with 5 x 3 min RunningIntervals, 3 min recovery between intervals	1:00 RecoveryRun	1:00 RecoveryRun	1:30 EnduranceRun with 4 x 3 min RunningIntervals, 3 min recovery between intervals	1:00 RecoveryRun	2:00 EnduranceRun
19	20	21	22	23	24	25
Rest Day	1:00 RecoveryRun	1:30 EnduranceRun with 4 x 3 min RunningIntervals, 3 min recovery between intervals	0:45 RecoveryRun	0:45 RecoveryRun	1:00 RecoveryRun	1:00 RecoveryRun

FIGURE 12.2 (A) A typical SteadyStateRun phase; (B) a typical RunningInterval phase. Note that the SteadyStateRun phase is longer and includes less recovery between the workouts than the RunningInterval phase.

MON	TUES	WED	THURS	FRI	SAT	SUN
5	6	7	8	9	10	11
Rest Day	1:30 EnduranceRun with 3 x 10 min TempoRun, 5 min recovery between intervals	1:30 EnduranceRun with 3 x 8 min TempoRun, 4 min recovery between intervals	1:00 RecoveryRun	1:00 RecoveryRun	1:30 EnduranceRun with 3 x 10 min TempoRun, 5 min recovery between intervals	1:30 EnduranceRun with 3 x 8 min TempoRun, 4 min recovery between intervals
12	13	14	15	16	17	18
Rest Day	1:00 RecoveryRun	1:30 EnduranceRun with 3 x 10 min TempoRun, 5 min recovery between intervals	1:30 EnduranceRun with 3 x 8 min TempoRun, 4 min recovery between intervals	1:00 RecoveryRun	1:30 EnduranceRun with 3 x 8 min TempoRun, 4 min recovery between intervals	2:00 EnduranceRun
19	20	21	22	23	24	25
Rest Day	1:00 RecoveryRun	1:30 EnduranceRun with 3 x 8 min TempoRun, 4 min recovery between intervals	1:30 EnduranceRun with 3 x 8 min TempoRun, 4 min recovery between intervals	1:00 RecoveryRun	1:00 RecoveryRun	1:30 EnduranceRun with 3 x 8 min TempoRun, 4 min recovery between intervals
26	27	28	29	30	31	1
Rest Day	1:00 RecoveryRun	1:00 RecoveryRun	1:00 RecoveryRun	1:30 EnduranceRun with 3 x 12 min TempoRun, 6 min recovery between intervals	1:30 EnduranceRun with 3 x 10 min TempoRun, 5 min recovery between intervals	2:00 EnduranceRun

FIGURE 12.3 A back-to-back-style training plan. There is one additional hard workout, as compared to Figure 12.4. Even in this example, the hardest workouts are still early in the phase.

phase it is important to focus on recovery, get proper sleep, try to reschedule big work projects, and avoid other life stressors. If they are trying to change body composition, it is best to do it at some other point in the season. During this hardest phase, all of their spare energy will be needed for hard training and purposeful recovery. Ninety percent of the time this is the TempoRun, or lactate threshold, phase. Although this phase is not the most intense and does not have the biggest volume, it hits the right balance of volume and intensity. That balance tends to grind an athlete down over the course of time more so than higher intensities (with less volume) or lower intensities (with higher volume).

MON	TUES	WED	THURS	FRI	SAT	SUN
5	6	7	8	9	10	11
Rest Day	1:30 EnduranceRun with 3 x 10 min TempoRun, 5 min recovery between intervals	1:00 RecoveryRun	1:30 EnduranceRun with 3 x 8 min TempoRun, 4 min recovery between intervals	1:00 RecoveryRun	1:30 EnduranceRun with 3 x 10 min TempoRun, 5 min recovery between intervals	2:00 EnduranceRun
12	13	14	15	16	17	18
Rest Day	1:30 EnduranceRun with 3 x 10 min TempoRun, 5 min recovery between intervals	1:00 RecoveryRun	1:30 EnduranceRun with 3 x 8 min TempoRun, 4 min recovery between intervals	1:00 RecoveryRun	1:30 EnduranceRun with 3 x 10 min TempoRun, 5 min recovery between intervals	2:00 EnduranceRun
19	20	21	22	23	24	25
Rest Day	1:30 EnduranceRun with 3 x 8 min TempoRun, 4 min recovery between intervals	1:00 RecoveryRun	1:30 EnduranceRun with 3 x 8 min TempoRun, 4 min recovery between intervals	1:00 RecoveryRun	1:30 EnduranceRun with 3 x 8 min TempoRun, 4 min recovery between intervals	2:00 EnduranceRun
26	27	28	29	30	31	1
Rest Day	1:00 RecoveryRun	1:00 RecoveryRun	1:00 RecoveryRun	1:30 EnduranceRun with 3 x 12 min TempoRun, 6 min recovery between intervals	1:00 RecoveryRun	1:30 EnduranceRun with 3 x 10 min TempoRun, 5 min recovery between intervals

FIGURE 12.4 A non-back-to-back-style training example. There are only nine hard workouts, as compared to the ten in the back-to-back style.

The Case for Back-to-Back Hard Days

Should you run on tired legs? Yes, but not for the reason you might think. Many ultrarunners have adopted a strategy with their long runs in which they intentionally run long and far on consecutive days. The theory is that this type of training teaches your body to "run when it is tired," mimicking the demands of an ultramarathon. I adopt the back-to-back training strategy with my athletes in nearly every phase, so needless to say, I'm a fan. However, I take it a step further. Although I have my athletes do back-to-back long runs, I also have them do back-to-back days with SteadyStateRuns, TempoRuns, and, in certain circumstances, RunningIntervals. While using this strategy, you will certainly be more tired on the second day than the first. Your legs will feel like bricks, and if you have done the first workout correctly, you can't perform quite up to the level that you did on Day 1.

But I do not have my athletes do back-to-back days to teach them to "run on tired legs." I do it because the effect on the aerobic engine is greater when you are concentrate your training load. In addition, at times back-to-back days allow you to fit in one or two more high-quality workouts per phase (compare the examples in Figures 12.3 and 12.4). This is important because athletes tend to look at training from the standpoint of weekly volume, but you also need to consider your total workload for an entire phase of training. When you can schedule an extra workout or two within a period while still maintaining appropriate amounts of rest, you can wring greater gains out of that period of time. In practice, much of this strategy is adopted from other sports such as cross-country skiing and cycling (Rønnestad, Hansen, and Ellefsen 2014; Rønnestad et al. 2015). Even though running is a different sport and should be treated as such, many of the same principles apply across all aerobic sports. Taking this into account, I've adopted this block-style, load-concentration training strategy for the athletes I work with. Without a doubt, it's tricky to get right, and it requires careful monitoring of fatigue and performance. If you are designing your own training, I encourage you to first try back-to-back workouts at the SteadyStateRun intensity to see how you react. Do it once in a phase, preferably at the beginning. If you react well, you can try it across the course of the entire phase and then try it at different intensities.

How to Schedule Recovery Phases

By now, you have almost all of the tools to design your own training plan. You have laid out your LRP in accordance with the principles in Chapter 10. Your short-range plan is nice and tidy and awaiting the next workout. Now you have to answer the questions "When is enough, enough?" and "When do I need to recover?"

You have likely heard time and time again that "you don't get better until you rest." While this is true, the first part of the story is that you have to do the work—and you have to do enough of it to make a difference. That work, followed by an adequate recovery phase, should be enough to make small incremental improvements in your fitness.

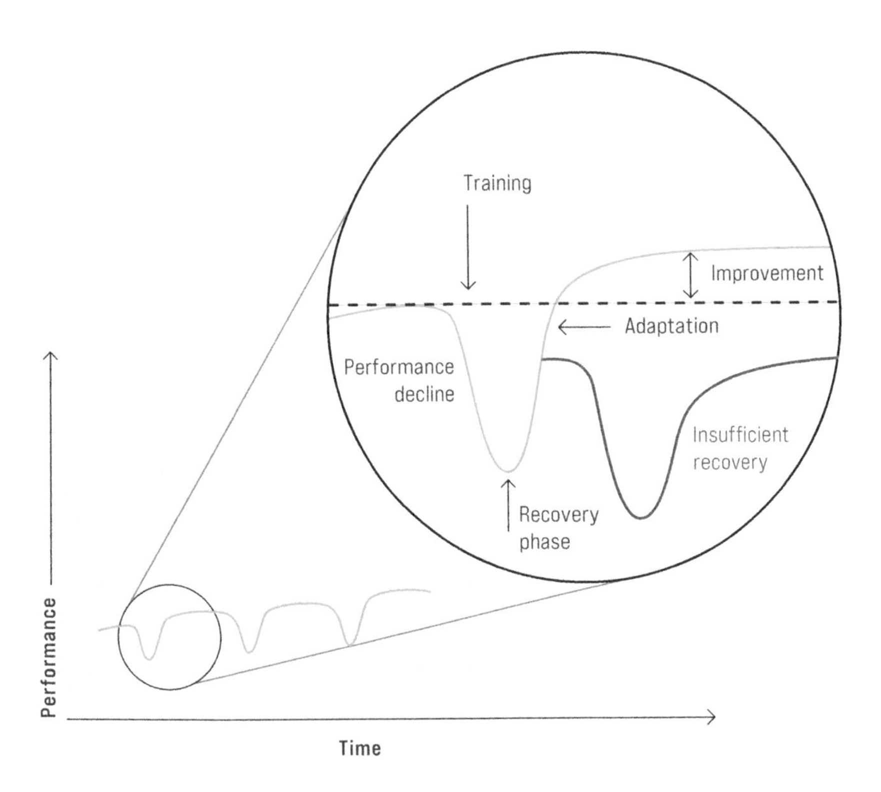

FIGURE 12.5 How fitness (green line) is affected over time from the applications of training stress and recovery.

So, what you should really be asking yourself is: "When have I done enough work?"

To answer that question, I've developed a three-point checklist I work through with every athlete when determining when to apply rest. It's based on physiology, practice, and, if available, wearable devices that can track things like sleep and HRV.

TRAINING MEANS YOUR PERFORMANCE WILL DETERIORATE BEFORE YOU GET BETTER

Before getting to the checklist, we all need to understand that, fundamentally, training makes your performance deteriorate in the short term (days and weeks) before you get better in the long term (weeks and months). You have to train hard enough that your body says, "Dang, this is hard. I better build up some more physiological stuff if I want to keep doing this and not die." Without a difficult-enough training stress *and then* the requisite recovery, you won't improve. You have to have both, not simply one or the other.

In this sense training can look like a good stock market chart with "performance" on the y-axis and "time" on the x-axis. The general trend over long periods of time will be upward, but it is certainly not trending up every single week.

The take-home message here is that you can't set PRs every week. If you are, congratulations! You are either new to the sport and/or your training is too easy and will stagnate at some point. Even if you have a moderate amount of training background, you should fully expect your performance to get moderately worse in some way before you apply rest and see further improvements.

POINT 1: PERFORMANCE DECLINES

The first and most powerful indicator that you need to rest is when your daily performance starts to decline past a certain threshold. If you are regularly doing intervals and harder runs, you will have some basis of performance to benchmark week to week. By comparing the Normalized Graded Pace or Grade Adjusted Pace for the intervals and/or your weekly hard runs, you can see if they are getting better, getting worse, or staying the same. When your performance drops off by 3 to 8 percent on more than two out of the last three workouts, it's time to give yourself a rest phase.

Any performance drop of less than 3 percent is within normal day-to-day variation. I would not even consider that a drop in performance, just noise in the measurement, so you can continue to train. Similarly, any one day where your performance drops by 3 to 8 percent should be expected, and I would not think twice about continuing to train.

However, stack two out of three sequential workouts that show a marked decline in performance, and that is a good indicator you have enough cumulative fatigue to warrant a rest phase. This is about finding the sweet spot between enough stress to make your body adapt and not so much that it will take an undue time to recover.

POINT 2: WHEN YOU FEEL WORSE FOR THREE DAYS IN A ROW

Besides performance decline indicating when you need to rest, how you feel day to day can also be an indicator of overall fatigue. Just like one difficult training day should not keep you from your next workout, one day where you feel worse than you did the day before should not deter you either. However, if you feel progressively worse during your runs for three days in a row, it's time to take some recovery.

So, how bad do you have to feel to classify it as a "worse" day? Unlike hard workouts where you will have consistent and quantifiable benchmarks to compare against, feeling "worse" for three days in a row is in the eye of the beholder. If you are tracking your

RPE (which you should), this could mean that RPE is a point or two higher for a normal EnduranceRun effort. Or you can scroll back through your training comments (which you should also be logging) and look for how you described each workout. If your comments indicate that you are "sluggish," "flat," or any similar vocabulary, these are written descriptors that you are feeling run-down. In any case, don't try to find hard and fast metrics. If you simply feel worse during your runs for a few days in a row, that's enough of an indicator that you should bring some needed recovery into the mix.

POINT 3: WHEN THE TRAINING PHASE GETS LONG

Even in the absence of measurable performance declines or simply feeling bad, training phases can't last forever. But if your training is on fire, you feel good day in and day out, and you keep seeing improvements week to week, is there even a need to apply some recovery? The answer is yes.

It might be tempting to keep extending training phases in the absence of feeling fatigued or seeing a performance decline. But even in these circumstances, a rest phase reset should occur every so often. While there is no exact science to determine when to cap off a training block that seems to be going swimmingly, I only let training phases last for six weeks, maximum, before applying rest. The six-week maximum time frame is based a bit on experience as well as science. When researchers look at the time it takes for training to make an impact on performance, the general time frame is four to six weeks—meaning when you do a hard workout or series of hard workouts, it takes your body four to six weeks to harvest that work into some meaningful improvement in performance and/or physiology. So, incorporating rest near the end of this time frame allows you to take advantage of your body's natural buildup and breakdown processes.

WHAT ABOUT MONITORING HEART RATE VARIABILITY, RESTING HEART RATE, AND SLEEP CYCLES?

More recently, various tools that measure physiological and lifestyle variables have become popular among athletes trying to gain a performance edge. Wearable technologies like the Whoop Strap and Oura Ring have emerged with a promise to determine when you are fatigued, whether your sleep is compromised, and when you should take a nap. I have seen and used these tools for decades, dating all the way back to taking a waking

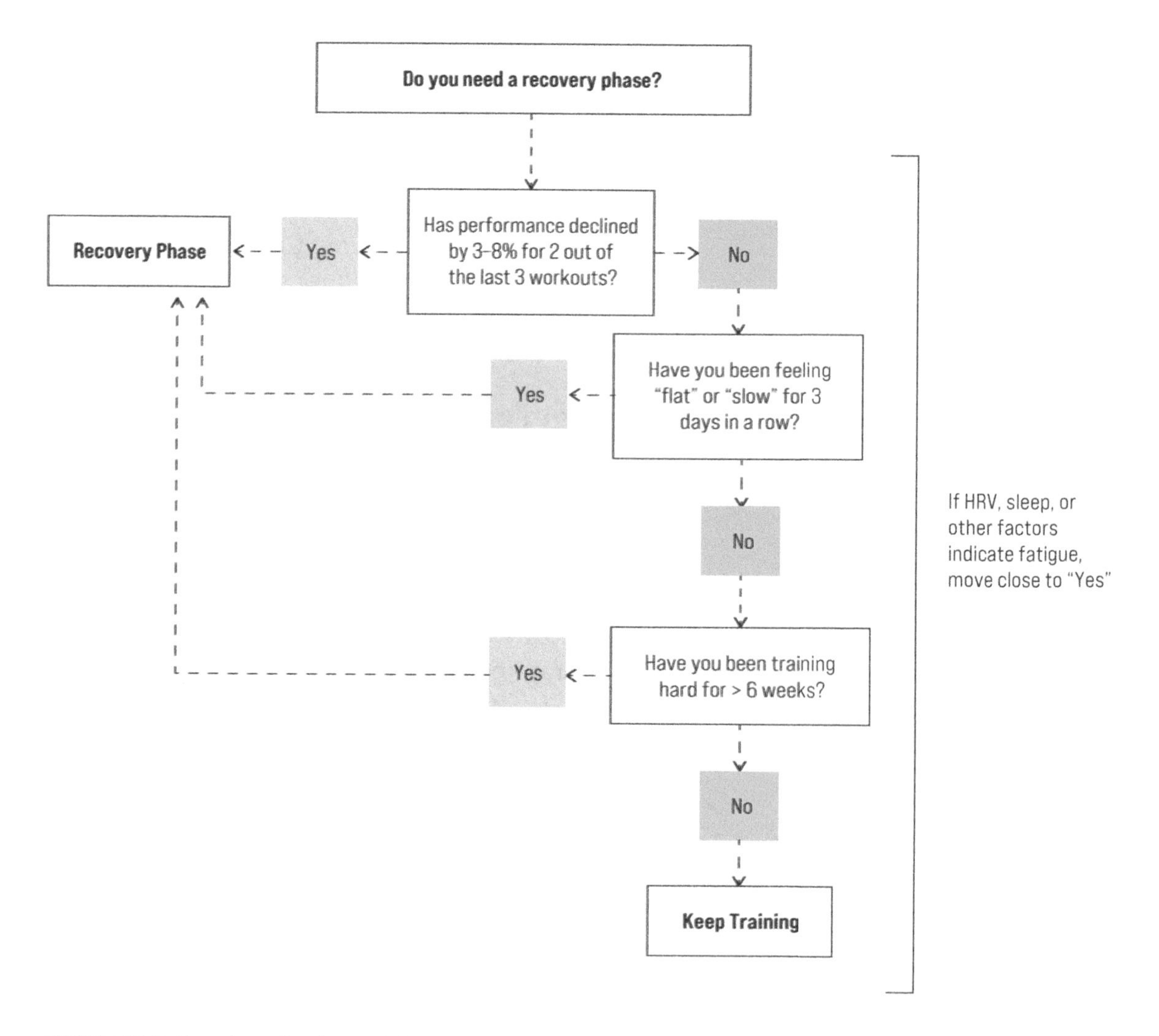

FIGURE 12.6 Flowchart for determining whether it is time to incorporate a recovery phase.

pulse on my wrist with no more technology than my fingers and a watch.

While these new devices can add value to the training process, it's important to keep context in mind and not let the data tail wag the performance dog. Performance, or lack thereof, will still be your best indicator of when to apply rest. Information from wearables simply adds detail to the picture. This information should ever so slightly nudge you to "yes, I need to rest" or "no, I can keep training," but it should not drive the process.

ARCHITECTURE OF THE RECOVERY PHASE

Don't overcomplicate this. Your recovery phase should consist of between four and six days of forty-five- to sixty-minute RecoveryRuns, with maybe an extra rest day thrown in for good measure. From the elite athletes I work with to the average Janes and Joes, this structure is almost universal. It's almost impossible to over-recover from runs being too short (duration) or workouts being too easy (intensity). You can, however, over-recover if you take seven or more days easy, because beyond that time frame the benefit of more rest won't outweigh the gradual decay of your fitness. So, rest hard for several days, get your legs back underneath you, maybe catch up on some sleep, and get back after it once the recovery phase is over.

DON'T BE AFRAID TO REST EARLY

When designing your short-range plan, realize that much of the time you will be guessing (in an educated way, of course). You will be forecasting how you will feel two to four or even six weeks from when you are creating your plan. Sometimes you are going to get that forecast right, and other times you will over- or undershoot how much training you can actually handle. Life adds nontraining stress to the mix in the form of working late, playing the soccer coach, and helping the kids out with schoolwork. Thus, you will also have to adapt to what is going on in real time.

When you are working through the aforementioned checklist, don't be afraid to rest early. Realize that your body can only handle so much stress over long periods of time, and it is usually advantageous to err on the side of resting early. If you slightly undershoot the length of the current training phase, you are going to give your body the ability to extend the next one. It will all come out in the wash as long as you are being reasonable phase to phase, working hard when you can, and backing off when you reach one of the three thresholds described above.

Tapering for Your Event

Iñigo Mujika, a highly regarded sports physiologist known for his work on tapering and detraining, has defined tapering as "a progressive nonlinear reduction of the training load during a variable period of time, in an attempt to reduce the physiological and psychological stress of daily training and optimize sports performance" (Mujika and Padilla 2000a).

Contrary to what most popular literature with clickbait headlines will tell you, tapering will not make or break your race. On average, you stand to gain 3 percent from a properly constructed taper (Mujika and Padilla 2003). However, the difference is minimized when you consider that the 3 percent increase is from the baseline of implementing no taper at all. With simple, reasonable rest before your event, you might gain 2 percent, whereas if you designed the most scientific and effective taper ever, you would gain 3 percent. That's a difference of 1 percent, which is not much for most athletes. Yes, you should still implement a taper before your event. But you should also be realistic about what you expect to gain from it, be reasonable about the duration of your taper, and not worry too much if things don't go perfectly to plan. Remember, Mujika talks about reduction of physiological and psychological stress as goals of a taper, so stressing about achieving the perfect taper is counterproductive.

BEFORE YOU TAPER

Train. One of the primary pitfalls of tapering occurs when athletes go into their goal event lacking confidence in their fitness. Remember Figure 10.4 and the time course for adaptation? Another point that chart illustrates is that after a period of time, if you are training properly, each subsequent workout results in fewer positive adaptations than the last. So, put in the work early. During the final two months of training, it's all about fine-tuning the fitness you have already built.

THE BASICS OF TAPERING

The purpose of a taper is to simultaneously reduce the negative aspects of training (fatigue) and enhance the positive ones (fitness). This combination will leave you more fit and psychologically prepared for race day. The great thing is, by reducing the negative aspects of training, you naturally enhance the positive ones. From a strategic standpoint, this is crucial. Tapering fundamentally revolves around first reducing certain training variables; then, as a consequence of that reduction, adaptation takes place. In this way, *tapering is not "maintenance,"* which is a word that is carelessly thrown around (as in "I am going to maintain my fitness"). No athlete has ever come to me in my coaching career with "maintenance" as a goal. It should not be yours during the tapering process. Tapering is not maintenance. Tapering improves your physiology, leaving you more fit and ready to perform.

Training is a combination of volume, intensity, frequency, and environment. These four variables can be used to describe nearly every workout for an ultrarunner. When talking tapering, it's best to break it down into how these four variables should be manipulated. Before breaking tapering down by these variables, though, we need to talk about perspective. I love science. It provides a platform from which we have the opportunity to work and explore. The fundamentals provide the base, and we get to build on top of it. Every so often, though, science gets too caught up in the minutiae. Tapering is one of those areas.

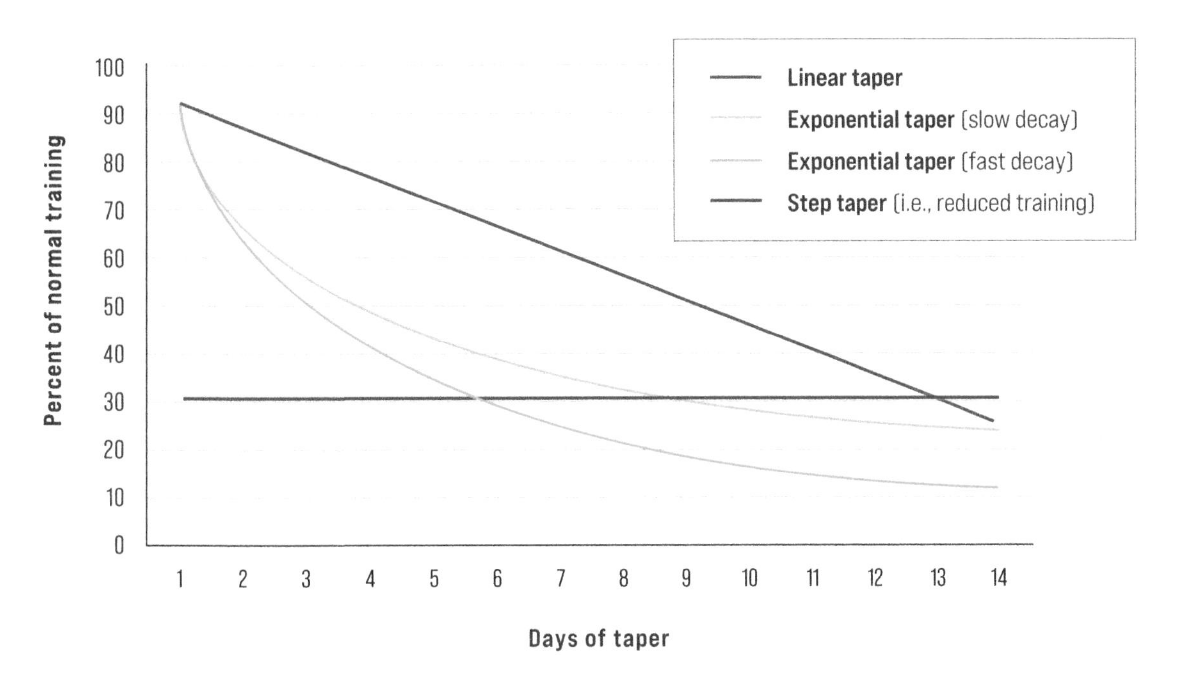

FIGURE 12.7 Schematic representation of the different types of tapers. Adapted from Mujika and Padilla 2003.

If you review the best literature on tapering, the research will recommend a "nonlinear, fast-decay reduction" of training load. This reduction takes the shape of the green line shown in Figure 12.7, which illustrates two types of nonlinear reduction, fast and slow decay, as well as a step reduction (reducing training load by a set percentage all at once) and a linear reduction (reducing training load at a fixed percentage day after day).

While I love the ingenuity of this graph and the countless hours spent on its development, this level of minutiae is impractical. For example, if you follow a "fast-decay" tapering process, on Day 5 your daily training volume is supposed to be at 32.5 percent. If you were normally doing a two-hour run, this means that your run for Day 5 should be thirty-nine minutes. Not forty or thirty-eight, but exactly thirty-nine. There's nothing magical about thirty-nine minutes of running on Day 5 of a taper or any other day. Athletes are human beings, not machines or lab rats. In my experience, it's best to understand the science and then find ways to use it practically.

Now, with a bit of perspective in hand, let's look at the best overarching strategies for tapering based on the current literature. For the purposes of calibration, in this discussion of the components of training, I am assuming a three-week tapering process for a runner who is training ten hours per week.

Volume: Reduce

Adjusting volume is your first step in the tapering process. Using a fast-decay tapering model, volume should decrease very quickly at first and then level off toward the end. Thus, if you start with an overall volume of ten hours per week, you should reduce that to four to five hours (40 to 50 percent of normal training volume) per week the first week, two to three hours (20 to 30 percent of normal training volume) the second week, and two hours maximum (<20 percent of normal training volume) in the last week.

Intensity: Reduce the Amount, Not the Type

Intensity is where things get a little tricky. The overarching strategy is to reduce the volume of intensity you do during the week but not the type of intensity. The amount that you reduce the intensity should follow the "fast-decay" strategy. Thus, similar to how you would reduce overall volume, you would reduce the volume of intensity quickly at first and then more slowly toward the end. For example, if in a normal training week you are doing four by ten-minute TempoRuns for a workout, during Taper Week 1 you would do three by five-minute TempoRuns (37.5 percent of the normal TempoRun volume). In Week 2 you would do two by five-minute TempoRuns (25 percent of the normal TempoRun volume), and in the last week one by five minutes (12.5 percent of the normal TempoRun volume).

Maintaining training intensity is a critical part of the tapering process. This is because the small amount of intensity that is done prevents a decline in the hard-earned benefits you have worked for in training (Hickson et al. 1985; Sheply et al. 1992).

Frequency: Maintain or Slightly Reduce

Frequency should be maintained or slightly reduced. This means that if you are running five days per week, continue running five days per week. If you are doing two specific workouts per week (TempoRun, SteadyStateRun, etc.), continue doing those two specific workouts per week using the guidelines above for reducing the volume of intensity for those workouts. If you decide to reduce the frequency of training, only do so by one day per week.

Environment: Maintain

Whatever terrain and vertical specificity you have been doing in training leading up to a race, maintain that during the taper. This means if you have been running on trails, continue to run on trails. If you have been running on roads, run on roads. One of the mistakes I see over and over again is athletes who are targeting mountainous trail events train on specific trails for those events but then change that specificity for their taper. They run around the track in Chamonix in preparation for the Ultra-Trail du Mont-Blanc, for instance. This violates the final tapering strategy of specificity.

THE TAPER TANTRUMS

The previously mentioned strategies are primarily (but not exclusively) aimed at improving your physiological state before an event. Your psychological state is just as important. And although the tapering strategies presented here have been demonstrated to also improve psychological qualities (Hooper, Mackinnon, and Howard 1999; Morgan et al. 1987; Raglin et al. 1996), many athletes still struggle with this aspect of race preparation. They feel as if they are losing fitness or missing out on training. The two to three weeks spent tapering seem to go on forever, and they doubt the process. They become antsy for the event, feel sluggish during their day-to-day life and runs, and become irritable and difficult to live with. This is normal, and it is important to understand that the "taper tantrums" are part of the process.

Angst and unease are normal psychological reactions to a taper. During the taper, you have more time and energy available than during your earlier training. That excess time and energy has to go somewhere, and many athletes utilize it simply to fret. To release their energy, they pack and repack their luggage, obsessively analyze splits, and second-guess their choice of socks. Any rational person observing these actions from the outside would probably get a chuckle, but these athletes aren't doing themselves any favors by expending their energy this way.

To better handle your taper, trust your training. If you have done the right things in training, the taper becomes easier to handle. Have confidence that the miles, vertical, and intensity you have put in over the previous months are going to pay off. Even if your training has not gone perfectly, if you have been conscientious and dedicated to the process, you should trust that you have done enough.

Create the right mindset for tapering. I routinely ask my athletes to review their training just in advance of their taper. Specifically I have them look at the sheer quantity of time they have dedicated to the process. The enormity of what they have done over the last several months puts the last few workouts in perspective. Those last workouts are a very, very small part of the entire process.

Avoid the taper tantrums by trusting your training and the tapering process. If you trust that you are going to come out the other side of a taper refreshed and ready for the event, the time you spend not running suddenly has purpose.

This is an excellent time to put your excess energy into rest. Yes, this takes just as much focus and energy as training, maybe even more so for ultrarunners. Take the time you had previously set aside for training and deliberately, intentionally set it aside for purposeful rest.

KEY POINTS FOR SHORT-RANGE PLANNING

- Do the hardest workouts when you are freshest. This is typically after a recovery week.
- Consequentially, the volume of intensity for your workouts should decrease as the training phase progresses.
- The higher the intensity of the training you are doing, the shorter any one phase can be.
- RunningInterval phases can be two to four weeks followed by a four- to five-day recovery phase.
- TempoRun phases can be three to four weeks followed by a four- to five-day recovery phase.
- SteadyStateRun phases can be three to six weeks followed by a four- to five-day recovery phase.
- Rest phases of four to six days should be incorporated when any of the following criteria are met:
  - Performance declines by 3 to 8 percent on two out of the last three workouts.
  - You feel worse during runs on three consecutive days.
- You are in the same phase for:
  - four weeks if doing RunningIntervals
  - four weeks if doing TempoRuns
  - six weeks if doing SteadyStateRuns
- Start tapering two to three weeks out from an event.
  - Reduce your overall training load (overall volume and volume of intensity, but not the intensity itself) quickly at first, then gradually toward the end.
  - Slightly reduce the frequency (days per week) or do not reduce the frequency at all.
  - Maintain specificity (environment and running surface).

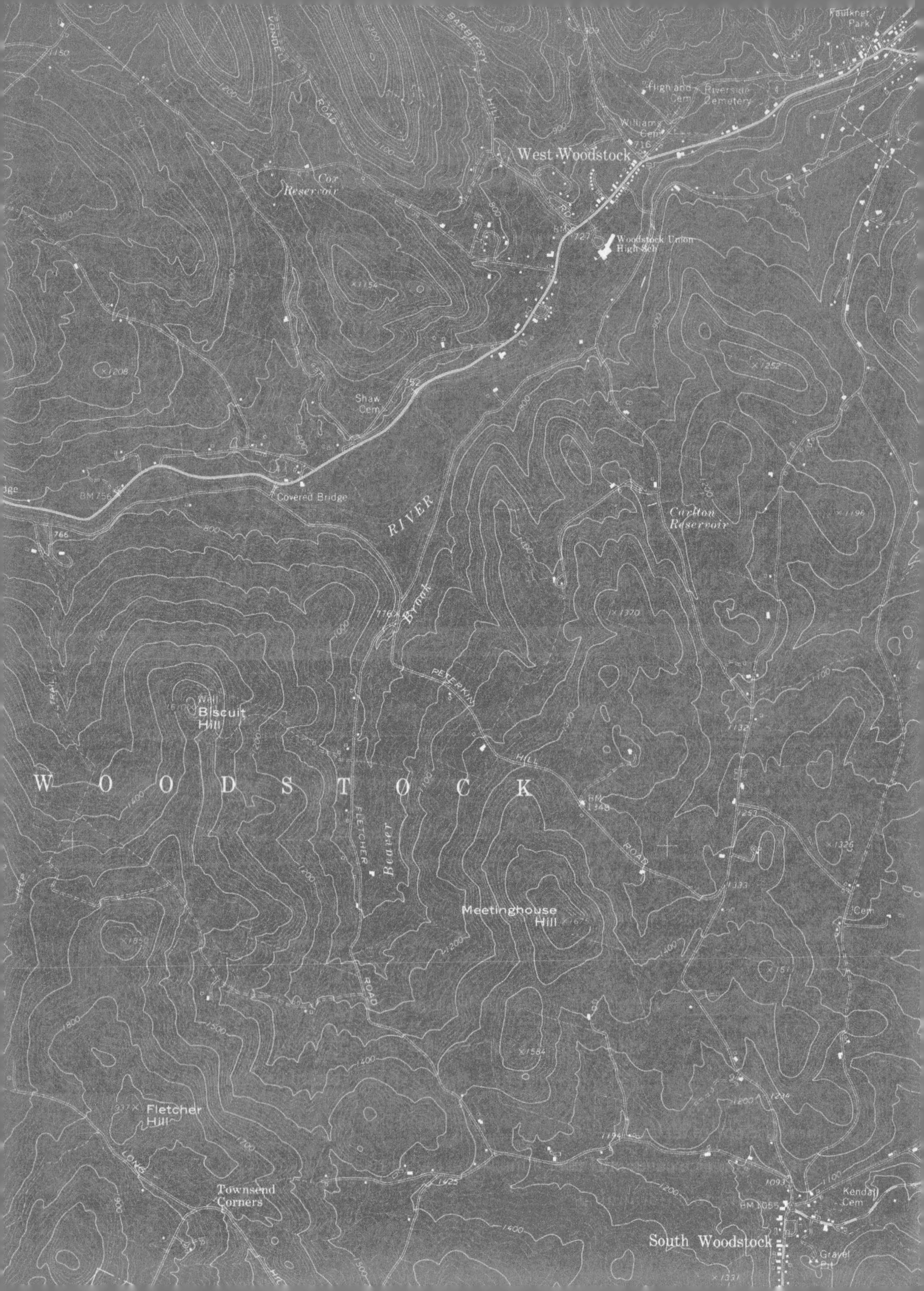

Faulkner Park
Highland Cem
Riverside Cemetery
Williams Cem
West Woodstock
Cox Reservoir
Woodstock Union High Sch
Shaw Cem
Covered Bridge
BM 756
RIVER
Carlton Reservoir
Brook
PETERKIN
HILL
ROAD
Biscuit Hill
W O O D S T O C K
FLETCHER
Beaver
Meetinghouse Hill
Cem
Fletcher Hill
Townsend Corners
Kendall Cem
BM 1055
South Woodstock
Gravel Pit

CHAPTER 13

Fueling and Hydrating for the Long Haul

Ultramarathon fueling is tricky. The duration and changing environmental conditions befuddle the nutrition programs of novice and experienced athletes alike. This assertion is supported by the fact that gastrointestinal distress is the leading reason athletes cite as the main cause of DNFs. I've already shown that your ability to physically complete the distance is not a limiting factor for success and that with structured training and smart planning you can overcome the challenges inherent in any ultramarathon course. But all that comes undone when your nutrition and hydration strategies fail. To optimize your performance and have the tools to work through adversity, you need a clear understanding of the fueling challenges specific to ultra-endurance sports, as well as nutrition and hydration strategies that work specifically for you.

Essential Elements of Sports Nutrition

Before we can talk about the nutrition challenges that are specific to ultramarathon athletes, we need to be on the same page in terms of the principles of sports nutrition. There are entire textbooks—and an entire profession—devoted to this topic, but in this book I'm going to cover only the essentials so we can move on to information that's more specific to ultrarunning.

MACRONUTRIENTS AND ENERGY PRODUCTION

Food is made up of three macronutrients: carbohydrate, protein, and fat. All the energy you expend comes from burning calories from these three sources, and you derive energy from all three sources at all times and at all levels of activity. The percentage of energy derived from each macronutrient depends on how quickly you need to produce energy and how much of a supply of each nutrient you have. Sitting and reading this book, you're deriving the vast majority of your energy from fat, although your brain (which is very engaged in learning, right?) is using carbohydrate. Not to be left out, protein is quietly working in the background repairing muscle damage from your last run, helping to maintain your immune system, growing skin and blood cells, and so forth. Protein contributes little to energy production, yet its role is still vital.

When you go for a run or increase your energy demand through any activity, your body responds by ramping up the rate at which macronutrients are broken down into usable energy. During aerobic exercise, energy production happens primarily in mitochondria, which are small organelles in cells (in this case, in muscle cells). Your mitochondria take broken-down carbohydrate and fat and produce carbon dioxide, water, and resynthesized adenosine triphosphate (ATP), the molecule that produces energy. Mitochondria are massively important for endurance performance; having more and bigger mitochondria gives you the ability to process more fuel per minute of exercise.

As you ramp up energy production in response to increased demand, the composition of your fuel mixture changes. The percentage of energy derived from carbohydrate exponentially increases, and this increase continues as exercise intensity rises from an endurance pace to lactate threshold and above. We'll get into the reason for this a bit later. For now, what's important to remember is that while the percentage of energy derived from carbohydrate increases dramatically with demand, the absolute amounts of fat and protein being used for energy also increase, and protein only minimally contributes to energy production.

There has long been a misconception that low-intensity exercise is fueled by fat, high-intensity exercise is fueled by carbohydrate, and there's a magical switch that gets thrown when you cross a certain pace. There's no switch. Absolute fat utilization increases as your exercise intensity increases from a RecoveryRun intensity to an

EnduranceRun intensity. As you reach higher intensities, near the upper end of your EnduranceRun or lower end of TempoRun intensities—or 60 to 70 percent of VO_2 max, depending on trainability (Maunder et al. 2018)—fat oxidation will begin to decline in order to support exercise at these higher intensities. But there is no all-or-nothing switch from one fuel source to another.

Another reason people misunderstand fat utilization is because they consider it to be a limitless source of available energy, without consideration of the physiological limitations on liberating energy from fat. Although fat is a great source of energy, it takes longer for your body to break down compared to carbohydrate. At rest and at low exercise intensities, you don't use much carbohydrate for energy. In fact, as you sit reading this book, 80 to 90 percent of your energy is coming from fat. At very low exercise intensities (20 to 25 percent of VO_2 max), you still rely on fat for about 70 percent of your energy because your body naturally conserves carbohydrate whenever it can. This conservation strategy is necessary because you can store only about 1,600 to 2,000 calories of carbohydrate onboard your body (primarily in your muscles and liver). In contrast, even a lean athlete (70 kg/154 lbs and 10 percent body fat) has more than 53,000 calories of stored fat.

MEASUREMENTS: IMPERIAL VS METRIC

AT TIMES IN THIS BOOK I use imperial units (feet of elevation, miles of distance), and at other times I use metric units (VO_2 expressed as milliliters per kilogram per minute or energy expenditure expressed as one calorie per kilogram per kilometer). In this chapter I will be using grams per kilogram to describe the amounts of a nutrient to consume based on your body weight. Why not stick with either imperial or metric throughout? I'm walking the fine line between using common terms for a US audience and correctly representing data used in the sports science and sports nutrition professions. It wouldn't make sense to translate grams per kilogram into ounces per pound or to create an imperial version of VO_2 max values.

As you read this chapter, there will be some sample conversions from kilograms to pounds. To determine your weight in kilograms, divide your weight in pounds by 2.2.

As you reach 60 to 70 percent of VO_2 max, fuel utilization comes equally from fat and carbohydrate. Better-trained athletes will reach and maintain this fifty-fifty balance at a higher percentage of their VO_2 max than athletes who are less fit. As exercise intensity increases above 60 percent of VO_2 max, the relative contribution from carbohydrate increases dramatically—but remember, even when you're burning a lot of carbohydrate at higher exercise intensities, you are still processing fat and carbohydrate using aerobic metabolism. For most athletes, once you exceed your lactate threshold intensity (70 to 90 percent of VO_2 max, depending on your fitness level), more than 80 percent of your energy is derived from carbohydrate. This, by the way, is one of the fatal flaws of extremely low-carbohydrate nutritional strategies for athletes. When you severely

FIGURE 13.1 (A) Fat and carbohydrate oxidation expressed in g/min. (B) Fat and carbohydrate oxidation represented as a percent of total energy expenditure (EE).

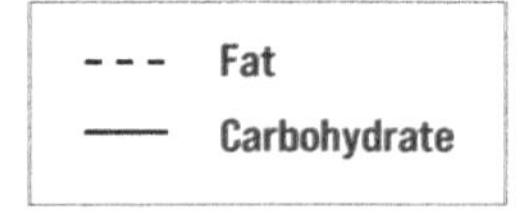

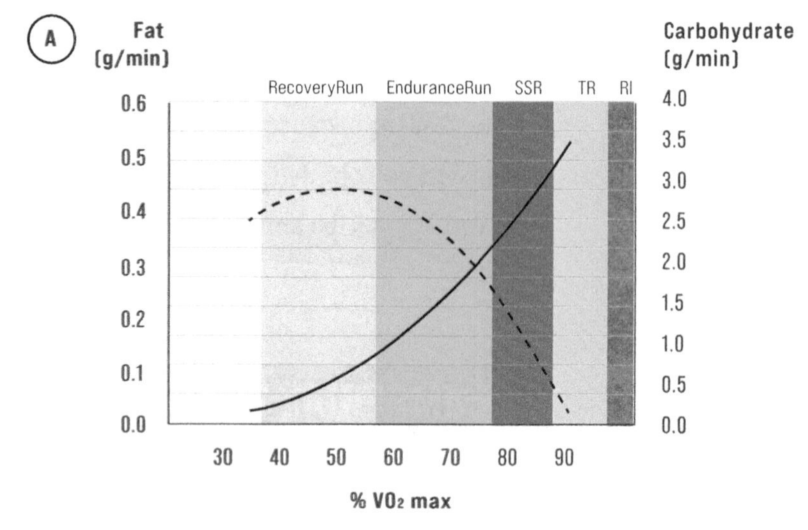

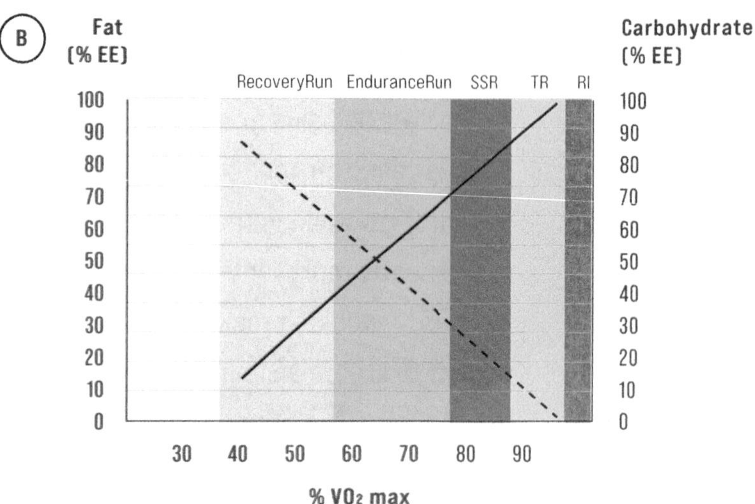

limit the amount of carbohydrate available to working muscles, you are limited by the rate at which your muscles can break down and process fat, which requires more oxygen (approximately 8 percent more than carbohydrate). As a result, you can keep moving forward, but you will be doing so at a slower pace at the same relative intensity.

As energy demand increases, carbohydrate can be broken down to release a portion of its potential energy quickly. This is called "glycolysis," and though it yields less energy per molecule of carbohydrate as compared to complete oxidation of carbohydrate, it provides energy to the working muscles faster.

What happens to the leftover metabolic byproducts from glycolysis? Well, the substrate that matters most in this discussion is lactate. This is the stuff that's unfairly developed a bad rap for years. It has been blamed for everything from the burning sensation in your muscles to delayed-onset muscle soreness. People have tried to massage it away, flush it out, and buffer it. Despite the lack of clarity on the subject, two things have become abundantly clear: (1) lactate is not the cause of fatigue we once thought it was, and (2) the best way to get rid of lactate is to reintegrate it as fuel into normal aerobic metabolism to complete the process of breaking it down into energy, water, and carbon dioxide. Endurance training, particularly when done at a variety of intensities, does this very well. The resulting training adaptations also enable you to recover from hard efforts more quickly, because deriving energy from glycolysis is like buying energy on credit: you have to pay the bill by slowing down, but when you can process lactate faster, you don't have to slow down as much or for as long.

So, where is protein in all this? Some people push protein as the preferred fuel, perhaps because high school biology taught us that muscle is made of protein, and therefore we need to eat protein in order to use our muscles. Protein is indeed necessary for building and maintaining muscle tissue, but it's not a very good fuel for exercise. For the most part, it has to be transported to the liver and converted into carbohydrate via gluconeogenesis so it can be transported back to muscles and burned as fuel. Protein plays important roles in sports nutrition (muscle protein synthesis, immune function, production of enzymes, etc.), but those roles don't include being a primary fuel source. Some protein does get broken down for energy, but regardless of exercise intensity, protein contributes only 10 to 15 percent of your total caloric expenditure.

MICRONUTRIENTS

Vitamins and minerals are micronutrients. Although you don't derive energy directly from them or need to consume them in quantities anywhere near as large as macronutrients (hence the name), they are essential for your health and performance because of their roles in producing energy, binding oxygen to red blood cells, maintaining bone density, producing muscle contractions, and much more. Because my focus here is sports nutrition for training and competition, in this section I focus on the vitamins and minerals that impact performance most directly.

Micronutrients like calcium, magnesium, zinc, and iron are important. So are vitamins A through K. But during training sessions and competitions, you neither lose very much of these micronutrients through sweat nor use very much to keep going. You are, however, eating quite a bit of food to replenish the calories you are expending. Micronutrient consumption, then, is not much of an issue for ultrarunners, because you are consuming plenty in the foods you are eating, and you are not losing or using much (relatively speaking) in the course of a training session or even an ultramarathon. In terms of performance, a normally healthy person—someone who does not have a condition causing a micronutrient deficiency—won't really improve performance by focusing on micronutrient intake or supplementation. Your body is already doing everything that needs to be done, provided you have a diverse diet that contains an adequate number of total calories and does not eliminate specific foods or macronutrients.

The Essential Roles of Fluids

When it comes to sports nutrition for ultra-endurance events, fluids are even more important than calories. During exercise, macronutrients have one essential job: to provide energy to working muscles. Water, in contrast, plays a wide variety of roles, and each of them is mission critical.

CORE TEMPERATURE REGULATION

Regulating your core temperature is water's most obvious role during exercise. As you exercise, some of the energy you burn produces the work that moves you forward, but unfortunately even more energy is wasted as heat. This is the price we pay for our overall lack of efficiency. The problem is that the human body operates properly only within a narrow temperature range, from 97°F to 104°F, with temperatures between 97°F and 100°F being optimal for performance (Gleeson 1998). Consequently, a lot of the heat generated from exercise has to be dissipated in order to maintain a core temperature within the optimal range.

Sweat is the body's primary cooling mechanism, with evaporative cooling carrying heat away from the body. As your core temperature rises, sweat glands all over your body start producing more sweat by drawing in fluid from the space around them and secreting sweat onto the surface of the skin. That fluid gets replaced by fluid from your blood plasma, making your blood volume a major reservoir of potential sweat.

As we'll cover in more detail later in this chapter, the amount of fluid an athlete needs to consume depends largely on sweat rate and body size, which can vary greatly depending on exercise intensity, air temperature, wind conditions, and humidity.

GUT MOTILITY AND DIGESTION

Without enough fluid, you cannot break down and absorb food effectively, which means your nutrition strategy is dependent on your hydration status. After food gets broken down in the stomach and travels to the small intestine, the nutrients, fluid, and everything else you want from that food has to be transported through the selective semipermeable membrane that makes up the wall of your intestine. To get carbohydrate from the intestine into the blood, you need to have enough water in the intestine to facilitate the transport. If you don't, the food sits there until enough water becomes available, either because you drink more or because it is pulled from your body into your intestine. This latter mechanism isn't ideal in any circumstance, but it is not a big problem when you are at rest and well hydrated. When you are exercising and pumping sweat onto your skin to cool off, however, your body prioritizes thermoregulation over digestion, and digestion slows dramatically. This is often the tipping point for gastrointestinal distress because once gut motility drops, it can take a long time for it to return to normal, and food that sits in the gut starts to ferment and is jostled around, leading to pressure, bloating, and a cascade of gastrointestinal issues you want to avoid.

BLOOD VOLUME

You have about 4.5 to 5.5 L of blood in your body, and it never stops moving. Athletes and coaches focus on blood's role in delivering oxygen to working muscles, but blood also delivers the nutrients your cells need to function and takes away the waste they produce. Blood also carries heat away from the core to the extremities and skin in order to maintain a healthy body temperature. Finally, blood plasma provides the fluid that ends up being excreted as sweat. One of the key responses to training and acclimation to heat and/or altitude is an increase in blood plasma volume. It's your body's way of filling the reservoir to be prepared for the anticipated activity and environment.

When you run low on fluids and plasma volume drops, your body starts prioritizing how to use what's left. In cold temperatures or in a cold summer rainstorm at high elevation, athletes with a better hydration status stay warmer longer. Dehydration hastens the onset of hypothermia. When it's hot outside and your plasma volume gets a little low, your resting and exercise heart rates increase. Your heart has to pump faster to deliver the same amount of oxygen using less fluid. When plasma volume gets even lower, your body prioritizes sweating over digestion, and if the situation gets dire, it prioritizes oxygen delivery over sweating, and you end up with heatstroke.

WASTE REMOVAL

Removal of metabolic waste products is another crucial role for fluids. This is of particular importance to ultrarunners because of the amount of muscle damage sustained during 50- and 100-mile events. The kidneys filter waste products out of your blood and excrete them in urine. With mild dehydration, urine production diminishes and the color of your urine starts to darken. More severe dehydration can damage your kidneys and alter the pH of your blood.

Day-to-Day Hydration Status

Fluid and electrolyte replenishment during exercise is heavily dependent on sweat rate and temperature. Fluid loss can range from 500 ml/hour to more than 2 L/hour, and electrolyte loss is greatly influenced by the composition of your sweat. Recommendations for fluid and sodium intake become far more complex during training and ultradistance competitions. I will cover those issues in more depth later in this chapter, but to start, let's examine recommendations that will help you stay well hydrated on a day-to-day basis.

Dehydration is often evaluated based on body weight. However, what many athletes don't realize is that they start their day or their workout already dehydrated. A 2 percent loss of body weight during your workout may not be truly 2 percent dehydration, but perhaps 4 percent dehydration if you started the day already low on body fluid.

Researchers Cheuvront and Sawka (2005) devised a simple Venn diagram that is useful for evaluating day-to-day hydration status (Figure 13.2). To use the diagram, you need to evaluate three things immediately after waking up: your weight (W), urine color (U), and thirst (T). If only one observation suggests dehydration but the other two are normal, dehydration is less likely. If two observations indicate dehydration, the condition is more likely. And if all three indicate dehydration, you're very likely to be dehydrated.

First, how thirsty are you? When you are low on body fluid, your body responds with the sensation of thirst. Although there is wide variability from person to person, research suggests dehydration of about 2 percent of body weight is associated with the sensation of thirst (Kenefick et al. 2012). Next comes urine color. The color of your urine is a common ballpark measure of urine concentration. Clear to straw-colored urine is

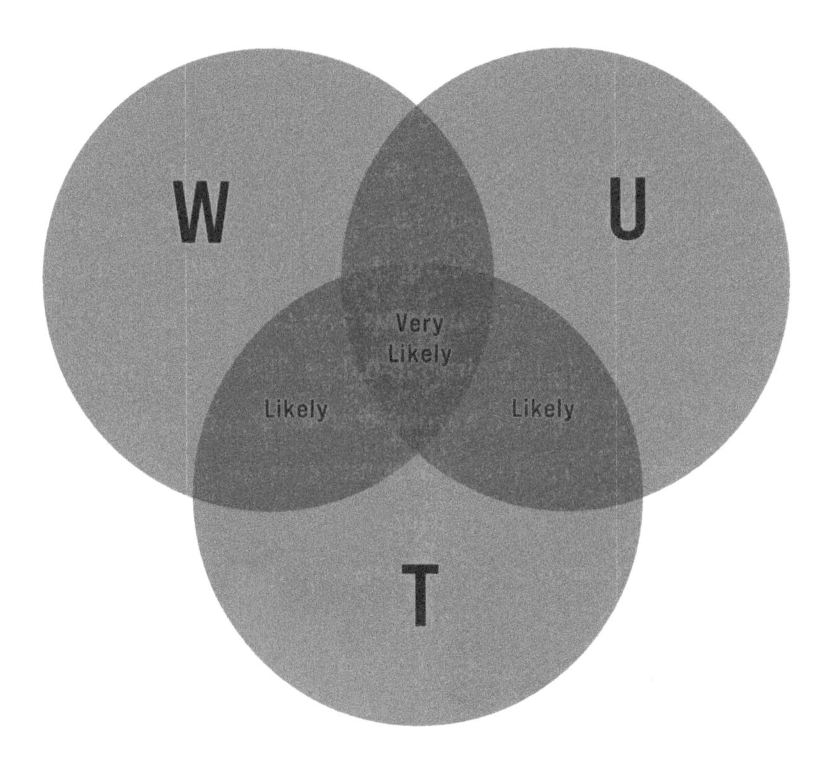

FIGURE 13.2 The WUT diagram helps you monitor your daily hydration status and the likelihood of dehydration. A change in two of the three areas—weight (W), urine color (U), and thirst (T)—indicates that you are likely dehydrated. A change in all three indicates that you are very likely to be dehydrated. Adapted from Cheuvront and Sawka 2005.

not suggestive of dehydration, but be careful not to automatically equate clear urine with ideal hydration. Urine will often be clear if you are hyperhydrated or hyponatremic, too. If your urine is the color of apple juice or darker, it is suggestive of dehydration. This color observation should also be from your urine stream or a collection cup rather than from diluted urine in a toilet bowl. After urinating, weigh yourself without clothing. From day to day, your weight should remain virtually unchanged. Even if you are gradually gaining or losing weight due to changes in fat or muscle mass, those changes will be very small within a twenty-four-hour period. A loss of 1 to 2 percent of body weight between one day and the next is more indicative of a change in total body fluid than in actual mass.

If two of the three or all three of these indices for evaluating body fluid indicate dehydration, then you have not done an adequate job of replenishing fluid losses over the preceding twenty-four hours. This doesn't necessarily mean you didn't drink enough during the previous day's workout. It also doesn't mean drinking copious amounts of fluid in the evening is the solution. (This method will increase first-morning urine volume and probably lighten its color, but much of that fluid is likely to pass right through rather than be stored onboard your body and rehydrate you.) It most likely means your overall daily fluid intake was inadequate to replenish combined losses from exercise, thermoregulation during normal activities (sitting outside on a warm day, working in a warm office, etc.), respiration, and water loss due to normal bodily function.

It's typically not a big issue if the WUT diagram indicates minor dehydration one day here and there, nor does one day of minor dehydration necessitate major changes in your habits. It is best to use the WUT diagram over a rolling three-day period. If you are consistently seeing indications of diminished hydration status over two or three days, you should make adjustments to your overall daily hydration habits. This often happens when athletes increase their training load, travel to a warmer climate or higher altitude, or experience a change in weather or seasons. The practical solution is to increase water consumption throughout the day rather than simply guzzling a large volume of water all at once. It is also important to use the recommendations later in this chapter to make sure you're consuming adequate fluids during training sessions.

If you can prevent two of the three (or all three) indices from indicating dehydration, you are starting your day in a better position to maintain ideal body fluid for the rest of the day. You are also more likely to start your workout with adequate body fluid so that when you see a 2 percent weight loss during a run it is an actual 2 percent loss due to dehydration, not a net 4 percent body-weight loss because you started the day and the workout already 2 percent down from day-to-day dehydration.

Sports Nutrition Guidelines for Ultrarunning

The three primary substances you can ingest before, during, and after running to support your activity level are calories, fluid, and electrolytes. More specifically, within these categories, it is most important to ingest carbohydrate, water, and sodium, which, when you distill sports nutrition to its essence, are the three consumables that make or break athletic performance. The key is to figure out how much you need of each, when you need them, and how to get them.

HOW SPORTS NUTRITION MOVES FROM MOUTH TO BLOODSTREAM

It is easy to get too caught up in trying to determine the ideal formula of a sports drink or the perfect ratio of carbohydrate to electrolyte. What many people overlook is that whatever you ingest gets combined in the stomach, and how it combines determines how quickly it gets into the small intestine, which then determines how quickly it gets into your bloodstream. This is particularly important for ultrarunners because long runs require frequent fueling from varied sources over many hours. The properties of an individual drink or food are less relevant than having a broader understanding of how carbohydrate, fluid, and electrolytes get from your mouth to your bloodstream. So, before we discuss specific recommendations on how many gels to eat, rates of fluid ingestion, and the like, let's take a moment to review how sports nutrition goes from a product wrapped up in a nice little pouch to ultimately fueling your run.

Digestion Starts in the Mouth

Before you even bite into the first piece of an energy bar, your body anticipates the incoming meal and prepares the body to digest it. The simple act of opening up a packet of chews or smelling the cheese quesadillas at an aid station will send signals to your body to anticipate a meal. Your salivary glands will secrete saliva, preparing your mouth for the first chemical process of food digestion, and gastric juices will begin to be secreted into the stomach. As you take a bite, saliva will moisten and to a small extent chemically break down whatever you are ingesting. If required, your teeth further macerate the food into a more swallowable form. All of this is in preparation to pass the foodstuff to the powerhouses of digestion: the stomach and small intestine.

From Stomach to Intestine

One of the primary roles of the stomach is to prepare food and fluid for entry into the small intestine. Your stomach doesn't just break food down from a mashed solid to a liquid slurry; it will hold on to that slurry until the mixture has the right chemical balance before opening the gates to the intestine. The rate at which this happens is called "gastric emptying," and as an athlete you want that process to be rapid.

A few things slow gastric emptying, including highly concentrated foods or solutions (think energy gels or highly concentrated sports drinks). These concentrated carbohydrates sit in your stomach until enough fluid is available to dilute the mixture, which is why it is recommended to consume 8 oz of water with an energy gel.

Taking in too much food and/or fluid can also slow gastric emptying. When you overload your system, gastric emptying can't keep up, and you get a sloshing belly. To a point, increased volume in the stomach accelerates gastric emptying, and you can train your system to go faster. However, even with training there is a limit, which is why consuming smaller volumes of fluid a few times per hour is preferable to guzzling the entire amount needed once an hour.

Absorption from the Intestine

Once the things you've eaten get to the small intestine, it's time to get them into the bloodstream! As with other systems in the body, there are several processes going on at the same time.

The wall of your intestine is a selective, semipermeable membrane, and water and other materials can pass through it in a number of ways. Some things move from the inside of the intestine into the cells of the intestinal wall and then out the other side to the interstitial space between the intestinal wall and the capillaries carrying blood.

Other things squeeze between the cells of your intestinal wall into this same interstitial space. When you consume plain water, you are likely to have a low-concentration solution in your intestine, meaning there's a bunch of fluid and not that much stuff dissolved in it. In contrast, the fluid in the interstitial space on the other side of the intestinal wall has a lot of stuff in it. The overall amount of stuff dissolved in a fluid is referred to as its osmolality; in this scenario, the fluid in the interstitial space has a higher osmolality than the fluid in the intestine. Water travels through a semipermeable membrane from an area of low osmolality to an area of high osmolality (it seeks to dilute the high-concentration area). Practically, this means water moves from the intestine to the interstitial space through the spaces between the cells of your intestinal wall, which is what you want.

Whereas water moves passively through the intestinal wall, carbohydrate has to be actively transported. You have distinct channels for different types of sugar: glucose uses door one, fructose goes through door two, and so forth. This is important for endurance athletes because it means you can take in energy faster when you consume

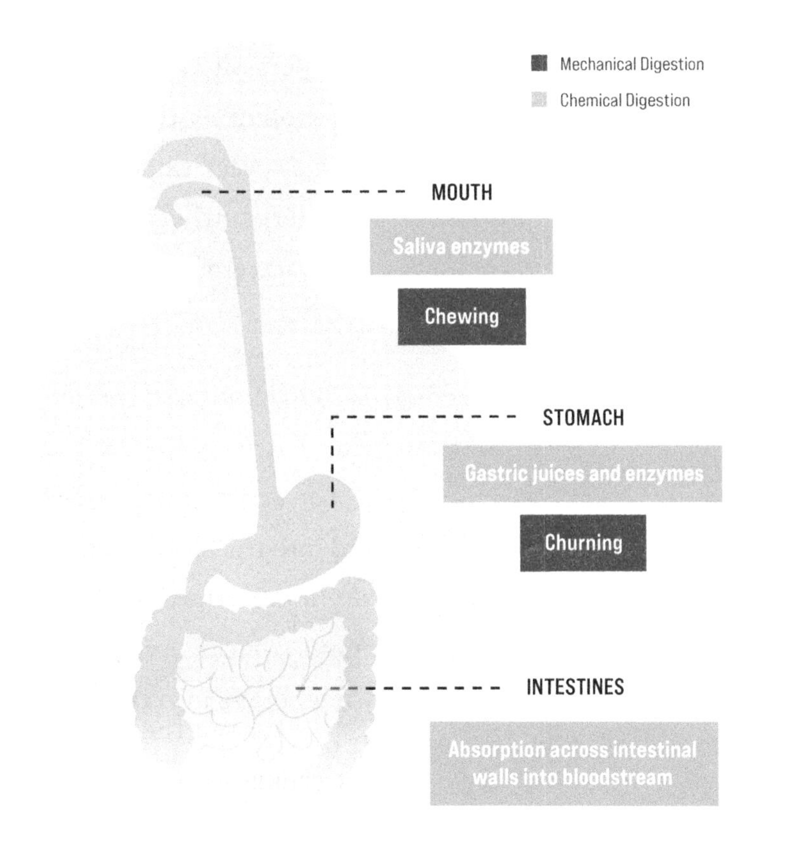

FIGURE 13.3 How and where digestion takes place.

multiple types of sugar. Think of it as trying to get into a football stadium: fewer doors mean longer lines and more waiting; more doors mean less waiting. Another benefit to the active transport of sugar is that sugar drags water with it, creating a second method for water to move from the intestine into the interstitial space.

There are also passive and active methods for getting sodium from the intestine to the interstitial space. Like water, sodium can be moved passively through the small spaces between the cells of your intestinal wall, but there are also two active transport methods for sodium. The first is a cotransport with carbohydrate. The cells in your small intestine have gates that enable cotransport of sugar and sodium together (one glucose molecule and two sodium ions) from the intestine into the cell of the intestinal wall. As a result, sodium and carbohydrate move into the bloodstream more quickly when they are present together, which is why even low-calorie electrolyte-rich sports drinks contain some sugar.

Once in the cell, glucose and sodium go their separate ways. Both end up in the interstitial space, but sodium uses a second active transport method: the sodium-potassium pump, which uses energy to pump three molecules of sodium out of the cell and bring two molecules of potassium in from the outside. The sodium-potassium pump is crucial because you are actively moving sodium from an area of low sodium concentration (inside the cell) to an area of higher concentration (the interstitial space), which is the opposite of what would happen normally. This movement of sodium further increases the osmolality of the interstitial fluid, which in turn draws more water from the intestine.

Getting into the Bloodstream

With all these passive and active methods moving fluid, carbohydrate, and sodium from the intestine into the interstitial space, the pressure in that space increases. At this point the pressure gradient becomes the active driver. The water in the space could go two ways: back to the interior of the intestine or forward into the bloodstream. The capillary membrane on the bloodstream side of the space is more permeable than the tighter membrane on the intestinal side. Because water moves from an area of higher pressure to lower pressure, it moves through the capillary membrane into the bloodstream, taking the sodium and carbohydrate with it.

As we discuss the ingredients of sports drinks, recommended foods for race day, and the balance of hydration status and sodium levels later in this chapter, understanding these mouth-to-bloodstream pathways helps you make decisions about the drinks and foods you're consuming.

During-Workout and Race Nutrition

The goal of sports nutrition during a workout or event is to supply your body with the energy, fluid, and electrolytes necessary for optimal performance. Consuming too little of any of them leads to underperformance, and consuming too much will generally lead to gastric distress, which in turn hinders performance. This requires a fine balancing act, one most athletes are inadequately prepared for because they often employ different rates of calorie consumption during events compared to their day-to-day training sessions. For example, they might only consume 100 calories per hour during a long training run yet try to take in 200–300 calories per hour in a race. This is the equivalent of training your legs, heart, and lungs at a 10 min/mi pace on a day-to-day basis and then asking them to operate at an 8- or 6-min/mi pace during the race. That would be absurd, and we need to think about training as not only preparing the legs, heart, and lungs for race day but also the stomach for race-day stressors. In that vein, I am going to present the following nutrition recommendations as strategies for both training and racing conditions.

CARBOHYDRATE

Over the course of the last several years, sports scientists have tried to pinpoint carbohydrate recommendation ranges that can be broadly applied to a variety of endurance athletes. They have studied tolerability of amounts and types of different carbohydrate sources, as well as the body's ability to use the ingested foodstuffs. The sum total of it all can be distilled down to a recommendation to consume 60 to 90 g/hour of carbohydrate for endurance activities lasting more than ninety minutes. This recommendation is based on the fact that you are able to absorb and utilize about 1 g of exogenous carbohydrate per minute during exercise. With training and a combination of carbohydrate sources (glucose and fructose), you may be able to increase this to about 1.4 g/min, or about 84 g/hr.

There is some emerging evidence that, with specific gut training, rates of over 90 g/hr can be utilized and could be of additional benefit (Costa et al. 2017; Cox et al. 2010; Urdampilleta et al. 2020). However, the utility of such high rates of carbohydrate intake is likely limited in an ultrarunning situation because the energy demand side of the equation does not require it. At ultramarathon distances the rate of caloric output, as well as the percentage of carbohydrate being utilized, are both less than what they would be in the more traditional endurance circumstances upon which many of these guidelines are based.

To get a better fix on this, let's do a little simple math based on some broad generalizations about ultramarathon intensity and the percentage of fat vs carbohydrate you would utilize in an ultra. In just about any ultramarathon, you are going to be running at an intensity of <65 percent of your VO_2 max. Sure, elite athletes can do the climbing portions of a 50-miler at slightly higher intensities, and maybe if you were trying to set a 50K world record you would be at 70 percent of your VO_2 max, but stay with me here. Earlier in this chapter I described the "crossover concept," which is a widely used physiological concept that describes the point at which you are deriving 50 percent of your calories from fat and 50 percent from carbohydrate (see Figure 13.1). A crossover point of 65 percent of VO_2 max is quite common for trained endurance athletes. (Plus, it makes the math easy in an ultramarathon, and I like easy math.) This means that at a normal ultramarathon intensity, roughly 50 percent of your fuel is coming from fat, of which you have a nearly unlimited reserve, and 50 percent is coming from carbohydrates, which you will need to replace. You could extend these percentages by ~10 points on either end based on the situation, but the gist would remain the same.

Now, how many calories are you burning per hour? This is actually a much bigger variable. It's based off of body weight and speed, but if we make some simple assumptions based on a normal person running at a normal intensity, we can once again get a general fix on the situation. A 70 kg person (154 lb) moving at 9:40 min/mi (10 K/hr) on flat terrain is going to utilize ~700 cal/hr. Since only 50 percent of these calories are derived from carbohydrate, this normal ultramarathon pace for a normal runner is going to cost them 350 cal/hr of carbohydrate based on our earlier assumptions. Now take into consideration that you have ~2,000–2,800 calories of glycogen and blood glucose on

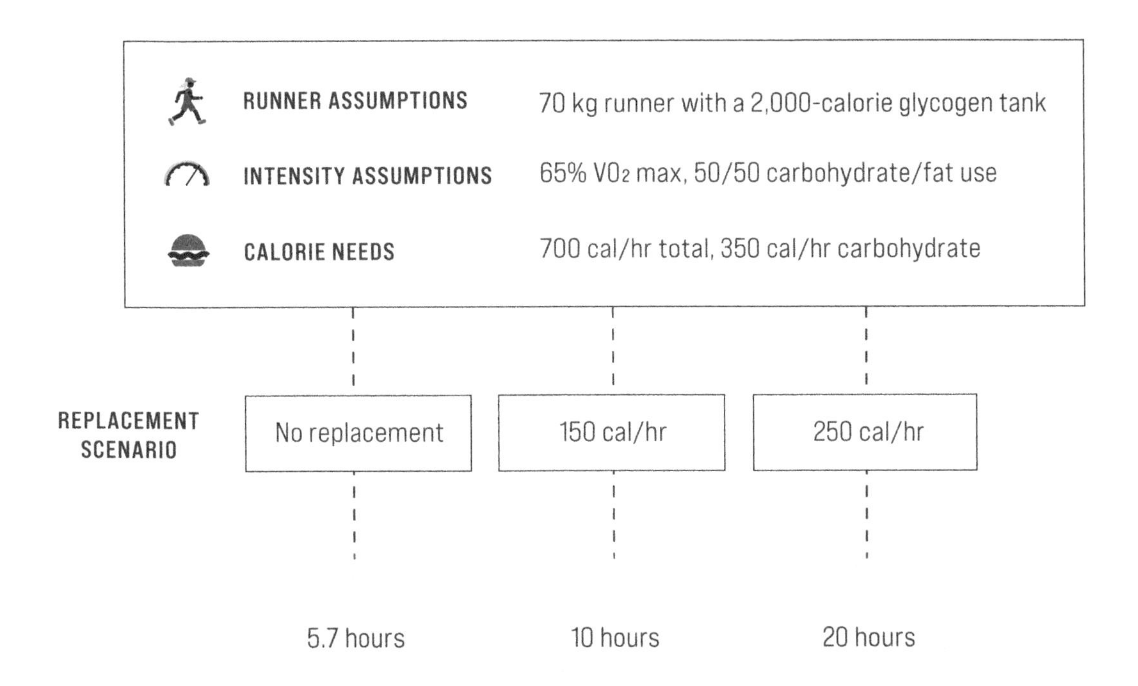

FIGURE 13.4 How long can you run with reasonable assumptions about intensity and caloric replacement?

board, provided that you are in a fed state (i.e., not fasting or doing a run immediately after waking up). This means that this normal runner running at a normal ultramarathon pace can run for over five hours and forty-two minutes or fifty-seven kilometers without any fuel. Increase the runner's size or pace, and the duration/distance goes down. Decrease the pace or size, and this goes up. Am I telling you to go out and run fifty-seven kilometers without food? Hell no. Please don't. That's stupid. But the simple math demonstrates that because most ultramarathon intensities are so low (<65 percent VO_2 max), higher rates of carbohydrate ingestion (up to 90 g/hr) are likely unnecessary.

So how much carbohydrate do you need for training and racing? The answer really depends on your performance goals. Generally speaking, the higher the intensity you need to maintain to accomplish your goal, the more carbohydrate you need. Subsequently, if you are a very fit runner interested in squeaking by the cutoffs, you will need less carbohydrate because you are operating at a lower percentage of your VO_2 max. What I advise athletes to do is to start at 60 g of carbohydrate per hour and move up and down from there based on the intensity of the race and what they can tolerate.

JASON KOOP'S SECRET RICE BALLS

ONE OF THE GREATEST TRUTHS about sports nutrition is that even the best foods are useless if they stay in your pocket. You have to put those calories, electrolytes, and fluids into your body for them to do you any good. That means you have to like how they taste, how they smell, how they feel in your mouth, and how easy they are to unwrap and get down your throat. When I was a novice endurance athlete, I loved Krispy Kreme doughnuts, and one of my early experiments in sports nutrition was to cram three or four into a sandwich bag and squeeze them out a torn corner, as you would a carbohydrate gel. My tastes and my cooking skills have improved since then, and I developed two variations of a rice ball that meet the during-workout and during-competition nutrition guidelines in this chapter and have the taste, texture, and convenience characteristics that make them a go-to favorite for several of my athletes.

BACON AND EGG RICE BALLS

makes about 12 rice balls

1½ cups uncooked basmati rice
2 eggs
2 strips bacon
2 oz grated Parmesan cheese
Salt to taste

1. Cook the rice.
2. Scramble and cook the eggs.
3. Cook the bacon. Drain excess fat and chop.
4. Combine rice, eggs, bacon, cheese, and salt in a large mixing bowl.
5. Scoop small portions into sandwich bags and tie the ends off.

Per ball: Calories: 133 / Carbohydrate: 18 g / Protein: 4 g / Fat: 5 g / Sodium: ~160 mg

SWEET AND SALTY RICE BALLS (VEGETARIAN)

makes about 12 rice balls

1½ cups uncooked basmati rice
2 eggs
2 Tbsp honey
1–1.5 Tbsp soy sauce to taste

1. Cook the rice.
2. Scramble and cook the eggs.
3. Combine rice, eggs, honey, and soy sauce in a large mixing bowl.
4. Scoop small portions into sandwich bags and tie the ends off.

Per ball: Calories: 115 / Carbohydrate: 20 g / Protein: 2 g / Fat: 3 g / Sodium: ~125 mg

PROTEIN

Protein's role in ultramarathon events is interesting. Although its role in energy metabolism is limited, there may be a role for protein as a way to mitigate the effects of muscle damage incurred during a race, although the research findings on this are still equivocal (Knechtle et al. 2011). Particularly during training, athletes would be well served to ingest ~40 g of protein every four hours throughout the day to aid in muscle protein synthesis (i.e., rebuild the muscle that you broke down). When your training runs are over four hours in duration, this recommendation carries particular weight in order to make the most out of the runs and facilitate recovery.

FAT

Simply put, fat's purpose in ultramarathon racing and training is to maintain the satiety of foods. Ingestion of fat will not materially add to your body's ability to oxidize fat as a fuel. Additionally, most individuals cannot consume more than 30 g (270 calories worth) of commercially available fat supplements like MCT oil without gastrointestinal distress.

FLUID CONSUMPTION

In addition to making sure you're consuming enough calories to support your workouts, you also have to make sure your fluid intake is adequate. The easiest way to determine whether your fluid consumption is keeping up with your fluid losses is to weigh yourself without clothing before and after your workouts (excluding runs of greater than 3 hours, because water released as a byproduct of oxidizing fuel will confound the results). Any weight you lose during this time is due to fluid loss. Although there is some evidence that athletes can lose 2 percent or more of their body weight due to dehydration with no decline in performance, and in some cases with an increase in competitive performance due to reduced body weight, in training there is no benefit to exceeding 2 percent weight loss during workouts.

Over the years, the notion of a 2 percent loss of body weight negatively impacting performance has become almost ubiquitous. This notion helped drive the now outdated recommendation to "consume as much fluid as tolerable" and likely has contributed to the rash of hyponatremia cases in ultrarunning (more on that later). In more recent years, that notion has been challenged, and "drink to thirst" has become a common moniker, suggesting that your sensation of thirst is all you need to tell you when to drink. These polar opposite recommendations (drink all you can vs drink to thirst) have befuddled race directors and athletes alike. I can vividly remember being at the pre-race meetings of two different 100-mile races that were separated by only six weeks and having the medical directors of each give these opposing recommendations on fluid consumption.

The fact of the matter is that if you ever try either of these strategies in a race, you will easily see how fallible they are. Weighing yourself at an aid station will contain far more error than the changes you are looking for (<2 percent) due to the sweat, dirt, and gunk stuck to your clothing. And don't even get me started on how accurate a scale is when placed on a patch of dirt next to your drop bags. Similarly, anyone who has run the Badwater Ultramarathon can attest to the fact that your perception of thirst is totally messed up by the many hours breathing in dry, hot desert air combined with copious amounts of sand and dust kicked up from your roadside crew. Both of these in-race ways of determining fluid replacement are ineffective, unsound, and likely to cause

1	Weigh yourself nude right before a run.
2	Go do a one-hour run at EnduranceRun intensity.
3	After the run, strip down, wipe down any sweat, and weigh yourself nude again.
4	Subtract your end weight from your beginning weight. Convert the weight to ounces (one pound equals 16 ounces). This is your hourly sweat rate in those specific conditions.
5	Aim to replace ~95–98% **(not 100%)** of those fluids during a race for those conditions. Why not 100%? Because in an ultra, weight loss from water stored in fat and carbohydrate are significant and does not need to be replaced. We don't quite know exactly how much fluid needs to be replaced, we just know it's not 100% as some of the fluid loss stems from metabolic processes not related to hydration status. Replacing 100% of the sweat loss in an ultra can lead to hyponatremia, or low blood sodium.
6	Repeat the test in different conditions. I recommend using steps of 10 degrees Fahrenheit.

FIGURE 13.5 The Sweat Test.

more harm than good in an ultramarathon setting. So, let's stop recommending them and get to a better solution.

The sweat test is a simple, effective tool you can use to get the best gauge on the fluids you will need to replace during training and racing. And the best thing about it is all you need is a scale.

Once you have done this across a range of conditions, it's easy to map your fluid replacement rate against the conditions of the race you are faced with by using a simple weather app that features hour-by-hour temperature conditions. It is worth noting that intensity affects your sweat rate as well (the more intense the exercise, the more you will sweat). However, given that most ultramarathons are performed around Endurance-Run intensity, the sweat test (Figure 13.5) covers a variety of ultramarathon scenarios and works as a good starting point.

SODIUM

Sodium is the last mission-critical nutrient in your racing and training arsenal. As with carbohydrate and fluid, sodium recommendations have ebbed, flowed, and changed over time. First off, the amount of sodium you require is a function of the amount of sodium lost in the sweat. Yes, you lose sodium through other sources, but sweat is the main one to focus on. Therefore, it's most useful to think about the amount of sodium you need to replace in terms of milligrams per unit of fluid you're ingesting to replace the fluid lost.

The next step in the equation is determining the concentration of sodium in your sweat. As with any other biological process, there is a tremendous amount of individual variation for sweat sodium losses (see Figure 13.6). As a testament to this, we all know the "salty sweater" who is caked in dried sodium after a run. Aside from putting up with a little teasing and maybe an extra wash cycle for their clothes, salty sweaters will also need a bit more sodium in their ultrarunning routine. A more scientific version of the salt-caked shirt can be found with commercially available sweat sodium testing. If you think you are a candidate for this, I encourage you to work with a registered dietitian who works with endurance athletes.

Finally, it is important to understand that you do not need to replace 100 percent of the sodium lost in sweat, as you have sodium reserves located in the body, namely in the skin. Current sports science is a bit conflicted on how much sodium you need to replace,

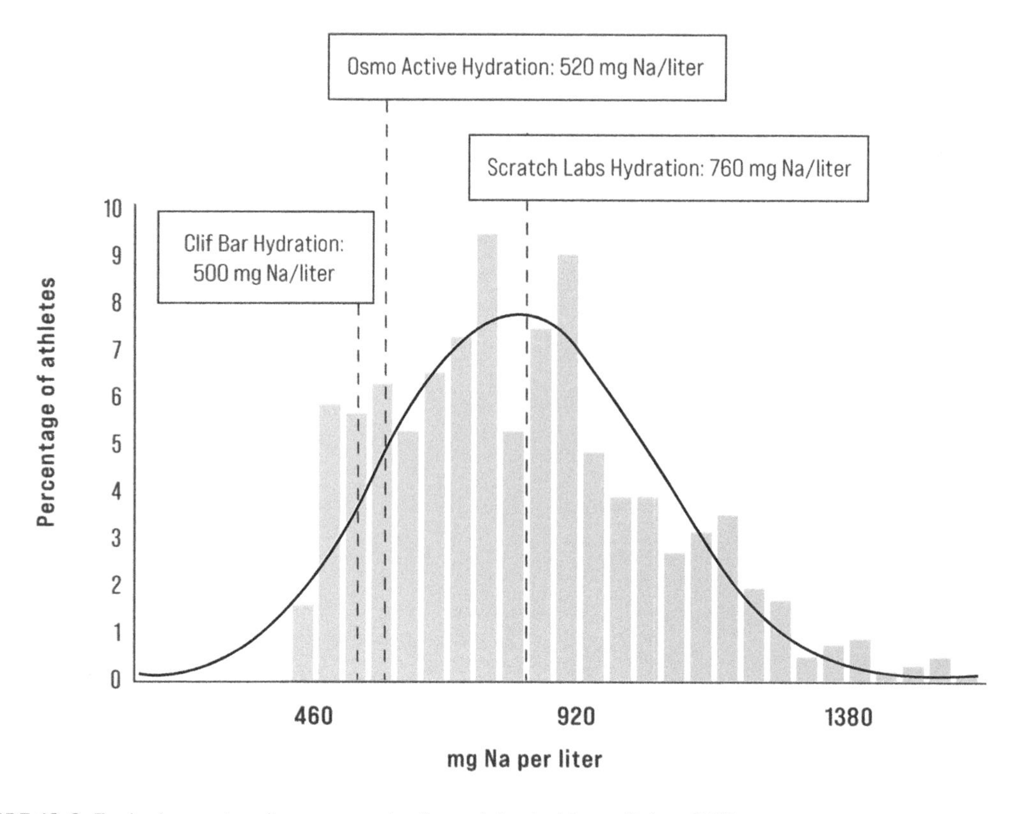

FIGURE 13.6 Typical sweat sodium concentrations. Adapted from Baker 2017.

but our best estimates are anywhere from 50 to 80 percent of the sodium lost in sweat. So, even if you have a precise sweat sodium test performed, realize that the goal is not 1:1 replacement, but rather to just get it close.

Confused yet? Don't worry, sports drink manufactures have made getting your sodium requirements easy for you, and most high-quality sports drinks will get you in the right ranges provided you mix the drink according to the manufacturer's recommendation. To meet your sodium needs, your goal should be to consume 600–800 mg of sodium per liter of fluid consumed. However, the sodium doesn't have to be in the drink; you can meet the requirement with plain water and sports nutrition products or real foods containing sodium, too. Even in the case where the sports drink you choose is a little light on sodium, it's pretty easy to get in the right range by adding normal sports nutrition products and other foodstuffs to your plan to make up the difference.

Lastly, what about those salt tablets? Salt tablets are generally not necessary and can encourage overdrinking due to the fact that they create an extremely hypotonic

WHAT THE HECK IS IN MY SPORTS DRINK?

A SPORTS DRINK IS ESSENTIALLY water with stuff dissolved in it. Some drinks have lots of different kinds of stuff dissolved in them, most of which just waste space. There is only so much room to dissolve solutes in a drink, and drinks with fewer ingredients can use more of that room for important things such as carbohydrate and sodium. The simplest drinks are the best because they are easiest on the gut and facilitate the transport of sugar and electrolyte across the semipermeable membrane of the intestinal wall better and faster.

The concentration of sports drinks is important. When you change the osmolality of the fluid (the total molecular concentration of everything in the drink—carbohydrate, electrolyte, flavoring, additives—per unit volume), it changes how the drink influences the overall mixture in your stomach and hence how that mixture makes it into the intestine. Sports drinks are formulated to optimize the absorption of carbohydrate, fluid, and electrolyte. If the osmolality of the sports drink is too high because of a bunch of additives, it may contribute to slower gastric emptying. When the osmolality of sports drinks is lower, it is more likely to contribute to faster gastric emptying (depending on what else you're eating and drinking), and if it's being consumed on an empty stomach it is formulated to get into the intestine quickly. If you are designing a sports drink to have a relatively low osmolality but you want it to deliver moderate to high amounts of sodium and/or carbohydrate, you have to eliminate anything that's not essential.

The primary ingredients, sugar, sodium, potassium, and flavoring, are in the drink for good reason. Putting electrolytes and flavoring into a fluid makes you want to drink more frequently and consume more fluid each time you drink. There's actually a lot more to the way your sports drink tastes than marketing mumbo jumbo. A lightly flavored drink is preferable to a stronger one because when you consume half a bottle in one long slug, the stronger-tasting drink becomes overwhelming and you stop drinking. A drink that tastes almost watered down when you are at rest will taste just about right when you are running. This is why athletes have long diluted commercial sports drinks like original Gatorade, which these days are often flavored to appeal to convenience store customers instead of athletes.

Even taste components and mouthfeel are important. A slightly tart drink will encourage you to drink more than an overly sweet one, and citrus flavors also increase the drive to drink. It should be no surprise, then, that almost every drink company has some version of lemon-lime and/or orange in its product line. In addition to the flavor, a sports drink needs to clear the mouth well. When a drink leaves a film in your mouth, as is often the case with overly sweet drinks, it's not only unpleasant, but you're not likely to drink again soon.

Rather than dilute sports drinks, it is better to find a drink with a lighter taste so you can comfortably consume it at full strength. If you are consuming a high-quality sports drink like Skratch Labs, Osmo, or Clif Hydration, it's generally unnecessary, and can be counterproductive, to dilute the drink.

environment in your stomach (too much sodium, not enough fluid). Therefore, it's better to avoid them and get your sodium from a combination of electrolyte drinks, gels, chews, and real food.

Making Sure You're Getting It Right

There's a simple way you can make sure your carbohydrate, fluid, and electrolyte intake is on target during workouts. An exercise I use at ultrarunning camps is to have athletes hold on to the wrappers from everything they consume during a four-hour EnduranceRun. After the run, we lay them all out and record the following for each item: carbohydrate calories, milligrams of electrolytes, and milliliters of fluid. We then give the athletes a report card outlining the results, where they did well, and where they might have failed.

After tallying up everything you have consumed, do some simple math. You are aiming for 200–300 calories per hour (with ~90 percent coming from carbohydrates; you can also subtract the first hour of the run if you have just eaten a meal), 16 to 32 oz of fluid, and 600 to 800 mg Na per 32 oz (about a liter) of fluid. The purpose of this exercise

CALORIES IN YOUR POCKET, HYDRATION IN YOUR BOTTLES

WHAT SHOULD BE IN YOUR BOTTLES during workouts: water or a high-carbohydrate and electrolyte sports drink?

For the vast majority of runs, a high-carbohydrate drink is not necessary. While high-carbohydrate drinks have a place in sports nutrition, separating calories from hydration is a better and more versatile strategy. What's in your bottle or hydration pack should serve the purpose of hydration, and the food in your pocket should serve the purpose of fueling.

As workload and temperature change, your fluid and calorie needs change independently. When it is hot, you need more fluid per hour, sometimes twice as much as during a cool run. This often happens during the course of an ultramarathon, where you start in the cool morning and run through the heat of the day. If your fluids contain 35 g or more of carbohydrate per 20 oz serving, you'll consume 35 g if you drink one bottle and 70 g if you drink two bottles in one hour. That's at the top end of the recommended range of 60 to 90 g of carbohydrate per hour; any further calories can lead to gastric distress. When you start to feel the initial stages of gastric distress, you delay drinking and start digging a dehydration hole that can take hours to recover from. Remember, you can come back from a caloric deficit easily and within minutes by eating. Returning to normal hydration status takes much longer, and being dehydrated during that time can have more deleterious effects on your performance.

Separating calories from hydration allows you to ratchet up fluid intake in response to high temperatures and dial it back in cooler conditions without greatly affecting your calorie supply. It also allows you to vary carbohydrate sources more easily because they are not tied to what you are drinking. This is important because your food choices can supply a large amount of the sodium you need to replenish. In many cases you can consume the recommended amount of sodium entirely through food sources while drinking plain water.

COSTA ET AL. 2019

CARBOHYDRATE RECOMMENDATIONS	Upwards of 90 g/hr (2:1 glucose to fructose) although such a high level likely unnecessary
FLUID RECOMMENDATIONS	Provided sufficient fluids/volumes are available, "drink to thirst," "ad libitum"
SODIUM RECOMMENDATIONS	Avoid excessive sodium supplementation during running. Consume sodium based on food cravings. Do not use highly visible salt losses as a signal for increasing sodium intake.
OTHER RECOMMENDATIONS	Use trial and error with foods/fluid quality/quantity to determine what is optimal. Try to simulate race day (and thus know what foods are available at race) by eating similar foods/fluids and in similar quantities in training that you will use in race. Use "B" or "C" races to determine how other contributing factors (travel, weather, pacing, competition, stress, changes in normal food availability) influence optimal nutritional strategy. Consume slightly more early (first 2 hrs) as GI symptoms tend to develop later. In longer (greater than 8 hrs) races, avoid excess protein, fat, fiber, or FODMAP-heavy foods; can mouth rinse with carbohydrate beverage in longer events when consuming enough becomes an issue.

TILLER ET AL. 2019

CARBOHYDRATE RECOMMENDATIONS	30–50 g/hr
FLUID RECOMMENDATIONS	450–750 ml/hr (by drinking every 20 min), greater in hot and humid conditions
SODIUM RECOMMENDATIONS	> 575 mg/L
OTHER RECOMMENDATIONS	In training: Individualized, periodized, food-first approach. Moderate-to-high carbohydrate diet (~ 60% of energy intake, 5–8 g/kg/d) to limit chronic glycogen depletion. Limit carbohydrate before occasional easy sessions and/or moderating daily carbohydrate intake, which may enhance fat oxidative capacity. This may compromise high-intensity efforts. Also, if doing this, implement with sufficient time to permit adaptations that enhance fat oxidative capacity. Protein intakes of ~ 1.6 g/kg/d up to 2.5 g/kg/d may be warranted during demanding training. In racing: 5–10 g/hr of protein. Eat (carbohydrate and protein) from variety of sources, more savory foods in longer races. Use progressive gut training and/or low-FODMAP diets to minimize GI distress. Ketogenic diets and/or ketone esters to improve ultramarathon performance are not currently evidence based, but further research needed. Strategically use caffeine in latter stages, particularly with sleep deprivation.

ACSM (AMERICAN COLLEGE OF SPORTS MEDICINE) POSITION STATEMENT 2016	
CARBOHYDRATE RECOMMENDATIONS	Up to 90 g/hr while exercising (ultra specific), 6–10 g/kg/d (for endurance athletes, not ultra specific)
FLUID RECOMMENDATIONS	Drink 5–10 ml/kg in the 2-4 hrs before exercise (pale yellow urine color). Drink enough during to limit day's weight loss to < 2% of body weight. Drink 1.25–1.5 L for every kg of weight lost after; none of these are specific for ultra-endurance.
SODIUM RECOMMENDATIONS	Keep blood sodium above 135 mmol/L; doesn't say how to achieve it, nor is it ultra specific
OTHER RECOMMENDATIONS	Nitrates improve exercise tolerance, economy, and performance in at least non-elite athletes.

TABLE 13.1 Nutrition recommendations for ultrarunning in scientific literature.

is to uncover what you are actually taking in and where you are deficient. You then can adjust your ranges based on your personal calorie, fluid, and sodium needs. The fluid side of the equation will be of particular importance, since as mentioned earlier it will vary tremendously based primarily on the environment.

An example of this nutrition report card, detailed in Figure 13.7, is a from a runner returning from a four-hour run having consumed 64 oz of total fluid, including three bottles of drink mix, as well as two gels and two bars.

Preworkout Nutrition

The most important aspect of the last full meal you eat before a training session is that it's out of your stomach and digested before you start training. This is especially important for interval workouts because higher-intensity efforts tend to be downright unpleasant on a full stomach. A relatively light meal that's rich in carbohydrate (preferably about 70 percent of total calories) is a good choice because meals that contain a lot of fat or protein stay in the stomach longer and are digested more slowly. That's a good thing if you're trying to feel full longer, but it's not good if you're about to go out for a hard workout. Examples of good meal choices are pasta, a turkey sandwich, or oatmeal with fruit.

	INVENTORY	FLUID	CALORIES	SODIUM
HOUR 1	1 BoBo Bar (peanut butter)	16 oz water	330 cal	95 mg Na
HOUR 2	1 GU (vanilla bean)	16 oz Skratch Hydration	180 cal	440 mg Na
HOUR 3	1 Clif Bar (blueberry crisp)	16 oz Skratch Hydration	340 cal	560 mg Na
HOUR 4	1 Clif Shot (razz)	16 oz Skratch Hydration	180 cal	475 mg Na
TOTAL		64 oz	1030 cal	1570 mg Na
TARGET		16-32 oz / hour	200-300 cal/hour (MINUS FIRST HOUR)	600-800 mg/ 32oz fluid
GRADE		A B C D F	A B C D F	A B C D F

Overall Grade: A

FIGURE 13.7 A nutrition report card.

When it comes to your preworkout or pre-race meal, a good rule of thumb is that meal size should get smaller the closer to the workout or race you get. For instance, you can consume 1.5 g of carbohydrate per kilogram of body weight when your final pre-workout meal is three hours before your run (Table 13.2), but this should be closer to 1 g/kg if you're going to train two hours after your last significant meal. Also, you shouldn't try to fill your daily fiber requirement at this time. The American Heart Association recommends 25 to 30 g of fiber a day to reduce LDL cholesterol (the bad kind) and lower the risk of heart disease, but fiber slows digestion, so it's better saved for other meals.

Postworkout Nutrition

Postworkout nutrition might be the most oversold concept in all of sports nutrition. Early on in my coaching career, I relentlessly pushed recovery shakes and concoctions

BODY WEIGHT (KG)	3-4 HOURS PRIOR	2-3 HOURS PRIOR	1-2 HOURS PRIOR	0-60 MINUTES PRIOR
	1.5-2.0 g/kg	1.0-1.5 g/kg	0.5-1.0 g/kg	0.25-0.5 g/kg
55 (121 lb.)	83-110	55-83	28-55	14-28
60 (132 lb.)	90-120	60-90	30-60	15-30
65 (143 lb.)	98-130	65-98	33-65	16-33
70 (154 lb.)	105-140	70-105	35-70	18-35
75 (165 lb.)	113-150	75-113	38-75	19-38
80 (176 lb.)	120-160	80-120	40-80	20-40
85 (187 lb.)	128-170	85-128	43-85	21-43

TABLE 13.2 Carbohydrate recommendations prior to exercise.

to my athletes after just about every workout. The theory was, the quicker your replaced what you lost, the more effective the workout and the more thorough your recovery. Furthering my bias was the fact that one of my coaching colleagues, Kathy Zawadzki, performed research that led to one of the original recovery drinks, Endurox R4. This drink was complete with what was thought at the time to be a magical ratio of 4 g of carbohydrate to 1 g of protein. The theory (again at the time) was that a beverage containing exactly 4 g of carbohydrate to 1 g of protein consumed within twenty minutes of exercise was the linchpin for attaining superhuman levels of recovery. (OK, maybe the fine folks over at Endurox didn't promise that you would leap over buildings in a single bound, but you get the picture.) While fluid, protein, sodium, and carbohydrate are important elements in your postworkout routine, we now know there's little need for such laser-guided precision.

In terms of carbohydrate, you want to start workouts and competitions with full glycogen stores. You can store about 1,600 to 2,000 calories of glycogen in your muscles and liver, with a bit more circulating in your blood. This carbohydrate energy will be burned alongside fat and a bit of protein in muscle cells as you exercise, but of the three, carbohydrate is the only one you can realistically deplete during a single bout of exercise, and it will certainly be depleted during an ultramarathon or a long training bout.

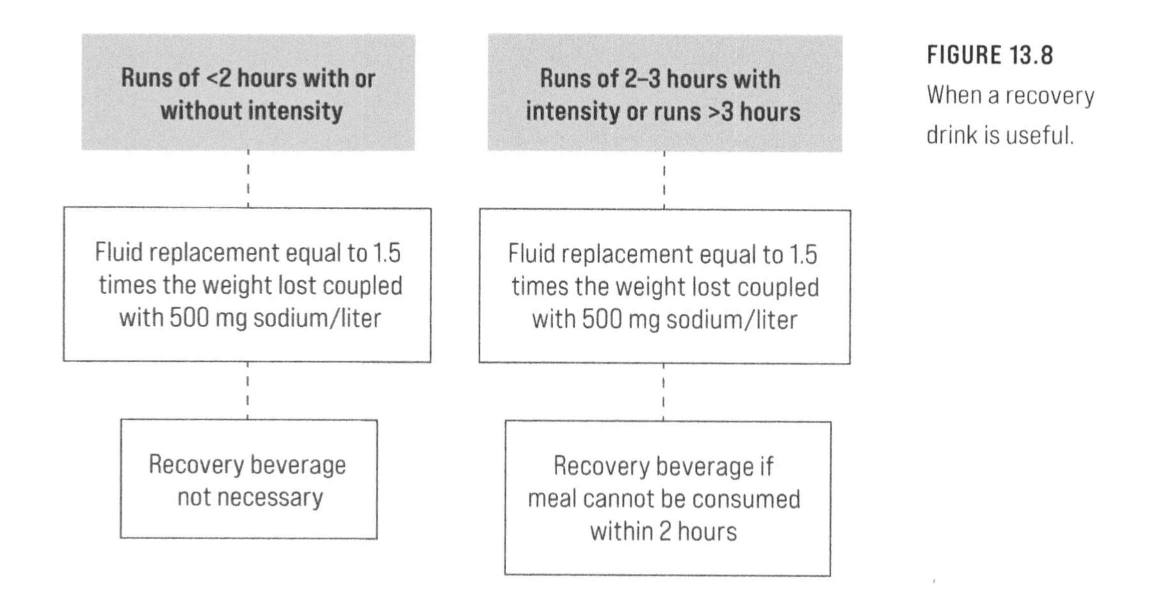

FIGURE 13.8
When a recovery drink is useful.

Fortunately it is relatively easy to ensure your glycogen stores are topped off before your next workout. Your body is primed to replenish muscle glycogen stores most rapidly within the first thirty to forty-five minutes following exercise. During this period, known as the "glycogen window," there literally are more gates or "windows" open to allow sugar to enter muscle cells.

The glycogen window is important, but it is also important to keep replenishment in perspective. We used to think immediate postworkout consumption of carbohydrate was absolutely crucial for maximizing glycogen replenishment. Nutrition companies capitalized on this concept by designing specific recovery shakes and beverages that were touted to "optimize recovery," and athletes started consuming these concoctions in large quantities, with little regard to their actual efficacy. While it is a good idea to get started with replenishment in the initial forty-five minutes after exercise because muscle cells are very receptive to taking in carbohydrate during that time, glycogen replenishment will reach 100 percent within twenty-four hours after exercise as long as you are consuming high-quality meals throughout the day. Therefore, I recommend that athletes optimize recovery with specific recovery beverages when both of the following conditions are met:

Your workout is over three hours OR your workout is over two hours and contains some structured intensity,

AND you don't have access to a high-quality meal immediately after the run (i.e., you have to drive for an hour to get home, or some other situation precludes you from sitting down to a good meal).

If you like drinking a postworkout shake just because you like it, that's great. Just don't think that it holds the key to your athletic future or that it is substantially more effective than eating a balanced meal.

Fluid and sodium are also important to replace post workout. Your goal within the first two hours after exercising should be to consume enough water to equal 1.5 times the water weight you lost during the session coupled with ~500 mg of sodium per liter of fluid. In other words, if you lost 2 lb (32 oz) during your workout, you should drink 48 oz of fluid within the two hours after you get back. This hydration rule of thumb applies to any run, not just runs over two hours or that contain intensity.

KEY POINTS FOR ESSENTIAL NUTRITION AND HYDRATION

- You are constantly using carbohydrate, fat, and protein for fuel when exercising.
- Protein is only used minimally for fuel, but it is important for repairing muscle damage, helping to maintain your immune system, and other necessary functions.
- As you increase intensity, you will also increasingly rely on carbohydrate as a fuel.
- Appropriate fluid is important for maintaining core temperature, gut motility, and blood volume.
- You can check your day-to-day hydration status by using a combination of body weight, urine color, and thirst, all examined first thing in the morning.
- Key nutrition targets for runs greater than two hours:
    - 16 to 32 oz of fluid per hour, adjusted to your individual needs, environmental conditions, and intensity
    - 200 to 300 calories per hour, adjusted per your tolerance
    - 600 to 800 mg of sodium per 32 oz of fluid ingested
- You can test your nutrition plan by using the nutrition report card.
- Recovery beverages are only beneficial in certain situations.

CHAPTER 14

Adapting Sports Nutrition Guidelines for Ultrarunning Events

Using the recommendations and strategies discussed earlier in this book, most ultrarunners can consistently fuel their workouts and maintain a good hydration status in training. It is during events that nutrition and hydration strategies frequently go off the rails. Gastrointestinal symptoms like nausea and vomiting are the top reasons athletes cite for dropping out (Hoffman 2011), and even athletes with in-depth knowledge and experience with the nutrition challenges of ultramarathons get knocked out of events by dehydration and upset stomachs.

Ultra-Specific Challenges of Ultradistance Events

One of my colleagues at CTS boiled the ultramarathoner's nutrition strategy down to this: develop the ability to simultaneously run and eat as much as you can without barfing. While that is a drastic oversimplification of the goals and challenges of fueling yourself through an ultramarathon, it is nonetheless true. It is especially true at the 100-mile distance, where caloric expenditure far exceeds the body's stored carbohydrate levels. You have to consume a lot of calories and a lot of fluid over the course of many hours in order to finish an ultramarathon, and you have to overcome several challenges that competitors in shorter events do not face.

PROLONGED DURATION

Challenge.

The simple fact of being outdoors, awake, and on your feet for many, many hours creates a nutritional challenge. Athletes in shorter events can eat a pre-race meal, consume calories and fluid to support their energy expenditure and thermoregulation needs, and then finish their event before needing another meal. They can deplete their energy stores faster and dig deeper into their reserves because postrace replenishment is only a few hours away. They can even race themselves into significant dehydration and gastrointestinal distress and reach the finish line before experiencing a significant decline in performance. Ultradistance competitors cannot be so cavalier or take as many risks because the duration and distance of the event will force them to deal with the consequences well before they reach the finish line.

Adaptation.

Ultramarathon runners must develop the ability to consume and digest a steady stream of calories over the course of many hours. Some of those calories need to be from solid foods with more bulk, more fat, and more protein than carbohydrate-only foods like gels and sports drinks. While the nutritional focus needs to be primarily on fueling with carbohydrate calories, it is important to realize your race foods are also taking the place of meals during longer events. Fat and protein are satiating, meaning they stave off feelings of hunger better than carbohydrate does. If you respond to feelings of hunger by overconsuming carbohydrate, you increase the likelihood of gastric distress. By incorporating solid foods containing fat and protein, you can continue to base your carbohydrate intake on your caloric expenditure rather than on a growling stomach.

LONG DISTANCES/TIMES BETWEEN AID STATIONS

Challenge.

Major urban marathons have aid stations nearly every mile. That's twenty or more aid stations in twenty-six miles, with food and fluids available at the finish line. At the Western States 100-Mile Endurance Run, there are twenty-one aid stations in 100 miles, with distances between stations ranging from five to seven miles in the first third of the race and from three to four miles in the final third. Depending on your pace and the terrain, that can mean well over an hour between aid stations. If you have trouble between aid stations that causes you to stop, that time can increase dramatically.

Adaptation.

With long distances between aid stations, you will require gear that allows you to fuel along the way. Train with the gear you plan to use on race day. If you rarely run with a hydration pack in training and then have to run with one during a 100-miler, it may become uncomfortable and a constant source of annoyance. The same goes for hydration bottles or that fuel belt you just picked up online. Some races mandate certain gear that you must carry at all times. Make sure you can fit it into your pack, that the pack is still comfortable, and that you can run effectively when the pack is fully loaded. If you will have pacers or support crews in aid stations, make sure they know how to quickly and efficiently refill your pack so you don't have to stop and wait.

DRAMATIC CHANGES IN ENVIRONMENTAL CONDITIONS

Challenge.

If your event starts in the dark and proceeds through an entire day and into the night, and perhaps even into the following morning, you are going to experience dramatic shifts in environmental conditions. Ultramarathon runners can face temperature swings of forty or more degrees and high-altitude rain or snowstorms (even in summer). These changes greatly impact your sweat rate and your perceptions of hunger and thirst.

Adaptation.

Use your equipment to minimize changes in your core temperature due to changes in environmental conditions. If it's going to get hotter, you want to take steps to stay cool: wear lighter clothing, remove layers, soak your clothing, drink cool beverages, and so forth. If it is going to get colder, use your equipment to stay warm by wearing more layers and swapping wet clothing for dry clothing. In both situations, you need to stay hydrated. As weather changes, be aware of changes in your sweat rate because that directly impacts your hydration strategy. As temperatures climb, you need to anticipate an increase in your sweat rate and start consuming more fluid. The longer you wait, the more behind you get in hydration status. In cold weather, your sweat rate will decline; it's important to recognize that and reduce fluid intake to avoid overhydration. If you are behind in hydration already, you can also take advantage of cooler temperatures to gradually get your hydration status back on track. If you anticipate dramatic changes in temperature during your event, know your sweat rate for a variety of temperature ranges. Dramatic environmental changes also disrupt your routine and strategy. You may forget to eat as you struggle through a thunderstorm or focus on staying warm through the predawn hours. This is where practice and a knowledgeable support crew can be invaluable.

GENERAL FATIGUE AND DIMINISHED DECISION-MAKING ABILITY

Challenge.

When you are very tired, you make decisions you would never make in a less-fatigued state. You might leave an aid station without refilling a hydration pack. You might zone out and not consume anything for miles. You might scrap your nutrition plan entirely and scarf down enough cookies to make you sick. I've seen all these things and many more, all caused by extreme fatigue.

Adaptation.

Habits and routines pay huge dividends for an ultradistance competitor. Develop habits that are consistent from everyday training sessions to your longest races so they become ingrained to the point that you stick to them even when you are unbelievably fatigued. Develop a routine you use every time you pick up your hydration pack: check for water, standard food choices, and standard equipment (like a rain shell). Make sure you at least have your bull's-eye foods (more on those later) with you whenever you leave an aid station. Keep these routines simple and minimal; you don't have to have everything all the time, but you always need to have something to eat, something to drink, and something to protect yourself from the elements. When you are fatigued and in the heat of battle, have a routine.

FOOD FATIGUE

Consuming small amounts of food and fluids over and over again during the course of many hours is exhausting. Many athletes reach a point where they don't want to expend the effort required to eat or they no longer have a taste for the food options available. This is rarely a problem in shorter events because less food is needed to complete the race. As a result, athletes competing in shorter events can utilize a narrower range of food options, whereas ultradistance athletes typically need to find a wider range of foods they are willing to eat and that work for them without causing an upset stomach. I have spent so much time working through the challenge of food fatigue with athletes that I have developed a specific strategy to deal with it.

The Bull's-Eye Nutrition Strategy

During training, particularly during longer runs, I have athletes experiment with different—and sometimes counterintuitive—foods to help them reach their target calorie ranges. Foods that work are easy to open and eat on the run. They taste good, don't get stuck in your teeth, and make you run as well as or better than you were running before eating them. Foods that don't work are difficult to open, messy, crumbly, and hard to hold in one hand. They get stuck in your mouth, are too dry, or are tough to swallow without choking. Most of all, they sit in your gut like a calorie bomb, make you feel bloated or full, and slow you down. Your goal is to find three to five foods you can count on to work in any situation. These are your bull's-eye foods.

All the food options you try can be categorized by where they fall on a target (picture an archery range—that kind of target). Your bull's-eye foods are your tried-and-true favorites. If these core foods begin to fail because you're tired of eating them, craving more sweetness or saltiness, or craving a different texture, then you can choose foods from the next ring of the target. These are foods you may not eat all the time, but you have tried them in training and know they work for you.

Beyond this ring are foods that you haven't tried but that are similar to foods you

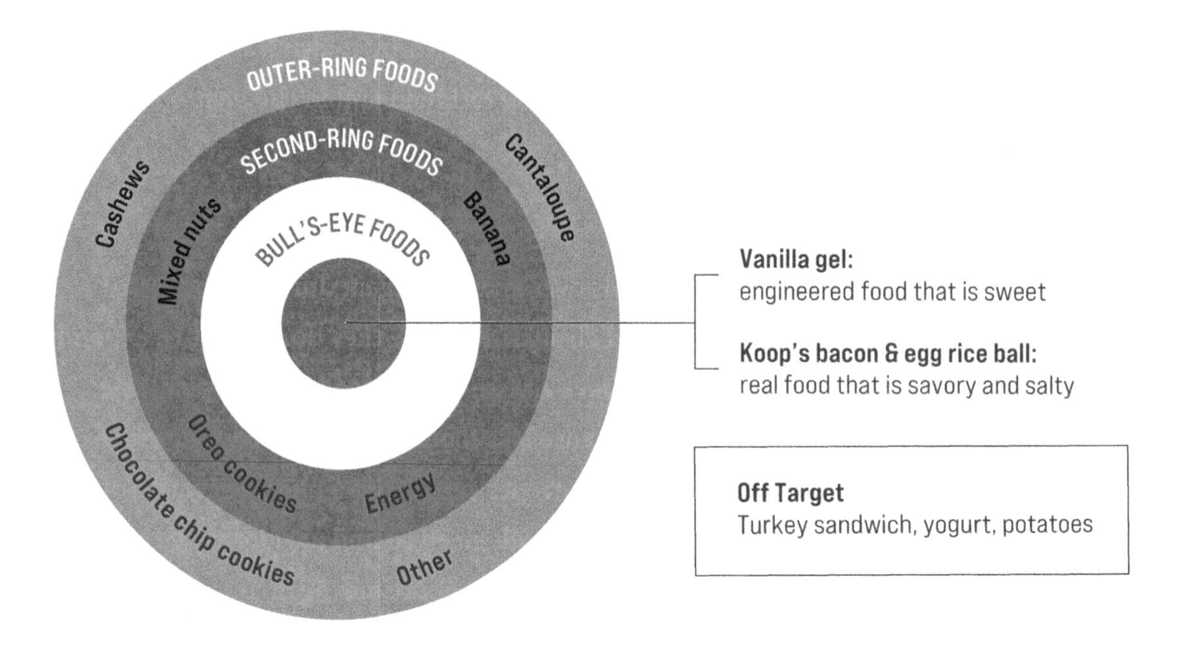

FIGURE 14.1 A sample bull's-eye nutrition strategy.

have tried. For instance, you may know that chocolate chip cookies work for you, but there are only oatmeal cookies in the aid station. Or you like regular potato chips, but only BBQ-flavored chips are available.

Anything beyond this ring is off target altogether. These are the foods you know don't work for you and foods similar to foods that don't work for you. It is important to list these foods out, as well, so that you and your crew are reminded of the things you have tried that have not worked in training.

Developing Your Bull's-Eye Foods

Variety is important in your short list of bull's-eye foods. The end goal is to find a combination of three to five foods that, together, meet all the following criteria:

- **AT LEAST ONE REAL FOOD**—something you make or assemble or that is not made specifically for running (rice ball, peanut butter and jelly sandwich, or pretzels)
- **AT LEAST ONE ENGINEERED FOOD** (gel, chewable, or sports drink)
- **SOMETHING SWEET**
- **SOMETHING SAVORY**
- **SOMETHING SALTY**

If you construct this combination correctly, these bull's-eye foods can be rotated and substituted during any race as needed, according to your target calorie range, which you identified earlier in this book. After these core foods have been fully vetted, experiment with backup (second-ring) foods. These backup foodstuffs are what you can confidently fall back on if you lose your taste or craving for your bull's-eye foods. The typical fall-back plan revolves around the aid station fare of cookies, soup, fruit, and sandwiches. Outer-ring foods will fall into this aid station assortment as well.

The bull's-eye strategy is easy to visualize and easy to explain to your support crew. Figure 14.1 is an actual example of one runner's bull's-eye strategy. At any point during a race, either the athlete or her support crew can quickly consult the target and make a good decision.

What about Strategies to Enhance Fat Metabolism?

Fat adaptation, or the ability to utilize more fat as fuel at higher intensities, has been a hot topic in the endurance sports world for the past decade. Some of the best minds in exercise science have dedicated the better parts of their careers to researching and writing seminal papers on the topic and helping athletes perform at their very best (see Louise Burke, Asker Jeukendrup, and others). Considering that gastrointestinal distress is one of the primary villains stopping ultrarunners in their tracks, the idea of becoming a better fat-burning machine is attractive. Additionally, the demands of ultramarathon racing involve running at lower intensities for long periods of time, which utilizes fat for energy to a greater extent than races like the 10K and marathon. Since you have a virtually unlimited source of energy stored in your body as fat and all the opportunity to use it at ultramarathon intensities, it makes sense to want to exploit this metabolic confluence of events. We also know that substrate metabolism is trainable and that with changes to diet and training, rates of fat oxidation can be as much as doubled for a given submaximal intensity (Purdom et al. 2018). However, what sounds like a relatively attractive strategy on the surface is a little less straightforward in practice.

A misnomer in the "fat-adapted" athlete world is that the only way to become more efficient at utilizing fat is by following a ketogenic, or extremely low-carbohydrate high-fat (LCHF) diet. The reality is that your body becomes fat adapted through a few different conduits. Normal endurance training improves fat oxidation by increasing your body's ability to produce energy aerobically. As you become more fit, you can utilize more oxygen at any given intensity, and thus you have a greater opportunity to utilize fat as a fuel. Dietary interventions such as a LCHF or ketogenic diet can further enhance this opportunity by upregulating fat oxidation pathways. You can also alter substrate metabolism to prioritize fat by changing fuel availably during specific training sessions. All of the aforementioned methods are effective. Remember, your body is smart. It is already a flex-fuel machine capable of burning multiple fuel sources and upregulating the fuel utilized based on training status and availability.

For many, optimizing fat metabolism to improve performance seems to be a win-win. You win by being able to tap into a nearly limitless fuel source and at the same time not rely on as much exogenous carbohydrate. You'll be more self-sufficient, less reliant on gels and aid station foods, and ultimately stave off gastrointestinal distress.

With so much going for it, what downsides could there possibly be from following an optimized approach to better fat utilization? The simplest answer is that you are compromising your ability to perform at higher intensities. This is because it takes approximately 8 percent more oxygen to liberate energy from fat as it does from carbohydrate. While fat is a nearly limitless energy source, it is also a more expensive fuel to use.

Some make the argument that the increased oxygen cost of liberating energy from fat is offset or justified by the fact oxygen delivery is at less of a premium at lower intensities, so the oxygen penalty for relying on fat for fuel is seemingly less important when running at 50 to 60 percent of your VO_2 max, as you have some bandwidth to spare. But it's not just less economical; it limits your capacity to utilize other substrates.

When you manipulate your diet in an attempt to optimize fat metabolism, carbohydrate becomes scarcer as a fuel source and your body also becomes less efficient at utilizing carbohydrates (Burke et al. 2016; Jeukendrup 2017). While theoretically a good-enough runner could run and walk slowly enough to complete 100 or even 200 miles on energy from stored fat alone, for mere mortals, even in the most fat-adapted state, ultramarathons are long and intense enough that athletes will need some exogenous carbohydrate. So yes, after a few weeks on a lower-carbohydrate diet you might now be a fat-metabolizing machine, but without the introduction of carbohydrates during and around training leading up to your event, you might not be able to effectively transport the carbohydrates you are trying to ingest (even in lower amounts), ironically making you more likely to experience gastrointestinal distress.

The economy penalty of relying on fat for energy doesn't just hurt race performance; training suffers, too. Reducing economy reduces performance, particularly at higher intensities. This means the amount of high-intensity work you can do is limited, either by a reduction in intensity (running slower during your intervals) or a reduction in the time you can spend at any intensity, or both. In any form, this reduces the training stress you can get out of an interval session like TempoRuns or RunningIntervals and therefore the benefits you can reap from those sessions. Furthermore, some training adaptations are attenuated in the absence of carbohydrate, meaning you quite literally get less bang for your hard-earned training buck.

Finally, a more recently explored drawback of following a LCHF strategy is the potentially increased risk of bone-stress injuries. In a first-of-its-kind study looking at LCHF diets and bone health, researchers found that even after three and a half weeks of a LCHF diet athletes showed changes in critical markers of bone health (Heikura et al. 2020). Specifically, subjects showed increased levels of CTX, a marker of bone resorption, and a decrease in P1NP, a marker of bone formation. These negative adaptations may have implications for injury risk and long-term bone health.

As with other areas of training and sports nutrition, fat adaptation is neither all good nor all bad. From a performance standpoint, I do not see compelling evidence for recommending a full-time LCHF nutrition strategy for ultramarathon runners, but I also understand that athletes make dietary decisions for a lot of reasons. If you choose to be a LCHF ultrarunner, that's fine as long as you accept the performance limitations that result from that decision. Alternatively, you can manipulate your diet to achieve specific goals.

DIETARY MANIPULATION

Dietary manipulations to enhance fat metabolism involve controlling the amount of carbohydrate you consume on a given day. These manipulations come in three main flavors:

DIETARY STRATEGY	CARBOHYDRATE CONTENT
Very low-carbohydrate ketogenic diet	<50g carbohydrate/day
Low-carbohydrate diet	15–30% of calories from carbohydrate
High-carbohydrate diet	60–65% of calories from carbohydrate
Consensus from International Society of Sports Nutrition	60% of calories from carbohydrate

TABLE 14.1 Carbohydrate content of different dietary strategies. Adapted from Burke 2020; Tiller et al. 2019; Wylie-Rosette 2016.

- **DIETARY KETOSIS:** The most restrictive is a ketogenic diet, which leverages the body's ability to produce and utilize ketones for fuel in the absence of carbohydrate. The diet garnered attention initially as a treatment for children with severe cases of epilepsy, before it was adapted into the nutrition and sports worlds as a way of manipulating substrate utilization and controlling weight. The diet consists of 75 to 85 percent calories from fat and 15 to 20 percent calories from protein, but the crucial parameter is restricting carbohydrate intake to fewer than 50 g per day (the equivalent of two to three bananas or two energy gels).
- **LOW-CARBOHYDRATE HIGH-FAT (LCHF):** A low-carbohydrate high-fat diet is next on the plate. While definitions vary, this diet is less restrictive than dietary ketosis and consists of 30 to 40 percent calories from carbohydrate. These two strategies run contrary to most sports science recommendations that call for 60 to 65 percent of an endurance athlete's calories to come from carbohydrate (Tiller et al. 2019).
- **PERIODIZED CARBOHYDRATE:** The third option is a periodized carbohydrate (PCHO) approach. The periodized approach can represent a blend of a ketogenic diet, LCHF diet, and high-carbohydrate low-fat diet, as well as approaching specific training sessions with low carbohydrate availability (more on that next). On a PCHO diet you would leverage high carbohydrate availability by

DIETARY STRATEGY	ADVANTAGES	DISADVANTAGES
Low-carbohydrate high-fat or Ketogenic (defined by less than 50g CHO/day)	Increased fat oxidation, sparing endogenous glucose Lower need for exogenous carbohydrates during activity Decreased body fat percentage	Inability to train and race at higher intensities Less efficient at transporting carbohydrates across gut membrane Increase risk of bone-stress injuries from hormonal changes affecting bone remodeling Restricted sources of food, specifically fruits and vegetables Can lead to low energy availability
High-carbohydrate low-fat	Consistently high training quality Trains the gut to facilitate more glucose absorption	Possible overreliance on carbohydrate as a fuel source
Periodized carbohydrates	Matches training intensity/duration to substrate needs Enhanced fat oxidation due to cellular changes in the muscle No diminished training quality	Logistically difficult to implement

TABLE 14.2 Advantages and disadvantages of dietary strategies to manipulate substrate utilization. Adapted from Burke 2020; Tiller et al. 2019; Wylie-Rosette 2016.

topping up muscle glycogen stores and fueling with carbohydrate during workouts for higher-intensity periods of training and/or specific workouts. Other less-intense workouts would be completed with intentionally low carbohydrate availability, either through diet manipulation, overnight fasting, or a low-carbohydrate day to delay postexercise glycogen replenishment. This "best of both worlds" strategy potentially allows you to reap the benefits of improving fat oxidation without limiting your ability to do higher-intensity work, thus maintaining quality throughout your training cycle so you are not shortchanging your fitness potential.

TRAINING MANIPULATION

Training manipulations for improving fat oxidation focus primarily on restricting carbohydrate availability for specific training sessions. The two primary strategies employed are:

1. Training twice per day and withholding carbohydrate intake after the first session. In this case, the first session of the day is a harder interval workout to deplete glycogen stores and the second session of the day is an EnduranceRun or RecoveryRun.
2. Fasted runs. In this case, the run starts with lower carbohydrate availability either due to an overnight fast (if the run is performed in the morning) or due to moderating carbohydrate throughout the day (if the run is performed in the evening). The training session is typically limited to less than two hours and performed without fuel.

Both of these strategies work on the premise that the low-carbohydrate training session amplifies your body's cellular signaling to produce more fat oxidizing machinery. This includes making more mitochondria as well as upregulating oxidative enzymes (Marquet et al. 2016).

Now all this feels a little bit like goldilocks and the three four bears. We want to find a situation that (1) leverages our fat-burning capabilities so we can utilize this nearly limitless yet expensive source of energy, (2) maintains performance at higher intensities, (3) promotes adaptation from all of our hard work in training, and (4) avoids any deleterious effects to bone health stemming from low energy availability. Is there a happy medium? It depends on who you ask. But since you are reading my book, I'll give you my humble opinion.

TRAINING STRATEGY	STEP 1	STEP 2	STEP 3	STEP 4
Two-a-day	Running interval session	Restrict carbohydrate immediately post run	Second session of 1.5–2-hour EnduranceRun performed without fuel	Refuel with carbohydrate post run
Fasted run	Overnight fast	EnduranceRun of 1.5–2-hour upon waking. Performed without fuel	Refuel with carbohydrate post run	

TABLE 14.3 Training strategies to enhance fat oxidation.

SHORT-TERM ENERGY DEFICITS AND RED-S

With any of these strategies, you are going to have to go through at least some short-term energy deficits, where you're consuming fewer calories than required for effective training. You might think, "No biggie, I'll just grab some more pizza for dinner to make up the balance." However, we're learning more and more that RED-S is problematic for endurance athletes. This normally happens when there is an energy deficit caused by a workout combined with and compounded by underfueling. Fat-adaptation strategies can further compound the negative effects, as they rely on short- or long-term energy deficits. The host of performance complications include decreased muscle strength, decreased performance, increased injury risk, and decreased training response, to name a few. In this sense, the negatives of most of the fat-adaptation strategies can quite quickly outweigh the positives.

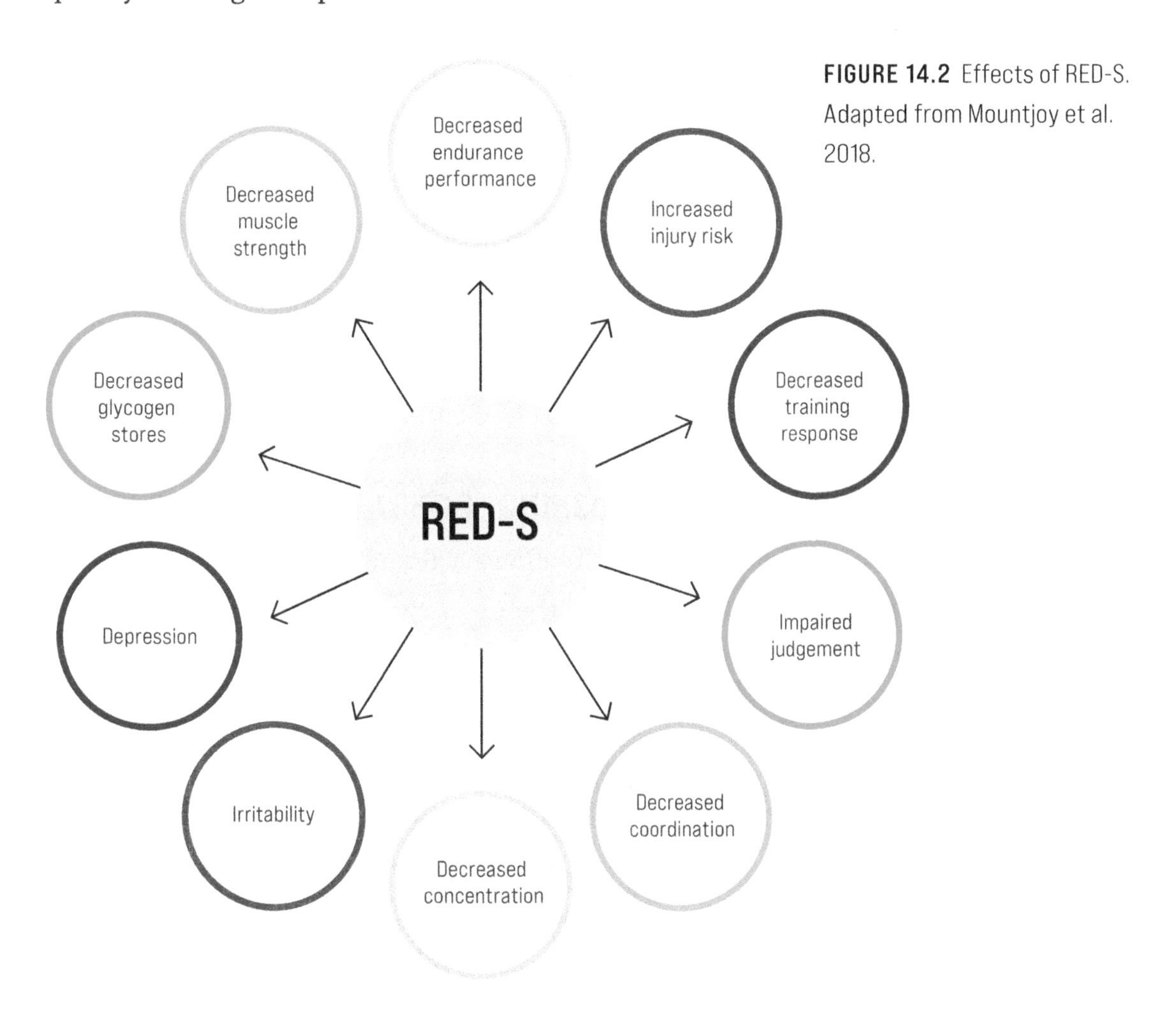

FIGURE 14.2 Effects of RED-S. Adapted from Mountjoy et al. 2018.

ULTRAMARATHONERS ARE ALREADY REALLY GOOD AT BURNING FAT

Simply by running copious hours at a relatively low intensity, ultrarunners are already really good at burning fat. As stated in the 2019 IAAF consensus statement on nutrition for athletes: "high fat oxidation rates also appear to be inherent in ultramarathon runners regardless of background macronutrient dietary modifications." Trying to double down on an effect you already have is a high-risk, low-reward (or no-reward) scenario.

ADHERENCE IS PROBLEMATIC, METABOLIC MANIPULATION IS TRANSIENT, AND EXPERTISE IS SCARCE

With any of these fat-adaptation strategies, adherence is difficult. We know from the work on the ketogenic diet that you need at least a few weeks of adherence before maximum benefits of fat oxidation start to appear. And after all that, the enhanced fat-burning effect loses its potency within a few days of reintroducing carbohydrates. While less studied, the transient nature of other fat-adaptation strategies is likely similar: they will take some time to show an effect, and that effect disappears quickly. Additionally, safe implementation requires technical knowledge from a registered dietician who can manage overall energy and micronutrient balance alongside the intended metabolic manipulation. Your fat-adapted friend and the athletes promoting these diets do not qualify as experts in this area, no matter their level of enthusiasm. Quite frankly, the level of expertise required is scarce and many athletes will not have access to the right support system.

WHAT ABOUT ATHLETES WHO ARE CRUSHING IT ON LOW-CARB DIETS?

It would be remiss of me not to discuss the numerous well-known and not-so-well-known athletes who have been able to improve their performances with fat-adaptation strategies. They are out there for sure, filling up your Instagram and Strava feeds with their latest accomplishments.

I will let you in on a not-so-secret: almost all of these performance benefits have nothing to do with the fat-adaptation side of the equation. They have almost entirely to do with the fact that the athlete lost weight. This point is driven home when I hear athletes advocate for using a ketogenic diet as a "tool". What this really means is that it's a tool for energy restriction, and the resulting weight loss leads to improvement.

I DON'T THINK IT'S A GOOD HEALTH MESSAGE

Finally, if you are spending lots of time figuring out how or where to skip your gel (or meal for that matter), you've got it all wrong. Much of the issue I have with fat-adaption strategies lies in the fact that there is too much fixation on what you are leaving out (breakfast, for example) and not enough on what you are putting in. If you want to be an athlete, the focus needs to be on the latter. High-quality foods, not the absence of them, are what athletes should focus on.

We need less obsession over calorie composition and more over calorie quality and adequate quantity.

When you focus on quality and adequate quantity over composition and restriction, the results are physically, emotionally, and psychologically healthier outcomes (see Figure 14.2 for psychological/emotional complications stemming from RED-S).

There is no greater example of poor judgement caused by intentionally fat adapting than the term "strategic tuber" or "strategic fruit," which I have seen pop up in the ketogenic and low-carb community. "Strategic" in this sense fits the narrow definition of a way of consuming carbohydrates (tubers and fruit in this case) to fuel intense workouts, but not so much that it violates some predetermined principle of carbohydrate restriction. Since when do we need to "strategically" use a food source that comes from the ground and is rich in vitamins and nutrients, tasty, and fulfilling? If a simple "not-so-strategic" banana—with all its vitamins and minerals—is going to destroy your nutrition strategy, there's something wrong with your nutrition strategy, not with the banana.

Just eat the sweet potatoes, bananas, and apples, people. They're good for you.

THERE IS ROOM FOR PERIODIZING CARBOHYDRATE AVAILABILITY AS WELL AS SESSIONS WITH LOWER CARBOHYDRATE AVAILABLY, WITH A TON OF CAVEATS

If you want to double down on your body's natural fat-burning machinery, there are a couple of low-risk, medium-reward tools in your tool belt. First, you can periodize your macronutrient composition so that during your EnduranceRun and SteadyStateRun phases, you are consuming ~50 percent of your daily calories from carbohydrate. For any TempoRun or RunningInterval phases, you should up this intake to ~60 percent. This is akin to the PCHO approach mentioned earlier. Second, doing an early morning

EnduranceRun of up to two hours after an overnight fast is likely another low-risk strategy. Finally, a two-a-day strategy where you perform an interval session (like TempoRun or RunningIntervals) with adequate carbohydrate availability followed by an EnduranceRun with lower carbohydrate availability can help promote fax oxidation without many deleterious effects, provided that you can carve out the time in your day for two sessions and the extra logistical work does not pile on additional nonworkout stress.

AVOID THESE THINGS

I realize that many of you reading this book will still be tempted by aggressive fat-optimization strategies. I get it. As I mentioned in the onset of this section, on the surface it seems an attractive proposition. If you do decide to undertake one of these, please avoid the following at all costs:

1. Low energy availability. Taking in too few calories, regardless of their macronutrient composition, will lead to a whole host of problems. Remember, with any fat-adaptation strategy the goal is to manipulate one macronutrient's availability, not total caloric availability.
2. Hard workouts in a fasted state or while restricting carbohydrate. Seriously, this is a terrible idea. You set yourself up for underperformance and overtraining all at the same time.
3. Hard workouts at the end of long runs. For whatever reason, I have seen this creep up from time to time in athletes' training, either as a means of "training on tired legs" or some sort of fat-adaptation strategy. Just don't do it. Like point #2 above, you are taking on a boatload of stress for little positive outcome.
4. Long runs without fuel. Don't go out and do your longest of long runs without fuel. A very long fasted run does not produce superior adaptations compared to some of the more reasonable strategies mentioned above. So, these activities have very little, if any, upside and a whole lot of downside. Sure, you can "get through it" by being tough, running slowly, and hydrating properly, but the reward for your effort is nil and might even result in maladaptation. The laurels of ultrarunning are littered with tales of well-intended athletes running 50 or even 100 miles without fuel and then wearing that accomplishment as a badge of honor. Last I checked, there are no awards for the lowest number of calories consumed in a race.

Balancing Hydration and Sodium: The Ultimate Challenge for Ultrarunning

Your total body water and your sodium concentration will affect performance in different ways. Further complicating the matter is the fact that at any point in time, your hydration and sodium balance can be normal or you could have too much or too little of either one.

Hydration state can be measured relative to your body weight, and your natremic state is measured by the concentration of sodium in your blood (measured in millimoles per liter). To understand how hydration status and sodium concentration change, it's important to first understand some terminology.

- **EUHYDRATED:** Normal level of hydration, typically less than 3 percent weight change
- **HYPOHYDRATED/DEHYDRATED:** Greater than 3 percent decrease in body weight
- **HYPERHYDRATED/OVERHYDRATED:** Increase in body weight
- **NORMONATREMIC:** Normal blood sodium concentration (135 to <145 mmol/L)
- **HYPONATREMIC:** Too little sodium in the blood: a blood sodium concentration of <135 mmol/L
- **HYPERNATREMIC:** Too much sodium in the blood: a blood sodium concentration of >145 mmol/L

Table 14.4 helps us to better visualize how these hydration and natremic states converge. It resembles a tic-tac-toe board, with the various hydration states on the horizontal rows and natremic states in the vertical columns. As with regular tic-tac-toe, occupying the center square puts you in a position of power. This is the desired physiological state in which you can run faster, run farther, and tolerate heat better.

Assuming you start your event euhydrated and normonatremic, during the course of an ultramarathon you are going to consume a lot of fluid, a lot of calories, and a lot of sodium. You will also be exposed to varying temperatures and weather conditions, and you will spend times at a variety of intensities. All these things, along with the sheer length of time you will be out on the course, will shift your hydration and natremic statuses.

No scenario is more advantageous than being euhydrated and normonatremic, but

Hydration State			Natremic States: Low Hyponatremic	Natremic States: Normal Normonatremic	Natremic States: High Hypernatremic
	Low	**Dehydrated**	Dehydrated and hyponatremic	Dehydrated and normonatremic	Dehydrated and hypernatremic
	Normal	**Euhydrated**	Euhydrated and hyponatremic	Euhydrated and normonatremic	Euhydrated and hypernatremic
	High	**Overhydrated**	Overhydrated and hyponatremic	Overhydrated and normonatremic	Overhydrated and hypernatremic

TABLE 14.4 How hydration and natremic states converge.

some of the other scenarios are worse than others. The one that gets the most media attention is the scenario in which an athlete is overhydrated and hyponatremic, specifically a slow marathoner who drinks way too much plain water and gains weight during the event. Hyponatremia happens in ultrarunning, too, but it can also manifest as euhydration and hyponatremia. This means the athlete is at normal body weight (less than 3 percent body-weight loss) but has not replenished enough sodium to offset losses from prolonged hours of sweating. It's dilution of the blood by removal of sodium, rather than dilution of the blood by the addition of too much water.

During an ultramarathon your sodium-hydration balance is one of the most important aspects of biofeedback to pay attention to. As you eat, drink, run, and spend more time in the elements, this balance is constantly shifting. Your goal is to stay in or get back to that center square!

The following sections represent the various combinations of hydration and natremic states you could end up in during the course of an ultramarathon. Some are more dangerous and affect your performance more than others. Similarly, some are easier to get into and easier to correct than others. To better explain them, each state is described by the level of hydration, level of sodium, the prevalence of the occurrence (extremely rare = less than 1 percent, rare = 3 to 6 percent, somewhat common = 10 to 15 percent, common = 30 percent or greater; adapted from Hoffman, Hew-Butler, and Stuempfle 2013), how you got there, what the symptoms are, and how you can get back to the center square (euhydrated and normonatremic).

COMBINATION 1: DEHYDRATED AND HYPONATREMIC

- **HYDRATION:** Low
- **SODIUM:** Low
- **OCCURRENCE:** Rare (3 to 6 percent of 100-mile finishers)

HOW YOU GOT HERE. You can get to this state if you have lost a lot of electrolytes through sweating and you have gradually fallen behind in both sodium and fluid replenishment. Rising temperatures during an ultramarathon can lead to this problem as well, because you have been losing sodium throughout the race, and then sweat rate increases dramatically and accelerates both fluid and sodium loss.

SYMPTOMS. Dry skin and mouth, thirst, craving for salty foods, dizziness on standing, weight loss, and low/no urine volume. At risk for heat stress in warm conditions.

HOW TO GET BACK TO THE CENTER SQUARE. Consume sports drink, salty broth, and/or a combination of water and salty foods. Don't consume only water. In warm/hot conditions slow down, wet your clothing, and douse with water to alleviate heat stress.

COMBINATION 2: EUHYDRATED AND HYPONATREMIC

- **HYDRATION:** Normal
- **SODIUM:** Low
- **OCCURRENCE:** Rare (3 to 6 percent of 100-mile finishers)

HOW YOU GOT HERE. This is a relatively easy state to reach in an ultramarathon, especially if you experience food fatigue and gradually start taking in less food or fewer sodium-containing drinks. Athletes who are salty sweaters can also end up in this state because they have higher sweat losses over time. This condition does not put you at elevated risk of heat stress, since you have plenty of body fluid for sweat; however, it can become much more serious if sodium balance is not corrected.

SYMPTOMS. Normal weight and thirst, moist mouth, craving for salty foods but nausea upon eating, and normal urine output.

HOW TO GET BACK TO THE CENTER SQUARE. Consume sports drink, salty broth, and/or a combination of water and salty foods. Try ginger or another remedy to alleviate nausea.

COMBINATION 3: OVERHYDRATED AND HYPONATREMIC

- **HYDRATION:** High
- **SODIUM:** Low
- **OCCURRENCE:** Rare (3 to 6 percent of 100-mile finishers)

HOW YOU GOT HERE. This dangerous condition requires immediate action. Athletes who consume too much plain water and not enough sodium are at risk. Even those who know better can end up in this situation when food fatigue and overall fatigue cause poor decision-making. Some stop eating due to nausea but continue consuming a lot of plain water in hopes of calming the nausea by getting the gut to start moving again. Hot conditions combined with frequent aid stations can make this worse, as sips of low-sodium fluids (cola, ginger ale, water) at aid stations add up.

SYMPTOMS. Increased weight, puffy hands, high output of clear urine, cognitive impairment, disorientation, sloshing stomach, nausea, and possible vomiting. Low risk of heat stress because there is plenty of fluid available for sweat.

HOW TO GET BACK TO THE CENTER SQUARE. If symptoms are mild and the condition is caught early, you may be able to return to a more euhydrated and normonatremic state by consuming salty foods and restricting fluid intake. Even if symptoms are mild, it is recommended that you stay in an aid station where medical professionals are present. The support crew needs to monitor the runner's condition closely because it can deteriorate quickly. A runner who is exhibiting frequent vomiting, seizures, or significant neurological impairment needs immediate attention from medical staff. When in doubt, seek medical help.

COMBINATION 4: DEHYDRATED AND NORMONATREMIC

- **HYDRATION:** Low
- **SODIUM:** Normal
- **OCCURRENCE:** Somewhat common (10 to 15 percent of 100-mile finishers)

HOW YOU GOT HERE. In this case, you are consuming plenty of sodium from a variety of foods but either are not consuming enough fluid or are underestimating your sweat rate. At high altitudes the air is dry and sweat evaporates quickly, so skin may seem pretty dry even though you are sweating profusely. You also lose more body fluid through respiration in dry air. This can lead runners to underestimate sweat rate and fail to replenish fluids adequately. In warm environments some athletes run low on fluids based on the amount they are carrying. Rationing fluid is better than running completely dry, but eventually it will lead to dehydration.

SYMPTOMS. Weight loss, dry mouth, strong thirst, normal appetite for food, possible dizziness upon standing, fatigue, loss of focus, low urine output, and urine may be the color of apple juice or darker. Elevated risk of heat stress in warm environments.

HOW TO GET BACK TO THE CENTER SQUARE. Consume water. Sports drink and/or salty broth can be consumed but are not necessary. In warm/hot conditions slow down, wet your clothing, and douse with water to alleviate heat stress.

COMBINATION 5: OVERHYDRATED AND NORMONATREMIC

- **HYDRATION:** High
- **SODIUM:** Normal
- **OCCURRENCE:** Common (>30 percent of 100-mile finishers)

HOW YOU GOT HERE. This scenario sometimes happens in cooler weather when sweat rates are relatively low and you are eating plenty of sodium-rich foods but also consuming more fluid than necessary. Sometimes athletes who follow a regimented fluid schedule will end up here because they don't reduce fluid intake when cool weather, rainstorms, and wet clothing reduce their sweat rate. However, even when the temperature rises, athletes can be susceptible to this issue. Simple paranoia about dehydration can lead them to overdrink. Research performed by Martin Hoffman during the Western States 100 and the Rio Del Lago 100 Mile Endurance Run has found that this scenario is the most common (aside from euhydration and normonatremia) for athletes (Hoffman, Hew-Butler, and Stuempfle 2013).

SYMPTOMS. Nausea, sloshing stomach, bloating, low thirst, slight weight gain or absence of expected minor weight loss, puffy hands, and normal taste for salty foods but diminished hunger due to feeling full.

HOW TO GET BACK TO THE CENTER SQUARE. Restrict fluid intake to just moisten the mouth. Consider just swishing fluid in the mouth and spitting it out. This is not a scenario that increases the risk of heat stress because there is plenty of fluid available for sweat.

COMBINATION 6: DEHYDRATED AND HYPERNATREMIC

- **HYDRATION:** Low
- **SODIUM:** High
- **OCCURRENCE:** Extremely rare (<1 percent of 100-mile finishers)

HOW YOU GOT HERE. The difference between this scenario and being dehydrated and normonatremic may be the absence of urination. With high sodium concentration in the blood, your body holds on to the water it has instead of making fluid available for urine. Athletes sometimes end up in this condition due to overconsumption of sodium through salt tablets or losing track of sodium intake from multiple sources (chips plus salt tablet plus electrolyte drink, etc.). The challenge with this scenario is that the high sodium consumption may lead to nausea, which reduces the appeal of drinking.

SYMPTOMS. Weight loss, dry mouth, dry skin, cessation of urination, strong thirst, and salty foods may taste bad. Athlete is at elevated risk of heat stress in warm environments.

HOW TO GET BACK TO THE CENTER SQUARE. Consume plain water and restrict sodium intake. If you need calories, seek low-sodium carbohydrate sources. Sip small amounts of water to mitigate nausea. In warm/hot conditions slow down, wet your clothing, and douse with water to alleviate heat stress.

COMBINATION 7: EUHYDRATED AND HYPERNATREMIC

- **HYDRATION:** Normal
- **SODIUM:** High
- **OCCURRENCE:** Extremely rare (<1 percent of 100-mile finishers)

HOW YOU GOT HERE. This state is caused by consuming too much sodium in too short a period of time. Athletes who use salt tablets when they don't need them can end up here easily, which is one of the reasons I recommend food and fluid sources of sodium rather than salt tablets.

SYMPTOMS. Normal weight, strong thirst, no dry mouth, salty foods may taste bad but appetite is generally normal, and normal urination frequency but urine is the color of apple juice or darker. Risk of heat stress is not elevated.

HOW TO GET BACK TO THE CENTER SQUARE. Restrict sodium intake and continue with normal consumption of water. If you need calories, seek low-sodium carbohydrate sources. The condition will improve as you lose sodium through sweat and urination, but be careful not to restrict sodium long enough to swing all the way to euhydrated and hyponatremic.

COMBINATION 8: OVERHYDRATED AND HYPERNATREMIC

- **HYDRATION:** High
- **SODIUM:** High
- **OCCURRENCE:** Extremely rare (<1 percent of 100-mile finishers)

HOW YOU GOT HERE. This is a scenario that's relatively hard to achieve. To get here you have to overconsume both fluid and sodium. It can happen, however, if an athlete is moving slowly in cool weather (low sweat rate) and consuming large amounts of salty food and/or large volumes of salty broth or high-sodium sports drinks. When you are moving slowly, it is easier to consume large volumes of food and fluids because the intensity is low and there is less jostling to upset the stomach.

SYMPTOMS. High thirst, slight weight gain, salty foods taste bad, high urine output, puffy hands, and possible confusion or poor decision-making. This scenario shares some characteristics with the more dangerous overhydration and hyponatremia, including puffy hands, possible confusion, weight gain, and high urine output. The key differences are that with this scenario you will be thirsty, salty foods will taste bad, and your urine will have more color (although it is still light).

HOW TO GET BACK TO THE CENTER SQUARE. Restrict fluid intake to just moisten the mouth. Consider just swishing fluid in the mouth and spitting it out. Restrict sodium intake. If you need calories, seek low-sodium carbohydrate sources. This is not a scenario that increases risk of heat stress because there is plenty of fluid available for sweat.

COMBINATION 9: EUHYDRATED AND NORMONATREMIC

- **HYDRATION:** Normal
- **SODIUM:** Normal
- **OCCURRENCE:** Common (>30 percent of 100-mile finishers)

HOW YOU GOT HERE. You're doing everything right and adjusting fluid and sodium intake appropriately for changing conditions. Congratulations! The important thing is to stay here, which requires foresight.

SYMPTOMS. Weight is stable or slightly low, but within 3 percent of starting weight. Normal appetite and sweating, and normal urine output. Mouth is moist, and you have no nausea.

HOW TO STAY IN THE CENTER SQUARE. Think about how the conditions are going to change in the next few hours and plan accordingly. If fluid loss is likely to accelerate based on rising temperature, higher elevation, or greater intensity, plan to carry more fluid and gradually increase sodium consumption (or at least have sources of sodium with you). With so many variables in play, there are bound to be errors that take you away from the center square. While continuing to move forward, the preferable hydration and sodium errors are slight dehydration and slight hypernatremia. As you head in the direction of overhydration and/or hyponatremia, running becomes uncomfortable because of nausea, puffy hands, bloating, and a sloshing stomach. Heading in the direction of dehydration and/or hypernatremia will be increasingly uncomfortable as well, characterized by increased thirst, dry mouth, and dry skin. While these symptoms are unpleasant, they are more easily solved (get water, wet skin to mitigate heat stress) and less likely to stop you completely.

Final Word

Your biggest takeaway from this chapter is this: sports nutrition is dynamic. There is no singular formula that will produce optimal results for all athletes in all conditions. This is an area where, as an athlete, you have to understand how to manipulate carbohydrate, fluid, and sodium based on exercise intensity, duration of activity, and environmental factors. Hopefully you now have a better understanding of how these three key ingredients interact with each other and are affected by numerous factors. Sports nutrition habits are also trainable. The first step is to determine the food and drink combinations that work best for you based on the ideas presented in this chapter. Then, over time, you can train to increase the amounts of those foods and drinks you can consume without upsetting your stomach.

KEY POINTS ON ADAPTING NUTRITION STRATEGIES FOR ULTRARUNNING

- Sports nutrition strategies need to be adapted to ultra-endurance events with consideration for event duration, environmental conditions, and access to aid stations.
- Athletes should develop a variety of foodstuffs that they can rely on in race situations.
- Enhanced fat metabolism is a natural byproduct of endurance training.
- Enhancing fat metabolism comes at a penalty in that it requires more oxygen to liberate an equivalent amount energy as compared to carbohydrate.
- Enhancing fat metabolism can be done through chronic dietary manipulation as well as acute training interventions. There are advantages and disadvantages to any of these strategies.
- If athletes choose to adopt a fat-metabolism-enhancing strategy, a low-risk approach is warranted, such as doing some EnduranceRun sessions with low carbohydrate availability.
- Athletes are best served to avoid extreme fat-adaptation strategies such as restricting carbohydrates on hard workouts and longer runs.
- Hydration can be extremely difficult to get right and problematic to diagnose when things go wrong.
- Ultramarathon nutrition is dynamic, and athletes should practice their nutrition in training multiple times under different conditions to account for variances in environmental conditions and intensity.

CHAPTER 15

Mental Skills for Ultrarunning

Don't let the relatively slow pace fool you—ultrarunning is a physically torturous sport. With every step, our feet impact the ground with force a few times greater than our own body weight. This collision with the earth reverberates from our feet through our legs, into our torso, and finally to the neck, shoulders, and head. Over the course of an ultramarathon, we take tens of thousands of steps, resulting in muscle damage so great it can be comparable to the physical trauma of a serious accident or illness. We are reminded of the physical brutality of the sport after races as we hobble around, unable to stand, sit, or walk without grimaces, grunts, and assistance. But the physical damage does not stop at the muscles. During an ultra, our gastrointestinal system is also damaged. The sheer volume of foods and fluids consumed, as well as all the jarring and jostling of running can cause physical damage to the gut that is characteristic of an acute infectious episode. Still, damaged muscles and a dysfunctional gastrointestinal system are not the end to the damage train. Ultrarunners also suffer injuries to their musculoskeletal system during the course of training and racing. Regardless of whether it's spraining an ankle, catching your toe on an unsuspecting rock and slamming onto the ground superman style, or suffering an overuse injury, these maladies are physical reminders of our interactions with the environment.

The volume and severity of physical insults are so great that we tend to give them our undivided attention. We want big strong quadriceps to withstand the torturous nature of downhill running. We want voluminous lungs and a powerful heart in order to deliver oxygen and blood to working muscles for hours on end. We measure and record things like cardiac output, VO_2 max, vertical gain, and mileage as physical reminders of the work we have done. The size, shape, and volume of these reminders serve as measuring sticks for improvement, the bigger the better. But the intense focus on the physical exposes our biggest blind spot as athletes: mental training.

Athletes generally give lip service to the idea that ultrarunning is a mental sport. Clichés like "the most important distance is the 6 inches in between your ears" and "running is 90 percent mental and the other 10 percent is mental" are found in magazines and podcasts and thrown around like cheap confetti. We revere the ideas of "grit" and "toughness" even though there is no way to encapsulate them on your Strava dashboard. We even get to see the manifestations of an athlete's mentality as they forge on after hours of not being able to eat, with macerated feet and with bloodied knees, leaving us to wonder, "How did she finish?"

Despite the clichés and visual reminders of the mental side of ultrarunning, most notions of training the mental aspects of the sport unfortunately stop there. We recognize that the space in between your ears is important, that athletes with better mental skills will outperform their physiologically equivalent peers, and that mental skills training can improve race outcomes, but we very rarely take the steps to make those improvements. Add that to the general dearth of mental skills training programs and professionals in the space (heck the first edition of this book missed this subject altogether, and many athletes do not have the first clue where to start.

Unlike traditional physiological improvements, mental skills development is difficult to measure directly, and progress is hard to track. With physiological improvements we can directly measure parameters like oxygen consumption, determine how changes in oxygen consumption relate to performance, and then design and deploy training interventions to test their ability to improve performance. The same is true with muscle strength, force production, and the formation of lactate and other metabolites: we can measure them, learn about their importance to performance, and then design interventions that hopefully impact those variables. As a result of all of this measuring, testing, and remeasuring, we know a tremendous amount about the physiology that drives effective interval design and training structure.

The causal relationship between developing mental skills and improving physical performance is less concrete, which unfortunately encourages an "if you can't measure it, it's not worth doing" way of thinking. Because it's difficult to directly tie the application of mental skills to specific physical improvements, coaches and athletes stick to what they can reliably measure. Indeed, much of the research on mental skill development is mechanistic in nature, rarely yielding clear performance outcomes. For example, we can trace the impact of mindfulness on brain function by using functional MRI images to see what areas of the brain exhibit greater activation when meditating. Yet the link from that brain activation to performance is what I would describe as an "extension of the mechanism."

On the whole, research findings in this area are equivocal between mental skills development having some effect and no effect on performance. Because of this conundrum, the first part of this chapter will be a primer on how your psychology interacts with your physiology to impact performance. My intention is to show you, using research, logic, and examples, that mental skills either enhance or limit your performance. After that, I will walk you through a few mental skills you can use during your day-to-day training and teach you to logically string them together, much the same way you would organize your physical training. In keeping with the rest of this book, there will be no golden answer! Just as I have intentionally omitted static physical training plans from this book, you will find no static program for mental skills development in this chapter. There are, however, common themes, strategies, and a general framework you can apply to your training to help you become a better ultrarunner.

Psychobiological Model of Fatigue

Earlier in this book I presented the concept of limiting factors in ultrarunning. These limiting factors included such things as musculoskeletal stress, thermal load, glycogen depletion, and the like. Undoubtedly all of these physiological phenomena impact performance. However, there's a growing understanding that what slows us down is not necessarily the physiological manifestation of any of these limiting factors; rather, it's how we psychologically perceive them. In this sense, our physiological capacity determines the upper limit of performance capacity, but our psychological skills are the deciding factor in how *much* of that capacity we ultimately utilize (Ikai and Steinhaus 1961). Figure 15.1 graphically illustrates this concept, as well as how improved mental skills can help you realize the most of your physiological capacity.

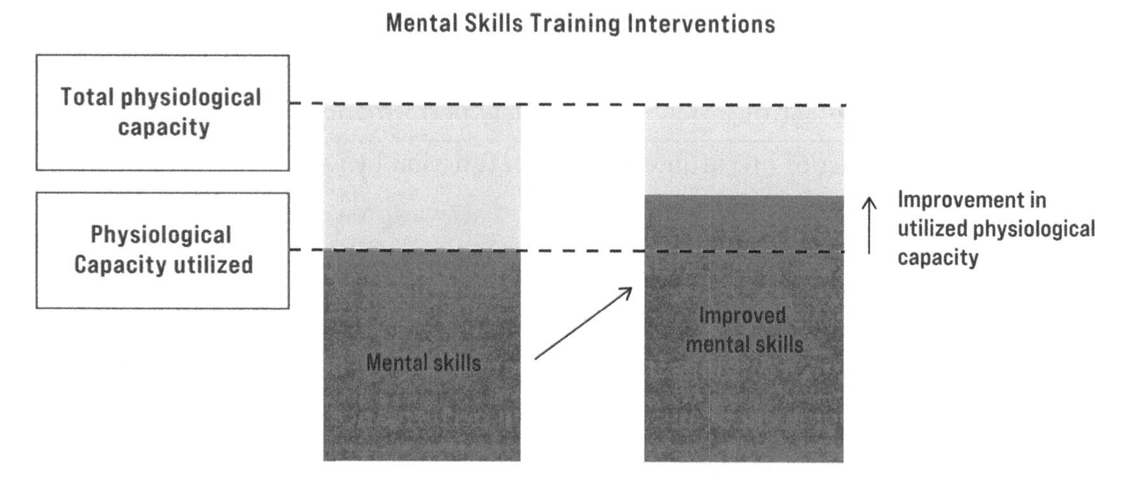

FIGURE 15.1 How improved mental skills can help you utilize more of your total physiological capacity.

This integrated model of physiology and psychology has been dubbed the psychobiological model of fatigue (PBM). In this sports psychology construction, an athlete's motivation and perception of effort are the primary drivers of performance. It differs from other psychological models, most notably Tim Noakes's central governor theory (Noakes 1997, 2012; Noakes et al. 2005). PBM recognizes that the brain and body act in concert to regulate performance, constantly modulating aspects of effort, pain, fatigue, and our perception of these sensations, whereas the central governor theory, as it was originally conceived, centered on the brain's role in protecting against catastrophe as the ultimate regulator of performance (though nuanced iterations of Noakes's model subtly changed this viewpoint over the years).

The difference is not inconsequential. Noakes's central governor theory designates the brain as the ultimate regulator whose only goal is to guard against catastrophe. Flowing from this theory, coaches and athletes have used psychological and physiological training strategies that were anchored around maximizing an athlete's ability to tolerate pain and discomfort. The "no pain, no gain" ethos found in many training strategies throughout the early 2000s paid homage to this. High-intensity training was all the rage for endurance athletes. Runners, cyclists, and triathletes alike pushed hard—often too hard—simply for the sake of improving the maximal amount of effort the regulator (brain) would tolerate before initiating shutdown. Athletes were taught to be "tough" and "gritty" and to persevere by whatever means necessary to achieve those ends. While toughness and grittiness are desirable traits for any athlete, they are not the only components of a comprehensive set of mental skills.

As opposed to the central governor theory's focus on the brain as the final arbiter of performance regulation, PBM puts the athlete and her regulatory skills in the driver's seat. PBM is anchored in the understanding that we psychologically interpret the physiological manifestations of things like pain, effort, drowsiness, fatigue, and discoordination and thus have the ability to voluntarily change regulatory strategies like pacing to optimize performance. PBM leaves room for the athlete to deliberately enhance aspects of motivation, consciously shift attention inward and outward, and even consume ergogenic aids like caffeine to alter the way we perceive the sensations that are telling us to slow down.

Perceived Exertion End Point Interactions

PBM can also explain why athletes drop out of races when there is plenty of physiological reserve to continue, through what is known as the "perceived exertion end point interaction." During any difficult task, we routinely and consistently monitor our effort in an attempt to correctly mete out our effort and achieve the best result (Figures 15.2 and 15.3). Think of an interval workout consisting of three by twelve-minute TempoRun intervals, for example. Typically, you pace the first interval in such a way that you can complete the next two. If, during the middle of the first interval, you think you are going too hard, you adjust your effort accordingly. In order to make these adjustments, you are drawing in your mind a line from your current effort level to what you *think* you can tolerate at the end of the task (the perceived exertion end point). As the workout goes on, you interpret new sensations of pain and fatigue and redraw this line over and over again, leading you to modulate your effort all the way to the end.

This process works very well in workouts and short races. We have a good sense of our maximum tolerable exertion level and how we can get to that maximum tolerable exertion over the course of a set of intervals, a 5K, or even a marathon. However, in an ultramarathon, this strategy backfires (Figure 15.4). Our predictive capabilities can only extend so far, and the sheer duration of an ultramarathon confounds our ability to accurately predict how this internal struggle will ultimately play out. As a consequence, you see athletes drop out halfway through an ultramarathon saying "I don't think I can finish" only to arrive at their hotel room moments later and immediately regret the decision. On the flip side, you can leverage knowledge of PBM and perceived exertion end point interactions to enhance ultramarathon race performance by "staying in the moment," which, although cliché, is an effective tool for bypassing your body's natural tendency to evaluate and predict effort (Figure 15.5). This will be discussed in more detail in the following chapter.

The message I want you to come away with is that your ultramarathon performance will be determined by a combination of your physiological capacity and your mental skills. Both can be enhanced by training. Your maximum capacity for performance is determined by your physiology, but how much of that maximum you actually utilize is determined by your mental skills.

Author's note: This interpretation of PBM is an amalgamation of several authors' descriptions of the phenomena, most notably Samuele Marcora. For further reading, please see Marcora 2008, Marcora 2009, and Marcora and Staiano 2010. Full references can be found at the back of the book.

Associative and Dissociative Focus Strategies

There is a lot of space in the sport of ultrarunning. There is linear space for miles on a ribbon of singletrack or miles of trail or road. There's the vertical space the mountains occupy as they jut out from the landscape. Finally, there is also the space in time ultrarunners experience, stemming from the duration of the event and various training activities. The last of these creates a lot of space within an ultramarathoner's mind, which can be filled with any number of things. We can calculate the time to the next aid station, focus inwardly on how our body feels, distract ourselves with music, take in the scenery, and occupy our wandering minds with any number of productive or counterproductive thoughts.

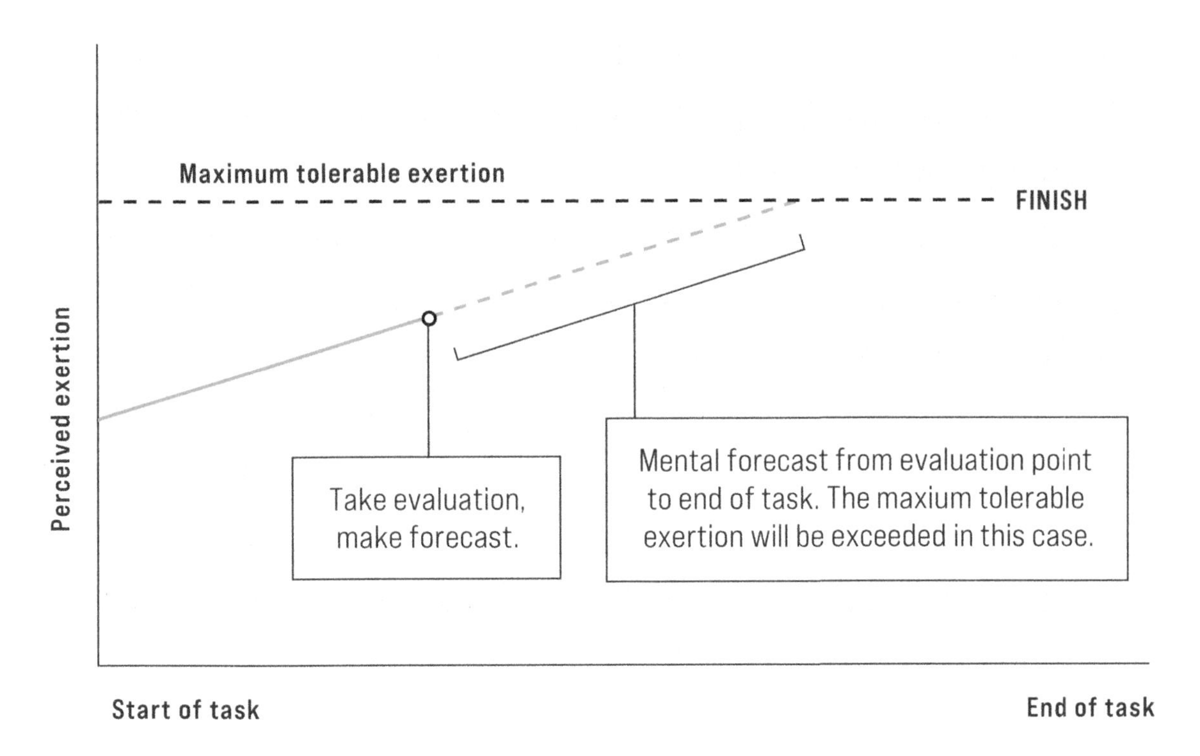

FIGURE 15.2 Schematic of the perceived end point interaction.

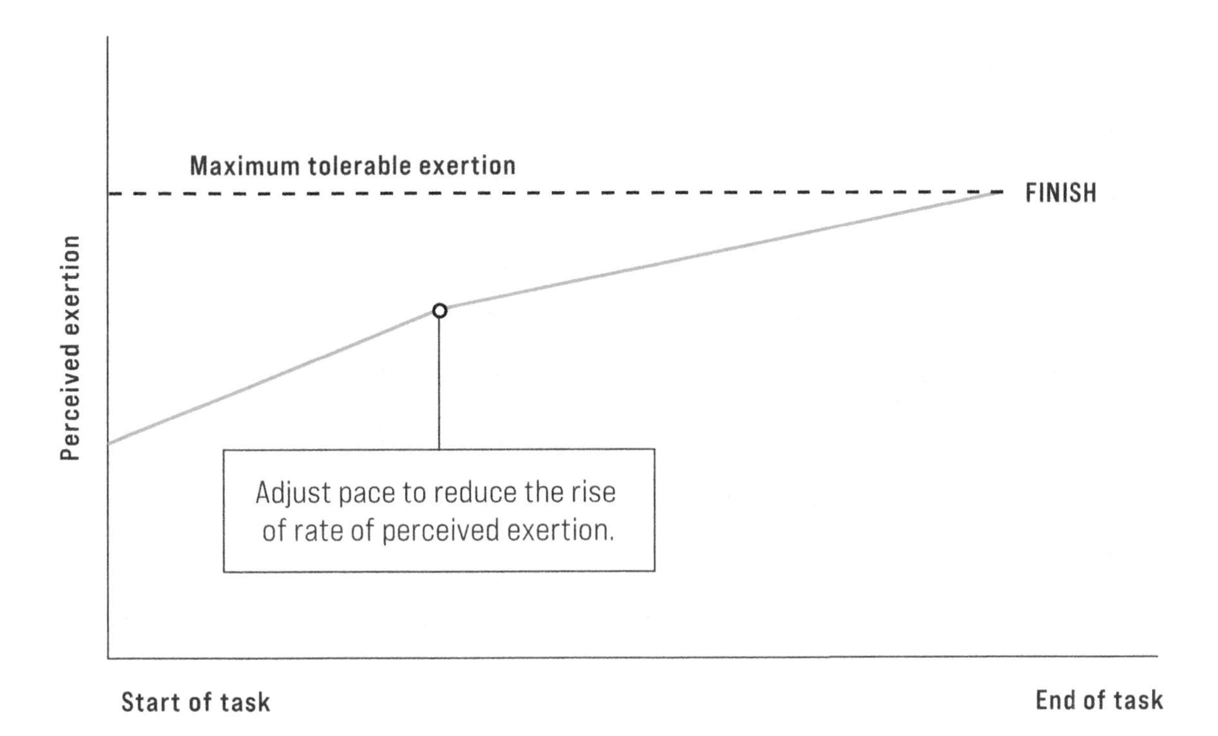

FIGURE 15.3 How an athlete adjusts pacing due to perceived end point interactions.

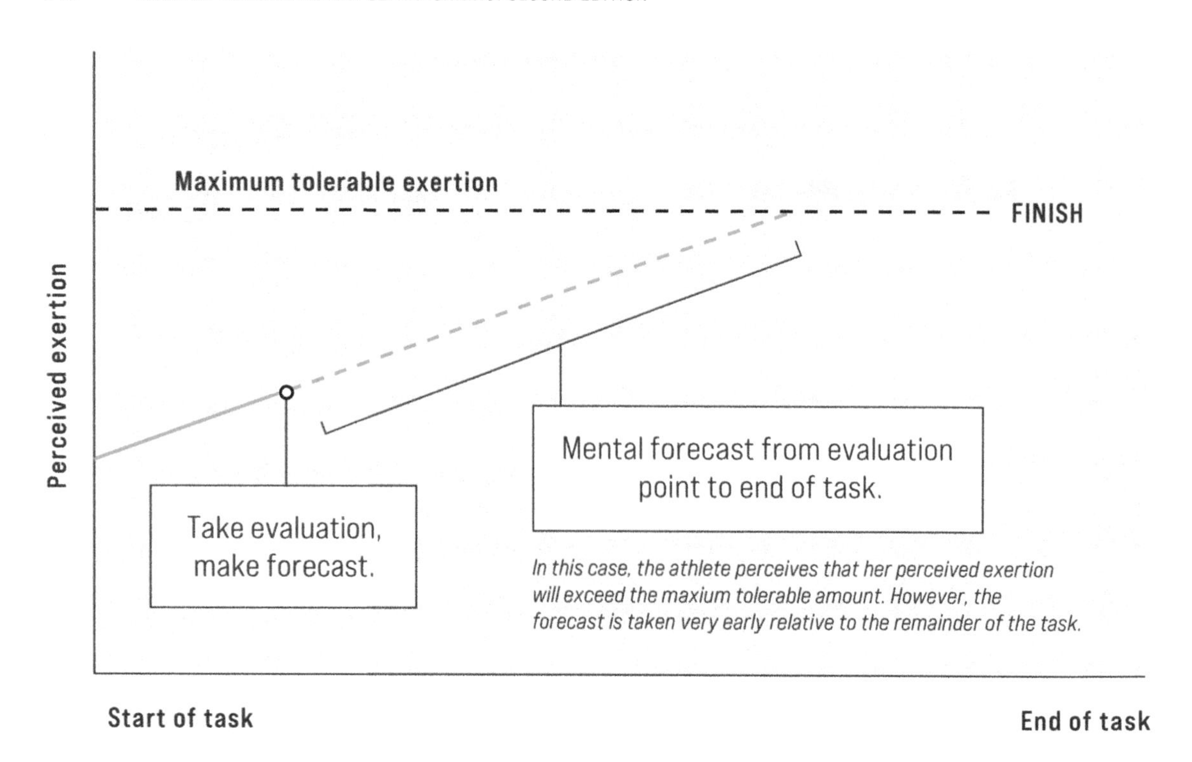

FIGURE 15.4 How an athlete can go awry with an early perceived end point interaction forecast.

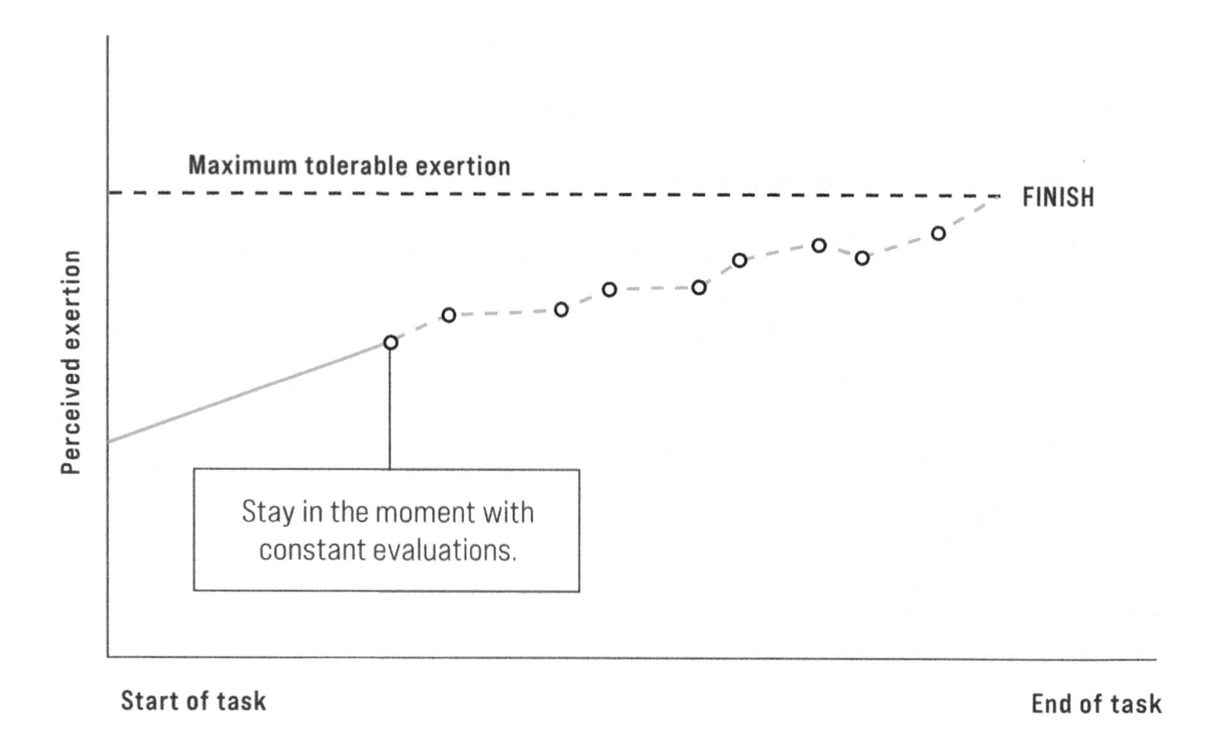

FIGURE 15.5 How staying in the moment avoids inaccurate forecasting.

In 1977, seminal research performed by Michael Pollock and William Morgan on focus and cognitive strategies revealed that, throughout the course of an event, elite marathon runners were more likely to focus on internal cues such as breathing rate and how their legs felt than their non-elite counterparts (Morgan and Pollock 1977). Non-elite athletes tended to turn their attention outward, choosing to distract themselves by thinking about uncompleted home projects, memories of the past, and other events unrelated to running as a way to distract them from the effort at hand. This bifurcation of focus has led the sports psychology field to frame focus strategies into two different categories, termed "associative" and "dissociative." As the adjectives imply, athletes using associative strategies direct their focus inward toward sensations and feelings they are presently experiencing. These strategies harness information derived from physiological sensory feedback in order to regulate performance. Dissociative strategies take the opposite approach, wherein the athlete temporarily removes himself from the present situation and redirects thoughts to something unrelated to the task. This can be as simple as counting or as complex as planning an elaborate meal, all in an effort to occupy the mind with anything other than what is happening with your physiology.

While this formative research created a distinction between elite athletes who focused inwardly and non-elite athletes who focused elsewhere, interventions should not be exclusively aimed at improving associative focus to be more like the elites, as Morgan and Pollock's original research implied. In the time since that research was performed, athletes, coaches, and sports psychologists have identified the need for athletes to move between associative and dissociative states depending on the particular situation.

In my view, the ability to move between associative and dissociative states is even more important in the sport of ultrarunning. For example, we know that dissociative techniques like counting or even conversing with your fellow runner can lower perceived exertion levels (Fillingim et al. 1989; Johnson and Siegel 1992). They can be effective during the middle stages of ultramarathons when fatigue is creeping in and perception of effort needs to be minimized, thus giving rise to the sentiment of "I have a long way to go but I feel fine." By contrast, we know that effort can be adjusted with associative strategies. For example, when you are climbing a hill early in the race and notice your breathing is becoming too labored, you can adjust your effort accordingly.

Being able to move between these two strategies is a skill that should be developed in training and then strategically deployed on race day.

STRATEGIES TO ENHANCE DISSOCIATIVE FOCUS

Being able to use dissociative focus strategies can be beneficial at times when feedback, like exertion and sensations of pain, needs to be reduced to improve or sustain performance. For example, in races like the Badwater 135 and Western States 100, where an athlete's feet become a particular pain point, you can choose to intentionally redirect your focus away from your ailing feet and toward something else. However, care must be taken when utilizing these strategies, as too much or reckless dissociation can cause you to miss important perceptual cues. How many of you reading this book have tripped over a rock or hit your head on a tree branch while off in la-la land instead of focusing on the task at hand? Probably everyone (including me). My point is that dissociative strategies need to be deployed in situations where they are actually useful, and there are many where they are not.

DISSOCIATIVE STRATEGY #1: COUNT THE PURPLE THINGS. Pick your favorite color (purple in this case) and, on your next run, count the number of times you see that color on your run. It's more difficult than you think, because you have to divert attention from spotting the next rock or the next turn or remembering when you need to take a gel in order to notice fellow trail runners decked out in an array of colors. Bonus points if you do this activity with a training partner and then compare notes after the run (ultrarunners are a competitive lot).

DISSOCIATIVE STRATEGY #2: PLAN A MEAL. The next time you want to practice utilizing dissociative strategies during a run, think of an elaborate meal you want to plan for your next dinner party or special occasion. Mentally rehearse getting the ingredients out of the refrigerator, carefully measuring each of them, combining the main ingredients with the perfect amount of salt and spice, and then cooking everything to perfection. If you do this in real time, it could take hours. And that's the key: be detailed and precise, and mentally rehearse the preparation so the experience is as vivid as possible.

I like to have athletes perform either of these strategies at deliberate times during the run, normally demarked by a time or feature like a turn from one trail to the next.

In this sense you force the dissociation to happen on your terms, not when your mind naturally wanders. Anybody can zone out, just ask a bored teenager during their least favorite class (English, for me). Ultimately, that's not what you are after; what you're after is the control to move to dissociation when you want to.

STRATEGIES TO ENHANCE ASSOCIATIVE FOCUS

Associate focus strategies are useful for times where you need to be in tune with what is going on with your physiology. Examples could include the beginning of a race when you are trying to pace your effort correctly, during the latter stages of a long climb as you push to the top, or while eating and drinking to ensure that you are consuming enough calories but not overloading your stomach. You can also use associative focus during fast and technical downhills to ensure precise placement of each step. In this way, many associative strategies become temporary "check-ins" with your internal physiology. Unlike dissociative strategies, they don't need to last long—just minutes for most, or maybe up to an hour if you have a very long technical downhill. Ultimately, your goal is still to be able to move between associative and dissociative strategies as the situation dictates.

ASSOCIATIVE STRATEGY #1: THE BODY SCAN. Borrowed from traditional mindfulness and meditation techniques (more on these later in the chapter), the body scan can be used as a formalized way of doing a systems check on your entire body during a workout or race. The procedure is simple. During your next run, pick a landmark or time marker to initiate your body scan. When you get to the marker, start at your head and take note of the different sensations. Can you feel your hat moving across your forehead? What about the buckle in back? Is your ponytail swishing back and forth across your neck? Gradually and systematically move down from your head to your neck, shoulders, arms, torso, abdomen, pelvis, upper legs, lower legs, and finally your feet. As you move down, take note and appreciate each sensation you come across. As you repeat this exercise, you will become more in tune with your body's feedback. As I will explain shortly, this can be integrated into a process to help you regulate effort, become aware of minor problems before they become larger issues, and adjust your plan accordingly.

The body scan can also be used in a passive setting alongside a meditation or mindfulness practice. In fact, it's prevalent in mindfulness apps like Headspace and Calm, which are great applications for those further interested in mindfulness practice. I encourage athletes to start with a passive body scan while sitting or lying down before moving to an active body scan during a run.

ASSOCIATIVE STRATEGY #2: FOLLOW YOUR BREATH. Your breath and respiration rate tell you a tremendous amount about your effort—so much so, that during intervals your simple respiration rate can serve as a near universal proxy for heart rate and oxygen consumption. This associative strategy is specifically focused on becoming more in tune with your breath so that you can regulate exertion, particularly during harder efforts. During your next run, take a moment to direct focus to your breath. Start with where the breath is coming from. Is it coming from your nose, from your mouth, or both? As you inhale, notice your chest expanding and subsequently contracting. You can put your hand on your chest if the physical touch helps you internalize this natural rise and fall. Do not force your breath to be long and deep or shallow and fast; just let it be however long or short it needs to be depending on the level of effort. This exercise can be performed while doing intervals as well, and the focus can assist in maximizing your effort, thus simultaneously improving the quality of the workout as well as your associative technique.

Associative strategies can be used across any physical sensation, from the whole-body scan to how your muscles and joints feel. Like dissociative strategies, they should be applied deliberately, depending on your desired outcome. Learning how to purposefully shift your focus between associate and dissociative strategies gives you more opportunity to direct your mind meaningfully in important moments, both in training and racing environments.

Mindfulness

Interventions in sport tend to borrow and steal lessons from other disciplines and redirect them in pursuit of improved performance. Take, for example, a pair of compression socks or pneumatic compression device (like the Normatec boots). These devices were originally developed for patients with poor circulation stemming from diseases such as diabetes. Compression interventions had been around for a long time before someone's

WHAT ABOUT MUSIC?

MANY ATHLETES CHOOSE to use music as a dissociative focus strategy and a motivational technique. Both of these would be viewed as passive ways of achieving either dissociation or motivation, but because it is a passive stimulus, using it during training is not effective for learning the skill of switching between associative and dissociative strategies. If you like to listen to music or your favorite podcast (or even the audio version of this book), that's great. But you should still carve out time during your training to deliberately work on active interventions and learn how to switch between associative and dissociative strategies.

entrepreneurial spirit kicked in and said, "Hey, athletes need better circulation, too. Let's adapt these for a different audience." Throw in some venture capital money, some Instagram influencers, and voilà, the compression garment industry and pneumatic compression devices were born. (Side note—we discussed the effectiveness of these tools in Chapter 8.)

Mindfulness for athletes is no different. Originating in ancient Buddhism, mindfulness practices have been around for centuries as part of meditation, simultaneous connection and detachment, and religious practice. At its core, mindfulness is a belief that all perceptions stemming from your thoughts, feelings, and the inside and outside world are impermanent. Perceptions can come and go as they please, and we can alter how we react (physically and/or psychologically) to them. Bringing this core belief into the sporting realm, athletes have used mindfulness techniques to better focus attention, perceive pain, become more accepting, reduce anxiety, and improve running economy (Bishop et al. 2006; Brown and Ryan 2003; Brown, Ryan, and Creswell 2007; De Petrillo et al. 2009; Hill et al. 2020).

Despite mindfulness's religious and spiritual background and the fact that it conjures images of long-haired meditating hippies sitting around a drum circle chanting "ommmmmmmm," the practice is not woo-woo pseudo-science fluffery at all. Neuroimaging studies performed on mindfulness practitioners have started to tease out exactly how the brain is impacted by different mindfulness interventions. Mindfulness can alter how the brain reacts to pain (Grant, Couremanche, and Rainville 2011) and affects body awareness (Hase et al. 2015; Mehling et al. 2009), both of which athletes can leverage to improve performance.

MINDFULNESS STRATEGIES

In 2004, researchers Frank Gardner and Zella Moore developed a multiphase mindfulness approach for athletes. Like any other area of athletic development, they suggest a "focus on the fundamentals" approach first, followed by a gradual ratcheting up of the mindfulness's difficulty and impact by applying it to real-world athletic scenarios. The original work, which is formally called the mindfulness-acceptance-commitment (MAC) approach to mindfulness, has been adopted and adapted by coaches, athletes, and sports psychologists to suit the needs of their particular situations. The following is my interpretation of their framework, which I have deployed with athletes. For greater detail on this work, please refer to the citation located in the references at the back of the book (Gardner and Moore 2004, 2015; Moore 2009).

STEP 1: Identifying What Matters in Competition and What Can Lead You Astray

Mindfulness for athletes does not necessarily begin with sitting on your favorite pillow in lotus position and focusing on belly breathing. Instead, take a moment and inventory what you need to be mindful about in the first place and what can distract you from those cues. For example, if you know you should be pacing your race off of your RPE, looking at your watch is a distraction. Seriously, what information salient to evaluating your RPE are you deriving from your current elevation? There can be a lot to inventory and, to be honest, it can be overwhelming. So, to start, pick a few and place the things that matter in one column and the things that can distract you from those in another.

While this is step one of your mindfulness journey, please feel free to revisit this as you move through the next three steps.

STEP 2: Becoming Acquainted with Mindfulness

Mindfulness in ultrarunning begins in a simple and unrelated setting. Acquainting oneself with mindfulness can be done during benign and routine events that are performed daily, such as cutting your food, brushing your teeth, and even folding your clothes.

THINGS TO BE MINDFUL OF	THINGS THAT WILL DISTRACT YOU
Rate of perceived exertion	Looking at the pace on your watch
Internal confidence	Where you are compared to others
Taking things one mile at a time	Calculating the distance to the next aid station

TABLE 15.1 An example inventory of attentional cues to be mindful of and what thoughts can be distractive.

Additionally, a host of apps like Calm and Headspace are available to introduce athletes to basic mindfulness concepts. If you are considering mindfulness as a tool in your mental skills arsenal, I highly encourage you to start with a basic subscription to one of these apps and have the narrator lead you though some of the fundamentals. If you want to take matters into your own hands (literally, in this case), I suggest the following exercise the next time you do a load of laundry:

The next time you set out to fold your laundry, set up the room and a time so that you will be in a quiet, uninterrupted space. As you pick up each article of clothing, take time to feel the textures of fabric, noticing if your fingers move along any buttons or seams. Take a breath and notice the residual fragrance of the detergent you used. Notice where your weight is balanced on your feet. As other thoughts seep into your mind (like what time you need to pick your kids up from soccer practice or what you have left to do on that work presentation), take note of them and when they come and go. Notice when your attention has turned back to the textures and smells of your laundry task.

The point of this simple exercise is to bring awareness to all of the thoughts you have flowing in and out of your consciousness. At this point you are not taking action on them, you're merely noticing these thoughts as they come and go. You can do a similar exercise while brushing your teeth, taking a walk, sitting down on the floor in a traditional meditative setting, or any other benign task that suits you.

STEP 3: Learning to Accept

The next step in your mindfulness journey is accepting your thoughts as neither good nor bad, but as they are. Being impermanent, thoughts entering into your consciousness can either stay or you can choose to redirect them somewhere else. In any case, they are what they are. They are not good or bad (as step one in this exercise could lead you to believe). Learning to accept these thoughts without judgement is the key in this next step of mindfulness. So, if during your routine task you notice that you are being judgmental about the thoughts entering your head (i.e., "this thought is bad/counterproductive"), notice the label, let it go, accept the thought for what it is, and redirect your attention to the task at hand.

Steps two and three of this exercise can be repeated daily, and I encourage athletes to spend at least two weeks on these simple exercises before moving on to the next step.

STEP 4: Moving to the Field

Now that you have a grasp on thoughts entering your head during routine tasks, it's time to take that strategy out into the field of practice during a normal training run. For this step, you will want to start small, preferably during one of your RecoveryRuns. Pick a section of the run bounded by two landmarks approximately two to three minutes apart. As you approach the first landmark, just as you did with the laundry exercise, make note of thoughts entering your mind. Once again, your goal is not to judge or place labels at this point, just notice as the thoughts come and go.

Repeat this process on subsequent RecoveryRuns for up to two weeks.

STEP 5: Putting Things into Play

This is the step where you integrate what is beneficial and detrimental to your focus into practice. For this step, you will need to review your list from step one. Pick a day where you have a particularly demanding run or set of intervals. Either during the intervals themselves or on a climb during the run, perform your mindfulness activity as you did during the previous step. Once again, you are taking note of thoughts as they enter your head, not judging them but accepting them as they are. This time, though, for the thoughts that are beneficial to optimizing performance, direct attention toward these to take action. If you notice that your breathing rate is climbing uncontrollably during a climb, you would direct that thought to action (slowing down, in this case). If you notice you feel the need to look at your watch (which is something that would distract you from your exertion), accept that thought as neither good nor bad but for what it is, and then redirect your mind to something that is productive (feeling the sensation in your legs, for example).

This final step integrates the previous steps into a cohesive strategy where you are considering the natural thoughts entering your mind without judgement and choosing what actions to take. This entire process takes a few months to get a handle on. So, I suggest moving through these steps slowly, a few weeks at a time. The fundamentals are always important, so feel free to integrate previous steps concurrently with the step you are on.

Imagery

Imagery has become an incredibly well-established field in sports psychology and athlete preparation. In fact, there is an entire journal devoted to imagery research in sport (*Journal of Imagery Research in Sport and Physical Activity*). Seminal research in this area performed by Terry Orlick and John Partington in 1988 studied the mental skills of 235 Canadian athletes who participated in the 1984 Olympic Games. They found that 99 percent of these athletes performed some sort of imagery in preparation (Orlick and Partington 1988). That's a staggering percentage of adoption for any type of intervention used in sport. You would have a hard time finding such a high rate of use for a category of training aids in any other area, such as strength training, nutritional supplementation, or working with a nutritionist. And don't think for a second that Canada has a secret lock on this intervention. Imagery is used by elite athletes in every sport, worldwide. Yet despite the widespread adoption of imagery at the elite level, for amateur and age-group athletes, imagery falls way down the list of priorities.

At its root, imagery is a way of mentally rehearsing a real-life scenario (like one you would encounter in a race, for example) during training so that when an athlete actually encounters that scenario in the field of competition, the movements, reactions, sensations, and psychological responses are more familiar. Thus, even if it's the first time you've actually experienced something in real life, you can take appropriate action because you have mentally rehearsed. Imagery is a multifaceted skill that can impact many areas of your ultrarunning game. For example, as a result of mentally rehearsing what to do in a traumatic situation, you can be calmer when you get lost (trust me, if you stay in ultrarunning long enough, this will happen to you). By imagining how you hike fluidly up a 4,000-foot pass, you will be more confident when you reach the foot of that pass on race day, even if you did not experience that type of terrain in training. You can also use imagery as a way to master technical skills, like running down a scrabbly descent.

DEVELOPMENT AND SEQUENCE OF IMAGERY TECHNIQUES

Like physical training, imagery training has a progression to it. Athletes initially undertaking imagery to sharpen their mental skillset should start simple and then gravitate toward more realistic, complex, and impactful imagery sessions. In this sense, you would begin imagery sessions at home, with the focus on simple scenarios encountered during training.

The setup here is simple: sit down in your favorite chair, think of the scenario that you want to work through, close your eyes, and then mentally rehearse what is going to happen. As you become more apt at taking these homegrown imagery skills out on your training runs (minus the closing your eyes part), you can use imagery during runs to mentally rehearse race scenarios.

EXAMPLES OF IMAGERY STRATEGIES

From a practical point of view, imagery strategies for ultrarunners can fall into two different categories. In one category, ultrarunners can use imagery to mentally rehearse critical sections of a race, like smoothly going through an aid station or grinding up

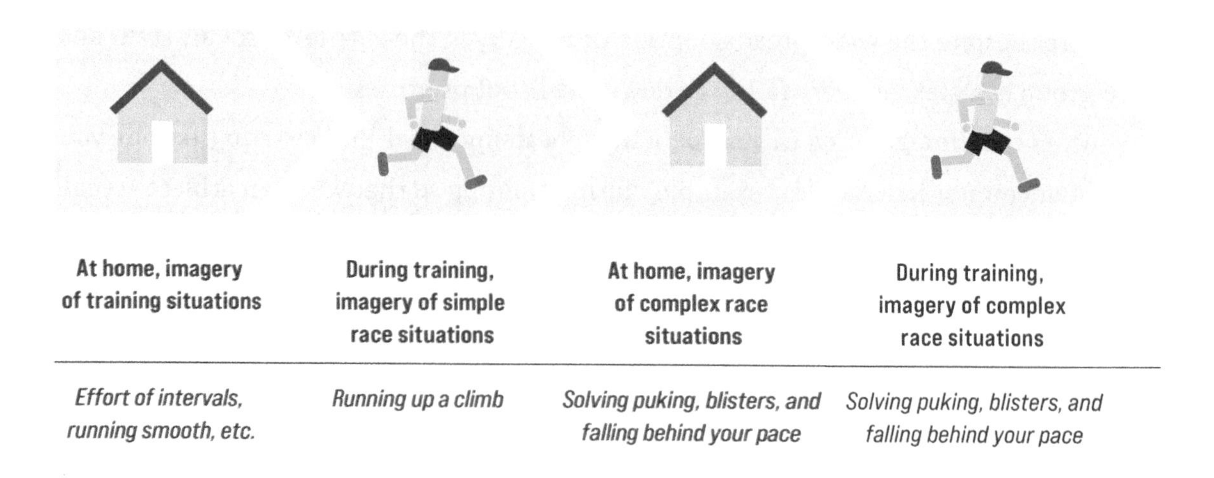

FIGURE 15.6 Sequence of imagery exercises.

a difficult climb. With these scenarios, you are attempting to improve your race-day effectiveness. Going back to our earlier principle that mental skills allow you to access a greater percentage of your maximum physiological capacity, imagery facilitates that through a "been there, done that" strategy. Here's an example:

> Athlete Jane is racing the Hardrock 100. She trains in Minneapolis and has never been on a 14,000-foot peak before. She has access to some small local climbs with 200 feet of elevation gain, and she will be running the Silver State 50 in preparation for Hardrock. Fortunately, she has done the Silver State 50 before and knows the climbs and descents. In order to prepare for Handies Peak, which is a 14,000-foot summit in the middle of the Hardrock course, Jane wants to use imagery strategies in training so that when she encounters the climb, it is not so foreign to her.
>
> Jane starts her imagery training at home, mentally rehearsing her next workout and how she is going to perform. Next, Jane uses her local 200-foot climb as a way of putting herself on the climbs of the Silver State 50. Each time she goes over her local climbs, she uses imagery to place herself back on the Silver State course, powerfully running and hiking each of the climbs. As Jane's training moves along, she does some research on YouTube to find out what Handies Peak is like. She mentally rehearses that climb at home, paying specific attention to the fact that there are two distinct pitches, separated by a talus field. The terrain moves from sharp rocks to loose gravel as the climb gets higher, and she imagines how her feet will feel as the surface changes. Finally, Jane moves these imagery sessions into the field of practice during training runs on her local 200-foot hill as well as during the Silver State 50.

The example above can be extrapolated to fit almost any race situation. The point of the whole exercise is to gradually move from simple imagery sessions that are relatively contrived to complex ones that will represent the real world.

The second category of imagery strategies is a form of contingency planning for when things inevitably go awry. As I have mentioned multiple times during the course of this book, if you stay in ultrarunning for any appreciable amount of time, it's not a matter of if, but rather when you will experience a catastrophic series of events that have the potential to take you out of a race you have trained so hard for. Particularly for things like 200-mile events and longer stage races, the duration and difficulty of the events result in unforeseen challenges that can throw even the most accomplished ultrarunners off their game. So, for athletes in this situation, I recommend imagery sessions that feature the absolute worst possible combination of things that can happen in a race. The exercise looks something like this:

STEP 1: Write Down the Worst Possible Race Situation You Can Imagine

We've all heard the horror stories of athletes breaking a headlamp, running out of an aid station without some critical piece of gear, getting lost, or bonking so hard that they swear they were abducted by aliens. Your first step in this exercise is to pick three or four of these horror stories, write them down, and then pick a point in your upcoming race where this cosmic misalignment of fortunes might actually happen all at once. Dialogue as much of the fictional narrative as you can, in as much detail as possible. Your situation might look like the following:

> I am running down Hope Pass, forty-four miles into the Leadville Trail 100. Suddenly I catch my toe on a rock and tumble down the trail. A few runners stop to help, and I notice my knee is split open and my hands have deep cuts from sliding down the scree. The bottles in the pack I was wearing broke in the whole ordeal, as did my trekking poles. As I continue to walk down the descent, I notice that all of my calories were somehow jettisoned out of my pack. I continue on toward the Winfield aid station without any fluid or food for the next two hours, and suddenly my stomach starts to feel nauseous. I throw up before getting to the aid station. As I enter the aid station, I realize that my crew has not made it there yet. So now I am only fifty miles into a 100-mile race, I have no crew, I have no way of carrying fluids, I am nauseated and bleeding from my knees, and I have a 2,000-foot climb right in front of me that I have to conquer.

STEP 2: Read Your Story. What Are You Going to Do about It?

Next, mentally rehearse what you are going to do to get out of that situation and keep running down the trail. Be specific; go step by step. For the example above, put yourself in the Winfield aid station. Realize that there are other crews and volunteers there to help. Go through each of your ailments and what you are going to do about it, step by step, one by one, as specifically as possible. If in your scenario you get patched up by medical personnel at the scene, visualize the color of their hair, make up a name for each of them, and imagine the conversation you will have. If in your scenario you have to borrow a pack from a pacer, what model was it and what were the colorways? The point of the exercise is to be as vivid and real as possible, rather than simply creating a counter-checklist to your series of mishaps described earlier. Your imagery exercise should end with you successfully continuing down the trail—perhaps with some bandages and a pack you borrowed from a volunteer, and without your poles, but you are continuing down the trail nonetheless, having turned what could have been a DNF into an epic comeback.

There's a lot going on in that scenario, but I have seen it happen exactly like that, as well as countless similar iterations. When faced with such scenarios, some athletes find the wherewithal to continue down the trail, and others throw in the towel. Using imagery to dig yourself out of a hole in practice can be the turning point for rescuing your race in real life.

Self-Talk

"Keep pushing." "You've got this!" "You've worked so hard for this." "I am going to make it to the finish."

All of these statements are forms of self-talk used by ultrarunners. Self-talk can take the form of instructional ("Plant your poles in line with your feet") or motivational ("You've got this"). In each of these cases, the talk should be matched to the desired outcome. If you need a pick-me-up, "You've got this" is going to be worth a whole lot more than "Plant your poles in line with your feet." To facilitate this alignment, as well as to give some framework for utilizing self-talk, psychology researcher Antonis Hatzigeorgiadis and his colleagues developed the IMPACT approach to self-talk.

- **IDENTIFY** what you want to achieve: Self-talk, like all training interventions, needs to have a specific goal in mind.

- **MATCH** self-talk to needs: What self-talk cues are going to facilitate the goals you identified?
- **PRACTICE** cues with consistency: In training, go try out your cues.
- **ASCERTAIN** what worked: Evaluate what cues worked and what cues did not work. Refine your plan accordingly.
- **CREATE A PLAN:** Create your self-talk plan from what worked in training. If you are using self-talk for a race, draw out what self-talk strategies might be helpful during different stages of the race.
- **TRAIN:** Like anything in life, you have to practice to get good!

If you have not caught on by now, the structure of designing self-talk interventions mirrors that of mindfulness, imagery, and training at large. In essence you are finding a self-talk plan that suits your needs, stress-testing that plan, and then training with that plan for eventual use during a race. Of particular note with self-talk, the type of self-talk you develop has to be specific to the outcome you want to achieve. Similar to the instructional vs motivational self-talk example, in an ultramarathon you are going to want different cues at different points of a race because your desired outcomes will change. For example, "You've got this" might be a poor self-talk cue in the beginning of a 100K race because it encourages you to dig deep or go harder when your goal at that point should be to conserve energy and relax. I've drawn out some of these scenarios in Table 15.2.

The remaining steps of the IMPACT self-talk strategy are relatively self-explanatory.

IDENTIFY WHAT YOU WANT TO ACHIEVE	MATCH SELF-TALK
Keep pushing when the race gets hard	"You've trained hard enough," "You've got this"
Run your own race	"Relax, focus on your effort"
Maximize effort during a training session	"Keep pushing, almost there"
Pole-strike effectively	"Plant your pole firmly, follow all the way through"

TABLE 15.2 Matching self-talk strategies to what you want to achieve.

You are testing out your self-talk strategies in training, seeing what works, modifying along the way, and ultimately determining a framework for what you will use during a race.

Purpose Through WHY

The societal, healthcare, and business responses to the COVID-19 pandemic will be studied for decades to come. The widespread disruption of established patterns and routines was totally unanticipated, and in the endurance community it tested the role of events for keeping athletes engaged. With most events cancelled, athletes lost the familiar guideposts they used to navigate through their training and competition seasons. Many athletes completely lost their way and went from being disciplined and goal-oriented to scattered and totally unmotivated in a matter of weeks. For some, this led to such frustration that they ended up throwing in the towel altogether. Maybe they stayed generally active, but they dropped any pretense of "training."

Other athletes never skipped a beat, even as their race calendars went up in smoke, gyms and offices closed, and stay-at-home orders were enacted. These athletes continued to train, had no problem with their daily 4:30 a.m. wake-up calls, continued to plug in their headlamps, and carried on with the daily grind. The difference between the two is that for the latter group, running served a purpose greater than collecting finisher medals and belt buckles.

Certainly, racing can be a powerful source of motivation. There's nothing wrong with competition as a part of the reason—or WHY—behind your commitment to running. But as we saw during the pandemic, there is a danger to overemphasizing races when considering the purpose running serves for you. Even in non-pandemic conditions, a strong purpose adds a turbocharger to your motivation engine fueled by competition.

Fortunately, I can almost guarantee you already have some underlying WHY for running besides the finish lines and belt buckles. Through more than twenty years of coaching runners, I can only recall a handful who only ran to race (and they didn't stick around in ultrarunning very long). You have to have a purpose, because running is not very glorious most of the time. There are times when it downright sucks. So, how do you find your WHY? I adapted the following framework from the renowned Simon Sinek, author of *Start with Why*, and include a personal example of going through the exercise myself.

STEP 1: Write Down All the Things You Do Consistently

Even gurus have to go grocery shopping. At the other end of the spectrum, people who feel like anonymous cogs in the machine often do things of great meaning—even if they don't realize it. You and I are somewhere in the vast middle between these extremes. Our lives contain a long list of basic tasks, but my guess is that you do some meaningful things on a consistent basis. Your first step in developing your individual WHY is to take an inventory of the things you voluntarily do on a regular basis. "Getting out of bed" or "fixing dinner for the kids" are both important but won't quite cut it at this stage. Think of the things that you look forward to, don't put off for later, and derive satisfaction from. Bonus points for activities you don't post on Instagram, that no one will know about, and for which no one will give you a lick of credit. These are activities you do for you. Don't try to assign meaning to them yet, just get them down on paper.

Figure 15.7 offers a simplified record from my brainstorming session for this step. I know that without fail I will run, coach, mentor other coaches, and build and help maintain trails in my local area. At the time I did the exercise, I actually had no idea why those were the things I did consistently and without much prompting. Nonetheless, I still do them. My guess is that many of you reading this book will have "running" as one of your consistent and nonnegotiable activities. If it is, then great. If not, don't worry, there's nothing wrong with you. This is just the first step in the process.

THINGS I DO CONSISTENTLY

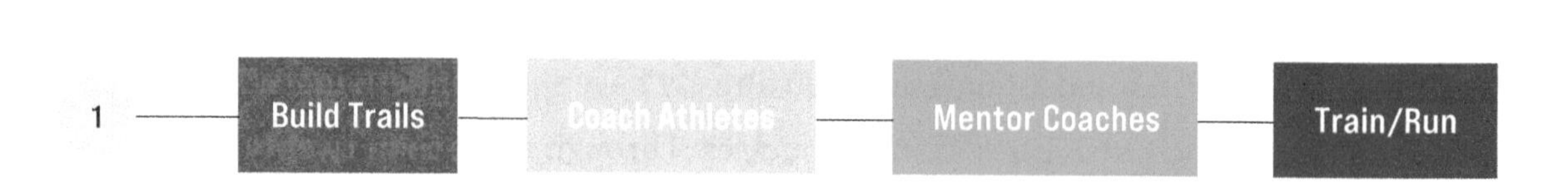

FIGURE 15.7 Step one in finding your why.

STEP 2: Find the Threads That Are Intertwined with Your Actions

The next step is to figure out the themes your most consistent activities have in common. This will likely take a while, so be patient. It took me a month to get through this step. I recommend setting aside time each week to come back to the exercise, review the connections you have already established, and search for the ones you haven't made quite yet. In my example, it became clear to me that after I worked on a trail, mentored a coach, or went for a run, something or someone was likely better off because of my effort. The themes of "betterment" and "improvement" started to resonate with me (as highlighted below).

When you do this for yourself, avoid simple truisms like "they make me feel good," "it's motivating," or "I love it." Dig deeper than superficial feelings and emotions. If it makes you feel good, why? If you love it, what about it do you love?

THINGS I DO CONSISTENTLY

1 — Build Trails — Mentor Coaches — Train/Run

2

After I do maintenance on a trail, it's in **better** shape. If I build a new trail, the entire network is better.

When I work with athletes, I get to see them **improve**.

When I mentor coaches, they are **better**, which in turn benefits their athletes.

I am a **better** person after I run. I am a bit **healthier** and **fitter** and can do my job **better**.

THE COMMON THEME IS IMPROVEMENT OR BETTERMENT

FIGURE 15.8 Step two in finding your why.

STEP 3: Phone a Friend

Sometimes we are not great at creating accurate depictions of ourselves. You know yourself well, and hopefully a bit better after the first two steps of this exercise, but at this stage some outside perspective is going to help. Up to this point you have been using self-evaluation, which can be biased toward telling the story of who we want to be or feel we should be rather than who we actually are at the present moment. This is normal, particularly for athletes, who are a naturally aspirational group.

So, now's the time to bring in one of your running friends, preferably one who knows you and is not afraid to tell it like it is. Don't waste time searching for the perfect person, just pick someone you can bounce ideas off of and who will offer up an external perspective. Their first role is to vet your "Things I do consistently" list. (Come on now, do you really volunteer at the soup kitchen all that often?) Next, encourage your friend to push you and poke holes in the themes you've identified as connections between your consistent activities. Outside perspective is helpful for separating what sounds good from what's real.

STEP 4: Craft Your Personal WHY

Now that you have your list of things you do without fail and the themes that connect them, it's time to craft your personal WHY. Simple is better, so try to keep it to one sentence and stick to the point. While you will have many interconnected themes between your consistent actions, choose the one (or two at the most) that are the most powerful. This is not a time for multilevel, choose-your-own-adventure-style plans. You need something concrete, actionable, and simple.

For me, that WHY boiled down to: "To leave things better than I found them." Yes, it's something you have heard hundreds of times, and admittedly it's a bit cliché. But that's fine, because it resonates with me. I can go for a run, work on a local trail, or help out a coach or athlete and know that at the end of the day my actions were aligned with my personal WHY.

STEP 5: Drilling Your WHY Back to the Beginning

Remember the PBM way back in the beginning of this chapter? The anchor points of this model are rooted in motivation and perception of effort. Your WHY is inherently tied to and reinforces your motivation. This matters in your day-to-day activities but is put under the magnifying glass during difficult athletic endeavors such as hard training and ultramarathon racing. The stronger your WHY, the more purposeful your motivation is, which in turn drives the entirety of the training process.

Sequence of Mental Skills Development

All endurance training is chronic. Measurable and meaningful improvement happens over the course of weeks and months rather than days or hours. Mental skills are similar. Just like you wouldn't train for a 100-mile event by doing a single ten-mile run, it is unrealistic to think that a single round of imagery, one five-minute mindfulness session, or a few sentences of self-talk will have a meaningful effect on your mental skills. It takes time and deliberate, repetitive practice to hone mental skills. There is also a preferred sequence to folding these into your training routine (much as I alluded to in the imagery strategies sections) that will enhance their effectiveness.

Earlier in this book, I presented a periodization scheme that begins with training that is least specific to the event and then moves deliberately to training that is most specific to the event. For most athletes training for ultramarathons, this leads to doing low-volume/high-intensity work early and then high-volume/low-intensity work as the race draws near. Designing training in this fashion optimally prepares you for whatever the race will throw at you. Physical training also gets harder over the course of time (remember the principle of progression?). While you first might start out with a five by three-minute set of RunningIntervals, during the next training phase that targets this intensity range you might be able to handle a greater load (seven by three, for example) and perhaps at a higher absolute intensity. Mental skills are no different. They can flow from general to specific and have a similar "loading" effect, where each subsequent task becomes gradually more challenging. You can even overlay your mental skills progression on your LRP in the "notes" or "other" section, if you like, which is something I do with my athletes to demonstrate how something as benign as sitting at home thinking about how you are going to pace your next interval set eventually leads to conquering something as arduous as Hope Pass on the Leadville course.

Below is a schematic that represents how the various mental skills can flow from the beginning to the end of a season, culminating in a race, as well an example of how each mental skill can "load" (increasing the difficulty and thus ultimate effectiveness). Starting with general associative and dissociative strategies, you lay the foundation of how to focus inward and outward and how to intentionally move between these states. During the planning process you may not know the details of the associative and dissociative thoughts that will be effective, you just know you will be using this time to hone the ability to shift focus on and off of yourself. Then, as you introduce mindfulness and self-talk, you will add meaning to what you are focusing on, creating greater depth and context. Finally, as you move to imagery, you will integrate all of these steps to mentally rehearse scenarios so you are ready to take actions and make decisions that impact your performance.

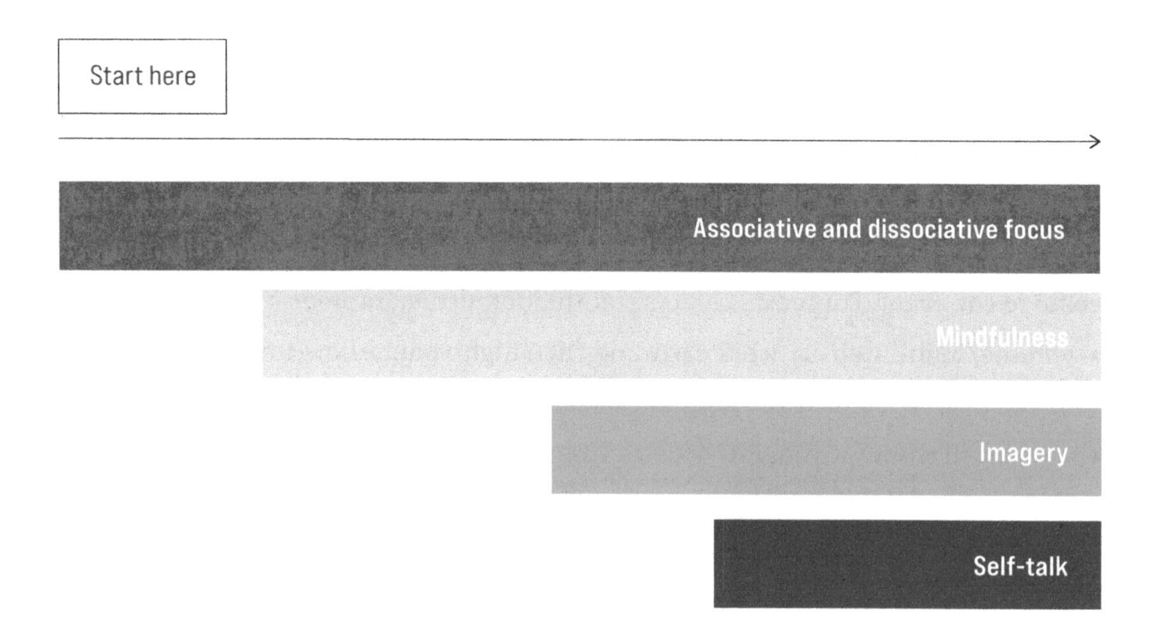

FIGURE 15.9 Where to start and how to incorporate mental skills.

KEY POINTS FOR MENTAL SKILLS TRAINING

- Ultrarunning is a very physical sport, but your mental skills are still important.
- Your physiological capacity determines the upper limit of performance, while your mental skills dictate how much of your physical capacity you ultimately use.
- Mental skills interventions have solid mechanistic rationale that has been demonstrated in research. However, translation to performance has been equivocal.
- The psychobiological model of fatigue states that how you interact with your body's physiology will regulate performance.
- Associative and dissociative strategies can both be used by ultrarunners to impact performance. Ultrarunners should learn to use and move between both of these types of strategies.
- A mindfulness practice can be useful to better manage the many impermanent thoughts flowing in and out of your head, homing in on those that are beneficial for performance while allowing those that are not beneficial to pass.

  Imagery can be used to mentally rehearse training and race scenarios in advance so that when the time comes, action is automated.
- Imagery techniques can be particularly effective in preventing a DNF when confronted with many confounding factors.
- Self-talk is another mental skills technique that can be used for motivation or for instructional purposes. Self-talk should be aligned specifically with the goals it is intended to achieve.
- Finding your larger purpose, or your WHY, can ground your everyday and athletic actions beyond outcome goals such as finishing a race or earning your next belt buckle.
- You should deploy mental skills interventions in a logical sequence for optimal performance. That sequence is: (1) associative and dissociative focus, (2) mindfulness, (3) imagery, and (4) self-talk.

Mt Whitney Cem
Gravel Pit
Cem
BM 1130.7
LONE PINE NARROW GAUGE
BM 1132.8
Lone Pine Park
BM 1135.5
Hospital
Lone
Corral
Prospects
ALABAMA HILLS
Mine
Prospects
BM 1144.4
BM 1190.2
Portagee Joe Campground
BM 1247.7
BM 1323.1
BM 1154.3
Grave
Cems
Borrow Pit
Locust Grove Campground
LONE PINE INDIAN RESER
INF
TUTTLE CREEK
White
BM
TION AREA
HILLS
BM 1152.9
RECREATION
Mt Whitney Golf Course
AREA
THUNDERCLOUD
LANE
SUNSET DRIVE
Corral
South Alabama Hills

CHAPTER 16

Creating Your Personal Race Strategies

Creating your personal race strategies is the final piece of the training process leading up to an event. Your personal race strategies bring your hard-earned training to life on race day. Setting race goals, deciding on nutritional strategies, and choosing your crew and pacers are the last pieces you complete in the weeks before the event. Many times, I have my athletes address the finishing touches during their taper, as a means of providing an outlet for their pent-up energy. In any case, last is certainly not least! By being clear on your goals, nutrition, and pacing, and by choosing the right crew (or not having one at all), you maximize the impact of the work you have done and the fitness you have attained.

Step 0: Review Your Training

Your personal race-day strategies start with a little homework: go review your training. Regardless of whether you keep a paper training log, work up your own spreadsheet, or use technology such as Strava, TrainingPeaks, Movescount, or Garmin Connect, pore over the last several months of training. Find where you were strong, and find the places where there were chinks in the armor. Look at the paces, grades, food, and fluids you utilized in training. This homework serves as the basis from which you will derive your race-day strategies. The effectiveness of your training sets a realistic framework for your goals. The nutrition you used in training is the platform you use to build your race-day nutrition strategy. The paces and workouts you accomplished in training provide a guide for meting out your race-day effort. Examine what you have done, and it will give you some boundaries for what you are capable of and what you need to do come race day.

What Is Your Race-Day Goal?

"What does success look like to you?" is the question I ask my athletes as the season is taking shape. The answer to this question helps me understand an athlete's goals for the season and for particular events. While I have some influence on shaping those goals, they ultimately belong to the athlete. After all, it's the athlete who has to put one foot in front of the other come race day. They should run, train, and race to accomplish goals they have created and own.

When narrowing down your race-day goals, I recommend using a similar philosophy. The goals you have on race day are not your partner's, your children's, your boss's, or your training buddy's. Your family, friends, and peers are key parts of your support network, but in the end your goals are yours and no one else's. This mindset may seem selfish, but starting from this reference point allows you to focus on you first.

Next, proceed to the practical steps of race-day goal setting. Whereas broad, early-season goal-setting questions about what success looks like are purposefully subjective and may seem hippie-dippie, the goals you establish for race day are concrete, actionable, and focused on the tasks at hand. This does not mean they need to be cold and formulaic. "Run with a smile" is just as concrete, actionable, and task-focused as "eat 200 calories an hour." Both of these are valid goals, and being creative with your goals helps personalize them. They do not have to fit into the stereotypical construct of a particular time, pace, or placing. They do, however, need to describe two things:

- **YOUR OUTCOME GOAL:** This is what you ultimately want to achieve.
- **YOUR PROCESS GOALS:** These are the things you need to do during the race to achieve your outcome goal.

OUTCOME VS PROCESS GOALS

Outcome goal: What you ultimately want to achieve.

Process goals: What you do along the way to support the outcome goal.

Example outcome goal: Finish the American River 50 in under eight hours.

Process goals:

- Eat a smart breakfast of 600 calories.
- Begin the race running 8:00 to 8:30 min/mi.
- Eat early and often, around 250 calories per hour.
- Stay positive.
- Tell the crew "thanks."

Example outcome goal: Finish the Vermont 100 having enjoyed the day.

Process goals:

- Keep the pace easy and manageable.
- Tell the crew to keep you smiling.
- Thank the volunteers at the aid station.
- Encourage other runners.
- Focus on gratitude that you get to run.

OUTCOME GOALS

I am a big fan of all sports. Although I have a particular affection for my hometown Dallas Cowboys, Dallas Mavericks, Texas Rangers, Texas A&M Aggies, and Dallas Stars, my love of sports and competition is expansive. My biggest fascination with sports is the simple outcome at the end of any sporting event. While I enjoy seeing how a particular play in football materializes and how all the plays throughout the game pile up to create a storyline by the fourth quarter, the outcome of the game is what fascinates me most.

Sports are inevitably an outcome-oriented affair. Wins and losses pile up at the top of the box score; the statistics are underneath. Particularly in running, where there is a starting line, a finish line, and a clock, there is always an outcome for every runner in the race. We can decide to place more or less importance on the outcome vs the process, but the outcome goal is the starting point for goal setting. All properly set outcome goals share three common characteristics that serve as a framework for formulating your particular goals:

- Outcome goals describe the outcome.
- Outcome goals are achievable.
- Outcome goals are challenging.

OUTCOME GOALS MUST DESCRIBE THE OUTCOME. Words matter, and so does specificity. The most important property of an outcome goal is that it must accurately describe the desired outcome. Outcomes can be times, places, or actions. They can be specific (such as a time or placing) or broad (such as a time range). Examples include:

- Place in the top third of the field.
- Finish the race.
- Run under nine hours for a 50-miler.

These are acceptable outcome goals that accurately describe some phenomenon that will occur at the conclusion of the event. Sounds simple? Apparently not. I consistently find athletes and coaches who use the wrong language to describe outcome goals. "I just want to finish" is a common way of expressing that you want to complete the race. I would never let an athlete express their goal this way, and you shouldn't do it either. The word "just" demeans the process, and "I want" is not an outcome of the event. "Finish the race" is the right goal; it describes the outcome you want to achieve.

RISKY BUSINESS: BALANCING CHALLENGING GOALS AND AFFINITY FOR RISK. Successful outcome goals strike a balance between being achievable and offering a challenge. Where you sit on the "achievability teeter-totter" depends on your individual tolerance for risk. As you set goals that are more challenging and closer to the limits of your capabilities, you must simultaneously accept a higher level of risk associated with those goals. However, goals beyond your capabilities are not well-constructed goals.

It is also important to realize that if you have a low tolerance for risk, an extremely challenging goal is just as inappropriate as a goal that is way beyond your capabilities. In other words, if you are risk averse, your goals will need to be more within your comfort zone. Being risk-averse is not a character flaw; nonetheless, your acceptance of or aversion to risk affects the way you need to set goals. A risk-averse athlete must put a premium on ensuring the goal is within his capabilities, even on a day when he underperforms for whatever reason.

Figure 16.1 illustrates the ideal balance. You have selected a goal that is challenging, and your affinity for risk is high enough that you will make the decisions and take the chances necessary to achieve your goal.

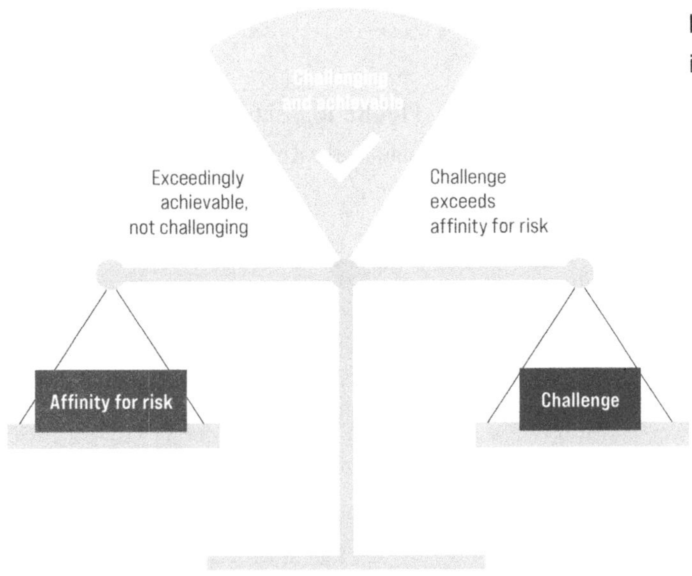

FIGURE 16.1 A goal where the challenge is balanced with the affinity for risk.

A goal that is more challenging requires more risk to remain in balance, as illustrated in Figure 16.2. Put another way, an athlete with greater affinity for risk can pursue goals that present greater challenges.

A goal that is less challenging remains highly achievable for athletes with less tolerance for risk, as shown in Figure 16.3. This can be a good scenario for a beginner because affinity for risk in endurance sports typically increases with experience, which consequently helps make more challenging events increasingly achievable over time.

Figure 16.4 illustrates a scenario in which your goal is highly challenging but you're

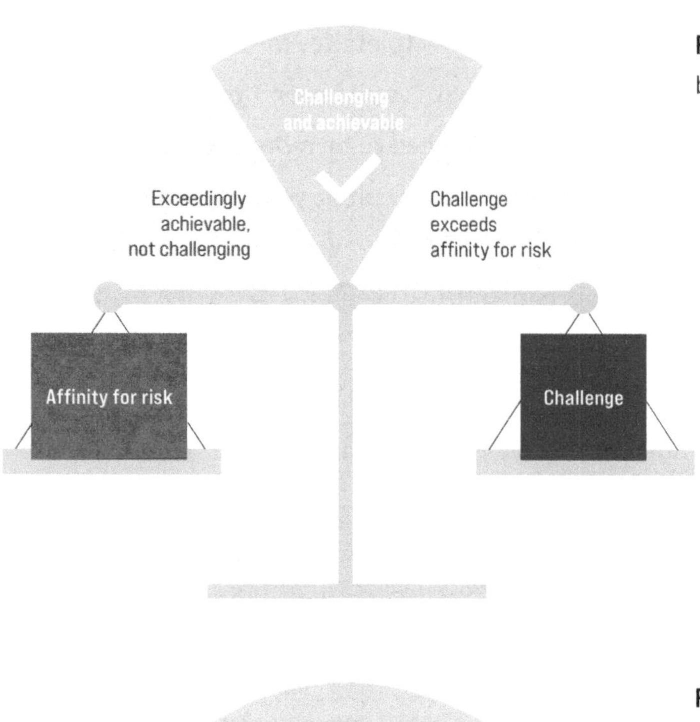

FIGURE 16.2 A bigger challenge that is balanced with a larger affinity for risk.

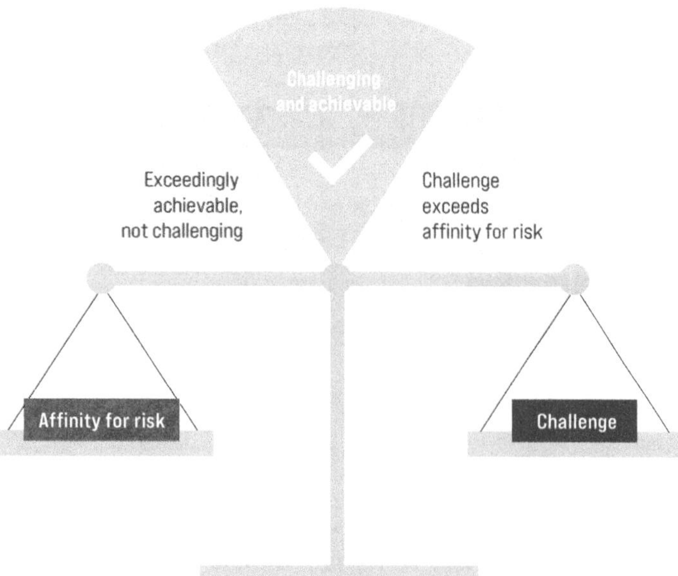

FIGURE 16.3 An easier challenge that is balanced with a smaller affinity for risk.

not tolerant enough of the risks necessary to make that goal achievable. In this situation it is highly unlikely you will achieve your outcome goal. While I encourage athletes to take on challenging goals, you can only push the challenge aspect of your goals as far as your risk tolerance will let you. You may be physically capable of achieving a more challenging goal, but you will fail over and over again unless your affinity for risk is high enough to enable you to fully apply that physical capacity to the goal.

FIGURE 16.4 A bigger challenge that is not balanced with a larger affinity for risk.

Finally, Figure 16.5 illustrates a scenario in which you have a high affinity for risk and your goal is highly achievable. It is virtually guaranteed that you will achieve your outcome goal. Although that may seem like a winning scenario, from a goal-setting perspective it is out of balance. The goal is simply not challenging enough.

FIGURE 16.5 An easy challenge that is thrown out of balance with a large affinity for risk.

What's wrong with an easy goal? Beyond the fact that you're disrespecting your own abilities, goals that are too easy lead to complacency, lack of focus, and big mistakes. Challenging goals force you to focus because many aspects of training, nutrition, and strategy have to go right in order for you to succeed. When the goal is too easy, you don't take it seriously, you don't prepare, and you can find yourself in a surprisingly dangerous position on race day.

HOW MANY OUTCOME GOALS CAN YOU HAVE? When setting outcome goals for an event, think simple and few. A large number of complex outcome goals is a recipe for chaos. I push, prod, and facilitate the narrowing process with my athletes, but in the end, it is their responsibility to craft their own outcome goals. Typically, after a few conversations, one singular outcome-based goal emerges. Any previous iterations of the outcome-based goal normally transition to process goals.

When an outcome goal is a placing or a time in the particular event, most athletes will choose to set A, B, and C goals for that time/place. For example, if your outcome goal is to run nine hours in the American River 50, you might have an A goal of 8:45, a B goal of 9:00, and a C goal of 9:15. These are all still challenging enough and within a normal range of performance. Other athletes will have an A goal of 9:00 and a B goal of finishing the race. Finally, some athletes will have only one goal: "I'm going to run 8:45 or bust!" When this is the case, my role as a coach is to first ensure that the goal is reasonable and balanced with the right affinity for risk. Then I offer 100 percent support for the athlete in that goal.

Once again, these are your goals. Take the time and care to craft them, and you will be on the right path.

Process Goals

I fully admit that I am a mixed martial arts (MMA) fanatic. A sport that started with obscure "last man standing" types of tournaments has now made its way into the mainstream, and I simply cannot get enough of it. I appreciate the sport for the entertainment; it's a good product and consistently fun to watch. But what really piques my interest is the way these athletes from varying backgrounds, much like ultrarunners, prepare to compete. Training for MMA involves mastery of many different fighting forms. Boxers, wrestlers, Muay Thai fighters, kickboxers, and jujitsu practitioners come together and do battle in the octagon. In these matches, victory can be won in a variety of ways. You can win by forcing your opponent to "tap out," which is the grown-up, professional version of crying uncle. You can win by decision, which puts the outcome in the hands of judges sitting ringside. You can win by knockout or a referee stoppage.

As these athletes prepare for competition, their different fighting styles converge. Strikers face wrestlers. Boxers face grappling artists. Muay Thai and jujitsu practitioners square off. As the saying in the sport goes, "Styles make fights."

Fighters are acutely aware of each other's strengths and weaknesses. They know whether their opponent has heavy hands (like Conor McGregor's famous left hand) or a penchant for a particular submission technique (like Ronda Rousey's storied armbar). Because of these different styles, fighters are forced to think about how they are going to win. They can't simply try harder. They must think about how they are going to use their strengths and exploit their opponent's weaknesses to achieve victory.

When you watch these athletes train, particularly as they enter a training camp in preparation for a big fight, their coaches home in on one question: "How do you see the fight ending?" The fighter, having already rehearsed the scenario in her head throughout practice, knows the answer: "I win by knockout," "I win by submission," or "I win by armbar." The "I win" part for MMA fighters is the outcome goal. The "by knockout," "by submission," or "by armbar" part peers into the process of achieving that goal. In training, MMA fighters rehearse how to control position, cut off angles, and physically wear out their opponent as different pieces of the process of accomplishing the outcome of winning. During the fight, pieces of the process they have rehearsed come to light as the fighters move, strike, and control position within the octagon. These fighters know it is not good enough to simply answer their coach's question with "I win." Their answer specifies how they will defeat their opponent.

As in MMA, defining the outcome goal in ultrarunning is only half the battle. The remaining part relies on setting process goals that will lead to success. Planning process goals is the actionable portion of your race-day goal-setting exercise. Unlike the outcome goal, which will be influenced by variables outside of your control, you have greater control over process goals come race day. They are the actions, thoughts, checkpoints, and supporting activities you do during the race to better ensure the outcome goal is achieved. In this way, process goals should dominate your thought process during the race. Thinking "I need to eat another gel to hit 200 calories an hour" at mile 30 of a 50-miler is going to do a lot more good than thinking "I need to finish in nine hours." As with outcome goals, process goals need to be personalized to suit you as an individual, your capabilities, and most importantly your personality.

When I have my athletes move through the process of goal planning, highly individualized paths emerge to support their outcome goals. Many times, even athletes with very similar outcome goals have wildly different process goals. Your process is your own, but all well-set process goals meet the following criteria:

- The process goal must directly support the outcome goal.
- The runner must be able to control the process.
- The process goals must suit the runner's individual needs.

PROCESS GOALS MUST SUPPORT THE OUTCOME GOAL. As you move through the development of your race-day process goals, the most important question to answer is, "Do the process goals support the outcome goal?" Accomplishing each process goal should bring you one step closer to your outcome goal. Goals related to pace, effort level, attitude, nutritional planning, and gear selection are all valid process goals as long as they directly improve the likelihood of accomplishing the outcome goal. Process goals that do not directly affect the outcome are frivolous and only suck valuable energy from your race. A great litmus test for a properly constructed set of process goals is to run them by your crew. If a process goal is well constructed, it should be something that your crew can easily reinforce while you are in an aid station, as well as something that makes an impact down the road.

PROCESS GOALS MUST BE UNDER THE RUNNER'S CONTROL. For a process goal to be effective, you must be able to execute it during the course of race day. Process goals such as eating a certain number of calories, running at a particular pace, and having a great attitude are all under your control. Process goals that fall outside of your control, particularly if they are dependent on another person, are not properly set process goals. "Run with Analisa for the first half" might sound like an easy goal to accomplish, but you are

HOW YOUR CREW CAN REINFORCE YOUR PROCESS GOALS

Outcome goal: Finish the American River 50.

Process goals: Eat 200 calories an hour.

List your process goals on a cue card and give it to your crew. Have them ask questions related to the specific process goals you need to go through, such as, "How many calories have you taken in? It's three hours into the race, so you should have consumed 600 calories by now."

not in control of Analisa's running. Avoiding the weather, staying in the top twenty, or beating a fellow runner are all similarly inappropriate; you as the runner are not in complete control.

PROCESS GOALS MUST SUIT THE NEEDS OF THE INDIVIDUAL. When setting process goals with my athletes, I am careful to help them tailor their goals to their individual needs, psychology, and personality. Many of the process goals you develop will include technical aspects (such as pace, calories per hour, and anything that can be quantified) and psychological facets of the event (such as "stay positive"). The emphasis on either technical or psychological aspects must be tailored to the individual, but I always encourage athletes to include at least one of each. If you run well when you track stats and numbers (such as calories and pace), you should have a larger proportion of those types of process goals. If you run well with more psychological cues (such as staying positive, having fun, interacting with the crew), these should constitute a larger proportion of your process goals. Similarly, when I am out at races encouraging athletes, I will provide the statistic-focused athlete with comments such as, "You ran that section right on your target time! Great job!" In contrast, an athlete who thrives more from psychological motivation will hear, "Stay positive! This next section is your strength, and your crew is right around the corner!"

Goal-Setting in Your First Ultra or First 100-Mile Event

The Leadville Trail 100 is notorious for having an extremely poor finish rate. Most years it hovers around 50 percent; some years, it's even lower. While the race is certainly difficult, there are no good reasons for this level of failure in the event. Some runners blame the altitude. Others say the climbing is just too much. Neither of these is true. As race founder Ken Chlouber would say, "These are crybaby excuses."

The real rationale for Leadville's poor finish rate revolves around the fact that there are no prerequisites to enter the race, as there are for many other 100-mile events. An athlete needs only to survive the lottery process, plunk down an entry fee, and show up in order to start the race. As a result, many athletes who enter the event are new to the sport or are using Leadville as their first 100-mile race. Many of the innocent rookies drop like flies. The effort required to complete 100 mountainous miles at high altitude torments runners as they attempt to locomote through the wee hours of the night and into the next day. The athletes struggle with cutoffs, calories, and a sense of what the hell they have gotten themselves into. Sadly, many who are struggling will refuse to continue. It's a tough race for sure, but not as tough as one would expect from a 50 percent finish rate.

Far more than 50 percent of the athletes entering the Leadville Trail 100 have the necessary fitness to complete the race. The athletes who don't finish rarely lack the physical ability, but rather a sense of purpose. Purpose is what will drive them in and out of the frigid Outward Bound aid station at mile 75 when a warm car ride back into town is oh so tempting. The rookie mistake is not a lack of training, it is a failure to understand the special feeling that comes from finishing one's first 100-mile race. They come to the race without that singular purpose, and it costs them.

It has taken me until this point in the book to insert a personal story about training and preparing for ultramarathons. All the earlier chapters are filled with anecdotes from my athletes, and this is on purpose in order to avoid introducing my own N-of-1 bias.

My first 100-mile event was the Leadville Trail 100 in 2008. An athlete's first ultra and first 100-mile race are special moments. These two accomplishments represent unique achievements that are unparalleled in the runner's athletic career. Because one's "first" is such a special moment, the goal-setting process for these events should revolve around getting to the finish line at all costs. Time, place, and performance in these circumstances are all secondary considerations.

I will always remember the year I first finished the Leadville Trail 100, because I proposed to my wife at the finish line. I chose to reinforce the "finish at all costs" mentality by carrying a ring in the pocket of my shorts for the entirety of the 2008 Leadville Trail 100. For the finish line proposal, I had no backup plan. I either finished the race and got on one knee, or . . . well, I didn't know what the hell I was going to do. For 100 miles, the ring was there, with the center stone occasionally pressing into my thigh. It was a constant reminder of how important the race was and how special the finish would be. That was my outcome goal—finish the race and have the chance to propose to my future wife. There were no B, C, or D goals, just one goal and one focus.

My process goals were similarly suited: run conservatively, take time in the aid stations, enjoy the company of my pacers, and take additional warm gear. All were aimed at finishing in any time under the thirty-hour cutoff. While the race was hard, the ending of the story was a happy one. Sure, I was well prepared and fit, and I had a fantastic support team (including this book's coauthor, Jim Rutberg). But the crucial aspect of preparation was setting the all-important outcome goal and its supporting process goals. Achieving that goal meant the world to me.

The Dreaded DNF

Ultramarathons are hard. Most experienced ultrarunners have at least one "Did Not Finish," or DNF, on their record. Sure, you may come across athletes without a DNF, but these individuals are at the edges of the bell curve. In my coaching career, I have had my fair share of athletes who have DNFed in an ultra. I have had several DNFs myself. Some could have been prevented, but others were unavoidable. While it's always heartbreaking to see an athlete underperform, I have never, not once, been upset with, ashamed by, mad at, or embarrassed by an athlete who takes a DNF.

There are three reasons for this:

- If a DNF results from some random act like rolling an ankle or getting off course, that's part of the game. No sense in agonizing over it. Injuries and mishaps can happen on any training day and on any training mile throughout the year. It's just dumb luck if it happens on race day.

- If a DNF results from a lack of preparation, either physical or mental, that's on me, provided the athlete did the work in training. It's my job to make sure the athlete gets to the starting line prepared for the event. Similarly, my hope in writing this book is to give you enough knowledge and tools so you will be well prepared when you reach the starting line for your event.
- Some athletes choose to race at the edges of their capabilities. That is their goal. For these athletes, a DNF may be the right personal choice once their aggressive goal slips away, even when completing the race is still a possibility. Reaching the finish line might require limping through the remaining miles or a three-hour nap at the aid station; they could still finish, yet they choose not to continue. These athletes have chased the goal they set and should have no shame in that DNF. If you are clear about your goals, then a DNF as a potential ramification of aggressive goal setting is just as gutsy as struggling to the end. As long as you are crystal clear on your goals, find the right balance of challenge and risk, and take the time to craft goals in a meaningful way, then you will always make the right decision if faced with the possibility of a DNF.

Creating an Effort-Based Race-Day Strategy

Pacing can make or break your race day. Wrist-top GPS technology can provide accurate information on pace, altitude, cadence, and heart rate to help guide the process. These data cues can be used to better prepare for race day, but reliance on this information can also ruin your plans if you apply it incorrectly.

Pacing data from athletes competing in the Western States 100 reveal that athletes who perform better and place higher generally have less speed variability overall and slow down less as the race progresses (Figure 16.6; Hoffman 2014). The easy conclusion to make is that these athletes paced the race better and thus slow down less and finish the race faster. However, could it be that the athletes who slowed down less were just more prepared? That question has yet to be answered.

In any case, there are three different strategies to properly gauge your effort and speed during a race: pace, heart rate, and perceived exertion. You can choose to utilize

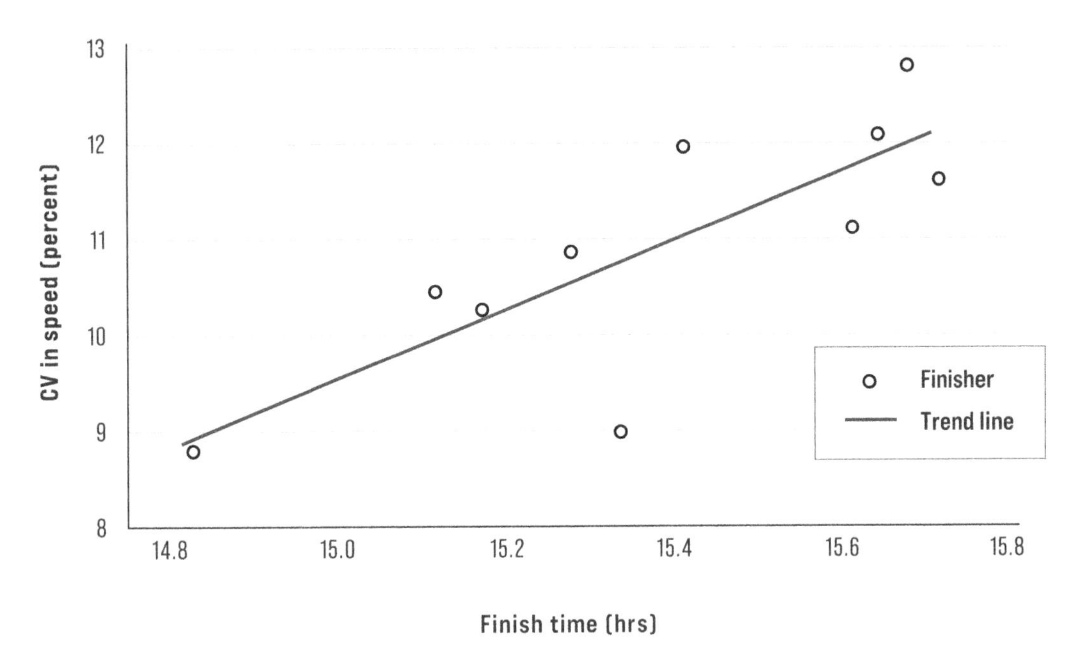

FIGURE 16.6 Relationship between coefficient of variation (CV) in speed and finish time for the ten fastest finishers of the Western States 100. The fastest finishers had the lowest variation in speed. Source: Hoffman 2014.

one or a combination that suits your needs and situation.

OPTION 1: Pace

The standard marathon race-day plan invariably revolves around hitting some sort of pace for specific segments of the race. Even before the advent of GPS watches, digital timing clocks lined the routes of the major marathon courses, sometimes appearing as often as every mile. As GPS watches evolved, runners started monitoring pace in real time. For athletes looking to set a particular pace or time standard for a marathon, this is a good solution. You have all the data you need at regular intervals to pace the race out properly. In many major marathons, you can even get customizable pacing bracelets, complete with splits for each and every mile.

As I've said already, ultramarathons are not simply long marathons. Thus, although pace can be a useful component of your race-day strategy, there are limitations that you will have to account for to determine if it is a useful tool for you and your goals.

Pace is a good tool on race day in the following scenarios:

- Race terrain is flat and level, without any technical elements for 50K and

50-mile distances. In this situation you can choose to base your race-day strategy entirely on pace. If you are keenly aware of your TempoRun, SteadyStateRun, and EnduranceRun paces, your race-day paces can mirror these when appropriate. Similarly, if there is an element of flat, level terrain somewhere within a trail race, you can incorporate pace in those sections to gauge your race-day intensity.

- You are able to train on the racecourse. In this situation, if you are aware of your pace on certain segments and during certain workouts, you can use that information to calibrate your race-day pace. For example, if you consistently do SteadyStateRun intervals up a climb in training and that climb is used during the race, you can check your GPS watch at various points during the climb to make sure you are at the right pace. For 50K and 50-mile races many athletes can climb segments at their SteadyStateRun or TempoRun intensities. Generally speaking, if the total number of climbing segments in the race matches the training interval lengths described in Chapter 9 (see Table 9.1), you can reproduce those same intensities during the race if you have trained properly for them.

Pace is a poor tool on race day in the following scenarios:

- The terrain is different than your home training ground. The terrain will slow you down if it is more technical than you're accustomed to, and the opposite is true if the race-day terrain is more benign. This is true at all race intensities and at all grades. Bottom line: if your race-day terrain is much more or less difficult than your home training ground, pace will be a poor tool for you come race day.
- The altitude is different than your home training ground. When you are at higher altitudes, your pace will be negatively affected. The opposite is true if you are racing at lower altitudes. These effects are highly individual, making it difficult or unwise to attempt to adjust pace based on a mathematical formula.
- For 100-kilometer and 100-mile events. Typically these events are so long that you will be running much slower and easier than your day-to-day training paces and intensities.

OPTION 2: Heart Rate

As discussed in Chapter 6, heart rate is generally a poor way for an ultrarunner to determine intensity. Factors such as sleep, temperature, hydration, fatigue, and time of day may affect heart rate at any particular point in time. Furthermore, because I am an advocate of training based on RPE, introducing heart rate on race day would violate the tried-and-true rule of "try nothing new on race day." Nevertheless, there is one limited scenario in which it is appropriate to use heart rate to gauge your race-day intensity.

Heart rate is a good tool on race day in the following scenario:

- When an athlete is consistently overenthusiastic at the start of races. In this case, I recommend using a heart rate monitor as a governor for the first 25 percent of the race. The simple procedure I use is to find the athlete's normal SteadyStateRun heart rate range during training (still using RPE to determine the intensity during the actual workouts) and then have them use that value as an upper limit that is not to be exceeded during the first 25 percent of the race. For example, if during training an athlete's heart rate range is normally 160 to 165 beats per minute for SteadyStateRun intervals, I will set 165 as the heart rate ceiling that the athlete cannot exceed for the first 25 percent of the race. Effectively this holds the athlete at the lower end of SteadyState intensity or higher end of EnduranceRun, because race-day heart rates are generally higher for the first 25 percent of the race due to freshness and adrenaline.

Heart rate is a poor tool on race day in the following scenarios:

- Just about everything else. Your race-day heart rate is going to be affected by a multitude of factors. Early in the race, adrenaline will artificially elevate heart rate. As fatigue sets in, your heart rate will be depressed. All in all, heart rate is a poor choice to use come race day.

OPTION 3: RPE

Racing should be a reflection of your training. Similarly, pacing during the race should revolve around how you pace your day-to-day efforts. With my athletes this means using RPE. Your internal RPE offers a calibration point that accurately identifies your intensity and is independent from factors that affect pace and heart rate. But the main reason my athletes use RPE on race day is because it is what they have used in training. Day in and day out, they are calibrating their efforts using a simple 1 to 10 scale. Race day should be no different. (For a detailed look at RPE, refer to Chapter 6.) The sidebar "Calibrating RPE for Race Day" illustrates how an athlete was able to take his efforts during day-to-day training and translate them into proper pacing on race day.

CALIBRATING RPE FOR RACE DAY

IF YOU HAVE TAKEN THE TIME to properly train and develop your fitness, you can race as you have trained. This means that during the race you should be able to recreate the time-at-intensities you accomplished in training. For example, if you were consistently doing four by ten-minute efforts at TempoRun intensity during training, you can accumulate forty to sixty minutes of the same intensity during the race. The same is true for EnduranceRun and SteadyStateRun intensities. Based on the attributes of the race you are preparing for, you can map out a plan of what RPE to target for different parts of the race.

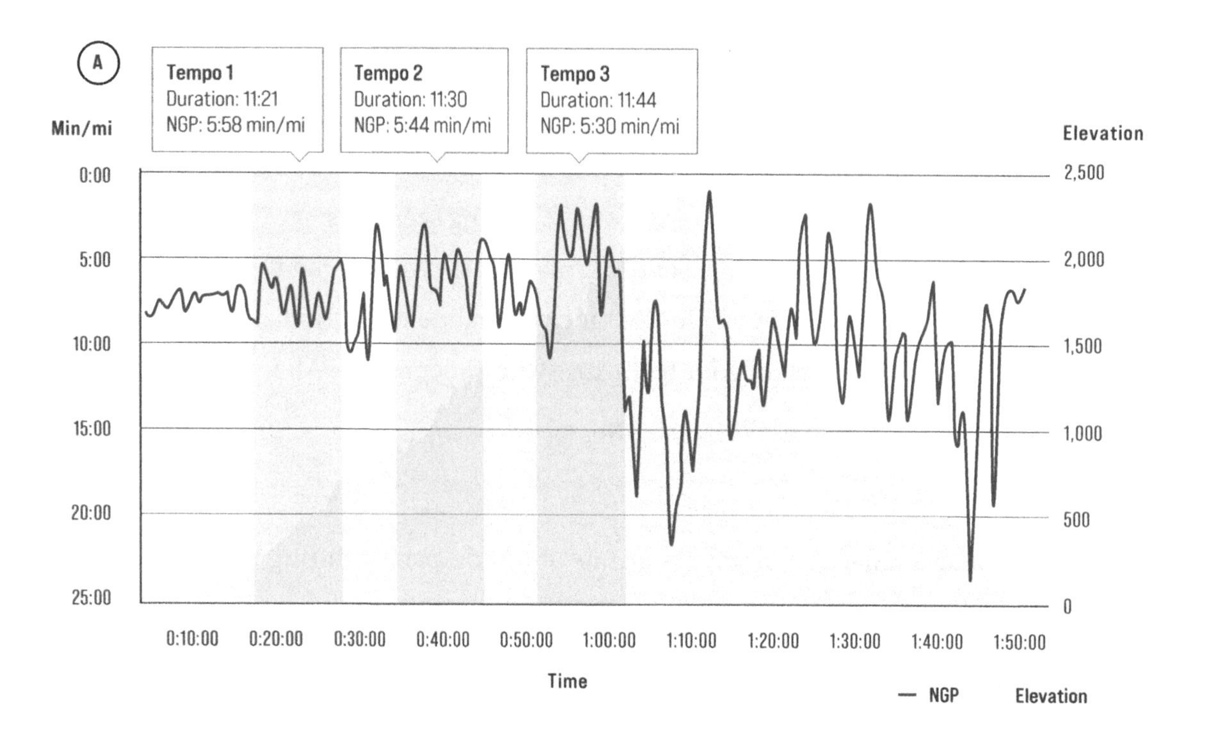

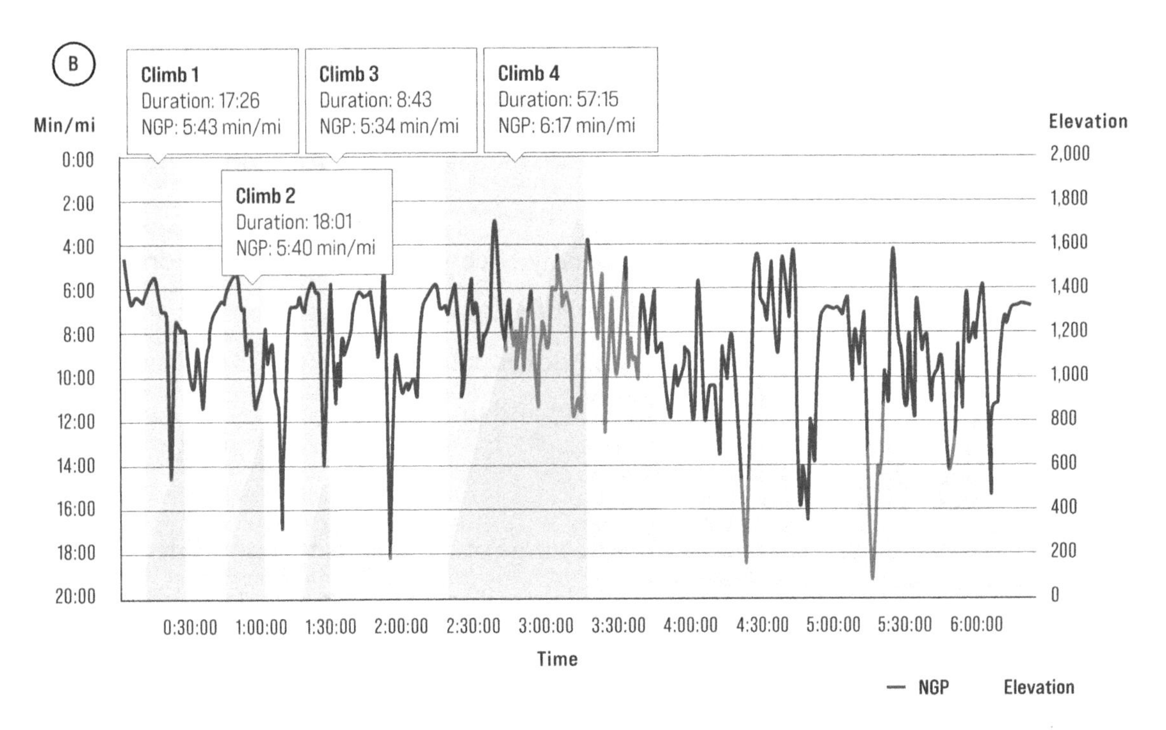

FIGURE 16.7 Comparison of Tempo intervals done in (A) in training to (B) the climbs in a race.

> The first figure (A) is a typical TempoRun that an athlete did in preparation for the 2014 North Face Endurance Challenge. It shows that he can average a Normalized Graded Pace (NGP) of 5:30–6:00 min/mi for three by eleven-to-twelve-minute intervals. The intervals for this workout would be at an RPE of 8 to 9.
>
> The second figure (B) is a GPS file from the same athlete's actual race. The first four major climbs of the race are highlighted with the NGPs the athlete was able to run. In this situation, he accurately calibrated his race-day effort from his training efforts because the climb segments were similar in length to what he was doing in training. The race data validate this strategy, as the NGP from the first three climbs is similar to his TempoRun NGP during training. The NGP from the fourth climb would be indicative of a SteadyStateRun effort because it is closer to sixty minutes in length.

Why Staying in the Moment Works

"Focus on the mile you are in." "Just take it one aid station at a time." "Be present." If you have been at an aid station during an ultra, you have almost certainly heard these strategies, and others, uttered by pacers and athletes as a means of psychologically coping during the race. They've been so overused that they are trite by now. At their roots, they are all trying to break up a long effort into more manageable shorter ones, otherwise known as "compartmentalizing the effort."

Few think about why this strategy is actually effective; they've just regurgitated it based off of an experience, anecdote, or tall tale. But it turns out there's a scientific rationale to compartmentalizing the effort. Additionally, this practice is well suited for ultrarunning because of the sport's complexity and uncertainty.

HOW WE PACE WORKOUTS

Ultrarunners have always adopted a wide range of pacing strategies. While I advocate for a perceived exertion–based strategy for trail and ultrarunners, I realize my opinion is not the only game in town. Some athletes choose to use heart rate, others utilize pace, and some runners are starting to use foot-based power meters. When I was in college, our coach would place orange cones every 50 m along the track and then program a beeper to broadcast over the loudspeakers at distinct intervals corresponding to the paces we were trying to achieve. All of these strategies have their merits: they provide feedback to the athlete, and the athlete can either adjust their effort or maintain it accordingly. However, when uncertainties enter the equation—as they do in ultrarunning—the athlete has to apply a more nuanced understanding of pacing.

A 2018 study out of Australia looked at athletes performing a 30K cycling time trial with and without cues about the distance remaining (Wingfield et al. 2018). Athletes who knew how far they had gone in the time trial were able to achieve higher power outputs (particularly in the last two minutes) despite no changes in heart rate or RPE (see Figure 16.8).

This makes a lot of sense. When you know how much farther you have to go, you can take an internal risk assessment to gauge how hard you can push (see Figure 16.9). This phenomenon is what is known as "perceived exertion end point interaction." It simply states that if given a task, let's say a workout or a race, athletes will pace themselves according to two facets: (1) how they feel at the moment and (2) how far they have to go. You constantly integrate those two points as you progress through the task and calibrate your effort so you are spent (or at least perceive that you are spent) at the very end. You are literally drawing and redrawing an internal line between where you feel right

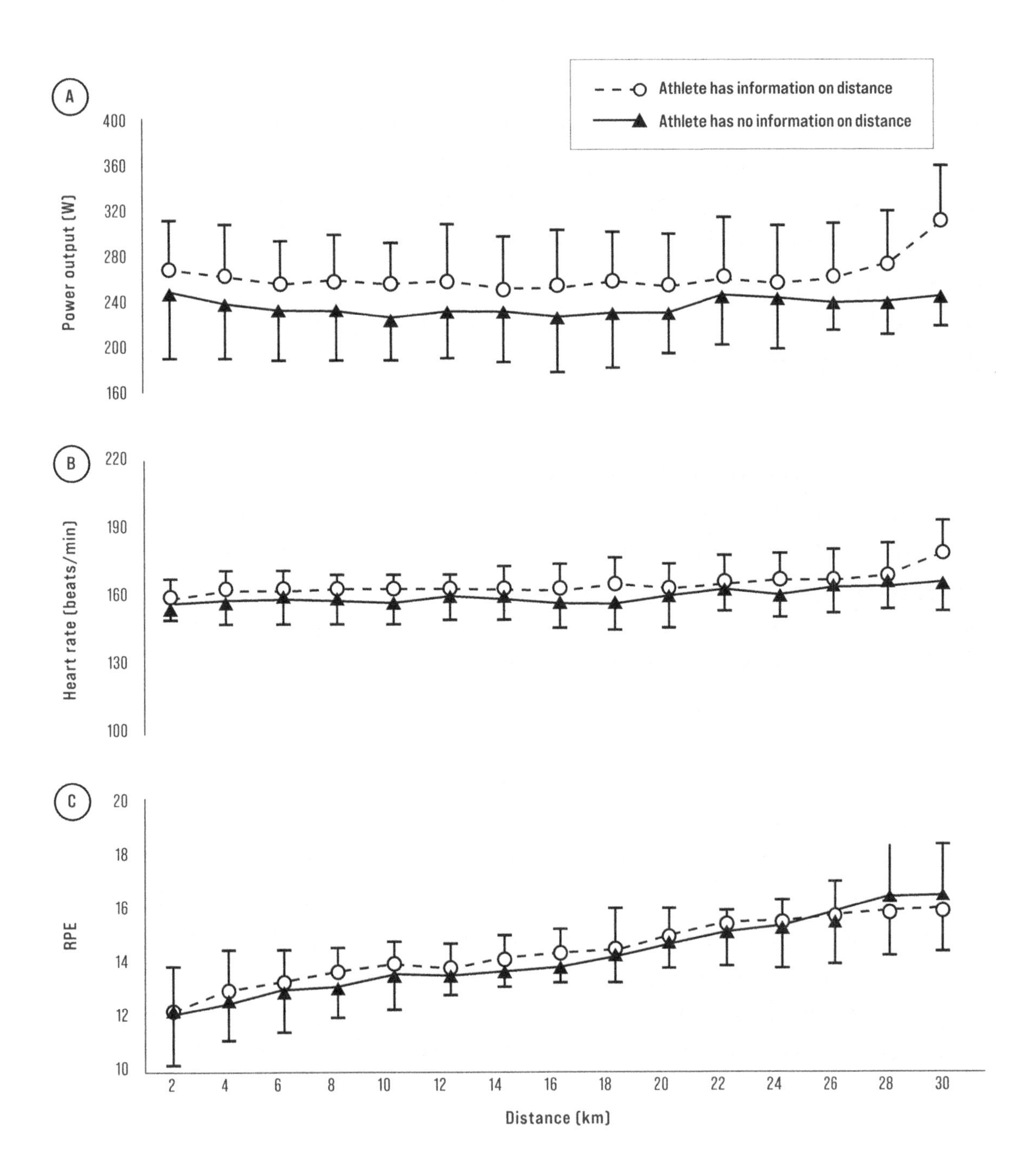

FIGURE 16.8 A 30K cycling time trial done with information on distance and without. Source: Wingfield 2018.

now and where you project you will feel at the end point.

Interestingly, this rationale has also been used to explain why novice athletes are so poor at pacing, because they don't know the end point well enough. It can explain how

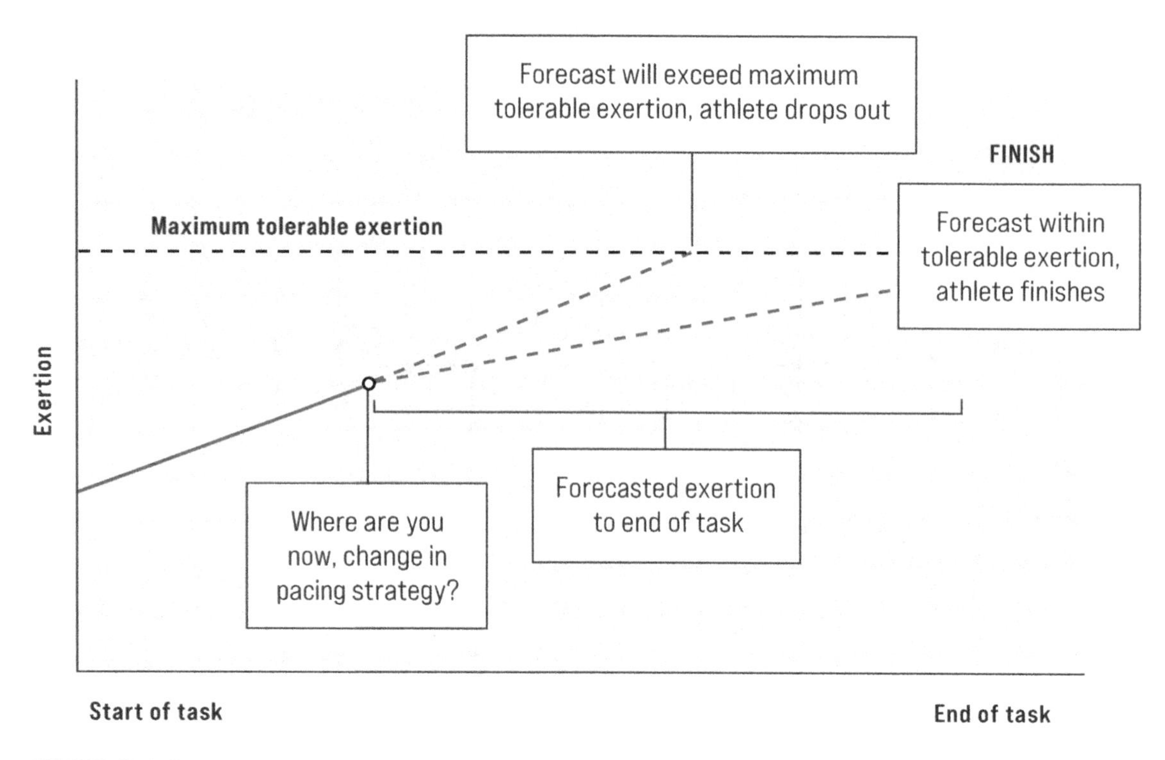

FIGURE 16.9 Perceived exertion end point interaction.

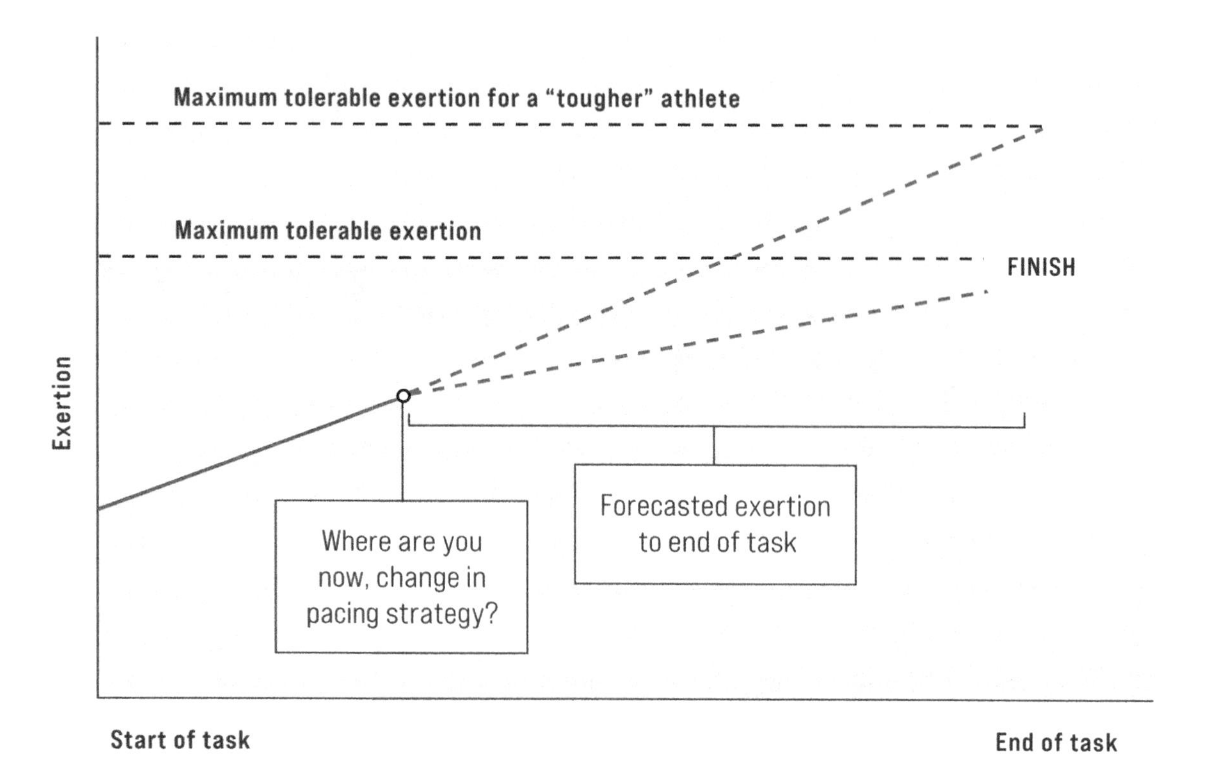

FIGURE 16.10 How a "tougher" athlete fares better.

"tougher" athletes can perform better; they are willing to risk a steeper slope and higher end point (see Figure 16.10). And it also explains why youth athletes have a tendency to start out too hard, as they have poor internal measurements of exertion. Flavors of this phenomenon have also made their way into famous models of performance regulation, such as Tim Noakes's central governor theory (Noakes, Peltonen, and Rusko 2001) and Ross Tucker's Anticipatory Regulation Model (Tucker 2009). I also feel there is a translational point in ultrarunning.

FORECASTING DNF DECISIONS

If you have been keeping track during this chapter, I've used the dreadful DNF rates at the Leadville Trail 100 as an example of poor goal setting. There's also much to be learned from observing how and where athletes make the choice to drop out. Every year I make it a point to spend several hours at the Outward Bound aid station at the Leadville Trail 100. Located at mile 75 of the race, it is a DNF decision point for many. Runners come into the aid station in all different states. Some look great, others awful. Despite their varying outward-looking conditions, there is no real correlation between the athletes' appearances and who drops out or continues on to the finish. There is, however, an internal calculation made by each and every person as they enter that aid station. Whether they realize it or not, they look at how they feel at the moment and extrapolate that to how they anticipate feeling while running the remaining twenty-five miles back to the town of Leadville—which include the infamous Powerline climb. According to the perceived exertion end point interaction concept, if the slope or the end point of that imaginary line exceeds what they perceive is tolerable to them, they get their wristband cut, head into their car, and take the short ride back to town. The athletes that forge on have imaginary lines that are within their preconceived limitations, whether through a higher exertion tolerance, a more accurate forecast, or a lower degree of instantaneous suffering. However, the potential for error in both of these strategies remains the same: you are forecasting for a long period of time with many unknowns.

IN THE MOMENT

The take-home message for ultrarunners is that there's some method to the madness of "being in the moment." Forecasting and predicting in ultrarunning can be a fool's errand, although we're naturally inclined to do it. We're even trained to incorporate perceived exertion end point interactions in workouts and hard runs. However, unlike in a workout or marathon, your ability to predict how you will feel hours down an ultramarathon trail is clouded by the sheer duration and your impaired ability to comprehend (because let's get real: are you smarter or dumber after eighty miles?). So, when you get to your own Outward Bound aid station and all seems hopeless, forget the forecasting. Stay in the moment, focus on your effort at the present time, and draw upon some of the mental skills that we covered in Chapter 15. The finish line will eventually show up—just give it time.

Sleep Considerations for Longer Events (200 miles, etc.)

Ultramarathons lasting more than 48 hours require some special planning, particularly in regard to sleep. This is an area where the research is pretty thin, and we are doing a lot of educated guesswork in terms of when, where, and how much to sleep during events. Rather than just leave it at "it depends," let's go over the basics of what we know about when, where, and why the sleep monster might jump on your back.

THE WITCHING HOUR

Ultrarunning folklore is riddled with tales of hallucinations, out-of-body experiences, paranormal activities, and even an alien sighting or two. Given enough time and sleep deprivation, ghouls and goblins, devils and demons, witches and wildlife will inevitably appear, haunting even the heartiest of souls. I've been there. Deep into the Tor des Géants I swore some random Italian at an aid station was one of my lifelong friends. The bewildered look on his face after I gave him a big giant bear hug was the only thing that snapped me back to the fact that I was on a mountain ledge at 8,000 ft. I've also seen it firsthand, like when an athlete I was pacing at the Badwater 135 was having a full-blown conversation with the Michelin Man, complete with an origin story and advice on electrolytes. But do you ever wonder why all of these tales of the supernatural happen around the same time? Why do the Care Bears magically appear at 3 a.m. and not 3 p.m.? Why is it called the "witching hour" and not the "witching ambiguous period in the middle of the night?" The fact is, the vast majority of these silly stories and tall tales occur during a very narrow window of time, between 2 and 4 a.m., and as it turns out, that's no cosmic coincidence.

The term "witching hour" actually has roots hundreds of years old. Many years ago, it was thought that the separation between the living and the dead was narrowest somewhere between the hours of 2 and 4 a.m. This thought became so prevalent that in the 1500s the Catholic Church actually banned activities during this time for fear of witches and warlocks ushering the dead into the living domain.

In ultrarunning terms, the phenomenon is similar. At some point in the wee hours of the morning, weird stuff starts to happen. Rocks turn into bears. Branches move and take the form of talking snakes. And more importantly, your performance declines.

A 2020 study published in the journal *Sleep Science* looked at runners during the Fort Clinch 100 Mile Endurance Run and tracked their pace and dropout rates during the

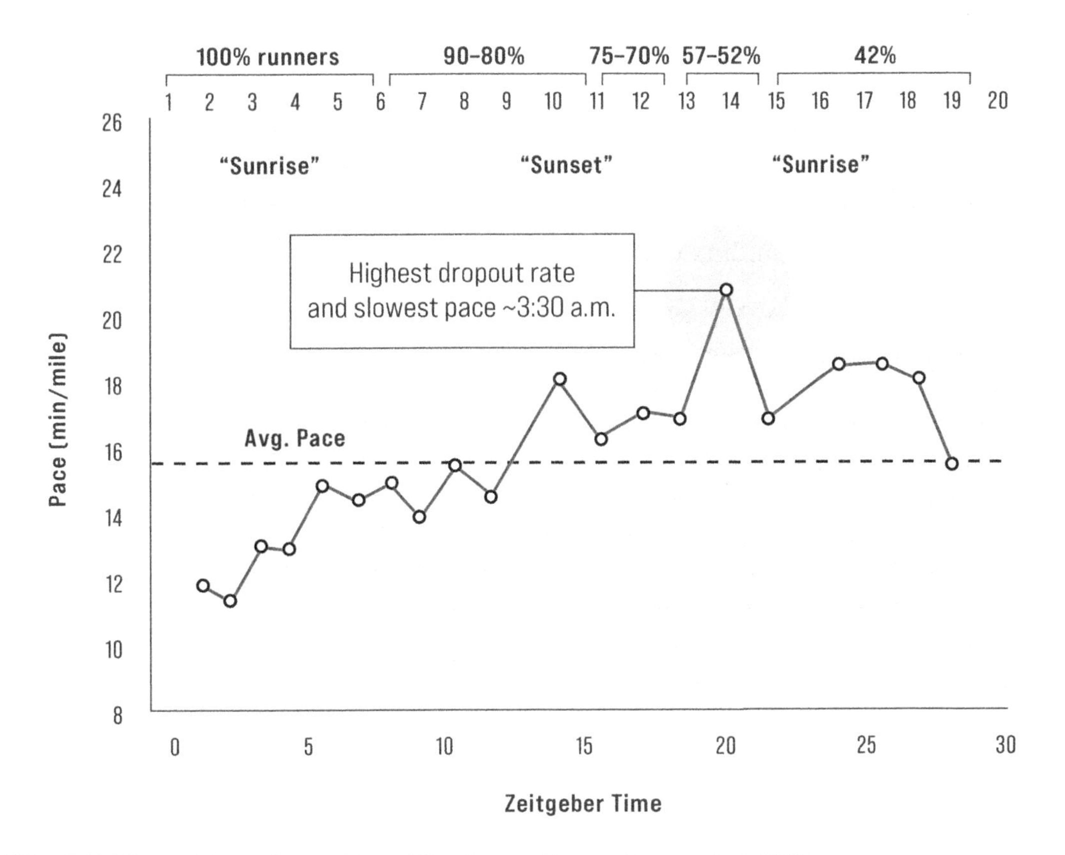

FIGURE 16.11 When athletes drop out in a 100-mile race. Source: Brager et al. 2020.

race, as well as their sleeping habits during the race (Brager et al. 2020). I was not surprised to learn the 100-mile runners had their slowest paces and highest dropout rates at exact same time, at about 3:30 a.m. (which is denoted by Zeitgeber time 20 on the x-axis in Figure 16.11).

This aligns with research looking at circadian rhythms showing that some people have more difficulty controlling core temperature when required to exercise in the early hours of the morning (Muginshtein-Simkovitch et al. 2015). So, there's some science to the fact that hallucinations and the sleep monster seem to show up for everyone at the same time.

SLEEP EXTENSION

Athletes try all manner of training strategies to avoid going zero miles an hour while curled up in a sleeping bag during a race. Some try overnight runs, while others simply stay up for a couple of days in a row, powering through life with a few extra cups of coffee. Many feel that the experience of being a new parent better prepares them for sleep deprivation. This begs the question: can you actually improve your tolerance for sleep deprivation? Meaning, is there some physiological improvement you can make in training that causes your body to adapt and perform better (or less badly) when sleep-deprived?

The answer is a resounding no. You can't train sleep deprivation simply by going on an overnight run, the way you train a muscle to be stronger by lifting heavier weights. The aforementioned strategies are experiential—they will help you get accustomed to and familiar with the sensation of sleep deprivation, which can be helpful, but it's hard to tell if those experiences actually improve future performances.

Therefore, I advocate that athletes only do one or two overnight runs at the very most, and sometimes not at all. The toll you pay for these bouts of sleep deprivation is high, and the benefit is slim to none.

While you might not be able to "train" sleep deprivation in a classic way, you can undertake strategies in advance of an overnight event to help mitigate the negative consequences. Sleep extension (sometimes referred to as sleep banking) is a simple and effective way to improve any performance where sleep deprivation might become an issue. Researchers have studied this strategy for decades and have found that, in general, one week of extending sleep by as little as an hour per night can improve cognitive function and performance. Additionally, and more relevant for longer ultramarathons, sleep extension appears to have a positive effect on performance during bouts of sleep deprivation that occur immediately after the extension, particularly from a cognitive perspective. This is great news for anyone going into a twenty-four-plus-hour event where decision-making, navigation, and mood will be important for success.

HOW TO DO IT

Fortunately, sleep extension is easy. Most research protocols have centered around a one- to two-week sleep extension protocol where total time in bed is ten hours per night (Vitale et al. 2019). If the time commitment is problematic for you, don't fret—there does appear to be a linear dose response for sleep extension protocols up to ten hours. This means that if you habitually sleep seven hours, even an extension of one hour per night for one week will have some positive effect.

While I would love for every athlete I work with to be able to sleep ten hours a night, let's face it, life happens. From a practical standpoint, I've had my athletes target nine to ten hours a night for two weeks leading up to a big overnight race. When adding sleep hours, it's preferable (and usually the most practical), but not necessary, to go to sleep earlier as opposed to waking up later. Nine hours of sleep a night for one week seems to have a moderate and tangible effect on their ability to stay awake and alert during an overnight event, provided they weren't chronically sleep-deprived to start out with. This strategy also leverages the efficacy of the sleep extension without being too intrusive on their daily schedule, so it's a win all the way around.

SLEEPING DURING A RACE

When and how long to sleep during races is one of those areas where few people agree. In addition, there's not a lot in the literature we can draw from to inform best practices. We do know that sleep restriction (withholding sleep for a few hours for at least a night) can negatively impact endurance performance by as much as 4 percent. Total sleep deprivation can impair performance by over 11 percent (Cullen et al. 2019; Fullagar et al. 2015). Taking a nap might help curb some of that deterioration, but it is unclear to what extent and how much it would apply during an ultramarathon. So, the general working philosophy I use with my athletes breaks races up into three segments:

1. RACES SHORTER THAN FORTY-EIGHT HOURS: NO SLEEP NEEDED

For these races, there might be no sleep needed, provided that you performed the sleep extension protocol mentioned earlier and you respond to short-term sleep deprivation normally.

2. RACES FROM FORTY-EIGHT TO SEVENTY-TWO HOURS: SHORT NAPS

For these races, I advise athletes to get short 20- to 40-minute trail-side naps (or in an aid station if it's convenient) close to sunrise on the second day, and each morning after. The theory (and this is just a theory pioneered by adventure racers) is that timing when you wake up to right when the sun rises will align with your body's natural circadian rhythms.

3. RACES LONGER THAN SEVENTY-TWO HOURS: 90- TO 120-MINUTE CHUNKS OF SLEEP

For races lasting longer than three days, I advise runners to get at least 90 to 120 minutes of sleep, beginning during the second night. For races of this length, very few people can remain awake for the entirety of the event. And even for those who can, performance normally deteriorates to the point where some sleep provides more than enough of a benefit to make up for the time not moving.

In general, for most athletes I advise sleeping more than less, as long as you have the time to make cutoffs. While this might increase your downtime at aid stations, you are better able to preserve your performance on the trail, sometimes dramatically (10 percent or more if you read into the literature). Being extremely sleep-deprived can cost you hours on the racecourse due to deteriorated performance, bad decision-making, forgotten nutrition, and even a fall. Getting some sleep might cost you time in the short run but will pay off later down the trail.

Creating a Race-Day Nutrition Strategy

If you have done everything right in training, you should not need an elaborate race-day nutrition plan because your race nutrition will be very similar to what you ate in training. A simple plan is just as effective and is much easier to remember and execute as compared to a complex plan. I've seen inordinately detailed plans and have always likened them to the biochemistry experiments I performed as a young student. In these

THE NAPPUCCINO

IF YOU ANTICIPATE SLEEPING at any point during the event, researchers have discovered a great strategy involving caffeine and short power naps. While the findings are not specific to an ultramarathon setting, they can be modified and applied if you anticipate needing sleep or if an unanticipated trail nap is a must. In these situations, if you expect to take a twenty- to forty-minute power nap, it is best to consume caffeine just prior to the slumber. Paradoxically, the crux of the benefit lies in the time it takes for the stimulant to take effect. When you wake up, you'll be more refreshed and alert (Hayashi, Masuda, and Hori 2003; Horne and Reyner 1996; Reyner and Horne 1997).

unnecessarily complicated plans, the required food and fluid are detailed in thirty-, twenty-, and sometimes even ten-minute increments. Puzzled and confused crew members wade through the details, asking, "Was this aid station supposed to be 8 oz of Coke with a Nutella cracker, or water with half a scoop of the red powder, half a scoop of the other powder, and a peanut butter and jelly sandwich?" When watching these real-life chemistry experiments unfold, I have always wondered, "Is this how that runner trains?" To date, in all my experience as a runner and a coach, I have yet to come across an athlete who maintains such elaborate nutrition planning during training. Why, then, do they do it in a race?

Table 16.1 presents an example of such an overcomplicated nutrition plan. I adapted it from many of the flawed race plans I have seen over the years. Although the plan is well intended, it is too complicated, and the concoctions utilized are impractical to replicate in training. I once read a nutrition plan developed for an athlete that included consuming exactly 83 oz of liquid during a twenty-one-mile section of race. Not 82, not 84, but 83.

DEVELOP A STRATEGY, THEN A PLAN

You don't want to leave your nutrition to chance in an ultramarathon, but what you want to develop is a race-day nutrition strategy, after which you may or may not choose to create a race-day nutrition plan. A strategy encompasses the target calories, fluid, and foodstuffs you have tried and tested in training. If you develop an actual written-down-on-paper plan

RACE SECTION	FOOD	FLUID	SUPPLEMENTS
Start to aid station 1	2 gels	1 drink mix in bottle 1	1 salt tab
		1 drink mix in bottle 2	1 amino acid capsule
Aid station 1 to aid station 2	2 gels	Water in bottle 1	1 salt tab
	1 energy bar	1 electrolyte tablet in bottle 2	
		Coke in aid station	
Aid station 2 to aid station 3	1 pack energy chews	½ drink mix, ½ scoop whey protein in bottle 1	2 salt tabs
	½ pack energy chews	Water in bottle 2	
		Ginger ale in aid station	
Aid station 3 to finish	2 gels	½ drink mix, ½ Coke in bottle 1	1 salt tab
	1 pack energy chews	1 electrolyte tablet in bottle 2	1 amino acid capsule

TABLE 16.1 An overcomplicated nutrition plan.

from that overarching strategy, it should take no more than an elementary school education to execute. If you have done a good job in training by experimenting with the right foodstuffs and drinks, the race-day strategy should naturally end up being simple.

Developing your nutrition strategy for race day should revolve around the following aspects:

- Eat and drink what you have tried in training.
- Target calories per hour.
- Target fluid per hour, adjusted for the temperature range of the event.
- Know when and how to incorporate things like caffeine or stomach-calming tricks like antacids and ginger.

FLUIDS FIRST. As discussed in Chapter 13, your nutrition strategy is largely dependent on your hydration status. When your hydration status is good, the foods you ingest stand a chance of being absorbed and metabolized into energy. Therefore, your race-day nutrition strategy starts with the fluid you plan to take in during various parts of the race. Consider factors such as time between aid stations, temperature, and intensity. If you plan to consume liquid with some form of calories, this also sets the beginning of your caloric range, which you need to determine next.

FIND YOUR TARGET CALORIE RANGE. As opposed to a strict "eat this at thirty minutes, eat that at sixty minutes" type of plan, I recommend first targeting a specific calorie range. Once that range is determined, the specific foodstuffs you plan to consume on race day are developed during day-to-day training. The calorie count is relatively standard: 200 to 300 calories per hour after the first sixty minutes for most people. Some elite athletes can push that up toward 400 calories per hour. This process is described in Chapter 13.

DEVELOP YOUR BULL'S-EYE AND OUTER-RING FOODS. During training, particularly during longer runs, use your target calorie ranges and then experiment with different foodstuffs. This is how you develop the core group of bull's-eye foods that are tried and true for you. As described in Chapter 14, you also need to develop foods that fit into the outer rings of your target—those you can use for backup if your core go-to foods begin to fail or aren't available. It is important to build your lists of target foods and foods that are off target, so you can make good choices in any race, under varying circumstances, and as your preferences change during an event.

Once the core foods have been fully tested in training, experiment with your backup foods. In theory, the three to five bull's-eye foodstuffs developed in training will be all you need, but in ultrarunning, things don't always go as planned. These outer-ring foodstuffs are what you can fall back on when all else fails. The typical fallback plan revolves around the aid station fare of cookies, soup, fruit, sandwiches, and the like.

An example of an athlete's bull's-eye nutrition strategy is shown in Figure 16.12. I recommend trying to stay on target and rotating through your three to five bull's-eye foods for as long as you can during the race. If you get tired of those foods, then move to the outer rings.

CUSTOMIZE INTAKE FOR YOUR RACE DISTANCE AND EFFORT. Your blood flow is always being balanced between digestion, cooling, and your working muscles. Different intensities will allow you to digest different combinations and amounts of your bull's-eye foodstuffs. In general, the higher the intensity of the race, the more you will need to rely on easily digestible calories. The converse is also true. The longer the race, the less the intensity, and therefore the more you can incorporate complex foods. The complete "food target" (bull's-eye plus outer rings) represents any of the things you can eat, not necessarily the specific or optimal ones for a particular race. For example, you might only use gels from your bull's-eye in a 50K, gels and pretzels for a 50-mile race, and the entire rotation for a 100-mile event.

Figure 16.13 depicts a target that is customized for a more intense race. Using only three foodstuffs, this athlete would still have a real food (rice ball) and an engineered food (gel), all while including sweet, salty, and savory taste profiles.

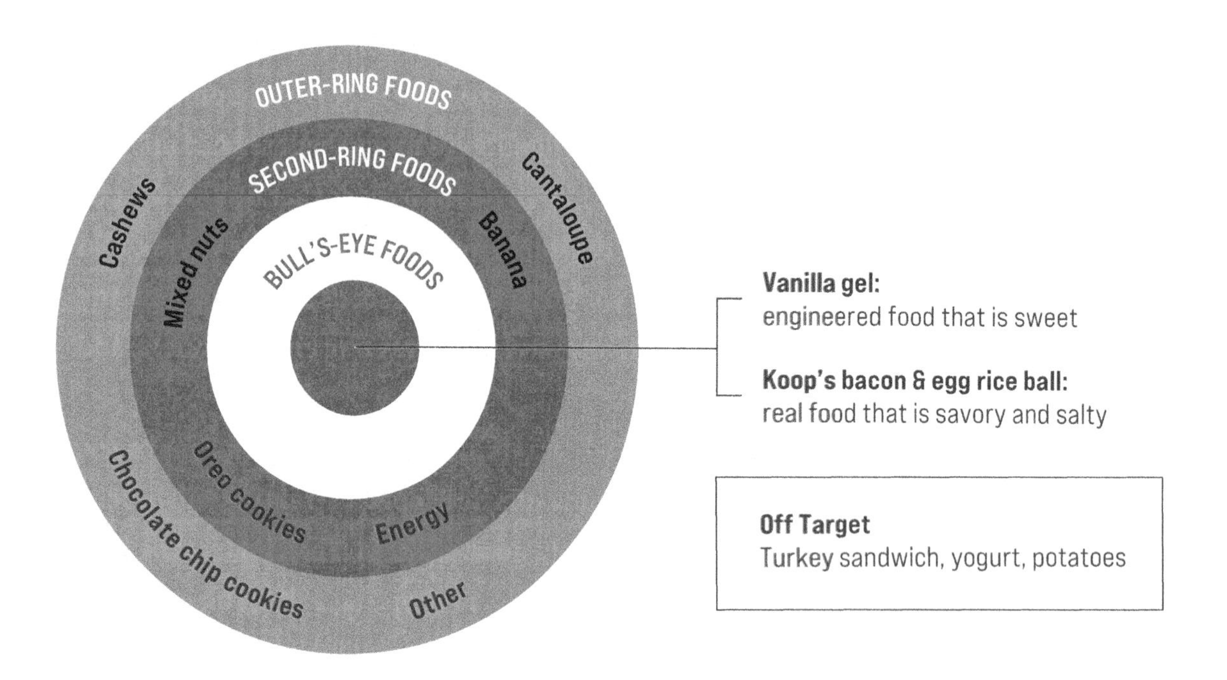

FIGURE 16.12 Example of a bull's-eye nutrition plan.

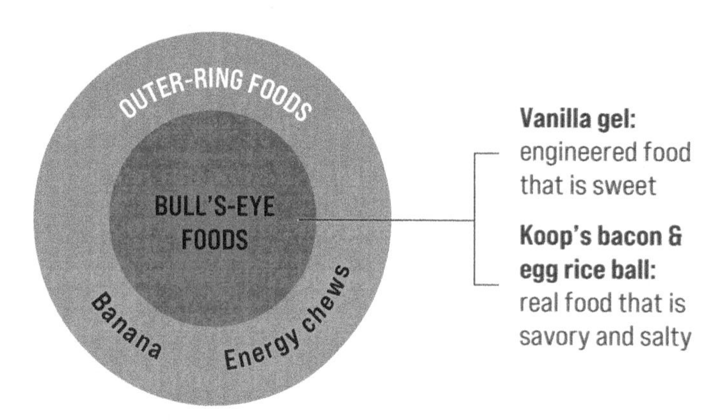

FIGURE 16.13 Target customization for a shorter, more intense ultra.

SUPPLEMENTS AND ERGOGENIC AIDS

Like bull's-eye nutrition, other supplements and ergogenic aids you anticipate using on race day should be tested in training. Yes, this means taking a caffeine pill or some crystallized ginger on a four-hour run when it is completely unnecessary! Your bull's-eye nutrition might be enough to get you to the finish line on race day. But because the distance and duration of the event are typically longer than any single training run, it's good to have a set of supplements and ergogenic aids that you can go to if (or when) the need arises.

Caffeine: The Original Performance-Enhancing Drug

Yes, caffeine is a drug. In fact, it is the most widely consumed psychoactive drug in the world today. Yes, it can enhance your performance. I vividly remember pacing my wife during the latter stages of the Run Rabbit Run 100 and stumbling upon a ream of a dozen 200 mg caffeine pills. I wondered whether the runner who dropped the package was simply being lazy by not cutting the foil pack down into more realistic chunks of a few pills or actually intended to use all 2,400 mg of caffeine over the last twenty miles of the race. Because ultrarunners are a somewhat obsessive group, I assumed the latter. That would have been a sight! I'm glad I found the pills, and not an amped-up arrhythmic runner.

Caffeine supplementation can be used in two ways: to acutely enhance your performance or as a stimulant specifically to stay awake and alert.

CAFFEINE AS A PERFORMANCE ENHANCER

Caffeine supplementation starts with your morning cup of coffee on race day. If you regularly drink a cup or two a day, feel free to enjoy a similar amount as you go through your pre-race routine. Supplementation starts from this baseline, based on the race distance you are about to undertake.

For shorter races lasting less than six hours, you can supplement with occasional caffeine, up to 50 mg per hour, for the entire race. The supplementation should mainly come from caffeinated gels, chews, tablets, and colas. If you typically have coffee in the morning, caffeine from the coffee should be enough for the first two to three hours of the race. Therefore, I suggest waiting until after the second or third hour to start supplementing with caffeine in other forms. Furthermore, the dose response from caffeine as it relates to endurance performance is not linear, meaning that moderate doses of caffeine are likely to have the same performance effect as higher doses (Graham and Spriet 1995; Pasman et al. 1995). More isn't always better. Thus, a cautious and conservative approach will likely be preferable to a more aggressive one.

CAFFEINE TO STAY AWAKE AND ALERT

Many ultrarunning events go into the night and through the following day. Runners are constantly battling the mythical-yet-real sleep monster, particularly in the wee hours of the morning, before sunrise and after twenty hours on their feet. Caffeine is one of the key pieces of ammunition against the sleep monster, whether you ingest it in the form of pills, colas, chocolate-covered espresso beans, energy drinks, or caffeinated sports nutrition products. However, when using caffeine as a stimulant to boost your alertness, the timing matters more than the form.

For athletes competing in events lasting longer than twenty-four hours, caffeine is best viewed as a stimulant to stay awake and alert. In these situations, you need to focus on when the stimulation will be needed most and then supplement at that point. This means starting the day with a normal routine, including pre-race breakfast and coffee if that is what you are accustomed to. As the race begins, however, take care to avoid caffeine. Gels, drinks, and foods at this point should all be noncaffeinated. Sometime after midnight, when you expect a visit from the sleep monster, begin your caffeine supplementation. Doses can be as high as 100 mg/hr for three to four hours and can cease shortly after the sun rises, which helps to reset your circadian rhythms.

Stomach Settlers

As was discussed in Chapter 4, gastrointestinal distress is one of the leading problems experienced by ultrarunners during races. Even though training runs provide few opportunities to test the efficacy of any of the typical stomach settlers, such as ginger, antacids, and hard candies, you may be able to rule them out by testing them during training, even when your stomach is not upset. You are doing this to make sure your settler of choice doesn't cause any unforeseen issues.

GINGER

Ginger is available in candy form, crystallized, or in a ginger beer or brew. It has long been recommended by herbalists and doctors and used by cancer patients and pregnant women as an alternative to drugs to treat nausea. The theory is that the chemicals and soothing flavor help to calm an upset stomach. Although much of the research either shows a benefit or is inconclusive, small doses are reported to have the most benefit (Lien et al. 2003; Lohsiriwat et al. 2010; Pongrojpaw, Somprasit, and Chanthasenanont 2007; Ryan 2012). You should note, however, that most of the generic ginger ales at aid stations contain no actual ginger!

ANTACIDS

These can be Tums or a generic alternative. When you eat, your body increases the amount of gastric acids in order to digest food. These acids can overflow up the esophagus and irritate and potentially damage the esophageal lining, as well as the lining of the stomach. To combat this increase in gastric acids, antacids provide a base in the form of calcium carbonate, which neutralizes the acid. Chew one or two at a time.

HARD CANDIES

Peppermints and butterscotch candies have long been used by runners to soothe sour stomachs. The theory is that the sucking motion of your mouth will relieve the distress. Although there is little scientific evidence to back up this claim, it's a home remedy that has been around for many years. In desperate times, it might be worth a shot. As an added bonus, you get the sugar from the candy. Butterscotch is my favorite.

This list of supplements and ergogenic aids is purposely very short. There should be no reason to incorporate anything other than real food, engineered sport-specific foods and sports drinks, and the items listed here. There are a lot of powders and packages in sports nutrition stores that promise to carry you farther and faster than ever before, but beware: supplements are not regulated by the Food and Drug Administration. They may contain ingredients that are not listed on the label, and the ingredients listed on the label may not be in the bottle or may be in the bottle in different amounts than listed. The combination of no regulation and inaccurate or deceptive manufacturing and labeling means that supplements from the corner store, grocery store, or specialized sports nutrition store may contain substances that are not only against the spirit of drug-free sport but are also prohibited by the US Anti-Doping Agency and World Anti-Doping Agency.

NSAIDs

Don't include NSAIDs (aspirin, ibuprofen, naproxen) in your race-day plan. Ever. They increase the risk of hyponatremia (Page et al. 2007; Wharam et al. 2006) and greatly increase the stress placed on the renal system, putting you at greater risk of renal injury and rhabdomyolysis (emptying of damaged or dead muscle tissue from muscles into the bloodstream). The desire to ache a little less isn't worth the risk of ending up in the hospital with renal failure. Pretty easy choice.

MODIFIED NUTRITION STRATEGY FOR RACE DAY

Table 16.1 showed a flawed, overcomplicated plan to demonstrate how not to develop a race-day nutrition plan. Now let's look at an example of what you should do. Table 16.2 shows a properly developed and streamlined race-day nutrition strategy. It is focused on target calorie and fluid ranges, not exact foodstuffs and specific scoops of powder. It gives the athlete the flexibility to choose to consume 100 calories of a prepackaged bar or the equivalent amount of energy from chews. The fluid is easy to manage, with target total consumption ranges from aid station to aid station. Finally, this is merely a replication

RACE SECTION	FOOD	FLUID	SUPPLEMENTS
Start to aid station 1 (2 hours)	100 calories total (1 gel)	20-30 oz. total (water)	None
Aid station 1 to aid station 1 (2 hours)	400-500 calories total (gels and prepackaged bar)	30-50 oz. total (water and drink mix)	None
Aid station 2 to aid station 3 (3 hours)	600-750 calories total (rice balls, gels, energy chews)	50-70 oz. total (water and drink mix)	1 salt tab
Aid station 3 to finish (2 hours)	400-500 calories total (gels and prepackaged bar)	~50 oz. total (water and drink mix)	Ginger chews or antacid if necessary

TABLE 16.2 A simplified nutrition plan.

of what the athlete would do in training. For a five-hour training run—similar to the five hours between aid stations 1 and 3—the athlete would take 80 to 120 oz of sports drink and water with 1,000 to 1,250 calories of gels, bars, rice balls, and energy chews.

Recruiting and Instructing Your Support Crew

Ultrarunning has a special community. Nearly every weekend in cities, parks, and wildlands all across the country, people are organizing and running ultramarathons. Aid stations are stocked, and volunteers arise in the wee hours of the morning to take their places. With comprehensive aid station support at most ultras these days, it is certainly not necessary to have a crew for your race, but it sure is nice to see a familiar face.

Given their vital role in providing personalized aid and encouragement, choosing your crew to support you on your ultramarathon adventure is not a decision to take lightly. When you choose the correct crew mates, they can push you to greater heights. They will know exactly what to say and what to give you, and they may even be able to anticipate what you will need next. Alternatively, when you choose the wrong crew, they can drag you down. The wrong crew can drain your energy, make mistakes in execution, and, worst of all, cause a DNF when you are able to move forward.

THE FIRST STEP: DETERMINE WHETHER YOU WANT A CREW AT ALL

Both new and experienced runners sometimes choose to forego crews entirely. Most races make this possible with bountiful aid stations and more than enough helpful volunteers to keep you moving. If, for whatever reason, your preferred crew (family, friends, etc.) cannot make the event, don't fret. The race will most likely be able to take care of you.

If you decide you want a crew, your next move is to determine who exactly you want out there. Husbands, wives, kids, friends, and running partners can all make up a good crew. If they care for you and can get away for the weekend, chances are they would jump at the chance to help. However, just because your friends and loved ones can be part of your crew does not mean that they should be. The best crew members are the people who know you as a runner and as a person . . . and have only a small amount of sympathy. After all, it's going to be tough out there, so it's best to have someone in your corner who does not mind telling you to suck it up.

ALIGN YOUR CREW WITH YOUR GOALS FIRST, AND THEN INSTRUCT THEM ON THE TACTICAL DETAILS

First and foremost, your crew is there to assist you in achieving your goals; handing off gels or a jacket and making soup are merely the means to that end. I consistently see crews with folders, spreadsheets, and labeled baggies in the aid stations of ultramarathon events. Any kid off the street could look at a highlighted portion of a worksheet, pull the food and gear listed on it, and lay them out for the runner. You don't need a supportive, caring, and engaged crew member for that. And if that's all you empower your crew to do, you are not leveraging the people around you to enhance your performance. The error people make is having crew members who are well instructed on what to do but poorly instructed on the crew's overall goals, as well as the runner's outcome and process goals. Make no mistake, these overall goals are far more important than the number of potatoes a crew member hands you at mile 30. Beginner racers and crews tend to rely more on worksheets and minute-by-minute instructions because the structure provides confidence. Your goal, however, should be to progress to the point where, if you have properly instructed and empowered your crew, they can do the job armed with an index card, a duffel bag full of your gear and nutrition, and driving directions.

DO YOU WANT A PACER?

Many ultramarathons, particularly at the 100K and 100-mile distances, allow the use of pacers to accompany the runner. In theory, the pacers can provide motivational support and offer a level of safety for their runner and other runners in the field. As an added benefit, serving as a pacer is a great way to get an introduction into the sport. Most pacers are well intended, but some end up undoing their runner's race. Personality conflicts, goal misalignments, and a lack of preparation have waylaid many an ultrarunner's best-laid plans. Using a pacer or choosing to go solo is entirely a personal preference. The decision ultimately lies with the runner.

SUCCESS IS ALWAYS THE RUNNER'S RESPONSIBILITY

Crew or no crew, pacer or no pacer, the responsibility of finishing the race and achieving your goals is yours alone. When you have this default mindset, your crew and/or pacer(s) merely catalyze the process; they are not the linchpins in the operation. Success will ultimately be up to you, your training, and the determination you put forth on race day. When you are choosing a crew or a pacer, remember that it is always your responsibility as a runner to succeed. Your crew or a pacer can help you thrive on race day, but you should not rely on them for your success.

The ADAPT System for Problem-Solving

Everyone has a plan until they get punched in the mouth. —Mike Tyson

If you do one single thing at a high enough intensity for long enough, every once in a while the shit hits the fan. As much as you have trained, as patiently as you have paced, as dialed as your race-day nutrition is, and as experienced as you are, you will eventually get punched in the mouth, and it is going to hurt. Your legs will feel like lead, your effort will feel unreasonable, you will start tripping over roots and rocks, and your stomach will be in knots. If you are especially unlucky, these infirmities will all happen at once and last for many miles. Maybe it won't happen in your next race or the one after that, but if you remain in the ultramarathon game for a long enough time, lady luck's evil doppelgänger will eventually find you.

Ultramarathons are long enough that you have the opportunity to go through (many) highs and (hopefully fewer) lows. Some of the highs will be amazing; some of the lows will be excruciating. For many athletes, that's part of the attraction to the sport. However, having things go wrong does not necessarily mean your race is over. Fortunately, most ultramarathon cutoffs are generous enough that you can have a bad patch (or two) and still complete the event. And the more fit you are, the more bandwidth you'll have to get through a rough patch.

Believe me, I would much rather my athletes never have to experience bad patches in their races. Ideally, ultramarathoners would just run and eat and run, and run and eat and run some more, and never have any issues. If you play your cards right and prepare well, this is usually the case. Nonetheless, it's wise to prepare yourself for some tough times. As the British writer and former Prime Minister Benjamin Disraeli said, "I am prepared for the worst, but hope for the best."

I have developed five simple steps you can apply to get yourself out of the proverbial hole, regardless of the situation you're in. These steps form the easy-to-remember and appropriate acronym ADAPT, which also serves as a reminder of what you need to do at your lowest of lows:

- **ACCEPT**
- **DIAGNOSE**
- **ANALYZE**
- **PLAN**
- **TAKE ACTION**

ACCEPT

Accept things as they are. We all live in the present. In the exact moment that things deteriorate, you have to be present. Sure, you can hope that Scotty will beam you up to another place and another time where your stomach is not tied up in knots, but that isn't going to happen. So, accept the fact that things suck at the moment. Accept that your primary outcome goal might go out the window. Accept that you might be stuck in the aid station for the next hour or even longer, or that you might need to curl up and take a trail nap (your water bottle or hydration pack can make for an outstanding pillow, by the way). Accept how you are right now, however bad that might be, and get over it.

Emotion clouds judgment. It pulls an opaque veil over the situation, effectively rendering you incapable of rational thought and action. Acceptance of the situation allows you to move forward. When you reach the point of acceptance, you forget the past. The rock you just stubbed your toe on for the fifth time? Gone. The trail marker you missed, costing you precious time and energy on the wrong path? In the past. You can't change the fact that you've tripped and fallen three times over the last hundred yards, but you can change your outlook. Acceptance of the situation moves you from the past into the present. It lifts the veil of emotion and enables you to think and act rationally. Accept first, and then you are ready to move forward.

DIAGNOSE

Make a quick and dirty assessment of what is going on. Don't try to solve your problems yet, just try to figure out what is going on. This step is easy. If you just rolled your ankle, then, duh, you have an injured ankle. If your stomach has turned, then your nutrition plan has gone awry. If you are frustrated because you have fallen, then you are simply frustrated. Don't worry about the specifics of the issue just yet or how to resolve it; just diagnose the problem. Keep this step simple and to the point. "I have an upset stomach," "I am lightheaded," or "I am frustrated" (or a combination of these) will work perfectly fine. It is also fine to identify more than one problem, but resist the urge to roll right to analysis or planning before clearly identifying the problem. When people fail at this step, they end up creating solutions to the wrong problems.

ANALYZE

Now it is time to apply some brain power to the problem and enlist whatever synapses you have that are still working. You have moved on and accepted that things suck. You have diagnosed what the issue is. It's now time to analyze the situation you are in. Where is the next aid station? How much time do you have until the next cutoff? What tools, food, supplies, and gear are available? Create a mental inventory, because these are the means you will use to get yourself out of the hole you are currently in. The outcome of the next step depends on the analysis you do!

PLAN

You have accepted the situation, diagnosed what is wrong, and analyzed your surroundings and tools. Now it's time to actually devise a plan. This is by far the most complicated step. The plan should not require Mensa-level analysis, but it will require some brainpower. Your plan incorporates your earlier analysis of the situation and the means at your disposal. It takes the wheres and whats and weaves them into concrete steps that can lift you out of the hole you have dug. Depending on the situation, a simple plan might be to get to the next aid station and figure it out from there. If this is the case, you can share the results of your diagnosis and analysis with your crew, and they can help you formulate a new plan. One step at a time.

TAKE ACTION

When it's all said and done, you have to take action. Problems do not fix themselves. You as the athlete have to do something deliberate to fix them. If you believe in magic, like the Disneyland type of magic, then ultrarunning is not for you. Put your plan into action. Take action—by force if necessary.

> **Situation:** "I have just rolled my ankle on a rock."
>
> **Accept:** "My ankle is going to hurt for a bit. I am going to be slower. This is fine. I'm over it."
>
> **Diagnose:** "I have an injured ankle."
>
> **Analyze:** "I was sixty minutes away from the next aid station. Now I am about ninety minutes away if I walk. I do not have enough food or water on me for that length of time. I have crew at the next aid station."
>
> **Plan:** "I am going to walk into the next aid station. If I see another runner, I will ask them for some food and fluid. When I get to the next aid station, I am going to see if there is medical help there or some other way to tape/brace my ankle. My crew is there, so they can help me with this."
>
> **Take action:** "I am going to walk down the trail now." As another runner approaches: "I am going to ask this runner for some fluid."

WHAT IS MISSING FROM THE ADAPT SYSTEM?

Admittedly, the acronym ADAPT is a bit contrived. It represents a series of steps that are analogous to problem-solving techniques that have been used by Boy Scouts, mountaineers, adventure racers, and the military, among others. The point of using the acronym is to identify a series of concrete steps you can focus on when you are at the lowest of low points. It is also important to understand what I intentionally left out of the ADAPT system.

Predict

Many runners are by nature analytical people. They are experts at doing easy math and determining their pace and how long it is going to take to get to the next aid station. While under normal circumstances it is a good thing to know when and how long it will take to locomote from place to place, when one is trying to climb out of a negative situation, it's best to keep that thinking to a minimum. You should absolutely figure out how long it is going to take you to get to the next aid station, but the math should end there; do not forecast the following aid station, or the one after that, and certainly not the finish line. One never knows how the day is going to turn out.

Radically Change Your Race Strategy

The acronym is ADAPT, not PANIC. Making small, incremental changes is always better than drastically revising your well-thought-out race strategy all at once. Many times, small changes (or adaptations) to your original plan are all that are necessary.

Guess

Simply taking a stab in the dark to fix a problem should be the last resort. If you do a thorough job of analyzing and planning, the steps to get out of the hole should be quite clear-cut. Fortunately for most of us, fixing problems in ultrarunning is not rocket science. There is typically a wealth of experience out on the course during race day. Your crew, aid station workers, and fellow runners can help if you get stumped. Use them if necessary!

KEY POINTS FOR PERSONALIZING YOUR RACE STRATEGY

- Personalizing your race-day strategy starts with reviewing your training.
- Race-day strategies should consist of both process and outcome goals.
- Race-day strategies should balance your current fitness levels with your affinity for risk.
- Your race-day strategy should be based on effort (as opposed to heart rate or pace) and be constructed from your training experience.
- Beware of forecasting how you will feel during a race. Staying in the moment works!
- Longer races such as 200-milers will require special strategies around sleep:
  - Pre-event "sleep banking" can be effective.
  - Sleep deprivation training is likely only beneficial for the experiential aspect.
  - Sleeping during longer races should prioritize preserving performance over limiting downtime.
- Race-day nutrition strategies should be simple and based on what you have done in training.
- You should try supplements and other ergogenic aids like ginger and caffeine in training before you try them on race day.
- When shit hits the fan, ADAPT: Accept, Diagnose, Analyze, Plan, Take action.

CHAPTER 17

Racing Wisely

Athletes frequently ask me about how many races they will need as they get set to start the journey toward their goal event. Particularly if their goal is challenging, athletes often feel the need to have some logical series of races in order to prepare. The question has always puzzled me. No one really "needs" a race. Yet many people think there is some magical formula that will tell them, "If you complete x and y races, you will be prepared for your goal."

Further confounding the issue is the fact that the number of ultrarunning events grows every year. It is quite easy to find a 50K, 50-mile, or 100-mile event on any given weekend. In certain areas, the travel required to reach an ultramarathon is minimal. Given that most ultrarunners are an outdoorsy group, George Mallory's oft-quoted rationale "because it's there" becomes a reason to race and race often.

Doing a race because you feel you "need" it or simply because "it's there" is a poor way to pick and choose events. Unfortunately, many athletes fall victim to this psychology. They endlessly chase the races they feel they need because they are there. They race too much, and they race without true purpose.

Statistics on ultrarunners tease this out as well. A greater percentage of ultrarunners run more than one race per year compared to their marathon, half marathon, 10K, and 5K counterparts. This is particularly interesting because the effort and recovery required for an ultra are far greater than for sub-ultra distances.

To better understand what racing means to each individual, I gathered several of

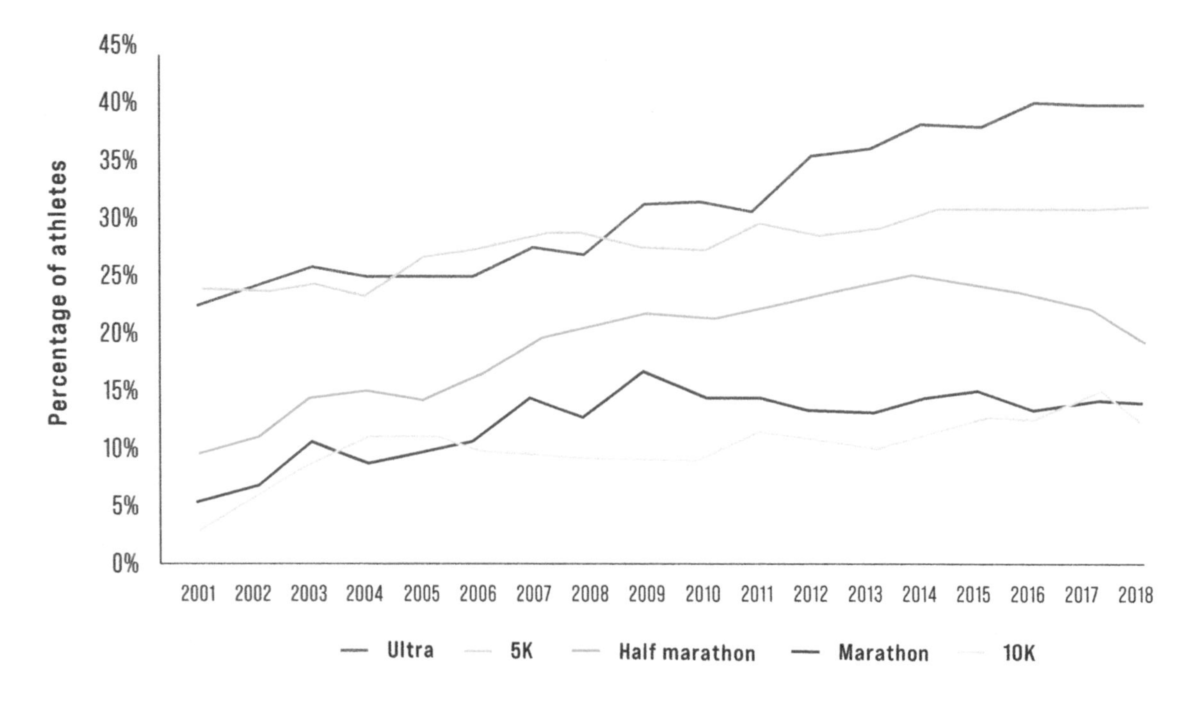

FIGURE 17.1 Percentage of racers competing in multiple races per year. Adapted from Andersen 2020.

my athletes on a conference call. Some of them race nearly every weekend. Others race only once in a calendar year. The conversation was fascinating. Interestingly, while the optimum quantity and types of races varied wildly from athlete to athlete, their viewpoints on why and when to race were equally dissimilar. What ultimately emerged was a different set of values each athlete placed on the racing process. That value system then set the construct for how many and what types of races each athlete did.

Racing and what it represents to you are rooted in your personal values. The values you put on the process of racing should determine what and when you choose (not need) to race. Like many other value systems, this one is entirely individual. The same series of races that works for one athlete might be counterproductive for another, even when they are preparing for the same goal event.

In the following sections, I have summarized the racing values for the various athletes I work with. Some might fit your own value set; some might not. Your values will ultimately determine what races you pick and how many of them end up on your calendar. I encourage you to use these as a starting point for your goals. The ultimate end point is up to you to craft.

Racing as the End of Means

For many, racing represents the simple end point of training. While from a coaching standpoint I always view training as continuous, some athletes bookend the process with the races they choose. Athletes put in miles, contrive different intervals, and sacrifice time with family and friends to make themselves better in order to race at their best. For these athletes, racing fulfills the training process. In some cases, much of the athletes' specific training is spent hammering up steep gravel roads. Many times, this is at the expense of climbing some breathtaking peak, rock climbing, or reading (yet another) book. For these athletes, racing validates the work and sacrifice necessary to achieve their goals. Racing is the ultimate point of what they do on a day-to-day basis. If you are an athlete who sees racing as the logical end point of a period of training or preparation, you may not feel the need to race very frequently. You are more likely to place greater value on particular races that are important to you, rather than racing for the sake of racing.

Racing as a Competitive Outlet

Many of us are competitive by nature, and this innate competitive psychology drives athletes to want to race. Running against fellow athletes or against oneself is what racing represents. These athletes enjoy seeing how their fitness and toughness stack up. When your competitive drive is what you're satisfying, it may make sense to incorporate more high-quality racing into your annual plan.

Racing as Part of the Training Process

Day-to-day training can only prepare you for so much. Managing aid stations, drop bags, foreign terrain, and event-day logistics is difficult to replicate in training. Racing can help to bridge the gaps that remain. Furthermore, racing can provide an opportunity for a big training stimulus. The duration and intensity of the race usually exceed what an athlete can accomplish in day-to-day training.

Some athletes place a similar value on the racing process. They race a lot, sometimes three out of four weeks a month throughout many months of the year. They race frequently because they value racing as part of the training process. I know this because I interact with athletes like this on a daily basis, and together we determine how much emphasis to place on different races throughout the year. This assessment is crucial for any athlete who is using races as part of the training process. There is only so much physical and emotional bandwidth available for racing. Determining each race's individual emphasis helps to manage that bandwidth.

For many athletes, races can help bridge the gaps between day-to-day training and the goal event. Sometimes they provide a great opportunity to put in a huge training day with aid station support rather than having to manage that support on your own. They provide a bigger training stimulus and an arena for athletes to work on the things they are going to face during their goal event.

Racing to Be Part of a Community

I often say that "it's the same group of idiots at every race." For many, racing involves community. In ultrarunning, we are lucky that the community is such a good one. The "idiots" I lovingly refer to are friends I have had the fortune of sharing the trails with on many Saturdays. Many ultrarunners find that racing allows them to touch base with the community of people they identify with, much like any other social group. This is why you see many ultrarunners become aid station volunteers and attend races simply to cheer other people on. They value the community of people who make up the sport. If it's the community that draws you to races, but you struggle with balancing your purposeful training with the preparation for and recovery from frequent races, you may benefit from volunteering at events. That way you can stay engaged with the community while still staying true to your overall long-range plan for the year.

Find Your Racing Values

The answer to the question "How many races do I need?" comes from first determining your racing values. The aforementioned examples are just a few. Racing can represent many things to you, and these can ebb and flow over time. When setting up your season and choosing races, first think about what those races represent to you. Is it the competition, a stepping-stone, the end point of your training, or something entirely different? Like any value system, your racing values are for you to determine. After you have done this, the distance, timing, and frequency of the races you choose can follow suit.

Optimal Racing for Maximum Performance

If your race values are rooted in achieving optimal performance, there is a range of race frequency that you can utilize to ensure that you are toeing the line in the best shape possible. For purposes of simplification, the following ranges assume that you are racing only at the specified distances in a twelve-month period. For example, if you want to maximize your performance at the 100-mile distance, you can do so one or two times per year if that is the only distance you race.

- **100-MILE:** one or two times per twelve months
- **100K AND 50-MILE:** two or three times per twelve months
- **50K:** three or four times per twelve months

Is Suboptimal Racing OK?

Yes! You can race four 100-milers in a calendar year (or in a few short months, as is the case with the Grand Slam of Ultrarunning). But that does not mean you can optimally prepare for each one. How suboptimal is the third, fourth, or fifth 100-mile race in a twelve-month period? That's a guessing game, and the answer is rooted in your own personal physiology and psychology. The point is, if your racing values are to optimize the training process, you will be most likely to fulfill those values by limiting your racing. This does not mean that racing more is bad (suboptimal ≠ bad). It only means that when you are determining your racing values, it is important to keep in mind the practical ramifications and possible drawbacks of choosing too many races.

Prerequisite Training Distances for Ultramarathons

One of the persistent concepts in run training is that you must be able to complete a specific percentage of your goal distance in training in order to be prepared for your race. This idea comes from marathon training, where people are convinced they need to complete a twenty-mile run as the final long run before their taper. But there is nothing magical about that twenty-mile run, and there is similarly nothing magical about running 50 miles before you attempt to run 100, or 30 miles before you attempt to run 100K. Ironically, this is one area in which marathon training is similar to ultramarathon training: the one long run is not a prerequisite for success.

Would it be ideal if you could do it? Sure. Completing very long runs helps to reinforce your pacing, nutrition, and hydration strategies. Very long runs give you the opportunity to face adversity and work through rough patches. But the physiology necessary to successfully complete an ultramarathon is not significantly impacted by whether or not you have completed one single very long run. If you cannot incorporate such a run into your training schedule, but you can focus on developing your cardiovascular system and creating the strategies to manage your effort level and fueling, you can still successfully complete an ultramarathon.

KEY POINTS FOR HOW MUCH TO RACE

- There are no prerequisite races necessary to be successful at any ultramarathon distance.
- Finding your racing values will help you determine how many races you want to do.
- You can race as the end of means, as a competitive outlet, as part of the training process, or to be part of the community.
- If you are looking to race optimally, limit your racing to one to two times per twelve months for a 100-miler, two to three times per twelve months for the 100K or 50-mile distance, and three to four times per twelve months for the 50K distance.
- Suboptimal racing is OK as long as you identify the goals of the race during the training process

FOREST BOUNDARY
American Lead and Zinc Mill
Pony Express Mine
Little Gem Mine
Rotary Park
American Nettie Mine
Schofield Mine
Jonathan Mine
Silvershield Mill
Wanakah Mine
Bridalveil
The Blowout
Elkhorn Ranch
UNCOMPAHGRE
Rock of the Ages Mine
Speedwell Mine
Radium Springs Swimming Pool
Twin Peaks
Sister Peak
Cascade Falls
OURAY
Oak Creek
Box Canyon
CITY BDY
Uncompahgre Gorge
Uncompahgre River
Mineral Farm
Angel Creek
Canyon Creek

CHAPTER 18

Coaching Guide to Major Ultramarathons

Never underestimate the value of course knowledge when it comes to racing an ultramarathon. The more you know about the terrain, weather, aid stations, gradients, durations of climbs, and landmarks, the better off you'll be on race day. Ultrarunning is an intellectual pursuit as much as it is a physical challenge, and having more knowledge enables you to create a better plan of attack.

Course reconnaissance is one way athletes gain knowledge about the demands of particular races, but that's not a realistic option for a lot of runners who travel significant distances to compete in their goal events. Some runners take the long view and race an event once as a recon mission with the idea they'll return a second time to pursue a performance goal. This is effective, but it's at least a two-year process! The most accessible way athletes learn about races is by talking with other athletes who have already done the event. As with training, however, this method suffers from the N-of-1 bias.

A benefit of coaching a large number of athletes over a long period is that I have been able to build a library of course-specific knowledge for major races. Based on input from athletes I work with, this coaching guide to major North American and international ultras is designed to supplement the information you'll find on the races' websites and in their race bibles. The goal here isn't to republish every detail about these well-known races but to provide the kind of insider advice and guidance that can only come from experience.

American River 50

The American River 50, held the first weekend of April, is one of the oldest and largest ultramarathons in the United States. The point-to-point course starts at Folsom Lake, east of Sacramento, California, and roughly follows the bike path around the lake and down the American River before doubling back on the other side and continuing into the Sierra Nevada foothills to the finish in Auburn, California.

The field of 800-plus runners enjoys a mostly flat course, especially for the first twenty-five miles. In fact, the race is frequently called "a road marathon followed by a trail run" thanks to its split personality. Experienced ultrarunners come to this race to notch PRs, while many newbies tackle it as their first ultra.

DID YOU KNOW? The American River 50 is known for one of the sweetest pieces of swag among ultra race finishers: a Patagonia jacket.

Course record: 5:32:18 (Jim Howard, 1981); 6:09:08 (Ann Trason, 1993)

Median time: 11:07

Cutoff time: 14 hours

Climbing:

Total elevation gain: 3,100 feet (half of which comes in the last five miles)

Total elevation loss: 2,100 feet

WEATHER. It's generally warm but not hot in the Sacramento Valley this time of year. The issue for many runners is that they aren't yet acclimated to the heat, even if that's only 75°F.

Rain is unlikely, but if it does rain, expect to spend the majority of the day in the wet because spring storms can take all day to move through the area.

UNIQUE WEATHER-RELATED CHALLENGE. The heat comes on in full force at the most difficult, final section of the race, which features the only long, sustained climb on the course over somewhat technical terrain (especially compared with the first half of the race).

EQUIPMENT. Despite the flat course and time spent on the bike trail, you'll want to wear trail running shoes to tackle the race's second half. You'll also need a headlamp for the first thirty minutes of the race, which you can then dump at the first aid station.

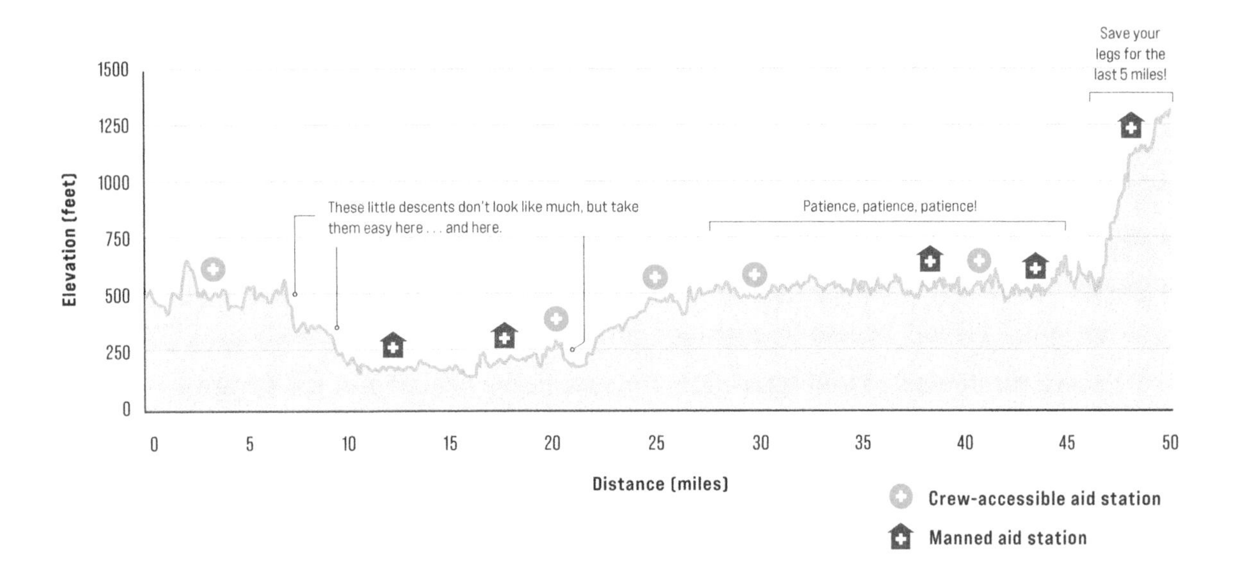

INDISPENSABLE GEAR. Carry two water bottles, as some aid stations are more than an hour apart.

CRUX OF THE RACE. The last five-mile section is a 1,500-foot climb that few are psychologically prepared for after cruising along for the first forty-five miles. The climb psyches many people out, so much so that some runners fail to finish the race even though they probably could.

CRITICAL MENTAL CHALLENGE. Runners who fail at the American River 50 tend to do so because they think it will be easier than it is. They find themselves loping along at marathon pace through the first couple of hours without even trying; they figure they're having a good day, not realizing that they're going too fast. Successful runners here have to force themselves to slow down during those first twenty-five miles, a challenging task when the field's size means there's always someone running faster around you.

TRAINING TIPS. You'll want to prepare to handle technical downhill sections. They're not long, but the race's relative speed can easily overmatch your agility—and state of fatigue—if you're not ready for them.

CRITICAL TRAINING PHASE. If you are using this race as a tune-up for your primary ultras later in the summer, feel free to do VO_2 max work in the months leading up to the race. Although you will not tap into that intensity too much, it will set the stage for those more important upcoming races. If this is your goal event or your first ultra, you should be doing SteadyStateRun work in the four to eight weeks before the race.

CREW TIPS. Crew access is considered very easy. The main difficulty for your crew will be dealing with other crews when searching for parking space at the aid stations. As a result, crews may underestimate travel and parking time and miss their runners. Plan out a strategy in which you only need to see your crew at certain, strategically chosen aid stations. This will be less stressful for you and them.

Pacers are allowed to join starting at mile 24.31, the Beal's Point aid station.

Badwater 135

This legendary 135-miler, which is run from the lowest and hottest point on the planet, Badwater, California, in Death Valley National Park (280 feet below sea level), to Whitney Portal at 8,300 feet, bills itself as "The World's Toughest Foot Race" for four main reasons: it is run at the end of July when daytime highs regularly exceed 110°F; it is run entirely on bone-crushing tarmac; it crosses three mountain ranges; and it is thirty-five miles longer than the more popular 100-mile ultramarathons.

The field for Badwater is capped at 100 runners per year, and racers must qualify by completing three 100-mile races, with the most recent occurring within the preceding twelve months. Applicants who complete Badwater's Salton Sea or Cape Fear races are given special consideration.

Course record: 21:33:01 (Yoshihiko Ishikawa, 2019); 24:13:24 (Patrycja Bereznowska, 2019)

Median time: 37:24

Cutoff time: 48 hours

Climbing:

Total elevation gain: 14,600 feet

Total elevation loss: 6,100 feet

Significant climbs:

Stovepipe Wells to Townes Pass; Panamint Springs to Father Crowley Point; Lone Pine to Whitney Portal

DID YOU KNOW? The original Badwater race in 1977 finished atop Mount Whitney, the highest spot in the continental United States at 14,505 feet in elevation. That was an extra eight miles from (and 6,205 feet higher than) the current finish line at Whitney Portal.

WEATHER. Think you know heat? You don't know heat until you try running in Death Valley, where the temperature can top 130°F, and it will stay above 100°F for significant portions of the race (minus a few "cool" respites of 70°F temps on top of the mountain passes in the middle of the night). Despite the recent change to a night start, the course is still hot throughout the evening. There's no rain, and you can pray for clouds, but don't expect them.

UNIQUE WEATHER-RELATED CHALLENGE. It comes down to surviving the heat and the sun. Run on the relatively cooler white stripe on the shoulder of the road because the black asphalt will be hot enough to melt your shoes

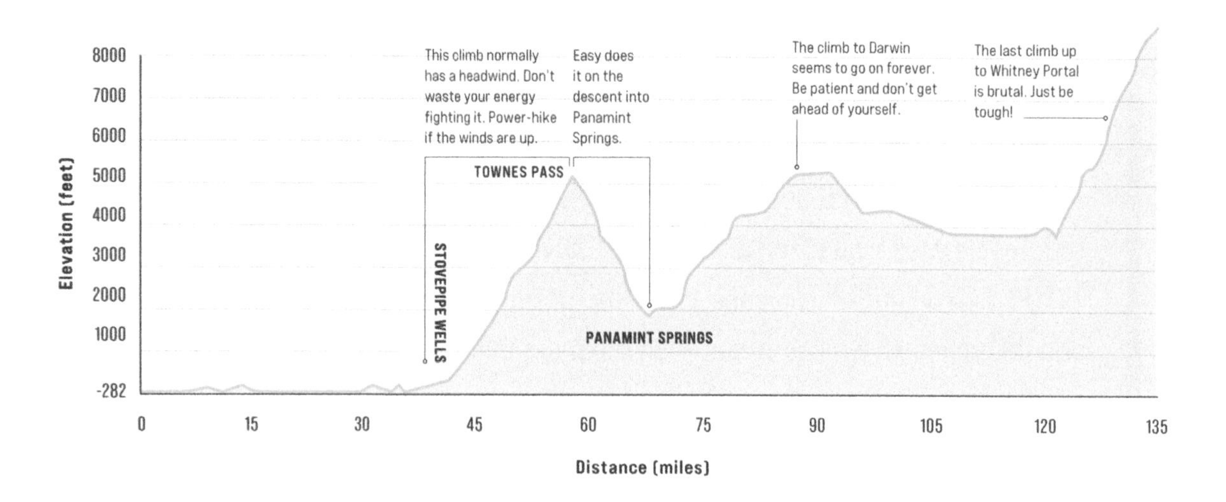

and blister the bottoms of your feet. There is usually a searing headwind, with gusts of twenty-five to thirty miles per hour, coming out of Stovepipe Wells at mile 41.5. It will suck the moisture right out of your nose and throat and make you choke. Consider applying saline solution inside your nose to keep it moist, and pop a steady supply of lozenges to help moisten your throat.

EQUIPMENT. With the extreme exposure and heat, proper clothing can make a big difference. You will want to wear clothes that will stay wet so you can enjoy some evaporative cooling effect. Therefore, avoid the fastest-drying and moisture-wicking fabrics. Ice sleeves are a must, as well as a hat that you can refill with ice every couple of miles.

INDISPENSABLE GEAR. Ice. Lots of ice. You'll need more than you ever thought you would, and keeping it frozen inside an armory of high-quality coolers is a huge challenge. Not helping matters: there are very few places to find ice along the route, and everyone else in the race is looking for a lot of ice, too.

CRUX OF THE RACE. The entire race is probably unlike anything you've ever put yourself through, but the last half-marathon of the course from Lone Pine to Whitney Portal is a 4,573-foot climb straight up the side of the mountain. Coming at mile 122, it hits most racers at a point where they've already pushed beyond anything they've done before (run more than 100 miles).

CRITICAL MENTAL CHALLENGE. Because the ultrarunners who make up the field at

Badwater are quite experienced, they are generally very good at heat acclimation and race-day planning. The time span and the sleep deprivation, not the heat, can be the hardest challenges. With the recent change to a night start, racers and crews can be out there for three consecutive nights, which is a first for many of them. Spending all that time in the race's extreme conditions can leave even well-prepared racers battling through a complete breakdown of their bodies' ability to thermoregulate. It's not the temperature itself but rather the amount of time you're exposed to it that eventually breaks you down.

THE PRO KNOWS. "Many ultrarunners can run all day and night on trails, but Badwater is a road race, not a trail race. Whereas a trail runner can do 75 percent of his training on dirt, training for Badwater means that more than 60 percent of your miles should be on pavement. It takes a long time to get the body used to that. I always tell people that running 200 miles anywhere else is nothing compared to finishing Badwater." *—Dean Karnazes, ten-time Badwater 135 finisher*

TRAINING TIPS. While for most hot-weather races a "minimum effective dose" strategy with heat acclimation is a good thing, Badwater is a different beast. Having a solid heat acclimation strategy is a good first step (described in depth in Chapter 7), but you will also want to do many of your training runs during the hottest parts of the day. This gives you the chance to test out some of your gear as well as familiarize your body with the rigors of running multiple hours in the heat.

CRITICAL TRAINING PHASE. Because the final few weeks of training should include critical heat acclimation, runners need to build their fitness and peak mileage six to eight weeks out from the race. Running your longest and hardest runs at the same time you are trying to acclimate to the heat is a recipe for disaster.

CREW TIPS. Your crew is vital to success in the Badwater 135—and also likely to suffer while offering assistance. In fact, more crew members than runners end up requiring medical attention for heat- and exhaustion-related emergencies. It's that brutal. Crew members need their own strict hydration and rest schedules to survive.

Successful teams need a minimum of two crew members to trade off duties, run resupply missions, and, most important, attend to their runner, who will need constant monitoring. Badwater is unique in that crews can help their runner at any time, anywhere on the course (except for certain sections of the race as specified by the race management). The only requirement is that they find a safe place to pull all four tires off the main road.

Pacers are allowed, but unlike other trail or road races, they can only run behind their runner, not in front or to the side.

Finally, read the rule book! No other ultramarathon in the United States, and perhaps the world, has more elaborate rules than Badwater. To protect the integrity of the race and ensure that future races happen, crews must be keenly aware of the rules.

Comrades Marathon

Held annually in June, the Comrades Marathon boasts the largest ultramarathon field in the world with approximately 25,000 runners participating annually. The renowned South African race is held on the roads between Durban and Pietermaritzburg in the KwaZulu-Natal province. The 55-mile point-to-point race alternates between "up" years and "down" years, yielding a net elevation gain or loss pending the direction. Due to the field size, the race infrastructure, and running on roads, the race will more closely resemble a large international road marathon than your run-of-the-mill trail ultra, complete with road running style aid stations spaced out every few kilometers. Should you choose to partake in the adventure, be prepared for enthusiastic crowds, starting corrals, and professional chip timing.

Course records:

Up: 5:24:39 (Leonid Shvetsov, 2008), 5:58:53 (Gerda Steyn, 2019)

Down: 5:18:19 (David Gatebe, 2016), 5:54:43 (Frith Van Merwe, 1989)

Median time: 10:42

Cutoff time: 12 hours

Climbing:

Total elevation gain: 6,300 feet for up years, 4,150 feet for down years

Total elevation loss: just the opposite of the gain!

DID YOU KNOW? Comrades was run for the first time in 1921, making it the oldest ultramarathon in the world. It has been run every year since, with the exceptions of during World War II and the COVID-19 pandemic. It attracts a stellar list of elite athletes competing for the richest ultrarunning prize purse (over $250,000). The race awards cash prizes for the top ten overall finishers, top age group finishers, winners of the team competition, top South African runners, and top KwaZulu-Natal athletes.

HOW TO GET IN. Athletes have to qualify for the race by running strict time standards. Qualifying times can be from a marathon, various ultramarathon distances, and even the marathon leg of an Ironman® triathlon. Your qualifying time will determine your seeding position for the race.

WEATHER. The race is held in the middle of June and typically has favorable conditions. For runners from

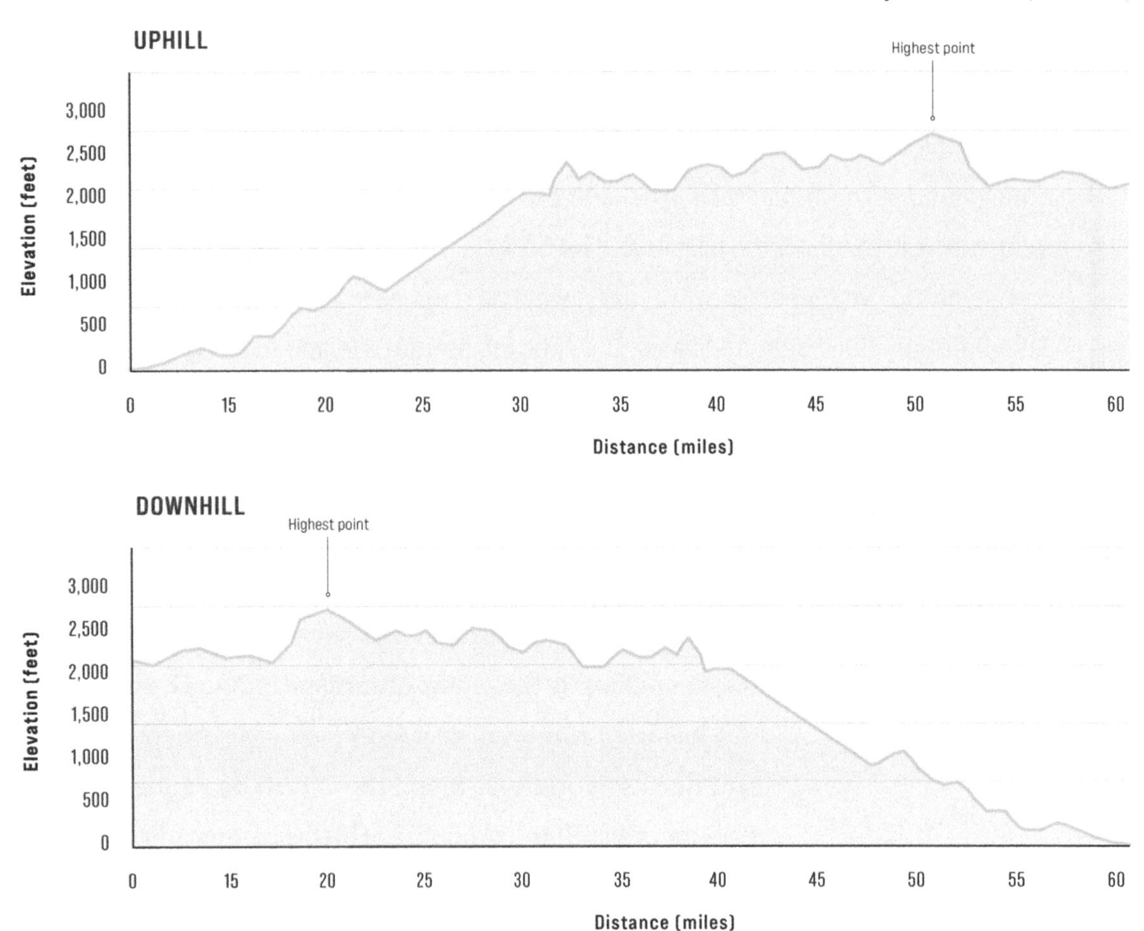

mountainous or cold-weather regions, it could be a touch warm. While no special heat acclimation is necessary, running in the afternoon in full sun for the last few weeks can help.

CRITICAL MENTAL CHALLENGE. The atmosphere of the race is more like a road marathon than a trail ultra. It is easy to get sucked into the crowd in the early miles and run too hard. Particularly in a downhill year, where your early pacing strategy should revolve around saving your legs, runners should pay attention to a pacing plan based off of their predicted finish time. This is an instance where relying on your watch and splits might be of more benefit than perceived exertion.

TRAINING TIPS. On uphill years, training for the Comrades can be similar to training for any flatter 50-mile or 100K trail ultra. April and May should consist of TempoRuns and maybe SteadyStateRuns for the back-of-the-packers. If you are normally a trail runner, running specifically on roads three times per week will need to be added in during the last several weeks. For runners training for a downhill year, realize that your race pace during portions of the event will be faster than your normal EnduranceRun pace or even SteadyStateRun pace. Because of this, you can do TempoRuns right up to the taper of the event. If you regularly train on trails, make sure you are picking more benign trails so you don't lose any footspeed. If you choose to do specific downhill work, sprinkle it in lightly; three or four sessions total during the last six weeks will be plenty.

For some mid- to back-of-the-packers, there will be some climbs that are more effective to walk vs run. Don't let the stigma of "walking on the road" get to you. If it's more effective to power-hike, then do it and save your legs for later in the race.

Hardrock 100

One of the toughest 100-mile races in the world, the Hardrock, held in mid-July, starts and finishes in the high alpine town of Silverton, Colorado, and sends competitors on a loop around the most remote and highest mountain passes in the state, including an ascent up and over 14,048-foot Handies Peak. The route's elevation averages 11,186 feet, topping 12,000 feet thirteen times.

Getting into the race is almost as difficult as finishing it. Runners must have completed a qualifying ultra run, and even then there are only forty-seven slots available for first-time participants. In addition, there is a service requirement: eight hours of volunteer work at an ultra race.

Course record: 22:41 (Kilian Jornet, 2014); 27:18 (Diana Finkel, 2009)

Median time: 40:31

Cutoff time: 48 hours

Climbing:

Total elevation gain/loss: 33,050 feet

Significant climbs: They are all hard! Hardrock is one of the most notoriously difficult 100-mile events. You are climbing or descending nearly the entire course.

DID YOU KNOW? On even years the race goes clockwise. On odd years it runs counterclockwise. Racers have to kiss the Hardrock, a large stone painted with a picture of a ram's head, to officially finish the race. This race also has one of the most detailed course descriptions available; read it.

WEATHER. Prepare for subfreezing nights in the high alpine sections and highs in the mid-70s in the town of Ouray. Because the race takes place in the middle of the Rocky Mountain summer monsoon season, expect late afternoon thunderstorms, some of them violent, with extreme drops in temperature and even snowfall. Fortunately, the storms move in and out quickly most of the time.

UNIQUE WEATHER-RELATED CHALLENGE. Be on the lookout for clouds developing into storms that can unleash a bone-chilling cloudburst of rain or hail. The route takes participants over multiple exposed ridgelines where lightning strikes are a very real concern. If you see or hear lightning nearby, work your way down to a lower

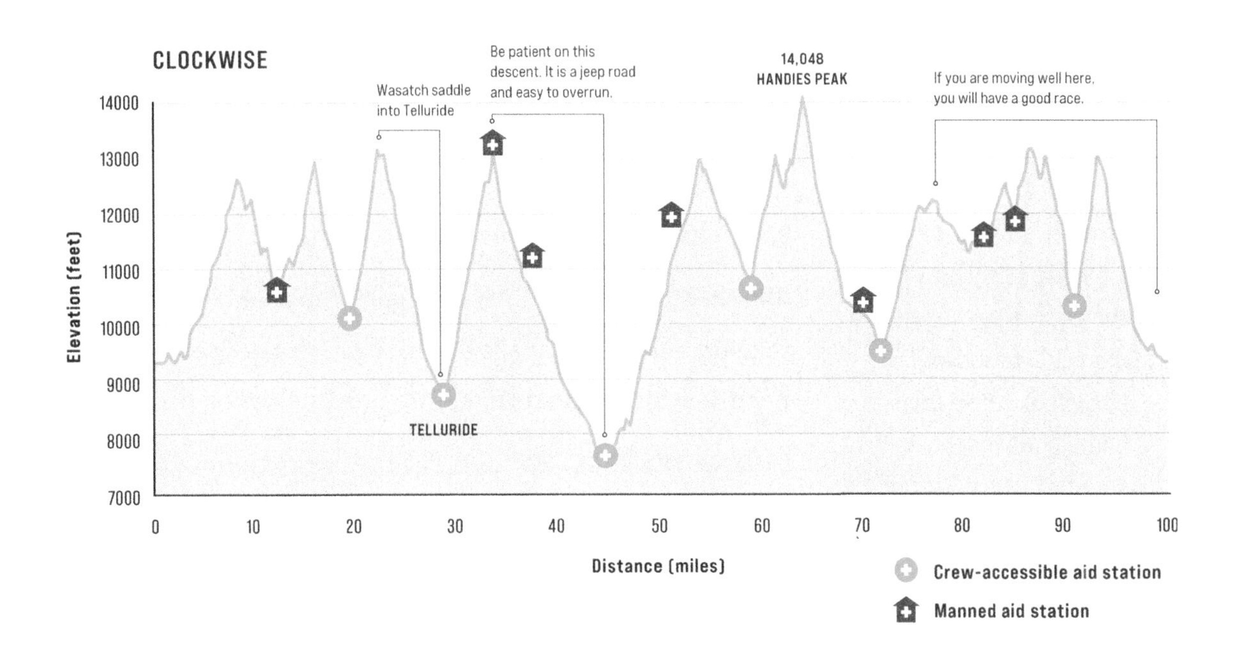
CLOCKWISE
Wasatch saddle into Telluride
Be patient on this descent. It is a jeep road and easy to overrun.
14,048
HANDIES PEAK
If you are moving well here, you will have a good race.
TELLURIDE
Elevation (feet)
14000
13000
12000
11000
10000
9000
8000
7000
0
10
20
30
40
50
60
70
80
90
100
Distance (miles)
Crew-accessible aid station
Manned aid station

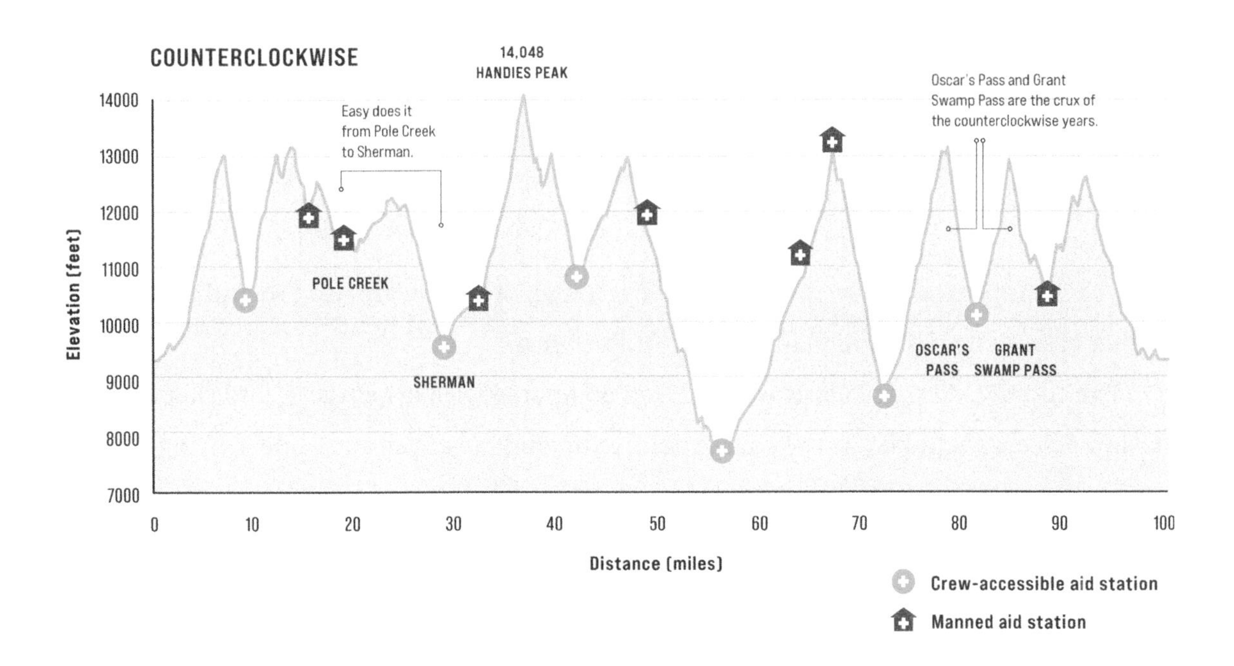
COUNTERCLOCKWISE
14,048
HANDIES PEAK
Easy does it from Pole Creek to Sherman.
Oscar's Pass and Grant Swamp Pass are the crux of the counterclockwise years.
POLE CREEK
SHERMAN
OSCAR'S PASS
GRANT SWAMP PASS
Elevation (feet)
14000
13000
12000
11000
10000
9000
8000
7000
0
10
20
30
40
50
60
70
80
90
100
Distance (miles)
Crew-accessible aid station
Manned aid station

elevation as quickly and safely as possible.

THE PRO KNOWS.

"On years when the race runs counter-clockwise, you have to watch your pace through the Pole Creek section. You can easily let yourself fly down the course to the Sherman aid station and blow your whole race. Same goes for the descent off the Wasatch saddle into Telluride in the clockwise years. People get so excited to see the town below that they blow out their quads by going too fast."

—Missy Gosney, fourth place, 2015

EQUIPMENT. Carry a packable waterproof, breathable rain jacket at all times. Wrap your mind around the fact that you might be out on the course for two nights, and pack accordingly. Pack a complete change of clothes in every drop bag (from underwear to outerwear). Trekking poles can help steady your pace on the downhills.

INDISPENSABLE GEAR. An emergency space blanket will take up hardly any space but may prove a godsend if you need to wait out a storm before heading over a pass.

CRUX OF THE RACE. Handies Peak, at more than 14,000 feet, is higher than many people have ever climbed before, much less in the middle of the night, which will be the case for many runners during clockwise years. The altitude can slow you down more than you expect, but pushing too hard at this altitude can take a lot out of you, so gauge your effort by exertion rather than speed.

CRITICAL MENTAL CHALLENGE. It's a long race. A good time is under thirty hours, which is the cutoff for other less challenging 100-milers. Even for experienced ultrarunners, the Hardrock will have you on your feet longer than you are used to and running at higher elevations than you may be comfortable with.

The course isn't particularly well marked compared with other races, and that is by design. Racers should know the course before showing up at the start line. During the race, participants (and their pacers) must pay attention to their whereabouts at all times.

TRAINING TIPS. Training for the Hardrock is about banking as much vertical in the legs as possible. Shoot for long runs with 4,000 to 5,000 feet of climbing/descending on successive days. And take any chance you have to run at altitude, not necessarily to acclimate but to understand how your body responds to it.

CRITICAL TRAINING PHASE. May and June, with lots of hiking and descending. Most athletes cannot match the 680 feet of elevation change per mile in training, but it is critical to do whatever you can. Even for the winners, nearly all the uphills will be hikes, so spend the majority of May and June hiking as much as possible.

CREW TIPS. Crews are allowed only at the designated aid stations, some of which are remote with no cellular phone service. Crew members need to prepare for a lot of driving on twisting mountain roads and Forest Service roads.

Pacers need to make sure to pack for a long time on the trail, as much as ten hours, and carry enough water and food accordingly. Because there are few, if any, bailouts between aid stations, pacers must understand that they have to be prepared to go the distance.

Javelina Jundred

The setup for the Javelina Jundred makes it unusual among ultras. The popular race with more than 600 participants takes place entirely inside McDowell Mountain Regional Park, which is situated just outside the sprawl of Scottsdale, Arizona. The race, either a 100K or a 100-miler, is relatively flat and consists of twenty-mile loops in the park. What's unique about the race is that with each lap, runners reverse direction to run the next loop, giving everyone multiple chances to see each other (and for those aiming to win the race, a chance to see where their competition is).

Relatively little elevation change, easy logistics, and timing at the very end of the running season make the Javelina Jundred attractive to ultrarunners looking to qualify for the Western States 100-Mile Endurance Run.

Course record:

100-mile: 13:01:14 (Patrick Regan, 2017); 14:52:06 (Devon Yanko, 2015)

100K: 7:58:43 (Christian Gering, 2019); 8:48:25 (Courtney Dauwalter, 2016)

Median time:

100-mile: 26:01:26

100K: 16:28:57

Cutoff time:

100-mile: 30 hours

100K: 29 hours

Climbing:

Total elevation gain/loss:
100-mile: 7,900 feet.
100K: 5,000 feet

DID YOU KNOW? Because the race occurs on or near Halloween, costumes are encouraged for runners and their crews, with awards given for the best male and female costumes. And because crews are allowed only at the start/finish line, they set up camp for the duration of the race and turn it into an all-day/all-night party. I have run as a Chippendale dancer.

WEATHER. As far as ultras go, the weather is relatively mild, with overnight temperatures in the high 50s to low 60s. Daytime highs can reach the mid-90s. Rain is rare, but it can happen.

UNIQUE WEATHER-RELATED CHALLENGE. The timing of the race at the end of October means that runners from farther north have already spent months running in much cooler fall weather. When they arrive in Arizona, they're not acclimated to running in 90-degree sun, with no shade anywhere on the course. As a result, expect to run slower than you may have planned

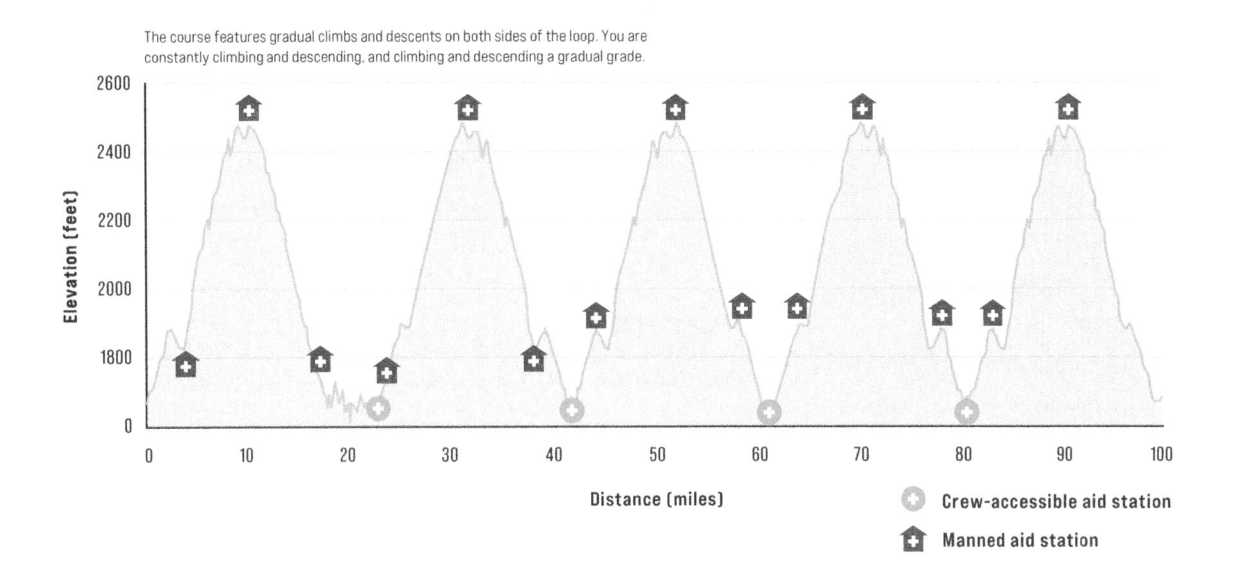

due to the heat. Sunset doesn't always bring relief either. Many runners (and crews) aren't prepared for the sudden 40-degree drop in temperature once the sun goes down.

EQUIPMENT. With minimal weather-related issues and regular aid station intervals (you're never more than six-and-a-half miles from the next aid station), there's no need to carry any special equipment beyond a water bottle or two. The race start/finish line is part aid station, part Woodstock with runner crews and their tents lining the course. So, have your crew bring a pop-up tent and some chairs to enjoy the event. Everyone needs to shuttle in from an off-site parking area.

INDISPENSABLE GEAR. Many runners wear gaiters to keep the grit and small pebbles from the sandy washes and trail out of their shoes.

CRUX OF THE RACE. The imperceptible descent from the backside of the course to the start/finish line lulls many runners into thinking they're going to have an A+ day, and they start running faster than they should. When they start the slog back up that incline, they pay the price. Although there is not a lot of elevation gain/loss, you are very rarely running on perfectly flat terrain.

CRITICAL MENTAL CHALLENGE. Despite its easy logistics and relatively flat course, the Javelina Jundred is a deceptively hard race, with a finishing rate of only roughly 50 percent. The reason, beyond the heat, is that with every twenty-mile lap, racers return to

THE PRO KNOWS.

"Many people start out this race too fast because of the cool morning temperatures and easy geography. After the first lap, at least a third of the field is usually running a sub-twenty-four-hour pace, which is unsustainable unless they're an elite pro. The key to finishing is to force yourself to go slow during the first couple of laps."

—Jamil Coury, race director

where all the crews' camps are set up. During the night, the start/finish turns into a party atmosphere, with music, beer trucks, disco balls—it's a hard environment to leave. Even the backside aid station is set up as a party. Help yourself by not sitting down and getting sucked into the scene.

TRAINING TIPS. If you live in a climate that features cool, crisp autumns, train during the heat of the day, not the mornings or evenings. Get comfortable running in sand and gravel—dry riverbeds work well. You don't need to do all of your runs in sand and gravel, but do enough to get used to them. Thanks to the terrain, it's possible to run the entire Javelina Jundred course, which makes pacing discipline a must.

CRITICAL TRAINING PHASE. Both the 100K and the 100-mile Javelinas are steady grinders, so EnduranceRun and SteadyStateRun intensity will be your bread and butter in September and October.

CREW TIPS. There may be no easier race to crew than the Javelina Jundred. The hardest part is shuttling in all your gear and camping equipment the afternoon or evening before the event starts. But after setting up camp, the crew doesn't need to move. Accordingly, make sure they—and you—have enough food, fluids, and creature comforts to last for the entire race, since they can't easily hop in a car to go get supplies or a meal.

As soon as the sun goes down on day one or after the third loop, whichever comes first, pacers are allowed to join their runners to the finish of the race.

JFK 50

The oldest ultra run in America, the JFK 50 started in 1962. The point-to-point race, held every November between Boonsboro and Williamsport, Maryland, is now the largest ultra in the country, with a cap of 1,000 runners. The course starts in western Maryland on the Appalachian Trail before connecting with the sublime C&O Canal Towpath along the Potomac River on the way to the finish. It's considered a fast and relatively easy course without much climbing (and nearly all the climbing is completed in the first five miles). But it's a different kind of race, as champions of western 100-mile races soon discover when they fail to crack the top ten.

Course record: 5:21:28 (Jim Walmsley, 2016); 6:11:59 (Ellie Greenwood, 2012)

Median time: 10:20

Cutoff time: 13 hours

Climbing: Total elevation gain/loss: 2,077 feet

DID YOU KNOW? The 50-mile distance came from a challenge to the US Marines by then president John F. Kennedy to hike fifty miles in under twenty hours, as Teddy Roosevelt's marines had done. That led a group of eleven civilians to try it on what is now the JFK 50 course. By 1970, seventy-three participants had finished. For comparison, the first New York City Marathon held in 1970 recorded only fifty-five finishers.

WEATHER. Expect crisp fall weather for the Appalachian Mountains: highs in the mid-50s and lows at start time in the high 30s. It can rain, though. It can even snow.

UNIQUE WEATHER-RELATED CHALLENGE. It's rarely uncomfortably hot for this race; it's usually a glorious running day with perfect temperatures. Or it could rain, sleet, or snow. Prepare for the latter by stocking your drop bags with plenty of dry clothes to change into.

INDISPENSABLE GEAR. A space blanket is a small insurance policy worth carrying in case your day goes south and the cold starts getting to you.

CRUX OF THE RACE. The majority of the climbing takes place within five miles of the start, with a lot of it on technical, rocky trail. It will be a conga line up and down the mountains.

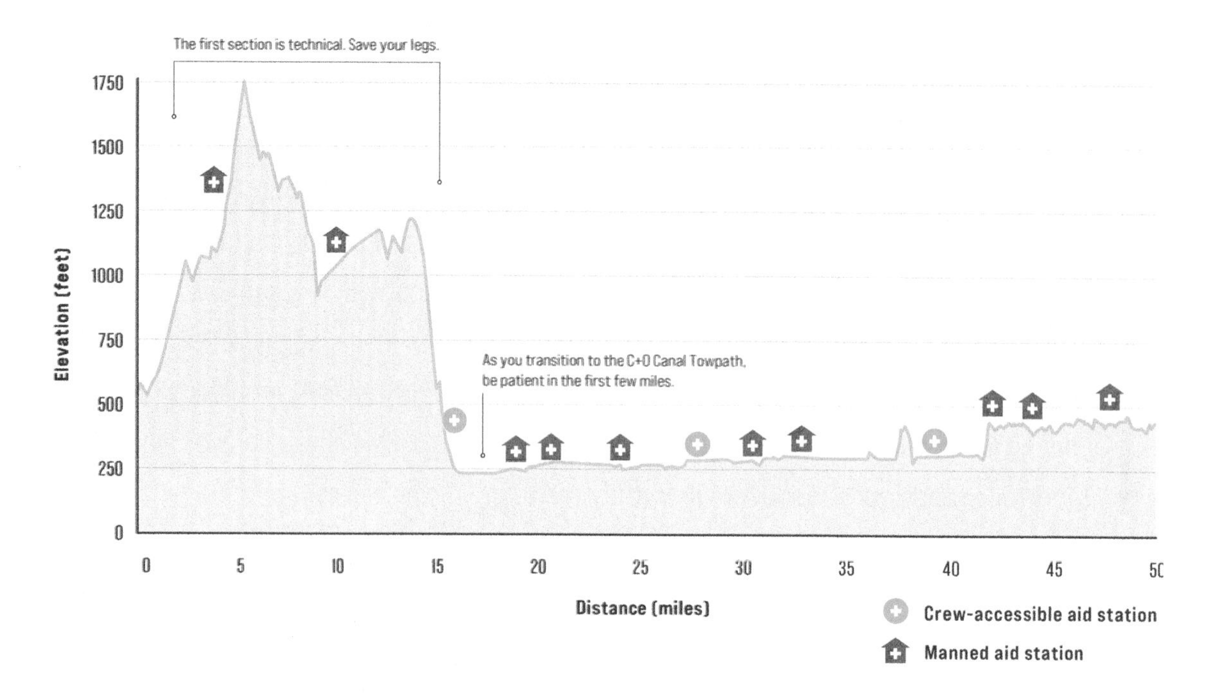

If you're not careful, this can become a giant energy suck as you're constantly trying to sprint around people on the trail. If you find yourself stuck in the pack, save your energy, settle in, and carefully pick spots where you can pass more people more easily.

CRITICAL MENTAL CHALLENGE. Once runners hit the flat, soft gravel of the C&O Canal Towpath, many unwisely figure the hard part's over and pour on too much speed in those first few towpath miles. Holding yourself in check and sticking with your race plan is critical here; you still have thirty-five miles to go.

TRAINING TIP. Except for parts of the roughly ten-mile stretch along the Appalachian Trail, the JFK 50 is a completely runnable event, and you can easily settle into a rhythm for the duration of the course. You have to train for the trails and for the flats. Versatility is key for success in this event.

CRITICAL TRAINING PHASE. This is a late-season race for many ultrarunners, so starting healthy is a priority. Training during July, August, and September should include TempoRuns and SteadyStateRuns, which will pay off in this race.

CREW TIPS. The horseshoe-shaped route of the race makes it relatively easy for crew members to support their runners. That said, with 1,000 participants, your crew will likely find themselves more stressed out over the battle for parking at aid stations than over helping you, especially for the first few aid stations when the field will still be relatively bunched up. Better to plan on a few strategic meeting points and a smart drop bag strategy for the other points to get you through the race.

Pacers are not encouraged, but they are allowed.

Lake Sonoma 50

This early-season 50-miler is held every April in the beautiful and lush (at that time of year) Sonoma Valley in Northern California. The out-and-back rolling trail course is considered fast and features many sections through forest shade, across twelve creeks, and around its namesake lake. Trail runners love it; 86 percent of the course is on relatively smooth, nontechnical singletrack trails. The race has a high finishing rate (approximately 90 percent) and is often used as a tune-up race for the Western States 100, which is held in June. Entry is via a blind lottery (i.e., there's no preferential treatment for past entrants or pros).

Course record: 5:51:16 (Jim Walmsley, 2018); 7:08:23 (Stephanie Howe, 2015)

Median time: 11:03

Cutoff time: 14 hours

Climbing: Total elevation gain/loss: 10,500 feet

DID YOU KNOW? The Island View aid station on the course is so remote that supplies and volunteers have to be delivered by boat.

WEATHER. April in the Sonoma Valley has near-perfect ultrarunning weather, with lows in the mid-40s and highs in the mid-70s. Even during the heat of the day, much of the trail is under the shade of tree cover. There's one caveat (it's a big one): if it's raining, there's a good chance that it will rain hard throughout the day and that the temperature will stay uncomfortably cool.

UNIQUE WEATHER-RELATED CHALLENGE. None, really. It's California. It's spring. Odds are it's going to be a nice day.

EQUIPMENT. There are no special equipment needs and no need to carry much beyond water and food. Also, water at the more remote aid stations will be limited to drinking, not dousing yourself to cool off; you'll want to do that at the creek crossings or at the lake.

INDISPENSABLE GEAR. Some aid stations are nearly seven and a half miles apart, a long distance during the hottest part of the race. As such, carry more water and food than you think you might need.

CRUX OF THE RACE. From mile 33 to the finish, the race can feel long and lonely, with

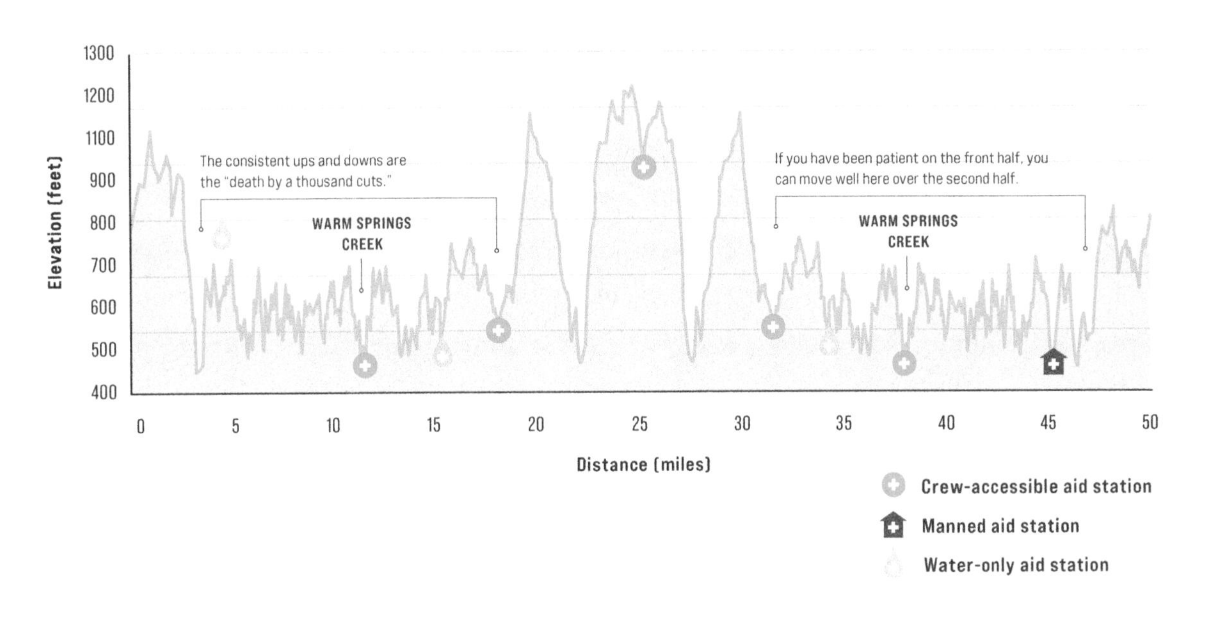

THE PRO KNOWS.

"To do well in this race, you've got to be able to run fast, yet deal with a lot of climbing. That combination is unique in the ultra world, which is why you want to train for running this race—not just speed-hiking—uphill and down."

—Dakota Jones, first place, 2012

roughly five to seven and a half miles between the last three aid stations. Not helping matters, you won't see many people due to the terrain and how spread out everyone is. For midpackers and those at the back, the race can suddenly feel like running through the middle of nowhere by yourself.

CRITICAL MENTAL CHALLENGE. For a 50-mile race with no mountains to climb, the Lake Sonoma 50 packs a serious dose of vertical into its punchy course. The relentless ups and downs with few flat sections or gradual inclines to rest can blow racers' quads apart well before the finish. The key, as with any ultra, is pacing, especially on the short downhill sections. "Death by a thousand cuts" is how former course record holder Alex Varner describes the multitude of ups and downs.

TRAINING TIPS. Work on your foot turnover to maintain your speed on the short flats and to mitigate some of the punishment (but not speed) on the downhill stretches. The race requires a lot of pace changes; work on that in training by including ups, downs, and flats in any specific interval work.

CRITICAL TRAINING PHASE. If you are using this race as a tune-up for your primary ultras later in the summer, some VO_2 max work leading up to the race is a good idea. Although you will not tap into that intensity much, it will set the stage for those more important upcoming races. If this is your goal event, or your first ultra, you should be doing SteadyStateRun work in the four to eight weeks leading up to the race.

CREW TIPS. Thanks to the usually mild weather, crewing this race is easy. However, getting to the remote Warm Springs Creek aid station involves a lot more driving on winding roads than many expect. Crews will need to be self-contained and have a full tank of gas for the day because fuel stations and grocery stores are too far away to dash off for a resupply.

Pacers are not allowed on the course.

Leadville Trail 100

Held in late August in the Colorado Rockies, the Leadville Trail 100 is one of the oldest and most iconic 100-mile races in North America. Known for its high altitude (the lowest point of the race is 9,200 feet) and relatively large race field, the race attracts a number of first-time 100-mile runners to the starting line due to the fact that there is no qualifying requirement to enter.

Course record:
15:42:59 (Matt Carpenter, 2005); 18:06:24 (Ann Trason, 1994)

Median time: 28:20

Cutoff time: 30 hours

Climbing: Total elevation gain/loss: 18,168 feet

Significant climbs:

Colorado Trail and Hagerman Pass Road: 5.65 miles, 1,338 feet

Hope Pass: 4.48 miles, 3,204 feet

Sheep's Gulch: 2.4 miles, 2,303 feet

Leaving Twin Lakes to the Colorado Trail: 2.7 miles, 1,222 feet

Powerline: 3.88 miles, 1,483 feet

Significant descents:

Powerline: 3.88 miles, 1,483 feet

Colorado Trail into Twin Lakes: 2.7 miles, 1,222 feet

Sheep's Gulch: 2.4 miles, 2,303 feet

Hope Pass: 4.48 miles, 3,204 feet

Hagerman Pass Road and the Colorado Trail: 5.65 miles, 1,338 feet

DID YOU KNOW? Leadville local Ken Chlouber started the race in 1983 as a way to generate tourism revenue for the town, which at the time had the highest unemployment rate in the nation.

WEATHER. Typically cool, crisp mornings in the low 40s give way to mild afternoon temps in the mid-70s. Fast-moving thunderstorms roll through this area of the Rocky Mountains in the late afternoon, so if you are up high, especially above the timberline, make sure you have gear for nasty weather.

UNIQUE WEATHER-RELATED CHALLENGE. Late August can offer a dry weather window in the Colorado Rocky Mountain monsoon season, but every few years the race falls on the edge of the rainy season. If this is the case, expect heavy rain throughout the day and snow and sleet at higher elevations and during the night. In addition, between 10 p.m. and 4 a.m., it can be quite cold. Combine that with late-race fatigue and difficulty generating body heat, and you have a recipe for hypothermia. Miles 87 to 95 around Turquoise Lake exaggerate this particular constellation of calamities, so bring extra clothes for that section.

EQUIPMENT. Leadville is unique in the world of ultras in that pacers, who can join after mile 50, can mule (or carry the equipment) for their runners. The race directors instituted this rule as homage to the area's mining heritage and the miners' essential companion, the noble burro. Take advantage of this rule and have your pacer carry extra clothes, water, food, headlamp batteries, and trekking poles should you need them.

INDISPENSABLE GEAR. A pacer/mule to lighten your load.

CRUX OF THE RACE. Although the Hope Pass (12,600 feet) double crossing in the middle of the race always receives the most attention, the crux of the course is the climb up Powerline over Sugarloaf Pass (11,071 feet) and then the descent into the May Queen aid station at mile 86.5. This section comes late in the race, and the Powerline climb, although not long, is steep and slow-going. The section of the Colorado Trail leading into the May Queen aid station is one of the more technical parts of the course. Add in the darkness of night and tired legs, and it can be a rough go.

It can also be the weirdest: one of my most notable ultra hallucinations occurred on the Hagerman Road descent, where all the rocks came to life and were dancing and twirling across the gravel road!

CRITICAL MENTAL CHALLENGE. With as many as 600 to 800 participants and an out-and-back course, the race can become quite crowded. Many find this a source of inspiration, but it can also backfire as runners struggle to relax and run their own race among the crowd. Worse, some runners struggling to beat the cutoffs tend to cluster into groups of shared misery around miles 60 to 85, producing a negative feedback loop that slows everyone down to the pace of the slowest runner in the group. The result is that some runners who could have easily beaten the cutoffs do not. The key is to realize when you're in such a group and accelerate out of it immediately.

TRAINING TIPS. Although the course isn't particularly challenging from a technical

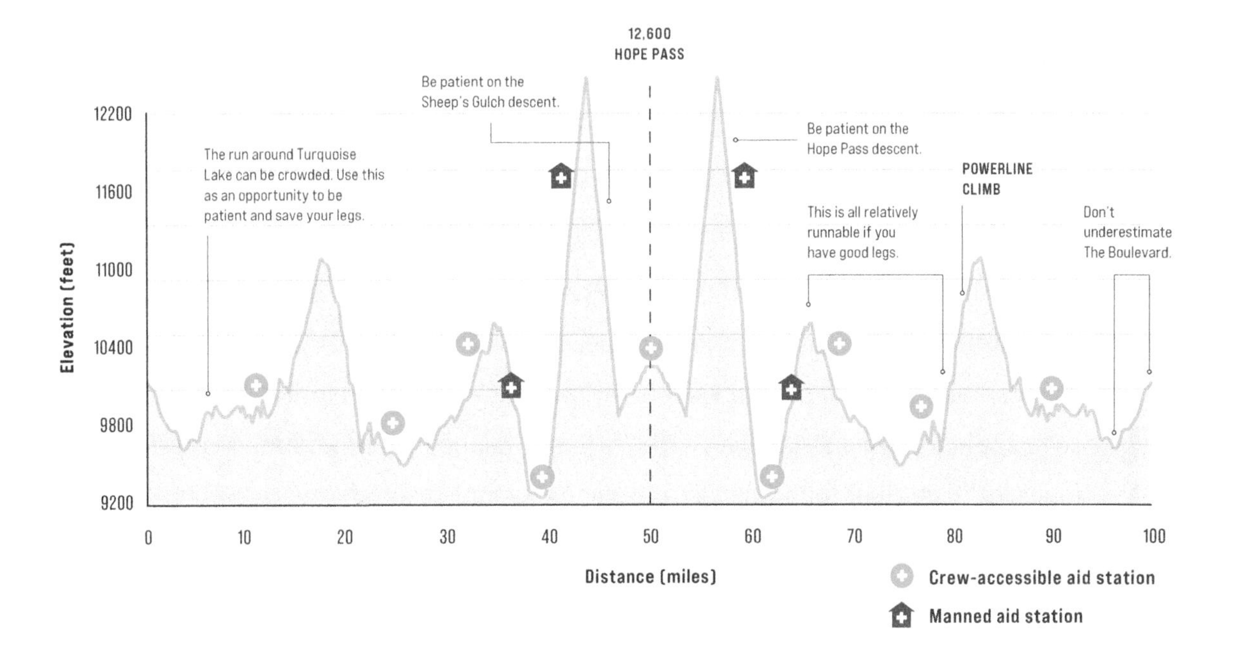

THE PRO KNOWS.

"There's a three-mile, gradual uphill finish into town called "The Boulevard." Coming at mile 97, it's more difficult than you'd expect. Don't think you are home free when you get to the Boulevard; continue pushing until you can see the finish line on 6th Street."

—Dylan Bowman, second place, 2011

perspective, many runners fear the altitude with good reason: it exaggerates any weakness in a runner's pacing and nutrition game plan. Thus, it's critical to practice and follow the hydration and nutrition plan you've mapped out for the race in the weeks and months leading up to the event. Come race day, slow and steady will pay off.

CREW TIPS. With the start/finish in Leadville and the course staying in one general area, logistics for the race are relatively easy. But with so many runners bringing so many crew members to the race, and with few access points to aid stations, tempers among crews can flare over parking spots and positioning at the aid stations. There's no need for it; whether you're right next to the aid station check-in or thirty yards down the trail, it isn't going to matter. Tell them to chill out.

Tor Des Géants

Tor des Géants (simply known as the Tor) is the Super Bowl of 200-mile ultramarathons. Literally translated to "Tour of the Giants," the tough, rugged, remote route attracts runners from around the world wishing to take a crack at one of the most difficult endurance races on the planet. The route lies in the Aosta Valley of northwestern Italy and employs the notoriously steep Italian Alps, which athletes must climb, traverse, and descend over at least a few days' time. The route utilizes two of the oldest trails in the region (Alta Via 1 and Alta Via 2); connects more than thirty different municipalities, cities, and villages; and climbs twenty-five different mountain passes.

Distance: 221 miles

Median time: 133 hours

Cutoff time: 150 hours

Climbing: 82,000 feet of climbing and descending

DID YOU KNOW? The Tor des Géants brings out the entire valley to support the event. In the week leading up to and the week during the race, the 1,260-square-mile region becomes completely immersed in all things Tor. The small towns and villages the Tor passes through are adorned with Tor banners and billboards, and every shop seems to have some trinket adorned with the Tor logo, including postcards, special edition beers, and stuffed animals. The central town of Aosta has festivals, movie screenings, and athlete panels which runners, crew, and locals alike attend.

HOW TO GET IN. The Tor des Géants has one of the more interesting lottery processes: they weight the field by proportionally allocating entries based on the percentage of applicants by country. In other words, if 10 percent of the applicants hail from the United States, 10 percent of the 750-person field that is selected will be from the US. This makes the race field a true representation of the worldwide interest. There are no other prerequisites for entry.

WEATHER. Weather around the Aosta Valley can change dramatically from one mountain pass to the next. Be prepared for anything, literally. You can get hail and snow up one climb and have temps in the 80s on the following descent. Fortunately, the race produces "zone forecasts" for each of the five major geographic regions of the course. These can be

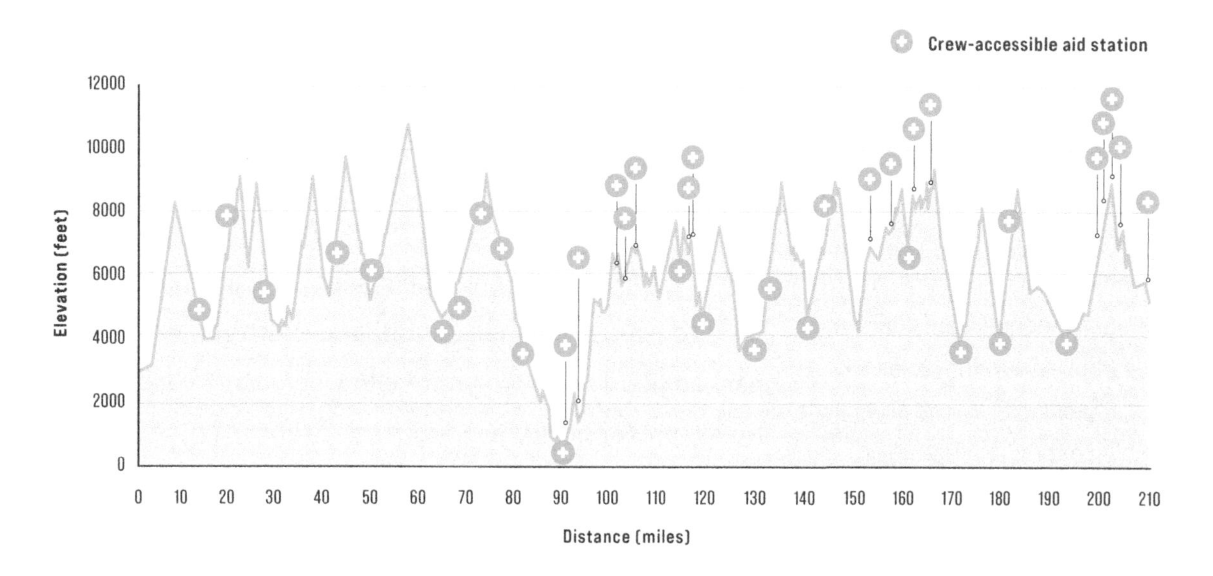

accessed via an app or at the major aid stations (which are known as "Life Bases").

AID STATIONS. Aid stations at the Tor des Géants are a combination of high alpine refugios (small mountain cabins or huts) approximately every 10K and major aid stations called "Life Bases" every 50K. The Life Bases are literally a lifeline, offering runners warm meals, a shower, medical support, places to sleep, and access to your all-important yellow duffle bag (see Equipment section next). If you have support crew coming over to the Tor, consider yourself lucky. While the Aosta Valley is a great getaway, crewing for the Tor is a big favor to ask and normally chews up over a week of precious time. If you want crew, get your brownie points in order so that you can cash them in!

EQUIPMENT. Mandatory equipment is handled a bit differently at the Tor. When you receive your race bib, you will also receive a giant yellow duffel bag that will soon become your lifeline and best friend (feel free to give it a pet name, as well). Depending on the conditions, race management can require you to physically carry any of the equipment from the mandatory list or they can leave you to your own devices. At a minimum you must always carry cold- and foul-weather gear, a hat, gloves, two headlamps with backup batteries, your phone, and a passport. All of the mandatory gear required by the race and not physically on you while out on the course is to be placed in your yellow bag and returned to the race officials before the start. Pay attention, as the list is extensive and includes things like crampons, a knife, and extra string for a broken shoelace, all of which you might actually need. Similar to how the airlines treat luggage, your giant yellow bag follows you around the course from Life Base to Life Base and magically appears from a volunteer's hands upon your arrival.

THE PRO KNOWS.

"Tor will test you like no other race. It is relentless. The climbs are long, hard, and seem to never end; and once you get though one of the high mountain passes, it's back down the other side for a quad-smashing descent. But it's all worth it. The return back to the start/finish line in Courmayeur will be one of, if not the most, memorable finishes of your ultra career. Whether or not you can remember the rest of the race is another question altogether. I only remember about 50 percent, so I will keep going back."

—Jason Koop, 2019 finisher

INDISPENSABLE GEAR. Poles. Just look at the elevation statistics. Poles are an indispensable tool at the Tor. Get used to using them both uphill and downhill. Bring a backup pair to stow in your yellow gear bag should you break one (or both). A cylindrical cardboard tube normally used for architecture drawings and large maps is a good way to pack foldable poles to ensure they don't get crushed in transit.

CRITICAL LOGISTICAL CHALLENGE. Sleep. The winners will finish the Tor in a little over seventy hours. With enough caffeine, they might be able to make it through the race with just a trail nap or two. For the rest of the field, when and where you sleep is critical. Aid stations will limit you to two hours, and most of the time they are very strict on this. Take advantage of whenever you can get a full two hours of sleep regardless of whether it is in a high alpine refugio or Life Base. Refer back to Chapter 16 for sleep strategies.

TRAINING TIPS. Hike, hike, and hike some more. There is hardly any uphill running at the Tor. The race selection lottery for the Tor happens in February, meaning you will have about seven months to train from the time you know you are in the race to when the gun goes off. Use all of this time. You can spend February, March, and April in a normal running routine full of intervals and the like, but once May rolls around, your focus should be on low-intensity hiking.

CREW TIPS. Many families like to go to the Tor as a vacation of sorts. It's a great destination, as the area is magnificent and filled with adventures and history. If you do have support crew, have them stay in the central town of Aosta rather than where the race starts and ends in Courmayeur. This will save them about an hour's worth of driving per Life Base they go to, which will start to stack up as the days move along. Getting around from town to town is not all that difficult, but be mindful of the speed traps and paid parking lots. Italy is renowned for their traffic enforcement! You won't know if you've been caught speeding in a rental car until four months later when you get a bill in the mail. Trust me on this.

UTMB/CCC/TDS

The Ultra-Trail du Mont-Blanc (UTMB), Courmayeur-Champex-Chamonix (CCC), and Sur les Traces des Ducs de Savoie (TDS) are the three most popular races occurring over the UTMB weekend. While they do not all occur on exactly the same trails, the trails are similar enough that preparation for any of these races will be similar.

Median time:

UTMB: 40:46

CCC: 22:18

TDS: 39:27

Cutoff time:

UTMB: 46:30

CCC: 26:30

TDS: 44:00

Climbing:

UTMB: Total elevation gain/loss: 32,808 feet

CCC: Total elevation gain: 20,132 feet

Total elevation loss: 20,769 feet

TDS: Total elevation gain: 29,855 feet

Total elevation loss: 30,492 feet

DID YOU KNOW? The UTMB races bring over 100,000 people and 10,000 runners to the Chamonix valley every year. The races are an enormous economic driver for the mountain town that sees all types of adventurers from BASE jumpers to backcountry skiers and, yes, ultrarunners. The UTMB races all revolve around the Mont Blanc massif, which spans the countries of France, Italy, and Switzerland.

HOW TO GET IN. The UTMB races are notoriously convoluted to enter. An elaborate system of qualifying points is necessary to apply for entry into each race. From there, the race organizers use a lottery system to fill each field. Every few years, different aspects of the points system change. Points are available in many countries, and more value is placed on longer races.

WEATHER. Weather around the Mont Blanc massif is notoriously moody. Particularly on the Italian side, clear and sunny skies can change to a hailstorm in an instant.

EQUIPMENT. The races all have mandatory gear that is periodically checked at aid stations. Don't be a weight weenie and try to skimp out on a more protective jacket or pants. Be prepared for bad weather if there is any hint of it in the weather forecast in the days leading up to the race.

INDISPENSABLE GEAR. Your pack. You must wear a pack

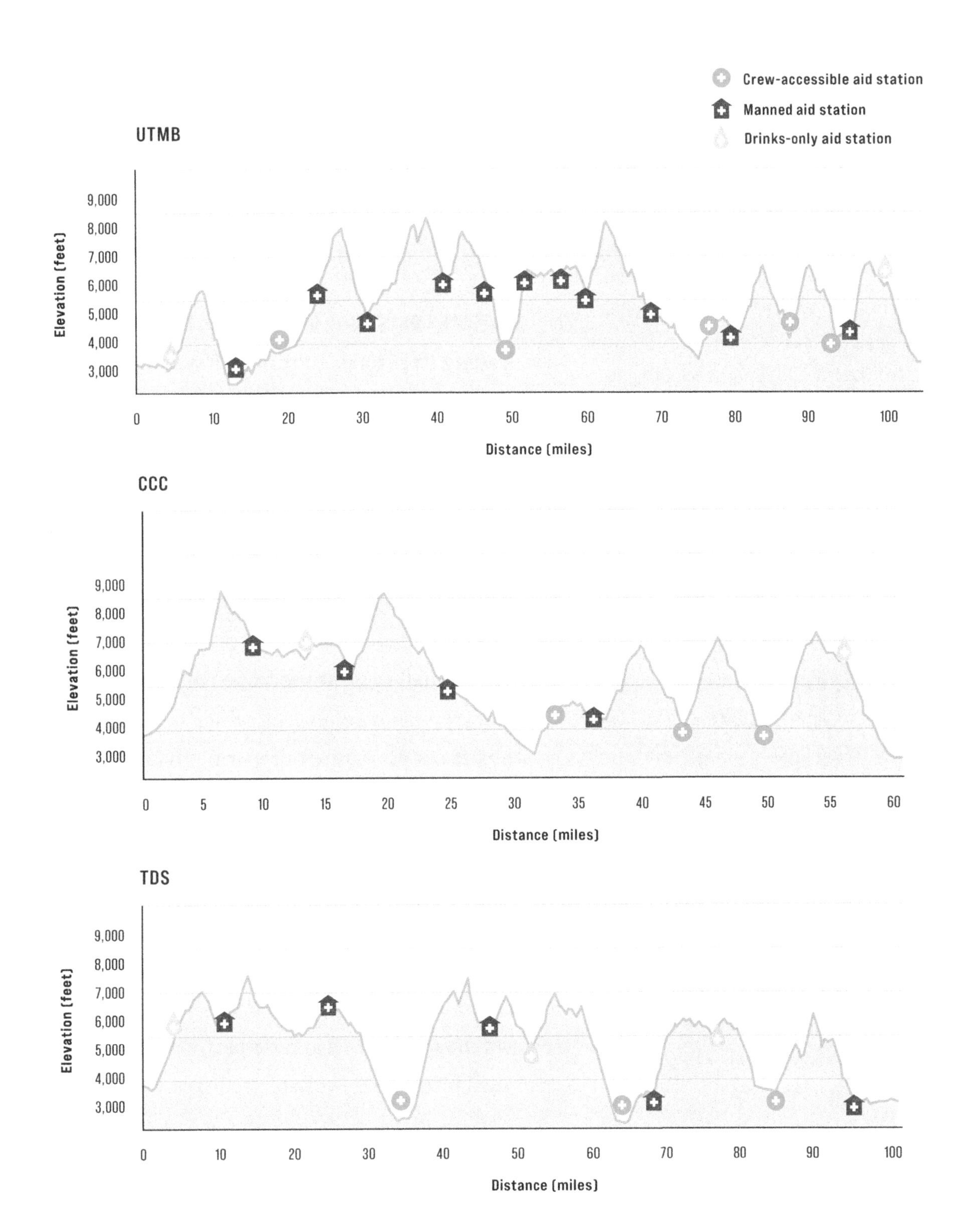
Crew-accessible aid station
Manned aid station
Drinks-only aid station
UTMB
Elevation (feet)
9,000
8,000
7,000
6,000
5,000
4,000
3,000
0
10
20
30
40
50
60
70
80
90
100
Distance (miles)
CCC
Elevation (feet)
9,000
8,000
7,000
6,000
5,000
4,000
3,000
0
5
10
15
20
25
30
35
40
45
50
55
60
Distance (miles)
TDS
Elevation (feet)
9,000
8,000
7,000
6,000
5,000
4,000
3,000
0
10
20
30
40
50
60
70
80
90
100
Distance (miles)

THE PRO KNOWS.

"UTMB is a magical race. The energy of the race, spectators, and the mountain conjure up some intense emotions. So, try to get over to Chamonix a week in advance. That will give you time to adjust to the time difference and get a couple days to relax before racing. Stay out of the heart of Chamonix. Staying just a mile or two up or down the valley is much quieter. The public transportation is great, so there's no need to get a car. Resist the urge to go explore the mountain once you arrive. The trails are stunning and hard to stay off, but curb your enthusiasm. Your legs will thank you on race day.

Play to your strengths. Are you good at descending? Flats? Uphills? UTMB is a race that really has it all. Know your strengths and weaknesses as a runner and use them to your advantage. Poles are a godsend, but make sure you know how to use them. Get your required gear ahead of time, and practice running with it.

Patience is key at UTMB. It's a long race, and hardly ever won over the first half of the race."

—Stephanie Howe, three-time UTMB and onetime CCC finisher

and carry mandatory gear per the race rules. Train with it at least three days per week, even if you don't need all of the gear. Packs will ride differently depending on how they are loaded. Finding out that your mandatory headlamp jabs into your ribs when placed into a particular pocket is not something to save for race day.

CRITICAL LOGISTICAL CHALLENGE. For UTMB, the evening start tends to throw off a lot of runners. Even for runners who get the opportunity to travel out to the race early and get adjusted to the time zone, sitting around all day twiddling your thumbs waiting for the start can be a gigantic waste of energy. Adding to the energy suck is the vibrancy of the town of Chamonix. With thousands of runners all converging on the small town at the same point in time, the city is a buzz of energy, which can drain the life out of a runner preparing to tackle the Mont Blanc. Staying slightly outside of the city is a good idea, as is ignoring all of your friends training too hard during their taper.

TRAINING TIPS. For many runners not accustomed to European trail running, the UTMB races will be a shock. The climbs are steep, and switchbacks are few and far between. Don't get lulled into a false sense of security by looking at the elevation gain/loss on paper; pay close attention to the grade and length of the individual climbs themselves. In North America, it is almost impossible to do too much climbing and descending to get prepared for this race. A training camp in the Rocky Mountains or Sierras would be a great addition to your program in the July or early August time frame. Additionally, if you do not run regularly with poles, get used to them. Using poles can be a big advantage at any of the UTMB races, and most runners would consider them indispensable.

CRITICAL TRAINING PHASE. July and early August should consist of a lot of low-intensity hiking on steep terrain (using your poles, of course). If you have done a good job building your intensity in earlier phases, you can get away with filling your last six weeks of training with EnduranceRuns (and hiking) and RecoveryRuns.

CREW TIPS. Many families like to go to UTMB with their runner as a vacation. Generally speaking, the race is very accessible to spectators yet difficult for crews, as there is a strict limit on when crew members can enter an aid station. Additionally, only one crew member is allowed to enter each station, so choose wisely. The race management will check for mandatory gear at aid stations, so crews should make sure their runner leaves with any mandatory equipment.

Vermont 100

One of the few 100-mile races on the East Coast and one of the oldest in North America, the Vermont 100 takes place every July on a large, looping course in eastern central Vermont. The well-marked, well-supported course follows country roads through bucolic, rolling farmland and New England forests. Unlike ultras out west, there are no sustained climbs or technical sections, but that doesn't mean it's easy. The oppressive humidity of a New England summer and the course can take their toll. Still, its easily accessed location, numerous aid stations and ample support, and lack of altitude make the Vermont 100 an attractive choice for many runners' first 100-miler.

Entrants to the 100-miler (there's a 100K race run on the same day) need to have completed a 50-mile ultra in under twelve hours or a 100K race in under fourteen hours, and to have completed a volunteer day at any ultra event that is 50K or longer.

Course record: 14:47:35 (Brian Rusiecki, 2014); 16:42:32 (Kami Semick, 2010)

Median time: 24:47

Cutoff time: 30 hours

Climbing: Total elevation gain/loss: approximately 14,000 feet

DID YOU KNOW? The Vermont 100 is run congruently with a 100-mile endurance horse race. Runners share the course with the horses, with many of the equine finishing times equaling those of the top runners.

WEATHER. Summer temperatures in Vermont range from 80°F to 85°F in the day to 55°F to 65°F at night. As far as ultramarathons go, the conditions are quite pleasant. If you're lucky, you'll get a couple of late afternoon showers to cool things off quickly.

UNIQUE WEATHER-RELATED CHALLENGE. The high humidity will present a struggle for runners who are not acclimated to it. The body's ability to cool itself is hindered by the humidity, and runners will have to get used to running in sweat-drenched gear and deal with the potential for chafing that goes with it.

EQUIPMENT. Runners don't need to haul much with them. The relatively mild weather, easy-access route, and

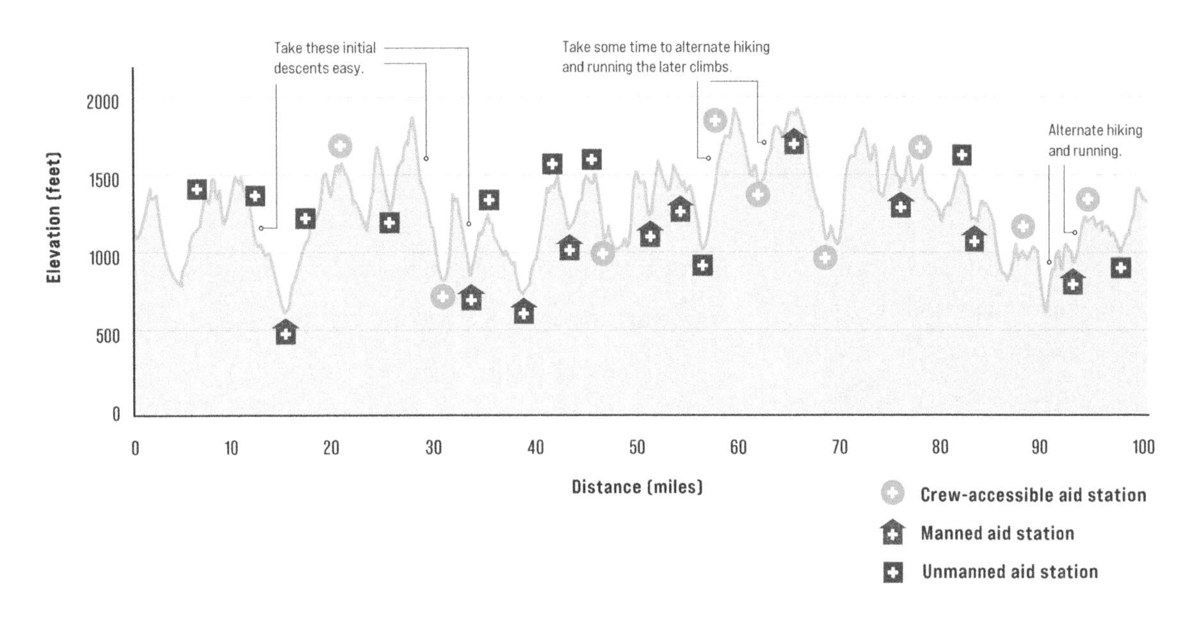

copious aid stations—the max distance between stations is five miles; the average distance between them is three and a half miles—mean that runners can get by with the bare necessities: a hat and a water bottle or two.

INDISPENSABLE GEAR. Cushioned road shoes, not trail shoes. Because the Vermont 100 travels along hard-packed gravel farm roads, jeep tracks, and short sections of pavement, it's a runnable course. Those dirt roads often surprise runners with how much pounding they dish out on their bodies. It's better to think of this event as a 100-mile road race rather than a trail run.

CRITICAL MENTAL CHALLENGE. On paper, the Vermont 100 doesn't look too hard—no giant climbs or technical sections—but the saw-edge course profile reveals a relentless series of short climbs and descents that never seem to end. It's difficult to find any sense of rhythm, the kind you might enjoy on the long climbs and descents of ultras out west. At first, running on country roads seems too easy, with sure footing, plenty of space to maneuver, and a well-marked course that's nearly impossible to get lost on. This causes many runners to start out too fast.

TRAINING TIPS. Heat training is vital, and if you can do it in a humid climate, so much the better. After that your priority should be preparing your quads for the relentless punchy downhill sections on a hard-packed surface. There's no need to worry about altitude; it's a nonfactor because the race tops out at under 2,000 feet in elevation.

CRITICAL TRAINING PHASE. Given that the race is generally rolling, expect to maintain a constant intensity, regardless of where you are in the pack. Endurance-Runs and SteadyStateRuns in the May–June time frame are advised, with your volume reaching its maximum in early June.

CREW TIPS. Because the course is a loop, you can camp out at the remote start/finish line the night before the race. This seems like it should be relatively easy, but keep in mind that the nearest town is thirty-five miles away. Arrive with everything you and your crew need for the race.

Follow the race bible to a T because it is very easy to get lost on the course. The race directors have it dialed to the 0.01th of a mile for a good reason: unmarked dirt roads head off in all directions, and your phone's GPS won't always work in this part of Vermont.

THE PRO KNOWS.

"The crux of the race is the Camp Ten Bear Loop between mile 43 and mile 70. During this section the climbs and descents are longer, the tree cover is far less consistent, and the road surfaces are grittier. As a result, this innocent twenty-seven-mile section can take a lot out of a runner. If you're not careful through here you run the risk of a real death slog over the final thirty miles when you get more singletrack, deeper tree cover, and the cool temperatures of the night."

—Andy Jones-Wilkins, three-time Vermont 100 winner

Wasatch Front 100

Held the weekend after Labor Day in September, this point-to-point race in Utah starts outside of Salt Lake City and traverses the Wasatch Mountains, heading southeast to finish in Soldier Hollow, Utah. Its unique feature is that the route, which runs between altitudes of 5,000 and 10,467 feet, stays high on the crest of the Wasatch, following various ridgelines, trails, and jeep roads until dropping down to the finish.

Applicants must complete eight hours of supervised trail maintenance work through a local Forest Service office and submit a verified work report to the race before being allowed to start.

DID YOU KNOW? The race ends at 5 p.m. on Saturday so that the vast majority of its volunteer force has plenty of time to get home in order to attend church on Sunday. The race also boasts one of the most professional and dedicated ham radio volunteer groups that tracks the runners throughout the race.

WEATHER. The Wasatch is known for extreme temperature swings, ranging from the mid-20s in the early morning to scorching mid-80s in the middle of the afternoon. Between mile 20 and mile 40, the dry heat kicks in.

UNIQUE WEATHER-RELATED CHALLENGE. Having the right gear to handle the 60-degree temperature range. You'll want ice sleeves and ice-filled bandanas to wear during the heat of the day, and double gloves, knit hat, and a down jacket for the nights in the mountains, where the technical trails don't allow you to move fast enough to generate sufficient heat to keep you warm. Some years have recorded snow on the mountain passes. Other years have seen temperatures top 100°F.

EQUIPMENT. Make sure you have enough gear to handle any weather conditions, from snow to triple-digit temperatures. Carry more water than you think you'll need, especially if you're at the front of the pack, because you'll be running through the hottest sections of the course at the hottest time of the day.

INDISPENSABLE GEAR. A packable down jacket that stuffs down to the size of a water bottle.

Course record: 18:30:55 (Geoff Roes, 2009); 22:21:47 (Bethany Lewis, 2014)

Median time: 31:32

Cutoff time: 36 hours

Climbing

Total elevation gain: 26,882 feet

Total elevation loss: 26,131 feet

Significant climbs:

Lamb's Canyon: 4 miles and 2,035 feet

Millcreek to Red Lovers Ridge: 6.5 miles and 2,000 feet

Catherine Pass: 3.6 miles and 1,761 feet

Significant descents:

Jeep road leading to the Francis Peak aid station: 4 miles and 1,715 feet

Bald Mountain to the Alexander Ridge aid station: 5.49 miles and 2,253 feet

Scott's Pass to Brighton Lodge: 3.14 miles and 1,135 feet

Catherine Pass to Ant Knolls aid station: 1.9 miles and 1,423 feet

"The glide" and "the plunge": short, steep plunges starting at mile 79, known as "Irv's Torture Chamber"

CRUXES OF THE RACE. The descents off of Catherine Pass and "Irv's Torture Chamber" are rooted in ultrarunning lore for good reason. They occur late in the race, are tough, and will shred even the most seasoned runner's quads with steep technical descending.

CRITICAL MENTAL CHALLENGE. Getting out of the Brighton Lodge aid station at mile 67.3. It's just before the big climb up to the highest point of the race, Point Supreme, at 10,467 feet. Many runners arrive in the middle of the night, cold and wasted. The check-in is located right inside the A-frame, but all the drop bags are fifty feet farther inside, where it's warm and cozy. Beyond that is a room referred to as "the morgue," so called because racers who enter it to rest often never leave. If you have a drop bag inside, grab it and then head immediately back outside, or have your crew wait for you outside to help you. Whatever you do, don't spend any more time inside than you have to.

TRAINING TIPS. Depending on your fitness, you can run approximately 70 percent of the course, much of which follows smooth roads and singletrack. That said, don't be lulled into thinking that it's easy. The relentless climbing and descending will take their toll, and you'll want to train your body accordingly. If running in heat is a known weakness, train for it by running in the hottest part of the day for some of your runs and perhaps using a sauna for additional heat acclimation. And although the altitude is not as extreme as

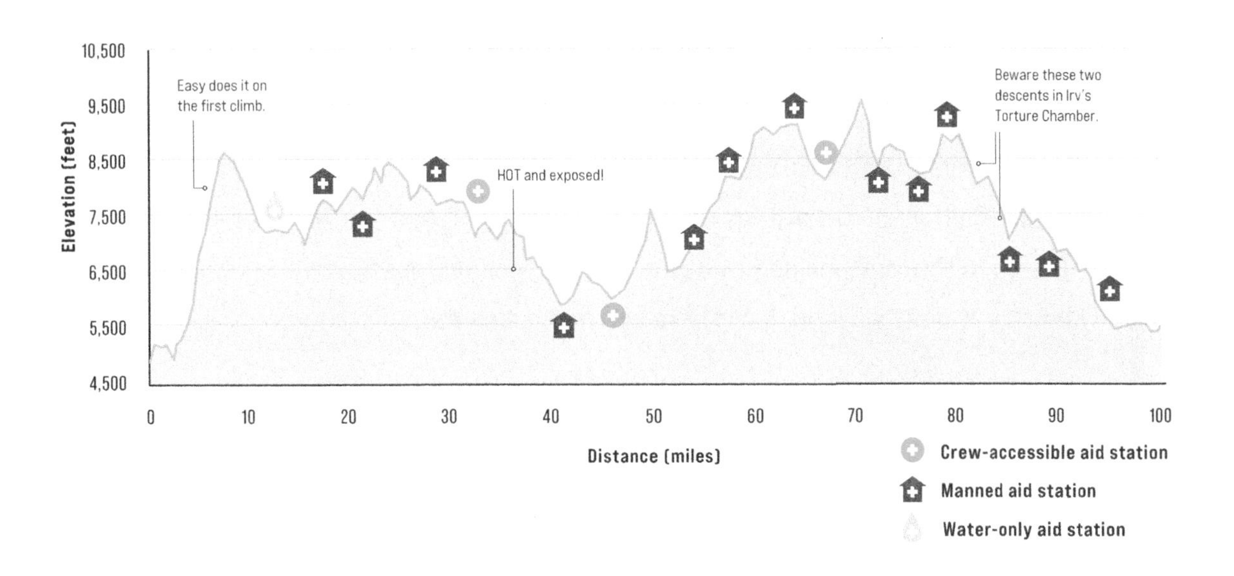

in races in Colorado, it tops out in the last third of the race and hits most runners in the early hours of the morning.

THE PRO KNOWS.

"The climb out of the Brighton aid station is one of lore. But in reality, it's really not that hard. The combination of the climb being late in the race, normally at night, and after an easy road descent will make you feel like it is harder than it actually is. When you get to the Brighton aid station, get your food and gear and get out!"

—Jason Koop, eleventh place, 2012

CRITICAL TRAINING PHASE. July and August you should be doing big EnduranceRun miles, lots of climbing and SteadyStateRun intensity.

CREW TIPS. Pacers can join runners at mile 45. Pacers running through the night, and especially those starting out of the Brighton Lodge aid station, should be dressed for hiking—not running—in subfreezing temperatures.

Western States 100

The granddaddy of North American ultramarathons, the Western States 100-Mile Endurance Run was first run officially in 1977. The point-to-point trail race starts in Olympic Valley, California, crosses the Sierra Nevada, and descends to the finish in Auburn, California. Its heritage and global prestige attract the world's best ultrarunners to the race, making this arguably the most competitive ultra race in North America, if not the world. A win here can make a career.

Competitors are chosen by lottery from a pool of those who've completed either a 100-mile or another qualifying ultra race within a year's time (November to November). The sub-100-mile qualifiers come with time cutoffs determined by Western States race officials.

Course record: 14:09:28 (Jim Walmsley, 2019); 16:47:19 (Ellie Greenwood, 2012)

Median time: 26:03

Cutoff time: 30 hours

Climbing:

Total elevation gain: 18,090 feet

Total elevation loss: 22,970 feet

DID YOU KNOW? The Western States 100-Mile Endurance Run originally began as a 100-mile endurance horse race, which was called the Tevis Cup, after several local horsemen completed the route in 1955. In 1974, Gordy Ainsleigh, a veteran Tevis Cup rider, decided to run the race just to see if he could, finishing in 23:42. In 1977, the run separated from the trail ride and became the first official Western States Endurance Run.

WEATHER. The race is held on the last full weekend in June. The timing, close to the summer solstice, means a short night of chilly temperatures in the high 20s and long days in the hot sun, with temperatures well into the 90s. Temperatures over 100°F are not uncommon. Even at altitudes of 6,000 to 8,000 feet, the heat will make its presence felt. Rain is unlikely, but it can occur.

UNIQUE WEATHER-RELATED CHALLENGE. Fast runners will encounter the most exposed section of the course—with no shade and the possibility of temperatures pushing 110+°F—during the hottest part of the day, between 2 p.m. and 5 p.m. But it's not just fast

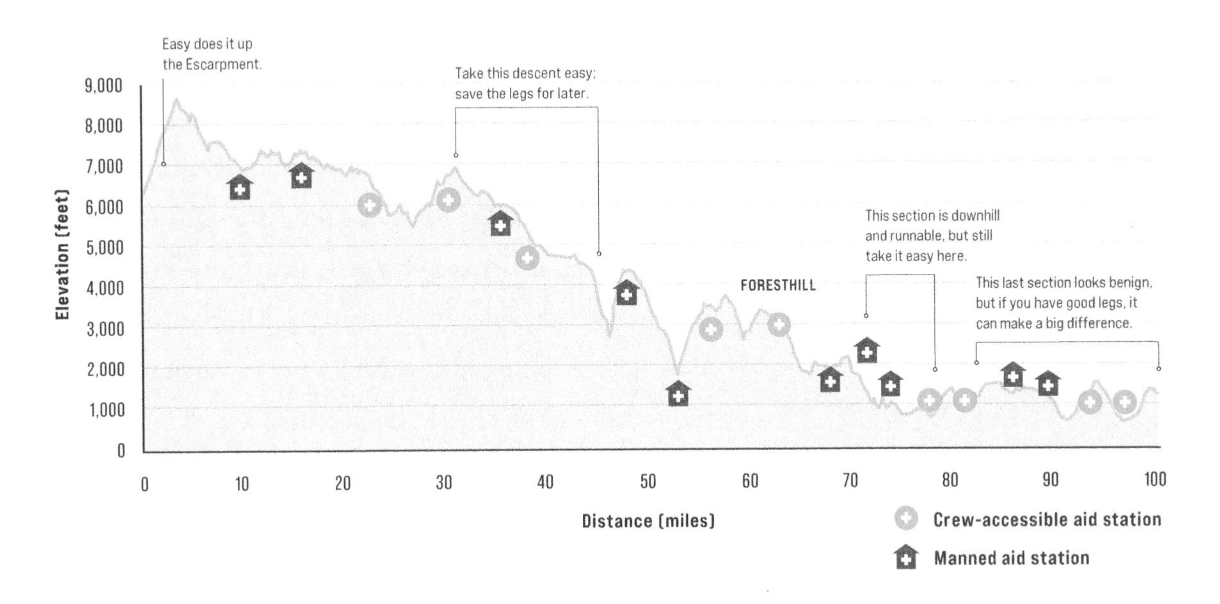

runners who need to worry; heat is cited as an issue across the pack.

EQUIPMENT. Due to the heat, bandanas, headbands, a hat, or ice sleeves that can be filled with ice will go a long way toward making your day tolerable. But thanks to the high number of aid stations (twenty-one), you don't necessarily need to haul extra gear beyond fluids.

INDISPENSABLE GEAR. A bandana you can soak in ice water, fill with ice, and wrap around your head or neck to cool you down.

CRITICAL MENTAL CHALLENGE. The roughly seventeen-mile descent down the Cal Street section out of Foresthill School, which starts at mile 62, can hit runners during the hottest parts of the day. The relatively gradual decline drops more than 3,000 feet, and it's deceptively easy to go too fast here and blow out your quads. You need to be conscious of when it feels easy during this stretch and hold your speed in check. That way, you'll have enough in your legs to get through the punchy climbs in the last twenty miles.

TRAINING TIPS. Acclimate to running in heat by doing some of your training runs during the hottest parts of the day, making sure to experiment with your fluid and nutrition intake to find out what works. If you can, take advantage of access to a sauna in the last several days leading up to the race. This will help you get used to the heat. In fact, this is so important that one of my colleagues has taken a thermal imaging camera out to the race to analyze runners' temperatures. Her results? The cooler runners fared better than the hotter ones.

THE PRO KNOWS.

"Every ultrarunner has this race on their bucket list. As a result, you end up with a very competitive international field. If you're not careful, you can get caught up in the competition, reacting to other racers' moves and eventually blowing yourself apart instead of sticking to your own race strategy."

—Dylan Bowman, three-time finisher, third place in 2014

CRITICAL TRAINING PHASE. April and early May with TempoRun work. Western States is one of the few races where I insist that runners find a dry sauna to help them acclimate to the heat. Therefore, it is critical that their cardiovascular fitness is built to a maximum before the sauna protocol starts.

CREW TIPS. Although there are a number of aid stations open to crews, some require shuttles. And because it's a point-to-point race through remote stretches of the Sierra Nevada, crew members spend a lot of time driving, often on twisting, narrow mountain roads.

Pacers can be used starting at the Foresthill aid station at mile 62.

References

Aguilera, Diana. 2017. "Ultrarunners May Want to Skip the Advil." *Medium*. Stanford Magazine. July 18. https://medium.com/stanford-magazine/ultrarunners-may-want-to-skip-the-advil-5f03fed055da.

Allan, J. R. 1964. "A Study of Foot Blisters" (research memorandum). United Kingdom: Army Operational Research Establishment.

Allan, J. R., and A. L. Macmillan. 1963. "The Immediate Effects of Heat on Unacclimatized Paratroops: Exercise 'Tiger Brew II'" (research memorandum). Report No. 16/62. United Kingdom: Army Operational Research Establishment.

"American College of Sports Medicine Opinion Statement on: The Participation of the Female Athlete in Long-Distance Running." 1979. *Current Sports Medicine Reports*: 1967–1981.

Andersen, Jens Jakob. 2020. "The State of Running 2019." Run Repeat: https://runrepeat.com/state-of-running.

Anderson, J. 2017. "Acclimatization To Altitude." *Sport Fitness Advisor*. September 16. https://www.sport-fitness-advisor.com/acclimatization-to-altitude.html.

Bailey, Stephen J., Jonathan Fulford, Anni Vanhatalo, Paul G. Winyard, Jamie R. Blackwell, Fred J. DiMenna, Daryl P. Wilkerson, Nigel Benjamin, and Andrew M. Jones. 2010. "Dietary Nitrate Supplementation Enhances Muscle Contractile Efficiency During Knee-Extensor Exercise in Humans." *Journal of Applied Physiology* 109 (1): 135–148.

Baker, Lindsay B. 2017. "Sweating Rate and Sweat Sodium Concentration in Athletes: A Review of Methodology and Intra/Interindividual Variability." *Sports Medicine* 47 (S1): 111–128.

Balsalobre-Fernández, Carlos, Jordan Santos-Concejero, and Gerasimos V. Grivas. 2016. "Effects of Strength Training on Running Economy in Highly Trained Runners." *Journal of Strength and Conditioning Research* 30 (8): 2361–2368.

Bam, Jenefer, Timothy D. Noakes, June Juritz, and Steven C. Dennis. 1997. "Could Women Outrun Men in Ultramarathon Races?" *Medicine and Science in Sports and Exercise* 29 (2): 244–247.

Banister, E. W., and T. W. Calvert. 1980. "Planning for Future Performance: Implications for Long Term Training." *Canadian Journal of Applied Sport Science* 5 (3): 170–176.

Barnes, K., A. Kilding, W. Hopkins, M. McGuigan, and P. Laursen. 2013. "Effects of Different Uphill Interval-Training Programs on Running Economy and Performance." *Journal of Science and Medicine in Sport* 15: S14.

Bartholomew, John R., Jonathan L. Schaffer, and Georges F. Mccormick. 2011. "Air Travel and Venous Thromboembolism: Minimizing the Risk." *Cleveland Clinic Journal of Medicine* 78 (2): 111–120. doi:10.3949/ccjm.78a.10138.

Bartlett, Jamie L., and Rodger Kram. 2008. "Changing the Demand on Specific Muscle Groups Affects the Walk-Run Transition Speed." *Journal of Experimental Biology* 211 (8): 1281–1288.

Basta, Maria, George P. Chrousos, Antonio Vela-Bueno, and Alexandros N. Vgontzas. 2007. "Chronic Insomnia and the Stress System." *Sleep Medicine Clinics* 2 (2): 279–291. doi:10.1016/j.jsmc.2007.04.002.

Beidleman, Beth A., Charles S. Fulco, Bruce S. Cadarette, Allen Cymerman, Mark J. Buller, Roy M. Salgado, Alexander M. Posch, et al. 2017. "Is Normobaric Hypoxia an Effective Treatment for Sustaining Previously Acquired Altitude Acclimatization?" *Journal of Applied Physiology* 123 (5): 1214–1227. doi:10.1152/japplphysiol.00344.2017.

Bellinger, Phillip, Ben Desbrow, Wim Derave, Eline Lievens, Chris Irwin, Surendran Sabapathy, Ben Kennedy, Jonathan Craven, Evan Pennell, Hal Rice, and Clare Minahan. 2020. "Muscle Fiber Typology Is Associated with the Incidence of Overreaching in Response to Overload Training." *Journal of Applied Physiology* 129 (4): 823–836. doi:10.1152/japplphysiol.00314.2020.

Berg, Kris. 2003. "Endurance Training and Performance in Runners." *Sports Medicine* 33 (1): 59–73.

Beuter, A., and F. Lalonde. 1989. "Analysis of a Phase-Transition in Human Locomotion Using Singularity Theory." *Neuroscience Research Communications* 3 (3): 127–132.

Bhasin, Shalender, Linda Woodhouse, Richard Casaburi, Atam B. Singh, Dimple Bhasin, Nancy Berman, Xianghong Chen, et al. 2001. "Testosterone Dose-Response Relationships in Healthy Young Men." *American Journal of Physiology-Endocrinology and Metabolism* 281 (6).

Bigland-Ritchie, B. 1981. "EMG and Fatigue of Human Voluntary and Stimulated Contractions." In Human Muscle Fatigue: Physiological Mechanisms, edited by Ruth Porter and Julie Whelan, 130–156. London: Pitman Medical.

Bijker, K., G. De Groot, and A. Hollander. 2002. "Differences in Leg Muscle Activity During Running and Cycling in Humans." *European Journal of Applied Physiology* 87 (6): 556–561.

Bishop, Scott R., Mark Lau, Shauna Shapiro, Linda Carlson, Nicole D. Anderson, James Carmody, Zindel V. Segal, et al. 2006. "Mindfulness: A Proposed Operational Definition." *Clinical Psychology: Science and Practice* 11(3).

Blagrove, Richard C., Glyn Howatson, and Philip R. Hayes. 2017. "Effects of Strength Training on the Physiological Determinants of Middle- and Long-Distance Running Performance: A Systematic Review." *Sports Medicine* 48 (5): 1117–1149.

Bongers, Coen C. W. G., Maria T. E. Hopman, and Thijs M. H. Eijsvogels. 2017. "Cooling Interventions for Athletes: An Overview of Effectiveness, Physiological Mechanisms, and Practical Considerations." *Temperature* 4 (1): 60–78. doi:10.1080/23328940.2016.1277003.

Bonn-Miller, Marcel O., Mallory J. E. Loflin, Brian F. Thomas, Jahan P. Marcu, Travis Hyke, and Ryan Vandrey. 2017. "Labeling Accuracy of Cannabidiol Extracts Sold Online." *Jama* 318 (17): 1708. doi:10.1001/jama.2017.11909.

Bontemps, Bastien, Fabrice Vercruyssen, Mathieu Gruet, and Julien Louis. 2020. "Downhill Running: What Are The Effects and How Can We Adapt? A Narrative Review." *Sports Medicine* 50 (12): 2083–2110. doi:10.1007/s40279-020-01355-z.

Bosquet, Laurent, and Inigo Mujika. 2012. "Detraining." In *Endurance Training: Science and Practice*, edited by Inigo Mujika, 100–106.

Bouchard, Claude. 2012. "Genomic Predictors of Trainability." *Experimental Physiology* 97 (3): 347–352. doi:10.1113/expphysiol.2011.058735.

Brager, Allison J, Sukru Demiral, John Choynowski, Jess Kim, Bill Campbell, Vincent F Capaldi, Guido Simonelli, and Steve Hammer. 2020. "Earlier Shift in Race Pacing Can Predict Future Performance during a Single-Effort Ultramarathon under Sleep Deprivation." *Sleep Science* 13 (1): 25–31. doi:10.5935/1984-0063.20190132.

Bramble, D. M., & Lieberman, D. E. (2004). "Endurance Running and the Evolution of Homo." *Nature*, *432*(7015), 345–352. https://doi.org/10.1038/nature03052.

Brooke, M. H., and K. K. Kaiser. 1970. "Muscle Fiber Types: How Many and What Kind?" *Archives of Neurology* 23 (4): 369–379.

Brooks, George A. 1986. "The Lactate Shuttle during Exercise and Recovery." *Medicine & Science in Sports & Exercise* 18 (3): 360–368.

Brown, Jim. 2011. "Detraining (Reversibility)." In *Encyclopedia of Sports Medicine*, edited by Lyle J. Micheli, 359–360. Thousand Oaks, CA: SAGE Publications. doi:10.4135/9781412961165.n140.

Brown, Kirk Warren, and Richard M. Ryan. 2003. "The Benefits of Being Present: Mindfulness and Its Role in Psychological Well-Being." *Journal of Personality and Social Psychology* 84 (4): 822–848. doi:10.1037/0022-3514.84.4.822.

Brown, Kirk Warren, Richard M. Ryan, and J. David Creswell. 2007. "Mindfulness: Theoretical Foundations and Evidence for Its Salutary Effects." *Psychological Inquiry* 18 (4): 211–237. doi:10.1080/10478400701598298.

Browning, Raymond C., Emily A. Baker, Jessica A. Herron, and Rodger Kram. 2006. "Effects of Obesity and Sex on the Energetic Cost and Preferred Speed of Walking." *Journal of Applied Physiology* 100 (2): 390–398.

Browning, Raymond C., and Rodger Kram. 2005. "Energetic Cost and Preferred Speed of Walking in Obese vs. Normal Weight Women." *Obesity Research* 13 (5): 891–899.

Browning, Raymond C., and Rodger Kram. 2007. "Effects of Obesity on the Biomechanics of Walking at Different Speeds." *Medicine and Science in Sports and Exercise* 39 (9): 1632.

Buchheit, Martin. 2014. "Monitoring Training Status with HR Measures: Do All Roads Lead to Rome?" *Frontiers in Physiology* 5.

Buczek, Frank L., and Peter R. Cavanagh. 1990. "Stance Phase Knee and Ankle Kinematics and Kinetics During Level and Downhill Running." *Medicine and Science in Sports and Exercise* 22 (5): 669–677.

Burke, Louise M. 2015. "Re-Examining High-Fat Diets for Sports Performance: Did We Call the 'Nail in the Coffin' Too Soon?" *Sports Medicine* 45 (S1): 33–49.

Burke, Louise M. 2020. "Ketogenic LowCHO, HighFat Diet: the Future of Elite Endurance Sport?" *The Journal of Physiology* 599: 819–843. doi:10.1113/JP278928.

Burke, Louise M., Megan L. Ross, Laura A. Garvican-Lewis, Marijke Welvaert, Ida A. Heikura, Sara G. Forbes, Joanne G. Mirtschin, et al. 2017. "Low Carbohydrate, High Fat Diet Impairs Exercise Economy and Negates the Performance Benefit from Intensified Training in Elite Race Walkers." *The Journal of Physiology* 595 (9): 2785–2807.

Byrne, Christopher, Craig Twist, and Roger Eston. 2004. "Neuromuscular Function After Exercise-Induced Muscle Damage." *Sports Medicine* 34 (1): 49–69.

Cappellini, Germana, Yuri P. Ivanenko, Richard E. Poppele, and Francesco Lacquaniti. 2006. "Motor Patterns in Human Walking and Running." *Journal of Neurophysiology* 95 (6): 3426–3437.

Carr, Amelia J., Philo U. Saunders, Brent S. Vallance, Laura A. Garvican-Lewis, and Christopher J. Gore. 2015. "Increased Hypoxic Dose After Training at Low Altitude with 9h Per Night at 3000m Normobaric Hypoxia." *Journal of Sports Science and Medicine* 14 (4): 776–782.

Carrio, I., M. Estorch, R. Serra-Grima, M. Ginjaume, R. Notivol, R. Calabuig, and F. Vilardell. 1989. "Gastric Emptying in Marathon Runners." *Gut* 30 (2): 152–155.

Casa, Douglas J. 1999. "Exercise in the Heat. I. Fundamentals of Thermal Physiology, Performance Implications, and Dehydration." *Journal of Athletic Training* 34 (3): 246–252.

Casa, Douglas J., Lawrence E. Armstrong, Susan K. Hillman, Scott J. Montain, Ralph V. Reiff, Brent S. E. Rich, William O. Roberts, and Jennifer A. Stone. 2000. "National Athletic Trainers' Association Position Statement: Fluid Replacement for Athletes." *Journal of Athletic Training* 35 (2): 212–224.

Casey, Ellen, Farah Hameed, and Yasin Y. Dhaher. 2014. "The Muscle Stretch Reflex throughout the Menstrual Cycle." *Medicine & Science in Sports & Exercise* 46 (3): 600–609.

Cavagna, G. A., and M. Kaneko. 1977. "Mechanical Work and Efficiency in Level Walking and Running." *Journal of Physiology* 268 (2): 467–481.

Cavanagh, Peter R., and Keith R. Williams. 1982. "The Effect of Stride Length Variation on Oxygen Uptake During Distance Running." *Medicine and Science in Sports and Exercise* 14 (1): 30–35.

Cavanagh, Peter R., and Mario A. Lafortune. 1980. "Ground Reaction Forces in Distance Running." *Journal of Biomechanics* 13 (5): 397–406.

Cermak, Naomi M., Martin J. Gibala, and Luc J. C. van Loon. 2012. "Nitrate Supplementation's Improvement of 10-km Time-Trial Performance in Trained Cyclists." *International Journal of Sport Nutrition and Exercise Metabolism* 22 (1): 64–71.

Chabbey, Elise, and Pierre-Yves Martin. 2019. "Renal Risks of NSAIDs in Endurance Sports." *Revue Médicale Suisse* 15 (639): 444–447.

Chang, Young-Hui, H. W. Huang, Chris M. Hamerski, and Rodger Kram. 2000. "The Independent Effects of Gravity and Inertia on Running Mechanics." *Journal of Experimental Biology* 203 (2): 229–238.

Chapman, D., M. Newton, P. Sacco, and K. Nosaka. 2006. "Greater Muscle Damage Induced by Fast versus Slow Velocity Eccentric Exercise." *International Journal of Sports Medicine* 27 (8): 591–598.

Chapman, Robert F., Jonathon L. Stickford, and Benjamin D. Levine. 2010. "Altitude Training Considerations for the Winter Sport Athlete." *Experimental Physiology* 95 (3): 411–421. doi:10.1113/expphysiol.2009.050377.

Chawla, Sonam, and Shweta Saxena. 2014. "Physiology of High-Altitude Acclimatization." *Resonance* 19 (6): 538–548. doi:10.1007/s12045-014-0057-3.

Cheung, Karoline, Patria A. Hume, and Linda Maxwell. 2003. "Delayed Onset Muscle Soreness." *Sports Medicine* 33 (2): 145–164.

Cheuvront, Samuel N., and Michael N. Sawka. 2005. "SSE#97: Hydration Assessment of Athletes." *Sports Science Exchange* 18 (2): 1–12.

Cheuvront, Samuel N., Robert Carter, Keith C. Deruisseau, and Robert J. Moffatt. 2005. "Running Performance Differences between Men and Women." *Sports Medicine* 35 (12): 1017–1024.

"Chronic Sleep Restriction Negatively Affects Athletic Performance." 2016. *ScienceDaily*. June 13. https://www.sciencedaily.com/releases/2016/06/160613130709.htm.

Clark, L. R., M. J. Dellongono, T. A. Wilson, and K. M. Mangano. 2018. "Clinical Menstrual Dysfunction Is Associated with Low Energy Availability but Not Dyslipidemia in Division I Female Endurance Runners." *Journal of Exercise Physiology Online* 21 (2): 265–276.

Clarkson, Priscilla M. 2007. "Exertional Rhabdomyolysis and Acute Renal Failure in Marathon Runners." *Sports Medicine* 37 (4–5): 361–363.

Clarkson, Priscilla M., Kazunori Nosaka, and Barry Braun. 1992. "Muscle Function After Exercise-Induced Muscle Damage and Rapid Adaptation." *Medicine and Science in Sports and Exercise* 24 (5): 512–520.

Clarkson, Priscilla M., and Monica J. Hubal. 2002. "Exercise-Induced Muscle Damage in Humans." *American Journal of Physical Medicine and Rehabilitation* 81 (11): S52–S69.

Cohen, Sheldon, William J. Doyle, Cuneyt M. Alper, Denise Janicki-Deverts, and Ronald B. Turner. 2009. "Sleep Habits and Susceptibility to the Common Cold." *Archives of Internal Medicine* 169 (1): 62–67. doi:10.1001/archinternmed.2008.505.

Constantini, Keren, Daniel P. Wilhite, and Robert F. Chapman. 2017. "A Clinician Guide to Altitude Training for Optimal Endurance Exercise Performance at Sea Level." *High Altitude Medicine & Biology* 18 (2): 93–101. doi:10.1089/ham.2017.0020.

Costa, Ricardo J. S., Atlanta Miall, Anthony Khoo, Christopher Rauch, Rhiannon Snipe, Vera Camões-Costa, and Peter Gibson. 2017. "Gut-Training: the Impact of Two Weeks Repetitive Gut-Challenge during Exercise on Gastrointestinal Status, Glucose Availability, Fuel Kinetics, and Running Performance." *Applied Physiology, Nutrition, and Metabolism* 42 (5): 547–557.

Costa, Ricardo J. S., Martin D. Hoffman, and Trent Stellingwerff. 2018. "Considerations for Ultra-Endurance Activities: Part 1- Nutrition." *Research in Sports Medicine* 27 (2): 166–181.

Cox, A. J. 1945. "Variations in Size of the Human Stomach." *California and Western Medicine* 63 (6): 267–268.

Cox, Gregory R., Sally A. Clark, Amanda J. Cox, Shona L. Halson, Mark Hargreaves, John A. Hawley, Nikki Jeacocke, Rodney J. Snow, Wee Kian Yeo, and Louise M. Burke. 2010. "Daily Training with High Carbohydrate Availability Increases Exogenous Carbohydrate Oxidation During Endurance Cycling." *Journal of Applied Physiology* 109 (1): 126–134.

Coyle, E. F., M. K. Hemmert, and A. R. Coggan. 1986. "Effects of Detraining on Cardiovascular Responses to Exercise: Role of Blood Volume." *Journal of Applied Physiology* 60 (1): 95–99. doi:10.1152/jappl.1986.60.1.95.

Cullen, Tom, Gavin Thomas, Alex J. Wadley, and Tony Myers. 2019. "The Effects of a Single Night of Complete and Partial Sleep Deprivation on Physical and Cognitive Performance: A Bayesian Analysis." *Journal of Sports Sciences* 37 (23): 2726–2734. doi:10.1080/02640414.2019.1662539.

Daanen, Hein A. M., Sebastien Racinais, and Julien D. Périard. 2017. "Heat Acclimation Decay and Re-Induction: A Systematic Review and Meta-Analysis." *Sports Medicine* 48 (2): 409–430. doi:10.1007/s40279-017-0808-x.

Datz, F. L., P. E. Christian, and J. Moore. 1987. "Gender-Related Differences in Gastric Emptying." *Journal of Nuclear Medicine* 28 (7): 1204–1207.

Davies, C. T. M., and M. W. Thompson. 1979. "Aerobic Performance of Female Marathon and Male Ultramarathon Athletes." *European Journal of Applied Physiology and Occupational Physiology* 41 (4): 233–245.

Davies, C. T., and M. W. Thompson. 1986. "Physiological Responses to Prolonged Exercise in Ultramarathon Athletes." *Journal of Applied Physiology* 61 (2): 611–617.

De Petrillo, Lillian A., Keith A. Kaufman, Carol R. Glass, and Diane B. Arnkoff. 2009. "Mindfulness for Long-Distance Runners: An Open Trial Using Mindful Sport Performance Enhancement (MSPE)." *Journal of Clinical Sport Psychology* 3 (4): 357–76. doi:10.1123/jcsp.3.4.357.

Desbrow, Ben, Caren Biddulph, Brooke Devlin, Gary D. Grant, Shailendra Anoopkumar-Dukie, and Michael D. Leveritt. 2012. "The Effects of Different Doses of Caffeine on Endurance Cycling Time Trial Performance." *Journal of Sports Sciences* 30 (2): 115–120.

DeVita, Paul, Joseph Helseth, and Tibor Hortobagyi. 2007. "Muscles Do More Positive Than Negative Work in Human Locomotion." *Journal of Experimental Biology* 210 (19): 3361–3373.

Di Prampero, Pietro E. 1992. "Energetics of Running." In *Endurance in Sport*, 2nd ed., edited by R. J. Shephard and P.-O. Åstrand, 813–823. Oxford: Blackwell Science.

Diedrich, Frederick J., and William H. Warren Jr. 1995. "Why Change Gaits? Dynamics of the Walk-Run Transition." *Journal of Experimental Psychology: Human Perception and Performance* 21 (1): 183–202.

Dong, Jin-Guo. 2016. "The Role of Heart Rate Variability in Sports Physiology." *Experimental and Therapeutic Medicine* 11 (5): 1531–1536.

"Drug Overdose Deaths." 2020. *Centers for Disease Control and Prevention*. March 19. https://www.cdc.gov/drugoverdose/index.html.

Ebbeling, Cara B., and Priscilla M. Clarkson. 1989. "Exercise-Induced Muscle Damage and Adaptation." *Sports Medicine* 7 (4): 207–234.

Ejaz, P., K. Bhojani, and V. R. Joshi. 2004. "NSAIDs and Kidney." *Journal of the Association of Physicians of India* 52: 632–640

Elliott-Sale, Kirsty J., Kelly L. Mcnulty, Paul Ansdell, Stuart Goodall, Kirsty M. Hicks, Kevin Thomas, Paul A. Swinton, and Eimear Dolan. 2020. "The Effects of Oral Contraceptives on Exercise Performance in Women: A Systematic Review and Meta-Analysis." *Sports Medicine* 50 (10): 1785–1812.

Enoka, Roger M. 2008. *Neuromechanics of Human Movement*, 4th ed. Champaign, IL: Human Kinetics.

Eston, Roger G., Jane Mickleborough, and Vasilios Baltzopoulos. 1995. "Eccentric Activation and Muscle Damage: Biomechanical and Physiological Considerations During Downhill Running." *British Journal of Sports Medicine* 29 (2): 89–94.

Fallon, K. E., G. Sivyer, K. Sivyer, and A. Dare. 1999. "The Biochemistry of Runners in a 1600 km Ultramarathon." *British Journal of Sports Medicine* 33 (4): 264–269.

Falls, Harold B., and L. Dennis Humphrey. 1976. "Energy Cost of Running and Walking in Young Women." *Medicine and Science in Sports* 8 (1): 9–13.

"The Female ACL: Why Is It More Prone to Injury?" 2016. *Journal of Orthopaedics* 13 (2).

Ferley, Derek D., Roy W. Osborn, and Matthew D. Vukovich. 2013. "The Effects of Uphill vs. Level-Grade High-Intensity Interval Training on VO2max, Vmax, V(L), and Tmax in Well-Trained Distance Runners." *Journal of Strength and Conditioning Research* 27 (6): 1549–1559.

Figard-Fabre, H., N. Fabre, A. Leonardi, and F. Schena. 2009. "Physiological and Perceptual Responses to Nordic Walking in Obese Middle-Aged Women in Comparison with the Normal Walk." *European Journal of Applied Physiology* 108 (6): 1141–1151.

Fillingim, Roger B., David L. Roth, and William E. Haley. 1989. "The Effects of Distraction on the Perception of Exercise-Induced Symptoms." *Journal of Psychosomatic Research* 33 (2): 241–248. doi:10.1016/0022-3999(89)90052-4.

Fitzgerald, Dominic, Christopher Beckmans, David Joyce, and Kathryn Mills. 2019. "The Influence of Sleep and Training Load on Illness in Nationally Competitive Male Australian Football Athletes: A Cohort Study over One Season." *Journal of Science and Medicine in Sport* 22 (2): 130–134. doi:10.1016/j.jsams.2018.06.011.

Fletcher, Jared R., Ted R. Pfister, and Brian R. Macintosh. 2013. "Energy Cost of Running and Achilles Tendon Stiffness in Man and Woman Trained Runners." *Physiological Reports* 1 (7).

Fogoros, Richard N. 1980. "'Runner's Trots': Gastrointestinal Disturbances in Runners." *Journal of the American Medical Association* 243 (17): 1743–1744.

Fullagar, Hugh H. K., Sabrina Skorski, Rob Duffield, Daniel Hammes, Aaron J. Coutts, and Tim Meyer. 2014. "Sleep and Athletic Performance: The Effects of Sleep Loss on Exercise Performance, and Physiological and Cognitive Responses to Exercise." *Sports Medicine* 45 (2): 161–186. doi:10.1007/s40279-014-0260-0.

Gandevia, S. C., R. M. Enoka, A. J. McComas, D. G. Stuart, and C. K. Thomas. 1995. "Neuro-biology of Muscle Fatigue." In *Fatigue Neural and Muscular Mechanisms*, edited by S. C. Gandevia, R. M. Enoka, A. J. McComas, D. G. Stuart, and C. K. Thomas, 515–525. New York: Springer Science and Business Media.

Garbisu-Hualde, Arkaitz, and Jordan Santos-Concejero. 2020. "What Are the Limiting Factors During an UltraMarathon? A Systematic Review of the Scientific Literature." *Journal of Human Kinetics* 72 (1): 129–139. doi:10.2478/hukin-2019-0102.

García-Pallarés, Jesús, Luis Sánchez-Medina, Carlos Esteban Pérez, Mikel Izquierdo-Gabarren, and Mikel Izquierdo. 2009. "Physiological Effects of Tapering and Detraining In World-Class Kayakers." *Medicine & Science in Sports & Exercise*, 42 (6): 1209–1214. doi:10.1249/mss.0b013e3181c9228c.

García-Pallarés, Jesús, Miguel García-Fernández, Luis Sánchez-Medina, and Mikel Izquierdo. 2010. "Performance Changes in World-Class Kayakers Following Two Different Training Periodization Models." *European Journal of Applied Physiology* 110 (1): 99–107.

Gardner, Frank L., and Zella E. Moore. 2004. "A Mindfulness-Acceptance-Commitment-Based Approach to Athletic Performance Enhancement: Theoretical Considerations." *Behavior Therapy* 35 (4): 707–723. doi:10.1016/s0005-7894(04)80016-9.

Gardner, Frank L., and Zella E. Moore. 2017. "Mindfulness-Based and Acceptance-Based Interventions in Sport and Performance Contexts." *Current Opinion in Psychology* 16: 180–184. doi:10.1016/j.copsyc.2017.06.001.

Garvican-Lewis, Laura. 2017. "Altitude: Friend or Foe?" *Journal of Science and Medicine in Sport* 20. doi:10.1016/j.jsams.2017.09.452.

Garvican-Lewis, Laura A., Iona Halliday, Chris R. Abbiss, Philo U. Saunders, and Christopher J. Gore. 2015. "Altitude Exposure at 1800 m Increases Haemoglobin Mass in Distance Runners." *Journal of Sports Science and Medicine* 14 (2): 413–417.

Gastin, Paul B. 2001. "Energy System Interaction and Relative Contribution During Maximal Exercise." *Sports Medicine* 31 (10): 725–741. doi:10.2165/00007256-200131100-00003.

Gazendam, Marnix G. J., and At L. Hof. 2007. "Averaged EMG Profiles in Jogging and Running at Different Speeds." *Gait and Posture* 25 (4): 604–614.

Giandolini, Marlène, Sébastien Pavailler, Pierre Samozino, Jean-Benoît Morin, and Nicolas Horvais. 2015. "Foot Strike Pattern and Impact Continuous Measurements During a Trail Running Race: Proof of Concept in a World-Class Athlete." *Footwear Science* 7 (2): 127–137.

Gibson, A. St. Clair, E. J. Schabort, and T. D. Noakes. 2001. "Reduced Neuromuscular Activity and Force Generation During Prolonged Cycling." *American Journal of Physiology—Regulatory, Integrative and Comparative Physiology* 281 (1): R187–196.

Gill, S. K., J. Hankey, A. Wright, S. Marczak, K. Hemming, D. M. Allerton, P. Ansley-Robson, and R. J. Costa. 2015. "The Impact of a 24-h Ultra-marathon on Circulatory Endotoxin and Cytokine Profile." *International Journal of Sports Medicine* 36 (8): 688–695.

Giovanelli, Nicola, Amanda Louise Ryan Ortiz, Keely Henninger, and Rodger Kram. 2016. "Energetics of Vertical Kilometer Foot Races; Is Steeper Cheaper?" *Journal of Applied Physiology* 120 (3): 370–375.

Glass, Stephen, Gregory Byron Dwyer, and American College of Sports Medicine. 2007. *ACSM's Metabolic Calculations Handbook*. Philadelphia, PA: Lippincott Williams and Wilkins.

Gleeson, M. 1998. "Temperature Regulation During Exercise." *International Journal of Sports Medicine* 19 (S2). doi:10.1055/s-2007-971967.

Goldfarb-Rumyantzev, A. S., and S. L. Alper. 2013. "Short-Term Responses of the Kidney to High Altitude in Mountain Climbers." *Nephrology Dialysis Transplantation* 29 (3): 497–506. doi:10.1093/ndt/gft051.

Gorski, T., E. L. Cadore, S. S. Pinto, E. M. Da Silva, C. S. Correa, F. G. Beltrami, and L. F. M. Kruel. 2009. "Use of NSAIDs in Triathletes: Prevalence, Level of Awareness and Reasons for Use." *British Journal of Sports Medicine* 45 (2): 85–90. doi:10.1136/bjsm.2009.062166.

Gottschall, Jinger S., and Rodger Kram. 2005a. "Energy Cost and Muscular Activity Required for Leg Swing During Walking." *Journal of Applied Physiology* 99 (1): 23–30.

Gottschall, Jinger S., and Rodger Kram. 2005b. "Ground Reaction Forces During Downhill and Uphill Running." *Journal of Biomechanics* 38 (3): 445–452.

Goudriaan, Anna E., Bruno Lapauw, Johannes Ruige, Els Feyen, Jean-Marc Kaufman, Matthias Brand, and Guy Vingerhoets. 2010. "The Influence of High-Normal Testosterone Levels on Risk-Taking in Healthy Males in a 1-Week Letrozole Administration Study." *Psychoneuroendocrinology* 35 (9): 1416–1421.

Goutianos, Georgios. 2016. "Block Periodization Training of Endurance Athletes: A Theoretical Approach Based on Molecular Biology." *Cellular and Molecular Exercise Physiology* 4 (2).

Grabowski, Alena M., and Roger Kram. 2008. "Effects of Velocity and Weight Support on Ground Reaction Forces and Metabolic Power During Running." *Journal of Applied Biomechanics* 24: 288–297.

Graham, T. E., and L. L. Spriet. 1995. "Metabolic, Catecholamine, and Exercise Performance Responses to Various Doses of Caffeine." *Journal of Applied Physiology* 78 (3): 867–874.

Grant, Joshua A., Jérôme Courtemanche, and Pierre Rainville. 2011. "A Non-Elaborative Mental Stance and Decoupling of Executive and Pain-Related Cortices Predicts Low Pain Sensitivity in Zen Meditators." *Pain* 152 (1): 150–56.

Grewer, Christof, Armanda Gameiro, Zhou Zhang, Zhen Tao, Simona Braams, and Thomas Rauen. 2008. "Glutamate Forward and Reverse Transport: From Molecular Mechanism to Transporter-Mediated Release after Ischemia." *IUBMB Life* 60 (9): 609–619. doi:10.1002/iub.98.

Gribok, Andrei, Jayme L. Leger, Michelle Stevens, Reed Hoyt, Mark Buller, and William Rumpler. 2016. "Measuring the Short-Term Substrate Utilization Response to High-Carbohydrate and High-Fat Meals in the Whole-Body Indirect Calorimeter." *Physiological Reports* 4 (12).

Griggs, R. C., W. Kingston, R. F. Jozefowicz, B. E. Herr, G. Forbes, and D. Halliday. 1989. "Effect of Testosterone on Muscle Mass and Muscle Protein Synthesis." *Journal of Applied Physiology* 66 (1): 498–503.

Groner, Cary. 2015. "The Mechanistic Mysteries of Foam Rolling." *Lower Extremity Review Magazine*, October 2015. https://lermagazine.com/cover_story/the-mechanistic-mysteries-of-foam-rolling.

Guo, Lan-Yuen, Fong-Chin Su, Chich-Haung Yang, Shu-Hui Wang, Jyh-Jong Chang, Wen-Lan Wu, and Hwai-ting Lin. 2006. "Effects of Speed and Incline on Lower Extremity Kinematics During Treadmill Jogging in Healthy Subjects." *Biomedical Engineering: Applications, Basis and Communications* 18 (2): 73–79.

Guth, Lisa M., and Stephen M. Roth. 2013. "Genetic Influence on Athletic Performance." *Current Opinion in Pediatrics* 25 (6): 653–658. doi:10.1097/mop.0b013e3283659087.

Haase, Lori, April C. May, Maryam Falahpour, Sara Isakovic, Alan N. Simmons, Steven D. Hickman, Thomas T. Liu, and Martin P. Paulus. 2015. "A Pilot Study Investigating Changes in Neural Processing after Mindfulness Training in Elite Athletes." *Frontiers in Behavioral Neuroscience* 9.

Hamill, Joseph, and Kathleen M. Knutzen. 2006. *Biomechanical Basis of Human Movement*. Philadelphia, PA: Lippincott Williams and Wilkins.

Handelsman, David J., Angelica L. Hirschberg, and Stephane Bermon. 2018. "Circulating Testosterone as the Hormonal Basis of Sex Differences in Athletic Performance." *Endocrine Reviews* 39 (5): 803–829.

Hannon, Patrick R., Stanley A. Rasmussen, and Carl P. Derosa. 1985. "Electromyographic Patterns During Level and Inclined Treadmill Running and Their Relationship to Step Cycle Measures." *Research Quarterly for Exercise and Sport* 56 (4): 334–338.

Hansen, Ernst A., and Gerald Smith. 2009. "Energy Expenditure and Comfort During Nordic Walking With Different Pole Lengths." *Journal of Strength and Conditioning Research* 23 (4): 1187–1194.

Harris, Alon, Alice K. Lindeman, and Bruce J. Martin. 1991. "Rapid Orocecal Transit in Chronically Active Persons with High Energy Intake." *Journal of Applied Physiology* 70 (4): 1550–1553.

Hashmi, Farina, Barry S. Richards, Saeed Forghany, Anna L. Hatton, and Christopher J. Nester. 2012. "The Formation of Friction Blisters on the Foot: the Development of a Laboratory-Based Blister Creation Model." *Skin Research and Technology* 19 (1). doi:10.1111/j.1600-0846.2012.00669.x.

Hatzigeorgiadis, Antonis, Nikos Zourbanos, Alexander T. Latinjak, and Yannis Theodorakis. 2014. "Self Talk." In *Routledge Companion to Sport and Exercise Psychology: Global Perspectives and Fundamental Concepts*, edited by Athanasios Papaioannou and Dieter Hackfort, 372–385. New York, NY: Routledge.

Hawley, John A., Carsten Lundby, James D. Cotter, and Louise M. Burke. 2018. "Maximizing Cellular Adaptation to Endurance Exercise in Skeletal Muscle." *Cell Metabolism* 27 (5): 962–976.

Hayashi, Mitsuo, Akiko Masuda, and Tadao Hori. 2003. "The Alerting Effects of Caffeine, Bright Light and Face Washing After a Short Daytime Nap." *Clinical Neurophysiology* 114 (12): 2268–2278.

Heer, M., F. Repond, A. Hany, H. Sulser, O. Kehl, and K. Jäger. 1987. "Acute Ischaemic Colitis in a Female Long Distance Runner." *Gut* 28 (7): 896–899.

Heikura, Ida A., Louise M. Burke, John A. Hawley, Megan L. Ross, Laura Garvican-Lewis, Avish P. Sharma, Alannah K. A. McKay, et al. 2020. "A Short-Term Ketogenic Diet Impairs Markers of Bone Health in Response to Exercise." *Frontiers in Endocrinology* 10.

Helge, J. W. 2017. "A High Carbohydrate Diet Remains the Evidence Based Choice for Elite Athletes to Optimise Performance." *The Journal of Physiology* 595 (9): 2775.

Herring, Kirk M., and Douglas H. Richie Jr. 1990. "Friction Blisters and Sock Fiber Composition. A Double-Blind Study." *Journal of the American Podiatric Medical Association* 80 (2): 63–71.

Hicheur, Halim, Alexander V. Terekhov, and Alain Berthoz. 2006. "Intersegmental Coordination During Human Locomotion: Does Planar Covariation of Elevation Angles Reflect Central Constraints?" *Journal of Neurophysiology* 96 (3): 1406–1419. doi:10.1152/jn.00289.2006.

Hicks, Audrey L., Jane Kent-Braun, and David S. Ditor. 2001. "Sex Differences in Human Skeletal Muscle Fatigue." *Exercise and Sport Sciences Reviews* 29 (3): 109–112.

Hickson, R. C., C. Foster, M. L. Pollock, T. M. Galassi, and S. Rich. 1985. "Reduced Training Intensities and Loss of Aerobic Power, Endurance, and Cardiac Growth." *Journal of Applied Physiology* 58 (2): 492–499.

Hill, Antje, Linda Schücker, Marvin Wiese, Norbert Hagemann, and Bernd Strauß. 2020. "The Influence of Mindfulness Training on Running Economy and Perceived Flow under Different Attentional Focus Conditions – an Intervention Study." *International Journal of Sport and Exercise Psychology*. doi:10.1080/1612197x.2020.1739110.

Hodges, G. R., T. W. DuClos, and J. S. Schnitzer. 1975. "Inflammatory Foot Lesions in Naval Recruits: Significance and Lack of Response to Antibiotic Therapy." *Military Medicine* 140 (2): 94–97.

Hoffman, Martin D. 2014. "Pacing by Winners of a 161-km Mountain Ultramarathon." *International Journal of Sports Physiology and Performance* 9 (6): 1054–1056.

Hoffman, Martin D., and Eswar Krishnan. 2013. "Exercise Behavior of Ultramarathon Runners: Baseline Findings from the ULTRA Study." *Journal of Strength and Conditioning Research* 27 (11): 2939–2945.

Hoffman, Martin D., and Eswar Krishnan. 2014. "Health and Exercise-Related Medical Issues Among 1,212 Ultramarathon Runners: Baseline Findings from the Ultrarunners Longitudinal TRAcking (ULTRA) Study." *PLoS ONE* 9 (1): e83867. doi:10.1371/journal.pone.0083867.

Hoffman, Martin D., Ian R. Rogers, Jeremy Joslin, Chad A. Asplund, William O. Roberts, and Benjamin D. Levine. 2015. "Managing Collapsed or Seriously Ill Participants of Ultra-endurance Events in Remote Environments." *Sports Medicine* 45 (2): 201–212.

Hoffman, Martin D., and Kevin Fogard. 2011. "Factors Related to Successful Completion of a 161-km Ultramarathon." *International Journal of Sports Physiology and Performance* 6 (1): 25–37.

Hoffman, Martin D., and Kristin J. Stuempfle. 2014. "Hydration Strategies, Weight Change and Performance in a 161 km Ultramarathon." *Research in Sports Medicine* 22 (3): 213–225.

Hoffman, Martin D., Kristin J. Stuempfle, Kerry Sullivan, and Robert H. Weiss. 2015. "Exercise-Associated Hyponatremia with Exertional Rhabdomyolysis: Importance of Proper Treatment." *Clinical Nephrology* 83 (4): 235–242.

Hoffman, Martin D., Tamara Hew-Butler, and Kristin J. Stuempfle. 2013. "Exercise-Associated Hyponatremia and Hydration Status in 161-km Ultramarathoners." *Medicine and Science in Sports and Exercise* 45 (4): 784–791.

Hoffman, M. D. 2008. "Anthropometric Characteristics of Ultramarathoners." *International Journal of Sports Medicine* 29 (10): 808–811.

Hoffman, M. D., D. K. Lebus, A. C. Ganong, G. A. Casazza, and Marta Van Loan. 2010. "Body Composition of 161-km Ultramarathoners." *International Journal of Sports Medicine* 31 (2): 106–109.

Hooper, Sue L., Laurel T. Mackinnon, and Alf Howard. 1999. "Physiological and Psychometric Variables for Monitoring Recovery During Tapering for Major Competition." *Medicine and Science in Sports and Exercise* 31 (8): 1205–1210.

Hooren, Bas Van, and Jonathan M. Peake. 2018. "Do We Need a Cool-Down After Exercise? A Narrative Review of the Psychophysiological Effects and the Effects on Performance, Injuries and the Long-Term Adaptive Response." *Sports Medicine* 48 (7): 1575–1595. doi:10.1007/s40279-018-0916-2.

Hopkins, Will G. 2005. "Competitive Performance of Elite Track-and-Field Athletes: Variability and Smallest Worthwhile Enhancements." *Sportscience* 9: 17–20.

Horne, Jim A., and Louise A. Reyner. 1996. "Counteracting Driver Sleepiness: Effects of Napping, Caffeine, and Placebo." *Psychophysiology* 33 (3): 306–309.

Hreljac, Alan. 1993. "Preferred and Energetically Optimal Gait Transition Speeds in Human Locomotion." *Medicine and Science in Sports and Exercise* 25 (10): 1158–1162.

Hubble, Calvin, and Jinger Zhao. 2016. "Gender Differences in Marathon Pacing and Performance Prediction." *Journal of Sports Analytics* 2 (1): 19–36.

Hunter, S. K. 2014. "Sex Differences in Human Fatigability: Mechanisms and Insight to Physiological Responses." *Acta Physiologica* 210 (4): 768–789.

Ikai, Michio, and Arthur H. Steinhaus. 1961. "Some Factors Modifying the Expression of Human Strength." *Journal of Applied Physiology* 16 (1): 157–163. doi:10.1152/jappl.1961.16.1.157.

Ingalls, Christopher P., Gordon L. Warren, Jay H. Williams, Christopher W. Ward, and R. B. Armstrong. 1998. "EC Coupling Failure in Mouse EDL Muscle After in Vivo Eccentric Contractions." *Journal of Applied Physiology* 85 (1): 58–67.

Irwin, Michael R. 2015. "Why Sleep Is Important for Health: A Psychoneuroimmunology Perspective." *Annual Review of Psychology* 66 (1): 143–172. doi:10.1146/annurev-psych-010213-115205.

Isacco, Laurie, and Nathalie Boisseau. 2016. "Sex Hormones and Substrate Metabolism During Endurance Exercise." In *Sex Hormones, Exercise and Women*, edited by Anthony C. Hackney, 35–38. New York, NY: Springer.

Issurin, Vladimir B. 2018. "Biological Background of Block Periodized Endurance Training: A Review." *Sports Medicine* 49 (1): 31–39.

Jeukendrup, A. E., and J. McLaughlin. 2011. "Carbohydrate Ingestion During Exercise: Effects on Performance, Training Adaptations and Trainability of the Gut." In *Nestlé Nutrition Institute Workshop Series Sports Nutrition: More Than Just Calories—Triggers for Adaptation*, edited by R. J. Maughan and L. M. Burkem, 1–17. Basel, Switzerland: Karger.

Jeukendrup, A. E., K. Vet-Joop, A. Sturk, J. H. Stegen, J. Senden, W. H. Saris, and A. J. Wagenmakers. 2000. "Relationship Between Gastro-intestinal Complaints and Endotoxaemia, Cytokine Release and the Acute-Phase Reaction During and After a Long-Distance Triathlon in Highly Trained Men." *Clinical Science* 98 (1): 47–55.

Jeukendrup, A. E., W. H. Saris, P. Schrauwen, F. Brouns, and A. J. Wagenmakers. 1995. "Metabolic Availability of Medium-Chain Triglycerides Coingested with Carbohydrates during Prolonged Exercise." *Journal of Applied Physiology* 79 (3): 756–762.

Jeukendrup, Asker E. 2017. "Training the Gut for Athletes." *Sports Medicine* 47 (S1): 101–110.

Jeukendrup, Asker E., Luke Moseley, Gareth I. Mainwaring, Spencer Samuels, Samuel Perry, and Christopher H. Mann. 2006. "Exogenous Carbohydrate Oxidation During Ultraendurance Exercise." *Journal of Applied Physiology* 100 (4): 1134–1141.

Johnson, James H., and Donald S. Siegel. 1992. "Effects of Association and Dissociation on Effort Perception." *Journal of Sport Behavior* 15 (2): 119–129.

Joyner, M. J. 1991. "Modeling: Optimal Marathon Performance on the Basis of Physiological Factors." *Journal of Applied Physiology* 70 (2): 683–687. doi:10.1152/jappl.1991.70.2.683.

Joyner, Michael J. 2017. "Physiological Limits to Endurance Exercise Performance: Influence of Sex." *The Journal of Physiology* 595 (9): 2949–2954.

Keay, Nicky. "Raising Awareness of RED-S in Male and Female Athletes and Dancers." *British Journal of Sports Medicine Blog* (blog), October 30, 2018. https://blogs.bmj.com/bjsm/2018/10/30/raising-awareness-of-red-s-in-male-and-female-athletes-and-dancers/.

Keller, T. S., A. M. Weisberger, J. L. Ray, S. S. Hasan, R. G. Shiavi, and D. M. Spengler. 1996. "Relationship Between Vertical Ground Reaction Force and Speed During Walking, Slow Jogging, and Running." *Clinical Biomechanics* 11 (5): 253–259.

Kenefick, Robert W., Samuel N. Cheuvront, Lisa Leon, and Karen K. O'Brien. 2012. "Dehydration and Rehydration." In *Wilderness Medicine*, 6th ed., edited by Paul S. Auerbach. Philadelphia, PA: Mosby.

Kiens, Bente, Carsten Roepstorff, Jan F. C. Glatz, Arend Bonen, Peter Schjerling, Jens Knudsen, and Jakob N. Nielsen. 2004. "Lipid-Binding Proteins and Lipoprotein Lipase Activity in Human Skeletal Muscle: Influence of Physical Activity and Gender." *Journal of Applied Physiology* 97 (4): 1209–1218.

Kiistala, U. 1972a. "Dermal-Epidermal Separation. I. The Influence of Age, Sex and Body Region on Suction Blister Formation in Human Skin." *Annals of Clinical Research* 4 (1): 10.

Kiistala, U. 1972b. "Dermal-Epidermal Separation. II. External Factors in Suction Blister Formation with Special Reference to the Effect of Temperature." *Annals of Clinical Research* 4 (4): 236–246.

Kim, Hyo Jeong, Yoon Hee Lee, and Chang Keun Kim. 2007. "Biomarkers of Muscle and Cartilage Damage and Inflammation During a 200 km Run." *European Journal of Applied Physiology* 99 (4): 443–447.

Kim, S. H., S. Kim, H. I. Choi, Y. J. Choi, Y. S. Lee, K. C. Sohn, Y. Lee, C. D. Kim, T. J. Yoon, J. H. Lee, and Y. H. Lee. 2010. "Callus Formation Is Associated with Hyperproliferation and Incomplete Differentiation of Keratinocytes, and Increased Expression of Adhesion Molecules." *British Journal of Dermatology* 163 (3): 495–501. doi:10.1111/j.1365-2133.2010.09842.x.

Knapik, Joseph J., Katy Reynolds, and John Barson. 1998. "Influence of an Antiperspirant on Foot Blister Incidence During Cross-Country Hiking." *Journal of the American Academy of Dermatology* 39 (2): 202–206.

Knapik, Joseph J., Katy L. Reynolds, Kathryn L. Duplantis, and Bruce H. Jones. 1995. "Friction Blisters." *Sports Medicine* 20 (3): 136–147.

Knapik, Joseph J., Murray P. Hamlet, Kenneth J. Thompson, and Bruce H. Jones. 1996. "Influence of Boot-Sock Systems on Frequency and Severity of Foot Blisters." *Military Medicine* 161 (10): 594–598.

Knechtle, Beat, Andrea Wirth, Patrizia Knechtle, Kanai Zimmermann, and Goetz Kohler. 2009. "Personal Best Marathon Performance Is Associated with Performance in a 24-h Run and Not Anthropometry or Training Volume." *British Journal of Sports Medicine* 43 (11): 836–839.

Knechtle, Beat, Brida Duff, Ulrich Welzel, and Götz Kohler. 2009. "Body Mass and Circumference of Upper Arm Are Associated with Race Performance in Ultraendurance Runners in a Multistage Race—The Isarrun 2006." *Research Quarterly for Exercise and Sport* 80 (2): 262–268.

Knechtle, Beat, and Pantelis T. Nikolaidis. 2018. "Physiology and Pathophysiology in Ultra-Marathon Running." *Frontiers in Physiology* 9.

Knechtle, Beat, Patrizia Knechtle, Claudia Mrazek, Oliver Senn, Thomas Rosemann, Reinhard Imoberdorf, and Peter Ballmer. 2011. "No Effect of Short-Term Amino Acid Supplementation on Variables Related to Skeletal Muscle Damage in 100 Km Ultra-Runners - a Randomized Controlled Trial." *Journal of the International Society of Sports Nutrition* 8 (1).

Knechtle, Beat, Patrizia Knechtle, Ingo Schulze, and Goetz Kohler. 2008. "Upper Arm Circumference Is Associated with Race Performance in Ultra-endurance Runners." *British Journal of Sports Medicine* 42 (4): 295–299.

Knechtle, Beat, Patrizia Knechtle, Thomas Rosemann, and Oliver Senn. 2011. "What Is Associated with Race Performance in Male 100-km Ultra-marathoners—Anthropometry, Training or Marathon Best Time?" *Journal of Sports Sciences* 29 (6): 571–577.

Knechtle, Beat, Thomas Rosemann, Patrizia Knechtle, and Romuald Lepers. 2010. "Predictor Variables for a 100-km Race Time in Male Ultra-marathoners." *Perceptual and Motor Skills* 111 (3): 681–693.

Kölling, Sarah, Rob Duffield, Daniel Erlacher, Ranel Venter, and Shona L. Halson. 2019. "Sleep-Related Issues for Recovery and Performance in Athletes." *International Journal of Sports Physiology and Performance* 14 (2): 144–148. doi:10.1123/ijspp.2017-0746.

Koop, J. (2019, February). UROY Winners: How They Did It. *Ultrarunning Magazine.*

Koopman, René, Daphne L. E. Pannemans, Asker E. Jeukendrup, Annemie P. Gijsen, Joan M. G. Senden, David Halliday, Wim H. M. Saris, Luc J. C. Van Loon, and Anton J. M. Wagenmakers. 2004. "Combined Ingestion of Protein and Carbohydrate Improves Protein Balance during Ultra-Endurance Exercise." *American Journal of Physiology-Endocrinology and Metabolism* 287 (4).

Kowalski, Erik, and Jing Xian Li. 2015. "Ground Reaction Forces in Forefoot Strike Runners Wearing Minimalist Shoes During Hill Running." *Footwear Science* 7 (S1): S40–42.

Kram, Rodger, Timothy M. Griffin, J. Maxwell Donelan, and Young Hui Chang. 1998. "Force Treadmill for Measuring Vertical and Horizontal Ground Reaction Forces." *Journal of Applied Physiology* 85 (2): 764–769.

Kramer, Patricia Ann, and Adam D. Sylvester. 2011. "The Energetic Cost of Walking: A Comparison of Predictive Methods." *PLoS ONE* 6 (6): E21290.

Kupchak, Brian R., William J. Kraemer, David R. Hooper, Cathy Saenz, Lexie L. Dulkis, Paul J. Secola, Lee E. Brown, et al. 2016. "The Effects of a Transcontinental Flight on Markers of Coagulation and Fibrinolysis in Healthy Men after Vigorous Physical Activity." *Chronobiology International* 34 (2): 148–161. doi:10.1080/07420528.2016.1247851.

Kushner, Abigail, William P. West, and Leela S. Pillarisetty. 2020. "Virchow Triad." In *StatPearls*. Treasure Island, FL: StatPearls Publishing.

Küster, Michael, Bertold Renner, Pascal Oppel, Ursula Niederweis, and Kay Brune. 2013. "Consumption of Analgesics before a Marathon and the Incidence of Cardiovascular, Gastrointestinal and Renal Problems: a Cohort Study." *BMJ Open* 3 (4). doi:10.1136/bmjopen-2012-002090.

Kyröläinen, Heikki, Janne Avela, and Paavo V Komi. 2005. "Changes in Muscle Activity with Increasing Running Speed." *Journal of Sports Sciences* 23 (10): 1101–1109.

Lacour, J., and C. Denis. 1982. "Detraining Effects on Aerobic Capacity." In *Medicine and Sport Science Physiological Chemistry of Training and Detraining*, edited by P. Marconnet and J. Poortmans, 230–237. doi:10.1159/000408790.

Laird, Robert H., and Don Johnson. 2012. "The Medical Perspective of the Kona Ironman Triathlon." *Sports Medicine and Arthroscopy Review* 20 (4): 239. doi:10.1097/jsa.0b013e3182736e8e.

Larson, Peter, Erin Higgins, Justin Kaminski, Tamara Decker, Janine Preble, Daniela Lyons, Kevin Mcintyre, and Adam Normile. 2011. "Foot Strike Patterns of Recreational and Sub-elite Runners in a Long-Distance Road Race." *Journal of Sports Sciences* 29 (15): 1665–1673.

Lauersen, Jeppe Bo, Thor Einar Andersen, and Lars Bo Andersen. 2018. "Strength Training as Superior, Dose-Dependent and Safe Prevention of Acute and Overuse Sports Injuries: A Systematic Review, Qualitative Analysis and Meta-Analysis." *British Journal of Sports Medicine* 52 (24): 1557–1563.

Laursen, Paul B., and David G. Jenkins. 2002. "The Scientific Basis for High-Intensity Interval Training." *Sports Medicine* 32 (1): 53–73.

Lebrun, C. M. 2003. "Decreased Maximal Aerobic Capacity with Use of a Triphasic Oral Contraceptive in Highly Active Women: a Randomised Controlled Trial." *British Journal of Sports Medicine* 37 (4): 315–320.

Lee, Chin, Walter L. Straus, Robert Balshaw, Suna Barlas, Suzanne Vogel, and Thomas J. Schnitzer. 2004. "A Comparison of the Efficacy and Safety of Nonsteroidal Antiinflammatory Agents versus Acetaminophen in the Treatment of Osteoarthritis: A Meta-Analysis." *Arthritis & Rheumatism* 51 (5): 746–754. doi:10.1002/art.20698.

Lepers, Romuald, Christophe Hausswirth, Nicola Maffiuletti, Jeanick Brisswalter, and Jacques van Hoecke. 2000. "Evidence of Neuromuscular Fatigue After Prolonged Cycling Exercise." *Medicine and Science in Sports and Exercise* 32 (11): 1880–1886.

Lepers, Romuald, Nicola A. Maffiuletti, Ludovic Rochette, Julien Brugniaux, and Guillaume Y. Millet. 2002. "Neuromuscular Fatigue During a Long-Duration Cycling Exercise." *Journal of Applied Physiology* 92 (4): 1487–1493.

Levine, Robert V., and Ara Norenzayan. 1999. "The Pace of Life in 31 Countries." *Journal of Cross-Cultural Psychology* 30 (2): 178–205. doi:10.1177/0022022199030002003.

Lewis, Nathan A., Dave Collins, Charles R. Pedlar, and John P. Rogers. 2015. "Can Clinicians and Scientists Explain and Prevent Unexplained Underperformance Syndrome in Elite Athletes: an Interdisciplinary Perspective and 2016 Update." *BMJ Open Sport & Exercise Medicine* 1 (1). doi:10.1136/bmjsem-2015-000063.

Lien, Han-Chung, Wei Ming Sun, Yen-Hsueh Chen, Hyerang Kim, William Hasler, and Chung Owyang. 2003. "Effects of Ginger on Motion Sickness and Gastric Slow-Wave Dysrhythmias Induced by Circular Vection." *American Journal of Physiology—Gastrointestinal and Liver Physiology* 284 (3): G481–G489.

Lievens, Eline, Malgorzata Klass, Tine Bex, and Wim Derave. 2020. "Muscle Fiber Typology Substantially Influences Time to Recover from High-Intensity Exercise." *Journal of Applied Physiology* 128 (3): 648–659. doi:10.1152/japplphysiol.00636.2019.

Lohsiriwat, Supatra, Mayurat Rukkiat, Reawika Chaikomin, and Somchai Leelakusolvong. 2010. "Effect of Ginger on Lower Esophageal Sphincter Pressure." *Journal of the Medical Association of Thailand* 93 (3): 366.

Loudin, Amanda. 2017. "Does Taking Ibuprofen for Pain Do More Harm than Good?" *ESPN*. July 19, 2017. http://www.espn.com/espnw/life-style/article/20105680/does-taking-ibuprofen-pain-do-more-harm-good.

Lucas, Wayne, and Paul C. Schroy. 1998. "Reversible Ischemic Colitis in a High Endurance Athlete." *American Journal of Gastroenterology* 93 (11): 2231–2234.

Mackenzie, I. C. 1983. "Effects of Frictional Stimulation on the Structure of the Stratum Corneum." In *Stratum Corneum*, edited by Ronals Marks and Gerd Plewig, 153–160. Berlin: Springer.

Maffetone, Phil. 2015. "The New Aerobic Revolution." *MAF*. May 1, 2015. https://philmaffetone.com/the-new-aerobic-revolution/.

Majed, Lina, Clint Hansen, and Ahmad Alkhatib. 2016. "Characteristics of Preferred Gait Patterns: Considerations for Exercise Prescription, Figure 2." In *Sedentary Lifestyle: Predictive Factors, Health Risks and Physiological Implications*, edited by Ahmad Alkhatib. Hauppauge, NY: Nova Science Publisher.

Marcora, Samuele. 2009. "Perception of Effort during Exercise Is Independent of Afferent Feedback from Skeletal Muscles, Heart, and Lungs." *Journal of Applied Physiology* 106 (6): 2060–2062. doi:10.1152/japplphysiol.90378.2008.

Marcora, Samuele. 2010. Effort: Perception of. In *Encyclopedia of Perception*, edited by E. Bruce Goldstein, 380–383. Los Angeles, CA: Sage.

Marcora, Samuele M. 2008. "Do We Really Need a Central Governor to Explain Brain Regulation of Exercise Performance?" *European Journal of Applied Physiology* 104 (5): 929–931. doi:10.1007/s00421-008-0818-3.

Marcora, Samuele Maria, and Walter Staiano. 2010. "The Limit to Exercise Tolerance in Humans: Mind over Muscle?" *European Journal of Applied Physiology* 109 (4): 763–770. doi:10.1007/s00421-010-1418-6.

Margaria, Rodolfo, 1976. *Biomechanics and Energetics of Muscular Exercise*. Oxford: Clarendon Press.

Margaria, R., P. Cerretelli, P. Aghemo, and G. Sassi. 1963. "Energy Cost of Running." *Journal of Applied Physiology* 18 (2): 367–370.

Marquet, Laurie-Anne, Jeanick Brisswalter, Julien Louis, Eve Tiollier, Louise M. Burke, John A. Hawley, and Christophe Hausswirth. 2016. "Enhanced Endurance Performance by Periodization of Carbohydrate Intake." *Medicine & Science in Sports & Exercise* 48 (4): 663–672.

Martin, Vincent, Guillaume Y. Millet, Alain Martin, Gaelle Deley, and Gregory Lattier. 2004. "Assessment of Low-Frequency Fatigue with Two Methods of Electrical Stimulation." *Journal of Applied Physiology* 97 (5): 1923–1929.

Martin, Vincent, Hugo Kerhervé, Laurent A. Messonnier, Jean-Claude Banfi, André Geyssant, Regis Bonnefoy, Léonard Féasson, and Guillaume Y. Millet. 2010. "Central and Peripheral Contributions to Neuromuscular Fatigue Induced by a 24-h Treadmill Run." *Journal of Applied Physiology* 108 (5): 1224–1233.

Martínez, Sonia, Antoni Aguiló, Carlos Moreno, Leticia Lozano, and Pedro Tauler. 2017. "Use of Non-Steroidal Anti-Inflammatory Drugs among Participants in a Mountain Ultramarathon Event." *Sports* 5 (1): 11. doi:10.3390/sports5010011.

Maughan, Ronald J., Louise M. Burke, Jiri Dvorak, D. Enette Larson-Meyer, Peter Peeling, Stuart M Phillips, Eric S. Rawson, et al. 2018. "IOC Consensus Statement: Dietary Supplements and the High-Performance Athlete." *British Journal of Sports Medicine* 52 (7): 439–455. doi:10.1136/bjsports-2018-099027.

Maunder, Ed, Daniel J. Plews, and Andrew E. Kilding. 2018. "Contextualising Maximal Fat Oxidation During Exercise: Determinants and Normative Values." *Frontiers in Physiology* 9.

Mcdermott, Brendon P., Cody R. Smith, Cory L. Butts, Aaron R. Caldwell, Elaine C. Lee, Jakob L. Vingren, Colleen X. Munoz, et al. 2018. "Renal Stress and Kidney Injury Biomarkers in Response to Endurance Cycling in the Heat with and without Ibuprofen." *Journal of Science and Medicine in Sport* 21 (12): 1180–1184. doi:10.1016/j.jsams.2018.05.003.

Mcnulty, Kelly Lee, Kirsty Jayne Elliott-Sale, Eimear Dolan, Paul Alan Swinton, Paul Ansdell, Stuart Goodall, Kevin Thomas, and Kirsty Marie Hicks. 2020. "The Effects of Menstrual Cycle Phase on Exercise Performance in Eumenorrheic Women: A Systematic Review and Meta-Analysis." *Sports Medicine* 50 (10): 1813–1827.

"Medical and Other Risks." 2020. *Western States Endurance Run*. Accessed December 29. https://www.wser.org/medical-and-other-risks/.

Mehling, Wolf E., Viranjini Gopisetty, Jennifer Daubenmier, Cynthia J. Price, Frederick M. Hecht, and Anita Stewart. 2009. "Body Awareness: Construct and Self-Report Measures." *PLoS ONE* 4 (5).

Melanson, Edward L., Teresa A. Sharp, Helen M. Seagle, Tracy J. Horton, William T. Donahoo, Gary K. Grunwald, Jere T. Hamilton, and James O. Hill. 2002. "Effect of Exercise Intensity on 24-h Energy Expenditure and Nutrient Oxidation." *Journal of Applied Physiology* 92 (3): 1045–1052.

Miller, A. E. J., J. D. Macdougall, M. A. Tarnopolsky, and D. G. Sale. 1993. "Gender Differences in Strength and Muscle Fiber Characteristics." *European Journal of Applied Physiology and Occupational Physiology* 66 (3): 254–262.

Millet, G. Y., R. Lepers, N. A. Maffiuletti, N. Babault, V. Martin, and G. Lattier. 2002. "Alterations of Neuromuscular Function After an Ultramarathon." *Journal of Applied Physiology* 92 (2): 486–492.

Millet, Grégoire P., and Guillaume Y. Millet. 2012. "Ultramarathon Is an Outstanding Model for the Study of Adaptive Responses to Extreme Load and Stress." *BMC Medicine* 10 (1): 77.

Millet, Guillaume Y. 2011. "Can Neuromuscular Fatigue Explain Running Strategies and Performance in Ultra-Marathons?" *Sports Medicine* 41 (6): 489–506.

Millet, Guillaume Y., Katja Tomazin, Samuel Verges, Christopher Vincent, Régis Bonnefoy, Renée-Claude Boisson, Laurent Gergelé, Léonard Féasson, and Vincent Martin. 2011. "Neuromuscular Consequences of an Extreme Mountain Ultra-marathon." *PLoS ONE* 6 (2): E17059.

Millet, Guillaume Y., and Romuald Lepers. 2004. "Alterations of Neuromuscular Function After Prolonged Running, Cycling and Skiing Exercises." *Sports Medicine* 34 (2): 105–116.

Millet, G. Y., J. C. Banfi, H. Kerherve, J. B. Morin, L. Vincent, C. Estrade, A. Geyssant, and L. Feasson. 2011. "Physiological and Biological Factors Associated with a 24 h Treadmill Ultra-Marathon Performance." *Scandinavian Journal of Medicine & Science in Sports* 21 (1): 54–61.

Minett, Geoffrey M., Melissa Skein, Francois Bieuzen, Ian B. Stewart, David N. Borg, Aaron Je Bach, and Joseph T. Costello. 2016. "Heat Acclimation for Protection from Exertional Heat Stress." *Cochrane Database of Systematic Reviews*. doi:10.1002/14651858.cd012016.

Minetti, A. E, L. P. Ardigo, and F. Saibene. 1994. "The Transition Between Walking and Running in Humans: Metabolic and Mechanical Aspects at Different Gradients." *Acta Physiologica Scandinavica* 150 (3): 315–323.

Minetti, Alberto E., Christian Moia, Giulio S. Roi, Davide Susta, and Guido Ferretti. 2002. "Energy Cost of Walking and Running at Extreme Uphill and Downhill Slopes." *Journal of Applied Physiology* 93 (3): 1039–1046.

Mirtschin, Joanne G., Sara F. Forbes, Louise E. Cato, Ida A. Heikura, Nicki Strobel, Rebecca Hall, and Louise M. Burke. 2018. "Organization of Dietary Control for Nutrition-Training Intervention Involving Periodized Carbohydrate Availability and Ketogenic Low-Carbohydrate High-Fat Diet." *International Journal of Sport Nutrition and Exercise Metabolism* 28 (5): 480–489.

Mitchell, Jere H., William Haskell, Peter Snell, and Steven P. Van Camp. 2005. "Task Force 8: Classification of Sports." *Journal of the American College of Cardiology* 45 (8): 1364–1367.

Modica, Jesse R., and Rodger Kram. 2005. "Metabolic Energy and Muscular Activity Required for Leg Swing in Running." *Journal of Applied Physiology* 98 (6): 2126–2131.

Mohler, Betty J., William B. Thompson, Sarah H. Creem-Regehr, Herbert L. Pick Jr., and William H. Warren Jr. 2007. "Visual Flow Influences Gait Transition Speed and Preferred Walking Speed." *Experimental Brain Research* 181 (2): 221–228.

Mølmen, Knut Sindre, Sjur Johansen Øfsteng, and Bent R Rønnestad. 2019. "Block Periodization of Endurance Training – a Systematic Review and Meta-Analysis." *Open Access Journal of Sports Medicine* 10: 145–160.

Monaco, Cynthia, Jamie Whitfield, Swati S. Jain, Lawrence L. Spriet, Arend Bonen, and Graham P. Holloway. 2015. "Activation of AMPK2 Is Not Required for Mitochondrial FAT/CD36 Accumulation during Exercise." *PLoS ONE* 10 (5).

Monash University. 2015. "Extreme Exercise Linked to Blood Poisoning." Press release, June 9, 2015.

Montgomery, William H., Marilyn Pink, and Jacquelin Perry. 1994. "Electromyographic Analysis of Hip and Knee Musculature During Running." *American Journal of Sports Medicine* 22 (2): 272–278.

Moore, Zella E. 2009. "Theoretical and Empirical Developments of the Mindfulness-Acceptance-Commitment(MAC) Approach to Performance Enhancement." *Journal of Clinical Sport Psychology* 3 (4): 291–302. doi:10.1123/jcsp.3.4.291.

Morgan, W. P., D. R. Brown, J. S. Raglin, P. J. O'Connor, and K. A. Ellickson. 1987. "Psychological Monitoring of Overtraining and Staleness." *British Journal of Sports Medicine* 21 (3): 107–114.

Morgan, William P., and Michael L. Pollock. 1977. "Psychologic Characterization of the Elite Distance Runner." *Annals of the New York Academy of Sciences* 301 (1 The Marathon): 382–403. doi:10.1111/j.1749-6632.1977.tb38215.x.

Mori, Hideki, Hidekazu Suzuki, Juntaro Matsuzaki, Kanami Taniguchi, Toshiyuki Shimizu, Tsuyoshi Yamane, Tatsuhiro Masaoka, and Takanori Kanai. 2017. "Gender Difference of Gastric Emptying in Healthy Volunteers and Patients with Functional Dyspepsia." *Digestion* 95 (1): 72–78.

Mountjoy, Margo, Jorunn Kaiander Sundgot-Borgen, Louise M. Burke, Kathryn E. Ackerman, Cheri Blauwet, Naama Constantini, Constance Lebrun, et al. 2018. "IOC Consensus Statement on Relative Energy Deficiency in Sport (RED-S): 2018 Update." *British Journal of Sports Medicine* 52 (11): 687–697.

Mountjoy, Margo, Jorunn Sundgot-Borgen, Louise Burke, Susan Carter, Naama Constantini, Constance Lebrun, Nanna Meyer, et al. 2014. "The IOC Consensus Statement: beyond the Female Athlete Triad—Relative Energy Deficiency in Sport (RED-S)." *British Journal of Sports Medicine* 48 (7): 491–497.

Muginshtein-Simkovitch, Evgenia, Yaron Dagan, Mairav Cohen-Zion, Barliz Waissengrin, Itay Ketko, and Yuval Heled. 2015. "Heat Tolerance after Total and Partial Acute Sleep Deprivation." *Chronobiology International* 32 (5): 717–24. doi:10.3109/07420528.2015.1030409.

Mujika, Iñigo, and Sabino Padilla. 2000a. "Detraining: Loss of Training-Induced Physiological and Performance Adaptations. Part I." *Sports Medicine* 30 (2): 79–87.

Mujika, Iñigo, and Sabino Padilla. 2000b. "Detraining: Loss of Training-Induced Physiological and Performance Adaptations. Part II." *Sports Medicine* 30 (3): 145–154.

Mujika, Iñigo, and Sabino Padilla. 2003. "Scientific Bases for Precompetition Tapering Strategies." *Medicine and Science in Sports and Exercise* 35 (7): 1182–1187.

Munro, Carolyn F., Doris I. Miller, and Andrew J. Fuglevand. 1987. "Ground Reaction Forces in Running: A Reexamination." *Journal of Biomechanics* 20 (2): 147–155.

Myburgh, Kathryn H. 2003. "What Makes an Endurance Athlete World-Class? Not Simply a Physiological Conundrum." *Comparative Biochemistry and Physiology Part A: Molecular and Integrative Physiology* 136 (1): 183–185.

Nacht, Sergio, Jo-Ann Close, David Yeung, and Eugene H. Gans. 1981. "Skin Friction Coefficient: Changes Induced by Skin Hydration and Emollient Application and Correlation with Perceived Skin Feel." *Journal of the Society of Cosmetic Chemists* 32 (2): 55–65.

Naylor, P. F. D. 1955. "The Skin Surface and Friction." *British Journal of Dermatology* 67 (7): 239–248.

Nazem, Taraneh Gharib, and Kathryn E. Ackerman. 2012. "The Female Athlete Triad." *Sports Health: A Multidisciplinary Approach* 4 (4): 302–311. doi:10.1177/1941738112439685.

Neufer, P. Darrell. 1989. "The Effect of Detraining and Reduced Training on the Physiological Adaptations to Aerobic Exercise Training." *Sports Medicine* 8 (5): 302–321. doi:10.2165/00007256-198908050-00004.

Nevill, Alan M., Damon Brown, Richard Godfrey, Patrick J. Johnson, Lee Romer, Arthur D. Stewart, and Edward M. Winter. 2003. "Modeling Maximum Oxygen Uptake of Elite Endurance Athletes." *Medicine and Science in Sports and Exercise* 35 (3): 488–494.

Newham, D. J., G. Mcphail, K. R. Mills, and R. H. T. Edwards. 1983. "Ultrastructural Changes After Concentric and Eccentric Contractions of Human Muscle." *Journal of the Neurological Sciences* 61 (1): 109–122.

Nicol, C., P. V. Komi, and P. Marconnet. 1991. "Fatigue Effects of Marathon Running on Neuromuscular Performance." *Scandinavian Journal of Medicine and Science in Sports* 1 (1): 10–17.

Nigg, B. M., H. A. Bahlsen, S. M. Luethi, and S. Stokes. 1987. "The Influence of Running Velocity and Midsole Hardness on External Impact Forces in Heel-Toe Running." *Journal of Biomechanics* 20 (10): 951–959.

Nilsson, Johnny, and Alf Thorstensson. 1989. "Ground Reaction Forces at Different Speeds of Human Walking and Running." *Acta Physiologica Scandinavica* 136 (2): 217–227.

Noakes, T. D., A. St. Clair Gibson, and E. V. Lambert. 2005. "From Catastrophe to Complexity: a Novel Model of Integrative Central Neural Regulation of Effort and Fatigue during Exercise in Humans: Summary and Conclusions." *British Journal of Sports Medicine* 39 (2): 120–124. doi:10.1136/bjsm.2003.010330.

Noakes, T. D., J. E. Peltonen, and H. K. Rusko. 2001. "Evidence That a Central Governor Regulates Exercise Performance during Acute Hypoxia and Hyperoxia." *Journal of Experimental Biology* 204 (18): 3225–3234.

Noakes, Timothy David. 2012. "Fatigue Is a Brain-Derived Emotion That Regulates the Exercise Behavior to Ensure the Protection of Whole Body Homeostasis." *Frontiers in Physiology* 3. doi:10.3389/fphys.2012.00082.

Nosaka, K., and P. M. Clarkson. 1996. "Variability in Serum Creatine Kinase Response After Eccentric Exercise of the Elbow Flexors." *International Journal of Sports Medicine* 17 (2): 120–127.

Nosaka, Kazunori, K. E. I. Sakamoto, Mike Newton, and Paul Sacco. 2001. "How Long Does the Protective Effect on Eccentric Exercise-Induced Muscle Damage Last?" *Medicine and Science in Sports and Exercise* 33 (9): 1490–1495.

Novacheck, Tom F. 1998. "The Biomechanics of Running." *Gait and Posture* 7 (1): 77–95.

Nummela, A., Heikki Rusko, and Antti Mero. 1994. "EMG Activities and Ground Reaction Forces During Fatigued and Nonfatigued Sprinting." *Medicine and Science in Sports and Exercise* 26 (5): 605–609.

O'Donnell, Shannon, Christopher Beaven, and Matthew Driller. 2018. "From Pillow to Podium: a Review on Understanding Sleep for Elite Athletes." *Nature and Science of Sleep* 10: 243–253.

Øktedalen, O., O. C. Lunde, P. K. Opstad, L. Aabakken, and K. Kvernebo. 1992. "Changes in the Gastrointestinal Mucosa After Long-Distance Running." *Scandinavian Journal of Gastroenterology* 27 (4): 270–274.

Oliver, Samuel J., Ricardo J. S. Costa, Stewart J. Laing, James L. J. Bilzon, and Neil P. Walsh. 2009. "One Night of Sleep Deprivation Decreases Treadmill Endurance Performance." *European Journal of Applied Physiology* 107 (2): 155–161.

Orlick, Terry, and John Partington. 1988. "Mental Links to Excellence." *The Sport Psychologist* 2 (2): 105–130. doi:10.1123/tsp.2.2.105.

Ortiz, Amanda Louise Ryan, Nicola Giovanelli, and Rodger Kram. 2017. "The Metabolic Costs of Walking and Running up a 30-Degree Incline: Implications for Vertical Kilometer Foot Races." *European Journal of Applied Physiology* 117 (9): 1869–1876.

Overgaard, Kristian, Tue Lindstrøm, Thorsten Ingemann-Hansen, and Torben Clausen. 2002. "Membrane Leakage and Increased Content of Na+-K+ Pumps and Ca2+ in Human Muscle After a 100-km Run." *Journal of Applied Physiology* 92 (5): 1891–1898. doi:10.1152/japplphysiol.00669.2001.

Padulo, Johnny, Douglas Powell, Raffaele Milia, and Luca Paolo Ardigò. 2013. "A Paradigm of Uphill Running." *PLoS ONE* 8 (7): E69006.

Page, A. J., S. A. Reid, D. B. Speedy, G. P. Mulligan, and J. Thompson. 2007. "Exercise-Associated Hyponatremia, Renal Function, and Nonsteroidal Antiinflammatory Drug Use in an Ultraendurance Mountain Run." *Clinical Journal of Sport Medicine* 17 (1): 43–48.

Paoloni, J. A., C. Milne, J. Orchard, and B. Hamilton. 2009. "Non-Steroidal Anti-Inflammatory Drugs in Sports Medicine: Guidelines for Practical but Sensible Use." *British Journal of Sports Medicine* 43 (11): 863–865. doi:10.1136/bjsm.2009.059980.

Papaioannides, D., C. Giotis, N. Karagiannis, and C. Voudouris. 1984. "Acute Upper Gastro-intestinal Hemorrhage in Long-Distance Runners." *Annals of Internal Medicine* 101 (5): 719.

Pasman, W. J., M. A. Van Baak, A. E. Jeukendrup, and A. De Haan. 1995. "The Effect of Different Dosages of Caffeine on Endurance Performance Time." *International Journal of Sports Medicine* 16 (4): 225–230.

Peake, Jonathan M., Llion A. Roberts, Vandre C. Figueiredo, Ingrid Egner, Simone Krog, Sigve N. Aas, Katsuhiko Suzuki, et al. 2016. "The Effects of Cold Water Immersion and Active Recovery on Inflammation and Cell Stress Responses in Human Skeletal Muscle after Resistance Exercise." *The Journal of Physiology* 595 (3): 695–711. doi:10.1113/jp272881.

Pellegrini, Barbara, Leonardo Alexandre Peyré-Tartaruga, Chiara Zoppirolli, Lorenzo Bortolan, Elisabetta Bacchi, Hélène Figard-Fabre, and Federico Schena. 2015. "Exploring Muscle Activation during Nordic Walking: A Comparison between Conventional and Uphill Walking." *PLoS ONE* 10 (9).

Périard, J. D., S. Racinais, and M. N. Sawka. 2015. "Adaptations and Mechanisms of Human Heat Acclimation: Applications for Competitive Athletes and Sports." *Scandinavian Journal of Medicine & Science in Sports* 25: 20–38. doi:10.1111/sms.12408.

Peter, Laura, Christoph Alexander Rust, Beat Knechtle, Thomas Rosemann, and Romuald Lepers. 2014. "Sex Differences in 24-Hour Ultra-marathon Performance—A Retrospective Data Analysis from 1977 to 2012." *Clinics* 69 (1): 38–46.

Pfeiffer, Beate, Trent Stellingwerff, Eric Zaltas, and Asker E. Jeukendrup. 2010a. "CHO Oxidation from a CHO Gel Compared with a Drink During Exercise." *Medicine and Science in Sports and Exercise* 42 (11): 2038–2045.

Pfeiffer, Beate, Trent Stellingwerff, Eric Zaltas, and Asker E. Jeukendrup. 2010b. "Oxidation of Solid versus Liquid CHO Sources During Exercise." *Medicine and Science in Sports and Exercise* 42 (11): 2030–2037.

Philp, Andrew, Louise M. Burke, and Keith Baar. 2012. "Altering Endogenous Carbohydrate Availability to Support Training Adaptations." In *Nestlé Nutrition Institute Workshop Series Sports Nutrition: More Than Just Calories – Triggers for Adaptation*, edited by R .J. Maughan and L. M. Burke, 19–37. Basel, Switzerland: Karger.

Pongrojpaw, Densak, Charinthip Somprasit, and Athita Chanthasenanont. 2007. "A Randomized Comparison of Ginger and Dimenhydrinate in the Treatment of Nausea and Vomiting in Pregnancy." *Journal of the Medical Association of Thailand* 90 (9): 1703–1709.

Probert, C. J., P. M. Emmett, and K. W. Heaton. 1993. "Intestinal Transit Time in the Population Calculated from Self Made Observations of Defecation." *Journal of Epidemiology & Community Health* 47 (4): 331–333.

"The Prohibited List." 2020. *World Anti-Doping Agency*. January 1, 2020. http://www.wada-ama.org/en/what-we-do/the-prohibited-list.

Proske, U., and D. L. Morgan. 2001. "Muscle Damage from Eccentric Exercise: Mechanism, Mechanical Signs, Adaptation and Clinical Applications." *Journal of Physiology* 537 (2): 333–345.

Proske, Uwe, and Trevor J. Allen. 2005. "Damage to Skeletal Muscle from Eccentric Exercise." *Exercise and Sport Sciences Reviews* 33 (2): 98–104.

Purdom, Troy, Len Kravitz, Karol Dokladny, and Christine Mermier. 2018. "Understanding the Factors That Effect Maximal Fat Oxidation." *Journal of the International Society of Sports Nutrition* 15 (1).

Pyne, David B., Cassie B. Trewin, and William G. Hopkins. 2004. "Progression and Variability of Competitive Performance of Olympic Swimmers." *Journal of Sports Sciences* 22 (7): 613–620.

Qamar, M. I., and A. E. Read. 1987. "Effects of Exercise on Mesenteric Blood Flow in Man." *Gut* 28 (5): 583–587.

Quinn, J. 1967. "The Effects of Two New Foot Powders on the Incidence of Foot Infection and Blisters in Recruits During Basic Training" (research memorandum). Report No. P/6. Farnborough, United Kingdom: Army Personnel Research Establishment.

Raglin, John S., David M. Koceja, Joel M. Stager, and Craig A. Harms. 1996. "Mood, Neuromuscular Function, and Performance During Training in Female Swimmers." *Medicine and Science in Sports and Exercise* 28 (3): 372–377.

Rebay, M., A. Arfaoui, and R. Taiar. 2008. "Thermo-mechanical Characterization of the Interaction Foot-Athletic Shoe During the Exercise." Paper presented at the Fifth European Thermal-Sciences Conference, Eindhoven, The Netherlands, May 2008.

Reyner, Luise A., and James A. Horne. 1997. "Suppression of Sleepiness in Drivers: Combination of Caffeine with a Short Nap." *Psychophysiology* 34 (6): 721–725.

Reynolds, Gretchen. 2017. "Bring On the Exercise, Hold the Painkillers." *The New York Times*. July 5, 2017. https://www.nytimes.com/2017/07/05/well/move/bring-on-the-exercise-hold-the-painkillers.html/.

Reynolds, Katy, Andre Darrigrand, Donald Roberts, Joseph Knapik, Jon Pollard, Kathryn Duplantis, and Bruce Jones. 1995. "Effects of an Antiperspirant with Emollients on Foot-Sweat Accumulation and Blister Formation While Walking in the Heat." *Journal of the American Academy of Dermatology* 33 (4): 626–630.

Ristolainen, L., J. A. Kettunen, B. Waller, A. Heinonen, and U. M. Kujala. 2014. "Training-Related Risk Factors in the Etiology of Overuse Injuries in Endurance Sports." *Journal of Sports Medicine and Physical Fitness* 54 (1): 78–87.

Rivas, Eric, Manisha Rao, Todd Castleberry, and Vic Ben-Ezra. 2017. "The Change in Metabolic Heat Production Is a Primary Mediator of Heat Acclimation in Adults." *Journal of Thermal Biology* 70: 69–79. doi:10.1016/j.jtherbio.2017.10.001.

Roberts, Spencer S. H., Wei-Peng Teo, Brad Aisbett, and Stuart A. Warmington. 2019. "Effects of Total Sleep Deprivation on Endurance Cycling Performance and Heart Rate Indices Used for Monitoring Athlete Readiness." *Journal of Sports Sciences* 37 (23): 2691–2701.

Roethenbaugh, Gary. 2019. "'Ohana' Theme throughout 2019 IRONMAN and IRONMAN 70.3 Events." *EnduranceBiz*. May 23, 2019. https://endurance.biz/2019/industry-news/ohana-theme-throughout-2019-ironman-and-ironman-70-3-events/.

Rønnestad, B. R., J. Hansen, and S. Ellefsen. 2014. "Block Periodization of High-Intensity Aerobic Intervals Provides Superior Training Effects in Trained Cyclists." *Scandinavian Journal of Medicine and Science in Sports* 24 (1): 34–42.

Rønnestad, Bent R., Joar Hansen, Vetle Thyli, Timo A. Bakken, and Øyvind Sandbakk. 2015. "5-Week Block Periodization Increases Aerobic Power in Elite Cross-Country Skiers." *Scandinavian Journal of Medicine and Science in Sports* 26 (2): 140–146.

Rønnestad, Bent R., Tue Rømer, and Joar Hansen. 2020. "Increasing Oxygen Uptake in Well-Trained Cross-Country Skiers During Work Intervals With a Fast Start." *International Journal of Sports Physiology and Performance* 15 (3): 383–389.

Ronto, Paul. 2020. "Which Runners Are the Most Obssessed?" *Run Repeat.* https://runrepeat.com/most-obssessed-runners-stats-page.

Rost, M., J. Jacobsson, Ö. Dahlström, M. Hammar, and T. Timpka. 2014. "Amenorrhea in Elite Athletics Athletes: Prevalence And Associations To Athletics Injury." *British Journal of Sports Medicine* 48 (7). doi:10.1136/bjsports-2014-093494.254.

Rowlands, Ann V., Roger G. Eston, and Caroline Tilzey. 2001. "Effect of Stride Length Manipulation on Symptoms of Exercise-Induced Muscle Damage and the Repeated Bout Effect." *Journal of Sports Sciences* 19 (5): 333–340. doi:10.1080/02640410152006108.

Ryan, Julie L., Charles E. Heckler, Joseph A. Roscoe, Shaker R. Dakhil, Jeffrey Kirshner, Patrick J. Flynn, Jane T. Hickok, and Gary R. Morrow. 2012. "Ginger (Zingiber officinale) Reduces Acute Chemotherapy-Induced Nausea: A URCC CCOP Study of 576 Patients." *Supportive Care in Cancer* 20 (7): 1479–1489.

Sakaguchi, Masanori, Haruna Ogawa, Norifumi Shimizu, Hiroaki Kanehisa, Toshimasa Yanai, and Yasuo Kawakami. 2014. "Gender Differences in Hip and Ankle Joint Kinematics on Knee Abduction During Running." *European Journal of Sport Science* 14 (S1): S302–S309.

Sanders, Joan E., Barry S. Goldstein, and Daniel F. Leotta. 1995. "Skin Response to Mechanical Stress: Adaptation Rather Than Breakdown—A Review of the Literature." *Journal of Rehabilitation Research and Development* 32 (3): 214–2164.

Saporito, Bill. 2012. "Who Is the Fittest Olympic Athlete of Them All?" *Time.* July 19, 2012.

Sarzynski, Mark A., Sujoy Ghosh, and Claude Bouchard. 2016. "Genomic and Transcriptomic Predictors of Response Levels to Endurance Exercise Training." *The Journal of Physiology* 595 (9): 2931–2939. doi:10.1113/jp272559.

Sawka, Michael N., C. Bruce Wenger, Andrew J. Young, and Kent B. Pandolf. 1993. "Physiological Responses to Exercise in the Heat." In *Nutritional Needs in Hot Environments: Applications for Military Personnel in Field Operations*, edited by Institute of Medicine, Committee on Military Nutrition Research, and Bernadette M. Marriott, 55–74. Washington, D.C.: National Academy Press.

Sawka, Michael N., Lisa R. Leon, Scott J. Montain, and Larry A. Sonna. 2011. "Integrated Physiological Mechanisms of Exercise Performance, Adaptation, and Maladaptation to Heat Stress." *Comprehensive Physiology*, 1883–1928. doi:10.1002/cphy.c100082.

Sawka, Michael N., Louise M. Burke, E. Randy Eichner, Ronald J. Maughan, Scott J. Montain, and Nina S. Stachenfield. 2007. "Exercise and Fluid Replacement." *Medicine and Science in Sports and Exercise* 39 (2): 377–390. doi:10.1249/mss.0b013e31802ca597.

Seiler, Stephen. 2006 "Time Course of Training Adaptations." Chapter in *EXERCISE PHYSIOLOGY, The Methods and Mechanisms Underlying Performance.*

Seiler, Stephen, and Jarl Espen Sjursen. 2004. "Effect of Work Duration on Physiological and Rating Scale of Perceived Exertion Responses during Self-Paced Interval Training." *Scandinavian Journal of Medicine and Science in Sports* 14 (5): 318–325.

Shea, Steven A., Michael F. Hilton, Kun Hu, and Frank A.j.l. Scheer. 2011. "Existence of an Endogenous Circadian Blood Pressure Rhythm in Humans That Peaks in the Evening." *Circulation Research* 108 (8): 980–984. doi:10.1161/circresaha.110.233668.

Shepley, B., J. D. MacDougall, N. Cipriano, J. R. Sutton, M. A. Tarnopolsky, and G. Coates. 1992. "Physiological Effects of Tapering in Highly Trained Athletes." *Journal of Applied Physiology* 72 (2): 706–711.

Shorten, Martyn R. 2000. "Running Shoe Design: Protection and Performance." In *Marathon Medicine*, edited by D. Tunstall Pedoe, 159–169. London: Royal Society of Medicine.

Sinex, Jacob A., and Robert F. Chapman. 2015. "Hypoxic Training Methods for Improving Endurance Exercise Performance." *Journal of Sport and Health Science* 4 (4): 325–332. doi:10.1016/j.jshs.2015.07.005.

Skein, Melissa, Rob Duffield, Johann Edge, Michael J. Short, and Toby Mündel. 2011. "Intermittent-Sprint Performance and Muscle Glycogen after 30 h of Sleep Deprivation." *Medicine & Science in Sports & Exercise* 43 (7): 1301–1311.

Sloniger, Mark A., Kirk J. Cureton, Barry M. Prior, and Ellen M. Evans. 1997. "Lower Extremity Muscle Activation During Horizontal and Uphill Running." *Journal of Applied Physiology* 83 (6): 2073–2079.

Smith, Judith L., Patricia Carlson-Kuhta, and Tamara V. Trank. 1998. "Forms of Forward Quadrupedal Locomotion. III. A Comparison of Posture, Hindlimb Kinematics, and Motor Patterns for Downslope and Level Walking." Journal of Neurophysiology 79 (4): 1702–1716.

Solli, Guro S., Espen Tønnessen, and Øyvind Sandbakk. 2017. "The Training Characteristics of the World's Most Successful Female Cross-Country Skier." *Frontiers in Physiology* 8.

Stanley, Christopher T., David Pargman, and Gershon Tenenbaum. 2007. "The Effect of Attentional Coping Strategies on Perceived Exertion in a Cycling Task." *Journal of Applied Sport Psychology* 19 (3): 352–363. doi:10.1080/10413200701345403.

Staron, Robert S., Fredrick C. Hagerman, Robert S. Hikida, Thomas F. Murray, David P. Hostler, Mathew T. Crill, Kerry E. Ragg, and Kumika Toma. 2000. "Fiber Type Composition of the Vastus Lateralis Muscle of Young Men and Women." *Journal of Histochemistry & Cytochemistry* 48 (5): 623–629.

Storer, Thomas W., Lynne Magliano, Linda Woodhouse, Martin L. Lee, Connie Dzekov, Jeanne Dzekov, Richard Casaburi, and Shalender Bhasin. 2003. "Testosterone Dose-Dependently Increases Maximal Voluntary Strength and Leg Power, but Does Not Affect Fatigability or Specific Tension." *The Journal of Clinical Endocrinology & Metabolism* 88 (4): 1478–1485.

"Supplements." *Sport Australia*. Accessed August 13, 2021. http://www.ais.gov.au/nutrition/supplements.

Swanson, Stephen C., and Graham E. Caldwell. 2000. "An Integrated Biomechanical Analysis of High Speed Incline and Level Treadmill Running." *Medicine and Science in Sports and Exercise* 32 (6): 1146–1155.

Talanian, Jason L., and Lawrence L. Spriet. 2016. "Low and Moderate Doses of Caffeine Late in Exercise Improve Performance in Trained Cyclists." *Applied Physiology, Nutrition, and Metabolism* 41 (8): 850–855.

Tarnopolsky, L. J., J. D. Macdougall, S. A. Atkinson, M. A. Tarnopolsky, and J. R. Sutton. 1990. "Gender Differences in Substrate for Endurance Exercise." *Journal of Applied Physiology* 68 (1): 302–308.

Telhan, Gaurav, Jason R. Franz, Jay Dicharry, Robert P. Wilder, Patrick O. Riley, and D. Casey Kerrigan. 2010. "Lower Limb Joint Kinetics During Moderately Sloped Running." *Journal of Athletic Training* 45 (1): 16.

Temesi, John, Pierrick J. Arnal, Thomas Rupp, Léonard Féasson, Régine Cartier, Laurent Gergelé, Samuel Verges, Vincent Martin, and Guillaume Y. Millet. 2015. "Are Females More Resistant to Extreme Neuromuscular Fatigue?" *Medicine and Science in Sports and Exercise* 47 (7): 1372–1382. doi:10.1249/mss.0000000000000540.

Thomas, D. Travis, Kelly Anne Erdman, and Louise M. Burke. 2016. "Position of the Academy of Nutrition and Dietetics, Dietitians of Canada, and the American College of Sports Medicine: Nutrition and Athletic Performance." *Journal of the Academy of Nutrition and Dietetics* 116 (3): 501–528. doi:10.1016/j.jand.2015.12.006.

Thompson, M. A. 2017. "Physiological and Biomechanical Mechanisms of Distance Specific Human Running Performance." *Integrative and Comparative Biology* 57 (2): 293–300. doi:10.1093/icb/icx069.

Thompson, Paul D., Erik J. Funk, Richard A. Carleton, and William Q. Sturner. 1982. "Incidence of Death During Jogging in Rhode Island from 1975 Through 1980." *Journal of the American Medical Association* 247 (18): 2535–2538.

Tiidus, Peter M., and C. David Ianuzzo. 1982. "Effects of Intensity and Duration of Muscular Exercise on Delayed Soreness and Serum Enzyme Activities." *Medicine and Science in Sports and Exercise* 15 (6): 461–465.

Tiller, Nicholas B., Justin D. Roberts, Liam Beasley, Shaun Chapman, Jorge M. Pinto, Lee Smith, Melanie Wiffin, et al. 2019. "International Society of Sports Nutrition Position Stand: Nutritional Considerations for Single-Stage Ultra-Marathon Training and Racing." *Journal of the International Society of Sports Nutrition* 16 (1).

Tiller, Nicholas B., Kirsty J. Elliott-Sale, Beat Knechtle, Patrick B. Wilson, Justin D. Roberts, and Guillaume Y. Millet. 2021. "Do Sex Differences in Physiology Confer a Female Advantage in Ultra-Endurance Sport?" *Sports Medicine* 51: 895–915. doi:10.1007/s40279-020-01417-2.

Tucker, R. 2009. "The Anticipatory Regulation of Performance: the Physiological Basis for Pacing Strategies and the Development of a Perception-Based Model for Exercise Performance." *British Journal of Sports Medicine* 43 (6): 392–400. doi:10.1136/bjsm.2008.050799.

Tyler, Christopher James, Caroline Sunderland, and Stephen S. Cheung. 2013. "The Effect of Cooling Prior to and during Exercise on Exercise Performance and Capacity in the Heat: a Meta-Analysis." *British Journal of Sports Medicine* 49 (1): 7–13. doi:10.1136/bjsports-2012-091739.

Ungprasert, Patompong, Wisit Cheungpasitporn, Cynthia S. Crowson, and Eric L. Matteson. 2015. "Individual Non-Steroidal Anti-Inflammatory Drugs and Risk of Acute Kidney Injury: A Systematic Review and Meta-Analysis of Observational Studies." *European Journal of Internal Medicine* 26 (4): 285–291. doi:10.1016/j.ejim.2015.03.008.

Ungprasert, Patompong, Wisit Cheungpasitporn, Daych Chongnarungsin, Napat Leeaphorn, Supawat Ratanapo, Chrystal Price, and Wonngarm Kittanamongkolchai. 2012. "What Is The 'Safest' Non-Steroidal Anti-Inflammatory Drugs?" *American Medical Journal* 3 (2): 115–123. doi:10.3844/amjsp.2012.115.123.

Urdampilleta, Aritz, Soledad Arribalzaga, Aitor Viribay, Arkaitz Castañeda-Babarro, Jesús Seco-Calvo, and Juan Mielgo-Ayuso. 2020. "Effects of 120 vs. 60 and 90 g/h Carbohydrate Intake during a Trail Marathon ON Neuromuscular Function and High Intensity RUN Capacity Recovery." *Nutrients* 12 (7): 2094. doi:10.3390/nu12072094.

Vacher, P., E. Filaire, L. Mourot, and M. Nicolas. 2019. "Stress and Recovery in Sports: Effects on Heart Rate Variability, Cortisol, and Subjective Experience." *International Journal of Psychophysiology* 143: 25–35.

Venables, Michelle C., Juul Achten, and Asker E. Jeukendrup. 2005. "Determinants of Fat Oxidation during Exercise in Healthy Men and Women: a Cross-Sectional Study." *Journal of Applied Physiology* 98 (1): 160–167.

Venter, Rachel. 2012. "Role of Sleep in Performance and Recovery of Athletes: A Review Article." *South African Journal for Research in Sport, Physical Education and Recreation* 34 (1): 167–184.

Vitale, Kenneth C., Roberts Owens, Susan R. Hopkins, and Atul Malhotra. 2019. "Sleep Hygiene for Optimizing Recovery in Athletes: Review and Recommendations." *International Journal of Sports Medicine* 40 (8): 535–43. Doi:10.1055/a-0905-3103.

Volek, Jeff S., Daniel J. Freidenreich, Catherine Saenz, Laura J. Kunces, Brent C. Creighton, Jenna M. Bartley, Patrick M. Davitt, et al. 2016. "Metabolic Characteristics of Keto-Adapted Ultra-Endurance Runners." *Metabolism* 65 (3): 100–110.

Volek, Jeff S., Timothy Noakes, and Stephen D. Phinney. 2015. "Rethinking Fat as a Fuel for Endurance Exercise." *European Journal of Sport Science* 15 (1): 13–20.

von Rosen, P., A. Frohm, A. Kottorp, C. Fridén, and A. Heijne. 2016. "Too Little Sleep and an Unhealthy Diet Could Increase the Risk of Sustaining a New Injury in Adolescent Elite Athletes." *Scandinavian Journal of Medicine & Science in Sports* 27 (11): 1364–1371. doi:10.1111/sms.12735.

Vonhof, John. 2011. *Fixing Your Feet: Prevention and Treatments for Athletes*. Birmingham, AL: Wilderness Press.

Vuorimaa, T., M. Ahotupa, K. Häkkinen, and T. Vasankari. 2008. "Different Hormonal Response to Continuous and Intermittent Exercise in Middle-Distance and Marathon Runners." *Scandinavian Journal of Medicine & Science in Sports* 18 (5): 565–572. doi:10.1111/j.1600-0838.2007.00733.x.

Wahl, P., S. Mathes, K. Köhler, S. Achtzehn, W. Bloch, and J. Mester. 2013. "Acute Metabolic, Hormonal, and Psychological Responses to Different Endurance Training Protocols." *Hormone and Metabolic Research* 45 (11): 827–833. doi:10.1055/s-0033-1347242.

Walsh, Neil P. 2018. "Recommendations to Maintain Immune Health in Athletes." *European Journal of Sport Science* 18 (6): 820–831. doi:10.1080/17461391.2018.1449895.

Warden, Stuart J. 2010. "Prophylactic Use of NSAIDs by Athletes: A Risk/Benefit Assessment." *The Physician and Sportsmedicine* 38 (1): 132–138. doi:10.3810/psm.2010.04.1770.

Waśkiewicz, Zbigniew, Barbara Kłapcińska, Ewa Sadowska-Krępa, Milosz Czuba, Katarzyna Kempa, Elżbieta Kimsa, and Dagmara Gerasimuk. 2011. "Acute Metabolic Responses to a 24-h Ultra-Marathon Race in Male Amateur Runners." *European Journal of Applied Physiology* 112 (5): 1679–1688.

Welle, Stephen, Rabi Tawil, and Charles A. Thornton. 2008. "Sex-Related Differences in Gene Expression in Human Skeletal Muscle." *PLoS ONE* 3 (1).

Wharam, Paul C., Dale B. Speedy, Timothy D. Noakes, J. M. Thompson, Stephen A. Reid, and Lucy-May Holtzhausen. 2006. "NSAID Use Increases the Risk of Developing Hyponatremia During an Ironman Triathlon." *Medicine and Science in Sports and Exercise* 38 (4): 618–622.

Whatmough, Steven, Stephen Mears, and Courtney Kipps. 2017. "The Use Of Non-Steroidal Anti-Inflammatories (Nsaids) At The 2016 London Marathon." *British Journal of Sports Medicine* 51 (4). doi:10.1136/bjsports-2016-097372.317.

Whatmough, Steven, Stephen Mears, and Courtney Kipps. 2018. "Serum Sodium Changes in Marathon Participants Who Use NSAIDs." *BMJ Open Sport & Exercise Medicine* 4 (1). doi:10.1136/bmjsem-2018-000364.

White, Tracie. 2017. "Pain Reliever Linked to Kidney Injury in Endurance Runners." *Stanford Medicine*. July 5, 2017. https://med.stanford.edu/news/all-news/2017/07/pain-reliever-linked-to-kidney-injury-in-endurance-runners.html.

Whitworth-Turner, Craig, Rocco Di Michele, Ian Muir, Warren Gregson, and Barry Drust. 2017. "A Shower before Bedtime May Improve the Sleep Onset Latency of Youth Soccer Players." *European Journal of Sport Science* 17 (9): 1119–28. doi:10.1080/17461391.2017.1346147.

Wickler, Steven J., Donald F. Hoyt, Andrew A. Biewener, Edward A. Cogger, and L. Kristin. 2005. "In Vivo Muscle Function vs Speed II. Muscle Function Trotting up an Incline." *Journal of Experimental Biology* 208 (6): 1191–1200.

Wilke, Jan, Robert Schleip, Werner Klingler, and Carla Stecco. 2017. "The Lumbodorsal Fascia as a Potential Source of Low Back Pain: A Narrative Review." *BioMed Research International* 2017: 1–6. doi:10.1155/2017/5349620.

Wilson, Patrick B. 2019. "'I Think I'm Gonna Hurl': A Narrative Review of the Causes of Nausea and Vomiting in Sport." *Sports* 7 (7).

Wingfield, Georgia, Frank Marino, and Melissa Skein. 2018. "The Influence of Knowledge of Performance Endpoint on Pacing Strategies, Perception of Effort, and Neural Activity during 30-Km Cycling Time Trials." *Physiological Reports* 6 (21). doi:10.14814/phy2.13892.

Worthing, Robert M., Raechel L. Percy, and Jeremy D. Joslin. 2017. "Prevention of Friction Blisters in Outdoor Pursuits: A Systematic Review." *Wilderness & Environmental Medicine* 28 (2): 139–49. https://doi.org/10.1016/j.wem.2017.03.007.

Wylie, Lee J., James Kelly, Stephen J. Bailey, Jamie R. Blackwell, Philip F. Skiba, Paul .G Winyard, Asker E. Jeukendrup, Anni Vanhatalo, and Andrew M. Jones. 2013. "Beetroot Juice and Exercise: Pharmacodynamic and Dose-Response Relationships." *Journal of Applied Physiology* 115 (3): 325–336.

Yack, H. John, Carole Tucker, Scott C. White, and Heather Collins. 1995. "Comparison of Overground and Treadmill Vertical Ground Reaction Forces." *Gait and Posture* 3 (2): 86.

Yeo, Wee Kian, Carl D. Paton, Andrew P. Garnham, Louise M. Burke, Andrew L. Carey, and John A. Hawley. 2008. "Skeletal Muscle Adaptation and Performance Responses to Once a Day versus Twice Every Second Day Endurance Training Regimens." *Journal of Applied Physiology* 105 (5): 1462–1470.

Yokozawa, T., N. Fujii, Y. Enomoto, and M. Ae. 2003. "Kinetic Characteristics of Distance Running on the Uphill." *Japanese Journal of Biomechanics in Sports and Exercise* 7: 30–42.

Yokozawa, Toshiharu, Norihisa Fujii, and Michiyoshi Ae. 2005. "Kinetic Characteristics of Distance Running on Downhill Slope." *International Journal of Sport and Health Science* 3: 35–45.

Zaleski, Amanda L., Kevin D. Ballard, Linda S. Pescatello, Gregory A. Panza, Brian R. Kupchak, Marcin R. Dada, William Roman, Paul D. Thompson, and Beth A. Taylor. 2015. "The Effect of Compression Socks Worn during a Marathon on Hemostatic Balance." *The Physician and Sportsmedicine* 43 (4): 336–41. doi:10.1080/00913847.2015.1072456.

Zaleski, Amanda, and Beth Taylor. 2016. "Compression and Clots in Athletes Who Travel." *Lower Extremity Review Magazine*. January 2016. https://lermagazine.com/article/compression-and-clots-in-athletes-who-travel.

Zaryski, Calvin, and David J. Smith. 2005. "Training Principles and Issues for Ultra-endurance Athletes." *Current Sports Medicine Reports* 4 (3): 165–170.

Zierath, Juleen R, and John A Hawley. 2004. "Skeletal Muscle Fiber Type: Influence on Contractile and Metabolic Properties." *PLoS Biology* 2 (10).

Zingg, Matthias Alexander, Klaus Karner-Rezek, Thomas Rosemann, Beat Knechtle, Romuald Lepers, and Christoph Alexander Rüst. 2014. "Will Women Outrun Men in Ultra-marathon Road Races from 50 km to 1,000 km?" *SpringerPlus* 3: 97.

AUTHOR BIOS AND ACKNOWLEDGMENTS

Jason Koop

JASON KOOP walks the walk—or runs the run, as the case may be—when it comes to ultras. His journey from a cross-country runner at Texas A&M to ultra coach started with a postgraduation internship at CTS in the summer of 2001. A runner in a company of predominantly cycling coaches, Koop was quickly drafted and trained to be the company's lead running coach. Over his career he has coached hundreds of athletes of all abilities for ultramarathons across the globe. In 2006 he traveled around the United States coaching and supporting Dean Karnazes as the "Ultramarathon Man" ran 50 marathons in 50 states in 50 days. Karnazes again tapped Koop's expertise in 2011 for "Regis and Kelly's Run Across America with Dean Karnazes," a nearly 3,000-mile cross-country run. Then in 2021 Koop accompanied Timothy Olson for his Fastest Known Time of the Pacific Crest Trail.

Over his coaching career, Koop has served many roles including Director of Regional Coaches, Director of Coaching, Director of Operations and now serves as the head coach for CTS-Ultrarunning, where he has helped to build a department of over 15 professional ultramarathon coaches. During his tenure, he has also developed CTS's quality assurance system for coaching, the CTS Coaching College, hiring, screening and training processes for new coaches and mentored hundreds of new endurance coaches.

Koop's personal ultrarunning resume includes two top-10 finishes at the Leadville Trail 100 Run and finishes at some of ultrarunning's most formidable events, including the Western States Endurance Run, the Badwater 135, the Wasatch 100, Tor de Geants and the Hardrock 100.

Acknowledgments

I am a very modest person from a humble background. I did not have a fancy education, was never at the top of my class, was not a very good athlete and if I am being honest, there's no reason I should be the one informing thousands on anything, let alone running and training. What I did have in life are fantastic coaches, teammates, educators, and mentors, all of whom have a tremendous impact on me personally and professionally. I would be remiss if I failed to mention them and how they have impacted my career.

The coaches I have had in my life, Lyndall Weaver, Tom Clark, Chuck Estill, Billy Cox, Terry Jessup, and Dave Hartman: There's a piece of each of you in this book.

Chris Carmichael, Jim Lehman and Jay T. Kearney: You took a kid who couldn't coach his way out of a wet paper bag and helped him become a pretty OK coach (jury is still out though). I am forever grateful for the initial risk you took in hiring me and the countless hours you each spent helping me develop as a coach and a man.

My coauthors, Jim Rutberg and Corrine Malcolm, thank you for believing in this project, giving me a nudge when I needed it and your immense contributions to the text.

To Stephanie Howe, PhD and Nick Tiller, PhD, thank you for your blunt, honest and direct feedback on the scientific portions of this book. Your contributions raised the level of the content beyond my wildest expectations.

To Rodger Kram, PhD, thank you for your guidance in the early development in the first edition of this book. More important, thanks for helping with the bloopers.

To Martin Hoffman, MD, thank you for your guidance in the early development in the first edition of this book. More important, thank you for being a leader in the ultraendurance community.

To the coaches at CTS: Many, if not all, the ideas represented in this book are ones we as a team have developed over the course of many years, debates, and continuing education sessions. I am proud to call you my colleagues and my friends.

To Jackson Brill for your endless reference wrangling and contributions to the biomechanics section. The future is bright for you!

Special thanks to Allison Goldstein for editing and proofing the copy of this book in what is always the most humbling experience of my year.

To Abby Hall for styling and illustrations, you made this book look good!

To my mother Linda, who gave me a role model on being a humble, servant based leader.

To my father Myron, for letting me make mistakes, yet never the same one twice.

To my brother who always lent me some of his boundless entrepreneurial spirit throughout my career.

Finally to my wife Liz, who is the best partner I could ever ask for.

AUTHOR BIOS AND ACKNOWLEDGMENTS

Jim Rutberg

JIM RUTBERG'S career has centered on helping coaches and sports scientists share their expertise and guidance with athletes. In addition to co-authoring *Training Essentials for Ultrarunning*, he co-authored *Ride Inside* with Joe Friel and seven books with Chris Carmichael: *The Time-Crunched Cyclist, The Time-Crunched Triathlete, The Ultimate Ride, Chris Carmichael's Food for Fitness, Chris Carmichael's Fitness Cookbook, The Carmichael Training Systems Cyclist's Training Diary*, and *5 Essentials for a Winning Life*. As the Media Director and a coach for CTS, Jim has written and contributed to innumerable web and magazine articles, and his work has appeared in *Bicycling, Outside, Road Bike Action, Men's Health, Men's Journal, Velonews, Inside Triathlon*, and more. A graduate of Wake Forest University and former elite-level cyclist, Rutberg lives in Colorado Springs.

Acknowledgments

As Jason is quick to acknowledge, this is largely my fault. Jason and I have been colleagues and friends since we were fresh out of college, and I have watched him develop into one of the most respected and knowledgeable coaches in ultrarunning. When I cajoled Jason into writing the first edition of this book, I knew he had the knowledge and passion to create ultrarunning's benchmark training book, but I underestimated the enthusiastic response from the ultrarunning community. This expansive second edition aims to address at least some of the queries and requests we received from readers, a feat that was only possible with the help of a great team. In addition to Jason Koop and Corrine Malcolm, I'd like to thank Stephanie Howe, Nick Tiller, Abby Hall, Allison Goldstein, Jackson Brill, and Tuviel Levi for contributing their time, expertise, and hard work on this project. I am extraordinarily proud to play a role in bringing this work to a larger audience.

I have had the pleasure and honor to co-author several books on training and sports nutrition, and I am thankful to Chris Carmichael, the entire coaching staff at CTS, and to Joe Friel for providing their knowledge and the opportunity to devote time, energy, and resources to writing books. And thank you to my sons, Oliver and Elliot, for putting up with me and eating frozen pizza when I have deadlines.

AUTHOR BIOS AND ACKNOWLEDGMENTS

Corrine Malcolm

CORRINE MALCOLM is an endurance coach for CTS, a science communicator, and a professional ultra-endurance athlete because her sense of direction is bad enough that she often runs far too long. Corrine became a coach because she fell in love with human physiology as a cross country skier, but had an evident disdain for basement lab work as a graduate student. A self-proclaimed 'ultra-nerd', she thrives in being a science hub for the CTS coaching team, breaking down new research in ways anyone can understand because, in her words, "Science should be for everyone." When Corrine isn't writing or reading, you'll find her chasing her husband, Stephen, or their dog, Petey, through the hills around their home. Corrine's personal ultra resume includes top ten finishes at the Leadville Trail 100, the Western States Endurance Run, and UTMB's TDS; and is the women's FKT record holder on the 171-mile Tahoe Rim Trail.

Acknowledgments

As a coach, writer, and runner I'd like to think I'm permanently somewhere between green and seasoned, and because of that I will always have mentors to thank. I'm forever grateful for my coauthors, Jason Koop and Jim Rutberg; getting tagged in on this project is a dream come true. To the coaches I've had, you each had a hand in shaping me into the human I am today, on and off the trails. I owe you so very much. To my CTS coaching team, there is a reason I came on with CTS as a graduate student. I wanted a place to grow, and you keep delivering on that initial promise. To my parents who have watched me write many incomplete run-on sentences over the years and still encouraged me to keep writing, thank you. Finally, to my husband Stephen, may you never stop humoring me as I insist on reading out loud to you.

Index

Made in the USA
Coppell, TX
01 June 2022